GALATIANS

GALATIANS

ZONDERVAN
Exegetical Commentary
ON THE
New Testament

THOMAS R. SCHREINER

CLINTON E. ARNOLD
General Editor

ZONDERVAN ACADEMIC

Galatians
Copyright © 2010 by Thomas R. Schreiner

ISBN 978-0-310-49216-0 (ebook)

Requests for information should be addressed to:
Zondervan, 3900 *Sparks Dr., Grand Rapids, Michigan 49546*

Library of Congress Cataloging-in-Publication Data

Schreiner, Thomas R.
    Galatians / Thomas R. Schreiner.
       p. cm. (Zondervan exegetical commentary series on the New Testament)
    Includes bibliographical references and index.
    ISBN: 978-0-310-24372-4 (hardcover, printed)
    1. Bible N.T. Galatians—Commentaries. I. Title.
  BS2685.53.S37 2010
  227'.4077—dc22   2010019091

All Scripture quotations from books other than Galatians (which is a translation by the author), unless otherwise indicated, are taken from The Holy Bible, *New International Version®, NIV®.* Copyright © 1973, 1978, 1984 by Biblica, Inc.® Used by permission of Zondervan. All rights reserved worldwide.

Any internet addresses (websites, blogs, etc.) and telephone numbers in this book are offered as a resource. They are not intended in any way to be or imply an endorsement by Zondervan, nor does Zondervan vouch for the content of these sites and numbers for the life of this book.

Cover design: *Tammy Johnson*
Interior design: *Beth Shagene*

Printed in the United States of America

---

21 22 23 24 25 26 27 28 29 30 /TRM/ 27 26 25 24 23 22 21 20 19 18 17 16 15 14 13 12 11 10

To Diane
You have filled me with joy (2 Tim. 1:4)

Contents

Series Introduction

This generation has been blessed with an abundance of excellent commentaries. Some are technical and do a good job of addressing issues that the critics have raised; other commentaries are long and provide extensive information about word usage and catalog nearly every opinion expressed on the various interpretive issues; still other commentaries focus on providing cultural and historical background information; and then there are those commentaries that endeavor to draw out many applicational insights.

The key question to ask is: What are you looking for in a commentary? This commentary series might be for you if

- you have taken Greek and would like a commentary that helps you apply what you have learned without assuming you are a well-trained scholar.
- you would find it useful to see a concise, one- or two- sentence statement of what the commentator thinks the main point of each passage is.
- you would like help interpreting the words of Scripture without getting bogged down in scholarly issues that seem irrelevant to the life of the church.
- you would like to see a visual representation (a graphical display) of the flow of thought in each passage.
- you would like expert guidance from solid evangelical scholars who set out to explain the meaning of the original text in the clearest way possible and to help you navigate through the main interpretive issues.
- you want to benefit from the results of the latest and best scholarly studies and historical information that help to illuminate the meaning of the text.
- you would find it useful to see a brief summary of the key theological insights that can be gleaned from each passage and some discussion of the relevance of these for Christians today.

These are just some of the features that characterize the new Zondervan Exegetical Commentary on the New Testament series. The idea for this series was refined over time by an editorial board who listened to pastors and teachers express what they wanted to see in a commentary series based on the Greek text. That board consisted of myself, George H. Guthrie, William D. Mounce, Thomas R. Schreiner, and Mark L. Strauss along with Zondervan senior editor at large, Verlyn Verbrugge, and former Zondervan senior acquisitions editor Jack Kuhatschek. We also enlisted a board of consulting editors who are active pastors, ministry leaders, and seminary professors to help in the process of designing a commentary series that will be useful to the church. Zondervan senior acquisitions editor David Frees has now been shepherding the process to completion.

We arrived at a design that includes seven components for the treatment of each biblical passage. What follows is a brief orientation to these primary components of the commentary.

Literary Context

In this section, you will find a concise discussion of how the passage functions in the broader literary context of the book. The commentator highlights connections with the preceding and following material in the book and makes observations on the key literary features of this text.

Main Idea

Many readers will find this to be an enormously helpful feature of this series. For each passage, the commentator carefully crafts a one- or two- sentence statement of the big idea or central thrust of the passage.

Translation and Graphical Layout

Another unique feature of this series is the presentation of each commentator's translation of the Greek text in a graphical layout. The purpose of this diagram is to help the reader visualize, and thus better understand, the flow of thought within the text. The translation itself reflects the interpretive decisions made by each commentator in the "Explanation" section of the commentary. Here are a few insights that will help you to understand the way these are put together.

1. On the far left side next to the verse numbers is a series of interpretive labels that indicate the function of each clause or phrase of the biblical text. The corresponding portion of the text is on the same line to the right of the label. We have not used technical linguistic jargon for these, so they should be easily understood.

2. In general, we place every clause (a group of words containing a subject and a predicate) on a separate line and identify how it is supporting the principal assertion of the text (namely, is it saying when the action occurred, how it took place, or why it took place?). We sometimes place longer phrases or a series of items on separate lines as well.

3. Subordinate (or dependent) clauses and phrases are indented and placed directly under the words that they modify. This helps the reader to more easily see the nature of the relationship of clauses and phrases in the flow of the text.

4. Every main clause has been placed in bold print and pushed to the left margin for clear identification.

5. Sometimes when the level of subordination moves too far to the right — as often happens with some of Paul's long, involved sentences! — we reposition the flow to the left of the diagram, but use an arrow to indicate that this has happened.

6. The overall process we have followed has been deeply informed by principles of discourse analysis and narrative criticism (for the Gospels and Acts).

Structure

Immediately following the translation, the commentator describes the flow of thought in the passage and explains how certain interpretive decisions regarding the relationship of the clauses were made in the passage.

Exegetical Outline

The overall structure of the passage is described in a detailed exegetical outline. This will be particularly helpful for those who are looking for a way to concisely explain the flow of thought in the passage in a teaching or preaching setting.

Explanation of the Text

As an exegetical commentary, this work makes use of the Greek language to interpret the meaning of the text. If your Greek is rather rusty (or even somewhat limited), don't be too concerned. All of the Greek words are cited in parentheses following an English translation. We have made every effort to make this commentary as readable and useful as possible even for the nonspecialist.

Those who will benefit the most from this commentary will have had the equivalent of two years of Greek in college or seminary. This would include a semester or two of working through an intermediate grammar (such as Wallace, Porter, Brooks and Winberry, or Dana and Mantey). The authors use the grammatical language that is found in these kinds of grammars. The details of the grammar of the passage, however, are only discussed when it has a bearing on the interpretation of the text.

The emphasis on this section of the text is to convey the meaning. Commentators examine words and images, grammatical details, relevant OT and Jewish background to a particular concept, historical and cultural context, important text-critical issues, and various interpretational issues that surface.

Theology in Application

This, too, is a unique feature for an exegetical commentary series. We felt it was important for each author not only to describe what the text means in its various details, but also to take a moment and reflect on the theological contribution that it makes. In this section, the theological message of the passage is summarized. The authors discuss the theology of the text in terms of its place within the book and in a broader biblical-theological context. Finally, each commentator provides some suggestions on what the message of the passage is for the church today. At the conclusion of each volume in this series is a summary of the whole range of theological themes touched on by this book of the Bible.

Our sincere hope and prayer is that you find this series helpful not only for your own understanding of the text of the New Testament, but as you are actively engaged in teaching and preaching God's Word to people who are hungry to be fed on its truth.

CLINTON E. ARNOLD
general editor

Preface

This commentary is written especially for pastors and students who want some help with the Greek text. It is not intended as a comprehensive commentary on Galatians. I have tried to keep the commentary brief and lucid so that it will be of help to the busy pastor and layperson. At the same time, I wanted to interact to some extent with competing views of Galatians, and I try to do this too in the introduction, the footnotes, and debated passages (like Gal 2:16 and 3:10–14). With the rise of the New Perspective on Paul, the meaning of Galatians is intensely debated. What was the situation Paul addressed, and what message does Paul communicate in the letter? A responsible interpreter must interact with other views, especially since so many question the Reformation view of the letter. Hence, I did not think I could simply convey my own interpretation without interacting with alternate viewpoints. I know it is out of fashion in some circles, but it seems to me that Martin Luther and John Calvin were substantially right in their interpretation of the letter and that their pastoral application of the letter still stands today.

My thanks to Clint Arnold, who invited me to be an associate editor for this series and who has served as an outstanding general editor. His comments on the first draft were of significant help in improving the manuscript for publication. George Guthrie provided constructive criticism on the diagrams, and I am thankful he took time out of his busy schedule to assist me. I am also grateful to Verlyn Verbrugge for his excellent editorial work and his assistance in seeing this work come to publication.

R. Albert Mohler Jr., the president of Southern Baptist Theological Seminary, and Russell Moore, the dean of the School of Theology and the senior vice-president for Academic Administration, also deserve thanks. I am grateful for their warm support of my scholarly endeavors and for the granting of a sabbatical, which enabled me to work on this commentary. Indeed, I stand in debt to Southern Baptists everywhere who support the Cooperative Program, for I would not have the time to write if they did not give generously.

Oren Martin also deserves thanks for his help in writing this volume. He chased down articles for me and was eager to assist me in whatever I asked him to do. I am also grateful for Rick Elzinga (a pastor near Portland, Oregon) who carefully read the manuscript, noting errors and suggesting corrections.

A rousing thank-you is due to Greg Van Court. As I wrote the commentary, I inserted works in the footnotes and bibliography without keeping track of whether they were cited before and without organizing what was included. Greg performed the huge task of sorting out and organizing my notes and bibliography, and his labors saved me countless hours. He also retrieved articles, helped conform the diagrams to the required style, and performed numerous other tasks that I asked him to do. I can scarcely thank Greg enough for his service of love and his careful work.

My colleague and friend Jim Hamilton read the entire commentary and made many invaluable suggestions. I am grateful that he took time out of his busy schedule to assist me with his sharp editorial eye.

I dedicate this volume to Diane. She has been my wife and beloved friend for thirty-four years. She shared with me the word of life when I was seventeen years old, which led to my salvation. I cannot imagine a better mother for our children. Her encouragement and support of my ministry cannot be expressed in words. Everyone who knows Diane will testify to her servant's heart and to her radical faith in God. "I thank my God in all my remembrance of you" (Phil 1:3 ESV).

Thomas R. Schreiner
January, 2010

Abbreviations

AB	Anchor Bible
ABD	*Anchor Bible Dictionary.* Edited by D. N. Freedman. 6 vols. New York, 1992.
Abraham	*On the Life of Abraham* (Philo)
ABR	*Australian Biblical Review*
Ag. Ap.	*Against Apion* (Josephus)
AGJU	Arbeiten zur Geschichte des antiken Judentums und des Urchristentums
Alleg. Interp.	*Allegorical Interpretation* (Philo)
AnBib	Analecta biblica
Ant.	*Jewish Antiquities* (Josephus)
ANTC	Abingdon New Testament Commentaries
ASV	American Standard Version
2 Bar.	*2 Baruch (Syriac Apocalypse)*
BBR	*Bulletin for Biblical Research*
BDAG	Bauer, W., F. W. Danker, W. F. Arndt, and F. W. Gingrich. *Greek-English Lexicon of the New Testament and Other Early Christian Literature.* 3rd ed. Chicago, 2000.
BDF	Blass, F., A. Debrunner, and R. W. Funk. *A Greek Grammar of the New Testament and Other Early Christian Literature.* Chicago, 1961.
BECNT	Baker Exegetical Commentary on the New Testament
BETL	Bibliotheca ephemeridum theologicarum lovaniensium
BEvT	Beiträge zur evangelischen Theologie
Bib	*Biblica*
Bib. Ant.	*Liber antiquitatum biblicarum* (Pseudo-Philo)
BIS	Biblical Interpretation Series
BJRL	*Bulletin of the John Rylands University Library of Manchester*
BNTC	Black's New Testament Commentaries
BSac	*Bibliotheca sacra*
BT	*The Bible Translator*
CBQ	*Catholic Biblical Quarterly*

CC	Continental Commentaries
Creation	*On the Creation of the World* (Philo)
CRINT	Compendia rerum iudaicarum ad Novum Testamentum
CTJ	*Calvin Theological Journal*
CurrBR	*Currents in Biblical Research*
Decalogue	*On the Decalogue* (Philo)
DPL	*Dictionary of Paul and His Letters.* Edited by G. F. Hawthorne, R. P. Martin, and D. G. Reid. Downers Grove, IL, 1993.
Dreams	*On Dreams* (Philo)
Eccl. Hist.	*Ecclesiastical History* (Eusebius)
EIN	Einheitsübersetzung-KBA (1980)
ELO	Unrevidierte Elberfelder (1905)
1 En.	*1 Enoch (Ethiopic Apocalypse)*
2 En.	*2 Enoch (Slavonic Apocalypse)*
ESV	English Standard Version
ETL	*Ephemerides theologicae lovanienses*
EvJ	*Evangelical Journal*
EvQ	*Evangelical Quarterly*
ExpTim	*Expository Times*
FBJ	French Bible Jerusalem
GNV	Good News Version
GTJ	*Grace Theological Journal*
HDR	Harvard Dissertations in Religion
HNT	Salkinson-Ginsburg Hebrew New Testament
HNTC	Harper's New Testament Commentaries
HRD	Herder Translation (Revised Version 2005)
HTKNT	Herders theologischer Kommentar zum Neuen Testament
HTR	*Harvard Theological Review*
ICC	International Critical Commentary
Int	*Interpretation*
ISBE	*International Standard Bible Encyclopedia.* Edited by G. W. Bromiley. 4 vols. Grand Rapids, 1979–1988.
IVPNTC	InterVarsity Press New Testament Commentary
JBL	*Journal of Biblical Literature*
JBMW	*Journal of Biblical Manhood and Womanhood*
JETS	*Journal of the Evangelical Theological Society*
JGRChJ	*Journal of Greco-Roman Christianity and Judaism*
Jos. Asen.	*Joseph and Aseneth* (Pseudepigrapha)
JSJ	*Journal for the Study of Judaism in the Persian, Hellenistic, and Roman Periods*
JSJSup	Journal for the Study of Judaism Supplements

JSNT	*Journal for the Study of the New Testament*
JSNTSup	Journal for the Study of the New Testament: Supplement Series
JTS	*Journal of Theological Studies*
Jub.	*Jubilees*
Jud	*Judaica*
J.W.	*Jewish War* (Josephus)
KEK	Kritisch-exegetischer Kommentar über das Neue Testament (Meyer-Kommentar)
KJV	King James Version
Lib. Ed.	*De liberis educandis* (Plutarch)
Life	*The Life* (Josephus)
LNTS	Library of New Testament Studies
LSG	Louis Segond, 1910
LUT	Lutherbibel, 1545
LUO	Lutherbibel, 1912
LXX	Septuagint
m. ʿAbod. Zar.	ʿAbodah Zarah (Mishnah)
m. ʾAbot	ʾAbot (Mishnah)
m. Demai	Demai (Mishnah)
Mem.	*Memorabilia* (Xenophon)
MNTC	Moffatt New Testament Commentary
Moses	*On the Life of Moses* (Philo)
m. Šabb.	Šabbat (Mishnah)
MT	Masoretic Text
NA	Nestle-Aland, *Novum Testamentum Graece*
NAC	New American Commentary
NACSBT	New American Commentary Studies in Bible and Theology
NCB	New Century Bible
NDBT	*New Dictionary of Biblical Theology.* Edited by T. Desmond Alexander and Brian S. Rosner. Downers Grove, IL, 2000.
Neot	*Neotestamentica*
NET	NET Bible
NICNT	New International Commentary on the New Testament
NICOT	New International Commentary on the Old Testament
NIDNTT	*New International Dictionary of New Testament Theology.* Edited by C. Brown. 4 vols. Grand Rapids, 1975 – 1985.
NIGTC	New International Greek Testament Commentary
NIV	New International Version
NIVAC	NIV Application Commentary
NovT	*Novum Testamentum*
NovTSup	Novum Testamentum Supplements

NSBT	New Studies in Biblical Theology
NRSV	New Revised Standard Version
NT	New Testament
NTM	New Testament Monographs
NTS	*New Testament Studies*
OT	Old Testament
Pesiq. Rab.	*Pesiqta Rabbati*
PNTC	Pillar New Testament Commentary
Prelim. Studies	*On the Preliminary Studies* (Philo)
Presb	*Presbyterion*
Pss. Sol.	*Psalms of Solomon*
RelSRev	*Religious Studies Review*
RevExp	*Review and Expositor*
Rhet.	*Rhetoric* (Aristotle)
RSV	Revised Standard Version
SBG	Studies in Biblical Greek
SBJT	*Southern Baptist Journal of Theology*
SBLABib	Society of Biblical Literature Academia Biblica
SBLDS	Society of Biblical Literature Dissertation Series
SBLSP	Society of Biblical Literature Seminar Papers
SBT	Studies in Biblical Theology
SCH	Schlachter Bibel, 2000
SEÅ	*Svensk exegetisk årsbok*
SJT	*Scottish Journal of Theology*
SNTSMS	Society for New Testament Studies Monograph Series
Spec. Laws	*On the Special Laws* (Philo)
SR	*Studies in Religion*
ST	*Studia theologica*
TBei	*Theologische Beiträge*
T. Benj.	*Testament of Benjamin*
TDNT	*Theological Dictionary of the New Testament.* Edited by G. Kittel and G. Friedrich. Translated by G. W. Bromiley. 10 vols. Grand Rapids, 1964–1976.
Tg. Onq.	*Targum Onqelos*
Tg. Ps.-J.	*Targum Pseudo-Jonathan*
THKNT	Theologischer Handkommentar zum Neuen Testament
T. Isaac	*Testament of Isaac*
TJ	*Trinity Journal*
T. Jud.	*Testament of Judah*
T. Reu.	*Testament of Reuben*
T. Sol.	*Testament of Solomon*

TynBul	*Tyndale Bulletin*
WBC	Word Biblical Commentary
WTJ	*Westminster Theological Journal*
WUNT	Wissenschaftliche Untersuchungen zum Neuen Testament
ZNW	*Zeitschrift für die neutestamentliche Wissenschaft und die Kunde der älteren Kirche*
ZTK	*Zeitschrift für Theologie und Kirche*

Introduction

Martin Luther captured the message of Galatians and the teaching of Jesus (Matt 5:3) when he wrote:

> Therefore, God accepts only the forsaken, cures only the sick, gives sight only to the blind, restores life to only the dead, sanctifies only the sinners, gives wisdom only to the unwise fools. In short, He has mercy only on those who are wretched, and gives grace only to those who are not in grace. Therefore no proud saint, no wise or just person, can become God's material, and God's purpose cannot be fulfilled in him. He remains in his own work and makes a fictitious, pretended, false, and painted saint of himself, that is, a hypocrite.[1]

Amazingly, Gordon Fee writes from quite a different perspective, saying that his goal is to help people read Galatians "as if the Reformation had never happened."[2] On the one hand, Fee's goal is laudable. He wants to read the text on its own terms. On the other hand, it is remarkably naïve and ahistorical, for he pretends that he can read Galatians as a neutral observer of the text apart from the history of the church. I am not suggesting that we must read Galatians *in defense* of the Reformation, nor am I denying that the Reformation may be askew in some of its emphases. But it must be acknowledged that none of us can read Galatians as if the Reformation never occurred. Such a reading is five hundred years too late. Nor can we read Galatians as if the twentieth century never happened or apart from the works of Ignatius, Irenaeus, Augustine, Anselm, Aquinas, and the like. We can consider whether Reformation emphases were wrong (I will argue that they were not), but what we cannot do is read Galatians as if we were the first readers.

Paul is engaged in a battle for the gospel in this letter, and his words still speak to us today. Vital issues for the Christian life are tackled in Galatians. Paul unpacks the heart of the gospel. We see the meaning and the centrality of justification by faith, which Luther rightly argued was the article by which the church stands or falls. How can a person stand before a holy God without being condemned? Paul answers that question in Galatians.

---

1. Martin Luther, "The Seven Penitential Psalms," trans. by Arnold Guebert, in *Selected Psalms III* from *Luther's Works* (ed. Jaroslav Pelikan; St. Louis: Concordia, 1958), 14:163.

2. Gordon D. Fee, *Galatians* (Pentecostal Commentary Series; Dorset: Deo, 2007), 1.

Jesus Christ is also central in Galatians. We will see that Jesus is fully divine and hence should be worshiped. And the cross of Christ plays a fundamental role in the letter, for no one is justified apart from the cross. Believers are right with God because Christ on the cross bore the curse that believers deserved, and Christ freed us from the power of sin through his death and resurrection.

Paul also emphasizes the power of the Holy Spirit in the lives of believers, for as Christians we please God only through relying on the Spirit. The Christian life is not an exercise in autonomy or self-effort but is lived in dependence on the Holy Spirit. The role of the law in the Christian life is also unpacked, so that we gain a sharper profile of the relationship between the old covenant and the new, between the law and the gospel, between the old age and the age to come. Galatians focuses on soteriology, but at the same time the nature of sin is set forth in the letter, and thereby we understand more clearly why the death of Jesus Christ is of supreme importance. Reading Galatians should not be merely an academic enterprise. The gospel Paul proclaims in it has often been used by the Lord to revive the church. We see from Paul's passion for the gospel that issues of life and death are at stake.

Author

No significant scholarly debate exists on whether Paul wrote Galatians.[3] Indeed, Galatians is often identified as quintessentially Pauline. I will assume, therefore, without further argumentation that Galatians was written by Paul.

Recipients

Was the letter to the Galatians written to south or north Galatia? Why does it even matter? It should be said at the outset that the destination of the letter does not fundamentally change its interpretation. Where it makes a difference is in terms of history. The destination of the letter determines how we correlate Galatians with Acts. For instance, did Paul's confrontation with Peter (Gal 2:11 – 14) take place before the apostolic council of Acts 15 (so most who support the south Galatian theory) or after that meeting (the north Galatian theory)? Now it does affect inter-pretation to some extent. Does Paul omit mentioning any of his visits to Jerusalem in the letter to the Galatians (see more on this below)? How do we correlate the Pauline visits to Jerusalem with his visits as they are recorded in Acts? The issue is of some importance because we have a historical faith and believe that the events of biblical history are significant. Still, the importance of the issue must not be

---

3. For a helpful history of interpretation of Galatians, see John Riches, *Galatians through the Centuries* (Blackwell Bible Commentaries; Oxford: Blackwell, 2008).

exaggerated, and some readers may want to skip to the next section and read about the situation of the letter.

Galatia became a Roman province in 25 BC, and the province included people from many ethnic groups, including the "Celts" or "Galatians," who had migrated to Asia Minor by 278 BC.[4] In Paul's day the province was a large area that touched the Black Sea in the north and the Mediterranean in the south. As time passed, however, the province changed. "Vespasian detached almost all of Pisidia from Galatia in AD 74 and about AD 137 Lycaonia Galatica was removed and added to an enlarged province of Cilicia. In AD 297 southern Galatia was united with surrounding regions to form a new province of Pisidia with Antioch as its capital."[5]

Hence, commentators in early church history naturally thought Galatians was written to the province as it existed in later Roman history, and therefore, virtually all scholars believed that Galatians was written to the ethnic Galatians in the northern part of the province. But the work of William Ramsey and others in the twentieth century has provoked scholars to reexamine the destination of the letter, for scholars are now apprised of the dimensions of the Galatian region during Paul's day. Therefore, the identity of the recipients of the letter has been debated intensely in the last century.

The north Galatian theory maintains that the letter was sent to ethnic Galatians located in the northern part of the Galatian province.[6] As Philip Esler remarks, the north Galatian theory could be described as "tribal" Galatia since on this view the letter was sent to those who were ethnically Galatians.[7] The south Galatian view proposes that the letter was sent to the cities Paul visited on his first missionary journey in Acts 13 – 14.[8] It is not the purpose of this commentary to discuss in detail the destination of the letter, but some of the major arguments for both views will

4. Ben Witherington III, *Grace in Galatia: A Commentary on Paul's Letter to the Galatians* (Grand Rapids: Eerdmans, 1988), 2 – 3.

5. Ibid., 5.

6. This view is accepted by most German NT scholars, though it is not limited to them. E.g., Hans Dieter Betz, *Galatians: A Commentary on Paul's Letter to the Churches in Galatia* (Hermeneia; Philadelphia: Fortress, 1979), 1 – 5.

7. Philip F. Esler, *Galatians* (New York/London: Routledge, 1998), 32. Esler supports the north Galatian theory (32 – 36).

8. For a defense of a south Galatian destination, see Rainer Riesner, *Paul's Early Period: Chronology, Mission Strategy, Theology* (trans. Doug Scott; Grand Rapids: Eerdmans, 1998), 286 – 91; F. F. Bruce, *The Epistle to the Galatians: A Commentary on the Greek Text* (NIGNT; Grand Rapids: Eerdmans, 1982), 43 – 56; Richard N. Longenecker, *Galatians* (WBC; Dallas: Word, 1990), lxiii – lxxxvii; Colin J. Hemer, *The Book of Acts in the Setting of Hellenistic History* (WUNT 49;

Tübingen: Mohr Siebeck, 1989), 247 – 51, 277 – 307; Stephen Mitchell, *The Rise of the Church* (vol. 2 of *Anatolia: Land, Men, and God in Asia Minor*; Oxford: Clarendon, 1993), 1 – 5; Cilliers Breytenbach, *Paulus und Barnabas in der Provinz Galatien: Studien zu Apostelgeschichte 13f.; 16,6; 18,23 und den Adressaten des Galaterbriefes* (AGJU; Leiden: Brill, 1996), 99 – 173; Richard Bauckham, "James, Peter, and the Gentiles," in *The Missions of James, Peter, and Paul: Tension in Early Christianity* (ed. Bruce Chilton and Craig Evans; NovTSup 115; Leiden: Brill, 2005), 135 – 36; James M. Scott, *Paul and Nations: The Old Testament and Jewish Background of Paul's Mission to the Nations with Special Reference to the Destination of Galatians* (WUNT 84; Tübingen: Mohr Siebeck, 1995), 181 – 215. But Scott's appeal to the table of nations fails to convince. For a critique of Scott, see Eckhard J. Schnabel, *Jesus and the Twelve* (vol. 1 of *Early Christian Mission*; Downers Grove, IL: IVP, 2004), 498 – 99; idem, *Paul and the Early Church* (vol. 1 of *Early Christian Mission*; Downers Grove, IL: IVP, 2004), 1298 – 99.

be presented, and I will argue that the south Galatian hypothesis is more likely. In any case, the interpretation of the letter is not affected significantly by whether one holds to a north or south Galatian hypothesis,[9] though one's view on the destination of the letter has major implications for Pauline chronology.

Support for the North Galatian Theory

I begin with arguments supporting the north Galatian theory, but will also note the counter-arguments of those who support the south Galatian theory.

(1) J. B. Lightfoot supports the north Galatian view by contending that the temperament of the Galatians fits with what we know about the Gauls, that is, that they were fickle and superstitious.[10] This argument is hardly convincing, for fickleness and superstition were not limited to Gauls.[11]

(2) Acts 16:6 and 18:23 likely refer to north Galatia. These two visits square with Gal 4:13, where Paul says that he preached to the Galatians when he was sick "formerly [the first time]" (πρότερον). Now if Paul visited the Galatians a first time, then he also was present a second time, and this fits with Acts 16:6 and 18:23. Again, this argument is hardly decisive. Acts 16:6 says nothing about founding new churches, and the Greek word can be translated "at first" and does not necessarily imply two visits. Further, even if there were two visits, Paul may have counted the retracing of his steps in Acts 13 – 14 as a second visit.[12] Finally, in Acts 16:6 the word "Phrygian [country]" is likely an adjective, specifying the part of Galatia in which Paul traveled, and Acts 18:23 describes Paul's travels in southern Galatia and Phrygian Asia.[13]

(3) It is important to observe that the churches visited in Acts 13 – 14 are not identified as Galatian churches by Luke. But we must be careful here, for Luke's terminology is not necessarily the same as Paul's. Paul typically refers to Roman provinces, whereas Luke refers to ethnic groupings in the provinces, though the issue is complex and cannot be resolved simplistically.[14]

(4) Paul would not use the term "Galatians" to describe those living in south Galatia, for they were not "Galatians" ethnically.[15] The ethnic Galatians were the Gauls who lived in the north, and secular writers regularly use the term "Galatians"

9. A number of scholars have supported a north Galatian destination, but at the same time defend the historical accuracy of the letter. See, e.g., Lightfoot (see the next note); J. Gresham Machen, *Machen's Notes on Galatians: Notes on Biblical Exposition and Other Aids to Interpretation of the Epistle to the Galatians from the Writings of J. Gresham Machen* (ed. John H. Skilton; Nutley, NJ: Presbyterian and Reformed, 1977), 22 – 26.

10. J. B. Lightfoot, *The Epistle of St. Paul to the Galatians with Introductions, Notes and Dissertations* (repr.; Grand Rapids: Zondervan, 1957), 4, 12 – 15.

11. So Bruce, *Galatians*, 8.

12. Ibid., 44.

13. Cf. Bruce, *Galatians*, 11 – 13; Hemer, *The Book of Acts in the Setting of Hellenistic History*, 280 – 85; Witherington, *Galatians*, 6.

14. Cf. Bruce, *Galatians*, 15; Riesner, *Paul's Early Period*, 289.

15. So J. Louis Martyn, *Galatians: A New Translation with Introduction and Commentary* (AB; New York: Doubleday, 1997), 16.

to refer to the north Galatians. But what other term would Paul use to describe the Galatians, for those living in the province of Galatia came from many ethnic groups?[16] Only the term "Galatians" would be sufficiently comprehensive to include all of them.

(5) If Galatians were addressed to churches founded on Paul's first journey, Paul would not have written in Gal 1:21, "Then I came into the regions of Syria and Cilicia," but instead, "Then I came to Syria and Cilicia and on to you." But this argument fails to recognize that 1:21 does not refer to the first missionary journey but to the interval between Acts 9:30 and 11:25.[17]

(6) One of the strongest arguments for supporting the north Galatian view is the relationship between Acts 15 and Gal 2:1 – 10. Those who support the north Galatian view argue that Acts 15 refers to the same events as Gal 2:1 – 10. On this view, the chronology of Paul's visits to Jerusalem was as follows: Acts 9:26 – 28 = Gal 1:18; Acts 11:30/12:25 is skipped in Galatians; Acts 15:1 – 35 = Gal 2:1 – 10.[18] The arguments for identifying Acts 15 with Gal 2:1 – 10 are quite impressive. First, the subject in both texts is the same: circumcision. Second, the place is the same: Jerusalem. Third, the people are the same: James, Peter, John, Paul, and Barnabas. Fourth, the decision was the same: circumcision was not required.[19] The response to this argument will be explained below.

(7) Paul in Gal 2:1 – 10 presents himself as the leader of the missionary team of Paul and Barnabas. But if Gal 2:1 – 10 is equivalent to Acts 11:27 – 30/12:25 (as most who support the south Galatian view claim),[20] Gal 2:1 – 10 occurred before the first missionary journey. Luke consistently lists Barnabas before Paul at the beginning of the first missionary journey (Acts 13), suggesting that Barnabas was the leader at the time. But if the south Galatian view is true, Barnabas should be listed before Paul in Gal 2:1 – 10. So, the mention of Paul first in 2:1 – 10 suggests that he is the leader of the team, and therefore (say those who support the north Galatian theory) 2:1 – 10 reflects the events after the first missionary journey.[21] But this argument also fails to convince, for Paul naturally relays the visit to Jerusalem from his perspective, and this accounts for Paul's prominence.

(8) According to Gal 2:1 – 10, Paul is recognized as an apostle. But if the south Galatian theory is true, on what basis was Paul acknowleged to be an apostle? For, according to the usual south Galatian theory, Paul had not yet been on the first missionary journey. If anybody would be called the apostle to the Gentiles, it would

16. So Bruce, *Galatians*, 16; Riesner, *Paul's Early Period*, 287 – 88; Hemer, *The Book of Acts in the Setting of Hellenistic History*, 290 – 305.

17. So Bruce, *Galatians*, 15 – 16; Schnabel, *Paul and the Early Church*, 1077.

18. Other scholars argue that the account in Acts is not historically reliable. For a response to this view, see Hemer,

The Book of Acts in the Setting of Hellenistic History.

19. See Lightfoot, *Galatians*, 123 – 28.

20. See Longenecker, *Galatians*, lxxvii – lxxxiii; Schnabel, *Paul and the Early Church*, 987 – 1003.

21. So Robert H. Stein, "The Relationship of Galatians 2:1 – 10 and Acts 15:1 – 35: Two Neglected Arguments," *JETS* 17 (1974): 241 – 42.

seem to be Barnabas, not Paul — if the south Galatian theory is true. Those who support the north Galatian destination point out that it makes perfect sense for Paul to be acknowledged as an apostle if the first missionary journey had already taken place (Acts 13 – 14), and Gal 2:1 – 10 is equivalent with Acts 15:1 – 35.[22] But those who support the south Galatian theory have a good counter-argument. An acknowledgment of Paul's apostleship in Gal 2:1 – 10 is scarcely surprising, for he had presumably done missionary work during his years at Tarsus. In any case, he and Barnabas had ministered together among the Gentiles in Antioch for a year, and Paul could have been identified as an apostle on the basis of his work in that city.

(9) The similarity of subject matter in Galatians and Romans suggests, according to the north Galatian hypothesis, that they were written at roughly the same time. If Galatians were written to north Galatia, it may have been written between AD 50 – 57 and Romans is probably between AD 55 – 57, and hence the two are rather close together. But trying to assign a date based on the similarity of subject matter is precarious. Indeed, there are some significant differences between Galatians and Romans as well, and hence trying to assign a date based on the similarity of content is arbitrary. Furthermore, even if the letters do overlap significantly in content, we can hardly establish a date on such a basis. We could just as easily argue that Paul's theology on the law remained stable over the ten to fifteen years that he wrote letters.[23] We all know people whose views have not changed in any significant way over twenty to thirty years, and there is no reason to doubt that Paul may have been the same, especially when we consider that he had served as a missionary for fifteen years or more before the writing of his first canonical letters.

(10) Most scholars throughout church history have argued that the letter was written to north Galatia. This argument loses much of its force when we realize that south Galatia was separated from north Galatia and incorporated into Pisida in AD 74. Those who lived in subsequent generations did not realize, therefore, that south and north Galatia were part of the same province when Paul wrote the letter, and this may explain the dominance of the north Galatian hypothesis historically.

Support for the South Galatian Theory

Though I favor a south Galatian destination, the supporting arguments are not clear enough to remove doubt. We are reminded here of the tentativeness of the historical task since we lack enough information to reach a secure conclusion. If Paul wrote to south Galatia, then he likely wrote to the churches evangelized in Acts 13 – 14. Here I focus on some of the remaining arguments supporting a south Galatian destination, but I note some of the weaknesses of these arguments as well.

---

22. Ibid., 242.

23. Indeed, it has been argued that Paul developed his view of the law extraordinarily early. See Seyoon Kim, _The Origin of Paul's Gospel_ (Grand Rapids: Eerdmans, 1982).

(1) Some support a south Galatian hypothesis by noting that Paul wrote in Greek, which was not the mother tongue of the north Galatians. This argument is not a strong one, however, since Greek was the lingua franca of the Greco-Roman world. In what other language would Paul write to communicate with all the Galatians?

(2) Paul normally uses Roman imperial terms when there are geographical references, and hence "Galatians" would refer to the Roman province of Galatians. Again, this observation, though true, does not prove a south Galatian destination, for the north Galatians were part of the province of Galatia as well.

(3) Acts 16:6 and 18:23 do not refer to the the founding of churches in north Galatia. Though it is possible that Paul established churches in north Galatia, we have no firm evidence that he did so, whereas we know that he planted churches in south Galatia. Furthermore, the reference to Phrygia may simply designate the ethnic area of Galatia that Paul traveled through according to Acts 16:6. This may be supported by the one article for both the Galatian and Phrygian region. In any case, both Acts 16:6 and 18:23 may not even report on any travels of Paul to north Galatia.

(4) Paul refers to Barnabas as if the Galatians know him personally (Gal 2:13), and we know that Barnabas traveled with Paul when the south Galatian churches were evangelized (Acts 13 – 14).[24] There is no indication, however, that Barnabas ever evangelized the north Galatian churches, and hence the personal reference seems superfluous. We must admit, however, that the argument presented here is from silence. Paul refers to Barnabas in 1 Cor 9:6, and yet we have no evidence that Barnabas visited Corinth either. Barnabas may have visited north Galatia, though there is no record of the visit.

(5) Acts 20:4 implies that the south Galatian churches contributed to the collection for the poor saints in Jerusalem (cf. Rom 15:25 – 28; 1 Cor 16:1 – 4; 2 Cor 8:1 – 9:15), but nothing is said about a contribution from north Galatian churches. It must be noted, however, that this also is an argument from silence, for it is possible that north Galatian churches participated, though it remains unmentioned.

(6) Some have pointed to the enthusiastic reception given to Paul at Lystra, where he was acclaimed as the Greek god Hermes (Acts 14:11 – 18), and the statement that Paul was received as an angel of God in Gal 4:14. This is surely a thin reed on which to base an argument, for in the same text in Acts the people turned against Paul and stoned him! Further, it seems difficult to believe that Paul recalled the people hailing him as the Greek god Hermes when he said that the Galatians received him as a messenger of Christ. According to Acts, Paul and Barnabas were dismayed that they were celebrated as gods. The response of the people was not identified as a mark of spiritual insight.

(7) Paul concentrated on main cities and trade routes in his evangelism, and north Galatia was far from these main trade routes. Once again, this argument is

---

24. So Riesner, *Paul's Early Period*, 288 – 89.

not compelling, for Derbe and Lystra were not large cities, and Ancyra and Pessinus in north Galatia were some of the most important cities in Asia Minor.

(8) The Jewish-Christian missionaries who opposed Paul would more likely have traveled to the nearer south Galatia than to the more inaccessible north Galatia.[25] Once again, however, it is difficult to determine what zealous proponents of a theology antagonistic to Paul would do. We must admit that they may have been motivated to travel to north Galatia as well.

(9) Peter's lapse in Galatians (2:11 – 14), it is claimed, makes better sense before the apostolic council of Acts 15 (AD 48),[26] for some think it unlikely that Peter would fail after matters were ironed out at the apostolic council in Acts 15. This argument has some merit, for it seems less likely that James would send messengers to the church after the council in Acts 15. Still, history is full of surprises, and debates have ensued after formal agreements many times in history. Further, we know that human beings are prone to fail and to live hypocritically even after formal agreements have been reached.

(10) The failure to mention Timothy may indicate that the letter was written before the events of Acts 16, since Timothy is mentioned in every letter except Ephesians and Titus, but this again is an argument from silence.

(11) One of the stronger arguments for the south Galatian hypothesis is that Paul would not have neglected any of his visits to Jerusalem in Gal 1 – 2 since he wanted to demonstrate his independence from the Jerusalem apostles. If he omitted any visit, he would open himself to the charge that he failed to mention an occasion when he was influenced by the apostles in Jerusalem. If this is the case, then Gal 1:18 is equivalent to Acts 9:26 – 28, and Gal 2:1 – 10 is matched by the visit to Jerusalem in Acts 11:27 – 30 and 12:25.[27] On this reading the visit to Jerusalem recorded in Acts 15:1 – 35 is omitted in Galatians because the council described in Acts had not yet occurred when Paul wrote the letter.[28]

We have seen above that the most serious objection to this scenario is that Acts 15:1 – 35 and Gal 2:1 – 10 are remarkably similar. At both meetings circumcision was debated and the apostles decided that circumcision was not required for the salvation of Gentiles. Is it possible that the same meeting took place on two occasions? Many defenders of the south Galatian hypothesis respond by emphasizing that the meeting in Gal 2:1 – 10 was of a different nature than the council in Acts 15. The former was a private meeting, while the latter was a public discussion.[29] In Acts we see official deliberations and a formal decision, while in Galatians we see

---

25. Ibid., 286 – 87.

26. Schnabel, *Paul and the Early Church*, 1077. Hemer dates it in early 49 (*The Book of Acts in the Setting of Hellenistic History*, 269).

27. In support of this view, see Schnabel, *Paul and the Early Church*, 987 – 92.

28. So Bauckham, "James, Peter, and the Gentiles," 136.

29. Bauckham points out that the private agreement of Gal 2:1 – 10 flamed into controversy again ("James, Peter, and the Gentiles," 136 – 37). He says, "Agreements reached on such controversial issues — in many spheres of life — frequently have to be negotiated again and again" (136). And,

an informal and private judgment.[30] Further, south Galatian proponents claim that Paul would have informed the Galatians what the council decided if the events of Acts 15 had already transpired. Why would he refrain from informing the Galatians about such an important decision?

We must admit that untangling the knots in deciphering the destination of Galatians is difficult.[31] It is possible that Acts 15:1 – 35 and Gal 2:1 – 10 record the same meeting from different perspectives. The debate over circumcision may have lasted several days or even longer, and we see a compressed summary of what occurred in both Galatians and Acts. Further, it is possible to hold to a south Galatian destination and to argue that Gal 2:1 – 10 and Acts 15:1 – 35 refer to the same event.[32] One could argue that Paul did not record every visit to Jerusalem but only included visits in which he had significant private discussions with the apostles. Hence, he may not have included visits to Jerusalem where he was with the apostles in public settings. We notice in Galatians that he limits his description to a private meeting with Peter and James (Gal 1:18 – 19), and to his private meeting with James, John, and Peter (2:1 – 10).

Further, it is possible that the substance of what was decided by the apostolic council of Acts 15 is summarized in a compressed form in Gal 2:6. Paul does not cite an official document but declares that nothing was added to his gospel, showing that the apostles agreed with his theology. Paul, in other words, relayed the events of the meeting from his perspective.

Identifying the recipients of Galatians is important for Pauline chronology and history, but it is not determinative for the interpretation of the letter, and the meaning of the letter does not change dramatically whether we opt for a north or south Galatian hypothesis. On balance, it seems that a south Galatian hypothesis is preferable, and I incline towards Gal 2:1 – 10 = Acts 11:27 – 30/12:25, though, as noted, a south Galatian destination is possible with Gal 2:1 – 10 = Acts 15:1 – 35 as well.

"It is inherently very likely that such a crucially important and unavoidably controversial issue as the status of Gentile believers and their relationship with Jewish believers should have sparked recurrent controversy over many years and have been discussed on various occasions" (137). We know from history that the Council at Nicea did not end controversy over the Trinity and that issues that were "resolved" at Nicea continued to be debated for many years afterwards.

30. So Hemer, *The Book of Acts in the Setting of Hellenistic*

History, 247 – 51. But Lightfoot suggests there was a private meeting on the same occasion before the public conference (*Galatians*, 103).

31. So also Matera, who leans slightly toward the recipients being in southern Galatia. See Frank J. Matera, *Galatians* (Sacra Pagina; Collegeville, MN: Liturgical Press, 1992), 19 – 24.

32. So Moisés Silva, *Interpreting Galatians: Explorations in Exegetical Method* (Grand Rapids: Baker, 2001), 129 – 38.

In Depth: The Cities on Paul's First Missionary Journey

If Galatians is addressed to south Galatia, then it was written to the cities Paul and Barnabas visited on their first missionary journey: Pisidian Antioch, Iconium, Lystra, and Derbe (Acts 13 – 14). Hence, it is of some value to consider briefly what we know about these cities, though the interpretation of the letter does not depend on such information since the south Galatian destination is only a hypothesis. Mitchell suggests that Paul visited Pisidian Antioch after his time in Cyprus because Sergius Paulus, the proconsul in Cyprus (Acts 13:5 – 12), was originally from Pisidian Antioch.[33]

Pisidian Antioch, a Phrygian city, "was founded under Seleukos I Nikator (358 – 281 BC) or Antiochus II (261 – 245 BC) by Greek colonists from Magnesia on the Maeander."[34] Under Augustus it became a Roman military colony in 25 BC. The Phrygian moon god, Men, had a temple there, which attracted people from far away.[35] The city was located strategically and was on the east-west road called the Via Sebaste. Roman influence in the city was significant, and the city "was supposed to be a new Rome at the border of Phrygia and Pisidia."[36] It is not surprising to learn, then, that a temple was built for Augustus.[37] Mitchell says the city "had emerged as the principal Roman colony in the Greek East."[38] The city was blessed with some wealth, and there was a significant Jewish presence in the city. Therefore, the city was complex in that Jewish, Roman, and local cultures coexisted and intermixed.

Iconium was an old city (inhabited ethnically by Phrygians); its existence is traced back to at least the third millennium BC.[39] The city was located strategically since important roads crossed through the city. Roman influence was apparent in the city, and the city prospered as a place for trade and agriculture. It was probably particularly favored by the emperor Claudius (AD 41 – 54). A temple for Zeus existed in the city, and we find evidence for the imperial cult there as well.[40]

Augustus founded Lystra in 25 BC. It was a military colony like Pisidian

---

33. Mitchell, *The Rise of the Church*, 6 – 7.

34. Schnabel, *Paul and the Early Church*, 1098. On Pisidian Antioch, see also Stephen Mitchell, "Antioch of Pisidia," *ABD*, 1:264 – 65; Schnabel, *Paul and the Early Church*, 1098 – 103; B. van Elderen, "Antioch (Pisidian)," *ISBE*, 1:142.

35. Mitchell, *The Rise of the Church*, 24 – 25.

36. Schnabel, *Paul and the Early Church*, 1100.

37. Stephen Mitchell, *The Celts and the Impact of Roman Rule* (vol. 1 of *Anatolia: Land, Men, and God in Asia Minor*; Oxford: Clarendon, 1993), 104. Mitchell says the imperial

cult must have been a competitor with Christianity, but he acknowledges that hard evidence is scarce (*The Rise of the Church*, 10).

38. Mitchell, *The Rise of the Church*, 7.

39. On Iconium, see Schnabel, *Paul and the Early Church*, 1111; W. Ward Gasque, "Iconium," *ABD*, 3:357 – 58; D. A. Hagner, "Iconium," *ISBE*, 2:792 – 93.

40. For the latter, see Mitchell, *The Celts and the Impact of Roman Rule*, 104.

Antioch and was also placed at a strategic crossroads.[41] A temple for Zeus existed in the city, and there are indications that the city was wealthy; hence the view that the city was of little consequence should be rejected. Even though Lystra was Lycaonian, the Roman presence affected the city's character.

Derbe, a Lycaonian city, was likewise on the road that linked it with the more important Iconium.[42] The city apparently had a special relationship with the emperor Claudius.

Date

The date of the letter is determined by the question of the recipients. If one espouses a south Galatian hypothesis and places the letter before the events of Acts 15:1–35, then Galatians is the earliest Pauline letter and may have been written ca. AD 48.[43] We have just noted, however, that one could support the south Galatian hypothesis and correlate Acts 15:1–35 with Gal 2:1–10. In such a scenario, the letter could be dated in the early 50s. If one accepts the north Galatian hypothesis, the letter was likely written somewhere between AD 50–57.

Situation

Mirror-Reading

The situation of Galatians must be discerned from the letter itself. But how can we reconstruct what occurred when we are separated from the letter by two thousand years and are limited to Paul's comments and perspective in detecting the historical circumstances that called forth the letter? It has often been said that we suffer from the disadvantage of hearing only one end of a phone conversation. There was no need for Paul to explain the situation thoroughly to the Galatians since they were obviously acquainted firsthand with what was happening. Therefore, we have to engage in mirror reading to determine the historical background of the letter. The method for such a mirror reading has been set forth in an important essay by John Barclay, with which I am in significant agreement.[44] I will begin by

---

41. On Lystra, see Schnabel, *Paul and the Early Church*, 1112–13; D. S. Potter, "Lystra," *ABD*, 4:426–27; D. A. Hagner, "Lystra, *ISBE*, 3:192–93.

42. John D. Wineland, "Derbe," *ABD*, 2:144–45; Schnabel, *Paul and the Early Church*, 1121.

43. Cf. here Bruce, *Galatians*, 43–56; Schnabel, *Paul and the Early Church*, 1077; Hemer, *The Book of Acts in the Setting of Hellenistic History*, 269. Witherington dates it in AD

49 (*Galatians*, 8–20). Still, an earlier date is not required on a south Galatian hypothesis. Matera thinks the letter was written to south Galatia and dates it in the mid-50s (*Galatians*, 26).

44. John M. G. Barclay, "Mirror-Reading a Polemical Letter: Galatians as a Test-Case," *JSNT* 31 (1987): 73–93 (see also his *Obeying the Truth: Paul's Ethics in Galatians* [Minneapolis: Fortress, 1988], 36–74). On mirror reading, see also Silva, *Interpreting Galatians*, 104–8. For an approach that is less

identifying the major elements Barclay sets forth for identifying opponents in a polemical letter.[45]

Barclay begins by warning us against overconfidence in reconstructing the situation when opponents are named since we are limited to Paul's perspective on the situation. In addition, he observes that the Pauline response is often polemical and emotional, and hence Paul inevitably distorts the character of the opponents. Barclay rightly perceives that Paul does not present the opponents as they would have presented themselves. Paul does not attempt to write an objective report of the theology of the agitators.

Still, it does not follow that Paul's portrayal is inaccurate. For if he had miscommunicated the views of his opponents, it is less likely that his response to them would have been effective in convincing the Galatians. Furthermore, it is certainly the case that no one has a "God's-eye" view of any situation. But if we accept the Scriptures as the Word of God, Paul's words in the letter represent the divine perspective of the opponents and cannot be restricted merely to his human judgment. In other words, Paul's view is privileged. Obviously, those who put the Scriptures on the same level as any other human writing will not accept this judgment.

Barclay warns of common pitfalls in historical reconstruction. For example, J. B. Tyson relies on Paul's defensive statements alone to establish the identity of the opponents, but in doing so he omits Gal 3 – 4.[46] Ignoring one third of the letter, which also contains the heart of Paul's argument, is methodologically flawed.[47] We must also beware of overinterpretation. Some scholars read too much into 5:11 in reconstructing the nature of the opposition.

In the same way, we must be cautious about identifying the slogans and catchphrases of the opponents and using such to sketch in the nature of the opposition. As Barclay observes, such a process demands that (1) Paul knew the "exact vocabulary" of the opponents; (2) Paul reused this vocabulary ironically or polemically; (3) we are able to discern where Paul borrows the vocabulary of opponents; and (4) we are able to reconstruct the meaning originally intended by the opponents.[48] Too often in the history of scholarship scholars have placed too much confidence in their ability to read between the lines.

I would suggest the following principles for discerning the opponents.[49] (1) We should begin by looking for explicit statements about the opponents or explicit statements about the recipients of the letter. (2) The frequency and clarity of Paul's

convincing, see B. H. Brinsmead, *Galatians — Dialogical Response to Opponents* (SBLDS 65; Chico, CA: Scholars Press, 1982), 23 – 33. Barclay notes the weaknesses in Brinsmead's reconstruction ("Mirror-Reading," 82 – 83).

45. For another helpful analysis of the opponents, see In-Gyu Hong, *The Law in Galatians* (JSNTSup 81; Sheffield: Sheffield Academic Press, 1993), 97 – 120.

46. J. B. Tyson, "Paul's Opponents in Galatia," *NovT* 10 (1968): 241 – 54.

47. Cf. also Hong, *Law in Galatians*, 102.

48. Barclay, "Mirror-Reading," 82.

49. Barclay lists seven principles (ibid., 85). I am citing the exact wording of some of his principles here.

statements may indicate the nature of the opposition. (3) The simplest and clearest reconstruction should be preferred, unless there is compelling evidence for more complexity. (4) The reconstruction that is the most plausible historically should be accepted. There is no fail-safe way to determine the nature of opponents, for interpretation of historical documents remains an art. Still, Barclay's principles are an important advance in deciphering the historical plausibility of various reconstructions.

The Evidence in Galatians

In applying these principles to Galatians, we begin with explicit features in the text. In 1:6–9 we learn that certain men were harassing the Galatians and preaching another gospel. It seems most likely from Paul's language (though certainty is impossible) that they have come from outside the congregation. In 4:17 Paul indicts the motives of these preachers. They evince zeal for the Galatians, but their zeal is stained by impure motives, for they actually want the Galatians to be entranced with them. Since the opponents are distinguished here from the Galatians themselves, it seems probable that they were not originally part of the congregation.

Galatians 5:7–10 refers to someone who has hindered the Galatians from obeying the truth and has persuaded them to adopt an alien course. Paul pronounces judgment on this one who is troubling the Galatians. Here "the one disturbing" (ὁ ταράσσων) the Galatians is described with a singular construction, whereas in 1:7 the plural is used ("some who are disturbing," οἱ ταράσσοντες). Indeed, the opponents are also spoken of in terms of a plurality in 5:12 and 6:12–13. It may be the case that the leader of the opposition is in view in 5:10. Alternatively, and more plausibly in my judgment, the singular is generic in 5:10, and if this is the case, Paul is not singling out any particular opponent in 5:10. Once again, however, the evidence suggests that outsiders attempted to persuade the Galatians of a new route; they cut in on the Galatians in the midst of the race (5:7).

Perhaps the most important piece of evidence about the opponents emerges in 6:12–13, for they insisted that the Galatians receive circumcision. The content of the remainder of the letter certainly suggests that the adversaries demanded circumcision, but 6:12–13 removes any doubt. Of course, the importance of circumcision in the letter is also suggested by 5:12, for there Paul sarcastically recommends that the agitators emasculate themselves.

After looking at the explicit features, the next step is to ask what can be justly inferred about the opponents from Galatians. (1) From Gal 1–2 we can infer that the opponents disputed the legitimacy of Paul's apostleship.[50] Some scholars have questioned this conclusion, maintaining that Paul presents himself autobiographically

---

50. Rightly Barclay, "Mirror-Reading," 87. In contrast to Hong, who thinks that their comments about Paul may have been "incidental statements" (*Law in Galatians*, 106).

as an exemplar of the truth of the gospel.[51] Still, the defensive tone of the text suggests that the legitimacy of his apostleship was under attack. The first verse of the letter has a defensive tone unlike the openings in all the other Pauline letters. Further, Paul explicitly defends himself against the charge of pleasing people (1:10), and this defensive statement is tied to the ensuing narrative argument (see the exegesis below). In addition, Paul's insistence that he had limited contact with the apostles and the Judean churches (1:18–24) suggests that he was defending the independence of his gospel. Finally, the account in 2:1–10 seems to indicate that the opponents claimed that the apostles in Jerusalem did not agree with the Pauline gospel.[52]

(2) Paul recounts the incident in Jerusalem when the false brothers tried to impose circumcision on Titus (2:3). He does so because what happened in Jerusalem mirrors the situation in Galatia. Paul does not specifically note that the opponents in Galatia demanded circumcision at this juncture in the letter, but he forecasts here the central issue in the debate.

(3) The long scriptural argument in Gal 3–4 is probably a response to the exegesis of the opponents. Indeed, the adversaries likely appealed to Abraham as a model, stressing that only those who were circumcised were the true sons of Abraham.[53] They likely threatened those who refused to be circumcised with an eschatological curse, saying that circumcision was the means to avoid the curse pronounced on Abraham's opponents (Gen 12:3).[54] As Hong says, the opponents likely saw salvation-historical continuity between the covenant with Abraham and the Sinai covenant, seeing the latter as "the fulfillment and completion" of the former.[55]

(4) The Galatians were observing various days of the calendar (4:9–10) at the behest of the opponents.[56]

(5) Finally, Paul warns the Galatians in no uncertain terms about the consequences of receiving circumcision (5:2–6). There is little doubt that the Galatians considered circumcision at the impetus of the agitators (6:12–13). Paul's extensive argument relative to the law suggests that the opponents contended for law observance in general.[57]

I am identifying the next category as probable. It seems likely that the opponents

---

51. Cf. G. Lyons, *Pauline Autobiography: Toward a New Understanding* (Atlanta: Scholars, 1985).

52. Esler is probably right in saying that 4:25 indicates that the opponents had a relationship with Jerusalem (*Galatians*, 74). Barclay says they likely appealed to Jerusalem even if they did not come from there (*Obeying the Truth*, 43, 59). Cf. also Bruce, *Galatians*, 25–26; Matera, *Galatians*, 10.

53. Barclay, *Obeying the Truth*, 53, 66; Hong, *Law in Galatians*, 105; Martyn, "Law-Observant," 357; B. C. Lategan, "The Argumentative Situation of Galatians," in *The Galatians Debate: Contemporary Issues in Rhetorical and Historical Interpretation* (ed. Mark D. Nanos; Peabody, MA: Hendrickson, 2002), 387–89.

54. Cf. Todd A. Wilson, *The Curse of the Law and the Crisis in Galatia: Reassessing the Purpose of Galatians* (WUNT 2/225. Tübingen: Mohr Siebeck, 2007), 53–62. Perhaps the Galatians also feared the curse because of cultural and religious factors they experienced growing up in Anatolia (ibid., 72–79).

55. Hong, *Law in Galatians*, 107, 113. The citation comes from 113.

56. Martyn's summary of the teaching of the opponents is probably close to what they taught ("A Law-Observant Mission to Gentiles," in *The Galatians Debate* [ed. Mark D. Nanos; Peabody, MA: Hendrickson, 2002]).

57. So Barclay, "Mirror-Reading," 86–87; cf. Bruce, *Galatians*, 28–29.

had links with the Jerusalem church, and they charged Paul with distorting the gospel proclaimed by the apostles in Jerusalem.[58] Further, they probably appealed specifically to Gen 17:9 – 14, where circumcision is required perpetually for both Abraham and his descendants.[59] Hearing those verses would likely have exerted a great impact on the Galatians. Perhaps the adversaries also appealed to the Sarah and Hagar narratives to buttress their position (cf. 4:21 – 30), arguing that the true sons of Abraham and Isaac were all circumcised.

The next category represents what is possible but much less certain. Perhaps the Galatians told Paul, according to 5:11, that Paul circumcised his converts in some circumstances. We lack enough information to determine precisely what they said. Perhaps they insisted that Paul proclaimed the necessity of circumcision in other contexts but failed to mention it in Galatia in order to please his hearers.[60]

Finally, some matters are conceivable and possible, but we must not base much upon them in determining the situation in Galatia. For instance, the adversaries may have spoken of completing Paul's work (3:3). And they may have used the expression "law of Christ" (6:2), though it is just as conceivable that Paul coined the phrase to counter the agitators. They may have also used the word "elements" (στοιχεῖα, 4:3, 9), though this seems difficult to confirm since the term is not prominent in the letter.

In Depth: What is the Role of the Empire in Galatians?

Justin Hardin has argued recently that Paul in Galatians responds to the imperial cult, which was threatening the churches.[61] Recently many scholars have argued that the imperial cult played a significant role in NT writings. N. T. Wright,

---

58. This view goes back at least to Saint Chrysostom, *Homilies on Galatians, Ephesians, Philippians, Colossians, Thessalonians, Timothy, Titus, and Philemon* (vol. 13 of *Nicene and Post-Nicene Fathers of the Christian Church*, 2nd series; ed. Philip Schaff; Grand Rapids: Eerdmans, 1983), 13:2. Martyn says that even if the opponents did not come from Jerusalem, they believed that they represented Jerusalem (Martyn, "Law-Observant," 357). Cf. also here Barclay, "Mirror-Reading," 88. F. C. Baur argues that the opponents were genuine representatives of the apostles in Jerusalem (*Paul the Apostle of Jesus Christ: His Life and Works, His Epistles and Teachings*, 2 volumes in one [repr.; Peabody, MA: Hendrickson, 2003], 1:124 – 33). But such a reading is at variance with what Paul actually says in Galatians, and it is more likely that the Judaizers were aligned with Pharisaic Jews (like the Pharisees of Acts 15:2, 5), and these Pharisaic Jews did not agree with the pillars. See here Lightfoot, *Galatians*, 350 (though Lightfoot suggests that the pillars did

not take quick action against the Judaizers). Cf. also Bruce, *Galatians*, 25 – 26; E. P. Sanders, *Paul, the Law, and the Jewish People* (Philadelphia: Fortress, 1983), 18; Hong, *Law in Galatians*, 118 – 20; Vincent M. Smiles, *The Gospel and the Law in Galatia: Paul's Response to Jewish-Christian Separatism and the Threat of Galatian Apostasy* (Collegeville, MN: Liturgical Press, 1998), 4 – 5, 7 – 8.

59. Paul's relatively long scriptural argument in Gal 3 – 4 renders improbable Harvey's view that the Galatian opponents were interested in observance of the law but were unconcerned about theology. See A. E. Harvey, "The Opposition to Paul," in *The Galatians Debate: Contemporary Issues in Rhetorical and Historical Interpretation* (ed. Mark D. Nanos; Peabody, MA: Hendrickson, 2002), 321 – 33.

60. See the exegesis of 5:11 in the commentary.

61. Justin K. Hardin, *Galatians and the Imperial Cult: A Critical Analysis of the First-Century Social Context of Paul's Letter* (WUNT 2/237; Tübingen: Mohr Siebeck, 2008).

for instance, has defended this view in what he calls the fresh perspective on Paul.[62] But the most significant defense of this perspective relative to Galatians comes from Hardin, who documents the role of the cult in the Julio-Claudian period and in Galatia, arguing from 6:12–13 that the opponents commended circumcision so that they could secure status for themselves and avoid persecution.[63] The newly converted Gentiles in Galatia would have ceased participating in the imperial cult since they were now devoted to Christ. The opponents tried to persuade them to accept circumcision so that they could align themselves with the Jewish community and deter those (esp. local Jewish residents) who tried to bring "civic reprisals" on the newly converted Gentiles.[64] Bruce Winter advances a similar thesis, arguing that by receiving circumcision the newly converted Gentiles would become part of Judaism, which was exempt from the requirements of the imperial cult.[65]

Hardin's monograph represents careful scholarship, but ultimately the view advanced by him and Winter must be judged to be unsuccessful. There is no clear evidence in Galatians that the imperial cult was an issue. If it played such a major role in the letter, it is astonishing that Paul never mentions it. Indeed, whether the imperial cult played such a major role in the Pauline writings is questionable. Both Denny Burk and Seyoon Kim have rightly argued that the evidence supporting a polemic against the imperial cult in the Pauline letters is unpersuasive.[66] Even if the imperial cult was a major factor in other Pauline writings (which is doubtful, as Burk and Kim show) or in other places in the NT, it plays no role in Galatians. Hardin rightly sees that the agitators were concerned about their status in 6:12–13, but it hardly follows from this that they worried about the requirements of the imperial cult. Paul does not breathe a word about governing authorities in Galatians (in contrast to Rom 13:1–7 and Titus. 3:1).[67]

One of the fundamental pieces of evidence Hardin adduces to support his thesis is his interpretation of 6:13. He wrongly says that the word "keep" (φυλάσσω) in 6:13 does not refer to keeping the Mosaic law but guarding the law "from being disregarded among the Gentiles."[68] Hardin is clearly mistaken here,

62. N. T. Wright, *Paul in Fresh Perspective* (Minneapolis: Fortress, 2005), 59–79.

63. Hardin, *Galatians and the Imperial Cult*, 24–81.

64. Ibid., 85–115 (esp. 115).

65. Bruce W. Winter, *Seek the Welfare of the City: Christians as Benefactors and Citizens* (Grand Rapids: Eerdmans, 1994), 123–43. The most significant difference between Hardin and Winter is that Hardin argues that the Jews in Galatia were still required to conform to the imperial cult.

66. Denny Burk, "Is Paul's Gospel Counterimperial? Evaluating the Prospects of the 'Fresh Perspective' for Evangelical Theology," *JETS* 51 (2008): 309–37; Seyoon Kim, *Christ and Caesar: The Gospel and the Roman Empire in the Writings of Paul and Luke* (Grand Rapids: Eerdmans, 2008), 3–71.

67. Even though Witherington sees some role for the imperial cult in Galatia, he rightly raises problems with seeing it in the background of 6:12 (*Galatians*, 448).

68. Hardin, *Galatians and the Imperial Cult*, 89.

for "keep" (φυλάσσω) is often used for observing what God has commanded in both the OT and the NT (cf. Gen 26:5; Exod 13:10; 15:26; 20:6; 31:13 – 14; Lev 18:4 – 5, 26; Matt 19:20; Acts 7:53; Rom 2:26, etc.), and that is the most natural meaning here. Hardin also argues that the observance of days, etc. (Gal 4:10) refers more naturally to the imperial festal calendar instead of the Jewish calendar.[69] His argument is again unpersuasive. Contrary to Hardin, the Jewish context of the remainder of the letter should influence how we read 4:10.[70] It makes the most sense to read the feasts and festivals here in terms of the OT law, especially since there is no hint in 4:10 that the feasts mentioned relate to the emperor.[71]

We need to be careful about overinterpreting what Paul says here relating to the observance of days. It is possible that the recipients of this letter had begun observing Sabbaths and new moons and intended to observe in the future Jubilee years and feasts like Passover and Pentecost.[72] We lack a precise understanding of what Paul says in 4:10, but such imprecision does not rule out a Jewish background. Hardin says that elsewhere Paul conforms to and follows the Jewish calendar, and hence he probably does not speak against such here.[73] Such a criticism misses the mark. Paul is not opposed to observing the OT law for cultural reasons (Acts 16:3; 1 Cor 9:19 – 23), but it goes beyond the evidence to say that Paul faithfully observed the Jewish calendar after he became a believer.

Moreover, Paul clearly argues in Galatians that believers are no longer under the Sinai covenant and the OT law (see the commentary). Hence, it fits nicely with the rest of Galatians if Paul, in 4:10, rebukes the Galatians for observing the OT calendar. In other words, Paul opposes the imposition of OT feasts and days in Galatians because they are required for salvation. To sum up, we can salute the stimulating work of Winter and Hardin, but their attempt to establish an imperial context for Galatians fails to convince.

In Depth: Is the Background in Galatians Paganism?

Troy Martin argues a rather idiosyncratic position relative to Galatians scholarship, contending that the Galatians were not tempted to return to Judaism but were actually falling back into their former paganism (4:8 – 11). When they learned from the opponents that circumcision was a requirement of the gospel,

---

69. Ibid., 116 – 47.

70. Ibid., 110.

71. Even if the feasts are pagan, there is no reason to see a reference to the imperial cult.

72. Against Hardin, *Galatians and the Imperial Cult*, 120.

73. Ibid., 120 – 21.

they relapsed into paganism since they would not want to submit to circumcision. Paul, therefore, tries to convince the Galatians that circumcision is not a requirement of his gospel.[74] Despite the creativity and ingenuity of Martin's reading, it is most plausible to conclude that the lengthy discussion on the law and circumcision is best explained by the Galatians' temptation to submit to such.

Martin can sustain his thesis only by claiming that Paul turns from the Galatians to address the opponents in 4:21 – 5:6.[75] Such a reading seems like a counsel of desperation. We have no other example in a Pauline letter where part of the letter is addressed directly to opponents. Most important, we lack clear evidence that Paul redirects his words to a distinct group in the congregation beginning with 4:21. Since Paul almost certainly addresses the whole congregation in 4:21 and asks them why they want to be under the law, Martin's claim that they desired to return to their pagan past should be rejected.

Similarly, since Paul threatens the readers with eschatological judgment if they submit to circumcision (5:2 – 4), it is clear that the Galatians were not tempted to return to their pagan past.[76] Paul, of course, identifies the Galatians' desire to observe the Mosaic law with returning to paganism (4:8 – 9), but this is quite different from saying that the Galatians were literally returning to their pagan ways.

Susan Elliott also supports a pagan connection, though in a different sense from Martin. Elliott claims that Paul opposed circumcision because of his "antipathy toward the cult of the Mother of the God and an abhorrence of self-castration."[77] Such a reading should be rejected since Paul says nothing whatsoever about any pagan cult in the letter, and circumcision is regularly linked with the observance of the Mosaic law in Galatians (2:3 – 5; 5:2 – 4; 6:12 – 13). Moreover, Hardin argues that 5:12 does not even refer to castration "but to severing the male member" per Deut 23:2 LXX.[78] Hardin rightly says that Elliott's link between "circumcision and the practice of castration among the *galli* is far fetched."[79]

Hardin also trenchantly observes that Elliott's choice of the Mother goddess as the background is speculative and too limiting since there were many deities in Anatolia during this time;[80] she needs to provide firmer evidence from

74. Troy Martin, "Apostasy to Paganism: The Rhetorical Stasis of the Galatian Controversy," in *The Galatians Debate: Contemporary Issues in Rhetorical and Historical Interpretation* (ed. Mark D. Nanos; Peabody, MA: Hendrickson, 2002), 73 – 94.

75. Ibid., 84 – 91.

76. Against Martin, see A. Andrew Das, *Paul and the Jews* (Peabody, MA: Hendrickson, 2003), 19 n. 4.

77. Susan Elliott, *Cutting Too Close for Comfort: Paul's Letter to the Galatians in Its Anatolian Cultic Context* (JSNTSup 248; London: T&T Clark, 2003), 13.

78. See Hardin, *Galatians and the Imperial Cult*, 7.

79. Ibid.

80. Ibid., 8.

Galatians itself for the Mother goddess theory. Hardin rightly says, "What she describes as the 'Anatolian zone' at the time of Paul's letter is actually evidence taken from over six centuries in scattered places across rural Anatolia (often outside of Galatia!) and then somehow all gathered together as evidence for the cities in which the Galatian readers lived in the middle of the first century."[81]

Clinton Arnold argues more generally that inscriptions from Anatolia help explain why the Galatians would have been disposed to accept the message of the opponents. The demand to keep certain cultic requirements and to do good works reflects their previous experience with local deities.[82] Arnold's reading usefully connects us to the cultural and religious background of the readers, and he may be correct in detecting one of the motivations that inspired the Galatians to consider Judaism. But once again we must beware of using evidence outside the letter to detect the situation in Galatians, particularly since Galatians itself focuses on Jewish practices and the OT law and makes no direct reference to pagan practices. As Hardin remarks, concern for divine forgiveness does not necessarily point to Anatolian concerns since the forgiveness offered in Christ is a staple of early Christian preaching. Furthermore, cursing in Galatians is naturally interpreted in light of the OT (Deut 27 – 29).[83]

In addition, Hardin notes that the inscriptions cited by Arnold stem mainly from western Anatolia in the second century AD, not from Galatia in the first century AD. And it is possible that Paul's readers "may have been Greeks or Romans and thus largely disconnected with these uniquely 'unhellenistic' ... religious practices."[84] What Paul does argue in Galatians is that the desire of the readers to submit to the OT law is comparable to returning to paganism (4:8 – 11).

Identity of the Opponents in Galatians

Many different theories have been proposed regarding the identity of the opponents. Here the various options are surveyed and critiqued. I will argue that the traditional view that the opponents were Judaizers is still the most satisfying. Readers may wonder why it is helpful to consider viewpoints that are ultimately rejected. It is important to see that almost every theory has some evidence in its favor, so even if a particular view is ultimately judged to be incorrect, it helps us sharpen our view as to what the letter teaches about the situation if we consider carefully other theories. Indeed, the theory we end up favoring must integrate all of the evidence in

---

81. Ibid.

82. Clinton E. Arnold, "'I Am Astonished That You Are So Quickly Turning Away!' (Gal 1.6): Paul and Anatolian Folk

Belief," *NTS* 51 (2005): 429 – 49.

83. Hardin, *Galatians and the Imperial Cult*, 9 n. 47.

84. Ibid., 10.

a more satisfactory manner than other solutions that are suggested. We gain greater confidence that the identity of the adversaries is accurate if it stands up against other proposed solutions.

Two-Front Theory of Opponents

It is not surprising that various views have emerged on the identity of the opponents since the evidence in the letter is ambiguous. Traditionally, the Galatian adversaries have been identified as Judaizers. In using the term *Judaizers* in this commentary, I mean that the opponents wanted to observe a Jewish way of life, a way of life prescribed in the OT law.[85] Lütgert challenged the conventional view in 1919 and argued that there were two different opponents in Galatia, i.e., Judaizers and libertines.[86] In 1929 Ropes adopted Lütgert's thesis, although he modified it at some points.[87] Crownfield recognized the major defect of the two-front hypothesis: the letter itself gives no indication that two different parties are being addressed.[88] However, Crownfield himself was influenced by the work of Lütgert and Ropes, for he abandoned the idea that the adversaries were Judaizers; instead, he suggested that the opponents in Galatia should be described as syncretists.[89] In other words, the agitators in Galatia, according to Crownfield, were Judaizers and pneumatics at the same time. Crownfield's essay did not affect NT scholarship greatly, for it lacked the detailed documentation necessary to establish his thesis.

---

85. For a brief historical survey, see F. F. Bruce, "Galatian Problems 3: The 'Other' Gospel," *BJRL* 53 (1970): 253–57. Martyn objects to the term because of the universal vision and mission of the opponents. See Martyn, "A Law-Observant Mission," 353–54. Martyn uses the neutral term "Teachers" to describe the opponents (*Galatians,* 117). Against Martyn, it seems appropriate to designate the opponents as Judaizers since they desired the Galatians to live in accord with the Jewish law (cf. Gal 2:14). Hays objects that the term "Judaizers" is unfitting because the dispute is among Jews, and the term refers to the adoption of Jewish practices and hence can only apply to Gentiles. See Richard B. Hays, *The Letter to the Galatians: Introduction, Commentary, and Reflections,* in *The New Interpreter's Bible,* vol. 11 (Nashville: Abingdon, 2000), 185. Hays rightly sees that the opponents are Jewish, but Paul writes to Gentiles who are tempted to conform to the Jewish way of life in accord with the law, and so using the terms "Judaizers" or "Judaizing" seems appropriate. Nanos argues that the term does not fit with Gentiles who seek to live as Jews and that the term has negative connotations. Mark D. Nanos, "The Inter- and Intra-Jewish Political Context of Paul's Letter to the Galatians," in *The Galatians Debate: Contemporary Issues in*

Rhetorical and Historical Interpretation (ed. Mark D. Nanos; Peabody, MA: Hendrickson, 2002), 400. Against Nanos, Paul himself uses the term in 2:14 in referring to the view of his opponents (even though he addresses Peter). I am not claiming here that the term "Judaizer" only has one meaning in every context, for Shaye J. D. Cohen rightly notes that the meaning of the term "Judaizer" must be discerned in context. See his "Crossing the Boundary and Becoming a Jew," *HTR* 82 (1989): 33.

86. Wilhelm Lütgert, *Gesetz und Geist: Eine Untersuchung zur Vorgeschichte des Galaterbriefes* (Gütersloh: Bertelsmann, 1919).

87. J. H. Ropes, *The Singular Problem of the Epistle to the Galatians* (Cambridge: Harvard Univ. Press, 1929). Ropes was heavily dependent on Lütgert, but his monograph received more attention because his essay was more carefully organized than Lütgert's.

88. Frederic R. Crownfield, "The Singular Problem of the Dual Galatians," *JBL* 64 (1945): 491–500.

89. Crownfield, 492; cf. Robert Jewett, "The Agitators and the Galatian Congregation," in *The Galatians Debate: Contemporary Issues in Rhetorical and Historical Interpretation* (ed. Mark D. Nanos; Peabody, MA: Hendrickson, 2002), 335.

Gnostic and Libertine Views of the Opponents

Schmithals took Crownfield's view a step further, although he was apparently unaware of Crownfield's article.[90] Schmithals maintained that the opponents in Galatia were a single group — Jewish Christian gnostics. The problem in Galatia was not one of nomism (i.e., devotion to the law) according to Schmithals; instead, the opponents were radical libertines (cf. 5:13 – 6:10). Schmithals used many of the same verses that Lütgert and Ropes employed (esp. 5:13 – 6:10) to show that the adversaries were libertines. Schmithals's reconstruction of the historical situation, however, is superior to theirs because he does not resort to the doubtful theory of two different opponents. Moreover, Schmithals's essay is superior to Crownfield's because it contains the detailed documentation lacking in the latter.

Before we evaluate Schmithals's hypothesis, we will examine Jewett's view of the opponents. Even though Jewett claims that the adversaries were Judaizers, his theory is in some respects similar to Schmithals's view.[91] Jewett maintains that the agitators were from Jerusalem and centered on the Mosaic law. They insisted that the Galatians had to be circumcised in order to attain perfection (3:3), but their motivation for advocating circumcision was to escape persecution from Zealot radicals who were terrorizing Palestine. These Zealot revolutionaries were hostile to Christian Jews who tolerated fellowship with uncircumcised Gentiles. Because of this persecution from Zealots, the agitators were provoked to visit Gentile congregations and campaign for the necessity of circumcision (6:12 – 13).[92]

The theory that the agitators were motivated by persecution to evangelize the Gentiles is foundational for Jewett's theory. Their desire to avoid persecution accounts for the antagonists not informing the Galatians that acceptance of circumcision and observance of the cultic calendar necessitated obedience to the whole law (5:3). The opponents, according to Jewett, would probably communicate the ramifications of circumcision later. This rather cavalier approach by the Judaizers

---

90. Walter Schmithals, *Paul and the Gnostics* (trans. John E. Steely; Nashville: Abingdon, 1972), 13 – 64.

91. Jewett, "Agitators," 334 – 47; cf. also Ralph P. Martin, *New Testament Foundations: A Guide for Christian Students* (rev. ed.; vol. 2, *The Acts, the Letters, the Apocalypse*; Grand Rapids: Eerdmans, 1978), 152 – 56.

92. Persecution was certainly involved, but Esler rightly notes that evidence is lacking to substantiate a Zealot hypothesis (*Galatians*, 74). More plausibly, John Muddiman argues that the persecution came from "a fanatical Diaspora brand of Pharisaism" ("Anatomy of Galatians," in *Crossing the Boundaries* [ed. Stanley E. Porter, Paul Joyce, and David E. Orton; BI 58; Leiden: Brill, 1994], 260), which was devoted to the law, and these Jewish opponents struck fear into the hearts

of the Jewish Christian agitators, who tried to persuade the Galatians to be circumcised. Muddiman remarks, "The root cause of the trouble in Galatia, then, is not those who advocate compromise from fear of persecution; it is those outside the Church who are willing to use all the means of synagogue discipline, namely, detention, fines, beatings and excommunication, to pressurize Jewish Christians into demanding that their fellow, non-Jewish, Christians accept circumcision" (261). But Muddiman wrongly rejects the idea that the opponents were also theologically motivated (264 – 70). The Pauline argument from the Scriptures (esp. 2:15 – 5:1) makes better sense if he counters an opposing theological view. Furthermore, the Pharisaism in view here probably came from Jerusalem itself.

led to an important result: the Galatian congregation understood these Jewish laws in terms of their Hellenism.[93] The Judaizers tolerated the Galatians' misunderstanding of the import of receiving circumcison, for they were interested in quick results to pacify the Zealots. Indeed, Jewett thinks that in the case of the calendar (4:10) the adversaries intentionally fused Jewish conceptions of the calendar with Hellenistic notions.

Significant differences exist between the interpretations proposed by Schmithals and Jewett. Jewett doubts the validity of describing the opponents as gnostics. Unlike Schmithals, he thinks the adversaries were focused on the Mosaic law. What happened is that the Galatians interpreted the Torah in libertinist terms because of their Hellenistic worldview. But despite the differences between Schmithals and Jewett, there are two significant similarities in the two interpretations. First, both scholars perceive that libertinism is the major problem in the congregation, and they depend on 5:13 – 6:10 to establish this point. Second, both argue that in the last analysis there was no problem with devotion to the law in Galatians. Circumcision was not observed as the initial step in obedience to the whole law. Instead, circumcision was submitted to because it liberated one from the demands of the rest of the law.

Both of these interpretations are stimulating and provocative, but they are ultimately not convincing because they do not adequately explain all the evidence from Galatians. Before we evaluate the points where Schmithals and Jewett agree, we will examine the arguments that are unique to Schmithals.

Evaluation of Arguments Supporting a Gnostic or Libertine View of the Opponents

Schmithals claims that Gal 3 – 4 contains typical Pauline theology that is unrelated to the Galatian situation. But it is methodologically flawed to select the parts of Galatians that harmonize with his theory as genuine evidence on the identity of the opponents (Gal 1 – 2; 5 – 6), while rejecting the section in Galatians that controverts his theory (Gal 3 – 4).[94] Schmithals does not offer a convincing reason for excluding Gal 3 – 4.[95] Indeed, it is improbable that the heart of the letter would be irrelevant to the position articulated by the adversaries.[96]

Schmithals also misunderstands Paul's defense in Gal 1 – 2. He thinks the adversaries could not be Judaizers because Paul's dependence on the apostles would be applauded and not criticized if the antagonists were Judaizers. But this reading of the evidence overlooks an important element of the antagonists' criticism of Paul.

93. Jewett, "Agitators," 342 – 43.

94. R. McL. Wilson, "Gnostics—in Galatia?" *Studia Evangelica* (Berlin: Akademie, 1968), 4:358 – 367, esp. 365 – 66.

95. Rightly Barclay, *Obeying the Truth*, 17 – 18.

96. Barclay also cogently remarks against Schmithals that "there is extremely little evidence for a positive evaluation of literal circumcision in any Gnostic movement" (*Obeying the Truth*, 48).

The criticism made by Paul's opponents was not only that Paul was *dependent* on Jerusalem but also that he had *distorted* the original message that he had received from the apostles.[97] Galatians 2:1 – 10 suggests that the opponents would not have objected to Paul's gospel if they thought it agreed with the kerygma of the pillars. The charge against Paul was twofold: (1) He was dependent on the pillars (1:10 – 24); and (2) he had distorted their message (2:1 – 10). To the charge that his gospel was derived from others, Paul replied that this was false — his gospel came through a revelation of Jesus Christ (1:11 – 17). To the charge that his gospel was a distortion of the original kerygma as proclaimed by the apostles in Jerusalem, Paul replied that this was patently false because the apostles recognized and ratified the authenticity of his gospel (2:1 – 10). Thus, Paul undercuts both the charge of dependence on the apostles and the charge of distorting the gospel.[98]

Against Jewett, it seems unlikely that Judaizers would agree to a Hellenistic libertine interpretation of their view of the Mosaic law. Jewett maintains that they would accept this fusion of nomism with Hellenism because they wanted quick results and would do anything to pacify the Zealots. But it is hard to see how such a profound distortion of Judaism would satisfy the Zealots.[99] Indeed, according to Jewett, the Galatians used circumcision and the cultic calendar as a cover for libertinism.[100] Although Jewett criticizes Schmithals because the latter argues that the antagonists denied the validity of the law, it is difficult to see how Jewett's view really differs from Schmithals on this matter,[101] for the Judaizers allowed and even encouraged their message to be interpreted syncretistically. Thus, the Galatians were not legalists, according to Jewett, but antinomians. They did not, according to Jewett, observe circumcision and the calendar as the first step in obeying the rest of the Torah. They did not observe these rites because they were devoted to the Torah.[102] Instead, the Galatians observed these rites because the latter were the first steps to perfection in a Hellenistic sense.

Jewett's understanding of the rationale for circumcision is practically indistinguishable from Schmithals's view that circumcision was observed in order to transcend fleshly experience. In both cases circumcision did not imply an obligation to obey the rest of the OT law. Instead, the rite symbolized one's perfection and liberation from law. This accounts for the libertinism in the congregation. Schmithals

---

97. See here Silva, *Interpreting Galatians,* 153 – 54; Timothy George, *Galatians* (NAC; Nashville: Broadman & Holman, 1994), 107; Smiles, *Gospel and Law in Galatia,* 34 – 35. Fee fails to see this latter point and hence misunderstands Paul's self-defense (*Galatians,* 38).

98. See John Bligh, *Galatians: A Discussion of St. Paul's Epistle* (London: St. Paul Publications, 1969), 33.

99. Further, it is unclear that the persecution truly stemmed from Zealots (see Barclay, "Mirror-Reading," 88).

100. It is also difficult to see how the opponents would

make inroads in Galatia along Hellenistic lines, for there is no evidence that Hellenists thought circumcision would lead to perfection. Rightly Terence L. Donaldson, "'The Gospel That I Proclaim among the Gentiles' (Gal 2:2): Universalistic or Israel-Centred?" in *Gospel in Paul: Studies on Corinthians, and Galatians and Romans for Richard N. Longenecker* (ed. L. Ann Jervis and Peter Richardson; JSNTSup 108; Sheffield: Sheffield Academic Press, 1994), 179.

101. See Jewett, "Agitators," 335.

102. Ibid., 347.

and Jewett are in agreement, then, on a major point. The problem in the Galatian *congregation* was not nomism (observance of the law) but libertinism.[103]

Contrary to Jewett and Schmithals, the evidence of the letter supports the notion that the central problem was devotion to the Mosaic Torah and not libertinism.[104] The argument that stretches from 2:16 – 5:12 is intended to prove that the Gentiles do not need to obey the law in order to be justified.[105] Paul argues that faith rather than the Torah makes one a child of Abraham (3:6 – 9); that the attempt to be justified by law places one under a curse (3:10 – 14); that the covenant of law was subsequent to the Abrahamic covenant of promise (3:15 – 20); that the Sinai covenant is abrogated now that the Messiah has come (3:15 – 4:11); that a return to the law spells a return to slavery (4:21 – 5:1); and that those desiring to be justified by the law cut themselves off from grace and Christ (5:2 – 12).

Galatians 3 – 5 is misinterpreted if one understands circumcision as the only part of the law the Galatians were attempting to obey. Indeed, Paul never even mentions circumcision in Gal 3 – 4. He attacks the problem of trying to be justified by the works of the law as a whole (3:10).[106] The Galatians were seeking to obey the law

---

103. One must separate Jewett's understanding of the opponents and how the congregation understood the opponents: the opponents were Judaizers according to Jewett, but the congregation interpreted the Judaizers' nomism to support a libertine lifestyle.

104. Brinsmead (*Galatians,* 29 – 30) criticizes Jewett for making such a sharp distinction between the opponents and the Galatian congregation. He emphasizes that the letter to the Galatians is a unity and that the identity of the false teachers should be ascertained from the genre of the letter. Galatians, according to Brinsmead, should be classified as a dialogical letter in which Paul is responding to his opponents. He argues that the opponents in Galatia are from "apocalyptic and sectarian Judaism, especially circles associated with Qumran" (195). Thus, there are many similarities between Galatians, Colossians, and 2 Corinthians (123 – 24, 142 – 43, 160 – 61, 196 – 200). The opponents are characterized by "nomistic enthusiasm" (198) and have a gnosticizing tinge. Brinsmead (*Galatians,* 20, 196 – 200) seems to be influenced by Georgi, arguing that both the opponents and the congregation encouraged law-obedience and circumcision in terms of "mystery initiation" (145). Circumcision, then, was viewed as a kind of mystery rite. It is seen "as the climactic sacrament, the completion of the mystery in which the Galatians became novices by baptism" (159). Brinsmead differs from Jewett in arguing that the congregation and the opponents should not be separated. However, his claim that the nature of the heresy relates to union with cosmic powers, that circumcision is an initiation rite into this mystery, and that the problem was some kind of enthusiastic nomism is remarkably

similar to Jewett's analysis. Of course, Brinsmead's reconstruction is more detailed than Jewett's because the former devotes a whole book to the topic. But the general orientation of the two scholars is the same. The criticisms raised against Jewett's theory basically apply to Brinsmead as well. Paul's persistent preoccupation with the Torah is not adequately explained by a theory that emphasizes the enthusiastic nature of nomism in Galatia. Reading Galatians in gnostic terms is unpersuasive, and what Brinsmead says about Galatians actually seems closer to the letter to the Colossians, though the identity of the opposition in Colossae is disputed as well. Finally, the idea that circumcision is related to mystery initiation is unconvincing. Barclay remarks, "But at no point do our sources give any clear indication of circumcision being interpreted as a rite of initiation into a mystery-cult" (*Obeying the Truth,* 49). Further, Brinsmead's method in discerning the teaching of the opponents is rife with errors (see Barclay, "Mirror-Reading," 82 – 83).

105. Augustine argued that Paul wrote Galatians to convince them that they were not under the law. See Eric Plumer, *Augustine's Commentary on Galatians: Introduction, Text, Translation, and Notes* (Oxford: Oxford Univ. Press, 2003), 125.

106. What is being said here is controversial of course, and the interpretation proposed here will be defended in the commentary proper. Bruce Longenecker rightly says that the opponents wanted the Galatians to keep the whole law and did not restrict themselves to circumcision. See Bruce W. Longenecker, *The Triumph of Abraham's God: The Transformation of Identity in Galatians* (Nashville: Abingdon, 1998), 30 – 33. See also Das, *Paul and the Jews,* 19 – 21.

because they wanted to be justified by the law (3:11).[107] Therefore, Paul argues not only that circumcision is abrogated but that the Mosaic law as a whole is annulled. The acceptance of circumcision represented the conviction that one desired to obey the whole law so that one could be justified by doing the law (5:3 – 4).[108]

Another indication that the Galatians were law-centered is 4:21. Here Paul characterizes the congregation as those "who want to be under the law." It is difficult to see how this description can apply to libertines. Such a statement is consistent, however, with the notion that the Galatians were trying to be justified by the law, that they were seeking to obey the whole Torah. It should be noted that Paul is not limiting himself to part of the law in 4:21. He speaks of wanting to be under the law in general terms, and thus it is most natural to conclude that the entire law is in view.[109]

If the primary problem in the congregation was libertinism, as Jewett and Schmithals claim, it is difficult to see why Paul devotes so much attention to the validity of the Torah for believers. Paul's emphasis on the believer's freedom from the reign of the law (Gal 3:15 – 4:7; 4:21 – 5:1) seems inapposite if the congregation were antinomian.[110] Schmithals appeals, as we have seen, to 5:3 and 6:13 to support the thesis that the antagonists did not intend to obey the whole law, but his interpretation of these verses is not compelling.[111] What Paul stresses here is the *obligation* (ὀφειλέτης) to obey the whole law in order to attain justification (cf. 5:3 – 4). In other words, Paul tries to wean them from law-oriented religion by indicating the impossibility of keeping the law.[112]

Jewett maintains that 4:8 – 11 supports the notion that the congregation synthesized the adversaries' nomism with their Hellenism because the feasts observed were Hellenistic and not Jewish.[113] The use of the word "elements" (στοιχεῖα) in 4:9 is also used to buttress his point, for the "elements" probably represent, according to Jewett, the astral spirits of the Hellenistic world. Against Jewett, it is more likely that the feasts described in 4:10 are Jewish.[114] Bruce claims the feasts are probably

---

107. Contra Nanos, "Political Context," 404 – 5.

108. Against Gordon, who says the focus is on inclusion of Gentiles instead of justification by faith. See T. David Gordon, "The Problem at Galatia," *Int* 41 (1987): 32 – 43.

109. Drane says: "But 4:21, both grammatically and logically seems to prove beyond the slightest possibility of doubt that the Galatian heretics were promoting the observance of the Law as well as circumcision." John W. Drane, *Paul, Libertine or Legalist? A Study in the Theology of the Major Pauline Letters* (London: SPCK, 1975), 47.

110. It is helpful to compare Galatians to Corinthians on this point, for there is evidence of antinomianism in Corinth. Thus, Paul does not emphasize Christian freedom as much as he does Christian responsibility. The case seems to be the opposite in Galatians.

111. Here Jewett rightly disagrees with Schmithals ("Agitators," 337 – 38).

112. Rightly Hong, *Law in Galatians*, 107.

113. Jewett, "Agitators," 343. For the view that the days and feasts listed here refer to the imperial cult, see the In Depth discussion of the imperial cult, above.

114. Donald Guthrie, *Galatians* (NCB; Grand Rapids: Eerdmans, 1973), 117; John J. Gunther, *St. Paul's Opponents and Their Background: A Study of Apocalyptic and Jewish Sectarian Teachings* (NovTSup 35; Leiden: Brill, 1973), 89; Ernest De Witt Burton, *A Critical and Exegetical Commentary on the Epistle to the Galatians* (ICC; Edinburgh: T&T Clark, 1920), 232 – 33; Lightfoot, *Galatians*, 171.

Jewish because the words used in 4:10 are similar to those found in Gen 1:14.[115] The emphasis on the desire to obey the OT law in Galatians (4:21) suggests that the Jewish calendar is in view. The fact that the "elements" (στοιχεῖα) are mentioned does not necessarily demonstrate that pagan feasts are being described, for the word may not refer to astral spirits.[116] Even if "elements" refers to astral spirits, Paul does not accuse the Galatians of literally reverting to the worship of astral deities. Instead, he compares their devotion to the OT law and circumcision to paganism. Paul's remarks in 4:8 – 11 do not indicate that the agitators were libertines. Instead, they reveal that Paul classed law-centered religion with idolatry.

The Role of Galatians 5:13 – 6:10 in the Letter

Those who argue that the Galatians were libertine make the methodological error of focusing on 5:13 – 6:10 to determine the life situation of the letter. It is a mistake to make a paraenetic section of a letter the primary datum in reconstructing the Galatians' life situation.[117] Paraenesis may be given to warn a congregation of a problem that is not yet present in the community so that Paul warns the congregation of a possible error instead of an actual one.[118]

The conventional view that the opponents were Judaizers has a good explanation for why 5:13 – 6:10 is placed at the end of the letter.[119] After Paul has emphasized so strongly the believer's freedom from the law, he wants to guard against a possible perversion or distortion of his message. Thus, he warns the congregation that freedom should not be used as an excuse for license. True freedom expresses itself in love and obedience to the Spirit.[120]

Furthermore, there are other explanations of 5:13 – 6:10 that are consistent with the opponents being Judaizers.[121] Betz suggests that Paul included 5:13 – 6:10 because the Galatians fell into libertinism before the Judaizers arrived.[122] According

---

115. Bruce, *Galatians*, 205 – 6. Betz thinks the observances mentioned cannot be confined to Judaism alone. He argues that the Galatians were not actually observing the days; rather, the indicative is used here to describe typical religious behavior. Just as they were about to fall prey to circumcision, so too they were about to participate in such observances. Betz, *Galatians*, 216 – 17. But this explanation seems artificial.

116. See the commentary under 4:3.

117. W. G. Doty, *Letters in Primitive Christianity* (Philadelphia: Fortress, 1973), 37 – 38; Morna Hooker, "Were There False Teachers in Colossae?" in *Christ and Spirit in the New Testament: Studies in Honour of Charles Francis Digby Moule* (ed. Barnabas Lindars and Stephen S. Smalley; Cambridge: Cambridge Univ. Press, 1973), 317.

118. For a typology of various views regarding the role of this section, see Wilson, *Curse of the Law*, 4 – 16.

119. Bernard O. Ukwuegbu argues that Gal 5:13 – 6:10

functions to give a separate social identity to the Christian community in Galatia. "Paraenesis, Identity-Defining Norms, or Both? Galatians 5:13 – 6:10 in the Light of Social Identity Theory," *CBQ* 70 (2008): 538 – 59. But social identity is only the consequence of, not the motivation for, the Pauline ethic.

120. This has been a common view in the history of scholarship. So e.g., W. G. Kümmel, *Introduction to the New Testament* (trans. A. J. Mattill Jr.; Nashville: Abingdon, 1975), 301; Franz Mussner, *Der Galaterbrief* (5th ed.; HTKNT; Freiburg: Herder, 1988), 364.

121. For a survey of the various explanations of the role of 5:13 – 6:10, see Barclay, *Obeying the Truth*, 9 – 23.

122. Betz, *Galatians*, 8 – 9. See also Martyn, "Law-Observant," 358; Lategan, "Argumentative Situation of Galatians," 395.

to Betz, Paul's gospel of freedom was distorted and misunderstood by the Galatians as a release from all law, and thus libertinism flourished. The congregation was ethically confused when the Judaizers arrived, and this confusion provided the Judaizers with a platform for their views. The Judaizers responded by saying that one could only overcome the flesh by obeying the law of God. Living in the Spirit alone is the path to license.[123] Barclay's view is not too far from Betz's, though he thinks the section is not written to counter libertinism but moral confusion.[124]

The views of Betz and Barclay are possible, but they suffer from at least two problems.[125] First, 5:21 indicates that Paul had already warned the Galatians about the danger of yielding to the flesh when he first visited them.[126] The arrival of the Judaizers did not propel Paul to offer advice regarding the flesh for the first time. Second, the emphasis of the letter is not on keeping the law but on freedom from the law, and hence it is questionable whether the Galatians had fallen into libertinism.

Borgen offers another possibility.[127] He argues that 5:13 – 6:10 is not directed against a possible libertinistic misunderstanding of Paul's message. Rather, the opponents viewed themselves as those who supplemented the Pauline gospel. Thus, in his view, we should understand 5:13 – 6:10 as the conclusion of the Pauline polemic against the opponents.[128] Paul demonstrates that he and the opponents are not allies, rejecting the idea that their teaching supplemented his gospel. Circumcision and life under the law do not restrain the flesh. The only way to overcome the flesh, according to Paul, is to live by the Spirit. Borgen may be partially correct in his analysis, but it is unlikely that the opponents presented themselves as Paul's allies.[129] Galatians 1 – 2, as I argue in that section, indicates that they sharply criticized Paul.

To sum up, the notion that the opponents were Judaizers is the most adequate explanation of all the evidence in Galatians. The presence of 5:13 – 6:10 in the letter does not show that the opponents were libertines. Most likely, Paul included this section to warn the Galatians against distorting his gospel.

Identifying the Opponents More Precisely

The theory that the opponents were Judaizers does not solve all the problems regarding the opponents. Munck points to the present participle in 6:13, "those who

---

123. As Leander E. Keck says, "They thought that by circumcision they were dealing effectively with the power of the flesh." See *Paul and His Letters* (Philadelphia: Fortress, 1979), 87.

124. Barclay, *Obeying the Truth*, 71 – 72, 106, 218.

125. Hong, *Law in Galatians*, 115 – 16.

126. Cf. Wilson, *Curse of the Law*, 14 – 15.

127. Peder Borgen, "Observations on the Theme 'Paul and Philo': Paul's Preaching of Circumcision in Galatia (Gal 5:11) and Debates on Circumcision in Philo," in *The Pauline Literature and Theology* (ed. S. Pederson; Göttingen: Vanden-

hoeck & Ruprecht, 1980), 92 – 102. For a similar view on the function of 5:13 – 6:10, see also George Howard, *Paul: Crisis in Galatia: A Study in Christian Theology* (2nd ed.; SNTSMS 35; Cambridge: Cambridge Univ. Press, 1990), 11 – 14.

128. There is certainly an element of truth in this view. See the argument of Matera that Gal 5 – 6 represents the culmination of Paul's argument. Frank J. Matera, "The Culmination of Paul's Argument to the Galatians: Gal 5.1 – 6.17," *JSNT* 32 (1988): 79 – 91.

129. Barclay, *Obeying the Truth*, 50.

are circumcised" (οἱ περιτεμνόμενοι), to determine the identity of the opponents.[130] The present tense must be taken seriously, according to Munck, and thus it refers to those who had been recently circumcised. Obviously, they could not be Jews since Jews were circumcised from birth; therefore, the opponents were Gentiles. Munck's interpretation is unlikely. It is improbable that a circumcision campaign would be started by Gentiles. Of course, one cannot rule out the possibility absolutely, but Munck bases his view on the tense of the participle. We should not press the tense of the participle in determining when the opponents were circumcised.[131]

It is probable, then, that the opponents were Jews, but it is more difficult to determine the precise identity of the Judaizers.[132] Tyson thinks that the adversaries were Christian Jews native to Galatia.[133] Ellis sees similarities between the opponents and the "Hebrews." The Hebrews are identified as Jews who took a strict attitude toward the Jerusalem cultus and may be similar to the Essenes.[134] Bruce argues the traditional position that the Judaizers were Pharisaic Jews.[135] The opponents, on this view, were similar to the Pharisaic Jews in Acts (15:1, 5), who insisted on the necessity of circumcision for salvation.[136]

Tyson's conviction that the opponents were native to Galatia is possible, but we lack enough information to determine the origin of the agitators. In any case, the cumulative evidence suggests they came from outside the congregation. (1) Paul often distinguishes between the opponents and the congregation, referring to the former in the third person and the latter with the second person (1:6 – 7; 4:17; 5:7 – 12; 6:12 – 13).[137] (2) Galatians 2 may suggest that the opponents were linked to

---

130. Johannes Munck, *Paul and the Salvation of Mankind* (trans. F. Clarke; Atlanta: John Knox, 1959), 89. So also Harvey, "Opposition to Paul," 326.

131. See here the commentary on 6:13. Kümmel says that Munck's view is "highly unlikely" (*Introduction*, 300).

132. Hurd argues the far-fetched notion that the opponents were the brothers from 2 Corinthians 8 – 9 who helped with the collection. See John C. Hurd, "Reflections concerning Paul's 'Opponents' in Galatia," in *Paul and His Opponents* (ed. Stanley E. Porter; Pauline Studies 2; Leiden: Brill, 2005), 129 – 48.

133. Tyson, "Opponents in Galatia," 248 – 52.

134. E. Earle Ellis, *Prophecy and Hermeneutic in Early Christianity: New Testament Essays* (Grand Rapids: Eerdmans, 1978), 110 – 12 and 118 – 22; cf. Gunther, *St. Paul's Opponents*, 315 – 17.

135. Bruce, *Galatians*, 30. Graham Stanton notes that in Justin's *Dialogue with Trypho*, Trypho's views show that some Jews believed that one entered into the covenant on the basis of obedience to the law (*Dialogue* 8:4; 10:3 – 4; 19:3). "The Law of Moses and the Law of Christ: Galatians 3:1 – 6:2," in *Paul and the Mosaic Law* (ed. James D. G. Dunn; Tübingen: Mohr Siebeck, 1996), 104 – 6.

136. Howard (*Paul: Crisis in Galatia*, 2 – 45) agrees that

the opponents were Judaizers from Jerusalem, but he moves in a different direction from Bruce. The problem, according to Howard, is that the Judaizers mistakenly thought that Paul also preached a circumcision gospel. They believed that Paul's message derived from the apostles at Jerusalem. Thus, the opponents were not enemies of Paul. In fact, they thought Paul left out the requirement of circumcision only because of his illness (4:13), so in good faith they completed his work. Paul's defense in Gal 1 – 2 is not a reaction to charges against the validity of his apostleship; rather, it explains why the apostles knew nothing of the content of his gospel. The issue, then, was simply a lack of information on the opponents' part; they had no particular animus against Paul. Against Howard, it is difficult to believe that Paul's defense of himself would be so pronounced if the adversaries simply lacked information. Paul's polemical language throughout the letter suggests that the issue was not merely a misunderstanding and lack of information. For critiques of Howard's view, see A. J. M. Wedderburn, "Review: *Paul: Crisis in Galatia*," *SJT* 33 (1980): 375 – 85; David Garland, "Review: *Paul: Crisis in Galatia*," *RevExp* 78 (1981): 114 – 15.

137. Cf. Bruce, *Galatians*, 19; Barclay, *Obeying the Truth*, 43; Martyn, "Law-Observant," 352; cf. Ellis, *Prophecy and Hermeneutic*, 110; Hong, *Law in Galatians*, 117.

Jerusalem in some way.[138] (3) Drane is probably right when he indicates that it is unlikely that people Paul converted would turn against him so quickly. It is more likely that agitators from the outside came in and confused the young believers.[139]

It is more difficult to decide between the views of Bruce and Ellis in terms of the identity of the adversaries. In either case the opponents would be ritually strict Jews from Palestine. At the end of the day, Bruce's interpretation seems more convincing because Ellis suggests that the opponents in Galatia may be similar in some respects to those in Colossae.[140] But the adversaries in Galatia were probably similar to the Pharisees in requiring circumcision (Acts 15:1, 5), while the Colossian heresy seems to stem from Jewish circles that did not emphasize circumcision to the same degree. Hence, in this commentary I will identify the opponents as Judaizers, and it seems probable that they were similar to the Pharisaic opponents in Acts 15.[141]

It is also probable that the adversaries considered themselves to be Christians.[142] They desired to correct the gospel that Paul proclaimed to the Galatians (1:6 – 9; 3:3) and to avoid persecution for the cross (6:12).[143] One key to the Judaizers' theology was their view of Paul; if Paul's gospel was apostolic, then the Judaizers were mistaken. From Paul's defense in Gal 1 – 2, we can infer that the Judaizers must have charged him with three things. (1) His gospel was derived from human beings, i.e., from the apostles. (2) Paul had *distorted* this gospel when he came to Galatia (1:6 – 10), since he did not insist on the validity of the law and the necessity of circumcision. (3) Paul's motive in doing this was to cater to Gentile wishes (1:1 – 10); he so wanted success that he abandoned the gospel that he usually preached (5:11).

The Viewpoint and Theology of the Opponents

The core of the opponents' theology was their focus on circumcision and the law. They probably claimed that circumcision was necessary for inclusion in the people of God.[144] After all, only those who were circumcised would receive the promises made to Abraham.[145] They almost certainly appealed to Gen 17, where

---

138. So Lightfoot, *Galatians*, 29; Kümmel, *Introduction*, 301.

139. Drane, *Libertine or Legalist*, 88.

140. So Ellis, *Prophecy and Hermeneutic*, 110 – 25.

141. Riches notes that most commentators until the nineteenth century believed that there was a polemic against Judaism in Galatians. See, *Galatians through the Centuries*, 67.

142. This is the majority view. See, e.g., Esler, *Galatians*, 73; Martyn, "Law-Observant," 353, 356 – 57; Barclay, "Mirror-Reading," 86. In defense of the idea that they were non-Christian Jews, see Nikolaus Walter, "Paul and the Opponents of the Christ-Gospel in Galatia," in *The Galatians Debate: Contemporary Issues in Rhetorical and Historical Interpretation* (ed. Mark D. Nanos; Peabody, MA: Hendrickson, 2002), 362 – 66. See the In Depth discussion below.

143. Jewett, "Agitators," 337.

144. Some have argued that circumcision was not always required to become a proselyte to Judaism. See, e.g., Neil McEleney, "Conversion, Circumcision, and the Law," *NTS* 20 (1974): 319 – 41. Perhaps a few Jews downgraded the necessity of circumcision for proselytes, but the mainstream view was that circumcision was required for proselytes. Rightly John Nolland, "Uncircumcised Proselytes?" *JSJ* 12 (1981): 173 – 94; Cohen, "Crossing the Boundary," 26 – 30.

145. Therefore, against Garlington, circumcision was not required to "maintain their covenant status." Don Garlington, *An Exposition of Galatians: A Reading from the New Perspective* (3rd ed.; Eugene, OR: Wipf and Stock, 2007), 11. Rather, the Judaizers contended that circumcision was required to *enter* the covenant.

circumcision is required as the sign of the covenant.[146] Circumcision was not restricted to the Jews; any foreigner who desired to attach himself to the congregation of Yahweh must be circumcised (Gen 17:11 – 13). Indeed, circumcision is linked with Abraham becoming the father of many nations (Gen 17:5 – 6). They likely reasoned that if a Gentile wanted to be a "son of Abraham," then he must receive the covenantal sign.

Furthermore, the necessity of circumcision was not temporally limited because God calls the covenant "everlasting" (Gen 17:7, 8, 13). The Judaizers may have emphasized their point with the words of Gen 17:14. "Any uncircumcised male, who has not been circumcised in the flesh, will be cut off from his people; he has broken my covenant." The Judaizers likely argued that circumcision was necessary for salvation. Burton sums up their opinion aptly: "Their whole argument may very well have been based on the seventeenth chapter of Genesis, and if their premise that the Old Testament is of permanent authority be granted, there is no escape from their conclusion."[147] Their interpretation of circumcision was inextricably related with their perspective on the Torah. Circumcision was the badge and symbol that one must obey the whole law. The law was God's inspired word and must never be violated, and as God's law it is in force forever. Thus, hermeneutically they understood Scripture in a straightforward, literal fashion.

Paul's self-defense in Gal 1 – 2 also leads us to the conclusion that the opponents criticized Paul, maintaining that he had no right to nullify the Torah. By way of contrast to Paul, the Judaizers likely said the apostles in Jerusalem agreed with them. Indeed, Paul's apostleship was suspect in their eyes since he was not an original apostle. They claimed that Paul's gospel was inferior to the gospel derived from the apostles in Jerusalem (2:1 – 10).[148] We can infer from Gal 3 – 4 that they argued strongly from Abraham. The emphasis on participation in Abrahamic blessing, sonship, and heirship indicates the center of their position. No one, claimed the Judaizers, could ever participate in the blessing of Abraham, could ever be called a son of Abraham, or could ever be an heir to the promise without being circumcised. Perhaps they even claimed that Paul did not deny this in his better moments (cf. 5:11). Perhaps, they reasoned, he did not want to disturb and upset the Galatian converts, so he simply omitted the requirement of circumcision (1:10). He wanted to mitigate and soften the demands of the gospel in order to attain success in winning converts.

This summary of the Judaizers' theological position suggests the simplicity, logic, and attractiveness of their view. Their solution was practical, definite, and theologically consistent. It was consistent with the lifestyle of the believers in

---

146. Cf. Smiles, *Gospel and Law in Galatia*, 64 – 65.

147. So Ernest De Witt Burton, "Those Trouble-Makers in Galatia," *Biblical World* 53 (1919): 557. See also Wilson, *Curse*

of the Law, 61 – 62.

148. So Bligh, *Galatians*, 29.

Jerusalem. Indeed, it was the way most believers lived before Paul came along. Thus, it is most natural that the Galatians began wondering about Paul's gospel. Paul had neglected to mention circumcision as the path to sharing in Abraham's blessing. The clear teaching of Scripture on first glance supported the Judaizers' contention: one must be circumcised to be included in the covenant community.

In Depth: Did the Galatian Opponents Believe Jesus Was the Christ?

I have argued that the opponents claimed to be Christians, that they confessed that Jesus was the Christ. The idea that the opponents claimed to be Christians has been the consensus of scholarship, but this consensus has been challenged recently. Muddiman argues that the false brothers did not claim to be Christians but wormed their way into the church to report back to Jewish authorities.[149] It is possible that the opponents did not claim to be Christians, but the traditional view that the adversaries professed faith in Jesus Christ is still preferable for three reasons. (1) Paul nowhere criticizes the opponents for failing to believe that Jesus is the Christ, which he would almost certainly have done if they denied such. We think of 1 – 2 John, where John criticizes the deficient Christology of his opponents.

(2) If the opponents denied that Jesus was the Christ, Paul would have countered by arguing at some length in Galatians that Jesus was indeed the Christ. This is evident since he counters their view of the law in some detail. But such a detailed defense of Jesus' messianic status is lacking, presumably because it was not disputed by the opponents.

(3) It seems more probable that the opponents would have made inroads in the Galatian congregation if they agreed significantly with Paul's gospel (and hence confessed that Jesus was the Christ), while also maintaining that Paul's gospel must be supplemented and improved by adding observance of the law to what they already believed.

The notion that the opponents were not believers in Christ has also been defended by Mark Nanos.[150] Nanos argues that the opponents should be identified as "influencers" (he says we must beware of negatively characterizing the opponents), that they were Jewish representatives of local synagogues, that the reference to "another gospel" should be interpreted ironically (1:6 – 7), and that their refusal to be persecuted for the sake of the cross (6:12) should not be

---

149. John Muddiman, "An Anatomy of Galatians," 262 – 63. See also Nikolaus Walter's view (n142).

150. Mark D. Nanos, *The Irony of Galatians: Paul's Letter in First-Century Context* (Minneapolis: Fortress, 2002).

understood to say that they claimed to be Christians. Nanos shows that the evidence for the opponents being outside Galatia is not as strong as is sometimes claimed, though it seems for the reasons stated earlier that the opponents most likely arrived from the outside.

Nanos strives to be fair to the opponents and hence shrinks back from negative language to characterize them. But for those of us who accept Paul's language as inspired Scripture and as God's viewpoint of the opponents, the Pauline stance regarding the opponents should be accepted as an accurate depiction, and hence it is legitimate to designate them as agitators, troublemakers, opponents of the gospel, and deserving God's eschatological curse (1:8–9).

The most creative dimension of Nanos's proposal is the argument that the opponents did not believe in Christ. But the same three arguments given above against Muddiman's proposal also speak against Nanos's view. Furthermore, it is unclear, contrary to Nanos, that the reference to the word "gospel" (1:6–7) should be understood ironically. We need more clues than are provided to detect irony. It is more probable that Paul designates their message as "gospel" because the opponents described it as such. And if the opponents used the word "gospel," it is also probable that they professed belief in Jesus as Messiah. Therefore, the opponents should not be classified as unbelieving Jews but as those who professed Jesus as the Messiah. What distinguished them from Paul was their desire to supplement the gospel with the requirement of circumcision and the observance of the OT law.

Structure[151]

Rhetorical Criticism

In recent years Paul's letters have been investigated from the standpoint of rhetorical criticism.[152] Did Paul use the patterns of argumentation and structure recommended in the Greco-Roman handbooks, especially in the works of Quintilian and Cicero?[153] Many scholars now answer such a question in the affirmative, and

---

151. The section on rhetorical criticism and epistolary features draws from my "Interpreting the Pauline Epistles," in *Interpreting the New Testament: Essays on Methods and Issues* (ed. David A. Black and David S. Dockery; Nashville: Broadman & Holman, 2001), 422–25.

152. For a useful introduction to Greek rhetoric see G. A. Kennedy, *New Testament Interpretation through Rhetorical Criticism* (Chapel Hill: Univ. of North Carolina, 1984); cf. also D. F. Watson and A. J. Hauser, *Rhetorical Criticism of the Bible: A Comprehensive Bibliography with Notes on History and Method* (Leiden: Brill, 1994).

153. For an analysis of the style of Galatians, see Terrance Callan, "The Style of Galatians," *Bib* 88 (2007): 496–516. Callan argues that the style is quite plain.

a growing body of literature reflects the attempt to comprehend Paul's letters as rhetorical compositions.

Rhetoric can be classified into three types: (1) judicial, (2) deliberative, and (3) epideictic. *Judicial rhetoric* is the language of the law court, where language of defense and accusation predominate, and guilt and innocence are under consideration. *Deliberative rhetoric* summons human beings to consider the future, seeking to persuade or dissuade them from a certain course of action. When speakers use *epideictic rhetoric*, they are celebrating common values or aspirations, or indicting something that is blameworthy.

Most rhetorical speeches have four elements: (1) the *exordium* (introduction), which introduces the speech and attempts to create empathy for what will follow; (2) the *narratio* (narration), which contains the main proposition and background information relevant to the argument; (3) the *probatio* (proofs to defend the main thesis), in which the arguments for the proposition are set forth; and (4) the *peroratio* (summary and conclusion), in which the whole argument is summarized and brought to a ringing conclusion so that the hearers will be persuaded.

The work that launched rhetorical criticism in Paul is Betz's commentary on Galatians.[154] He divides Galatians as follows, identifying it as a judicial apologetic letter:[155]

> Prescript 1:1 – 5
> Body 1:6 – 6:10
> *Exordium* (Introduction) 1:6 – 11
> *Narratio* (Narration) 1:12 – 2:14
> *Propositio* (Main Thesis) 2:15 – 21
> *Probatio* (Proofs) 3:1 – 4:31
> *Paraenesis* (Exhortation) 5:1 – 6:10
> Postscript (containing *Peroratio* — Summary) 6:11 – 18

Betz's work is enormously interesting, and we can immediately see the plausibility of the structure proposed. Indeed, one of the benefits of rhetorical criticism is that it reminds us that the Pauline letters are carefully structured and written. Nonetheless, there are serious questions that finally render Betz's proposal doubtful.[156] (1) The *exordium* (introduction) in Galatians hardly creates goodwill with the audience. Instead of thanking God for his work in their lives, Paul expresses

---

154. See Betz, *Galatians*, esp. 14 – 25. Betz summarized his work in an article before the commentary appeared. See his "The Literary Composition and Function of Paul's Letter to the Galatians," *NTS* 21 (1975): 352 – 79. Others have basically concurred with Betz. See Brinsmead, *Galatians*, 37 – 55; J. D. Hester, "The Rhetorical Structure of Galatians 1:1 – 2:14," *JBL* 103 (1984): 223 – 33. But Hester has since classified the letter as epideictic. J. D. Hester, "Epideictic Rhetoric and Persona in Galatians 1 and 2," in *The Galatians*

Debate: Contemporary Issues in Rhetorical and Historical Interpretation (ed. Mark D. Nanos; Peabody, MA: Hendrickson, 2002), 181 – 96.

155. The English words in the parentheses are mine.

156. For an evaluation of Betz, see G. Walter Hansen, *Abraham in Galatians: Epistolary and Rhetorical Contexts* (JSNTSup 29; Sheffield: Sheffield Academic Press, 1989), 25 – 27, 57 – 71.

astonishment at their departure from the gospel (1:6–11). No attempt to establish rapport with the readers is evident here. (2) Much of Galatians is comprised of paraenesis (5:1–6:10), but paraenesis has no place in the rhetorical handbooks. (3) Betz does not provide any literary examples of an actual apologetic letter that would function as a comparison with Galatians.[157] (4) Paul's Jewish background is completely ignored in the analysis of the letter.[158] (5) Betz also sees the letter as modeled after magic letters in antiquity, but such a comparison is improbable since magical letters are remarkably different from Galatians.

Some scholars have responded to Betz by suggesting that Galatians should be classified as deliberative rather than judicial rhetoric.[159] Seeing Galatians as fundamentally persuasive in intent seems correct, and yet it is still questionable whether it conforms so precisely to the pattern of Greek rhetoric, for a letter that intends to persuade does not necessarily fall into a precise rhetorical category. Rhetorical schemas have been suggested now for virtually every Pauline letter. The detailed suggestions seem to suffer from the problem of imposing a form on the Pauline letters that does not fit them precisely, and the same judgment applies to Galatians.[160] The unique features of Galatians are extinguished by a prefabricated pattern that squelches what the letter actually says.[161]

This is not to say that the new rhetorical approaches are without value. They remind us that the letters are carefully structured and crafted, for the new proposals would not be worthy of serious consideration if Paul's letters were organized poorly. Moreover, Paul was probably familiar with such rhetoric to some extent, for he was an educated person, and the impact of Hellenism was evident even in Palestine.[162] Even if he was unaware entirely of Greek rhetoric (which is unlikely), it still follows that we could detect some rhetorical features in his letters since the rhetorical hand-

---

157. Rightly Paul W. Meyer, "Review: *Galatians: A Commentary on Paul's Letter to the Churches of Galatia,* by Hans Dieter Betz," *RelSRev* 7 (1981): 319; David E. Aune, "Review: *Galatians: A Commentary on Paul's Letter to the Churches of Galatia,* by Hans Dieter Betz," *RelSRev* 7 (1981): 324.

158. W. D. Davies observes that Betz does not account sufficiently for the scriptural practices of the synagogue, especially in Galatians 3–4. The Jewish background of the letter and its messianic situation are neglected. See "Review: *Galatians: A Commentary on Paul's Letter to the Churches of Galatia,* by Hans Dieter Betz," *RelSRev* 7 (1981): 314–17.

159. See, e.g., Kennedy, *Rhetorical Criticism,* 145–47; R. G. Hall, "The Rhetorical Outline for Galatians: A Reconsideration," *JBL* 106 (1987): 277–88; W. B. Russell, "Rhetorical Analysis of the Book of Galatians," *BSac* 150 (1993): 341–58 and 416–39; François Vouga, "Zur rhetorischen Gattung des Galaterbriefes," *ZNW* 79 (1988): 291–92; Joop Smit, "The Letter of Paul to the Galatians: A Deliberative Speech,"

NTS 35 (1989): 1–26. For a more flexible solution where it is argued that Paul uses judicial, deliberative, and epideictic rhetoric in the introduction, see R. M. Berchman, "Galatians (1:1–5): Paul and Greco-Roman Rhetoric," in *The Galatians Debate: Contemporary Issues in Rhetorical and Historical Interpretation* (ed. Mark D. Nanos; Peabody, MA: Hendrickson, 2002), 60–72.

160. Scholars have suggested a number of different schemes for Galatians. For a survey, see D. François Tolmie, *Persuading the Galatians: A Text-Centred Rhetorical Analysis of a Pauline Letter* (WUNT 2/190; Tübingen: Mohr Siebeck, 2005), 1–19.

161. So Robert A. Bryant, *The Risen Crucified Christ in Galatians* (SBLDS 185; Atlanta: SBL, 2001), 52–54.

162. This point is disputed. For an entrée into the discussion see Jeffery A. D. Weima, "What Does Aristotle Have to Do with Paul? An Evaluation of Rhetorical Criticism," *CTJ* 32 (1997): 464–65.

books identify elements of effective communication that are used even by those who know nothing of Greek rhetoric.[163]

Nevertheless, we must seriously question whether Paul actually structured entire letters in accordance with the rhetorical handbooks.[164] The rules of rhetoric in these handbooks were designed for *speeches,* not for written discourse.[165] Rhetorical handbooks rarely refer to *letters,* and they do not contain prescriptions in terms of the type of argument employed (judicial, deliberative, or epideictic), nor do they recommend the following of a certain outline (*exordium, narratio, probatio, peroratio*). Porter concludes his study of the impact of the rhetorical handbooks upon letters by saying, "There is, therefore, little if any theoretical justification in the ancient handbooks for application of the formal categories of the species and organization of rhetoric to analysis of the Pauline epistles."[166] It is also instructive that early church fathers did not identify the Pauline letters as conforming to Greek rhetoric.[167] A number of the fathers were familiar with or trained in rhetoric, and yet they do not give any indication that they understood Paul's letters to be patterned after such rhetoric. If anything, they sometimes seemed embarrassed by the rudeness of his style.

As has been mentioned, the most serious problem with classifying Galatians is that the detailed schemes appear to be imposed upon the letter, but such a conclusion does not exclude the use of some rhetorical features in the Pauline letters.

Epistolary Features

Other scholars argue that we must examine epistolary features of Paul's letters along with rhetorical criticism.[168] All of Paul's letters consist of the opening, the

163. Esler, e.g., argues that Galatians is deliberative in a broad sense, even if it does not formally conform to deliberative rhetoric as explained in the handbooks (*Galatians,* 19, 59–61).

164. For the view that applying rhetorical categories to Galatians is mistaken, see Philip H. Kern, *Rhetoric in Galatians: Assessing an Approach to Paul's Epistle* (SNTSMS 101; Cambridge: Cambridge Univ. Press, 1998). See also the article by Weima, "What Does Aristotle," though I am less certain that Paul was uninstructed in Greek rhetoric. In contrast to Weima, I also think it is possible that Paul's negative comments about rhetoric in 1 Cor 2:1–5 should be restricted to his preaching, so that they do not rule out the use of rhetoric in his writings. Still, I think Weima is correct when he says that evidence is lacking to substantiate the use of such rhetoric in Paul. See also the questions raised by Tolmie, *Persuading the Galatians,* 24–27.

165. For a balanced assessment of the role of rhetoric in Galatians, see Janet Fairweather, "The Epistle to the Galatians and Classical Rhetoric: Parts 1–2," *TynBul* 45 (1994): 2–38; idem, "The Epistle to the Galatians and Classical Rhetoric: Part 3," *TynBul* 45 (1994): 213–43. Fairweather emphasizes that rhetorical features may be present, even if Paul was not educated in Greek rhetoric.

166. S. E. Porter, "The Theoretical Justification for Application of Rhetorical Categories to Pauline Epistolary Literature," in *Rhetoric and the New Testament: Essays from the 1992 Heidelberg Conference* (ed. S. E. Porter and T. H. Olbricht; Sheffield: JSOT Press, 1993), 115–16.

167. For this point see Weima, "What Does Aristotle," 467.

168. See Nils A. Dahl, "Paul's Letter to the Galatians: Epistolary Genre, Content, and Structure," in *The Galatians Debate: Contemporary Issues in Rhetorical and Historical Interpretation* (ed. Mark D. Nanos; Peabody, MA: Hendrickson, 2002), 117–42; Hansen, *Abraham in Galatians,* 21–54; G. Walter Hansen, "A Paradigm of the Apocalypse: The Gospel in the Light of Epistolary Analysis," in *The Galatians Debate: Contemporary Issues in Rhetorical and Historical*

body, and the closing.[169] The opening of letters usually has four elements: (1) the sender (e.g., Paul); (2) the recipients (e.g., the Galatians); (3) the salutation (e.g., grace and peace to you); and (4) a prayer (usually a thanksgiving). Interpretive significance can be discerned from Paul's variation from the pattern and from what he emphasizes in the opening. For example, the defensive tone of 1:1 is unparalleled in the Pauline letters, suggesting that the opponents called into question the legitimacy of his apostleship.

Paul not only lists himself as the sender in 1:2 but also mentions "all the brothers with me." With these words he communicates the truth that the gospel he preaches is not merely his private opinion. All the believers with Paul acknowledge it as well, and so the Galatians are renouncing Christian tradition if they repudiate his gospel.

Since Paul typically begins with a thanksgiving, the lack of the same in Gal 1 is significant.[170] Paul is not thankful but astonished by the defection in the church. Usually the opening of the letter is brief, two or three verses. Again Galatians stands out since the opening consists of five verses. The longest opening of all is found in Romans, where Paul writes to a church that he did not establish, and so he emphasizes from the inception of the letter his unique apostolic role and the gospel he proclaims to establish a common bond and understanding.

The substance of Pauline letters is found in the body, displaying remarkable creativity with no consistent pattern. The task of the interpreter is to trace Paul's argument carefully, letting the text itself dictate the structure.[171] The body of the letters highlights the distinctive nature of the Pauline epistles. Despite some overlap with other letters in the Greco-Roman world, they also have unique features that demand thorough and careful interpretation. Epistolary features and rhetorical

---

Interpretation (ed. Mark D. Nanos; Peabody, MA: Hendrickson, 2002), 143–54. These scholars emphasize that Galatians is a rebuke-request letter, where the Galatians are reproved and encouraged to follow the Pauline gospel. Understanding epistolary conventions certainly assists us in understanding the structure of the letter. Still, the approach adopted by these scholars is not entirely satisfactory. They rely on nonliterary letters from papyri in discerning the epistolary character of Galatians. But such letters are quite different from Galatians. The papyri letters are personal in nature and remarkably brief. So Bryant, *Crucified Christ in Galatians*, 43–44; Graham N. Stanton, "Review of *Abraham in Galatians: Epistolary and Rhetorical Contexts*," *JTS* 43 (1992): 614–15. It seems that the structure of the letter is not unlocked entirely by paying attention to its epistolary conventions. Galatians has a unique structure that must be discerned by careful attention to the unfolding of the argument of the letter. As Bryant says, "Since Paul's letters do not match other writings in these respects, genre comparisons of Paul's letters with other existent letters

cannot be exact; they can only be approximate at best" (*Crucified Christ in Galatians*, 44).

169. Bligh in his commentary arranges Galatians chiastically (*Galatians*, 37–42), but the scheme is forced upon the letter. Rightly C. K. Barrett, "The Allegory of Abraham, Sarah, and Hagar in the Argument of Galatians," in *Rechtfertigung: Festschrift für Ernest Käsemann* (ed. J. Friedrich, W. Pöhlmann, and P. Stuhlmacher; Tübingen: Mohr Siebeck, 1976), 3–5.

170. The prayer section often foreshadows important themes in the letter. See P. Schubert, *Form and Function of Pauline Thanksgivings* (Berlin: Töpelmann, 1939); P. T. O'Brien, *Introductory Thanksgivings in the Letters of Paul* (Leiden: Brill, 1977); G. P. Wiles, *Paul's Intercessory Prayers: Prayer Passages in the Letters of St. Paul* (London: Cambridge Univ. Press, 1974).

171. For a method of tracing the argument in Paul, see Thomas R. Schreiner, *Interpreting the Pauline Epistles* (Grand Rapids: Baker, 1990), 97–126.

characteristics may assist in interpreting the letter, but we must recognize that Galatians does not conform to any structure precisely.

The closing of letters is also interpretively significant, though the pattern varies, and discerning where the closing begins may be difficult.[172] The following elements are often present, and I will cite only two examples for each, though more could be given: (1) travel plans or personal situation (Rom 15:22 – 29; 1 Cor 16:5 – 9), but such is lacking in Galatians; (2) prayer (Rom 15:33; 1 Thess. 5:23), once again lacking in Galatians; (3) commendation of coworkers (Rom 16:1 – 2; 1 Cor 16:10 – 12), lacking in Galatians; (4) prayer requests (Rom 15:30 – 32; Col. 4:2 – 4), lacking in Galatians; (5) greetings (Rom 16:3 – 16; 1 Cor 16:19 – 21), lacking in Galatians; (6) final instructions and exhortations (Rom 16:17 – 20a; 1 Cor 16:13 – 18); in Galatians final instructions are found in 6:11 – 17 and are of importance in interpreting the letter; (7) holy kiss (1 Cor 16:20; 2 Cor 13:12); (8) autographed greeting (1 Cor 16:21; Gal 6:11); and (9) a grace benediction (Rom 16:20; Gal 6:18).

The contribution of the closing in interpreting letters is aptly illustrated from 6:11 – 18, though it must be observed that the importance of the closing varies from letter to letter.[173] The autograph formula (6:11) signals the weight of the closing, for Paul writes with large letters to emphasize the significance of what follows. What is most striking are the contrasts between the opponents and Paul.

- They boast in the circumcision of the Galatians (6:12 – 13), but Paul boasts in the cross of Christ only (6:14).
- The agitators "avoid persecution for the cross" (6:12), but Paul "accepts persecution … for the cross" (6:17) and bears the marks of that persecution upon his body.[174]
- The adversaries were attempting to force circumcision on the Galatians (6:12 – 13), but Paul views both circumcision and uncircumcision as optional, as *adiaphora* (6:15).
- The opponents live under the power of this world (6:14), but Paul has been inducted into the age to come, the "new creation" inaugurated by Christ (6:15).

A careful reading of the closing discloses that the fundamental issue in Galatians is the cross of Christ. Paul summarizes the major issue in the letter by reminding his readers of the significance of the cross (see also 1:4; 2:19 – 21; 3:1, 13; 4:4 – 5; 5:1, 11, 24). Since the closing reprises central themes of the letter, we are also given help in defining "the Israel of God" (6:16). Paul labors throughout the letter to emphasize that all those who belong to Christ are children of Abraham and share the blessing of Abraham. It is likely, then, that he uses the term "Israel of God" to designate both Jewish

---

172. See Jeffery A. D. Weima, *Neglected Endings: The Significance of Pauline Letter Closings* (JSNTSup 101; Sheffield: Sheffield Academic Press, 1994).

173. My comments here depend especially on the essay by

Jeffrey A. D. Weima, "Gal 6:11 – 18: A Hermeneutical Key to the Galatian Letter," *CTJ* 28 (1993): 90 – 107.

174. Ibid., 94.

and Gentile believers in Christ, summarizing one of the major themes of the letter at its conclusion. Reading the closing of the letter may cast significant light on the rest of the letter, especially when the closing is more extended, as in Galatians and Romans.

Outline[175]

I. Introduction: Desertion from Paul's Gospel Is Desertion from the Gospel (1:1 – 2:21)
  A. Greeting: Paul's Apostolic Authority (1:1 – 5)
  B. Problem Explained: Desertion from the Gospel (1:6 – 10)
  C. Paul's Gospel Derived from God, Not People (1:11 – 2:21)
    1. Thesis: Source of His Gospel Was Revelation (1:11 – 12)
    2. Thesis Support (1:13 – 2:21)
      a. His Past Hostility (1:13 – 14)
      b. His Call from God (1:15 – 17)
      c. His Relative Obscurity in Judea (1:18 – 24)
      d. Recognition of Paul's Authority by Pillars (2:1 – 10)
      e. Rebuke of Peter Substantiates Paul's Authority (2:11 – 21)
        i. Rebuke (2:11 – 14)
        ii. Transition: The Nature of the Gospel (2:15 – 21)
II. Paul's Gospel Defended from Experience and Scripture (3:1 – 4:11)
  A. Argument from Experience: Reception of Spirit by Means of Faith, Not Works (3:1 – 5)
  B. Argument from Scripture: Blessing of Abraham by Faith (3:6 – 14)
    1. Members of Abraham's Family by Faith (3:6 – 9)
    2. Curse of Law Removed Only in Christ (3:10 – 14)
  C. Argument from Salvation History: Priority of Abrahamic Covenant and Temporary Nature of Mosaic Covenant (3:15 – 4:11)
    1. Addition of Law Does Not Nullify Promise to Abraham (3:15 – 25)
      a. Interim Nature of Mosaic Covenant (3:15 – 18)
      b. The Purpose of the Law (3:19 – 25)
    2. Sons of God Are Abraham's Offspring (3:26 – 29)
    3. Argument from Slavery to Sonship (4:1 – 7)
    4. The Folly of Reverting to the Law (4:8 – 11)
III. A Call to Freedom from the Law and Freedom in the Spirit (4:12 – 6:10)
  A. Live in Freedom from the Law: Argument from Friendship (4:12 – 20)
  B. Stand in Freedom: Argument from Allegory (4:21 – 5:1)
  C. Resist the Dangerous Message of Bondage (5:2 – 12)
    1. It Involves the Requirement of Circumcision (5:2 – 6)
    2. Its Perpetrators Will Be Judged (5:7 – 12)

---

175. For similar outlines in some respects, see Dahl, "Paul's Letter to the Galatians," 141 – 42; Longenecker, *Galatians,* c – cix; G. Walter Hansen, *Galatians* (IVPNTC; Downers Grove, IL: IVP, 1994), 29 – 30.

Select Bibliography

Armitage, D. J. "An Exploration of Conditional Clause Exegesis with Reference to Galatians 1,8 – 9." *Bib* 88 (2007): 365 – 92.

Arnold, Clinton E. "'I Am Astonished That You Are So Quickly Turning Away!' (Gal 1.6): Paul and Anatolian Folk Belief." *NTS* 51 (2005): 429 – 49.

———. "Returning to the Domain of the Powers: *Stoicheia* as Evil Spirits in Galatians 4:3, 9." *NovT* 38 (1996): 55 – 76.

Avemarie, Friedrich. "Erwählung und Vergeltung: Zur optionalen Struktur rabbinischer Soteriologie." *NTS* 45 (1999): 108 – 26.

———. "Paul and the Claim of the Law according to the Scripture: Leviticus 18:5 in Galatians 3:12 and Romans 10:5." Pages 125 – 48 in *The Beginnings of Christianity: A Collection of Articles*. Edited by Jack Pastor and Menachem Mor. Jerusalem: Yad Ben-Zvi Press, 2005.

Baasland, Ernst. "Persecution: A Neglected Feature in the Letter to the Galatians." *ST* 38 (1984): 135 – 50.

Bachmann, Michael. *Anti-Judaism in Galatians? Exegetical Studies on a Polemical Letter and on Paul's Theology*. Translated by Robert L. Brawley. Grand Rapids: Eerdmans, 2008.

Barclay, John M. G. "Mirror-Reading a Polemical Letter: Galatians as a Test Case." *JSNT* 31 (1987): 73 – 93.

———. *Obeying the Truth: Paul's Ethics in Galatians*. Minneapolis: Fortress, 1988.

Barrett, C. K. "The Allegory of Abraham, Sarah, and Hagar in the Argument of Galatians." Pages 1 – 16 in *Rechtfertigung: Festschrift für Ernest Käsemann*. Edited by J. Friedrich, W. Pöhlmann, P. Stuhlmacher. Tübingen: Mohr Siebeck, 1976.

———. *Freedom & Obligation: A Study in the Epistle to the Galatians*. Philadelphia: Westminster, 1985.

———. "Paul and the 'Pillar' Apostles." Pages 1 – 19 in *Studia Paulina in honorem Jr. de Zwaan*. Edited by J. N. Sevenster and W. C. van Unnik. Haarlem: Bohn, 1953.

Bauer, Walter, Frederick W. Danker, William F. Arndt, and F. Wilbur Gingrich. *A Greek-English Lexicon of the New Testament and Other Early Christian Literature*. Revised and edited by Frederick W. Danker. 3rd ed. Chicago: University of Chicago Press, 2000.

Belleville, Linda. "'Under Law': Structural Analysis and the Pauline Concept of Law in Galatians 3:21 – 4:11." *JSNT* 26 (1986): 53 – 78.

Betz, Hans D. *Galatians: A Commentary on Paul's Letter to the Churches in Galatia*. Hermeneia. Philadelphia: Fortress, 1979.

———. "The Literary Composition and Function of Paul's Letter to the Galatians." *NTS* 21 (1975): 352 – 79.

Bird, Michael F. *The Saving Righteousness of God: Studies on Paul, Justification, and the New Perspective*. Eugene, OR: Wipf & Stock, 2007.

Bird, Michael F., and Preston Sprinkle, eds. *The Faith of Jesus Christ: Exegetical, Biblical, and Theological Studies*. Peabody, MA: Hendrickson, 2009.

Blass, F. and A. Debrunner. *A Greek Grammar of the New Testament and Other Early Christian*

Literature. Translated and revised by Robert W. Funk. Chicago: University of Chicago Press, 1961.

Blinzer, Josef. "Lexikalisches zu dem Terminus τὰ στοιχεῖα τοῦ κόσμου bei Paulus." Pages 429–43 in *Studiorum Paulinorum Congressus Internationalis Catholicus*. Vol 2. AnBib 17–18. Rome: Pontifical Biblical Institute, 1961.

Brinsmead, B. H. *Galatians—Dialogical Response to Opponents*. SBLDS 65. Chico: Scholars Press, 1982.

Bruce, F. F. *The Epistle to the Galatians: A Commentary on the Greek Text*. NIGTC. Grand Rapids: Eerdmans, 1982.

Bryant, Robert A. *The Risen Crucified Christ in Galatians*. SBLDS 185. Atlanta: Society of Biblical Literature, 2001.

Burke, Trevor J. *Adoption into God's Family: Exploring a Pauline Metaphor*. NSBT 22. Downers Grove, IL: IVP, 2006.

Burton, Ernest De Witt. *A Critical and Exegetical Commentary on the Epistle to the Galatians*. ICC. New York: Scribner's, 1920.

Carson, D. A., Peter T. O'Brien, and Mark A. Seifrid, eds. *Justification and Variegated Nomism*. Vol. 1: *The Complexities of Second Temple Judaism*. WUNT 2/140. Tübingen/Grand Rapids: Mohr Siebeck/Baker, 2001.

Charlesworth, James H., ed. *The Old Testament Pseudepigrapha: Apocalyptic Literature and Testaments*. Vol. 1. Garden City, NY: Doubleday, 1983.

———. *The Old Testament Pseudepigrapha: Expansions of the "Old Testament" and Legends, Wisdom and Philosophical Literature, Prayers, Psalms, and Odes, Fragments of Lost Judeo-Hellenistic Works*. Vol. 2. Garden City, NY: Doubleday, 1985.

Ciampa, Roy E. *The Presence and Function of Scripture in Galatians 1 and 2*. WUNT 2/102. Tübingen: Mohr Siebeck, 1998.

Collins, C. John. "Galatians 3:16: What Kind of Exegete Was Paul?" *TynBul* 54 (2003): 75–86.

———. "A Syntactical Note (Genesis 3:15): Is the Woman's Seed Singular or Plural?" *TynBul* 48 (1997): 139–48.

Danby, Herbert. *The Mishnah*. New York: Oxford University Press, 1933.

Das, A. Andrew. "Another Look at ἐὰν μή in Galatians 2:16." *JBL* 119 (2000): 529–39.

———. *Paul and the Jews*. Peabody, MA: Hendrickson, 2003.

———. *Paul, the Law, and the Covenant*. Peabody, MA: Hendrickson, 2001.

Davis, Anne. "Allegorically Speaking in Galatians 4:21–5:1." *BBR* 14 (2004): 161–74.

Davis, Basil S. *Christ as Devotio: The Argument of Galatians 3:1–14*. Lanham: University Press of America, 2002.

Debanné, Marc J. *Enthymemes in the Letters of Paul*. LNTS 303. London: T&T Clark, 2006.

De Boer, Martinus C. "The Meaning of the Phrase τὰ στοιχεῖα τοῦ κόσμου in Galatians." *NTS* 53 (2007): 204–24.

———. "Paul's Quotation of Isaiah 54.1 in Galatians 4.27." *NTS* 50 (2004): 370–89.

———. "Paul's Use and Interpretation of a Justification Tradition in Galatians 2.15–21." *JSNT* 28 (2005): 189–216.

Donaldson, Terence L. "The 'Curse of the Law' and the Inclusion of the Gentiles: Galatians 3:13–14." *NTS* 32 (1986): 94–112.

Doty, W. G. *Letters in Primitive Christianity*. Philadelphia: Fortress, 1973.

Duncan, George S. *The Epistle of Paul to the Galatians*. MNTC. New York: Harper & Brothers, 1934.

Dunn, James D. G. *The Epistle to the Galatians*. BNTC. Peabody, MA: Hendrickson, 1993.

———. "The Incident at Antioch (Gal 2:11–18)." *JSNT* 18 (1983): 3–57.

———. *Jesus, Paul and the Law: Studies in Mark and Galatians*. Louisville: Westminster/John Knox, 1990.

———. *The New Perspective on Paul: Collected Essays*. WUNT 185. Tübingen: Mohr Siebeck, 2005.

———. "The New Perspective on Paul." *BJRL* 65 (1983): 95–122.

———. "Once More, *Pistis Christou*." SBLSP 30 (1991): 730–44.

———. *The Theology of Paul the Apostle*. Grand Rapids: Eerdmans, 1998.

———. "Works of the Law and the Curse of the Law (Galatians 3:10–14)." *NTS* 31 (1985): 523–42.

———. "Yet Once More — 'The Works of the Law': A Response." *JSNT* 46 (1992): 99–117.

Eastman, Susan G. " 'Cast Out the Slave Woman and Her Son': The Dynamics of Exclusion and Inclusion in Galatians 4.30." *JSNT* 28 (2006): 309–36.

———. "The Evil Eye and the Curse of the Law: Galatians 3.1 Revisited." *JSNT* 83 (2001): 69–87.

———. *Recovering Paul's Mother Tongue: Language and Theology in Galatians*. Grand Rapids: Eerdmans, 2007.

Eckstein, Hans-Joachim. *Verheissung und Gesetz: Eine exegetische Untersuchung zu Galater 2,15–4,7*. WUNT 86. Tübingen: Mohr Siebeck, 1996.

Elliott, Mark A. *The Survivors of Israel: A Reconsideration of the Theology of Pre-Christian Judaism*. Grand Rapids: Eerdmans, 2000.

Elliott, Susan. *Cutting Too Close for Comfort: Paul's Letter to the Galatians in Its Anatolian Cultic Context*. JSNTSup 248. London: T&T Clark, 2003.

Ellis, E. Earle. *Paul's Use of the Old Testament*. Grand Rapids: Baker, 1957.

———. *Prophecy and Hermeneutic in Early Christianity: New Testament Essays*. Grand Rapids: Eerdmans, 1978.

Esler, Philip F. *Galatians*. New York/London: Routledge, 1998.

Fee, Gordon D. *Galatians*. Pentecostal Commentary Series. Dorset: Deo, 2007.

Fitzmyer, Joseph A. "Crucifixion in Ancient Palestine, Qumran Literature, and the New Testament." *CBQ* 40 (1978): 493–513.

———. "Paul's Jewish Background and the Deeds of the Law." Pages 18–35 in *According to Paul: Studies in the Theology of the Apostle*. New York: Paulist, 1993.

Fung, Ronald Y. *The Epistle to the Galatians*. NICNT. Grand Rapids: Eerdmans, 1988.

Gaffin, Richard B. Jr. *"By Faith, Not By Sight": Paul and the Order of Salvation*. Waynesboro, GA: Paternoster, 2006.

Garlington, Don. *An Exposition of Galatians: A Reading from the New Perspective*. 3rd ed. Eugene, OR: Wipf and Stock, 2007.

———. Paul's " 'Partisan ἐκ' and the Question of Justification in Galatians." *JBL* 127 (2008): 567–89.

———. "Role Reversal and Paul's Use of Scripture in Galatians 3.10–13." *JSNT* 65 (1997): 85–121.

Gordon, T. David. "A Note on παιδαγωγός in Galatians 3.24–25." *NTS* 35 (1989): 150–54.

———. "The Problem at Galatia." *Int* 41 (1987): 32–43.

Guthrie, Donald. *Galatians*. NCB. Grand Rapids: Eerdmans, 1973.

Hahn, Scott W. "Covenant, Oath, and the Aqedah: Διαθήκη in Galatians 3:15–18." *CBQ* 67 (2005): 79–100.

Hall, R. G. "The Rhetorical Outline for Galatians: A Reconsideration." *JBL* 106 (1987): 277–88.

Hansen, G. Walter. *Abraham in Galatians: Epistolary and Rhetorical Contexts*. JSNTSup 29. Sheffield: Sheffield Academic Press, 1989.

———. *Galatians*. IVPNTC. Downers Grove, IL: IVP, 1994.

Hardin, Justin K. *Galatians and the Imperial Cult: A Critical Analysis of the First-Century Social Context of Paul's Letter.* WUNT 2/237. Tübingen: Mohr Siebeck, 2008.

Harmon, Matthew S. "She Must and Shall Go Free: Paul's Isaianic Gospel in Galatians." PhD diss. Wheaton, IL: Wheaton College Graduate School, 2006.

Harrisville III, Roy A. "Before ΠΙΣΤΙΣ ΧΡΙΣΤΟΥ: The Objective Genitive as Good Greek." *NovT* 41 (2006): 353 – 58.

Hays, Richard B. "Christology and Ethics in Galatians: The Law of Christ." *CBQ* 49 (1987): 268 – 90.

———. *The Faith of Jesus Christ: An Investigation of the Narrative Substructure of Galatians 3:1 – 4:11.* 2nd ed. Grand Rapids: Eerdmans, 2002.

———. *The Letter to the Galatians: Introduction, Commentary, and Reflections.* Pages 181 – 348 in *The New Interpreter's Bible*, vol. 11. Nashville: Abingdon, 2000.

———. "*Pistis* and Pauline Christology: What is at Stake?" SBLSP (1991): 714 – 29.

Hengel, Martin, and Anna Maria Schwemer. *Paul between Damascus and Antioch: The Unknown Years.* Translated by John Bowden. Louisville: Westminster John Knox, 1997.

Hofius, Otfried. *Paulusstudien I.* WUNT 51. Tübingen: Mohr Siebeck, 1989.

Hong, In-Gyu. "Does Paul Misrepresent the Jewish Law? Law and Covenant in Gal 3:1 – 14." *NovT* 36 (1994): 164 – 82.

———. *The Law in Galatians.* JSNTSup 81. Sheffield: Sheffield Academic Press, 1993.

Houlden, J. L. "A Response to James D. G. Dunn." *JSNT* 18 (1983): 58 – 67.

Hove, Richard W. *Equality in Christ? Galatians 3:28 and the Gender Dispute.* Wheaton: Crossway, 1999.

Howard, George. *Paul: Crisis in Galatia. A Study in Early Christian Theology.* 2nd ed. SNTSMS 35. Cambridge: Cambridge University Press, 1990.

Hübner, Hans. *Law in Paul's Thought.* Trans. James G. Greig. Edinburgh: T&T Clark, 1984.

Hunn, Debbie. "PISTIS CHRISTOU in Galatians 2:16." *TynBul* 57.1 (2006): 23 – 33.

———. "Ἐὰν μή in Galatians 2:16: A Look at Greek Literature." *NovT* 49 (2007): 281 – 90.

Jewett, Robert. "The Agitators and the Galatian Congregation." Pages 334 – 47 in *The Galatians Debate: Contemporary Issues in Rhetorical and Historical Interpretation.* Edited by Mark D. Nanos. Peabody, MA: Hendrickson, 2002.

Jobes, Karen H. "Jerusalem, Our Mother: Metalepsis and Intertextuality in Galatians 4:21 – 31." *WTJ* 55 (1993): 299 – 320.

Johnson, H. Wayne. "The Paradigm of Abraham in Galatians 3:6 – 9." *TJ* 8 (1987): 179 – 99.

Kern, Philip H. *Rhetoric in Galatians: Assessing an Approach to Paul's Epistle.* SNTSMS 101; Cambridge: Cambridge University Press, 1998.

Kilgallen, J. J. "The Strivings of the Flesh ... (Galatians 5:17)." *Bib* 80 (1999): 113 – 14.

Kim, Seyoon. *Paul and the New Perspective: Second Thoughts on the Origin of Paul's Gospel.* Grand Rapids: Eerdmans, 2002.

———. *Christ and Caesar: The Gospel and the Roman Empire in the Writings of Paul and Luke.* Grand Rapids: Eerdmans, 2008.

Köstenberger, Andreas. "The Identity of the ἸΣΡΑΗΛ ΤΟΥ ΘΕΟΥ (Israel of God) in Galatians 6:16." *Faith and Mission* 19 (2001): 3 – 24.

Kuck, David W. " 'Each Will Bear His Own Burden': Paul's Creative Use of an Apocalyptic Motif." *NTS* 40 (1994): 289 – 97.

Kümmel, W. G. *Introduction to the New Testament.* Translated by A. J. Mattill Jr. Nashville: Abingdon, 1975.

Kwon, Yon-Gyong. *Eschatology in Galatians: Rethinking Paul's Response to the Crisis in Galatia.* WUNT 2/183. Tübingen: Mohr Siebeck, 2004.

Lambrecht, Jan. "Abraham and His Offspring: A Comparison of Galatians 5,1 with 3,13." *Bib* 80 (1999): 525–36.

———. "Critical Reflections on Paul's 'Partisan ἐκ' as Recently Presented by Don Garlington." *ETL* 85 (2009): 135–41.

———. *Pauline Studies: Collected Essays by Jan Lambrecht.* BETL 115. Leuven: Leuven University Press, 1994.

Lightfoot, J. B. *The Epistle of St. Paul to the Galatians with Introductions, Notes and Dissertations.* Reprint. Grand Rapids: Zondervan, 1957.

Longenecker, Bruce W. *The Triumph of Abraham's God: The Transformation of Identity in Galatians.* Nashville: Abingdon, 1998.

———. "'Until Christ Is Formed in You': Suprahuman Forces and Moral Character in Galatians." *CBQ* 61 (1999): 92–108.

Longenecker, Richard N. *Galatians.* WBC. Dallas: Word, 1990.

Lull, D. J. "'The Law Was Our Pedagogue': A Study in Galatians 3.19–25." *JBL* 105 (1986): 481–98.

Luther, Martin. "The Freedom of a Christian." In *Three Treatises.* Translated by W. A. Lambert. Revised by Harold J. Grimm. Philadelphia: Fortress, 1970.

———. *Lectures on Galatians 1535: Chapters 1–4.* Vol. 26 of *Luther's Works.* Edited by Jarislov Pelikan. St. Louis: Concordia, 1963.

———. *Lectures on Galatians, 1535: Chapters 5–6. Lectures on Galatians 1519: Chapters 1–6.* Vol. 27 of *Luther's Works.* Edited by Jarislov Pelikan. St. Louis: Concordia, 1964.

Lutjens, Ronald. "'You Do Not Do What You Want': What Does Galatians 5:17 Really Mean?" *Presb* 16 (1990): 103–17.

Lyons, G. Pauline *Autobiography: Toward a New Understanding.* Atlanta: Scholars, 1985.

Machen, J. Gresham. *Machen's Notes on Galatians: Notes on Biblical Exposition and Other Aids to Interpretation of the Epistle to the Galatians from the Writings of J. Gresham Machen.* Edited by John H. Skilton. Nutley, NJ: Presbyterian and Reformed, 1977.

Martin, Troy W. "The Covenant of Circumcision (Genesis 17:9–14) and the Situational Antitheses in Galatians 3:28." *JBL* 122 (2003): 111–25.

Martyn, J. Louis. "Apocalyptic Antinomies in Paul's Letter to the Galatians." *NTS* 31 (1985): 410–24.

———. *Galatians: A New Translation with Introduction and Commentary.* AB. New York: Doubleday, 1997.

———. "A Law-Observant Mission to Gentiles." Pages 348–61 in *The Galatians Debate: Contemporary Issues in Rhetorical and Historical Interpretation.* Edited by Mark D. Nanos. Peabody, MA: Hendrickson, 2002.

Matera, Frank J. "The Culmination of Paul's Argument to the Galatians: Gal 5.1–6.17." *JSNT* 32 (1988): 79–91.

———. *Galatians.* Sacra Pagina. Collegeville, MN: Liturgical Press, 1992.

Matlock, R. Barry. "Detheologizing the πίστις Χριστοῦ Debate: Cautionary Remarks from a Lexical Semantic Perspective." *NovT* 42 (2000): 1–23.

———. "'Even the Demons Believe': Paul and πίστις Χριστοῦ." *CBQ* 64 (2002): 300–318.

———. "πίστις in Galatians 3:26: Neglected Evidence for 'Faith in Christ'?" *NTS* 49 (2003): 433–39.

———. "The Rhetoric of πίστις in Paul: Galatians 2.16, 3.22, and Philippians 3.9." *JSNT* 30 (2007): 173–203.

McEleney, Neil. "Conversion, Circumcision, and the Law." *NTS* 20 (1974): 319–41.

McKnight, Scot. *Galatians.* NIVAC. Grand Rapids: Zondervan, 1995.

Metzger, Bruce M. *A Textual Commentary on the Greek New Testament.* 2nd ed. Stuttgart: Deutsche Biblelgesellschaft, 2002.

Meyer, Jason. *The End of the Law: Mosaic Covenant in Pauline Theology.* Nashville: Broadman & Holman, 2009.

Mijoga, Hilary B. P. *The Pauline Notion of Deeds of the Law.* Lanham: International Scholars, 1999.

Moo, Douglas J. "'Law,' 'Works of the Law,' and Legalism in Paul." *WTJ* 45 (1983): 73–100.

Morland, Kjell Arne. *The Rhetoric of the Curse in Galatians: Paul Confronts Another Gospel.* Atlanta: Scholars Press, 1995.

Morris, Leon. *Galatians: Paul's Charter of Christian Freedom.* Downers Grove, IL: IVP, 1996.

Mussner, Franz. *Der Galaterbrief.* 5th ed. HTKNT. Freiburg: Herder, 1988.

Nanos, Mark D. *The Irony of Galatians: Paul's Letter in First-Century Context.* Minneapolis: Fortress, 2002.

———, ed. *The Galatians Debate: Contemporary Issues in Rhetorical and Historical Interpretation.* Peabody, MA: Hendrickson, 2002.

Neyrey, Jerome H. "Bewitched in Galatia: Paul and Cultural Anthropology." *CBQ* 50 (1988): 72–100.

Nolland, John. "Uncircumcised Proselytes?" *JSJ* 12 (1981): 173–94.

O'Brien, Peter T. "Was Paul Converted?" Pages 361–91 in *Justification and Variegated Nomism.* Vol. 2: *The Paradoxes of Paul.* WUNT 2/181. Edited by D. A. Carson, Peter T. O'Brien, and Mark A. Seifrid. Grand Rapids: Baker, 2004.

Oepke, Albrecht. *Der Brief des Paulus an die Galater.* 3rd ed. THKNT. Berlin: Evangelische Verlagsanstalt, 1973.

Owen, Paul L. "The 'Works of the Law' in Romans and Galatians: A New Defense of the Subjective Genitive." *JBL* 126 (2007): 553–77.

Plumer, Eric. *Augustine's Commentary on Galatians: Introduction, Text, Translation, and Notes.* Oxford: Oxford University Press, 2003.

Rainbow, Paul A. *The Way of Salvation: The Role of Christian Obedience in Justification.* Waynesboro, GA: Paternoster, 2005.

Räisänen, Heikki. "Galatians 2:16 and Paul's Break with Judaism." *NTS* 31 (1985): 543–53.

———. *Paul and the Law.* Philadelphia: Fortress, 1986.

Ramsey, William M. *Historical Commentary on Galatians.* Edited by Mark Wilson. Reprint. Grand Rapids: Kregel, 1997.

Rapa, Robert Keith. *The Meaning of "Works of the Law" in Galatians and Romans.* Studies in Biblical Literature 31. New York: Peter Lang, 2001.

Richardson, Peter. *Israel in the Apostolic Church.* SNTSMS 10. Cambridge: Cambridge University Press, 1969.

———. "Pauline Inconsistency: I Corinthians 9.19–23 and Galatians 2.11–14." *NTS* 26 (1979–80): 347–62.

Riches, John. *Galatians through the Centuries.* Blackwell Bible Commentaries. Oxford: Blackwell, 2008.

Ridderbos, Herman N. *The Epistle of Paul to the Churches of Galatia.* Translated by Henry Zylstra. NICNT. Grand Rapids: Eerdmans, 1953.

Riesner, Rainer. *Paul's Early Period: Chronology, Mission Strategy, Theology.* Translated by Doug Scott. Grand Rapids: Eerdmans, 1998.

Roo, Jacqueline C. R. de. *"Works of the Law" at Qumran and in Paul.* NTM 13. Sheffield: Sheffield Phoenix Press, 2007.

Sanders, E. P. *Judaism: Practice and Belief. 63 BCE — 66 CE.* Philadelphia: Trinity Press International, 1992.

———. *Paul, the Law, and the Jewish People.* Philadelphia: Fortress, 1983.

———. *Paul and Palestinian Judaism: A Comparison of Patterns of Religion.* Philadelphia: Fortress, 1977.

Schlier, Heinrich. *Der Brief an die Galater.* 12th ed. KEK. Göttingen: Vandenhoeck & Ruprecht, 1965.

Schmithals, Walter. *Paul and the Gnostics.* Translated by John E. Steely. Nashville: Abingdon, 1972.

Schnabel, Eckhard J. *Early Christian Mission.* 2 vols. Downers Grove, IL: IVP, 2004.

Schoeps, H. J. *Paul: The Theology of the Apostle in the Light of Jewish Religious History.* Translated by Harold Knight. Philadelphia: Westminster, 1961.

Schreiner, Thomas R. "Circumcision." *DPL*, 137 – 39.

———. *The Law and Its Fulfillment: A Pauline Theology of Law.* Grand Rapids: Baker, 1993.

———. "Law of Christ," *DPL*, 542 – 44.

———. *New Testament Theology: Magnifying God in Christ.* Grand Rapids: Baker, 2008.

———. "Paul and Perfect Obedience to the Law: An Evaluation of the View of E. P. Sanders." *WTJ* 47 (1985): 245 – 78.

———. *Romans.* BECNT. Grand Rapids: Baker, 1998.

———. "'Works of Law' in Paul." *NovT* 33 (1991): 217 – 44.

Scott, James M. *Adoption as Sons of God: An Exegetical Investigation into the Background of υἱοθεσία in the Pauline Corpus.* WUNT 2/48. Tübingen: Mohr Siebeck, 1992.

Seifrid, Mark A. *Christ Our Righteousness: Paul's Theology of Justification.* Downers Grove, IL: IVP, 2000.

———. "Paul, Luther, and Justification in Gal 2:15 – 21." *WTJ* 65 (2003): 215 – 30.

Silva, Moisés, "Faith versus Works of Law in Galatians." Pages 217 – 48 in *Justification and Variegated Nomism.* Vol. 2: *The Paradoxes of Paul.* WUNT 2/181. Edited by D. A. Carson, P. T. O'Brien, and M. A. Seifrid. Grand Rapids: Baker, 2004.

———. "Galatians." Pages 785 – 812 in *Commentary on the New Testament Use of the Old Testament.* Edited by G. K. Beale and D. A. Carson. Grand Rapids: Baker, 2007.

———. *Interpreting Galatians: Explorations in Exegetical Method.* 2nd ed. Grand Rapids: Baker, 2001.

Smiles, Vincent M. *The Gospel and the Law in Galatia: Paul's Response to Jewish-Christian Separatism and the Threat of Galatian Apostasy.* Collegeville, MN: Liturgical Press, 1998.

Sprinkle, Preston. *Law and Life: The Interpretation of Leviticus 18:5 in Early Judaism and Paul.* WUNT 2/241. Tübingen: Mohr Siebeck, 2008.

Stanley, Christopher D. "'Under a Curse': A Fresh Reading of Galatians 3.10 – 14." *NTS* 36 (1990): 481 – 511.

Stanton, Graham N. "The Law of Moses and the Law of Christ: Galatians 3:1 – 6:2." Pages 99 – 116 in *Paul and the Mosaic Law.* Edited by James D. G. Dunn. Tübingen: Mohr Siebeck, 1996.

———. "Review of Abraham in Galatians: Epistolary and Rhetorical Contexts." *JTS* 43 (1992): 614 – 15.

Stendahl, Krister. *Paul among Jews and Gentiles and Other Essays.* Philadelphia: Fortress, 1977.

Stott, John R. W. *The Message of Galatians.* London: IVP, 1968.

Stuhlmacher, Peter. *Reconciliation, Law, and Righteousness.* Philadelphia: Fortress, 1986.

Thielman, Frank. *From Plight to Solution: A Jewish Framework for Understanding Paul's View of the Law in Galatians and Romans.* NovTSup 61. Leiden: Brill, 1989.

———. *Paul and the Law: A Contextual Approach.* Downers Grove, IL: IVP, 1994.

Tolmie, D. Francois. *Persuading the Galatians: A Text-Centred Rhetorical Analysis of a Pauline Letter.* WUNT 2/190; Tübingen: Mohr Siebeck, 2005.

Tomson, Peter J. *Paul and the Jewish Law: Halakah in the Letters of the Apostle to the Gentiles.* CRINT 3/1. Minneapolis: Fortress, 1990.

VanLandingham, Chris. *Judgment and Justification in Early Judaism and the Apostle Paul.* Peabody, MA: Hendrickson, 2006.

Vermes, Geza. *The Dead Sea Scrolls in English.* 3rd ed. New York: Penguin, 1987.

Vouga, François. "Zur rhetorischen Gattung des Galaterbriefes." *ZNW* 79 (1988): 291 – 92.

Wakefield, Andrew H. *Where to Live: The Hermeneutical Significance of Paul's Citations from Scripture in Galatians 3:1 – 14.* SBLABib 14. Atlanta: Society of Biblical Literature, 2003.

Wallace, Daniel B. "Galatians 3:19 – 20: A *Crux Interpretum* for Paul's View of the Law." *WTJ* 52 (1990): 225 – 45.

———. *Greek Grammar beyond the Basics.* Grand Rapids: Zondervan, 1996.

Wallis, Ian G. *The Faith of Jesus Christ in Early Christian Traditions.* SNTSMS 84. Cambridge: Cambridge University Press, 1995.

Watson, Francis. *Paul and the Hermeneutics of Faith.* London: T&T Clark, 2004.

Watts, Rikki E. "'For I Am Not Ashamed of the Gospel': Romans 1:16 – 17 and Habakkuk 2:4." Pages 3 – 25 in *Romans and the People of God.* Edited by Sven K. Soderlund and N. T. Wright. Grand Rapids: Eerdmans, 1999.

Weima, Jeffrey A. D. "Gal 6:11 – 18: A Hermeneutical Key to the Galatian Letter." *CTJ* 28 (1993): 90 – 107.

———. *Neglected Endings: The Significance of Pauline Letter Closings.* JSNTSup 101. Sheffield: Sheffield Academic Press, 1994.

———. "What Does Aristotle Have to Do with Paul? An Evaluation of Rhetorical Criticism." *CTJ* 32 (1997): 458 – 68.

Westerholm, Stephen. *Israel's Law and the Church's Faith: Paul and His Recent Interpreters.* Grand Rapids: Eerdmans, 1988.

———. "On Fulfilling the Whole Law (Gal 5:14)." *SEÅ* 51 – 52 (1986 – 87): 229 – 37.

———. *Perspectives Old and New on Paul: The "Lutheran" Paul and His Critics.* Grand Rapids: Eerdmans, 2004.

Wilcox, Max. "The Promise of the 'Seed' in the New Testament and the Targumim." *JSNT* 5 (1979): 2 – 20.

———. "'Upon the Tree' — Deut 21:22 – 23 in the New Testament." *JBL* 96 (1977): 85 – 99.

Williams, Sam K. *Galatians.* ANTC. Nashville: Abingdon, 1997.

———. "Justification and the Spirit in Galatians," *JSNT* 29 (1987): 91 – 100.

Willitts, Joel. "Context Matters: Paul's Use of Leviticus 18:5 in Galatians 3:12." *TynBul* 54 (2003): 105 – 22.

———. "Isa 54,1 and Gal 4,24b – 27: Reading Genesis in Light of Isaiah." *ZNW* 96 (2005): 188 – 210.

Wilson, Todd A. *The Curse of the Law and the Crisis in Galatia: Reassessing the Purpose of Galatians.* WUNT 2/225. Tübingen: Mohr Siebeck, 2007.

———. "The Law of Christ and the Law of Moses: Reflections on a Recent Trend in Interpretation." *CurrBR* 5 (2006): 123 – 44.

———. "'Under Law' in Galatians: A Pauline Theological Abbreviation." *JTS* 56 (2005): 362 – 92.

———. "Wilderness Apostasy and Paul's Portrayal of the Crisis in Galatians." *NTS* 50 (2004): 550 – 71.

Winger, Michael. "Act One: Paul Arrives in Galatia." *NTS* 48 (2002): 548 – 67.

———. "The Law of Christ," *NTS* 46 (2000): 537 – 46.

Wisdom, Jeffrey R. *Blessing for the Nations and the Curse of the Law: Paul's Citation of Genesis and Deuteronomy in Gal 3.8 – 10.* WUNT 2/133. Tübingen: Mohr Siebeck, 2001.

Witherington, Ben, III. *Grace in Galatia: A Commentary on Paul's Letter to the Galatians.* Grand Rapids: Eerdmans, 1998.

———. "Rite and Rights for Women — Galatians 3.28." *NTS* 27 (1981): 593 – 604.

Yeung, Maureen W. *Faith in Jesus and Paul: A Comparison with Special Reference to "Faith That Can Move Mountains" and "Your Faith Has Healed/Saved You."* WUNT 2/147. Tübingen: Mohr Siebeck, 2002.

Young, Norman H. "*Paidagogos:* The Social Setting of a Pauline Metaphor." *NovT* 29 (1987): 150 – 76.

———. "Pronominal Shifts in Paul's Argument to the Galatians." Pages 205 – 15 in *Ancient History in a Modern University.* Vol. 2 in *Early Christianity in Late Antiquity and Beyond.* Edited by T. W. Hillard, R. A. Kearsley, C. E. V. Nixon, and A. M. Nobbs. Grand Rapids: Eerdmans, 1998.

Ziesler, J. A. *The Meaning of Righteousness in Paul: A Linguistic and Theological Enquiry.* SNTSMS 20. Cambridge: Cambridge University Press, 1972.

Galatians 1:1 – 5

Literary Context

Most Greco-Roman letters consisted of an opening, a body, and a closing. Paul's letters have the same elements, but the body of the letter is much longer in the Pauline letters than the typical Greco-Roman letter. Galatians begins with the typical Pauline structure: (1) identification of author ("Paul," 1:1); (2) the recipients ("the churches of Galatia," 1:2); and (3) the salutation ("grace and peace," 1:3). The usual salutation in Greco-Roman letters was "greetings" (χαίρειν). The use of the term "grace" (χάρις) by Paul represents an adaptation of the typical style, and in using the word "grace," he introduces a prominent theme in his gospel. The term "peace" (εἰρήνη) probably hails from Jewish letters that used the word "peace" (2 Macc 1:1; *2 Bar* 78:3) in the greeting.

In most instances in the Pauline letters the initial greeting is remarkably brief (1 Cor 1:1 – 3; 2 Cor 1:1 – 2; Eph 1:1 – 2; Phil 1:1 – 2; Col 1:1 – 2; 1 Thess 1:1; 2 Thess 1:1 – 2; 1 Tim 1:1 – 2; 2 Tim 1:1 – 2; Phlm 1 – 3), but the initial greeting in Galatians is a bit longer. The unique features in the greeting are particularly crucial, for the distinctive elements foreshadow important themes in the letter:[1]

1. Paul's apostleship derives from God rather than from human beings (1:1), so that he is defending himself against the objections of the opponents.
2. Other believers concur with the Pauline gospel (1:2).
3. The new age of salvation has broken into time by Christ's death and resurrection, which has delivered believers from this present evil age (1:1, 4).
4. The Pauline gospel brings glory to God (1:5).

---

1. On the importance of the introduction here, see David Cook, "The Prescript as Programme in Galatians," *JTS* 43 (1992): 511 – 19.

→ **I. Introduction: Desertion from Paul's Gospel Is Desertion from the Gospel (1:1 – 2:21)**
   A. Greeting: Paul's Apostolic Authority (1:1 – 5)
   B. Problem Explained: Desertion from the Gospel (1:6 – 10)
   C. Paul's Gospel Derived from God, Not People (1:11 – 2:21)

Main Idea

The main point in the opening of the letter is Paul's desire for the Galatians to enjoy grace and peace. He was called as an apostle so that they would enjoy such blessings, and Christ died and has been raised from the dead so that grace and peace would be theirs.

Translation

Galatians 1:1-5

1a	author	**Paul, an apostle,**
b	source	not from human beings
c	agency	neither through human beings, but
d	agency	through Jesus Christ and
e	list	God the Father,
f	description	who raised him from the dead,
2a	introduction	**and** **all the brothers with me,**
b	addressees/place	**to the churches of Galatia.**
3a	desire/prayer	**May grace and peace be yours**
b	source	from God our Father and
c	list	the Lord Jesus Christ,
4a	description	who gave himself for our sins
b	purpose	to deliver us from the present evil age according ⤴ to the will of our God and Father.
5	exclamation/inference *(from 4a-b)*	**To him be the glory for the ages of the ages, amen.**

Structure

Galatians, though it has a unique opening in some respects, has the three main elements of letter openings: (1) Paul identifies himself as the author; (2) the recipients of the letter are specified (the Galatians); and (3) Paul utters a prayer wish.

(1) The letter opens with Paul identifying himself as the author, but he immediately adds that his apostleship is not from or through human beings. Rather, he was called as an apostle through Jesus Christ on the Damascus road and through God the Father, who is identified as the one who raised Jesus from the dead. The letter is not from Paul alone, but also represents the views of all the fellow believers who are with him.

(2) The recipients of the letter are identified as those who are in "the churches of Galatia."

(3) The main and second point of the opening is relayed in the prayer wish, where Paul prays that the Galatians will know God's grace and peace that come from God the Father and the Lord Jesus Christ. After mentioning Christ, Paul identifies him in a confessional statement as the one who gave himself for sins, and the purpose of his atoning work was to rescue believers from the present evil age. Christ's redemptive work has been carried out by the Father's will, and hence Paul closes with a doxology emphasizing that all the glory for the salvation accomplished goes to him.

Exegetical Outline

I. Introduction: Desertion from Paul's Gospel Is Desertion from the Gospel (1:1 – 2:21)

→ **A. Greeting: Paul's Apostolic Authority (1:1 – 5)**

    1. Sender: Paul and fellow believers (1:1 – 2)

    2. Prayer wish (1:3)

    3. Purpose of Christ's death (1:4)

    4. Glory to God (1:5)

Explanation of the Text

1:1a Paul, an apostle (Παῦλος ἀπόστολος). One of the most important themes in Galatians is Paul's apostolic authority, and he affirms it from the outset. Paul regularly, though not always (cf. Phil 1:1; Phlm 1), affirms his apostolic authority at the beginning of his letters (Rom 1:1; 1 Cor 1:1; 2 Cor 1:1; Eph 1:1; Col 1:1; 1 Tim 1:1; 2 Tim 1:1; Titus 1:1). Paul was called as an apostle on the Damascus road when the Lord Jesus appeared to him (Gal 1:12; 1 Cor 9:1; cf. Acts 9:1 – 7). He was particularly called to proclaim the gospel to the Gentiles (Rom 11:13; Gal 1:16; 1 Tim 2:7; cf. Acts

9:15). His apostleship was verified by the churches he established (1 Cor 9:2) and by the signs he performed (2 Cor 12:12).[2]

1:1b-c Not from human beings neither through human beings (οὐκ ἀπ' ἀνθρώπων οὐδὲ δι' ἀνθρώπου). Paul emphasizes, somewhat surprisingly, that his apostleship does not have a human origin. The defensive statement regarding his apostleship indicates that he responds to charges about the legitimacy of his apostleship.[3] Such an apologetic is not found in any of the other Pauline letter openings. Indeed, Paul anticipates a major theme of the first two chapters in defending his apostleship.[4] Apparently some opponents doubted the credibility of Paul's apostleship, arguing that his gospel had a human origin. We should probably not press the distinction between "from" (ἀπό) and "through" (διά), for the two prepositions emphasize that Paul did not derive his gospel from any human source.[5]

1:1d-e But through Jesus Christ and God the Father (ἀλλὰ διὰ Ἰησοῦ Χριστοῦ καὶ θεοῦ

πατρός). Paul's apostleship does not stem from human beings, but he was called as an apostle through Jesus Christ and God the Father. We have confirmation here that the prepositions should not be unduly pressed, for Paul uses "through" (διά) but not "from" (ἀπό). It is unlikely that Paul intends to say that his apostleship was "through" Jesus Christ and God the Father, but not "from" them. Rather, the general point is clear. Paul's apostleship derives from Jesus Christ and God the Father.

His is a divine appointment and a divine commission, and hence the gospel he proclaims is authoritative and true. The text also suggests that Jesus Christ and the Father are both divine beings, for Paul was not called merely by human beings.[6] To say that Jesus Christ is divine, of course, does not deny that he was also human. Indeed, the name "Jesus" points to his humanity, as does the title "Christ." It is common in scholarship to say that the title Christ bears no significance in Paul, but this common view is almost certainly mistaken.[7]

---

2. Karl H. Rengstorf maintained that apostleship derived from the Jewish institution of the *shaliach* ("ἀπόστολος," *TDNT*, 1:414 – 20), but there are also some differences between the two institutions, and hence we must note the discontinuities as well. The *shaliach* was a temporary delegate, in contrast to the lifelong calling of apostles. In addition, the *shaliach* typically served as an envoy in matters of business rather than religious matters. See the discussion in Longenecker, *Galatians*, 2 – 4. Martyn says the late development of the tradition rules it out as a source for the Pauline conception (*Galatians*, 93).

3. So Bruce, *Galatians*, 72; Longenecker, *Galatians*, 4; Silva, *Interpreting Galatians*, 153; Bryant, *Crucified Christ in Galatians*, 113; Esler, *Galatians*, 70. Esler remarks (71) that in a culture marked by competition we would expect that the opponents would criticize Paul (cf. 1:8 – 9; 5:12).

4. Contra Johan S. Vos, "Paul's Argumentation in Galatians 1 – 2," in *The Galatians Debate: Contemporary Issues in Rhetorical and Historical Interpretation* (ed. Mark D. Nanos; Peabody, MA: Hendrickson, 2002), 171, 179 – 80. Beverly R. Gaventa stresses that Gal 1 – 2 should not be limited to apologetic purposes, for Paul also functions as an example for the

Galatians in these chapters ("Galatians 1 and 2: Autobiography as Paradigm," *NovT* 4 1986. : 309 – 26). Gaventa underestimates the apologetic function of Gal 1 – 2, but she does call attention to other themes that join Gal 1 – 2 to the remainder of the letter. Barclay notes the weakness of Gaventa's analysis: "that Paul presents himself in these chapters as a paradigm for the Galatians ... can only be true to a very limited extent since most of what Paul recounts is wholly unlike the Galatians' experience" (*Obeying the Truth*, 76, n. 1).

5. Rightly Silva, *Interpreting Galatians*, 53 – 54; Garlington, *Galatians*, 45. But see Longenecker, who takes the prepositions as denoting source and agency (*Galatians*, 4).

6. Therefore, we have an allusion to Paul's Damascus road calling (Longenecker, *Galatians*, 5).

7. Contra J. D. G. Dunn, *The Epistle to the Galatians* (BNTC; Peabody, MA: Hendrickson, 1993), 26 – 27. Rightly N. T. Wright, *The Climax of the Covenant: Christ and the Law in Pauline Theology* (Minneapolis: Fortress, 1992), 41 – 55; Craig Blomberg, "Messiah in the New Testament," in *Israel's Messiah in the Bible and the Dead Sea Scrolls* (ed. Richard S. Hess and M. Daniel Carroll; Grand Rapids: Baker, 2003), 125 – 32.

1:1f Who raised him from the dead (τοῦ ἐγείραντος αὐτὸν ἐκ νεκρῶν). Paul often notes that it was God's will that he serve as an apostle, but only here in an introduction does he mention that God raised Jesus Christ from the dead. What is the significance of the resurrection here? The resurrection signifies that the new age has dawned (cf. Isa 26:19; Ezek 37:1 – 14; Dan 12:1 – 3), in which God will fulfill all his saving promises to Israel and to the entire world.[8] One of the major themes of the letter emerges here. The Galatians were turning the clock back in salvation history by submitting to circumcision and the Mosaic law. Since Jesus has been raised from the dead, believers are no longer under the Mosaic covenant. Once again Paul anticipates one of the central themes of the letter (the fulfillment of God's eschatological promises).

1:2 And all the brothers with me, to the churches of Galatia (καὶ οἱ σὺν ἐμοὶ πάντες ἀδελφοὶ ταῖς ἐκκλησίαις τῆς Γαλατίας). The letter is not sent by Paul alone but also comes from fellow believers who are with Paul. By "brothers" Paul could be referring to fellow Christian leaders who traveled with him,[9] but more probably he refers to the fellow believers who are with him as he writes the letter. Paul's gospel cannot be dismissed as idiosyncratic, as if he were the only one who proclaimed it. On the contrary, the brothers with him affirm the very gospel Paul proclaims,[10] and that gospel does not include the requirement to be circumcised.[11] The letter was written to not only one church but

to all the churches in Galatia (cf. 1 Cor 16:1, 19; 2 Cor 8:1; Gal 1:22; 1 Thess 2:14). As argued in the introduction, the Galatian churches probably refer to the churches located in south Galatia.

1:3 May grace and peace be yours from God our Father and the Lord Jesus Christ (χάρις ὑμῖν καὶ εἰρήνη ἀπὸ θεοῦ πατρὸς ἡμῶν καὶ κυρίου Ἰησοῦ Χριστοῦ).[12] Paul prays here that God the Father and Jesus Christ will shower grace and peace upon believers. As noted previously, Paul adapts the greeting that characterized typical Hellenistic letters. God's grace in Paul refers to his free mercy that is lavished on all who believe in Jesus Christ. Grace in Paul must not be limited to unmerited favor but also refers to God's transforming power.[13] The reference to grace is particularly significant in Galatians, for the Galatians are in danger of accepting a "gospel" that denies the grace of God.

Grace comes from the OT words "grace" (*ḥēn*) and "steadfast love" (*ḥesed*), denoting God's loyal love. God's grace and mercy are featured in the words of Exod 34:6 – 7, which are repeated often in the OT (e.g., Neh 9:17; Ps 103:8; 145:8; Joel 2:13; Jonah 4:2), denoting his forgiveness of his sinful people. The OT often celebrates the Lord's loyal and steadfast love (*ḥesed*). See, for example, the refrain in Ps 136.

The order in the greeting ("grace," then "peace") may be significant, for peace with God and with fellow human beings is a result of God's grace.[14] Indeed, grace and peace are both gifts of

---

8. See also here Cook, "Prescript as Programme," 512 – 15.

9. So Hays, *Galatians*, 202. Ellis argues that Paul often uses the word "brothers" (ἀδελφοί) to refer to Christian leaders (*Prophecy and Hermeneutic*, 13 – 22, see esp. 15). It seems instead that Paul typically uses the term to refer to all fellow believers (male and female). Rightly Dunn, *Galatians*, 30.

10. So Chrysostom, *Galatians*, 4; Longenecker, *Galatians*, 5; Dunn, *Galatians*, 29; Bryant, *Crucified Christ in Galatians*, 115.

11. Cf. Garlington, *Galatians*, 49.

12. There is strong external evidence for putting "our" (ἡμῶν) with "Lord Jesus Christ" (κυρίου Ἰησοῦ Χριστοῦ) instead of "God the Father" (θεοῦ πατρός) (𝔓[46], B, D, 1739, Byz). But Pauline style supports the reading adopted here (cf. Rom 1:7; 1 Cor 1:3; 2 Cor 1:2; Eph 1:2; Phil 1:2; Phlm 3). Furthermore, some solid external evidence supports this reading as well (ℵ, A, P, Ψ, 33, 81, 326, 1241), and it is accepted here as original.

13. See Dunn, *Galatians*, 31.

14. So Fee, *Galatians*, 17.

God. They are given by God, who is the Father of believers and the Lord Jesus Christ. The peace enjoyed by believers is a fulfillment of the covenant promise of peace promised in Ezekiel (Ezek 37:26; cf. Ps 72:7; Isa 54:10), and it comes through the proclamation of the gospel (Isa 52:7).[15] Such peace becomes a reality only through the coming of the Messiah (Isa 9:6 – 7) and his suffering for his people (Isa 53:5), as Paul will clarify in Gal 1:4.

Paul anticipates a major theme of the letter, for believers are God's sons and daughters through Jesus Christ (3:26). They are adopted into his family (4:1 – 7). Grace and peace do not come only from God the Father but also from Jesus Christ. Such a statement betrays a high Christology, for nowhere in the NT does grace and peace come from an angelic being or a human being.[16] Such gifts come only from God, and hence we have some of the raw materials from which the church hammered out the doctrine of the Trinity.

1:4a Who gave himself for our sins (τοῦ δόντος ἑαυτὸν ὑπὲρ[17] τῶν ἁμαρτιῶν ἡμῶν). The grace and peace that come from Jesus Christ are rooted in his self-giving at the cross, where he suffered in the place of believers so that they would be forgiven of their sins. The reference to Jesus Christ leads Paul to the theme of the cross. The statement has a confessional ring, and some scholars believe that a confessional or hymnic statement is cited here (cf. also Eph 5:2, 25; 1 Tim 2:6; Titus 2:14).[18] A number of criteria have been specified

for detecting pre-Pauline tradition, but the criteria are not objective enough to be decisive, for it is equally possible that Paul himself formulates the significance of Jesus' death here.[19]

In any case, even if Paul cites tradition, it must be interpreted in the context of Galatians. Again, the opening signals a central theme in the entire letter.[20] The Galatians are only entranced by circumcision because they have forgotten the significance of the cross (2:20 – 21; 3:1, 13; 4:4 – 5; 5:11, 24; 6:12, 14, 17). A right relationship with God is not obtained by circumcision but only through trusting in the cross of Jesus Christ. The term "gave" (δόντος) anticipates 2:20, where Paul speaks of the Son of God as the one "who loved me and gave (παραδόντος) himself for me." The love of Jesus manifests itself in his voluntary death on behalf of his people. Jesus' death was necessary because of human sin, and he gave himself so that those who trust in him would receive forgiveness of sins. The death of Christ is also substitutionary, for death is the consequence of sin (Rom 6:23), but Jesus Christ surrendered his life to atone for sins, and hence believers are spared final separation from God.

1:4b To deliver us from the present evil age according to the will of our God and Father (ὅπως ἐξέληται ἡμᾶς ἐκ τοῦ αἰῶνος τοῦ ἐνεστῶτος πονηροῦ κατὰ τὸ θέλημα τοῦ θεοῦ καὶ πατρὸς ἡμῶν). The purpose (ὅπως) of Jesus' self-giving is now explained. Jesus died to rescue believers from

15. So Roy E. Ciampa, *The Presence and Function of Scripture in Galatians 1 and 2* (WUNT 2/102; Tübingen: Mohr Siebeck, 1998), 49; cf. also Matthew S. Harmon, "She Must and Shall Go Free: Paul's Isaianic Gospel in Galatians," PhD diss. (Wheaton, IL: Wheaton College Graduate School, 2006), 65 – 70.

16. Rightly Machen, *Galatians*, 27.

17. The preposition "for" (ὑπέρ) has stronger external support (ℵ¹, B, H, 6, 33, 81, 326, 630, 1241ˢ, 2464), but the insertion of "concerning" (περί) in some manuscripts (𝔓⁴⁶ᵛⁱᵈ, ℵ*,

A, D, F, G, Ψ, 𝔐) attests to the overlap of the two prepositions in Koine Greek (so also Fee, who favors "concerning" [περί], *Galatians*, 19 – 20, n. 21).

18. E.g., Bruce, *Galatians*, 75; Martyn, *Galatians*, 88.

19. It is likely that we have an echo of Isa 53:4, 12, where the Servant of the Lord gives his life for the sake of his people. See Ciampa, *The Presence of Scripture in Galatians 1 and 2*, 51 – 60; Hong, *Law in Galatians*, 76 – 77; Fee, *Galatians*, 19.

20. Cf. Bryant, *Crucified Christ in Galatians*, 163 – 94; Cook, "Prescript as Programme," 516.

the evil of this present age, which the Galatians were succumbing to by considering circumcision. Jesus' death is located in the will and purpose of God the Father, and hence it represents the fulfillment of God's saving purposes and thus fulfills OT prophecy. The verb "deliver" (ἐξαιρέω) hearkens back to the OT and probably recalls the Lord's work in rescuing his people from Egypt (Exod 3:8; 18:4, 8, 9, 10 LXX); hence, it points to God's promise to deliver his people in the future (Isa 31:5; 60:16; Ezek 34:27).[21]

The eschatological character of Galatians emerges here, for Jesus came to rescue believers "from the present evil age."[22] Jewish thought distinguished between "this age" and "the coming age."[23] We find such a distinction in Jesus' teaching as well (Matt 12:32; 13:39, 40, 49; 24:3; 28:20; Mark 10:30; Luke 18:30; 20:35). Paul also uses the language of this age and the age to come (Eph 1:21). This age is also designated as "the present world [age]" (τῷ νῦν αἰῶνι, 1 Tim 6:17), and believers are not to be conformed to this age (Rom 12:2) as Demas was (2 Tim 4:10), for the world dominates the lives of unbelievers (Eph 2:2). Believers have been granted grace to live the life of the age to come in the midst of the present age (τῷ νῦν αἰῶνι, Titus 2:12). The rulers of this age crucified Jesus Christ because they were unaware that he was the glorious Lord (1 Cor 2:6, 8).

The intellectual worldview that controls the mindset of unbelievers is limited to this age (1 Cor 1:20; 3:18), and Satan rules as the god of this age (2 Cor 4:4). The present evil age is not the only reality, for the "fulfillment [ends] of the ages" (τὰ τέλη τῶν αἰώνων) has now dawned in Jesus Christ (1 Cor 10:11). The cross of Christ represents the intrusion of the new age,[24] or as Paul says in Gal 6:14–15, the new creation. Indeed, the reference to the new creation at the close of the letter functions as an inclusio with the text here, so that at the beginning and end of the letter the arrival of the last days in Christ is featured. The world in its present form is passing away (1 Cor 7:31). Jesus reigns in the present evil age, and his rule will reach its climax in the age to come (Eph 1:21; cf. 1 Cor 15:24–28), so that in the coming ages all will marvel over the grace of God displayed in Jesus Christ (Eph 2:7).

Again a major theme in Galatians is foreshadowed,[25] for Paul clarifies in Gal 3–4 that the law belongs to the old age, and the promise of Abraham is now being fulfilled in Christ. Hence, those who receive circumcision fall back into the old evil age after being delivered from it through Christ's death.[26] We see as well here the eschatological tension of Paul's thought, for even though the new age has come in Jesus Christ, the old age has not vanished entirely.[27] Believers live in the interval

---

21. So Ciampa, *The Presence of Scripture in Galatians 1 and 2*, 61–62, n. 104; Todd A. Wilson, "Wilderness Apostasy and Paul's Portrayal of the Crisis in Galatians," *NTS* 50 (2004): 555–57. Harmon argues that Paul draws on Isa 53 here as well, maintaining that Isa 53:10 is particularly in view ("She Must and Shall Go Free," 71–84).

22. For the importance of eschatology or what Martyn calls apocalyptic, see J. Louis Martyn, "Apocalyptic Antinomies in Paul's Letter to the Galatians," *NTS* 31 (1985): 410–24.

23. See here the discussion in Ciampa, *The Presence of Scripture in Galatians 1 and 2*, 61, n. 103.

24. So Bruce, *Galatians*, 76. Contra Yon-Gyong Kwon, *Eschatology in Galatians: Rethinking Paul's Response to the*

Crisis in Galatia (WUNT 2/183; Tübingen: Mohr Siebeck, 2004), 156–61.

25. For the view that Gal 1:4 plays a fundamental role in Galatians, see Smiles, *Gospel and Law in Galatia*, 68–75.

26. Cf. Cook, "Prescript as Programme," 516–18. Dunn says, "Presumably he [Paul] intended the appended clauses as something of a rebuke to his readers" (*Galatians*, 34).

27. For the eschatological tension in the verse, see Martyn, *Galatians*, 98; Witherington, *Galatians*, 76–77; Dunn, *Galatians*, 36. Betz formulates this incorrectly when he says, "It does not say that the coming aeon has already begun" (*Galatians*, 42). On the contrary, the new age has been inaugurated but not consummated. For a view similar to Betz's, see Kwon, *Eschatology*, 156–57.

between the already and not yet. God's promises are already realized in Christ, but "the present evil age" still exists, so that believers must remain vigilant and keep putting their trust in the cross of Christ.

1:5 To him be the glory for the ages of the ages, amen (ᾧ ἡ δόξα εἰς τοὺς αἰῶνας τῶν αἰώνων, ἀμήν). The saving work of God in Christ leads Paul to doxology. God's glory and honor and praise are displayed supremely in Christ and in the cross. I would define the glory of God as the beauty, majesty, and greatness of who he is, and therefore in all he does, whether in salvation or in judgment, the greatness of his being is demonstrated. Indeed, God will be praised forever because of his saving work in Christ.

Theology in Application

Paul's Apostleship

The first theme we see in the letter is Paul's authority as an apostle. How do we apply such a theme today? Christians have differed on this issue throughout history. Roman Catholics have believed in apostolic succession, and hence apostolic authority is supremely expressed in the pontiff, the pope of the Roman Catholic Church. As a Protestant in the free church tradition, I believe that church officers today do not have the same status or authority as the original apostles. There is no indication in the NT that apostles were replaced after Pentecost. When James was put to death (Acts 12:2), nothing is said about a replacement being appointed.

Apostolic authority is now enshrined in apostolic writings. In other words, the authority for the church is not found in any living human beings but in the NT canon. We are interested in studying Scripture carefully and reading commentaries on the biblical text because we believe that the Scriptures (including the OT) are God's authoritative Word to us today. Therefore, we measure everything by the Scriptures and attempt to be careful and wise in interpreting them.

Some charismatic groups believe that there are still apostles today. We must carefully sort out what they mean by "apostle." If they mean that there are apostles in the same sense in which Paul and the Twelve were apostles, we should reject such an interpretation. No person today has the authority of a Paul or Peter or John. To say that there is such authority in any living person is dangerous and can easily lead to authoritarianism and spiritual abuse. It should be said that such authoritarianism and spiritual abuse is not confined to charismatic groups that claim apostolic authority. Unfortunately some pastors are tyrannical and domineering and act as if they are apostles, even if they believe there are no apostles today!

Others understand the word "apostle" in a derivative sense, interpreting it to refer to one who serves as a missionary. Paul does not have such a definition of apostle in mind in Gal 1:1, but we do see this meaning elsewhere in Paul (e.g., Rom 16:7). To say that the word "apostles" refers to one who serves as a missionary does not lead to the same kind of authoritarianism that so easily creeps in if one thinks he is an apostle on the same level as Peter and Paul. Still, it seems that using the word "apostle" to designate missionaries should be avoided since many are apt to misunderstand what that term means, and Paul almost always uses the word in a technical sense for those who have a unique and unrepeatable authority.

All the Brothers with Me

It is instructive that in 1:2 Paul refers to the other brothers who are with him, suggesting thereby that they agree with his gospel. Paul was not the only person in the world who understood the truth of the gospel. We see from chapter 2 that the apostles affirmed Paul's gospel as well. If we are propounding a view that has never been articulated throughout the history of the church, we are almost certainly wrong. If someone thinks he or she has discovered a new doctrine after two thousand years of church history, we can be quite confident that such a person is mistaken. We are not isolated as believers. We live in community and hence we learn from brothers and sisters of our day and from believers who have gone before us.

Therefore, we can be quite sure that a doctrine such as open theism is unbiblical.[28] No branch of the Christian church — whether Catholic, Orthodox, or Protestant — has ever endorsed such a theology. It is not enshrined in any confessional statements, nor has any significant theologian ever espoused such a teaching. The universal teaching of the church throughout history is a reliable guide that should not be jettisoned.

Grace and Peace

One of the fundamental prayers that we can pray for others is that they will know God's grace and peace (1:3). One of the greatest human needs is grace since we are all sinners, and sin brings conflict and anguish into our lives. Hence, we pray that God's grace will also secure peace, both in our own hearts and in our churches. Sometimes we don't know what to pray for others, but everyone needs God's grace and peace everyday. How does grace affect us practically?

- It reminds us of the danger of religion and morality: We can so easily think of ourselves as noble people.
- We too quickly become smug and satisfied with our accomplishments.
- We comfort ourselves by comparing ourselves with others and thinking that we are better.
- We compare our families with others and take refuge in the goodness of our children.

---

28. See Bruce A. Ware, *God's Lesser Glory: The Diminished God of Open Theism* (Wheaton: Crossway, 2000).

- I know I am not resting in Christ if I become defensive when I am criticized.
- It is better to feel desperate and weak like a child and to hide ourselves in Christ's righteousness than it is to feel strong and confident in ourselves.

Christ Crucified

The gospel proclaimed focuses on Christ crucified as the one who delivers us from our sins. The wonder and beauty of the gospel is forgotten if we fail to see the depth and gravity of our sin, for then the death of Christ seems unnecessary. When we actually see and feel the weight of our sin, our joy in the forgiveness granted us is inexpressible and full of glory. Paul implies here that Christ died as a substitute for our sin, for in giving himself for our sins he took upon himself the death we deserved.

Astonishingly, some who claim to be evangelicals have said that penal substitution is "cosmic child abuse."[29] Others have diminished its significance by consistently downplaying its centrality,[30] but it clearly functions as the heart of the atonement, for our greatest need is to have a substitute who died in our place so that we can be saved.[31]

The New Age — Already but Not Yet

The new age has dawned in Christ but it is not yet consummated. As Christians we live between the times. We are rescued from the present evil age through Christ's death (1:4), and yet we must be warned not to revert back to the old era. We are delivered from sin but are not sinless. We are perfect in Christ but not yet perfected. Hence, we must remain vigilant so that we do not become captive to a false gospel that actually panders to our selfishness and pride, even after we have become Christians.

God's Glory

God's saving work in Christ is for the glory of his name. Speaking of God's glory has become commonplace for many believers, but its significance must not be slighted. When Paul thinks of Christ's great work on the cross, his humiliation and exaltation, he concludes by saying that all that occurred in these events was

---

29. Steve Chalke, *The Lost Message of Jesus* (Grand Rapids: Zondervan, 2003), 182 – 83. D. A. Carson shows the weaknesses in Chalke's claim, so that what Chalke says about penal substitution does not qualify as serious scholarship (*Becoming Conversant with the Emergent Church: Understanding a Movement and Its Implications* [Grand Rapids: Zondervan, 2005], 185 – 87).

30. Joel B. Green and Mark D. Baker, *Recovering the Scandal of the Cross: Atonement in New Testament and Contemporary Contexts* (Downers Grove, IL: IVP, 2000).

31. In defense of this view, see Thomas R. Schreiner, "Penal Substitution View," in *The Nature of the Atonement: Four Views* (ed. J. Beilby and P. R. Eddy; Downers Grove, IL: IVP, 2006), 67 – 98.

"to the glory of God the Father" (Phil 2:11). Paul sketches out God's purpose in salvation history in Rom 9 – 11, relaying his plan to save both Jews and Gentiles. He breaks into a praise-filled doxology at the conclusion, affirming that "from him and through him and to him are all things. To him be the glory forever! Amen" (Rom 11:36). When Paul thinks of God's saving work in election and redemption, in uniting all things in Christ, and in giving the Holy Spirit, he offers praise to God's grace at three points in the argument (Eph 1:6, 12, 14).

At the conclusion of his greatest letter, Paul gives glory to God (Rom 16:27). He tells the Corinthians that all things must be done to glorify God (1 Cor 10:31). The root sin is the failure to thank and honor and glorify God, so that the creature is exalted rather than the Creator (Rom 1:21 – 25). Faith pleases God because it glorifies him and looks to him as one who can be trusted (Rom 4:20). Believers are to accept one another because such actions bring glory to God (Rom 15:7). One practical example will suffice. How do we glorify God when we play sports? We honor him when we thank him for the ability he gave us to play, when we treat our opponents with respect, and when we do not argue and become contentious when we disagree with those on the other team.

Paul reminds us in Galatians that God's saving work brings glory and praise and honor to God. As believers we need to be Christ-centered, God-focused, and Spirit-filled. We must focus not on human beings first and foremost but on God himself. We love other human beings most when we do everything for God's glory and praise. We were made as human beings to enjoy and find awe in greatness, and nothing fills our hearts more than God himself. He is to be the sun, the moon, and the stars in our lives. May his praise fill our lives and spill over to others.

CHAPTER 2

Galatians 1:6 – 10

Literary Context

Paul typically includes a thanksgiving after the opening of the letter (Rom 1:8 – 15; 1 Cor 1:4 – 9; Phil 1:3 – 11; Col 1:3 – 8; 1 Thess 1:2 – 10; 2 Thess 1:3 – 10; 1 Tim 1:12 – 17; 2 Tim 1:3 – 7; Phlm 4 – 7) or after the blessing (Eph 1:15 – 23). It is striking in Galatians, then, that the thanksgiving is omitted.[1] Instead, we find an expression of astonishment in Gal 1:6 since the Galatians are turning to another gospel. This expression of astonishment in terms of epistolary features may be construed as the opening of the rebuke section of the letter.[2] The body of the letter commences here, and the main issue in Galatians is introduced to the readers. Paul writes because the Galatians are veering away from Christ. Their defection is due to outside influences, and a curse is pronounced on those who proclaim any other gospel.

I. Introduction: Desertion from Paul's Gospel Is Desertion from the Gospel (1:1 – 2:21)

    A. Greeting: Paul's Apostolic Authority (1:1 – 5)

➡   **B. Problem Explained: Desertion from the Gospel (1:6 – 10)**

    C. Paul's Gospel Derived from God, Not People (1:11 – 2:21)

        1. Thesis: Source of His Gospel Was Revelation (1:11 – 12)

        2. Thesis Support (1:13 – 2:21)

Main Idea

The central idea is Paul's astonishment that the Galatians are turning from the grace that is theirs in the gospel of Christ. The remainder of the paragraph explicates why desertion from the gospel is a fatal decision.

---

1. So O'Brien, *Introductory Thanksgivings*, 141, n. 1.
2. Dahl, "Paul's Letter to the Galatians," 117 – 22; Vos,

"Paul's Argumentation in Galatians 1 – 2," 171; cf. Betz, *Galatians*, 46.

Translation

Galatians 1:6-10

6a	exclamation	**I am astonished that you are so quickly turning away** from the one who called you into the grace of Christ for another gospel.
b	separation	
7a	assertion	**In fact, it is not another gospel,**
b	contrast *(to 7a)*	but there are some who are disturbing you and
c	progression *(from 7a)*	wanting to alter the gospel of Christ.
8a	condition	**Indeed,** even if we or an angel from heaven preach a gospel to you contrary to that which we preached to you,
b	exclamation	**let him be accursed.**
9a	condition	As we have said before and I am again saying now, "If anyone preaches a gospel to you contrary to that which you have received,
b	exclamation	**let him be accursed."**
10a	rhetorical question/ inference *(from vv. 6-9)*	Therefore, **am I pleasing human beings now or God?**
b	rhetorical question/ restatement (of 10a)	Or, **am I seeking to please people?**
c	assertion/basis *(of 10a-b)*	For if I were still attempting to please people, I would never have become a slave of Christ.

Structure

The body of the letter commences with an expression of astonishment ("I am astonished" [θαυμάζω]) that the Galatians are departing so quickly from the gospel of grace for another gospel (1:6). Verses 7 – 9 explain, starting with a relative clause, why the new gospel is not a gospel at all. The intruders into the Galatian churches are not proclaiming the gospel truly but are altering the gospel. Nevertheless, Paul dogmatically insists in 1:8 – 9 with two conditional clauses that the gospel cannot be changed. Indeed, even if Paul or an angel were to proclaim a new gospel, they would be cursed by God. Verse 10 represents a transitional verse in the argument and functions as an inference from vv. 8 – 9. The pronouncement of a curse on those who proclaim a false gospel demonstrates that Paul does not please people. In 1:10c Paul explains why it is clear that he is not pleasing people, for if such were his goal, he would never have become a slave of Jesus Christ.

Exegetical Outline

> **I. Introduction: Desertion from Paul's Gospel Is Desertion from the Gospel (1:1 – 2:21)**
>   A. Greeting: Paul's Apostolic Authority (1:1 – 5)
> ➡ **B. Problem Explained: Desertion from the Gospel (1:6 – 10)**
>   1. Turning to a gospel that is no gospel (1:6 – 7)
>   2. A curse on those who proclaim or receive a false gospel (1:8 – 9)
>   3. Paul does not seek to please people (1:10)
>   C. Paul's Gospel Derived from God, Not People (1:11 – 2:21)

Explanation of the Text

1:6 I am astonished that you are so quickly turning away from the one who called you into the grace of Christ for another gospel (Θαυμάζω ὅτι οὕτως ταχέως μετατίθεσθε ἀπὸ τοῦ καλέσαντος ὑμᾶς ἐν χάριτι Χριστοῦ[3] εἰς ἕτερον εὐαγγέλιον). The body of the letter introduces the situation that called forth Paul's urgent letter. Paul is shocked that the Galatians are departing from the gospel Paul preached to them.[4] Elsewhere in Jewish literature the verb "turn" (μετατίθημι) can describe departure or apostasy from the Jewish way of life (e.g., 2 Macc 7:24).

Paul is distressed that the Galatians are moving away from the only hope they have for the

---

3. There is some evidence for the omission of Χριστοῦ since it is lacking in 𝔓[46] and in the Western text. At the same time the external evidence for inclusion is remarkably strong. A decision is difficult, but the external evidence favors including the title (so Fee, *Galatians*, 23, n. 27).

4. The Galatians are in the process of departing from the gospel, but some lean too heavily on the present tense to defend this notion (e.g., Longenecker, *Galatians*, 14; Dunn, *Galatians*, 40). What indicates a process is the context of the letter as a whole.

forgiveness of sins, and hence the expression of astonishment also functions as a rebuke.[5] The words "so quickly" (οὕτως ταχύς) echo Exod 32:8 (cf. also Judg 2:17) and the golden calf incident.[6] Israel had just been liberated from Egypt, received the law at Mount Sinai, and entered into covenant with the Lord. When Moses ascended the mountain, they fashioned and worshiped the golden calf, turning aside from the Lord. As Exod 32:8 says, "They have turned aside quickly (παρέβησαν ταχύ) out of the way that I commanded them" (ESV). The Galatians seem to be repeating the error of the wilderness generation by departing from the Lord shortly after being delivered.

The Galatians' departure is shocking, for they are abandoning the gift of grace that is theirs in Christ. Paul emphasizes that God called them into the realm of Christ's grace.[7] The word group for "calling" (καλέω, κλῆσις, κλητός) is a Pauline favorite. The gospel is "preached" (κηρύσσω) to all, whether Jews or Greeks (1 Cor 1:22 – 23), but only some among all those who hear the message are "called" (κλητός, 1 Cor 1:24). Indeed, in subsequent verses the term "called" is explained in terms of those whom God has *chosen* (ἐκλέγομαι, 1 Cor 1:26 – 28).

It seems, then, that calling occurs *through* the proclaimed word, and yet calling is not absolutely coterminus with the word proclaimed since only *some* of those who hear the word are called. Calling, then, cannot be the same as being *invited* to be saved, for all those who hear the word preached are summoned to faith and obedience. Since calling overlaps with being chosen in this context, it seems that calling refers to God's effective work in bringing some who hear the gospel to saving faith (cf. Rom 8:30).[8]

The efficacy of God's call is a repeated theme in Pauline writings. God "calls into existence the things that do not exist" (Rom 4:17 ESV).[9] In context this refers to God's granting Abraham and Sarah the ability to have children. He calls life into being where no ability to produce life exists. Similarly, it was God's call that turned Paul from being a persecutor of the church to an apostle of Jesus Christ (Gal 1:13 – 16). In Rom 9 God's call is closely associated with his electing work, indicating that God effectively saves (Rom 9:7, 11, 24, 25, 26). Those whom God has chosen are called to faith through the proclamation of the gospel (2 Thess 2:13 – 14).[10] The God who has powerfully called believers to himself will also complete his sanctifying work (1 Thess 5:24). God's call stands in contrast to works (Rom 9:11; 2 Tim 1:9), for human works do not and cannot save, but only the grace of God. The power of God's call is evident, for "the gifts and the calling of God are irrevocable" (Rom 11:29 ESV).

---

5. Kwon rightly sees how crucial the issue of apostasy is in his work (*Eschatology*), but he goes beyond the evidence in saying that Paul maintains that the Galatians have already apostatized. Instead, according to Paul, the Galatians are on the verge of apostasy. See the exegesis of 5:2 – 4, where Paul warns the Galatians of apostasy rather than asserting that they have already committed it.

6. Israel's sin with the golden calf was etched upon its consciousness and is often recalled in Jewish tradition. See Scott J. Hafemann, *Paul, Moses, and the History of Israel* (WUNT; Tübingen: Mohr Siebeck, 1995), 195 – 204, 227 – 31; Ciampa, *The Presence of Scripture in Galatians 1 and 2*, 76 – 77; Wilson, "Wilderness Apostasy," 557 – 58.

7. The phrase "in grace" (ἐν χάριτι) may mean "by means of the grace" of Christ, but it is more likely that he refers to the realm of grace here. So Fee, *Galatians*, 23.

8. Against L. Michael White, who thinks that Paul rather than God is the one who called the Galatians. "Rhetoric and Reality in Galatians: Framing the Social Demands of Friendship," in *Early Christianity and Classical Culture: Comparative Studies in Honor of Abraham J. Malherbe* (ed. John T. Fitzgerald, Thomas H. Olbricht, and L. Michael White; NovTSup 110; Leiden: Brill, 2003), 326.

9. Rightly Martyn, *Galatians*, 109.

10. So also C. A. Wanamaker, *The Epistles to the Thessalonians* (NIGTC; Grand Rapids: Eerdmans, 1990), 267.

It is clear, then, that "calling" in Paul is inseparable from the gospel of grace. The Galatians by turning to the law and circumcision have departed from such a gospel to one based on human achievement rather than a divine gift. The word "gospel" (εὐαγγέλιον) hearkens back to the promise of return from exile in the OT (Isa 40:9; 52:7; 60:6; 61:1).[11] In Isa 40 – 66 the return from exile is linked with the fulfillment of God's promises to Israel and the inauguration of the new creation (Isa 65:17; 66:22). Paul sees this gospel — the fulfillment of God's saving promises — as realized in the ministry, death, and resurrection of Jesus Christ. The forgiveness of sins accomplished in the cross represents the fulfillment of God's eschatological promises.

1:7a In fact, it is not another gospel (ὃ οὐκ ἔστιν ἄλλο). Paul clarifies that the so-called gospel of the intruders is no gospel at all. Scholars of a former era tended to distinguish between the two Greek words for "another" (ἕτερος and ἄλλος), with the former Greek word (ἕτερος) meaning another of a different kind and the latter term (ἄλλος) meaning another of the same kind.[12] We have no clear evidence that the two different words for "another" had such technical definitions when the NT was composed.[13] Paul simply emphasizes in 1:7 that the so-called good news proclaimed by the intruders is no gospel at all.

1:7b But there are some who are disturbing you and wanting to alter the gospel of Christ (εἰ μή τινές εἰσιν οἱ ταράσσοντες ὑμᾶς καὶ θέλοντες μεταστρέψαι τὸ εὐαγγέλιον τοῦ Χριστοῦ). The reason for the Galatians' defection is now provided. Others were troubling them and causing them to doubt the validity of the gospel Paul proclaimed. It is likely that these troublemakers came from outside and argued that the gospel preached by Paul was seriously defective.[14] Here the phrase "some who are disturbing" (οἱ ταράσσοντες) is in the plural, indicating a number of opponents. In 5:10 the same word is used in the singular. "The one disturbing (ὁ ταράσσων) you will bear his judgment, whoever he is."[15] The use of the singular in 5:10 may indicate the leader among those who are annoying the Galatians, but it is more probable that the singular is generic in 5:10, so that the latter verse refers to the same group identified in 1:7.

Those disturbing the Galatians are criticized for desiring "to alter" (μεταστρέψαι) Christ's gospel. The word "alter" (from μεταστρέφω) is often used to denote strong contrasts, "denoting a radical change, as of water into blood, or fresh water into salt, or feasting into mourning, or daylight into darkness."[16] The opponents have been trying to seduce the Galatians to turn from the light of the true gospel to the darkness of a false gospel. How did the troublemakers alter Christ's gospel?[17]

---

11. See here Bruce, *Galatians*, 81 – 82; Garlington, *Galatians*, 67. Harmon provides a fuller explication of the Isaianic background ("She Must and Shall Go Free," 85 – 90).

12. J. B. Lightfoot, *Galatians*, 76; Burton, *Galatians*, 420 – 22; George, *Galatians*, 93; Bruce, *Galatians*, 80 – 81, though Bruce recognizes that Paul does not consistently maintain this distinction.

13. Martyn, *Galatians*, 110; Silva, *Interpreting Galatians*, 54 – 56. Garlington notes that the two words (ἕτερος and ἄλλος) are evidently synonymous in 2 Cor 11:4 (*Galatians*, 68)

14. See the section on the situation of the letter in the introduction.

15. The reference to the opponents as "troublers" may echo Achan's sin in Israel (cf. 1 Chr 2:7; Ps 107:27). So Longenecker, *Galatians*, 16; Ciampa, *The Presence of Scripture in Galatians 1 and 2*, 79 – 82. Stephen Anthony Cummins, from the parallels in 1 Macc 3:5 and 7:22, sees a parallel to the persecution in Maccabean times. *Paul and the Crucified Christ in Antioch: Maccabean Martyrdom and Galatians 1 and 2* (SNTSMS 114; Cambridge: Cambridge Univ. Press, 2001), 101.

16. Dunn, *Galatians*, 43.

17. Longenecker is likely correct in reading the genitive "of Christ" (τοῦ Χριστοῦ) as both objective and subjective (*Galatians*, 16).

We know from the remainder of the letter that they tried to persuade the Galatians to accept circumcision and submit to the OT law to become members of the people of God (cf. 5:2 – 6; 6:12 – 13; cf. 2:3 – 5). Such requirements, according to Paul, amounted to a distortion of the gospel, for it compelled Gentiles to adopt the Mosaic covenant for salvation.

1:8 Indeed, even if we or an angel from heaven preach a gospel to you contrary to that which we preached to you, let him be accursed (ἀλλὰ καὶ ἐὰν ἡμεῖς ἢ ἄγγελος ἐξ οὐρανοῦ εὐαγγελίζηται ὑμῖν[18] παρ' ὃ εὐηγγελισάμεθα ὑμῖν, ἀνάθεμα ἔστω). The truth of the message depends on its content (whether it accords with the gospel), not the credentials of the messenger. Therefore, even if Paul or an angel proclaimed a false gospel, they would stand under God's curse. The word ἀλλά, which introduces 1:8, does not signify a contrast here, but should be translated as "yet" or "indeed."[19] Verses 8 – 9 indicate that proclaiming another gospel is not a minor defect. Paul does not view the other gospel as a trivial departure from what he taught and preached in Galatia. Note that curse and blessing frame the letter (cf. 6:16).[20]

Paul uses hyperbolic language to exclude any source that might claim divine authority.[21] There is no suggestion here that the Galatian agitators actually claimed to have received revelation from an angel.[22] Paul uses conditional clauses in both 1:8 – 9, and he includes himself and angels, not because either was preaching a false gospel or alleged to do so, but to highlight the unchangeable nature of the gospel.[23] Furthermore, the inclusion of Paul demonstrates that Paul "is rebuking the Galatians, not in order to further his own agenda, but for the sake of the gospel, and for their sake."[24] The troublemakers did not appeal to angels but to the OT to argue for the necessity of circumcision (Gen 17:9 – 14). Still, the reference to angels demonstrates that preaching another gospel cannot be defended, even if the proclamation is defended by appealing to a heavenly source or a heavenly revelation.

Those proclaiming a false gospel are "accursed" (ἀνάθεμα). The term refers here to final destruction and condemnation. For example, in 1 Cor 16:22 those who fail to love the Lord Jesus are accursed. And Paul could almost wish to be cursed so that Jews who are separated from Christ will be saved (Rom 9:3). The word has its roots in the OT word "destruction" (*ḥērem*), which refers to something devoted to God (e.g., Lev 27:28 – 29; Num 18:14; Deut 7:26).[25] Paul draws on OT contexts where the word means destruction. For instance, those who sacrifice to other gods will be devoted to destruction (*ḥrm*, Exod 22:20). The cities within the land of promise were devoted to destruction and wiped out entirely (e.g., Num 21:2 – 3; Josh 6:17). Therefore, irrevocable punishment will be meted out to those who proclaim another gospel.

Excommunication by the church is not in view

18. Perhaps "to you" (ὑμῖν) is omitted in some manuscripts to make the statement a general one. The external evidence supports including the pronoun, and this seems to be slightly more likely.

19. Cf. D. J. Armitage, "An Exploration of Conditional Clause Exegesis with Reference to Galatians 1,8 – 9," *Bib* 88 (2007): 383.

20. So Wilson, *Curse of the Law*, 23.

21. Cf. Armitage, "Conditional Clause Exegesis," 375.

22. Against Betz, *Galatians*, 53; Martyn, *Galatians*, 113 (speaking through the false teachers); Witherington, *Gala-tians*, 83 (via the Mosaic law); Clinton E. Arnold, "Returning to the Domain of the Powers: *Stoicheia* as Evil Spirits in Galatians 4:3, 9," *NovT* 38 (1996): 75. George suggests that an angel may be mentioned since angels mediated the law (*Galatians*, 98).

23. Armitage notes that the word "even" (καί) demonstrates that it is unlikely that the condition would be fulfilled ("Conditional Clause Exegesis," 377). Cf. also Hays, *Galatians*, 206.

24. Armitage, "Conditional Clause Exegesis," 390.

25. For an examination of the term, see Kjell Arne Morland, *The Rhetoric of the Curse in Galatians: Paul Confronts Another Gospel* (Atlanta: Scholars Press, 1995), 81 – 96.

here[26] but eschatological punishment meted out by God.[27] It is evident from the strong language used that Paul does not consider the Galatian opponents to be believers, for they preach a different gospel. The curse Paul pronounces may also hearken back to Deut 13:1–11, where a false prophet who preaches apostasy is to be put to death.[28] But such an allusion does not indicate that church discipline is in view. Rather, end-time destruction from God himself will be the destiny of those who proclaim a false gospel.

1:9 As we have said before and I am again saying now, "If anyone preaches a gospel to you contrary to that which you have received, let him be accursed" (ὡς προειρήκαμεν καὶ ἄρτι πάλιν λέγω, εἴ τις ὑμᾶς εὐαγγελίζεται παρ' ὃ παρελάβετε, ἀνάθεμα ἔστω). Paul reaffirms the curse pronounced in v. 8 but applies it more broadly. Here Paul likely has in mind the Judaizers who were proclaiming a false gospel, and he pronounces a curse on them or anyone else who preaches a message contrary to what he previously preached.

Before pronouncing the curse, Paul reminds the Galatians that he is not saying anything new. He had instructed them that the gospel could not be altered when he first evangelized them.[29] The argument progresses from 1:8 to 1:9. If a curse falls on an apostle like Paul or even an angel if they proclaim a deviant gospel, then surely anyone else

who propagates a false gospel will be cursed.[30] Paul uses a conditional clause to summon the readers to consider whether the condition is fulfilled. The conditional clause here differs from 1:8, for now an indicative is used rather than a subjunctive. The use of the indicative here "invites an altogether less hypothetical application."[31] In other words, the opponents who proclaim another gospel are likely in view, and Paul affirms that those who promote a divergent gospel will be cursed.

Paul reaffirms, then, that the Galatians had already heard and received the true gospel when he first preached to them. Therefore, anyone who evangelizes in Galatia must proclaim the same gospel taught by Paul. If they teach a gospel contrary to Paul's, they will face an eschatological curse. By repeating the threat of God's curse in v. 9, the gravity of the offense of those who proclaim another gospel is underlined.

1:10a-b Therefore, am I pleasing human beings now or God? Or, am I seeking to please people? (Ἄρτι γὰρ ἀνθρώπους πείθω ἢ τὸν θεόν; ἢ ζητῶ ἀνθρώποις ἀρέσκειν). Paul uses rhetorical questions to emphasize that he is not trying to please people. The function of 1:10 in the argument is disputed. Does it stand alone, or does it belong with the previous paragraph, or the next one? Probably it is best to see the verse as transitional.[32] The conjunction in this context should be translated

---

26. Betz, *Galatians*, 54.

27. So Longenecker, *Galatians*, 17; Armitage, "Conditional Clause Exegesis," 376.

28. So Karl O. Sandnes, *Paul — One of the Prophets? A Contribution to the Apostle's Self-Understanding* (WUNT 2/43; Tübingen: J. C. B. Mohr, 1991), 71–72; Ciampa, *The Presence of Scripture in Galatians 1 and 2*, 83–88; Wilson, *Curse of the Law*, 25–26. Morland suggests as well that the covenantal curses of Deuteronomy 27–30 are in view (*The Rhetoric of the Curse in Galatians*, 151–53).

29. Alternatively, Armitage argues that the placement of the words "as we have said before" (ὡς προειρήκαμεν) indicates that Paul recalls 1:8, not what he said to the Galatians

orally on a previous occasion ("Conditional Clause Exegesis," 381).

30. So Morland, *The Rhetoric of the Curse in Galatians*, 150.

31. Armitage, "Conditional Clause Exegesis," 383, 389. So also Morland, *The Rhetoric of the Curse in Galatians*, 149; Martyn, *Galatians*, 114.

32. So George, *Galatians*, 100; Fee, *Galatians*, 32–33; Betz, *Galatians*, 54 (who also includes 1:11 as part of the transition). Garlington identifies 1:10 as "the climax" of 1:6–9 (*Galatians*, 71). Brian J. Dodd rightly sees the importance of 1:10, but I am not persuaded by his claim that Gal 1–2 are not apologetic ("Christ's Slave, People Pleasers and Galatians 1.10," *NTS* 42 [1996]: 90–104).

as "therefore" (γάρ).[33] The meaning of this term must be discerned in context, and in 1:10 it does not provide a *reason* for what is stated in 1:8 – 9 but a *conclusion*. Because Paul pronounces a curse on those who preach a false gospel (1:8 – 9), *therefore* it follows that he is not attempting to please people but only God himself (1:10).[34] The definition "therefore" falls within the semantic range of the conjunction (γάρ).[35]

The word πείθω usually means "persuade," but in this context it refers to the desire to please human beings or God.[36] Apparently, the Jewish opponents claimed that Paul failed to preach the whole gospel, which included the requirement of circumcision. Paul omitted circumcision to curry favor with the Gentiles in Galatia (cf. 5:11). Paul began the letter defending his apostolic authority, and here he rebuts the notion that he is pleasing people. Hence, it seems that Paul engages in an apologetic of his apostleship.

1:10c For if I were still attempting to please people, I would never have become a slave of Christ (εἰ ἔτι ἀνθρώποις ἤρεσκον, Χριστοῦ δοῦλος οὐκ ἂν ἤμην). We have a second class, contrary-to-fact condition here. If Paul had desired to please people (but he did not so desire), then he would never have become Christ's slave. Paul's curse on those who proclaim another gospel demonstrates that his aim is to please God rather than people. He clinches the case here by affirming that if he longed for the praise of fellow human beings, he would not have become a follower of Christ.

In the subsequent verses Paul will explain further how this is so, for he will argue shortly (1:13 – 14) that he was respected in Judaism for his zeal and learning. Conversely, as a Christian he is persecuted (5:11) and beaten (6:17). His suffering as an apostle verifies that he had become a "slave" (δοῦλος) of Christ, that he was vilified and attacked just like his Lord. Paul's willingness to suffer supports the truth that his goal in life is not to please people but God, that he is committed, as a slave of Christ, to do whatever the Lord commands.

Theology in Application

Proneness to Wander

We see from 1:6 that even after we become believers, we are prone to wander from God and the good news of free grace in Christ. Various influences may draw us away, including the sinfulness of our own hearts. In Galatians we see the influence of false teachers, who probably swayed the Galatians with their knowledge of the OT. An effective antidote against false teaching is both a head and heart knowledge of the gospel. When we truly understand that our righteousness is only in Christ, we will not be deceived by any other gospel. One of the practical ways to

---

33. On the other hand, it could be read as a loose connective. So Martyn, *Galatians,* 137.

34. Rightly Lategan, "Argumentative Situation of Galatians," 389 – 90; Dunn, *Galatians,* 49.

35. BDAG, s.v. 3 under γάρ. Longenecker sets off 1:10 as a separate paragraph (*Galatians,* 18).

36. Cf. Longenecker, *Galatians,* 18; Fee, *Galatians,* 33. Perhaps Paul contrasts himself here with religious charlatans. So Bruce, *Galatians,* 84 – 85; Martyn, *Galatians,* 138 – 40; Matera, *Galatians,* 47 – 48. The parallels are not clear enough to construct a link with the Maccabean period. Against Cummins, *Crucified Christ,* 112 – 13.

ensure that we stay true to the gospel is to join and become involved in a church that proclaims the gospel. Thereby we are accountable to other believers and do not try to live the Christian life on our own.

Only One Gospel

Paul also underscores in these verses that there is only one gospel and only one way of salvation. The severity of his language is striking. Paul pronounces an eternal curse on any who preach another gospel. He dogmatically rejects the gospel taught by the Judaizers and says that it is no gospel at all. The weightiness of Paul's judgment against the false teachers strikes home when we realize that the Judaizers most likely proclaimed that Jesus was the Christ. Nowhere in this book does Paul criticize the Galatians for a defective Christology. They are indicted for *adding* to the gospel by insisting that one cannot be a believer without being circumcised and keeping the OT law. Paul does not conceive of the difference between him and the Judaizers as a mere difference of opinion. On the contrary, he is convinced that they are not saved, that they will face eternal destruction, even though they accept Jesus as the Messiah.

Any theology, then, that posits works as the basis of our relationship with God is not the gospel of Christ. We must continue to uphold the gospel of grace that was formulated so clearly by Luther, Calvin, and the other Reformers. The clarity and the truth of the gospel could easily be lost. So many other things may clutter our minds, hearts, and lives that we may forget about the gospel, thinking all the while that we have not strayed from it. In our churches we may begin to concentrate on what it means to be good parents, to have a good marriage, to form meaningful relationships, and to make an impact in the world (all good things of course!), so that we slowly and inadvertently drift away from the gospel of free grace.

The Exclusivism of the Gospel

We also see in Paul's bracing words the exclusivism of the gospel. Many in our world today embrace pluralism (salvation may be gained through all religions) or inclusivism (people may be saved through Christ, even though they have never heard the gospel). Obviously, I cannot deal with the complexities of such a topic here or do it justice in such brief remarks. I can only point the reader to a discussion of this matter elsewhere[37] and register my opinion that exclusivism accords with the biblical witness. In a world where tolerance is valued and the rigidity of the past generations is rejected, we are inclined to go to the other extreme.

37. See the very fine treatment, *Faith Comes by Hearing: A Response to Inclusivism* (ed. Christopher W. Morgan and Robert A. Peterson; Nottingham, England: IVP, 2008). See also James M. Hamilton Jr., "Who Can Be Saved? A Review Article," *TJ* 28 (2007): 89 – 112.

Is it the case that Paul's anathemas here seem to be ill-mannered and unloving? Such sentiments reveal how far we have strayed from the biblical witness, indicating that our churches have not rightly balanced the doctrines of God's holiness and his love. We must beware of becoming cranks, and it is hoped that we do not adopt such a theology because we are judgmental, negative, and cynical. We must have courage to proclaim that there is only one way to salvation, that one is saved not by living a good life but only through faith in Jesus Christ. If we fail to proclaim that there is only one name by which we can be saved (Acts 4:12) and that human beings come to God only through Jesus (John 14:6), we will doubtless give assurance of salvation to people who are heading for final judgment. Nothing can be more unloving than granting false assurance to the perishing.

How does this apply practically? We must have courage to tell those with whom we work and those who live in our neighborhoods that if they are not trusting in Jesus Christ as the crucified and risen one, they are not saved. How much easier it is to smile and to say nothing and to think we just show we are Christians by how nice we are.

Pleasing God

Paul also warns us in this text about the danger of trying to please people instead of pleasing God. What slavery we live under when we long for the good opinion of others! It is far better to be a slave of Christ than to be enslaved to human opinions of us. Fear of human beings can be deadly. The reason many did not believe in Jesus was because they lusted for the glory and praise of people more than the glory of God (John 5:43 – 44). The parents of the blind man in John 9 were intimidated by the Pharisees and so refused to acknowledge Jesus' healing work in their son (John 9:22). In chapter 12 John sums up Jesus' public ministry: "Yet at the same time many even among the leaders believed in him. But because of the Pharisees they would not confess their faith for fear they would be put out of the synagogue; for they loved praise from men more than praise from God" (John 12:42 – 43).

I understand these verses to teach that such people did not have genuine saving faith (cf. John 2:23 – 25). Again, the reason for their failure to follow Jesus was fear of human beings. Such fear cannot be dismissed as trivial, for we have seen that fear of people may prevent us from putting our trust in Christ. What conquers such fear? God's promise that he will give to us everything we need, that he does not withhold any good thing from those who fear him (Pss 34:9; 84:11). We need a work of God's grace and Spirit to trust his great promises and to be liberated from the fear of people. Perhaps we fear to tell someone else at work what it means to be a Christian. Or perhaps we fear to share our struggles with other Christians because we are worried that they will think less of us. But we must fear God rather than people and be willing to be courageous and vulnerable.

CHAPTER 3

Galatians 1:11 – 17

Literary Context

Paul has opened the letter by affirming his apostolic authority, praying that grace and peace would be given to the Galatians by God and Jesus Christ (1:1 – 5). Such grace has been manifested supremely in the death of Christ, by which believers are inducted into the age to come, even while the present evil age continues. The introduction to the body of the letter shows why the Galatians need grace and peace so desperately (1:6 – 10). Outside teachers have come in, so that the Galatians have turned to (or are about to turn to) another gospel. Such a shift is no idle matter, according to Paul, for the gospel given by the Judaizers is no gospel at all, and any who proclaim it or receive it will be cursed by God forever.

Verse 10 is transitional in the argument. The anathema Paul proclaims (1:8 – 9) demonstrates that he is not attempting to please people. If that were his design, he would never have become a believer in Christ (1:10). Verse 11, with the rather formulaic words "I want to make known to you," may be identified as the opening to the remainder of the letter after the introduction.[1] Indeed, this verse itself functions as a thesis statement that supports the claim from 1:10 that Paul is not pleasing people.[2] He does not please people because the gospel he proclaims is not a human gospel.

In the remainder of 1:12 – 17 Paul supports the thesis that his gospel is not human by appealing to the revelation of that gospel on the Damascus road (1:12), his past life in Judaism (1:13 – 14), and his conversion and call apart from human mediation (1:15 – 17). Verse 11 commences an autobiographical and apologetic defense of the Pauline gospel that extends to the close of 2:21. The narrative character of the text is indicated by the temporal words that link the various sections together: "when" (ὅτε, 1:15); "then" (ἔπειτα, 1:18); "then" (ἔπειτα, 1:21); "then" (ἔπειτα, 2:1); "when" (ὅτε, 2:11).

What is evident, then, is that Paul is telling a story. Most scholars have understood Paul here to be engaging in a defense of his apostleship, which was questioned

---

1. Longenecker identifies this as a disclosure formula (*Galatians*, 20).

2. Longenecker sees 1:11 – 2:12 as the thesis for 1:13 – 2:14 (ibid.). Jean-Noël Aletti identifies 1:11 – 12 as the *proposition* for all of 1:11 – 21 and thinks 2:16 is the thesis for Galatians 3 – 4. "Galates 1 – 2: Quelle function et quelle démonstration?" *Bib* 86 (2005): 305 – 23.

by the Jewish false teachers. Lyons argues, however, that such a view misreads Paul's intention.[3] He argues that Paul provides a narrative of his own life so that the readers will see a concrete example of the freedom they are to embrace. Lyons's reading of this section is unpersuasive.[4] I argued in the introduction that there are clear indications that Paul responds in Galatians to opponents.[5] Further, Paul appears to respond to those who criticized his apostolic authority from the very first verse in the letter (1:1) and counters the claim that he pleases people in 1:10.

The reference to false brothers who tried to impose circumcision on Titus (2:3 – 5) also suggests that Paul is defending his apostolic authority. Lyons rightly reminds us that we must be careful in articulating the situation in the letter, but, as was argued in the introduction, there are solid reasons for thinking that Paul defends his apostleship in 1:1 – 2:21 and that he responds to a false gospel in Galatians. Hence, chapters 1 – 2 are rightly understood as narrative in which Paul defends his apostleship.[6]

I. Introduction: Desertion from Paul's Gospel Is Desertion from the Gospel (1:1 – 2:21)

  A. Greeting: Paul's Apostolic Authority (1:1 – 5)

  B. Problem Explained: Desertion from the Gospel (1:6 – 10)

➡   **C. Paul's Gospel Derived from God, Not People (1:11 – 2:21)**

    1. Thesis: Source of His Gospel Was Revelation (1:11 – 12)

    2. Thesis Support (1:13 – 2:21)

      a. His Past Hostility (1:13 – 14)

      b. His Call from God (1:15 – 17)

      c. His Relative Obscurity in Judea (1:18 – 24)

Main Idea

The central truth in 1:11 – 17 is that Paul's gospel is not from human beings but was received through a revelation of Jesus Christ (1:11 – 12). Therefore, the charge that he was pleasing people (1:10) is groundless. Galatians 1:13 – 17 supports the divine origin of Paul's gospel.

---

3. Lyons, *Pauline Autobiography*, 96 – 112. See also Hansen, "Paradigm of the Apocalypse," 145 – 46; Witherington, *Galatians*, 25, 38; Cummins, *Crucified Christ*, 114 – 35.

4. Rightly Esler, *Galatians*, 64 – 68. Esler comments that Lyons's reading is "socially unrealistic" (68) and is guilty of reading Paul from an overly intellectual standpoint. For further criticisms of Lyons, see Silva, *Interpreting Galatians*, 105 – 6; Smiles, *Gospel and Law in Galatia*, 5 – 7.

5. Therefore, Garlington's claim that "Paul is essen-

tially on the offensive, not the defensive" (*Galatians*, 75) is misconceived.

6. Timothy Wiarda mainly concurs with this reading. "Plot and Character in Galatians 1 – 2," *TynBul* 55 (2004): 231 – 52. He thinks, however, that 2:1 – 10 only supports the thesis in 1:11 – 12 "indirectly," and 2:11 – 14 "scarcely at all" supports it (246). His judgment on 2:11 – 14 is incorrect, for the independence of the Pauline gospel is revealed by his public rebuke of Peter. See comments on 2:1 – 14 for further explication.

Translation

Galatians 1:11-17

11	assertion	For I want to make known to you, brothers, that the gospel which is preached by me is not according to human beings.
12a	basis *(of 11)*	For I did not receive it from a human being,
b	series *(to 12a)*	nor was I taught it,
c	contrast *(to 12a-b)*	but I received it through a revelation of Jesus Christ.
13a	explanation	For you have heard
		of my former conduct in Judaism,
b	description *(of 13a)*	that I was persecuting the church of God exceedingly, and
c	progression *(of 13b)*	I was trying to destroy it, and
14a	progression *(of 13c)*	I was advancing in Judaism
b	extent	beyond many of my contemporaries among my nation,
c	cause *(of 13b-14a)*	because I was exceedingly zealous for my ancestral traditions.
15a/		But
16a	time *(of 17)*	when God was pleased to reveal his Son to me
15b	description *(of 15a/16a)*	the one who separated me from my mother's womb and
	series *(from 15b)*	called me through his grace
16b	purpose	so that I should preach him among the Gentiles,
c	assertion	I did not immediately consult with flesh and blood,
17a	series *(from 16c)*	neither did I go up to Jerusalem to those who were apostles before me,
b	contrast *(to 16c-17a)*	but I went away to Arabia,
c	sequence *(with 17b)*	and I returned again to Damascus.

Structure

As noted above, 1:11 – 2:21 supports the argument that Paul is not pleasing people but lives to honor God (1:10). The fundamental support and basis for the claim that Paul does not please people is the truth that the gospel he preaches is not a human gospel (1:11). The words, "for I want to make known to you" (γνωρίζω γὰρ ὑμῖν) represent a disclosure formula introducing a new section.

How can Paul verify that his gospel is not merely human? He answers this question in 1:12, using a "for" (γάρ) to support his claim. The gospel he proclaimed was not transmitted to him by a human being, nor was he taught it by another human being. Instead, he received the gospel supernaturally when he saw Jesus Christ on the Damascus road. Therefore, there is no doubt about the divine origin of his gospel.

Verses 13 – 17 support further (see again the "for" [γάρ]) the assertion that Paul received his gospel from God. In vv. 13 – 14 he argues that he was devoted to human teachings while he was still a part of Judaism. Paul's life in Judaism is described in terms of his zeal: he persecuted the church, he attempted to destroy it, and he advanced among his contemporaries. In other words, there was no human reason for Paul to become a slave of Christ. He was utterly convinced that the gospel was wrong and opposed it adamantly and passionately.

The text moves in a dramatically different direction in vv. 15 – 17 with the adversative conjunction and a temporal clause ("but when," ὅτε δέ). The word "when" is the first of many temporal words that carry the narrative along through 2:21. The only explanation for the change in Paul's life was the intervention of God when he revealed Jesus Christ to Paul on the Damascus road. Paul emphasizes the divine character of his conversion and call: God was pleased to reveal the Son to him; he had planned this from his conception; and he called Paul effectively through his grace. The purpose of this calling was so that Paul would proclaim the gospel to the Gentiles.

The evidence of Paul's independent reception of the gospel (1:17) is that he did not consult with any humans regarding the content of the gospel, nor did he travel to Jerusalem to consult with the apostles. Instead, Paul immediately went to Arabia to proclaim the gospel and returned to Damascus to do the same.

Exegetical Outline

    I. Introduction: Desertion from Paul's Gospel Is Desertion from the Gospel (1:1 – 2:21)

        A. Greeting: Paul's Apostolic Authority (1:1 – 5)

        B. Problem Explained: Desertion from the Gospel (1:6 – 10)

➡   **C. Paul's Gospel Derived from God, Not People (1:11 – 2:21)**

           1. Thesis: source of his gospel was revelation (1:11 – 12)

               a. Not a human gospel (1:11)

               b. Received through a revelation of Jesus Christ (1:12)

> **2. Thesis support (1:13 – 2:21)**
> > a. His past hostility (1:13 – 14)
> > > i. His persecution of the church (1:13)
> > > ii. His zeal in Judaism (1:14)
> > b. His call from God (1:15 – 17)
> > > i. A work of God's grace (1:15)
> > > ii. Purpose: proclamation among the Gentiles (1:16)
> > > iii. No need for validation (1:17)
> > c. His relative obscurity in Judea (1:18 – 24)

Explanation of the Text

1:11 For I want to make known to you, brothers, that the gospel which is preached by me is not according to human beings (Γνωρίζω γὰρ ὑμῖν, ἀδελφοί, τὸ εὐαγγέλιον τὸ εὐαγγελισθὲν ὑπ' ἐμοῦ ὅτι οὐκ ἔστιν κατὰ ἄνθρωπον). The introductory declarative statement, "I want to make known to you" (Γνωρίζω … ὑμῖν), as noted above, is a disclosure formula and also indicates the fundamental nature of what follows. The thesis of the following section is unveiled: Paul's gospel is not merely human but has a divine origin. Significantly, Paul uses the same verb when he reminds the Corinthians of the gospel he proclaims in 1 Cor 15:1: (lit.) "Now I make known to you (Γνωρίζω … ὑμῖν), brothers."

Indeed, the content of both declarations is remarkably similar, for in Corinthians he makes known "the gospel which I proclaimed to you" (τὸ εὐαγγέλιον ὃ εὐηγγελισάμην ὑμῖν), and in Galatians "the gospel which is preached by me" (τὸ εὐαγγέλιον τὸ εὐαγγελισθὲν ὑπ' ἐμοῦ). It is difficult to determine whether the superior textual reading here is "for" (γάρ) or "now" (δέ), but "for" (γάρ) has more support.[7] In either case, the meaning of the text does not change dramatically, for Paul either explains or grounds what he has said about not

pleasing people in 1:10. It seems, however, that the evidence favors "for" (γάρ), and hence 1:11 should be understood as a support or ground of 1:10.

The truth Paul communicates is that his gospel is divine in origin. It cannot be dismissed as merely a human gospel. Paul's statement here probably reflects an accusation made against him by his Jewish opponents. They contended that Paul's gospel was human in nature and that it had no independent authority or validity. Hence, according to the intruders who had entered the Galatian churches, Paul's gospel was one that pleased people by omitting some of the essential elements of the gospel, i.e., the need to be circumcised and to keep the OT law. As noted previously, from the first verse of the letter Paul defends the divine origin of his gospel, something he does not do in such explicit terms in any other letter.

1:12a-b For I did not receive it from a human being, nor was I taught it (οὐδὲ γὰρ ἐγὼ παρὰ ἀνθρώπου παρέλαβον αὐτό οὔτε ἐδιδάχθην). Paul supports here the theme that his gospel was not derived from human beings, for human beings did not pass it on to him or instruct him in the gospel. The word "received" (παραλαμβάνω) is used elsewhere for the transmission of tradition

---

7. See the careful discussion in Silva where he convincingly supports "for" (γάρ). Silva, *Interpreting Galatians*, 44 – 49. Against Longenecker (*Galatians*, 20, 22).

(cf. 1 Cor 11:23; 15:1, 3), and the term reflects a Jewish background.[8] Here Paul affirms that he did not receive the gospel from a chain of human tradition, nor was he taught it.

At first glance the affirmation here seems to contradict 1 Cor 15:3, for in the latter text Paul includes elements that were handed down to him via tradition. How can he say that the gospel was independently given to him, while affirming elsewhere that the gospel was transmitted to him by others? The contradiction is more apparent than real. In Galatians Paul affirms that the central elements of the gospel were given to him by Jesus Christ on the Damascus road. Indeed, many of the tenets in his theology may have been derived from this event in his life.[9] This is not to deny that Paul was familiar with the content of the gospel when he was persecuting the church.

Still, when Paul was an unbeliever he did not fully grasp or understand the message he rejected. For instance, he did not understand the substitutionary atonement (3:13), which teaches that Christ died in our place. He believed instead that Jesus' crucifixion proved that he could not be the Messiah. Paul also grasped as an unbeliever that the Christian faith threatened the centrality of the law, but he understood only after his conversion how the end of the law did not threaten OT teaching but actually fulfilled what the OT taught.

The independence of Paul's gospel does not lead to the conclusion that he learned nothing from the other apostles or that none of the Jesus traditions were conveyed to him by others. Such radical independence is not the point Paul makes here. Rather, he asserts that the fundamental truths of the gospel and his calling as an apostle to the Gentiles took place on the Damascus road.

1:12c But I received it through a revelation of Jesus Christ (ἀλλὰ δι᾽ ἀποκαλύψεως Ἰησοῦ Χριστοῦ).

Paul did not receive his gospel from any human source. Rather, the gospel was supernaturally revealed to him on the Damascus road. Is the genitive "Jesus Christ" (Ἰησοῦ Χριστοῦ) objective or subjective here?[10] Was the revelation given to him *by* Jesus Christ or did Paul *see* Jesus Christ? The relationship of genitives to nouns is imprecise and must be discerned by the context. It is possible that the genitive should be construed as both objective and subjective. In this instance, Jesus gave the revelation and is the object of the revelation.

But 1:16 suggests that the genitive here should be read as objective, for we read in 1:16 that God revealed his Son to Paul.[11] If 1:16 is accepted as parallel (and it makes good sense to do so since it is in the same context), God is the revealer and the Son is the object of the revelation. Paul did not receive his gospel from a human being, for he saw the risen Christ on the Damascus road, and the gospel in all its glory and beauty was disclosed to him. In seeing Jesus Christ he was also called to be an apostle (1 Cor 9:1 – 2; cf. also Acts 9:17, 27; 22:18) — an authoritative messenger of the crucified and risen Lord.

---

8. See Gerhard Delling, "παραλαμβάνω," *TDNT*, 4:12 – 13.

9. So George, *Galatians*, 112; Dieter Lührmann, *Galatians* (trans. O. C. Dean Jr.; CC; Minneapolis: Fortress, 1992), 17 – 18. Kim argues that the substance of the Pauline gospel was revealed to Paul on the Damascus road (*Origin of Paul's Gospel*). James D. G. Dunn questions the viability of Kim's thesis at a number of points. See "'A Light to the Gentiles' or 'The End of the Law'? The Significance of the Damascus Road Christophany for Paul," in *Jesus, Paul and the Law: Studies in Mark and Galatians* (Louisville: Westminster/John Knox,

1990), 93 – 100. For Kim's response to Dunn, see Seyoon Kim, *Paul and the New Perspective: Second Thoughts on the Origins of Paul's Gospel* (Grand Rapids: Eerdmans, 2002), esp. 1 – 35.

10. Some commentators defend a subjective genitive (e.g., Longenecker, *Galatians*, 23 – 24; Lightfoot, *Galatians*, 80; Machen, *Galatians*, 58 – 59), whereas others support an objective genitive (Bruce, *Galatians*, 89; Betz, *Galatians*, 63).

11. See the helpful discussion in Silva, *Interpreting Galatians*, 65 – 68.

1:13a For you have heard of my former conduct in Judaism (Ἠκούσατε γὰρ τὴν ἐμὴν ἀναστροφήν ποτε ἐν τῷ Ἰουδαϊσμῷ). Paul reflects here on his former life in Judaism before he met Christ on the Damascus road. Longenecker maintains that we have an "epistolary disclosure formula" here.[12] The word "for" (γάρ) supports the theme that Paul received the truth of the gospel through a revelation given by Jesus Christ, since only a revelation from God could turn Paul away from his devotion to Judaism.

Paul contrasts his past life in Judaism with his call and conversion. Some scholars argue that Paul was called on the Damascus road but not converted.[13] Such a view is attractive in that Paul believed faith in Christ fulfills what the OT promised. Still, it is clear that Paul was both called and converted when Christ appeared to him.[14] The first piece of evidence in support of Paul's conversion and call surfaces here. He describes his pre-Christian life as his "former conduct in Judaism." The term Judaism should be defined in terms of following Jewish beliefs and practices, especially as they are codified in the Mosaic law and in traditions developed from the Torah (see 2 Macc 2:21; 8:1; 14:38; 4 Macc 4:26).[15]

Paul remained Jewish ethnically, but he no longer considered himself to be part of Judaism. In this respect Paul differed from the opponents, who believed that faith in Christ was compatible with adherence to the Mosaic law.[16] Paul, by contrast, pronounced an anathema (1:8 – 9) on anyone who proclaimed a gospel other than the one he preached in Galatia. Obviously, Paul did not proclaim freedom from the law before he met Jesus on the Damascus road, and hence up until that time he was destined to be cursed on the last day.

1:13b-c That I was persecuting the church of God exceedingly, and I was trying to destroy it (ὅτι καθ᾽ ὑπερβολὴν ἐδίωκον τὴν ἐκκλησίαν τοῦ θεοῦ καὶ ἐπόρθουν αὐτήν). We have Paul's self-testimony with respect to his persecution of the Christian church before Christ was revealed to him. The imperfect tenses come to the forefront in verses 13 – 14, emphasizing ongoing action in past time. Paul's persecution accords with what we read in the book of Acts (Acts 7:58 – 8:3; 9:1 – 2, 13 – 14, 21; 22:3 – 5, 19 – 20; 26:4 – 5, 9 – 11, 14 – 15), and Paul confirms the same elsewhere in his letters (1 Cor 15:9; Phil 3:6; 1 Tim 1:13 – 16). Therefore, we have further evidence that Paul was both converted and called on the Damascus road.

To persecute God's church means that one is opposed to the assembly of God's people. The term Paul typically uses to designate the communities he established is "church" (ἐκκλησία) The word "church" derives from the OT, where the people of Israel were the "assembly of Yahweh" (e.g., Deut 23:2, 8;[17] 1 Chr 28:8), or "the assembly of Israel" (e.g., Lev 16:17; Deut 31:30; 1 Kgs 8:14, 22). The former phrase occurs in the LXX as the "assembly of the Lord" (ἐκκλησίαν κυρίου). Obviously Paul persecuted local churches, but here he thinks of the church in universal terms.[18] Paul elsewhere uses the phrase "church of God" (e.g., 1 Cor 1:2; 10:32; 11:22; 2 Cor 1:1; 1 Thess 2:14), suggesting

---

12. Longenecker, *Galatians*, 26.

13. Krister Stendahl, *Paul among Jews and Gentiles and Other Essays* (Philadelphia: Fortress, 1977), 1 – 23; Dunn, *Galatians*, 65; Hays, *Galatians*, 215.

14. See Peter O'Brien, "Was Paul Converted?" in *Justification and Variegated Nomism*; vol. 2: *The Paradoxes of Paul* (ed. D. A. Carson, Peter T. O'Brien, and Mark A. Seifrid; Grand Rapids: Baker, 2004), 361 – 91.

15. Cf. Ciampa, *The Presence of Scripture in Galatians 1 and 2*, 107; Garlington, *Galatians*, 80.

16. Rightly Ciampa, *The Presence of Scripture in Galatians 1 and 2*, 107 – 8.

17. Deut 23:9 in MT and LXX.

18. So Machen, *Galatians*, 60; Longenecker, *Galatians*, 28; Fee, *Galatians*, 41.

that he conceived of the church as the true Israel, the new people of God, and the fulfillment of what God intended with Israel.[19] Clearly, while Paul was persecuting the new Israel, he did not belong to "the Israel of God" (Gal 6:16).

Before Paul was converted, he was convinced that his persecution demonstrated his zeal for God and his righteousness (Phil 3:6). But he came to understand that what he thought was righteousness was actually the climax of his sinfulness, so that he was unworthy to be called as an apostle (1 Cor 15:9; cf. Eph 3:8). He designated himself as "a blasphemer and a persecutor and a violent man" (1 Tim 1:13) and as the "worst" of sinners (1 Tim 1:15).[20] Hence, God demonstrated his merciful grace in saving him (1:13 – 16) and calling him to proclaim the gospel to the Gentiles.

In persecuting the church Paul's goal was to destroy it. The phrase "I was trying to destroy it" (ἐπόρθουν) is in context voluntative, expressing an attempt that was not fully realized (cf. Acts 9:21). Garlington indicates the intensity communicated in the verb "destroy," pointing out that Josephus uses the same verb (*J.W.* 4.534) to denote "the burning of the villages and towns of Idumaea by Simon bar Giora."[21] Paul's efforts to exterminate the church did not spring from guilt. Before he was converted, he was utterly convinced that Jesus was not the Messiah and that the sect that promulgated such teachings was seriously mistaken.

Therefore, when God revealed Jesus to him on the Damascus road, he was totally astonished that his zeal and passion were misdirected.

1:14a-b And I was advancing in Judaism beyond many of my contemporaries among my nation (καὶ προέκοπτον ἐν τῷ Ἰουδαϊσμῷ ὑπὲρ πολλοὺς συνηλικιώτας ἐν τῷ γένει μου). Paul was a young and rising star in the Judaism, advancing beyond many of his fellow students. We learn from Acts that Paul was a pupil of Gamaliel (Acts 5:34; 22:3). He was trained as a Pharisee and ardently sought to please God in every arena of his life (23:6; 26:5; Phil 3:5).[22] The term "Judaism" is again used (see 1:13) to denote Paul's past, describing what occupied him before he met Jesus Christ on the Damascus road.

1:14c Because I was exceedingly zealous for my ancestral traditions (περισσοτέρως ζηλωτὴς ὑπάρχων τῶν πατρικῶν μου παραδόσεων). Paul's persecution of the church and his progress in Judaism are traced to his zeal for "my ancestral traditions." The word "traditions" should not be equated with the OT Scriptures. It denotes the way of life promulgated by the Pharisees, which Paul, once he became a Christian, no longer equated with the teachings of the OT Scriptures (cf. Mark 7:3, 5, 8, 9, 13). Such traditions developed over time (cf. Sir 8:9; 1 Macc 2:19 – 22; 2 Macc 6:1; 3 Macc 1:3; Josephus, *Ant.* 11.140; 13.297, 408; 19.349; Philo, *Spec. Laws* 2.253) and were eventually codified in

---

19. Such a view does not lead to the conclusion that ethnic Israel is now outside God's saving purposes (see Rom 9 – 11). For my reading of those chapters, see Thomas R. Schreiner, *Romans* (BECNT; Grand Rapids: Baker, 1998), 469 – 638.

20. Some scholars exclude the evidence from 1 Timothy since they believe the letter is inauthentic. Even if one thinks the letter is non-Pauline, it would still show how one of the earliest Pauline disciples understood Paul's past, confirming that Paul was both converted and called.

21. Garlington, *Galatians*, 82.

22. Neusner has argued that the goal of the Pharisees was to extend temple purity to every realm of life. Jacob

Neusner, *The Rabbinic Traditions about the Pharisees before 70* (3 vols.; Leiden: Brill, 1971). E. P. Sanders questions whether the Pharisees were the most influential sect in Judaism during Paul's day (*Judaism: Practice and Belief, 63 BCE – 66 CE* [Philadelphia: Trinity Press International, 1992], 380 – 412). For a defense of the view that the Pharisees were the dominant sect, see Roland Deines, "The Pharisees between 'Judaisms' and 'Common Judaism,'" in *Justification and Variegated Nomism*; vol. 1: *The Complexities of Second Temple Judaism* (ed. D. A. Carson, Peter T. O'Brien, and Mark A. Seifrid) (Tübingen/Grand Rapids: Mohr Siebeck/ Baker, 2001), 443 – 504.

Jewish writings after the close of the NT, such as the Mishnah, the Tosephta, and the Jerusalem and Babylonian Talmuds.[23]

Doubtless Paul, before his conversion (Acts 22:3; Phil 3:6), conceived of himself as part of a venerable Jewish tradition that stood for observance of the law. For instance, Phinehas, by slaying the Israelite man and Midianite woman engaging in sexual relations, displayed his zeal for the Lord (Num 25:11). So too Elijah demonstrated his zeal for the Lord in the slaying of the prophets of Baal (1 Kgs 19:10, 14). Matthias also manifested the same zeal when Antiochus Epiphanes (175 – 164 BC) tried to repress the Jewish religion. Matthias slew the Jew who was about to offer an illegitimate sacrifice along with the king's officer and then proceeded to tear down the altar (1 Macc 2:23 – 25). Matthias and those who followed him clearly saw themselves as exercising the same kind of zeal as Phinehas and Elijah (1 Macc 2:24, 26, 27, 50, 54, 58). The persecution of the church and the slaying of believers was, to Paul's way of thinking before his conversion, not an indication of his sin, but revealed the depth of his commitment and piety. Paul probably saw himself as a new Phinehas or Elijah, and a modern-day Hasmonean.

1:15a, 16a But when God was pleased to reveal his Son to me (ὅτε δὲ εὐδόκησεν [ὁ θεός] … ἀποκαλύψαι τὸν υἱὸν αὐτοῦ ἐν ἐμοί). The dramatic change in Paul's life can only be ascribed to God,[24] for there was no human reason why Paul, who was an ardent opponent of Jesus of Nazareth, would suddenly embrace him as Lord and Christ[25] apart from God's supernatural intervention.[26] Paul's call and conversion, therefore, find their explanation in God's will and his good pleasure. The infinitive "to reveal" (ἀποκαλύψαι) hearkens back to "the revelation of Jesus Christ" (ἀποκαλύψεως Ἰησοῦ Χριστοῦ) in 1:12, supporting the notion that God revealed Jesus Christ to Paul on the Damascus road.

The prepositional phrase (ἐν ἐμοί) could be translated "in me" rather than "to me."[27] Deciding between these two options is remarkably difficult, and a good case could be made for either interpretation. In context, however, the translation "to me" makes better sense, for Paul recalls Jesus' appearance to him on his way to Damascus, and hence he does not focus on the internal dimension of the revelation.[28]

Paul designates Jesus as God's "Son" here, and he uses this title on seventeen occasions in his letters.[29] Jesus' sonship implies his preexistence,

---

23. Against Witherington, who confines what Paul says here to the OT (*Galatians*, 104).

24. The word "God" (θεός) is rather evenly divided textually. The decision is not crucial exegetically, for it is obvious in any case that God is the subject, even if it is unstated. Probably the addition is scribal (so Fee, *Galatians*, 44, n. 25).

25. Therefore, there was no psychological preparation for Paul's conversion (rightly Machen, *Galatians*, 62).

26. I am following those who date Paul's conversion in AD 31/32. Riesner, *Paul's Early Period*, 64 – 74; Schnabel, *Paul and the Early Church*, 1037.

27. So Bruce, *Galatians*, 93; Longenecker, *Galatians*, 32; Sam K. Williams, *Galatians* (ANTC; Nashville: Abingdon, 1997), 47; B. Longenecker, *Triumph of Abraham's God*, 149 – 50; Garlington, *Galatians*, 83 – 84; Fee, *Galatians*, 45 – 46.

28. So Martyn, *Galatians*, 158. Cf. John Calvin, *Commentaries on the Epistles of Paul to the Galatians and Ephesians*, in

Calvin's Commentaries (trans. William Pringle; repr.; Grand Rapids: Baker, 2005), 21:42.

29. Some scholars have argued that the term was borrowed from Hellenism. See Wilhelm Bousset, *Kyrios Christos: A History of Belief in Christ from the Beginnings of Christianity to Irenaeus* (trans. John E. Steely; repr.; Nashville: Abingdon, 1970), 91 – 98; 206 – 10; Hans Joachim Schoeps, *Paul: The Theology of the Apostle in the Light of Jewish Religious History* (trans. Harold Knight; Philadelphia: Westminster, 1961), 150 – 60. It has been demonstrated, however, that such a view lacks compelling evidence and that the term derives from Jewish circles. So Martin Hengel, *The Son of God: The Origin of Christology and the History of Jewish-Hellenistic Religion* (trans. John Bowden; Philadelphia: Fortress, 1976); cf. Larry Hurtado, *Lord Jesus Christ: Devotion to Jesus in Earliest Christianity* (Grand Rapids: Eerdmans, 2003), 102 – 8.

contrary to the view of some scholars (cf. Rom 1:3, 9; 8:3; Gal 4:4). Often the term "Son" is used in contexts in which Jesus' atoning work is featured (Rom 5:10; 8:3, 32; Gal 2:20; 4:4; Col 1:13); hence, it is closely linked with the gospel.[30] Jesus' sonship suggests his unique and special relationship to God.

1:15b The one who separated me from my mother's womb and called me through his grace (ὁ ἀφορίσας με ἐκ κοιλίας μητρός μου καὶ καλέσας διὰ τῆς χάριτος αὐτοῦ). Paul continues to emphasize that his transformation was wholly the work of God, for God had destined him from the time he was in his mother's womb to be an apostle, and he called him to be such at a particular time in history, i.e., on the way to Damascus. It has been noted previously that Paul was both called and converted on this occasion, but the emphasis here is on Paul's call as an apostle, since the teachers in Galatia questioned the legitimacy of his apostleship.

The language Paul uses here alludes to the calling of Isaiah and Jeremiah as prophets.[31] Isaiah declares that the Lord called him from the womb of his mother (Isa 49:1).[32] Further, the Lord knew Jeremiah before he was in his mother's womb, and he appointed and set him apart as a prophet before his birth (Jer 1:5). Just as Isaiah and Jeremiah were called to be prophets, so too the Lord appointed Paul to be an apostle. Paul emphasizes that he was divinely appointed, for the Lord had appointed him to such a task before he was born (cf. Rom 1:1).

Further, God "called" (καλέσας) him "through his grace." The word "calling" here clearly means a call that is effective, a call that convinces the one who is summoned.[33] The reference to grace confirms such an idea. Paul did not volunteer to serve as an apostle, but he was summoned by God in a compelling way. Hence, his service as an apostle can be ascribed only to the grace of God, pointing to the forgiveness of his sins committed before his conversion.[34]

1:16b So that I should preach him among the Gentiles (ἵνα εὐαγγελίζωμαι αὐτὸν ἐν τοῖς ἔθνεσιν). This purpose clause (ἵνα) confirms that Paul emphasizes his call as an apostle. He does not focus on the personal benefit he derived, but on what God called him to do, i.e., to preach the good news of Jesus Christ to the Gentiles. The distinctive feature of Paul's apostleship emerges here, for he was intensely conscious of his unique commission to go to the Gentiles. Though the account of Paul's call in Acts also includes a reference to his call to Israel (Acts 9:15), the focus is clearly on his task to proclaim the gospel to the Gentiles (cf. Acts 22:21; 26:16–20).

Concentrating on the Gentiles never meant for Paul the exclusion of the Jews. Indeed, as Romans 11 indicates, Paul believed the two missions were interrelated (Rom 11:11–32). The proclamation of the gospel to the Gentiles is bound up with the Pauline understanding of the gospel, and in particular the truth that the Gentiles were not required to observe the law in order to be saved.

---

30. So Hengel, *Son of God*, 8–9.

31. So Sandnes, *Paul — One of the Prophets?* 61–65; Ciampa, *The Presence of Scripture in Galatians 1 and 2*, 111–12; Bruce, *Galatians*, 92.

32. Indeed, Paul may be implying here that he has taken up the vocation of the Servant of the Lord, since Christ, the Servant of the Lord par excellence, lives in him (cf. Acts 13:47; Gal 2:20). See here the discussion in Harmon, "She Must and Shall Go Free," 104–7, 138–60.

33. See the discussion of "calling" in comments on 1:6.

34. Sandnes says that the reference to grace "is certainly a reference to God's forgiveness of Paul's prior life as a persecutor of the church (vv. 13–14; cf. 1 Cor. 15:9–10). Without this act of grace Paul was completely inadequate to be a preacher of the gospel" (*Paul — One of the Prophets?* 64). Strangely, Fee tries to make a disjunction between theology and Paul's "worldview" here (*Galatians*, 44), which ends up blunting what Paul communicates about God's calling.

Paul's law-free gospel was revealed to him on the road to Damascus. He did not derive his gospel from any human authority.

1:16c I did not immediately consult with flesh and blood (εὐθέως οὐ προσανεθέμην σαρκὶ καὶ αἵματι). When God called Paul as an apostle and revealed the gospel to him, Paul did not hurry off to ask others about the legitimacy of the revelation.[35] The false teachers in Galatia may have questioned the legitimacy of Paul's apostleship, but Paul knew from the outset, without any outside confirmation, that he had been called to serve as an apostle.

Dunn argues that the verb "consult" (προσανατίθημι) does not merely mean "take counsel with someone." Rather, it means to "consult in order to be given a skilled or authoritative interpretation." The term is used of those who were qualified interpreters of dreams, signs, or omens.[36] So, according to Dunn, Paul did not consult with others about the "significance" of the revelation.

Silva rightly questions the legitimacy of Dunn's reading with three observations.[37] (1) Dunn puts too much emphasis on the meaning of the individual term, when the context itself should be granted more weight in coming to an interpretive conclusion. (2) The evidence in favor of taking "consult" (προσανατίθημι) as a technical term is lacking, for the verb does not always have a technical meaning. (3) Dunn does not assign a technical meaning for the same verb in 2:6, which reflects the weakness of his interpretation. To sum up: Paul's point is that he did not query others about the legitimacy of the revelation he received. He knew, without

a doubt, that he had been called as an apostle of Jesus the Christ.

1:17a Neither did I go up to Jerusalem to those who were apostles before me (οὐδὲ ἀνῆλθον εἰς Ἱεροσόλυμα πρὸς τοὺς πρὸ ἐμοῦ ἀποστόλους). Paul did not verify the truth of the revelation he received from others, nor did he immediately plan a trip to Jerusalem to discern whether the apostles in Jerusalem validated the revelation he received. He did not need or desire an apostolic imprimatur on the gospel he proclaimed.[38] Since he received his gospel by a revelation of Jesus Christ, he did not need anyone else to confirm its truth.

1:17b-c But I went away to Arabia, and I returned again to Damascus (ἀλλὰ ἀπῆλθον εἰς Ἀραβίαν καὶ πάλιν ὑπέστρεψα εἰς Δαμασκόν). Paul's confidence in the independence and validity of his gospel manifested itself in his traveling to Arabia after he had spent some time in Damascus.[39] The information contained in Galatians nicely supplements what we read in Acts. After Paul's conversion, he immediately proclaimed in the synagogues that Jesus was the Messiah (Acts 9:20). The account in Acts is incomplete, omitting any mention of Paul traveling to Arabia. Galatians fills out the historical record by informing us that Paul, after spending some time in Damascus, traveled to Arabia, and then returned later to Damascus. Acts telescopes the entire period by restricting itself only to what occurred in Damascus (9:19–25).

Many scholars postulate that Arabia refers to the Nabatean kingdom.[40] Most likely Paul also

---

35. Some scholars take "immediately" (εὐθέως) with the verb "go up" (ἀνῆλθον) (Bruce, *Galatians*, 94; Martyn, *Galatians*, 159), but it makes better sense to take it with the verb "consult" (προσανεθέμην) (cf. Longenecker, *Galatians*, 33).

36. James D. G. Dunn, "The Relationship between Paul and Jerusalem according to Galatians 1 and 2," *NTS* 28 (1982): 462–63.

37. Silva, *Interpreting Galatians*, 59–61.

38. Cf. here Wiarda, "Plot and Character," 240–41.

39. Schnabel dates Paul's time in Arabia as AD 32/33 (*Paul and the Early Church*, 1038).

40. E.g., Martin Hengel and Anna Maria Schwemer, *Paul between Damascus and Antioch: The Unknown Years* (trans. John Bowden; Louisville: Westminster John Knox, 1997),

proclaimed the gospel in Arabia, for there is no reason to think that he preached the gospel immediately in Damascus and then ceased to do so when he arrived in Arabia.[41] The account in 2 Cor 11:32 – 33 confirms such a reading as well, for Aretas IV was the King of Nabatea (9 BC to 40 AD), and the governor under Aretas attempted to arrest Paul in Damascus. Such an arrest is best accounted for by Paul's preaching of the gospel in Arabia.[42] Therefore, the view that Paul went to Arabia merely to study the OT Scriptures in light of the revelation given to him on the Damascus road is likely mistaken.[43] Instead, Paul verifies the truth of the gospel given to him by appealing to his preaching, without consulting anyone, both in Arabia and Damascus.

Theology in Application

Derived from God

We learn from these verses that the gospel is ultimately derived not from human beings but from God himself. In other words, the gospel represents a transcendent word from God — a word from above that speaks authoritatively and infallibly to human beings. Hence, rejection of the gospel amounts to a repudiation of what God himself has communicated. Paul labors to teach here that the gospel did not originate with him, and indeed it was contrary to his own view of reality, since he was convinced that faith in Christ was a perilous delusion.

Indeed, Paul's call and conversion function as significant evidence for the truth of the Christian faith. What can account for the radical transformation of a man who was implacably opposed to Jesus Christ and early Christians? As Paul explains here, there was no human reason for him to subscribe to the Christian faith. He thought he was like Phinehas and Elijah of old — a valiant warrior contending in God's name for the truth. He envisioned himself as a modern manifestation of the Maccabean heroes, who resisted apostasy with zeal in their own day. More than that, he was celebrated for his zeal and prowess in Judaism. Therefore, the only explanation for his call and conversion is the miraculous intervention of God. Paul's conversion has only one explanation: God himself. From a human standpoint, it was exceedingly unlikely.

---

110 – 13; Schnabel, *Paul and the Early Church*, 1033 – 34; Mussner, *Galaterbrief*, 91 – 92.

41. So Bruce, *Galatians*, 96; Hengel and Schwemer, *Paul between Damascus and Antioch*, 106 – 20; Schnabel, *Paul and the Early Church*, 1032 – 38. George thinks he preached and meditated, so that we do not have an either-or here (*Galatians*, 124). Riesner, on the other hand, questions whether Arabia refers to the Nabatean territory and doubts that Paul proclaimed the gospel there (*Paul's Early Period*, 256 – 60).

42. So also Chrysostom, *Galatians*, 12; Schnabel, *Paul and the Early Church*, 1036 – 37; Witherington, *Galatians*, 102.

43. But see Lightfoot, *Galatians*, 90; Burton, *Galatians*, 55 – 57; Machen, *Galatians*, 72 – 73 (mainly); Longenecker, *Galatians*, 34; Guthrie, *Galatians*, 71; Fee, *Galatians*, 51; N. T. Wright, "Paul, Arabia, and Elijah (Galatians 1:17)," *JBL* 115 (1996): 683 – 92. Wright argues that Paul, like Elijah, traveled to Arabia and returned with the realization that his previous zeal for the Torah was misguided. So also Hays, *Galatians*, 217. Garlington suggests that Arabia is mentioned because that is where Mount Sinai is located, and hence "Paul may well have gone to Mount Sinai to contemplate the law in the light of Christ" (*Galatians*, 92).

It is important to realize that our zeal and sincerity do not mean that we are necessarily right. We can be zealous for something and yet be zealously wrong. I remember as a young boy I was one of the last to disbelieve in Santa Claus! I was zealous for the truth of his existence, but I was wrong. Furthermore, we can become zealous for a cause and get out of balance. I know of a pro-life activist who was incredibly committed to life. But he ended up leaving his wife for another woman and moved to another state and bought an expensive house. His zeal for the cause of life was not truly rooted in the gospel, and he ignored his responsibility to his wife.

We also learn from this text that the gospel we proclaim is a divine gospel. It is a heavenly gospel in that it comes from the Father. We can be assured that a gospel that comes from God himself is true, that it cannot be dismissed as a human invention. Why should we believe in the Christian faith? We should believe in it because it is true. It reflects God's view of reality, and God's view is indisputably true since he is the creator of all reality.

The Power of Grace

Paul's conversion and call also point to the power of grace. If we had met Paul before his conversion, we doubtless would have been persuaded that he would never be converted. Maybe we would have even thought he had blasphemed against the Holy Spirit. Paul's conversion, then, reminds us of God's power to turn around the most unlikely people. We should never give up praying for those who seem impossible to reach, for salvation is of the Lord. Salvation is ultimately a miracle; it is a work of God. It cannot be calculated or manipulated.

God in his sovereignty desired to reveal his Son to Paul on the Damascus road, and in his grace and mercy he still saves today. No one deserves to be called by God. All of us, without exception, rightly stand under his judgment. Still, God calls us effectively to salvation by his stunning and mysterious grace. Let us, then, be filled with thanks and praise for his merciful and transforming grace. Let us marvel that he saves sinners who are filled with hatred toward him.

In other words, we cannot take credit for our salvation! Ultimately and finally we did not choose God but he chose us. We are no better than others. We were not wise enough to see what they didn't. The Lord opened our hearts to believe. When we consider that the Lord saved us by his grace, our hearts will be filled with praise and thanksgiving.

Calling

Finally, we learn that Paul was not only converted but also called. He was summoned to preach the gospel to the Gentiles. None of us is the apostle Paul. None of us is called to be an apostle, and not all of us are called to a paid ministry. But we are all called to serve the Lord wherever he puts us. We are all called to declare his glory where we live. We have the privilege of sharing the Word of life with those who are in darkness. We are not only to live in a way that manifests Christ, but we are also to proclaim the message of the gospel to others in our neighborhoods and workplaces. We are not called to "beat others over the head" with the gospel, but it isn't enough to simply "live out the gospel" before others. We must also declare and announce to others the message of the gospel. May God grant all of us courage to do so!

CHAPTER 4

Galatians 1:18 – 24

Literary Context

This text is joined with the previous sections with the word "then" (ἔπειτα, Gal 1:18 and 21). Paul continues to defend the theme that his ministry was not motivated by a desire to please people (1:10), which in turn is the conclusion drawn from the argument in 1:6 – 9. In support of the notion that pleasing people was not Paul's aim is the fact that his gospel is not a human one (1:11). Rather, it was given to him by a revelation of Jesus Christ on the Damascus road (1:12). Before Paul was called, he was a fierce opponent and persecutor of the gospel and committed to Judaism (1:13 – 14). But God supernaturally summoned him to proclaim Christ to the Gentiles (1:15 – 16). His gospel clearly came directly from God since he did not consult with the apostles or anyone else but immediately began to proclaim the gospel (1:17).

Verses 18 – 24 continue to support the theme that Paul did not please people and that his gospel was independent of the apostles. When he finally came to Jerusalem, the only apostles he saw were Peter and James (1:18 – 20), and he did not seek out the approval of the apostles. Further, most of the churches in Judea did not even know Paul face-to-face, which shows that he did not spend much time in Israel. They heard only about the remarkable change God had accomplished in him (1:21 – 24).

Main Idea

Paul's gospel is truly from God, and he was not pandering to people in his ministry. He did not derive his gospel from the apostles, for the only apostles he saw were Peter and James, and he only spent a limited amount of time with them. Nor did he spend much time in Judea, for most of the churches there did not know him personally but only heard about his ministry.

Translation

Galatians 1:18-24

18a	event	Then after three years **I went up to Jerusalem**	
b	purpose	to inquire of Cephas,	
c	sequence *(to 18a)*	and **I remained with him fifteen days.**	
19a	contra-expectation	But **I did not see any of the other apostles except**	**James,**
b	identification		the brother of the Lord.
20	exclamation/explanation *(of 1:10-19, and* *perhaps 1:20-2:21)*	**Behold,** before God, in the things I am writing to you **I am not lying.**	
21	sequence *(from 1:18-20)*	Then **I came into the regions of Syria and Cilicia.**	
22	simultaneous *(to 21)*	And **I was unknown personally to the churches of Judea,** which were in Christ.	
23	concession *(to 22)*	But **only they were hearing that the one who**	**persecuted us formerly** **is now preaching the faith** ↩ **that he was once attempting to destroy,**
24a	result *(of 23)*	and **they glorified God**	
b	cause *(of 24a)*	because of me.	

Structure

The argument in these verses is not terribly complicated. Paul continues to argue for his independence as an apostle, showing that his gospel did not come from a human source and that he was not motivated by a desire to please people. Since we have a narrative here in which Paul chronicles the timing of certain events, the narrative is marked by the repetition of "then" (ἔπειτα), which commences both 1:18 and 1:21.

In 1:18 – 20 Paul claims that his limited contact with the apostles demonstrates that he did not derive the gospel from them. He did not meet with Peter until three years had elapsed after his conversion and call, and then he only spent fifteen days with him. At the same time he saw James, the Lord's brother, but he had no contact with the rest of the apostles. We receive a hint from 1:20 that Paul is under attack by opponents in Galatia, for he insists in an oath formula before God that he is telling the truth. The oath formula could be restricted to what Paul says about his contact with the apostles (1:18 – 19), but it is also possible that it includes the entire narrative of events in 1:10 – 2:21.

Paul's independence is confirmed by the limited period of time he spent in Judea. He ministered in Syria and Cilicia, but the churches in Judea did not know him face-to-face (1:21 – 22). He had conducted his ministry independently of them. The Judean churches only heard about Paul's preaching of the gospel, and they praised God for his work (1:23 – 24).

Exegetical Outline

I. Introduction: Desertion from Paul's Gospel Is Desertion from the Gospel (1:1 – 2:21)

   A. Greeting: Paul's Apostolic Authority (1:1 – 5)

   B. Problem Explained: Desertion from the Gospel (1:6 – 10)

   C. Paul's Gospel Derived from God, Not People (1:11 – 2:21)

      1. Thesis: source of his gospel was revelation (1:11 – 12)

         a. Not a human gospel (1:11)

         b. Received through a revelation of Jesus Christ (1:12)

      2. Thesis support (1:13 – 2:21)

         a. His past hostility (1:13 – 14)

         b. His call from God (1:15 – 17)

         ➡ **c. His relative obscurity in Judea (1:18 – 24)**

            i. Relatively unknown to apostles (1:18 – 20)

               (1) Limited contact with Peter (1:18)

               (2) Limited contact with James (1:19)

               (3) Oath formula (1:20)

            ii. Relatively unknown in Judea (1:21 – 24)

               (1) Limited contact in Judea (1:21 – 22)

               (2) Known by report only (1:23 – 24)

         d. Recognition of Paul's authority by pillars (2:1 – 10)

         e. Rebuke of Peter substantiates Paul's authority (2:11 – 21)

Explanation of the Text

1:18 Then after three years I went up to Jerusalem to inquire of Cephas, and I remained with him fifteen days (Ἔπειτα μετὰ ἔτη τρία ἀνῆλθον εἰς Ἰεροσόλυμα ἱστορῆσαι Κηφᾶν,[1] καὶ ἐπέμεινα πρὸς αὐτὸν ἡμέρας δεκαπέντε). Paul's gospel was not dependent on the apostles, for he did not even see any apostles until three years after his conversion. As Longenecker says, "The Judaizers were evidently claiming that Paul was dependent on and subordinate to the apostles at Jerusalem."[2] In the time before he met Peter, Paul was not waiting for further instruction but was proclaiming the good news to the Gentiles in both Arabia and Damascus.

By three years here Paul probably means three years after his conversion.[3] In Jewish circles time could be reckoned inclusively. We see this clearly in terms of Jesus' death, for he was put to death on Friday and raised on Sunday, and this interval is described in terms of three days. Hence, if Paul was converted in AD 31/32, he may have visited Peter in AD 33/34. The visit here accords with Acts 9:26 – 30. The variants in the two accounts are explicable from the different perspective of Luke in Acts and Paul in Galatians.[4]

The word "Cephas" represents Peter's Aramaic name, which Paul most often uses when naming Peter (cf. 1 Cor 1:12; 3:22; 9:5; 15:5; Gal 2:9, 11, 14). The only exceptions are in Gal 2:7 – 8 (see below). The word "inquire" (ἱστορῆσαι) is disputed. In classical Greek it indicates an interview of someone else. Dunn argues that Paul visited Peter to derive information from him.[5] Hofius, however, maintains that the word simply means "get to know," with no thought of acquiring information.[6] Whatever view is preferred, we should not miss the main point here: Paul's independence from Peter in his proclamation of the gospel. Hence, Paul did not go to Peter to acquire information about the gospel since he received it independently on the Damascus road.

The independence of Paul's gospel is important because the Judaizers likely charged that Paul got his gospel from the Jerusalem apostles (he was dependent on them), and that he subsequently distorted what he received from them.[7] Still, Dunn rightly cites Dodd's famous words. "At that time he [Paul] stayed with Peter for a fortnight, and we may presume they did not spend all the time talking about the weather."[8] Surely Paul asked Peter during these two weeks for information about the historical Jesus and was grateful to learn more about the traditions of Jesus' words and deeds.[9] Doubtless, Paul learned from Peter, but it is also

---

1. The Majority Text favors "Peter," but Cephas is almost certainly original.

2. Longenecker, *Galatians*, 36.

3. So ibid., 37.

4. So Lightfoot, *Galatians*, 91 – 92; cf. also Bruce, *Galatians*, 97.

5. Dunn, "Paul and Jerusalem," 463 – 66; Dunn, *Jesus, Paul, and the Law*, 126 – 28; see also Witherington, *Galatians*, 119.

6. O. Hofius, "Gal 1:18: ἱστορῆσαι Κηφᾶν," *ZNW* 75 (1984): 73 – 85; cf. George S. Duncan, *The Epistle of Paul to the Galatians* (MNTC; New York: Harper, 1934), 31; Betz, *Galatians*, 76. Augustine argued that Paul visited Peter to

"build up brotherly love between them" (*Augustine's Commentary on Galatians*, 135; cf. also Calvin, *Galatians*, 44). Nor is the point that Paul did not tell Peter about the gospel he proclaimed to the Gentiles (Howard, *Paul: Crisis in Galatia*, 35 – 37). Against Howard, it is difficult to believe that Paul would not tell Peter about his gospel during the fifteen days they spent together.

7. For this theme, see the discussion of the situation of the letter in the introduction.

8. C. H. Dodd, *The Apostolic Preaching and Its Developments* (2nd ed.; London: Hodder & Stoughton, 1944), 16.

9. So Bruce, *Galatians*, 98. Hays wrongly underestimates what Paul likely learned from Peter (Hays, *Galatians*, 217).

probable that Peter learned much from Paul about the gospel given to him by Jesus.[10]

Indeed, the gospel for the Gentiles given to Paul on the Damascus road remained untouched.[11] Peter did not counter Paul's insistence that the law was not required for the salvation of the Gentiles. Paul specifies that he and Peter spent fifteen days together. Why does he mention this detail? Presumably to emphasize how limited the time period was. He did not see Peter for three years after his conversion, and when he did see him, the time was relatively short. Both temporal references, then, underline the independence of Paul's gospel.

1:19 But I did not see any of the other apostles except James, the brother of the Lord (ἕτερον δὲ τῶν ἀποστόλων οὐκ εἶδον εἰ μὴ Ἰάκωβον τὸν ἀδελφὸν τοῦ κυρίου). The independence of Paul's gospel continues to be the theme. Not only did he not see Peter for three years and spend only fifteen days with him, but he did not see the remaining apostles at all.[12] The only other apostle he saw was James, the brother of the Lord. The other prominent James, the brother of John, was executed by Herod Agrippa I in AD 44 (Acts 12:2).

Most scholars agree that the person in view here is James, the brother of Jesus.[13] James played an important role in the history of the early church. His ministry was to the Jewish people in Palestine, and he became the leader of the Jews in Jerusalem as Acts attests (Acts 12:17; 15:13 – 21; 21:18 – 25). This same James is likely also the author of the letter of James in the NT.[14] He did not believe Jesus was the Messiah during the latter's earthly ministry (Mark 3:21, 31 – 35; John 7:1 – 9). Presumably he came to faith when Jesus appeared to him after he was raised from the dead (1 Cor 15:7). James's prominence in Israel is attested by Josephus's account of his death in AD 62 (*Ant.* 20.9.1 §§197 – 203). James plays a central role in Paul's argument in Gal 2:1 – 14 as a representative of the church in Jerusalem and as one of the pillars of the church.

Does Paul identify James as an apostle here? One could render the Greek, "Other than the apostles I saw none, except James, the Lord's brother."[15] On this reading James is excluded from the apostolic circle. It is more likely, however, that the word "except" (εἰ μή) modifies the word "other" (ἕτερον).[16] If this is the case, James is included among the apostles. A parallel construction in 1 Cor 1:14 supports the idea that James is counted as one of the apostles (cf. also Luke 8:51; Phil 4:15), "I thank God that I baptized none of you except Crispus and Gaius" (ESV, εὐχαριστῶ τῷ θεῷ ὅτι οὐδένα ὑμῶν ἐβάπτισα εἰ μὴ Κρίσπον καὶ Γάϊον). It is clear that Crispus and Gaius are included among the baptized here, and in the

---

10. See here the convincing discussion in Hengel and Schwemer, *Paul between Damascus and Antioch*, 144 – 50.

11. Rightly Dunn, "Paul and Jerusalem," 465.

12. Hengel and Schwemer suggest that Paul did not want to attract attention to himself during this visit. Therefore, it is not the case that all the other apostles were absent from Jerusalem or that he refused to see the other apostles. They postulate that Paul wanted to keep a low profile (*Paul between Damascus and Antioch*, 135 – 36). They reject the Lukan report as "unhistorical" that Paul saw all the apostles (*Paul between Damascus and Antioch*, 138).

13. Against Calvin, who believed the person was James the son of Alphaeus (*Galatians*, 44).

14. So Douglas J. Moo, *The Letter of James* (PNTC; Grand Rapids: Eerdmans, 2000), 9 – 22; Luke T. Johnson, *The Letter of James* (AB; New York: Doubleday, 1995), 89 – 123; Richard Bauckham, *James: Wisdom of James: Disciple of Jesus the Sage* (New York: Routledge, 1999), 11 – 25. Peter H. Davids argues that traditions from James are incorporated into the letter (*The Epistle of James* [NIGTC; Grand Rapids: Eerdmans, 1982], 2 – 22).

15. Cf. here L. Paul Trudinger, "ἕτερον δὲ τῶν ἀποστόλων οὐκ εἶδον, εἰ μὴ Ἰάκωβον: A Note on Galatians i 19," *NovT* 17 (1975): 200 – 202; Machen, *Galatians*, 77 – 79.

16. George Howard, "Was James an Apostle? A Reflection on a New Proposal for Gal i 19," *NovT* 19 (1977): 63 – 64; Bruce, *Galatians*, 100 – 101; Martyn, *Galatians*, 174.

same way James is reckoned as one of the apostles. The apostles likely included more than the Twelve, for Paul distinguishes between Jesus' appearances to the apostles and to the Twelve in 1 Cor 15:5 – 7. Furthermore, James's status, both in Gal 2:1 – 10 and in Acts 15:13 – 21; 21:18 – 25, seems to be of an apostolic nature. Hence, I conclude that Paul considers him to be one of the apostles.

If we correlate what Paul says here with Acts, the visit described here fits with Acts 9:26 – 30. There we are told that Barnabas introduced Paul to the apostles since some feared that Paul was still an opponent. The biggest point of tension with Gal 1:18 – 19 is that Paul says that he visited only Peter and James, and Luke gives the impression that Paul saw many of the apostles. Probably Luke uses the plural somewhat loosely, so that strictly speaking Paul saw only two apostles. Luke's wording does not contradict such a restriction. Or, alternatively, perhaps Paul saw all the apostles, but had significant conversations only with Peter and James.

Another question that surfaces is what it means to say that James is "the Lord's brother." Three interpretations exist in the history of interpretation. (1) James was the literal son of Joseph and Mary. (2) James was the son of Joseph from a previous marriage. (3) James was a cousin of Jesus. The most natural interpretation is that James and the other brothers and sisters of Jesus that are named (Matt 13:55; Mark 6:3) are the literal sons of Joseph and Mary. Meier makes this case convincingly in a thorough and careful discussion of the matter.[17] We should not miss the main point Paul teaches here. Seeing only Peter and James indicates his independence from the rest of the apostles.

1:20 Behold, before God, in the things I am writing to you I am not lying (ἃ δὲ γράφω ὑμῖν, ἰδοὺ ἐνώπιον τοῦ θεοῦ ὅτι οὐ ψεύδομαι). This oath formula demonstrates the importance of this discussion to Paul and supports the idea that the Judaizers were disputing the legitimacy of his apostolic authority.[18] Otherwise, the strong protest that Paul writes the truth is superfluous. Perhaps the Judaizers charged him with being dependent on the apostles in Jerusalem. If so, the oath pertains to what is said in 1:18 – 19. Others restrict the oath formula to 1:15 – 19 or even to 1:13 – 19.[19] It is also possible that the oath is interjected into the middle of the argument and that it relates to all of 1:10 – 2:21.

Elsewhere Paul uses oath formulas where he wants to underline the importance of what he says (Rom 1:9; 9:1; 2 Cor 1:23; 11:10; 1 Tim 2:7). In particular, Paul interjects statements regarding the truthfulness of what he says when he thinks it will be disputed or doubted. Thus, we have further evidence that the Judaizers questioned Pauline authority, and he was compelled to offer an account defending his calling and commission.[20]

1:21 Then I came into the regions of Syria and Cilicia (ἔπειτα ἦλθον εἰς τὰ κλίματα τῆς Συρίας καὶ τῆς Κιλικίας). Paul delineates his itinerary with care to defend the independence of his gospel. He was in Jerusalem for a limited period of time, and it was three years after his conversion. After a short time in Jerusalem he left Palestine and ministered in Syria and Cilicia. Both Syria and Cilicia constituted a single Roman province at the time Paul wrote Galatians. Therefore, the plural "regions" is used in a loose sense and does not

---

17. John P. Meier, "The Brothers and Sisters of Jesus in Ecumenical Perspective," *CBQ* 54 (1992): 1 – 28. His article also contains a valuable history of interpretation.

18. There is no basis for the view that Paul restricted his visits to Peter and James because of persecution. Against Cummins, *Crucified Christ*, 127.

19. Cf. the discussion in Longenecker, *Galatians*, 39 – 40.

20. Indeed, it is difficult to account for this verse if Paul is not engaging in a defense of his apostleship. Note here that Witherington has to resort to the improbable idea that Paul interjects an oath just in case he is being criticized (*Galatians*, 122 – 23).

technically denote Roman provinces, for when Paul wrote Galatians, Syria and eastern Cilicia belonged to one Roman province (Syria-Cilicia).[21] Paul's relocation to Syria and Cilicia matches Acts 9:30, where he was sent off to Tarsus (in Cilicia) after a short time in Jerusalem (ca. AD 35).[22] Our knowledge of Paul's movements in those years is fragmentary, but we know that Barnabas (Acts 11:25 – 26) found Paul in Tarsus and persuaded him to minister in Syrian Antioch with him (ca. AD 42 – 46).

1:22 And I was unknown personally to the churches of Judea, which were in Christ (ἤμην δὲ ἀγνοούμενος τῷ προσώπῳ ταῖς ἐκκλησίαις τῆς Ἰουδαίας ταῖς ἐν Χριστῷ). This statement is included to emphasize the limited time Paul spent in Palestine.[23] He was not seeking out others within Israel to validate his gospel. Indeed, most of the believers in Judea did not know Paul personally. Judea was constituted as a Roman province when Galatians was written and included both Galilee and Samaria. Therefore, Paul refers here to a rather large area.[24] What we have here is a generalization, for it is likely that some believers knew him personally from his days in Jerusalem.[25] The point is that the majority of believers in Palestine and Jerusalem were unacquainted with him.[26] The plural "churches" here (see Gal 1:2) is modified by the phrase "in Christ" (ἐν Χριστῷ). The words "in Christ" may simply mean "Christian" here, but it is likely the meaning is deeper, pointing to union with Christ, to incorporation in him.

1:23 But only they were hearing that the one who persecuted us formerly is now preaching the faith that he was once attempting to destroy (μόνον δὲ ἀκούοντες ἦσαν ὅτι Ὁ διώκων ἡμᾶς ποτε νῦν εὐαγγελίζεται τὴν πίστιν ἥν ποτε ἐπόρθει). The Judean churches did not know of Paul through seeing but through hearing. They had no firsthand contact with him, but the report about him was circulating throughout Judea. The substance of the report was the dramatic change in Paul's life, which was already conveyed in 1:13 – 16. We have a typical then-now contrast here. The former persecutor who had tried to stamp out the Christian faith had now become one who proclaimed the gospel (εὐαγγελίζεται). Believers in Judea, then, functioned as witnesses to Paul's conversion and call.

The message Paul declared is designated here as "the faith" (τὴν πίστιν). Usually in Galatians the word "faith" means "trust in God," but that meaning does not fit here. Instead, the term is perhaps best defined as "the Christian religion" or "body of doctrine," referring to the Christian faith as a whole. If we compare the construction to 1:11, where Paul also uses a verbal form of the word "preach the gospel" (εὐαγγελίζω), there the thing preached is the "gospel" (τὸ εὐαγγέλιον)

---

21. So Bruce, *Galatians*, 103; Hengel and Schwemer, *Paul between Damascus and Antioch*, 157.

22. Cf. Hemer, *The Book of Acts in the Setting of Hellenistic History*, 267. Schnabel suggests AD 34 – 42 as the time period Paul spent in Syria and Cilicia (*Paul and the Early Church*, 1047).

23. As Witherington insightfully points out, this statement stands in tension with not only Acts 8:3 but also Gal 1:13, for in the latter text Paul says he persecuted the Jewish church, which sits awkwardly with the idea that they did not know him (*Galatians*, 124). Therefore, since we find the same tension within Galatians that we also find between Acts and

Gal 1:22, it is likely that the alleged contradiction between what we read here and in Acts can be reconciled.

24. In support of a reference to the Roman province here, see Bruce, *Galatians*, 103; Longenecker, *Galatians*, 41.

25. Rightly Machen, *Galatians*, 82. Therefore, there is no need to see a contradiction with Acts (against Martyn, *Galatians*, 175). See the helpful and more detailed discussion in Witherington, *Galatians*, 124 – 25. Machen suggests that Paul brought up Judea because the apostles were likely ministering in Judea (*Galatians*, 83 – 84).

26. Bruce notes that others who worked under Paul may have had direct contact with the churches (*Galatians*, 104).

itself (cf. 1 Cor 15:1; 2 Cor 11:7).[27] It seems, then, that "faith" here falls into the same semantic range so that it refers to the gospel in terms of what one believes in.[28]

A particularly illuminating parallel exists in Phil 1:27, where we find the words "the faith of the gospel" (τῇ πίστει τοῦ εὐαγγελίου). There the word "faith" seems to be used in the same fashion as in Galatians, and "the gospel" is appositional to "the faith." Though Paul typically uses the word "faith" to mean trust in God, there are some instances that match what we find here in Galatians (2 Cor 13:5; Eph 4:5), particularly in the Pastoral Epistles (1 Tim 3:9; 4:1, 6; 5:12; 6:10, 12(?), 21; 2 Tim 3:8; 4:7).

1:24 And they glorified God because of me (καὶ ἐδόξαζον ἐν ἐμοὶ τὸν θεόν). The churches in Judea function as witnesses to the transformation that occurred in Paul, even though they did not know him personally. They did not doubt his conversion and call, nor did they question what had occurred on the Damascus road. Rather, they praised and honored God for Paul's conversion and call. They recognized that only God in Christ deserves the glory, for he rescued Paul from the "present evil age" (1:4 – 5). The Greek prepositional phrase (ἐν ἐμοί) can be translated "in me" or "because of me."[29] The two renderings are not necessarily incompatible, though the latter is slightly more preferable since the focus is not on an interior work in Paul.

Theology in Application

This paragraph is probably the least significant theologically in Galatians, for Paul delineates his travels, underlining the truthfulness of his words. The legitimacy of his ministry is tied to his integrity. We often rightly remind ourselves that the power of the gospel is located in its message, not in ourselves. We are fallible and sinful vessels whom the Lord uses. But the power of our ministries cannot be separated from our godliness. If the way we live brings disrepute on the gospel, the message we proclaim is weakened. Paul's ministry was powerful because the transforming grace of God was evident in his life. People glorified God when they heard or saw what God had accomplished in him. May we live up to the same high calling!

Paul emphasizes his integrity in these verses. How are we living as Christians? Are we spending our money in a way that brings glory to God? Do we claim that Christ is central in our lives but spend our money and live just like unbelievers? In practice, do we live for a bigger house, longer vacations, and acquiring a boat? Or, do we spend our lives consumed in entertainment? We can waste our lives surfing the internet, watching sports, soap operas, and movies. Now, I am not saying that the latter are inherently wrong (though one wonders if soap operas are ever edifying!). My point is that we can end up living no different from unbelievers so that we spend our lives on what is trivial instead of what is eternal. Our treasure, as Jesus said, is where our heart is (Matt 6:21).

---

27. In Eph 3:8 to preach the gospel is to proclaim the inexhaustible riches of Christ.

28. Rightly Bruce, *Galatians*, 105; Hays, *Galatians*, 217;

Fee, *Galatians*, 53 – 54.

29. Cf. Bruce, *Galatians*, 105; Longenecker, *Galatians*, 42.

Galatians 2:1 – 10

Literary Context

The argument that began in 1:10 continues, and hence the autobiographical section of Galatians continues. Paul was not living to please people (1:10), and 1:11 – 2:21 supports this truth. After all, his gospel was not derived from human beings but given through a revelation of Jesus Christ (1:11 – 12). He defends the validity and independence of his gospel in 1:13 – 2:21. The appearance of Jesus Christ on the Damascus road verifies that Paul received his gospel by revelation (1:13 – 17) and that he was commissioned to preach to the Gentiles. Paul did not scurry off to consult with any others, including apostles, about the truth of that revelation. Indeed, he did not visit with Peter for three years and had limited contact with the apostles (1:18 – 20). Nor did he have any extensive contact with churches in Judea (1:21 – 24).

The next visit to Jerusalem was fourteen years later (probably fourteen years after Paul's conversion (ca. AD 44 – 46),[1] showing again his independence from the apostles (2:1 – 10). On this occasion he communicated his gospel to the pillars of the Jerusalem church (Peter, James, and John). Some false brothers in the church raised the issue of whether Titus as a Gentile should be circumcised. The leaders of the Jerusalem church, however, ratified the Pauline gospel. Paul insisted that he did not need their ratification, for his gospel stood apart from the view of the Jerusalem leaders. Nevertheless, when hearing Paul's gospel, they validated it as true.

---

1. For AD 46, see Hemer, *The Book of Acts in the Setting of Hellenistic History*, 267. For AD 44, see Schnabel, *Paul and the Early Church*, 900.

I. Introduction: Desertion from Paul's Gospel Is Desertion from the Gospel (1:1 – 2:21)

A. Greeting: Paul's Apostolic Authority (1:1 – 5)

B. Problem Explained: Desertion from the Gospel (1:6 – 10)

C. Paul's Gospel Derived from God, Not People (1:11 – 2:21)

  1. Thesis: Source of His Gospel Was Revelation (1:11 – 12)

  2. Thesis Support (1:13 – 2:21)

    a. His Past Hostility (1:13 – 14)

    b. His Call from God (1:15 – 17)

    c. His Relative Obscurity in Judea (1:18 – 24)

    d. Recognition of Paul's Authority by Pillars (2:1 – 10)

      i. Gospel Explained to Pillars (2:1 – 2)

      ii. Circumcision Not Required (2:3 – 5)

      iii. Nothing Added to Paul's Gospel (2:6 – 9)

      iv. Request to Remember the Poor (2:10)

    e. Rebuke of Peter Substantiates Paul's Authority (2:11 – 21)

Main Idea

When Paul traveled to Jerusalem fourteen years after his conversion, the Jerusalem leaders did not require Titus to be circumcised, even though some false brothers tried to insist on it. Indeed, the Jerusalem pillars added nothing to Paul's gospel. On the contrary, they ratified it and gave the right hand of fellowship to Paul and Barnabas as missionaries to the Gentiles.[2]

Translation

(See next page.)

Structure

The text is joined with the previous sections by the word "then" (ἔπειτα), just as 1:18 and 1:21 begin with "then" (ἔπειτα). Paul continues to relay the narrative of his relationship with the Jerusalem apostles. He did not see Peter for three years after his conversion (1:18), and then he did not return to Jerusalem for fourteen years.

---

2. Wiarda says that the main point here is "that Paul and his gospel are approved by the Jerusalem apostles" ("Plot and Character," 243).

Galatians 2:1-10

1a	sequence *(from 1:21)*	Then
		after fourteen years
		I went up again to Jerusalem with Barnabas,
b	simultaneous *(to 1a)*	taking along Titus also.
2a	explanation *(of 1a)*	And **I went up according to revelation,**
b	sequence *(to 2a)*	and **I communicated before them the gospel**
		that I preach among the Gentiles,
c	specific from general *(of 2b)*	that is, **I communicated it privately**
		before those of reputation,
d	basis *(of 2b-c)*	lest somehow I am running or
		had run in vain.
3a	resolution to problem *(in 1-2)*	But **not even Titus …**
		who was with me
		… was compelled to be circumcised,
b	concessive *(to 3a)*	even though he was a Greek.
4a	explanation *(from 3)*	**It was because of the false brothers**
		who sneaked in,
		who had slipped in
b	restatement *(of 4a)*	
c	purpose *(of 4a-b)*	to spy out our freedom
d	expansion *(of 4c)*	that we have in Christ Jesus,
e	purpose *(of 4c)*	in order to enslave us.

5a	contrast (to 4a)	But **we did not yield in subjection to them for an hour,**
b	purpose (of 5a)	in order that the truth of the gospel might remain with you.
6a	source	From those thought to be of reputation
b	explanation (of 6a)	(indeed, of what sort they were formerly makes no difference to me;
c	basis (of 6b)	God does not pay attention to human stature),
d	6a-d restates 1-5	that is, **those of reputation contributed nothing to me.**
7a	basis (of 9d)	But on the contrary,
		because they saw that I had been entrusted with the gospel for the uncircumcision,
b	comparison (to 7a)	just as Peter had been entrusted with the gospel for the circumcision
8	basis (of 7b)	(for the one who worked in Peter for the apostleship for the circumcision also
		worked in me for the Gentiles),
9a	basis (of 9d)	and
		because they recognized the grace given to me,
b	list	**James and Cephas and John,**
c	apposition (to 9b)	**those reputed to be pillars,**
d	inference (from 7a and 9a)	**gave to me and to Barnabas the right hand of fellowship,**
e	purpose (of 9d)	in order that we should go to the Gentiles, and
f	series (to 9e)	they to the circumcision.
10a	series (to 9d)	And **(they asked) that we should remember the poor,**
b	explanation (of 10a)	which indeed was the very thing I had been eager to do.

So, there was an interval of ten years or more between his two visits (since Jews reckoned time inclusively).[3]

Paul arrived in Jerusalem by revelation and brought Titus with him. While in Jerusalem he communicated the gospel with those of reputation (Peter, James, and John). Verse 3 represents the main point of 2:1 – 5. The men of repute did not think Titus should be circumcised, even though he was a Gentile. Verses 4 – 5 represent an anacoluthon, which as a sort of aside explains why the issue of Titus's circumcision even arose. False brothers had infiltrated the church with the demand for circumcision, which would bring believers into bondage. Paul explains in 2:5, however, that these false brothers did not win the day, and hence the integrity of the gospel was preserved.

The main point in 2:6 – 10 is that the men of repute added nothing to Paul's gospel (2:6). This truth restates the main point of 2:1 – 5, where it was decided that Titus would not be circumcised. In other words, the pillars of the church did not add to Paul's gospel by requiring circumcision. Not only did the pillars refuse to add anything to Paul's gospel, they also (2:7 – 9) specifically gave to Paul and Barnabas the right hand of fellowship. In other words, they ratified the validity of Paul's gospel — for two reasons (marked by causal paraticiples). (1) They recognized that he had been entrusted by God with the gospel for the Gentiles (2:7). Indeed, Paul's calling to the Gentiles was on the same plane as Peter's calling to preach the gospel to the Jews (2:8). (2) They recognized Paul had been endowed by God with grace for ministry (2:9).

In 1:11 – 24 Paul emphasizes the independence of his gospel. He received it directly from Jesus Christ and did not need any human validation to ratify his gospel. In 2:1 – 10 the argument advances. Even though Paul did not need human validation, the pillar apostles ratified Paul's gospel when he presented it to them. It seems likely that the Judaizers claimed that Paul's gospel was *derived* from Jerusalem and was later *distorted* by him. Paul counters in 1:11 – 2:10 that his gospel was *independent* from Jerusalem and later *ratified* by Jerusalem. The text concludes with an additional statement. The pillars asked Paul to remember the poor, and he concurred since he was already involved in such an endeavor (2:10).

Exegetical Outline

I. Introduction: Desertion from Paul's Gospel Is Desertion from the Gospel (1:1 – 2:21)

A. Greeting: Paul's Apostolic Authority (1:1 – 5)

B. Problem Explained: Desertion from the Gospel (1:6 – 10)

C. Paul's Gospel Derived from God, Not People (1:11 – 2:21)

1. Thesis: source of his gospel was revelation (1:11 – 12)

---

3. See commentary on 1:18.

2. Thesis support (1:13 – 2:21)

    a. His past hostility (1:13 – 14)

    b. His call from God (1:15 – 17)

    c. His relative obscurity in Judea (1:18 – 24)

➡   **d. Recognition of Paul's authority by pillars (2:1 – 10)**

        i. Gospel explained to pillars (2:1 – 2)

            (1) Fourteen years after Paul's conversion (2:1)

            (2) Visit in accord with revelation (2:2)

        ii. Circumcision not required (2:3 – 5)

            (1) In the case of the Gentile Titus (2:3)

            (2) Issue raised by false brothers (2:4)

            (3) Rejected to maintain gospel's truth (2:5)

        iii. Nothing added to Paul's gospel (2:6 – 9)

            (1) By those of reputation (2:6)

            (2) Because Paul's calling was recognized (2:7)

            (3) Because Paul's apostleship on same level as Peter's (2:8)

            (4) Because they recognized Paul was endowed with grace (2:9)

        iv. Request to remember the poor (2:10)

    e. Rebuke of Peter Substantiates Paul's Authority (2:11 – 21)

Explanation of the Text

2:1 Then after fourteen years I went up again to Jerusalem with Barnabas, taking along Titus also (Ἔπειτα διὰ δεκατεσσάρων ἐτῶν πάλιν ἀνέβην εἰς Ἱεροσόλυμα μετὰ Βαρναβᾶ, συμπαραλαβὼν καὶ Τίτον). The text is linked with 1:18 and 1:21 by the repetition of "then" (ἔπειτα), as Paul chronicles his relationship with the apostles in Jerusalem and the churches in Judea. The fourteen-year interval before traveling again to Jerusalem underscores the independence of Paul's gospel. He had spent fifteen days with Peter on his previous visit and the only other apostle he saw was James. Clearly, Paul did not need the Jerusalem apostles to endorse his gospel, for he did not travel to Jerusalem again for fourteen years.

The fourteen years could be reckoned from Paul's visit with Peter (1:18)[4] or from his conversion.[5] Resolving this matter does not affect the main point of the text, but it concerns scholars because of Pauline chronology. We have no information in the text that would compel us to choose one over the other.[6] If one favors a south Galatian theory, as I do, then it is likely that Paul reckons the fourteen years from his conversion in AD 31/32. Once again, the years may be reckoned inclusively, and hence this event may have taken place in about AD 44 – 46. Of course, certainty is impossible since we lack enough information to come to a definite conclusion.

When Paul traveled to Jerusalem, Barnabas

---

4. So Lightfoot, *Galatians*, 102; Fee, *Galatians*, 57.

5. So Martyn, *Galatians*, 189; Longenecker, *Galatians*, 45.

6. Betz suggests that the fourteen years should be dated

from Paul's visit to Syria and Cilicia (*Galatians*, 83), but the time span is too compacted for this to be likely.

traveled with him, and they brought Titus along.[7] One argument supporting the south Galatian hypothesis is that Barnabas and Paul together evangelized the south Galatian churches on the first missionary journey (Acts 13 – 14). So, the Galatians would have known Barnabas personally. Such a personal knowledge of Barnabas is less likely on the north Galatian hypothesis, for he did not travel with Paul on the second and third missionary journeys.[8]

The Galatians' knowledge of Barnabas's character is hinted at as well in the words "even Barnabas" (2:13). Barnabas played a vital role in the early church. He was given the moniker "Son of Encouragement" (Acts 4:36) and sold a field and generously gave the proceeds to the church (4:37). He played a central role in encouraging Paul in his ministry, for he convinced the other apostles of Paul's legitimacy (9:27) and recruited Paul some years later for the work in Syrian Antioch (11:25 – 26). Paul and Barnabas traveled together on the first missionary journey (Acts 13 – 14), defending a law-free gospel at what is typically called the Jerusalem Council (15:1 – 29). They had a sharp and famous disagreement about whether they should take John Mark on the second mission (15:35 – 39), and the dispute led to a parting of the ways. In the final analysis, however, Barnabas's faith in Mark was vindicated, as Paul later acknowledged (Col 4:10; 2 Tim 4:11; Phlm 24).

Titus was one of Paul's coworkers, and he played a major role in Corinth (cf. 2 Cor 2:13; 7:6, 13, 14; 8:6, 16, 23; 12:18). Paul later wrote a letter to him (cf. also 2 Tim 4:10). We know from Gal 2:3

that he was a Gentile. Did Paul bring Titus intentionally to Jerusalem as a test case regarding the requirement for circumcision?[9] Or, does Gal 2:4 suggest that the issue came up at the prompting of the false brothers? Since Paul's purpose is not to detail the history of what occurred in Jerusalem, certainty eludes us.

2:2a And I went up according to revelation (ἀνέβην δὲ κατὰ ἀποκάλυψιν). Paul went up to Jerusalem, not because he felt he needed validation for his gospel from the Jerusalem apostles, but because of a divine revelation directing him to do so. Such a revelation fits better with the Acts 11:27 – 30 visit of Paul and Barnabas to Jerusalem than the visit in Acts 15. According to Acts 15:2 Paul and Barnabas traveled to Jerusalem at the behest of the church in Syrian Antioch. But this directive for Paul and Barnabas does not necessarily preclude the giving of a divine revelation to Paul. It is possible, for instance, that Paul persuaded the church in Antioch to send him and Barnabas by appealing to a revelation that God had given him that instructed him to go to Jerusalem. Nevertheless, after the controversy over circumcision boiled over in Syrian Antioch, a visit of Paul and Barnabas to Jerusalem seems rather commonsensical. It seems more probable that a revelation was given to visit Jerusalem for the famine relief visit of Acts 11:27 – 30,[10] for the funds could have been sent to Jerusalem apart from Paul and Barnabas, and it may have seemed wiser for them to continue in their fruitful ministry in Antioch. But we can understand why Paul and Barnabas would travel

---

7. Stein sees the secondary role of Barnabas as evidence in support of the north Galatian hypothesis ("Two Neglected Arguments," 242) since Barnabas was the leader of the team during the famine visit of Acts 11:27 – 30. Such an argument is not decisive. Paul naturally records what happened from his perspective (cf. Longenecker, *Galatians* 46).

8. It is possible, of course, that Barnabas traveled to north

Galatia on another occasion apart from Paul, since we do not know the extent of Barnabas's movements.

9. Cf. Esler, *Galatians*, 130; Betz, *Galatians*, 85. Against this, see Bruce, *Galatians*, 111.

10. So Bruce, *Galatians*, 108 – 9. Riesner dates the famine collection to AD 41 – 45 (*Paul's Early Period*, 127 – 36).

to Jerusalem if God divinely revealed that they should do so.

Was the revelation given to Paul directly, or did Agabus receive it and communicate it to Paul, since Agabus was the person who informed the church in Antioch about the famine through a prophetic revelation?[11] Such questions interest scholars today, but we must confess that we lack enough information to posit a certain answer. In any case, the revelation was given by God, and Paul made the trip to Jerusalem in accord with God's will.

2:2b And I communicated before them the gospel that I preach among the Gentiles (καὶ ἀνεθέμην αὐτοῖς τὸ εὐαγγέλιον ὃ κηρύσσω ἐν τοῖς ἔθνεσιν). When Paul visited Jerusalem, he laid before the apostles the gospel he proclaimed among the Gentiles.[12] The reference to the Gentiles echoes Paul's call in 1:16 to proclaim to the Gentiles the gospel revealed to him on the Damascus road. The verb "communicate" (ἀνεθέμην) does not suggest that Paul referred his gospel to the men of repute and awaited their verdict, as if he was unsure about its validity.[13] Longenecker suggests that "them" (αὐτοῖς) refers here to the Jerusalem community in general,[14] but the flow of the argument as a whole suggests that the pillars

are in view. Paul knew his gospel was from Jesus Christ, and yet he also knew it was crucial for the Jerusalem pillars to agree with the gospel he proclaimed. As we consider the conclusion of 2:2, we will see why the ratification of the Jerusalem apostles was important.

2:2c That is, I communicated it privately before those of reputation (κατ᾽ ἰδίαν δὲ τοῖς δοκοῦσιν). The meeting held in Jerusalem was not public but private. The private character of the meeting suggests that it should be differentiated from the public council held in Acts 15,[15] though we cannot rule out that the private discussion described here preceded the public debate found in Acts 15.

Four times in this text Peter, James, and John are described as "those of reputation" (οἱ δοκοῦντες, 2:2, 6 [2x], 9). How should we understand this appellation? It could be understood as a dismissive comment: the leaders in Jerusalem have a name that is unwarranted.[16] Alternatively, the term can be read positively: Peter, James, and John deservedly enjoyed a high reputation.[17] Perhaps an interpretation between these two options is best. Paul did not doubt the stature and position of these leaders. Nevertheless, he cautioned against overestimating their authority.[18] Final

---

11. For tentative support of Agabus's revelation, see Longenecker, *Galatians*, 47. In support of a personal revelation, see Bruce, *Galatians*, 108.

12. Howard suggests (*Paul: Crisis in Galatia*, 38 – 39) that the Jerusalem apostles heard Paul's gospel for the first time on this occasion, but such a view is doubtful. It was noted earlier that Paul almost certainly shared the gospel he proclaimed when he was with Peter many years earlier (see Gal 1:18 above).

13. Dunn says the word does not imply that one party has a relatively higher status than another ("Paul and Jerusalem," 466 – 67; so also Martyn, *Galatians*, 190). Cf. Acts 25:14, where Festus lays his message before Agrippa, but there is no suggestion that Agrippa is superior to Festus, since the latter is the Roman procurator. Bruce (*Galatians*, 109) points to the incident in 2 Macc 3:9, "where Heliodorus [the emissary of the king] 'communicated' (ἀνέθετο) to the high priest the

information he had received about the wealth stored in the temple treasury."

14. Longenecker, *Galatians*, 47.

15. So Bruce, *Galatians*, 110. Bruce rejects the idea that a private meeting preceded a public one and suggests that the private meeting was held so that Paul and Barnabas could try to persuade the pillars of their view apart from the pressure of a public discussion.

16. Betz says that the pillars have authority, but Paul accepts "God and Christ" as his "only authority" (*Galatians*, 87; see also 92 – 93).

17. Burton, *Galatians*, 71; Bruce, *Galatians*, 109.

18. Paul uses the term because the opponents overestimated the apostles, and hence he does not criticize the Jerusalem apostles per se but those who exaggerated their importance (so Lightfoot, *Galatians*, 103; Longenecker, *Galatians*, 48).

authority does not reside in any person but only in the gospel (1:8).[19] Leaders are to be respected but not venerated, honored but not exalted above the gospel.[20]

2:2d Lest somehow I am running or had run in vain (μή πως εἰς κενὸν τρέχω ἢ ἔδραμον). Why did Paul privately disclose his gospel in Jerusalem? He says he did so in case his labor in the ministry was in vain. What we read here is surprising. Does Paul confess doubts here about the legitimacy of his gospel? Is he suggesting that he counseled in private with the Jerusalem leaders because he harbored private reservations about what he preached? Did he spend his first ten plus years in ministry in suspense, wondering if his gospel was truly given to him by God? All interpretations of this sort should be rejected, for they contradict the whole of Paul's argument up to this point. Paul entertains no doubts about his gospel since it was supernaturally revealed to him by God through Christ on the Damascus road. He insists that any other "gospel" deserves a divine curse (1:8 – 9). He did not need to consult with the apostles or anyone else since the gospel was unmistakably disclosed to him.

So, why did Paul confer behind closed doors with the apostles if he was not plagued with doubts about the veracity of his gospel? And why does he concede here that his efforts in proclaiming the gospel would be in vain if the apostles differed from him on the content of the gospel? The most satisfying answer is that Paul addresses the issue from a pragmatic standpoint here. He considers the practical ramifications that would follow if the apostles disagreed with him.[21] The truth of his gospel would not be affected by the decision of the apostles, for Paul's gospel was authoritative regardless of what the apostles said since it was revealed to him by God himself. Nevertheless, if the pillar apostles sent out an edict declaring that Paul's gospel was untrue, then his efforts in ministry would be practically nullified.

Such nullification would not, according to Paul, invalidate the truth of his gospel, for that was independently established by the revelation of Jesus Christ to him on the Damascus road. Rather, his gospel would not flourish if messengers visited every church he established with the word that the Jerusalem apostles disagreed with Paul. Such a judgment from the apostles in Jerusalem would wreak havoc in the churches he planted, and would sometimes reverse and often weaken the work accomplished.[22]

On the one hand, therefore, Paul did not need the imprimatur of Jerusalem to establish the truth of his gospel. On the other hand, their agreement with Paul was crucial from a practical standpoint. For if they diverged from Paul, his work would likely unravel when the view of Jerusalem became known in the Pauline churches. Indeed, it may have been tempting for the pillar apostles to compromise with the Judaizers on circumcision, for their ministry was mainly to Jewish Christians, who were circumcised.[23]

2:3 But not even Titus who was with me was compelled to be circumcised, even though he was a Greek (ἀλλ᾽ οὐδὲ Τίτος ὁ σὺν ἐμοί, Ἕλλην ὤν, ἠναγκάσθη περιτμηθῆναι). When Paul was in Jerusalem, the Jerusalem leaders did not require Titus to get circumcised. The explanation of the

---

19. Cf. here Smiles, *Gospel and Law in Galatia*, 37 – 38.

20. For an excellent summary of Paul's relations to the pillars in Gal 2:1 – 10, see Lightfoot, *Galatians*, 350 – 51.

21. Cf. Martyn, *Galatians*, 193; Smiles, *Gospel and Law in Galatia*, 40 – 42.

22. Cf. also Lightfoot, *Galatians*, 103 – 4; C. K. Barrett,

Freedom and Obligation: A Study in the Epistle to the Galatians (Philadelphia: Westminster, 1985), 11; Bruce, *Galatians*, 111; Longenecker, *Galatians*, 49.

23. So Lightfoot, *Galatians*, 104; Silva, *Interpreting Galatians*, 151.

Pauline gospel to them seems to have precipitated a discussion about the status of Titus (see 2:1 on Titus). Paul describes Titus as a "Greek," and the word "Greek" here does not necessarily mean that Titus was Grecian ethnically. It is simply another way of saying that Titus was a Gentile (cf. Rom 1:14, 16; 2:9, 10; 3:9; 10:12; 1 Cor 1:22, 24; 10:32; 12:13; Gal 3:28; Col 3:11). Should Titus then be circumcised? For the first time in the letter circumcision is mentioned. Note that Paul does not discuss here the situation in the Galatian churches but what took place when he arrived in Jerusalem. Nonetheless, he obviously relays what occurred in Jerusalem because it speaks to the state of affairs in Galatia (5:2 – 6; 6:12 – 13).

What is the import of circumcision here? According to the OT circumcision was required to be part of God's people. Those who refused circumcision did not belong to God's covenant people (Gen 17:9 – 14). Was circumcision still required for Gentile converts to Judaism in Paul's day? Apparently there was some debate in Second Temple Judaism over whether circumcision was mandatory, but the majority view subscribed to the clear teaching of the OT and required it.[24] Even some Jews who believed Jesus was the Messiah insisted that Gentiles were required to receive circumcision and to observe the law of Moses to be saved (Acts 15:1, 5). Since Titus was a Gentile, some contended that he could not belong to the people of God apart from circumcision.

Paul relays here the outcome of the private meeting in Jerusalem. They did not compel Titus to receive circumcision. Some have argued that Titus was circumcised voluntarily, but he was *not forced* to receive circumcision.[25] According to this reading, Titus is akin to Timothy in Acts 16:3. Timothy consented to circumcision, not in order to be saved, but to avoid conflict and to permit him to enter the synagogues with Paul for the preaching of the gospel. We should reject the idea that the situations of Titus and Timothy were similar. It is much more natural to understand Paul to say that Titus did not receive circumcision at all.

Verse 5 especially supports this reading, for if Titus was circumcised as a Gentile, then he subjected himself to the view of the false brothers. How would the truth of the gospel be preserved for the Galatians if Titus agreed to be circumcised? If Titus was circumcised, then the Galatians should be as well. What Paul emphasizes here is that Titus was not compelled to be circumcised by the Jerusalem leaders, even though he was a Gentile.[26] Lightfoot suggests that the pillars probably encouraged Paul as a concession to circumcise Titus, but Paul's arguments finally convinced them.[27]

In any case, Paul's ministry was not — for practical purposes — in vain, for the pillars ended up agreeing with the Pauline gospel as it was presented to them. Even though the pillars agreed with Paul, the distinctiveness of Paul's gospel

24. Rightly Nolland, "Uncircumcised Proselytes?" 173 – 94; Cohen, "Crossing the Boundary," 26 – 30. Against McEleney, "Conversion, Circumcision, and the Law," 319 – 41.

25. F. C. Burkitt, *Christian Beginnings* (London: Univ. of London Press, 1924), 118. He remarks, "for who can doubt that it was the knife which really did circumcise Titus that has cut the syntax of Gal ii 3 – 5 to pieces?" (118); so also Duncan, *Galatians*, 41 – 45. Nor is it clear, contra Dunn ("Paul and Jerusalem," 472), that the apostles could have compelled Titus to be circumcised. Augustine misunderstands this as well, thinking that it would not threaten

Paul's gospel to circumcise Titus (*Augustine's Commentary on Galatians*, 139).

26. Interestingly, the verb "compel" (ἀναγκάζω) is often used in Second Temple literature of Gentiles compelling the Jews to violate their laws (cf. 2 Macc 6:1, 7, 18; 7:1; 4 Macc 4:26; 5:2, 27; 18:5). See Cummins, *Crucified Christ*, 102.

27. Lightfoot, *Galatians*, 105 – 6; cf. also Dunn, *Galatians*, 96; Smiles, *Gospel and Law in Galatia*, 79 – 80. Presumably a long discussion probably preceded the decision. But it goes beyond the evidence here to see Paul "as something of a martyr figure" (against Cummins, *Crucified Christ*, 131).

should be noted.[28] The implications of a law-free gospel were grasped most clearly by Paul, though it is clear by Peter's comments in Acts 15:7 – 11 that he shared the same view as Paul.

Nor should we streamline the cases of Timothy and Titus as if they are the same. Timothy was considered to be a Jew because he was the son of a Jewish mother, though he had a Gentile father (Acts 16:1, 3).[29] Titus, by contrast, was a Gentile. Paul circumcised Timothy for cultural reasons: to advance the mission among the Jews. He consented to circumcise Timothy precisely because he was considered to be Jewish. Titus was in a completely different category as a Gentile. If Paul circumcised Titus, then he would have no basis for saying that circumcision was not required for the Gentiles in Galatia.

2:4a-b It was because of the false brothers who sneaked in, who had slipped in (διὰ δὲ τοὺς παρεισάκτους ψευδαδέλφους, οἵτινες παρεισῆλθον). Paul breaks into the argument here and refers to false brothers who surreptitiously entered the meeting. The Greek here is awkward, and Paul violates normal grammatical rules.[30] Perhaps Paul's emotional revulsion to the false brothers accounts for the sudden disruption in the text. We wish we had more information about what occurred at the meeting, and we must acknowledge that our information about what took place in Jerusalem is sketchy. Some have interpreted the text to say that the issue of Titus's circumcision

did not come up in his private meeting with the Jerusalem leaders and that it arose on a later occasion when the false brothers arrived.[31] It is more likely, however, that the events took place at the same time. The issue of Titus's circumcision had come to the forefront because of the influence of the false brothers.

Paul describes those who incited the controversy in pejorative terms. Most strikingly, they are designated as "false brothers" (ψευδαδέλφους; cf. 2 Cor 11:26). Those who advocated the circumcision of Titus claimed to be Christians. Apparently they believed Jesus was the Messiah, and yet Paul concludes that they were not genuinely brothers in the Lord.[32] Requiring circumcision and the observance of the law for salvation, in Paul's mind, puts one outside the circle of the redeemed.

What Paul says about the false brothers in Jerusalem applies also to the Judaizers who bedeviled the Galatians. Paul has already said that anyone who preaches another gospel is cursed (1:8 – 9). Those who desired to impose the law, according to Paul, were not merely mistaken on a minor matter. Requiring observance of the law changes salvation from being a work of God to a work accomplished by human beings. So, salvation is no longer of the Lord.

Paul also uses two words that suggest that the false brothers had insidiously entered into the church. The word "sneaked in" (παρεισάκτους) indicates that these men had snuck into the church, and the word "slipped in" (παρεισῆλθον) suggests

---

28. See especially here Silva, *Interpreting Galatians*, 154 – 58.

29. See Thomas R. Schreiner, "Circumcision," *DPL*, 139.

30. Nigel Turner says we have an anacoluthon here (*A Grammar of New Testament Greek*; vol. 3: *Syntax* [Edinburgh: T&T Clark, 1963], 343).

31. Indeed, some have maintained that Paul reflects in 2:4 – 5 on what took place on another occasion, not while he was in Jerusalem. For example, Bruce thinks what is relayed here took place in Antioch after the meeting in Jerusalem

(*Galatians*, 115 – 17; cf. also Guthrie, *Galatians*, 78; Schnabel, *Paul and the Early Church*, 996 – 97). It is possible that Paul does not follow chronology here, but it seems more likely that he relates what happened when he was in Jerusalem (so Longenecker, *Galatians*, 49; Dunn, *Galatians*, 97; Witherington, *Galatians*, 136).

32. Against Fee (*Galatians*, 62), who thinks that what is said here does not relate to "eternal salvation," but he surprisingly fails to see the implications of Gal 1:8 – 9 for this verse.

that they were interlopers. We find a similar reference to the false teachers in Jude 4, where the verb "crept in" (παρεισδύω) is used to denote the crafty work of opponents in worming themselves into the life of the congregation. So too in Jerusalem the false brothers had infiltrated the church, but they were not authentic Christians, and their presence created dissension.

2:4c-e To spy out our freedom that we have in Christ Jesus, in order to enslave us (κατασκοπῆσαι τὴν ἐλευθερίαν ἡμῶν ἣν ἔχομεν ἐν Χριστῷ Ἰησοῦ, ἵνα ἡμᾶς καταδουλώσουσιν). The insidious character of the false brothers continues to occupy Paul. They were infiltrators and interlopers and seducers, and hence their purpose in being part of the church was "to spy" (κατασκοπῆσαι). This word has the negative sense of spying in the two instances in which it is found in the LXX (2 Sam 10:3; 1 Chr 19:3). Betz points out that we have "military language turned into political metaphors," so that the false brothers are "like undercover agents and conspirators."[33]

The false brothers in Paul's view were still stuck in bondage, for like prisoners they came to see what freedom in Christ is like. But they did not arrive as prisoners who longed to be free but as those who desired to bring others into bondage with them. The word "enslave" (καταδουλώσουσιν) is future tense, and we would expect a subjunctive here after the Greek word used (ἵνα). Still, the use of the future instead of the subjunctive should not be assigned any exegetical significance. The meaning is the same as if a subjunctive were used (see 1 Pet 3:1).[34]

Obviously, the false brothers themselves did not think they were advocating slavery. What we find here is Paul's perspective on their theology, and Paul's view, for Christians who accept the

Scriptures as the Word of God, is authoritative and infallible. What believers enjoy, if they do not submit to the law, is freedom (ἐλευθερία). Freedom is a major theme in Galatians (cf. 4:22, 23, 26, 31; 5:1, 13), and it stands in contrast to slavery (4:1, 7, 22, 23, 24, 25, 31; 5:1). In every context, including here, freedom means freedom from the law. More specifically, bondage exists when circumcision and the law are required for salvation.

The freedom/slavery contrast points to the fulfillment of God's eschatological promises in Christ, signifying that the new exodus promised in Isaiah has now been become a reality.[35] Those who live under the old age of the law are enslaved, whereas those who are in Christ live in the new era in which God's saving promises are being fulfilled. The false brothers insisted that Titus had to be circumcised to belong to the people of God. It is remarkable that Paul, who had observed the Torah his entire life, now views such a requirement as the imposition of slavery.

In Galatians 3 – 4 Paul argues that subjection to the law does not bring freedom but enslaves. Requiring the law for salvation does not free people from sin but places them under the reign of sin. Reverting to the law is a yoke of slavery because human beings cannot keep the demands of the law. Hence, they groan under the law's demands, which they cannot fulfill. The freedom and liberty of the gospel were at stake when the opponents in Jerusalem tried to insist that Titus be circumcised.

2:5 But we did not yield in subjection to them for an hour, in order that the truth of the gospel might remain with you (οἷς οὐδὲ πρὸς ὥραν εἴξαμεν τῇ ὑποταγῇ, ἵνα ἡ ἀλήθεια τοῦ εὐαγγελίου διαμείνῃ πρὸς ὑμᾶς). The false brothers made no headway with Paul. He resisted the

---

33. Betz, *Galatians*, 90.
34. Rightly Longenecker, *Galatians*, 52.
35. See here Ciampa, *The Presence of Scripture in Galatians*

1 and 2, 138 – 42. Wilson emphasizes this same theme in 5:1 ("Wilderness Apostasy," 563 – 65).

pressure to circumcise Titus in order to preserve the truth of the gospel message.

The theme of slavery and subjugation continues in the use of the word "subjection" (τῇ ὑποταγῇ). Paul was adamant in the face of the insistence that Titus receive circumcision. He did not tolerate such a demand even for a minute. He recognized it as a false gospel and utterly repudiated it. A few Western witnesses omit the words "to whom not" (οἷς οὐδέ) here, as do Tertullian and Irenaeus, so that the verse reads, "We yielded in subjection for an hour, in order that the truth of the gospel might remain with you." Those who support this view maintain that Paul conceded that Titus be circumcised, so that he could preach his gospel among the Gentiles (1 Cor 9:19 – 23).

Such an interpretation should be rejected.[36] First, the variant reading should be rejected on external grounds. The vast majority of the witnesses and the best ones all support the inclusion of the words "to whom not" (οἷς οὐδέ). Second, the interpretation proposed should be rejected on the basis of internal evidence as well. How would the truth of the gospel be preserved if Paul capitulated and agreed to circumcise Titus?[37] The false brothers would surely trumpet such a decision and say that the Gentile believers in Galatia must be circumcised as well. If Paul agreed to circumcise Gentiles when pressured in Jerusalem, then the charge that he pleased people and waffled on circumcision would certainly be true (1:10; 5:11). It passes all understanding how yielding to the false brothers would preserve the truth of the Pauline gospel!

Paul holds himself up as an authority and a model for the Galatians. Just as he refused to relent when the false brothers demanded the circumcision of Titus, so they should refuse to listen to the words of the Judaizers who insisted that they should observe the law and be circumcised. To buckle under such pressure constitutes a denial of the gospel, which includes the truth that Gentiles are justified in the same way as Jews, by faith in Jesus Christ.[38] And it was not the Jerusalem apostles who imposed, or tried to impose, circumcision but the false brothers.

2:6a-c From those thought to be of reputation (indeed, of what sort they were formerly makes no difference to me; God does not pay attention to human stature) (ἀπὸ δὲ τῶν δοκούντων εἶναί τι – ὁποῖοί ποτε ἦσαν οὐδέν μοι διαφέρει· πρόσωπον ὁ θεὸς ἀνθρώπου οὐ λαμβάνει). The Jerusalem leaders are again described in terms of their stature. Paul warns against overestimating the pillars. They should not be venerated simply because they were disciples of Jesus during his earthly ministry. Presumably the false brothers (and the Judaizers in Galatia) argued that they were reliable authorities rather than Paul. One must beware of granting them too much authority, since final authority resides in the gospel, not human beings.

Paul was certainly not dazzled by the Jerusalem leaders, for their former status meant nothing to him.[39] Paul did not reject the apostolic authority of the pillars, but he rejected an obsequious veneration of them. Perhaps the Judaizers in Galatia are

---

36. So most interpreters. Cf. Longenecker, *Galatians*, 50; Betz, *Galatians*, 91 – 92; Bruce, *Galatians*, 113 – 15; Burton, *Galatians*, 76.

37. See here Metzger, *Textual Commentary*, 522 – 23.

38. J. R. Wisdom rightly emphasizes that the truth of the gospel is linked with the blessing of all nations (cf. Gal 3:8). See Jeffrey R. Wisdom, *Blessing for the Nations and the Curse of the Law: Paul's Citation of Genesis and Deuteronomy in*

Gal 3.8 – 10 (WUNT 2/133; Tübingen: Mohr Siebeck, 2001), 134 – 38.

39. The former status here refers to what they were before they met Paul (i.e., their stature as apostles of Jesus Christ who were called by him), and in James's case, his stature as a brother of the Lord. Therefore, Paul does not reflect here on their status at the time of the meeting in 2:1 – 10 but their status as apostles. So Calvin, *Galatians*, 54; Burton, *Galatians*,

subtly criticized here since they desired to make a good showing in the flesh (6:12). One should not become preoccupied with the pillars because God is not partial to any person, nor is he impressed with the reputation of anyone. Paul continues to support the claim that his ministry is not motivated by a desire to please people (1:10), and here he supports it by showing that the high status of the pillars does not lead to any alteration of his gospel.

The shift in tense between the imperfect "they were" (ἦσαν) and the present tense "differs" (διαφέρει) has spawned some discussion. The most probable view of the imperfect tense of "they were" (ἦσαν), as noted above, is that it refers to the relationship the pillars had with the historical Jesus during his ministry, and James's experience with Jesus by virtue of being from the same family. Paul was not starry-eyed and did not venerate the pillars on the basis of their past experiences.

Dunn emphasizes the present tense of the verb "differs" (διαφέρει) in his interpretation of the verse. He sees here a change of Paul's attitude toward the pillars since the meeting recorded in Galatians 2. At the time of the meeting in Jerusalem (ἦσαν) Paul thought more highly of the Jerusalem leaders, but *now* their stature *makes no difference to him*.[40] According to Dunn, we have a hint here of the split that occurred between Paul and Jerusalem *after* the meeting described in these verses. Dunn's reading of the text, however, should be rejected, as he puts too much weight on the present tense of the verb "differs" (διαφέρει).

We must beware of trying to tease more history out of the text than is warranted.[41] Otherwise we end up with speculation rather than exegesis. Recent studies of verbal aspect have rightly emphasized aspect rather than time in understanding verbs.[42] So, the present tense of a verb does not necessarily indicate present time, unless there are other contextual features to warrant such a reading. It is probable that both present tense verbs here (διαφέρει and λαμβάνει) represent general truths. The stature of apostles never mattered to Paul, and God is never moved by human status.[43]

2:6d That is, those of reputation contributed nothing to me (ἐμοὶ γὰρ οἱ δοκοῦντες οὐδὲν προσανέθεντο). Paul now restates the main point from 2:1 – 5. We saw earlier that the Jerusalem leaders did not require Titus to be circumcised, and hence the truth of the Pauline gospel was preserved. In other words, as Paul explains here, those of high stature added nothing to his gospel. They did not mandate circumcision for salvation, and hence they ratified the truth that salvation is not dependent on keeping the law.[44] Paul's gospel was independently true regardless of the view of the pillars, and yet when they were confronted with Paul's law-free gospel, they did not reject it but confirmed it. They saw no deficiency whatsoever in his gospel.

Thus, the Judaizers in Galatia, who presumably appealed to the Jerusalem apostles to validate their

---

87; Longenecker, *Galatians*, 53 – 54; Simon Gathercole, "The Petrine and Pauline *Sola Fide* in Galatians 2," in *Lutherische und Neue Paulusperspektive: Beiträge zu einem Schlüsselproblem der gegenwärtigen exegetischen Diskussion* (ed. Michael Bachmann; WUNT 182; Tübingen: Mohr Siebeck, 2005), 317.

40. Dunn, "Paul and Jerusalem," 473; idem, *Galatians*, 102 – 3.

41. Betz sees the present as "proverbial" (*Galatians*, 94 – 95); so also Longenecker, *Galatians*, 54; Martyn, *Galatians*, 199.

42. For some important studies on verbal aspect, see

Stanley E. Porter, *Verbal Aspect in the Greek of the New Testament, with Reference to Tense and Mood* (SBG 1; New York: Peter Lang, 1989); K. L. McKay, *A New Syntax of the Verb in New Testament Greek: An Aspectual Approach* (SBG 5; New York: Peter Lang, 1994); Buist M. Fanning, *Verbal Aspect in New Testament Greek* (Oxford: Clarendon, 1990).

43. Against Dunn, see also Witherington, *Galatians*, 139.

44. Against Martyn, who sees major issues relating to the law as unresolved at the conference so that some at Jerusalem believed that the Gentiles would eventually observe the law (*Galatians*, 220 – 22).

gospel, were profoundly mistaken in referring to the latter, for the apostles agreed with Paul, not with the Judaizers. The argument here is delicately handled. For on the one hand, Paul cannot compromise his gospel by granting that the Jerusalem apostles have ultimate authority. On the other hand, their ratification of his gospel functions as a powerful rebuttal of the view of the Judaizers in Galatia.

2:7 But on the contrary, because they saw that I had been entrusted with the gospel for the uncircumcision, just as Peter had been entrusted with the gospel for the circumcision (ἀλλὰ τοὐναντίον ἰδόντες ὅτι πεπίστευμαι τὸ εὐαγγέλιον τῆς ἀκροβυστίας καθὼς Πέτρος τῆς περιτομῆς). Rather than adding to or contributing anything to the Pauline gospel, the pillars ratified it and gave the right hand of fellowship to Paul and Barnabas (2:9). Here we have the first of two causal participles ("seeing," ἰδόντες) which explains why the Jerusalem leaders gave the right hand of fellowship to Paul and Barnabas. The second causal participle is the word "knowing" (γνόντες) in 2:9.

Why did the pillars ratify the Pauline gospel? They saw that Paul had been entrusted with the gospel for the uncircumcision. The word "entrusted" (πεπίστευμαι) should be understood here as a divine passive, and hence it is *God* who entrusted Paul with the gospel for those who were uncircumcised. Therefore, the Jerusalem leaders did not *establish* Paul's authority; they only *recognized* that God had given him such authority. Stein argues that the event here matches with Acts 15 rather than Acts 11:27 – 30 since the apostles would have no basis to recognize Paul's ministry if he had not been on the first missionary journey yet (Acts 13 – 14).[45] This argument is not decisive,

for the apostles would have heard reports about Paul's labors when he was in Syria and Cilicia (1:21 – 24).[46] Furthermore, Paul's work in Antioch with Barnabas would have been no secret to them (Acts 11:25 – 26).

The phrase "gospel for the uncircumcision" (τὸ εὐαγγέλιον τῆς ἀκροβυστίας) focuses on the truth that the gospel Paul proclaimed was for the Gentiles. I take it that the genitive "uncircumcision" (ἀκροβυστίας) is objective. There is also a hint here that circumcision is not required for salvation. Nevertheless, such an observation cannot be pushed too far since Paul also speaks of the gospel that Peter was entrusted with "for the circumcision" (τῆς περιτομῆς). Clearly, Paul would not endorse a gospel that required circumcision.[47]

Furthermore, in both 2:8 and 9 the contrast is between "the Gentiles (τὰ ἔθνη) and "the circumcision" (τὴν περιτομήν), indicating that when Paul uses the word "uncircumcision," it is another way of referring to Gentiles, and "circumcision" refers to Jews. Paul does not speak of two different gospels in content but of two different cultures in which the one gospel was proclaimed. Indeed, the last clause of this verse demonstrates that Peter was entrusted by God with the gospel as well, but his field of service was to the circumcision, i.e., the Jews. Paul emphasizes here that both he and Peter shared the same authority as apostles; they simply labored in different spheres. It should be noted as well that Paul does not question Peter's apostolic authority. He too was entrusted with the gospel, which suggests that Paul believed that Peter preached the same gospel he did.

2:8 (For the one who worked in Peter for the apostleship for the circumcision also worked in

---

45. Stein, "Two Neglected Arguments," 242.

46. Cf. Longenecker, *Galatians*, 40 – 41.

47. "In these parallel clauses, then, Paul in no way suggests that there are two gospels. There are, rather, two missions in

which the one gospel is making its way into the whole of the cosmos" (Martyn, *Galatians*, 202). So also Bruce, *Galatians*, 37, 120.

me for the Gentiles) (ὁ γὰρ ἐνεργήσας Πέτρῳ εἰς ἀποστολὴν τῆς περιτομῆς ἐνήργησεν καὶ ἐμοὶ εἰς τὰ ἔθνη). This verse is parenthetical to the argument, but it supports the claim in 2:7 that both Peter and Paul were entrusted by God with the same gospel. Peter was called as an apostle for the circumcision, i.e., for the Jews, because God had worked in Peter so that he was qualified to serve as an apostle to the Jews. In the same way, God worked in Paul so that he was qualified to serve as an apostle to the Gentiles.

Actually, Paul does not specifically use the word "apostle" of himself here. Paul's main point in the argument is not whether he was identified as an apostle but whether he was recognized as one who proclaimed the true gospel. Some scholars argue from the omission of the word "apostle" that Paul's apostolic status was not recognized in Jerusalem.[48] Such an interpretation is improbable, for we should not read between the lines and see an implicit criticism of Paul. It is more likely that even though the word "apostleship" is omitted, Paul's apostolic authority is implied (see 2:9 below).[49] Even though his apostleship is not specifically mentioned, validating Paul's gospel also validates his apostolic authority.

2:9a And because they recognized the grace given to me (καὶ γνόντες τὴν χάριν τὴν δοθεῖσάν μοι). The second reason is now given for the recognition by the Jerusalem leaders of Paul's ministry to the Gentiles. Not only did they see that Paul was entrusted with the gospel, but they also acknowledged that the grace of God was operative in Paul's life. When Paul reflected on his ministry, he often

spoke of the grace of God that called him into service (Rom 1:5; 15:15; 1 Cor 3:10; 15:10; Gal 1:15; Eph 3:2, 7, 8), and such grace is linked to his call to serve as an apostle. Therefore, it seems probable that the pillars recognized Paul's apostolic ministry in acknowledging the grace that was bestowed on him. Paul does not boast about his ministry here, for the focus is on the grace of God, which was "given" (δοθεῖσαν) to him.

2:9b-d James and Cephas and John, those reputed to be pillars, gave to me and to Barnabas the right hand of fellowship (Ἰάκωβος καὶ Κηφᾶς[50] καὶ Ἰωάννης, οἱ δοκοῦντες στῦλοι εἶναι, δεξιὰς ἔδωκαν ἐμοὶ καὶ Βαρναβᾷ κοινωνίας). The pillars ratified the gospel proclaimed by Paul and Barnabas, expressing their agreement by giving them the right hand of fellowship. At this juncture Paul names the three men of high reputation who functioned as leaders in Jerusalem. James and Peter were mentioned in 1:18 – 19, but they were not identified as the men of reputation there. Paul returns here (cf. 1:18) to identifying Peter by his Aramaic name, Cephas, in contrast to 2:7 – 8. The John mentioned here is almost certainly the son of Zebedee, who plays such a major role in the gospels. This is the only occasion in which he is mentioned in the Pauline letters, and he does not play a central role in Galatians.

What does Paul mean in saying that they were "reputed to be pillars"? Aus calls attention to traditions in Second Temple Judaism where the three patriarchs (Abraham, Isaac, and Jacob) are the three pillars for the nation and even the world.[51] Therefore, it seems that the term "pillars" (στῦλοι)

---

48. Longenecker, *Galatians*, 56; Betz, *Galatians*, 98 – 99; Dunn, "Paul and Jerusalem," 473.

49. See Bradley H. McLean, "Galatians 2.7 – 9 and the Recognition of Paul's Apostolic Status at the Jerusalem Conference: A Critique of G. Luedemann's Solution," *NTS* 37 (1991): 67 – 76; Ronald Y. K. Fung, *The Epistle to the Galatians* (NICNT; Grand Rapids: Eerdmans, 1988), 78; Gathercole,

"Galatians 2," 318; Hays, *Galatians*, 115.

50. 𝔓46 and mainly Western witnesses support "Peter," but "Cephas" is almost certainly original.

51. Roger D. Aus, "Three Pillars and Three Patriarchs: A Proposal Concerning Gal 2:9," *ZNW* 70 (1979): 252 – 61. But it is unlikely that the three were intentionally chosen as pillars to correspond to Abraham, Isaac, and Jacob as pillars.

in a Jewish context suggests that these three were the foundation of God's new temple, i.e., the new people of God.[52] Such a sentiment fits with Eph 2:20, where the church is "built on the foundation of the apostles and prophets." Further, there may also be a hint here that the new people of God, the true Israel, is established on a new foundation. Therefore, the true family of Abraham (Gal 3:6–9, 14), the true Israel of God (6:16), consists of those who belong to the new temple.

But how, then, do we account for Paul's statement that the three were "reputed" (δοκοῦντες) to be pillars?[53] Aus says that Paul cannot fully endorse the pillars since they teach a theology of merit.[54] This interpretation should be rejected, for the context here indicates a recognition of Paul's apostolic authority, and Paul's point in 2:3–5 is that the pillars did not compel Titus to be circumcised. Hence, they did not share the opinion of the false brothers in Jerusalem or the opponents in Galatia. What we have here, then, is Paul's recognition of the authority of the pillars, while at the same time he cautions against an undue veneration of them.[55] Paul does not reject the leadership of the three but warns against overestimating them.

The main point here is that the pillars of the Jerusalem church extended the right hand of fellowship to Paul and Barnabas.[56] In other words, they recognized the validity of the gospel proclaimed by Paul. They did not require Titus to be circumcised (2:3), nor did they add anything to the Pauline gospel (2:6). Instead, they realized that they were partners with Paul and Barnabas in proclaiming the same gospel.

Hence, the second major theme in the argument from 1:11–2:10 is enunciated. In 1:11–24 Paul trumpeted the independence of his gospel. He received it directly from Jesus Christ on the Damascus road. The Judaizers who traveled to Galatia probably argued that Paul derived his gospel from Jerusalem and that he distorted the gospel. Paul counters their claims in both areas. His gospel did not stem from Jerusalem, for he received it from a revelation of Jesus Christ himself (1:11–24). Furthermore, he did not distort the gospel. Even though he received it independently, the pillars recognized and ratified it when they heard it. They did not call for the circumcision of Gentiles, as is evident in the case of Titus (2:1–10).

2:9e-f In order that we should go to the Gentiles, and they to the circumcision (ἵνα ἡμεῖς εἰς τὰ ἔθνη, αὐτοὶ δὲ εἰς τὴν περιτομήν). The pillars recognized that Paul and Barnabas had a special calling to proclaim the gospel to the Gentiles, while

---

52. For a similar idea, see Matt 16:18. Cf. Ulrich Wilckens, "στῦλος," *TDNT*, 7:735; Martyn, *Galatians*, 205; Garlington, *Galatians*, 118. For the expectation of a new temple in Judaism, see, e.g., Ezek 40–48; *Jub.* 1:17–18; *1 En.* 90:28–29; *T. Benj.* 9:2; *2 Bar.* 32:3–4. For the new temple theme in all of Scripture, see G. K. Beale, *The Temple and the Church's Mission: A Biblical Theology of the Dwelling Place of God* (Downers Grove, IL: IVP, 2004).

53. C. K. Barrett argues that the term "pillars" originally denoted the eschatological status of Peter, James, and John, but their eschatological position was twisted into an institutional and ecclesiastical superiority by some of those who supported them ("Paul and the 'Pillar' Apostles," in *Studia Paulina in honorem Jr. de Zwaan* [ed. J. N. Sevenster and W. C. van Unnik; Haarlem: Bohn, 1953], 1–19).

54. Aus, "Three Pillars," 257–61.

55. So Longenecker, *Galatians*, 57–58; Matera, *Galatians*, 77.

56. Esler argues that the right hand of fellowship here designates the superiority of the pillars (*Galatians*, 133–34). The expression ("giving one's hand") in some contexts in the OT denotes devotion of an inferior to a superior (1 Chr 29:24; 2 Chr 30:8; Lam 5:6). In Second Temple Jewish literature the idea of a superior granting the right hand of fellowship to an inferior continues (1 Macc 6:58; 11:50, 62, 66; 13:50; 2 Macc 11:26; 12:11; 13:22; Josephus, *J.W.* 6.318–20, 345, 356, 378; *Ant.* 8.387; 18.328–29; 20.62). Still, the context of Galatians makes such an interpretation unlikely. The addition of the word "fellowship" indicates the equality of Paul/Barnabas and the pillars. Rightly Betz, *Galatians*, 100; Longenecker, *Galatians*, 58; Matera, *Galatians*, 77; Smiles, *Gospel and Law in Galatia*, 48.

they were focused on the circumcision, i.e., the Jews (see 2:7 above). Some understand the spheres geographically, so that Paul and Barnabas would preach in Gentile lands, whereas the pillars would proclaim the gospel in Jewish territory.[57] The agreement should be understood ethnically instead of geographically: Paul and Barnabas would minister to Gentiles and the pillars to the Jews.[58]

The spheres delineated here should not be understood rigidly, as if the pillar apostles would be violating the agreement if they ever participated in the Gentile mission.[59] Nor does the wording suggest that the evangelization of the Jews was off-limits for Paul, for he regularly evangelized Jews when preaching in synagogues according to Acts (cf. 1 Cor 9:19 – 23). What we have here is a recognition of the primary sphere of ministry for both Paul/Barnabas and the pillars at the time of the agreement, and an encouragement to continue in the sphere of ministry the Lord had allotted to each.[60] We should not read it as if it were an encyclical defining the boundaries of their ministries forever.

2:10 And (they asked) only that we should remember the poor, which indeed was the very thing I had been eager to do (μόνον τῶν πτωχῶν ἵνα μνημονεύωμεν, ὃ καὶ ἐσπούδασα αὐτὸ τοῦτο ποιῆσαι). The only request made by the Jerusalem leaders was that Paul would assist poor believers,

and Paul notes that such a request was nothing new, for he had already been raising money to assist the poor. Paul emphasizes that his gospel was already ratified and validated by the pillars. Therefore, they added nothing to what he proclaimed, and so Paul assures the Galatians that his gospel is the same one preached by the Jerusalem apostles. The only request made of Paul was that he should remember the poor[61] and continue to help them.[62]

The poor here refer to Jewish Christians. Elsewhere we see in Jewish literature that the poor are God's people (cf. 1QM 14.7; 1QpHab 12.3, 6; *Pss. Sol.* 5:2, 11; 10:6; 15:1; 18:2). The request to assist the poor was scarcely an addition to the Pauline gospel. Furthermore, Paul remarks that care for the poor was already his practice.[63] Indeed, if this trip to Jerusalem is the famine relief visit of Acts 11:27 – 30, then assistance for the poor constituted the reason for Paul's visit. Even if we identify Gal 2:1 – 10 with Acts 15:1 – 35, the visit of Acts 11:27 – 30 was now in the past, and hence Paul's support for the poor was already established.

Nor did his solicitation for the needy abate in the following years, for one of Paul's prime concerns was the collection for the poor saints in Jerusalem (cf. Rom 15:22 – 29; 1 Cor 16:1 – 4; 2 Cor 8:1 – 9:15). Indeed, Paul's enthusiasm for the collection may have also stemmed from the signal it sent to others of the unity of Jew and Gentile in Christ.[64]

---

57. E.g., Burton, *Galatians*, 97 – 99; 122; Scott, *Paul and the Nations*, 151 – 57.

58. Betz, *Galatians*, 100; Longenecker, *Galatians*, 58 – 59; Martyn, *Galatians*, 213. Longenecker cautions against overemphasizing the difference between these two interpretations.

59. Rightly Witherington, *Galatians*, 141. For a full discussion of the strengths and liabilities of both interpretations, see Schnabel, *Paul and the Early Church*, 992 – 1000. Schnabel suggests that the issue relates to the effectiveness of the missions of Paul and Peter, not the sphere of their activity. His solution fails to convince, for the purpose clause in 2:9 most naturally refers to different foci for missionary work.

60. Rightly Machen, *Galatians*, 131.

61. Turner sees the word "that" (ἵνα) as introducing an imperative here (*Syntax*, 95). So also Martyn, *Galatians*, 206.

62. Contra Larry W. Hurtado, evidence is lacking that Paul's ministry to the poor in Jerusalem was used against him to suggest his inferiority to the Jerusalem apostles ("The Jerusalem Collection and the Book of Galatians," *JSNT* 5 [1979]: 46 – 62).

63. Burton understands the verb "I was eager" (ἐσπούδασα) to refer to a future activity (*Galatians*, 99 – 100). It seems more likely, however, that the verb denotes an action already being carried out by Paul. So Bruce, *Galatians*, 126; Longenecker, *Galatians*, 60 – 61.

64. So Matera, *Galatians*, 83 – 84; Lührmann, *Galatians*, 41.

Theology in Application

False Teachers in the Churches

We learn from these verses that false teachers who claim to be fellow believers may worm themselves into churches (2:4). Apparently these people professed belief in Jesus as Messiah and Lord; yet Paul identifies them as false brothers! Probably many evangelicals today would be satisfied with someone claiming to believe Jesus is both Messiah and Lord. Why then does Paul say that they are not truly believers? Almost certainly because they taught that people were justified on the basis of works. They required circumcision and the observance of the law for salvation.

It seems unlikely that they are called false brothers merely for salvation-historical reasons, in that they desired to impose the old covenant on those who were in the new. Obviously, demanding that people live in the old era of salvation history is a mistake, but why would Paul say that anyone who holds such a position is damned? It makes better sense to say that the salvation-historical error is tied to an anthropological error. In other words, those who teach that salvation is ultimately based on works are false brothers.

We must be exceedingly careful to make sure we understand someone's theology before branding anyone as a false brother or sister. To say works are a necessary evidence of salvation is not the same as saying that works are the ultimate basis of our salvation. As we will see in the rest of Galatians, to base our salvation on our works denies what Christ did on the cross. Any theology that ultimately locates salvation in ourselves and what we do or accomplish is a false gospel. Salvation is no longer the work of God but represents our work, and hence we become idolaters who are praised for our contribution.

Do false brothers worm their way into our midst today? Clearly they do. The history of American universities testifies to such. So many of our great universities began as evangelical colleges, but they slowly became subverted. We think of Harvard and Yale.[65] And the story goes on and on. I am a Southern Baptist, and schools like Wake Forest, Stetson, Furman, and Mercer were once evangelical schools, but those days are over. False teachers came in and the gospel was lost.

Naturally I am not saying that there are not any Christians at such schools! The point is that the schools themselves are no longer evangelical. And is that happening at our evangelical colleges and universities today? Indeed, it is. Once again some schools are drifting from the gospel while claiming to be faithful to it. The first step in such a drift is almost always a denial of the inerrancy of Scripture. Sadly, the story has been repeated over and over again. Pray for our evangelical schools. And if you send your children to such schools, find out what they really teach. This may

---

65. See the study by James Tunstead Burtchaell, *The Dying of the Light: The Disengagement of Colleges and Universities* *from Their Christian Churches* (Grand Rapids: Eerdmans, 1998).

take some effort, but it it is well worth the time it will take. And if God has put you in a position to have an influence, be brave and take a stand. You will be vilified for being narrow-minded, but ask God to give you the courage to please him rather than people.

The Gospel of Grace Brings Freedom

A second theme here is that the gospel of grace brings freedom while devotion to the law results in bondage. Such a contrast shows again that Paul does not only restrict himself to a redemptive-historical disjunction between the old era and the new. Of course, what Paul says here is informed by salvation history as well, but the redemptive-historical contrast cannot be severed from anthropology. Living under the law brings bondage in the sense that it does not free people from the slavery of sin. Grace brings freedom, for it does not depend on human beings for righteousness. Therefore, we are freed from depending on what we do as the basis of salvation. We look to Christ alone for his redeeming work.

How easy it is to get our security and significance from what we do. We may be driven to activity by a deep-seated insecurity that longs for approbation from others. Our activity, both in our employment and at church, may appear to be an indication of our commitment to God. But at its root we may actually be seeking the approval of others, so that what we do does not flow from being accepted and loved in Christ but from a desire to obtain praise from others. O how easily we (I!) stray from the gospel. May we meditate daily on the truth that we are accepted not because of our work but because of what Christ has done for us.

The Proper Attitude toward Those in Authority

Finally, Paul's attitude toward the Jerusalem apostles is instructive. On the one hand, he recognizes their leadership and respects the position God has given them. On the other hand, he also recognizes their fallibility; hence, final authority is located in the gospel rather than in any human being. Leadership must be respected, but we must beware of servility or obsequiousness. We must beware of a rebellious and stubborn spirit that refuses to allow anyone to function as an authority over us. God has appointed leaders in our lives for our good and our sanctification. At the same time, no human being takes the place of God. Every leader, no matter how holy, is still a sinner and remarkably flawed.

Therefore, we should not venerate any human leader. We are to love the leaders God has placed over us without worshiping them. We should not despise them when we see their faults, for we all fall short in many ways (Jas 3:2). We must find the balance between unhealthy adulation of leaders and unloving and harsh criticism of them. If we know ourselves, we are keenly conscious of our many sins. Hence, we should not be surprised to find that our leaders are fallible. Such a recognition does not mean that we cease to respect them, though it does mean that we do not grant them an unquestioned authority. May God grant us the balance of respecting authority without idolizing it.

Our evangelical subculture (and larger culture as well!) tends to be dazzled by our religious superstars. How thankful we are for the ministries of pastors like John McArthur, John Piper, Mark Driscoll, and Tim Keller! And yet we must not venerate them. Some virtually become the disciples of these pastors (and others), and hence they fiercely and dogmatically defend every opinion of such men. Unfortunately, they buy into our celebrity culture and the word of famous pastors in effect becomes more important than the Word of God. We can unwittingly become incredibly secular even when we are talking about the Word of God. Paul warns us of the danger of venerating any human being. The gospel of Christ and the Word of God are our authority, and the pastors I named would agree that is not their word but the gospel that must be prized. May the Lord keep us from venerating evangelical superstars, so that our praise and adoration and wonder are directed to God in Christ alone.

Galatians 2:11 – 14

Literary Context

The argument for the independence and authority of the Pauline gospel continues. Paul's gospel was not received from human beings but given to him via a revelation of Jesus Christ (1:11 – 12). Paul's conversion and calling support the thesis that his gospel was given to him by God himself, for the only explanation for his change from persecutor to proclaimer of the gospel was the supernatural appearance of Christ on the Damascus road (1:11 – 17). Paul could not have derived his gospel from Peter, for he did not see him until three years after his conversion, and even then spent only two weeks with him (1:18 – 20). Nor did he receive it from the churches of Judea, for they did not even know Paul face-to-face (1:21 – 24). When the Jerusalem leaders heard the Pauline gospel fourteen years after his conversion, they did not demand the circumcision of Titus, nor did they add anything to Paul's gospel (2:1 – 10). Instead, they agreed his gospel was truly from God.

In the present paragraph (2:11 – 14), the narrative continues ("when," ὅτε), and Paul vindicates further the independence of his gospel in his rebuke of Peter. Not only did the Jerusalem leaders ratify the Pauline gospel (2:1 – 10), but his gospel stands as an authority over these apostles when they depart from it. Paul's independence from Jerusalem and his authority are reflected in his rebuke of Peter when the latter failed to live in accord with the truth of the gospel. Thus, Paul's gospel is authoritative not only in Galatia, but everywhere — even in Jerusalem.

Main Idea

The central idea here is that Paul had the boldness to rebuke Peter, demonstrating thereby that his gospel functioned as an authority over Peter. Hence, the Pauline gospel was not just Paul's personal opinion. It is *the* gospel in all times and in all places.

Translation

(See next page.)

Structure

Paul's authority as an apostle is demonstrated by his rebuke of Peter.[1] The narrative continues with another temporal word, but the temporal word is joined with an adversative since Paul rebukes Peter ("But when," [ὅτε δέ]). The main proposition in 2:11 – 14 comes to the forefront in 2:11. Paul resisted Cephas when the latter was in Antioch, and his rebuke of Peter was justified since Peter was in the wrong.

The remainder of the paragraph (2:12 – 14) explains the rebuke, marked by a "for" (γάρ). When Peter first arrived in Antioch, he freely ate with Gentiles. When "certain ones from James" came, however, he ceased to do so because he feared

---

1. Rightly Fung, *Galatians*, 105.

Galatians 2:11-14

11a	time *(of 11b-c)*	But when Cephas came to Antioch,
b	event	**I resisted him face-to-face**
c	basis *(of 11b)*	because he stood condemned.
12a	time *(of 12b)*	For before certain ones came from James,
b	event	**he was eating with the Gentiles.**
c	time *(of 12d)*	But when they came,
d	event	**he drew back**
e	sequence *(from 12d)*	and **separated himself**
f	basis *(of 12d-e)*	because he feared those of the circumcision.
13a	result *(of 12c-f)*	And as a result **the rest of the Jews joined him in hypocrisy,**
b	result *(of 13a)*	so that even Barnabas was carried away by their hypocrisy
14a	resolution to problem *(of 12-13)*	But when I saw that they were not walking straight in accordance with the truth of the gospel,
b	event	**I said to Cephas before them all,** "If you live like a Gentile and not like a Jew,
c	concession *(to 14b)*	even though you are a Jew,
d	fulfillment of condition *(of 14b-c)*	how can you compel the Gentiles to live like Jews?"

persecution from unbelieving Jews. The consequence of Peter's hypocrisy is relayed in 2:13. The remaining Jewish Christians and even Barnabas were swayed by Peter's hypocrisy and refrained from eating with Gentiles. This situation — i.e., Peter's hypocrisy and its impact on others — comprises 2:11 – 13. Paul's response begins in 2:14, for he perceived that Peter did not live in accord with the gospel. Paul focuses on the inconsistency of Peter's actions. Since Peter was already living like a Gentile, it made no sense for him now to coerce the Gentiles to live like Jews.

Exegetical Outline

I. Introduction: Desertion from Paul's Gospel Is Desertion from the Gospel (1:1 – 2:21)

A. Greeting: Paul's Apostolic Authority (1:1 – 5)

B. Problem Explained: Desertion from the Gospel (1:6 – 10)

C. Paul's Gospel Derived from God, Not People (1:11 – 2:21)

1. Thesis: source of his gospel was revelation (1:11 – 12)

2. Thesis support (1:13 – 2:21)

a. His past hostility (1:13 – 14)

b. His call from God (1:15 – 17)

c. His relative obscurity in Judea (1:18 – 24)

d. Recognition of Paul's authority by pillars (2:1 – 10)

e. Rebuke of Peter substantiates Paul's authority (2:11 – 21)

➡   **i. Rebuke (2:11 – 14)**

(1) Paul's opposition to Peter (2:11)

(2) Peter's withdrawal from Gentiles (2:12)

(3) Consequences of Peter's actions (2:13)

(4) Paul's response to Peter (2:14)

ii. Transition: The Nature of the Gospel (2:15 – 21)

Explanation of the Text

2:11 But when Cephas came to Antioch, I resisted him face-to-face because he stood condemned (Ὅτε δὲ ἦλθεν Κηφᾶς[2] εἰς Ἀντιόχειαν, κατὰ πρόσωπον αὐτῷ ἀντέστην, ὅτι κατεγνωσμένος ἦν). The narrative continues with the word "when" (ὅτε). Peter's arrival in Antioch cannot be dated definitely, but perhaps it occurred sometime after

his miraculous deliverance from prison and before the Jerusalem Council (Acts 12:17; 15:1 – 35). Syrian Antioch was probably the third largest city of the Roman Empire, and it is estimated to have had a population of 250,000.[3] The Jewish population may have been 25,000.[4]

Most likely the event recounted here took place

---

2. In this case the Majority Text and Western witness support the reading "Peter," but again "Cephas" is supported by external evidence.

3. Cf. Schnabel, *Jesus and the Twelve*, 784.

4. Ibid., 785.

after the account in 2:1 – 10, though some scholars think 2:11 – 14 preceded 2:1 – 10.[5] If 2:1 – 10 is identified with the famine relief visit in Acts (Acts 11:27 – 30), then the Antioch incident would likely have preceded the Jerusalem Council in Acts 15.[6] Peter's defection on this issue makes more sense previous to the Jerusalem Council, though given human fallibility, Peter could have transgressed after the council as well.

Paul is not interested here in relating the biography of his relationship with Peter, nor is he trumpeting himself as superior to Peter. Rather, he refers to his rebuke of Peter because it proves the independence and authority of his gospel. Paul did not reprove Peter because of a personal pique against him or because he suddenly lost his temper.[7] He reprimanded him because he was condemned before God for his actions.[8] Some early church fathers interpreted Peter's sin here as feigned, so that Peter pretended to be doing wrong so that Paul could correct him and all would be instructed.[9] Clement of Alexandria suggested the Cephas mentioned here was not the apostle Peter.[10] Such interpretations are desperate attempts to salvage Peter's reputation. It is better to acknowledge that even apostles sinned and fell short of God's glory.

Some have also asked whether Paul sinned in admonishing Peter publicly rather than in private. Should he have followed the instructions of Jesus and spoken to Peter individually instead of reprimanding him before all (cf. Matt 18:15 – 17)? A public rebuke in this instance was warranted because Peter's sin was committed in the public sphere, and it had public consequences in that others followed his example.[11] Therefore, a public reprimand was necessary, given the widespread impact of Peter's sin.[12]

2:12a-b For before certain ones came from James, he was eating with the Gentiles (πρὸ τοῦ γὰρ ἐλθεῖν τινας ἀπὸ Ἰακώβου μετὰ τῶν ἐθνῶν συνήσθιεν). Paul relates more specifically what led to his reprimand of Peter. Peter's eating with the Gentiles was apparently an ongoing activity (see the imperfect verb "he was eating with" [συνήσθιεν]) before the men from James arrived.[13] Apparently Peter regularly ate foods forbidden by the OT law before these men arrived. Modern readers wish that Paul had provided a more detailed record of the events recounted here, for his terse rehearsal leaves many questions unanswered. We are reminded of the historical distance that separates us from the original readers.

---

5. In support of the precedence of 2:11 – 14, see Munck, *Paul and the Salvation of Mankind*, 100 – 102. But most scholars rightly argue that Gal 2:1 – 10 preceded 2:11 – 14 (so Longenecker, *Galatians*, 63 – 64; Dunn, *Galatians*, 116, n. 1; Bruce, *Galatians*, 128; Matera, *Galatians*, 88 – 89; Witherington, *Galatians*, 149).

6. So Bruce, *Galatians*, 128 – 29; Longenecker, *Galatians*, lxxxi – lxxxii, 71.

7. Peter Richardson argues that Paul wrongly condemned Peter, for Peter followed the principle of accommodation set out by Paul himself in 1 Cor 9:19 – 23. "Pauline Inconsistency: I Corinthians 9.19 – 23 and Galatians 2.11 – 14," *NTS* 26 (1979 – 80): 347 – 62. But Richardson's argument is seriously flawed. See D. A. Carson, "Pauline Inconsistency: Reflections on I Corinthians 9.19 – 23 and Galatians 2.11 – 14," *Churchman* 100 (1986): 6 – 45.

8. In support of the idea of being condemned before God, see Longenecker, *Galatians*, 72; Ulrich Wilckens, "ὑποκρίνομαι," *TDNT*, 8:568, n. 51. He was not merely self-condemned (against Guthrie, *Galatians*, 84).

9. E.g., Chrysostom, *Galatians*, 18 – 20. For a summary of the views of the early church fathers, see Bruce, *Galatians*, 133 – 34.

10. According to Eusebius, who records Clement's view here, *Eccl. Hist.* 1.12.

11. Cf. here *Augustine's Commentary on Galatians*, 145; Bruce, *Galatians*, 132; George, *Galatians*, 179.

12. It may be the case that Paul's rebuke of Peter was grounded in his understanding of Lev 19:17 and Deut 19:15. For a discussion of this matter, see Ciampa, *The Presence of Scripture in Galatians 1 and 2*, 172 – 76.

13. So Betz, *Galatians*, 107.

"Certain ones ... from James,"[14] the Lord's brother, arrived in Antioch. Most likely they came to Antioch because James had instructed them to do so. Apparently news had reached Jerusalem about the actions of Peter and other Jewish Christians in Antioch. What message did James entrust to his emissaries? Did they convey it accurately to Peter?[15] Presumably they expressed concern about Peter and other Jews eating with Gentiles, fearing the consequences that would follow from not observing OT food laws. We can imagine that James and other Jewish Christians in Palestine would be troubled upon hearing that Peter and his friends were abandoning dietary regulations. Such news would have been scandalous to unbelieving Jews in Jerusalem, and it presumably troubled many Christian Jews in the homeland as well.

Still, it overreads the evidence to conclude that James demanded that Peter cease eating with the Gentiles since Paul does not criticize James here but only Peter. Indeed, Paul had just written that James agreed with his gospel (2:1 – 10). We must finally confess uncertainty about what James told the couriers to say.

What does it mean to say that Peter was eating with Gentiles?[16] The most natural reading suggests that Peter was no longer observing the OT food laws and was eating meals with Gentiles. Such behavior on his part fits with the vision he received in Acts 10:9 – 16, when God declared all foods clean, Peter visited Cornelius and his Gentile friends, and he proclaimed the gospel to them (cf. Mark 7:19). Most likely Peter ate Gentile food during his visit with Cornelius. Such behavior would be troubling and even scandalous to most Jews. Jews who were devoted to their religion took seriously the admonitions regarding clean and unclean foods (Lev 11; Deut 14). For example, Daniel and his cohorts restricted themselves to vegetables and water so that they would not be defiled with the king's food (Dan 1:8, 10, 12, 16).

From the Maccabean period onward, the boundary markers of Judaism (circumcision, Sabbath, and food laws) were at the forefront of Jewish consciousness. A hellenizing movement attempted to suppress Jewish distinctives, and those who observed the law were persecuted (cf. 1 Macc 1:47, 62; 4 Macc 7:6; Josephus, *Ant.* 11.8.7 §346). The Pharisees, according to Neusner, tried to regulate all of life according to the rules of purity.[17] Josephus mentions priests who ate only figs and nuts so that they could abstain from meat

---

14. D. W. B. Robinson argues that the correct reading here is "certain things" (τινα), referring to the stipulations of the decree (neuter plural indefinite pronoun) in Acts 15 ("The Circumcision of Titus and Paul's 'Liberty,'" *ABR* 12 [1964]: 40 – 42). This reading is improbable in terms of the relationship between Acts 15 and Galatians 2, since according to Acts Paul was present and agreed with the stipulations of the decree. In any case (see end of this note), the variant "certain things" (τινα) is not original. Enno Edzard Popkes accepts the same reading, maintaining that a single person (the masculine singular indefinite pronoun) is in view. "'Bevor *Einer* von Jakobus Kam ...': Anmerkungen zur Textkritischen und Theologiegeschichtlichen Problematik von Gal 2,12," *NovT* 46 (2004): 253 – 64. The variant should be rejected since it is supported only by 𝔓[46], it[d r], and Irenaeus (cf. Bruce, *Galatians*, 129).

15. Lightfoot suggests that they "abused" the authority James gave them (*Galatians*, 112; cf. Fee, *Galatians*, 74, n. 69).

Schoeps identifies the men from James with the false brothers of 2:4 (Schoeps, *Paul*, 67 – 68). Betz says that they accurately communicated James's sharp disapproval of Peter's actions (*Galatians*, 108 – 9).

16. Some argue that only the Lord's Supper is in view here. So Schlier, *Der Brief an die Galater* (KEK; Göttingen: Vandenhoeck & Ruprecht, 1965), 83, or only ordinary meals with Gentiles (Burton, *Galatians*, 104), but it is probable that both regular meals and the Lord's Supper are in mind. So Bruce, *Galatians*, 129; George, *Galatians*, 173; Fee, *Galatians*, 72 – 73; Robert Jewett, "Gospel and Commensality: Social and Theological Implications of Galatians 2.14," in *Gospel in Paul: Studies on Corinthians, Galatians and Romans for Richard N. Longenecker* (ed. L. Ann Jervis and Peter Richardson; JSNT-Sup 108; Sheffield: Sheffield Academic Press, 1994), 248.

17. See Neusner, *The Rabbinic Traditions about the Pharisees before 70*.

they considered unclean (*Life* 3 §13 – 14). Judith refrained from eating the meat and wine of the Gentiles (Jdt 12:1 – 2).

Indeed, concern for observing OT purity laws was a common theme in Jewish literature (Add Esth 4:17; Tob 1:10 – 12; *T. Reu.* 1:10; *T. Jud.* 15:4;

T. Isaac 4:5 – 6; 2 Macc 5:27; 4 Macc 1:33 – 34; 4:26; *Jos. Asen.* 7:1; 8:5; 1QS 5.16 – 18; *m. ʿAbod. Zar.* 2.3 – 4; 4.8 – 12).[18] Peter's eating with Gentiles, which in my view involved the eating of unclean foods, would be offensive to most Jews, and we can understand why he was pressured to desist.

In Depth: Eating with Gentiles

We should consider further here what it means to say that Peter was eating with the Gentiles. There is considerable debate among NT scholars on the matter. First, consider the background. Sanders is probably correct in saying that in some instances Jews who followed purity laws ate with Gentiles, as long as purity laws were observed.[19] Esler argues that Jews who conformed to the OT law did not share the same vessels of food and wine with Gentiles. They may have eaten in the same location (parallel eating), but they did not partake of food from the same vessels.[20] He points out that in the Lord's Supper believers shared from the same cup and same loaf (1 Cor 10:16 – 17).

Esler also observes that Jews may have abstained from sharing at table with Gentiles for several reasons: (1) They may have feared that the vessels used by Gentiles when they prepared foods were defiled because these vessels were also used for unclean foods; (2) Gentile food was unclean because of their idols; (3) Jews wanted to erect a boundary against outsiders; (4) their abstention may have stemmed from their understanding of OT laws regarding idolatry (Exod 23:13, 24, 32 – 33; 34:12 – 16; Deut 7:1 – 6, 23 – 26; 12:2 – 3; *m. Demai* 6.10; *m. ʿAbod. Zar.* 5:3 – 7; Acts 10:28; 11:3).[21] Probably there were different stances among Jews. Some thought that even eating with Gentiles (even if Jews ate separately) was prohibited (*Jub.* 22:3), while others believed that they could eat with Gentiles as long as they observed OT purity laws.

I argued above that the simplest and most natural reading of Gal 2:11 – 14 is that Peter actually ate unclean food — food prohibited by the OT law — before the men from James came. But some scholars disagree. Dunn, for instance, argues that before the men of James came, Peter and the Gentiles in Antioch were already observing the basic food laws of the Torah, and the men from James

---

18. All Mishnaic texts are from *The Mishnah* (ed. Herbert Danby; New York: Oxford Univ. Press, 1933).

19. E. P. Sanders, "Jewish Association with Gentiles and Galatians 2:11 – 14," in *The Conversation Continues: Studies in Paul & John in Honor of J. Louis Martyn* (ed. Robert T.

Fortna and Beverly R. Gaventa; Nashville: Abingdon, 1990), 170 – 88.

20. Esler, *Galatians*, 88 – 116.

21. Ibid., 96 – 97.

advocated an even stricter observance.[22] Dunn's view should be rejected, for we have no evidence that Christian Gentiles in Antioch were substantially observing food laws. Cohn-Sherbok rightly remarks, "Dunn does not provide any explicit demonstration to support his hypothesis that table-fellowship before the arrival of men from James involved a fair degree of observance of the dietary laws, including even some of the halachic elaborations concerning tithes and ritual purity."[23]

Paul describes Peter as *living like the Gentiles* (2:14), not as significantly keeping the food laws before the men of James arrived. The parallel with 4 Macc 4:26 is illuminating, for the "renunciation of Judaism" (ἐξόμυσθαι τὸν Ἰουδαϊσμόν) involves the eating of unclean food. In Galatians Paul probably identifies "judaizing" (ἰουδαΐζειν, 2:14) with the imposition of food laws on the Gentiles. But it is unlikely that Peter required Gentiles to conform in part to Judaism when he ate with them, or that the Christian Gentiles were gladly observing some of the dietary regulations before the men from James came on the scene. Therefore, it seems reasonable to conclude that Peter and the Gentiles in Antioch ate the "food of the Gentiles" (Tob 1:10 RSV), since Peter was living like a Gentile (2:14) and eating with Gentiles (2:12) until the men from James appeared.

Furthermore, even if there were some situations where Jews and Gentiles ate together and Jews conformed to their food laws, it is likely that such situations were relatively rare for practical reasons. Diodorus of Siculus confirms that typically Jews did not enjoy table fellowship with others (*Bibliotheca Historica* 34.1.2; cf. Philostratus, *Life of Apollonius* 5.33; Tacitus, *Histories* 5.5.2), presumably to avoid eating defiled food. And Gal 2:11 – 14 gives no indications that Peter observed food laws when eating with Gentiles.[24]

---

22. James D. G. Dunn, "The Incident at Antioch (Gal 2:11 – 18)," *JSNT* 18 (1983): 12 – 37; so also Matera, *Galatians*, 89. Peter J. Tomson argues that Peter and Paul did not violate purity laws but were considered liberal because they ate with Gentiles. See *Paul and the Jewish Law: Halakah in the Letters of the Apostle to the Gentiles* (CRINT 3/1; Minneapolis: Fortress, 1990), 227 – 36. Cf. also Mark D. Nanos, "What Was at Stake in Peter's 'Eating with Gentiles' at Antioch?" in *The Galatians Debate: Contemporary Issues in Rhetorical and Historical Interpretation* (ed. Mark D. Nanos; Peabody, MA: Hendrickson, 2002), 282 – 318; Howard, *Paul: Crisis in Galatia*, xix – xxii; Hays, *Galatians*, 232; Cummins, *Crucified Christ*, 163 – 69. Sanders thinks that Paul exaggerated what was going on at Antioch, and so the view that Peter actually violated the food laws is mistaken. What actually concerned James, says Sanders, was that Peter had too much contact

with Gentiles and was endangering his reputation. See Sanders, "Galatians 2:11 – 14," 185 – 87.

23. Dan Cohn-Sherbok, "Some Reflections on James Dunn's 'The Incident at Antioch (Gal 2:11 – 18),'" *JSNT* 18 (1983): 70 – 71. His whole critique is valuable (68 – 74). J. L. Houlden also shows that Dunn's position is not plausible in terms of its reconstruction of earliest Christianity ("A Response to J. D. G. Dunn," *JSNT* 18 [1983]: 58 – 67). See also the discussions in Burton, *Galatians*, 104; Betz, *Galatians*, 107.

24. Ciampa rightly argues that we should conclude that abstention from Gentile food would normally also involve not eating with Gentiles, even though, strictly speaking, abstention from unclean food is what is prohibited (*The Presence of Scripture in Galatians 1 and 2*, 162 – 63, n. 17); see also Witherington, *Galatians*, 153, n. 99. Contra, Bauckham, "James, Peter, and the Gentiles," 124; Michael F. Bird, *The Saving*

2:12c-f But when they came, he drew back and separated himself because he feared those of the circumcision (ὅτε δὲ ἦλθον,[25] ὑπέστελλεν καὶ ἀφώριζεν ἑαυτόν φοβούμενος τοὺς ἐκ περιτομῆς). Peter ate with the Gentiles and partook of unclean food until the men from James arrived. They likely informed him that James and other Jewish believers expressed concerns over his eating of unclean food. Peter responded by withdrawing and separating from the Gentiles. The imperfect verbs here (ὑπέστελλεν καὶ ἀφώριζεν) could be interpreted more than one way. Perhaps Peter slowly and gradually withdrew from the Gentiles.[26] Or, the verbs could be read as inceptive, which would mean that he suddenly stopped eating with Gentiles. Certainty on the meaning of the verb is impossible. In any case, Peter ceased eating with the Gentiles, presumably so that those from James could no longer accuse him of being defiled by foods that were unclean according to the OT (Lev 11:1 – 44).

Peter's withdrawal was not prompted by a change in his theology. He was spurred on by fear of those of the circumcision. The participle "fearing" (φοβούμενος) is causal, giving the reason why Peter separated himself. But who were "those of the circumcision" (τοὺς ἐκ περιτομῆς)? The phrase "those of the circumcision" (οἱ ἐκ περιτομῆς) is used in a variety of ways in the NT (Acts 10:45; 11:2; Rom 4:12; Col 4:11; Titus 1:10).[27] In some contexts it merely denotes those who are Jews (Rom 4:12). It seems in Acts that it denotes Jewish Christians, perhaps particularly emphasizing those who were conservative relative to the OT law (Acts 10:45; 11:2). In Colossians, however, the term refers to Jewish Christians (Col 4:11), without any implication that they were conservative relative to the law.[28] In Titus, "those of the circumcision group" refers to false teachers, who were almost certainly Jewish (Titus 1:10). Nonetheless, there is no evidence in Titus or the other Pastoral Letters that circumcision was required by the Pauline opponents. In conclusion, the meaning of the phrase "those of the circumcision" must be discerned contextually, for it is used in different ways depending on the situation addressed.

In Gal 2:12 "those of the circumcision" could refer to Jewish Christians[29] or, alternatively, to Jews who were not believers.[30] Some who think they were Jewish Christians maintain that they are equivalent with the men from James.[31] If this is the case, then Peter feared what James and his friends

---

Righteousness of God: Studies on Paul, Justification, and the New Perspective (Eugene: Wipf & Stock, 2007), 119 – 40.

25. The reading "he came," or "it came," or "certain things [plural neuter subject of third singular verb] came" (ἦλθεν) has significant textual support from diversified textual witnesses (𝔓[46vid], ℵ, B, D*, F, G, 33, 330, 2492, *al*). Therefore, it becomes the basis for Popkes ("Bevor *Einer* von Jakobus Kam," 253 – 64) favoring "someone" (τινα) in 2:12. Other manuscripts support the plural "they came" (ἦλθον) (A, C, D², H, K, P, Ψ, 81, 614, 1739, etc.). As Metzger observes, a scribe could have easily used the singular since the singular "he came" (ἦλθεν) occurs in 2:11, and three verbs in 2:12 have -εν endings: "he was eating" (συνήσθιεν), "he withdrew" (ὑπέστελλεν), and "he separated" (ἀφώριζεν). Therefore, seeing assimilation here is plausible (cf. Metzger, *Textual Commentary*, 523 – 24).

26. Longenecker, *Galatians*, 75; Matera, *Galatians*, 90.

27. The phrase is not exactly the same in all these passages, but it is similar enough to warrant placing them together here.

28. Against Ellis, who thinks they had a strict attitude toward the law (*Prophecy and Hermeneutic*, 121, 124). Contrary to Ellis, we should not conclude that the phrase has the same meaning everywhere it appears. We must discern the meaning of the phrase in context.

29. So Lightfoot, *Galatians*, 112; Burton, *Galatians*, 107; Betz, *Galatians*, 109; Matera, *Galatians*, 86; Hays, *Galatians*, 234; Bird, *Saving Righteousness of God*, 125 – 26.

30. Munck departs from both these views and sees a reference to Gentile Christians (*Paul and the Salvation of Mankind*, 106 – 8), but such a view is clearly mistaken, and it has not gained many adherents.

31. Burton, *Galatians*, 107; Martyn, *Galatians*, 236 – 40 (but he also equates them with the false brothers of 2:3 – 5); Betz, *Galatians*, 107 – 9; Smiles, *Gospel and Law in Galatia*, 89 – 91.

would say about his eating with Gentiles. Such a view is certainly possible but seems unlikely for two reasons. (1) It is doubtful that Paul thought James was responsible for Peter's lapse, even though concerns were likely raised about Peter's actions by James.[32] (2) Such a view would require that Peter feared James, which seems unlikely.[33]

Another possibility is that the circumcision party refers to Jewish Christians who were analogous to or even identical with the men of Antioch who required circumcision (Acts 15:1). Ellis says that "those of the circumcision are best understood as a faction of Jewish Christians."[34] But why would Peter fear those whom Paul calls "false brothers" in Gal 2:4? In 2:1 – 10 Peter sides with Paul against them on the matter of circumcision, and if the account in Acts 15 refers to a later situation, Peter again opposes such Jewish "Christians." Hence, it is difficult to believe that he feared such here.

Still another possibility presents itself: those of the circumcision refers to unbelieving Jews. Some identify them as politically active Jews who persecuted those who did not conform to their view of Torah.[35] It seems that in Acts 11:1 – 18 Peter did not fear Jewish Christians, who advocated circumcision. Instead, he explained to them why his actions were justified. But if those of the circumcision were unbelieving Jews who were persecuting Christians and who would intensify their persecution if

Jewish Christians departed from the Torah, then Peter's fear seems more likely.[36] Perhaps the men from James arrived and said that the threat of persecution against Jewish Christians was increasing because of reports that Jewish Christians in Antioch were departing from food laws and eating with Gentiles.[37] Peter feared the consequences of his actions for fellow Jews, who were believers, and thus he ceased eating with Gentiles to protect Jewish believers in Christ and, perhaps, to prevent a schism among Jewish believers.[38]

2:13 And as a result, the rest of the Jews joined him in hypocrisy, so that even Barnabas was carried away by their hypocrisy (καὶ συνυπεκρίθησαν αὐτῷ καὶ οἱ λοιποὶ Ἰουδαῖοι, ὥστε καὶ Βαρναβᾶς συναπήχθη αὐτῶν τῇ ὑποκρίσει). The impact of Peter's behavior was immediate and palpable. The remaining Jewish Christians also ceased eating with the Gentiles. Indeed, Peter's influence was so dramatic that even Barnabas, one of the prime movers behind the Gentile mission, stopped eating with the Gentiles. Paul identifies the motives of Peter and those influenced by him to be hypocritical.[39] In other words, Peter and his friends did not act out of conviction but were motivated by fear.

Many NT scholars depart from the text here and argue that Peter disagreed with Paul theologically.[40] Many posit a parting of the ways between Peter and Paul from this point on, and we

---

32. Cf. Guthrie, *Galatians*, 84.

33. Rightly Bruce, *Galatians*, 131. Cf. Longenecker, *Galatians*, 74; Fung, *Galatians*, 108.

34. Ellis, *Prophecy and Hermeneutic*, 117.

35. Jewett, "Agitators," 340 – 41; Bruce, *Galatians*, 130 – 31; Longenecker, *Galatians*, 74 – 75; Witherington, *Galatians*, 154 – 56. Nanos argues that Zealot activity commenced only later, and that it is doubtful in any case that they could affect what was happening in Antioch ("What Was at Stake?" 291). But the opponents could be Jewish and devoted to the law without being Zealots (so Muddiman, "Anatomy of Galatians," 263).

36. Jewett, "Agitators," 340 – 41. Cf. here Leonard Goppelt,

Apostolic and Post-Apostolic Times (trans. Robert A. Guelich; London: Adam & Charles Black, 1970), 59.

37. Dunn helpfully summarizes the tense social situation for Jews in the first century ("Incident at Antioch," 7 – 11).

38. See here, D. A. Carson, *Love in Hard Places* (Wheaton: Crossway, 2002), 150 – 60.

39. Bruce points out that the verb "I behave hypocritically" (ὑποκρίνομαι) is used in classical Greek to denote the work of actors (*Galatians*, 131).

40. E.g., Howard, *Paul: Crisis in Galatia*, 24 – 28, 41 – 45; Dunn, *Galatians*, 125 – 26, 130 – 31; Betz, *Galatians*, 108 – 10; Matera, *Galatians*, 90. Against this view, see Lightfoot's wise comments from long ago on this matter (*Galatians*, 354, n. 1).

are reminded of F. C. Baur's well-known division between Pauline and Petrine Christianity. Such theories, of course, disagree with the text of Galatians and provide an alternative historical reconstruction. Paul does not say that Peter changed his behavior relative to eating with Gentiles on the basis of new convictions. Rather, he charges that Peter and those who joined him acted *out of fear*.[41] According to the text, Peter and Paul still agreed *theologically*. Paul rebukes Peter because the latter acted *against* his convictions.[42]

Modern scholars who posit a different scenario are at a great disadvantage. They can do so only on the basis of doubting Paul's portrayal of the event, while they themselves lack any other historical access to what happened. Interestingly enough, some early church fathers argued from the use of the word "hypocrisy" that Peter and Paul were play-acting to teach the church a lesson.[43] In other words, Peter did not truly sin and act out of fear; he only pretended to do so, so that Paul's rebuke would give instruction to the others present. Again, such a reconstruction departs from the text and is an obvious attempt to spare Peter from any criticism.

We need to say a bit more about the view that Peter and Paul remained unreconciled after this event, for many scholars claim that the Antioch church repudiated Paul and that he struck out on his own from this point forward.[44] Indeed, they argue that the dissension between Peter and Paul here indicates that the agreement trumpeted in 2:1 – 10 was later severely qualified, if not nullified. Such a historical reconstruction, however, is unlikely, given the argument in Galatians. If the agreement in 2:1 – 10 with the Jerusalem apostles was later repudiated to a significant extent, then Paul's inclusion of such an agreement in the letter is deceptive.

Moreover, such an attempt to paper over the differences that allegedly came to the forefront later would never succeed. Paul was not foolish. He knew that if the pillars differed from him, his Jewish opponents would surely discover the truth and would proclaim it from the rooftops. Paul's appeal to the Jerusalem apostles in 2:1 – 10 is senseless and useless if they ended up nullifying the agreement relayed in 2:1 – 10. Paul's rebuke of Peter works in the argument only if Peter truly received it as a rebuke.

In other words, there is every reason to believe that Peter responded positively to Paul's reprimand since Peter acted out of fear, and not based on his convictions. Of course, the reaction of Peter is not the main point, for Paul's purpose was not to record the history of his relations with Peter but to defend his gospel to the Galatians. Still, we have already seen from 2:2 that if the pillars denied the Pauline gospel, then, practically speaking, Paul's gospel was in vain, and hence Paul likely referred to his rebuke of Peter because it demonstrated the authority of his gospel and because Peter responded positively to the rebuke.[45]

---

41. Ciampa points out important parallels in 2 Macc 6:24 – 26 and 4 Macc 6:17 – 22, where hypocrisy leads others astray. In both of these texts hypocrisy is tempting because of the persecution that will come for conforming to the law (see Ciampa, *The Presence of Scripture in Galatians 1 and 2*, 167 – 68).

42. Howard argues (*Paul: Crisis in Galatia*, 26 – 27) that Paul called Peter a hypocrite for changing his mind, but the text says that Peter altered his behavior because of fear, not out of conviction.

43. Clement of Alexandria argued that another Cephas besides the apostle Peter is in view here! Origen defended the idea that the confrontation was simulated, as did Jerome. But Augustine, in correspondence with Jerome, uncovered the weaknesses of such a view. For a survey of the early church debate, see Lightfoot, *Galatians*, 128 – 32.

44. This view has been common in NT scholarship since the work of F. C. Baur, *Paul the Apostle*, 270, 274 – 80, 303 – 5 (see, e.g., Betz, *Galatians*, 104; Martyn, *Galatians*, 15, 222 – 28, 236; Lührmann, *Galatians*, 44 – 45).

45. Contra Howard, *Paul: Crisis in Galatia*, 22.

Furthermore, as Schnabel points out, we have significant evidence that Peter and Paul were unified in letters written after Galatians.[46] Paul introduces Peter in 1 Corinthians without any mention of problems in his theology (1:12; 3:22; 9:5; 15:5), and in 1 Cor 15:3 – 11 he explicitly declares that he, Peter, and James proclaim the same gospel. Furthermore, in 2 Pet 3:15 – 16 we have further evidence that the division between Peter and Paul was not permanent.[47]

2:14a-b But when I saw that they were not walking straight in accordance with the truth of the gospel, I said to Cephas before them all (ἀλλ' ὅτε εἶδον ὅτι οὐκ ὀρθοποδοῦσιν πρὸς τὴν ἀλήθειαν τοῦ εὐαγγελίου, εἶπον τῷ Κηφᾷ[48] ἔμπροσθεν πάντων). Paul's response to the actions of Peter and those who followed his example confirms his authority as an apostle, since he corrects Peter for deviating from the gospel. We will discuss in the next section how far the quotation marks extend in this section.

It should be noted here that Peter's actions were viewed as compromising "the truth of the gospel" (τὴν ἀλήθειαν τοῦ εὐαγγελίου). In 2:5 Paul informs the Galatians that he resisted pressure from false brothers to circumcise Titus "in order that the truth of the gospel might remain with you" (ἵνα ἡ ἀλήθεια τοῦ εὐαγγελίου διαμείνῃ πρὸς

ὑμᾶς). The repetition of the phrase "the truth of the gospel" reveals that the imposition of food laws on the Gentiles by Peter cannot be differentiated from the attempt to force Titus to be circumcised. For Paul the gospel itself was at stake, for in effect Peter was requiring the Gentiles to observe the food laws to be saved. If Peter would only eat with Gentiles on the condition that they observed the food laws, he was saying in effect that they were not true believers unless they observed the purity laws. Hence, he was deviating, "not walking straight" (οὐκ ὀρθοποδοῦσιν) with reference to the truth of the gospel. And since Peter's sin was public in nature, it was necessary for Paul to correct him in the presence of all, and therefore he did so openly.

2:14b-d "If you live like a Gentile and not like a Jew, even though you are a Jew, how can you compel the Gentiles to live like Jews?" (Εἰ σὺ Ἰουδαῖος ὑπάρχων ἐθνικῶς καὶ οὐχὶ Ἰουδαϊκῶς ζῇς,[49] πῶς τὰ ἔθνη ἀναγκάζεις ἰουδαΐζειν;). Paul shines the spotlight on Peter's hypocrisy. Peter was Jewish, which means here that he was from the Jewish people ethnically. He was born and raised as a Jew, and hence for many years of his life he devoted himself to observing the Torah. Nonetheless, Peter no longer lived as a Jew but as a Gentile.

In other words, when Peter was in Antioch he

---

46. Schnabel, *Paul and the Early Church*, 1005 – 6.

47. In support of Petrine authorship, see Thomas R. Schreiner, *1, 2 Peter, Jude* (NAC; Nashville: Broadman & Holman, 2003), 255 – 76. Even if one sees the letter as pseudonymous, we have early Petrine tradition that salutes Paul, which is hard to square with the idea that there was a permanent break between Peter and Paul.

48. Once again many witnesses replace "Cephas" with "Peter," but the former has strong external and early support and is original.

49. A variety of variant readings exist for the phrase "and you do not live like Jews" (καὶ οὐχὶ Ἰουδαϊκῶς ζῇς). The reading in NA[27] has the most support textually (ℵ, A, B, C, H, P, Ψ, 33, 81, 104, 1175, *pc*). Most of the other

readings involve a change in word order and do not affect the meaning. Even if "you live" (ζῇς) alone is to be preferred (𝔓[46], 1881, *pc*, a, b, d), which is unlikely given the limited support (contra Tomson, *Paul and the Jewish Law*, 229), the text still affirms that Peter lived like a Gentile in contrast to his Jewish upbringing. Tomson, as noted, adopts the shorter reading and argues that Peter did not formerly eat unclean food. Instead, even though Peter observed food laws before the men from James came, after their arrival he was not trying to compel the Gentiles to adopt a Jewish way of life (227 – 30). But this reading is unlikely, for 2:12 – 14 emphasizes that Peter previously ate with the Gentiles and lived liked the Gentiles, which most naturally means that he ate unclean food.

did not observe the Jewish purity laws. He did not focus on the boundary markers that separated Jews from Gentiles. Gentiles who believed in Christ were considered to be equally members of the people of God, and Peter placed no emphasis on Jewish distinctives like circumcision or food laws. He enjoyed table fellowship with Gentiles and ate their food, and hence implicitly taught that observing purity laws was irrelevant for belonging to the people of God. Therefore, Paul is incredulous that Peter was suddenly requiring Gentiles to observe Jewish purity laws in order to dine with them.

One possibility is to interpret the word "live" (ζῆς) to denote the life of the age to come, as is typical in Paul. In that case, Paul emphasizes that Peter enjoys new life in Christ, even though he followed Gentile customs and did not observe the Jewish law. In other words, Peter had eternal life because of his trust in Jesus Christ and not by virtue of his observance of the law. This interpretation certainly makes sense, but it seems more likely that Paul is using the word "live" here in a more ordinary sense, referring to how Peter conducted himself in everyday life.

There are other examples in Paul where the word "live" refers to how one conducts one's life (Rom 7:1), even if such is not the normal meaning of the term. Context is decisive in assigning the meaning of a word, and Paul seems to describe here how Peter conducted himself in his everyday association with Gentiles. It could be objected that Paul could hardly use the present tense, for now Peter was no longer eating with the Gentiles.

But the present tense likely reflected Peter's normal practice, and the tense should not be pressed to say that he was living as a Gentile at that very moment.[50]

Peter's change of behavior, however, was sending a new message. He was now implying that Gentiles had to live like Jews to become part of the people of God. The verb "to judaize" (ἰουδαΐζειν) is also used in Esth 8:17, where Gentiles, because of their fear of the Jews, converted to Judaism and received circumcision. Josephus uses the verb in a similar way of a certain Metilius who saved his life by promising to become a Jew and be circumcised (*J.W.* 2.454; cf. also *Ant.* 13.257 – 58).[51] To live as a Jew means that one observes the Jewish law, and the parts of the law that were controversial (Sabbath, circumcision, and purity laws) came to the forefront since they distinguished Jews from Gentiles. Peter by refusing to eat with the Gentiles if they did not keep the food laws was in effect compelling (ἀναγκάζεις) the Gentiles to live like Jews in order to be part of the people of God.

The word "compel" (ἀναγκάζεις) forges a link with the false brothers of 2:3 – 5.[52] We saw above that Peter, like the false brothers, endangered "the truth of the gospel." Now we see that Peter is in effect compelling the Gentiles to become Jews to belong to the people of God, just as the false brothers tried to compel (ἠναγκάσθη, 2:3) Titus to be circumcised. Peter's actions, then, put him in the same category as the false brothers. He was deviating from the truth of the gospel and compelling Gentiles to adopt the Jewish law in order to be saved.

---

50. Contra Howard, *Paul: Crisis in Galatia*, xxii. On the meaning of "live" and the tense, see Machen, *Galatians*, 141 – 42, though Machen does not clearly come down on the meaning of the verb.

51. Harvey draws too sharp of a distinction between "living as Jew" (which is how he interprets "to judaize," ἰουδαΐζειν) and holding Jewish beliefs ("Opposition to Paul," 323 – 24), for

the latter surely informed the former. Longenecker argues that "to judaize" (ἰουδαΐζειν) focuses on becoming a Jew rather than living like a Jew, so that the term points to conversion to Judaism (*Galatians*, 78). It seems that we should not push the distinction too far, for those who take the step of becoming Jews are pledging to live like Jews from that time on.

52. Rightly Martyn, *Galatians*, 235.

Still, Paul does not identify Peter as a false brother, for Peter was acting hypocritically, not in accord with his convictions. Those who tried to force Titus to be circumcised were not genuine Christians, because they believed that one had to be circumcised to be saved. Peter, however, was a genuine believer, for his actions contradicted his beliefs. We have here another piece of evidence supporting the idea that Peter repented at Paul's rebuke, for if he did not, Paul would have considered him to be a false brother like those described in 2:3 – 5. It is clear from 1:18 and 2:1 – 10 (and later Pauline writings, as noted earlier) that Paul was convinced that Peter was a genuine Christian. Nevertheless, Paul severely reprimands Peter, for his behavior had the inadvertent effect of compromising the gospel, of suggesting that Gentiles had to observe the food laws to belong to the people of God.

Theology in Application

We All Stumble in Many Ways

We learn from this text that even the most spiritual and advanced Christians, like the apostle Peter, are still liable to sin. As James says, "We all stumble in many ways" (Jas 3:2). No Christian reaches a point where he or she is without sin, and even if we are experienced Christians, we may sin in significant ways. Such a realization humbles us, for we realize that apart from Jesus we can do nothing (John 15:5), and that our strength does not come from ourselves but the Lord. We are utterly dependent on the grace of God for every step of growth we take. None of us can boast about anything we have attained, for everything we have attained is a gift (1 Cor 4:7). So, we must continue to be vigilant in our spiritual lives. I know of pastors who have ministered for a long time and have had an affair at the end of their ministry. We cannot live on yesterday's grace; we need fresh grace for each new day, and so we are called upon every day to rely on God's grace in Christ.

Sin's Impact on Others

We also see from this text that our sins have an impact on others, especially if we are Christian leaders. The remaining Jews and even Barnabas were swept away by Peter's sin and imitated his behavior. None of us lives a solitary life. Our sins always have an effect on others. Those of us who are parents know that our sins shape our children. And all of us as Christians live in society with other believers. We are the body of Christ, not merely individual entities. Our sins in private affect others, even if we do not see how that can be so.

Conversely, it follows that our goodness plays a positive role in the lives of others. If sin is infectious, goodness has the same quality. Those who launch out in faith inspire others to do the same. Those who are fearless in preaching the gospel embolden others to share the good news without fear (Phil 1:12 – 14).

As Christians in the West we are prone to focus on our own spirituality. Are we reading our Bible devotionally and spending time in prayer with the Lord? And these activities are important. We tend, however, to downplay the importance of the church. Too often Western believers wander from church to church without really becoming committed to a body of believers. We tend to leave churches for consumeristic reasons, and often we only join a church if it can use our gifts. God calls on us to become part of the body and to love the believers who are part of the body. We don't gather with other believers fundamentally to fulfill our gifts but to help others grow. So, we should be asking ourselves, "How can I serve others in the body of Christ? How can I encourage my brothers and sisters in the faith? How can I influence them to walk faithfully with the Lord?"

Encouraging and Rebuking Other Believers

As believers we are responsible to both encourage and rebuke fellow believers. We hesitate to correct others, for we are keenly conscious of our own sins. Still, God calls us to restore gently those who have wandered from the right way (6:1). So many in our culture define love as leaving others alone, but the Scriptures teach that love has the courage to confront, that we rebuke others in humility because we love them and want them to know God deeply.

Paul's rebuke of Peter was not a fit of temper but a reminder that Peter had strayed from the truth of the gospel. Indeed, it took great courage because Paul stood alone in reproving Peter. He admonished Peter because the latter had compromised the gospel. Did Paul fail to follow the rules of Jesus when he corrected Peter publicly instead of privately (Matt 18:15 – 17)? Not at all. Peter's sin was a public matter that had public consequences. Therefore, a public rebuke was warranted. Elsewhere Paul teaches that elders who sin need public correction (1 Tim 5:20), presumably because their sin has an effect on the congregation as a whole.

We are also reminded by this text to accept correction humbly. When others correct us, we must bring the criticism before God to see if it accords with the truth or to see if there are elements of truth in the rebuke. We must beware if we think we have a special ministry of admonishing and correcting others, while at the same time we reject any criticism of ourselves!

CHAPTER 7

Galatians 2:15 – 21

Literary Context

The first question to be asked is where Paul's words to Peter, which began in 2:11, end. Since quotation marks are lacking in the original manuscripts, certainty eludes us. Possibly the words directed to Peter conclude after 2:14,[1] 2:15, 2:16,[2] 2:18, or 2:21. I personally argue that it makes most sense to see all of 2:14 – 21 as addressed to Peter.[3] At least four pieces of evidence support this conclusion. (1) Verse 15 is not clearly set off from 2:11 – 14. (2) The first person plural pronouns in 2:15 – 17 most naturally refer to Jewish Christians and would speak to such people in Antioch. (3) Verse 17 may reflect the charges against Peter. (4) A new subject commences in 3:1, where the Galatians are addressed directly.[4] As Matera notes, the lack of a reply from Peter also plays a rhetorical role, showing he has no answer to Paul's gospel.[5]

Paul sketches out in his reply to Peter the fundamental reason why Peter's behavior has compromised the gospel. In one sense it is not vital to resolve the issue where the words to Peter conclude, for the words recorded here are not intended for Peter but for the Galatian readers. Betz summarizes where scholars find agreement in saying, "Paul addresses Cephas formally, and the Galatians materially."[6]

This paragraph concludes the argument that began in 1:11 regarding the independence and authority of Paul's gospel. He has argued that his gospel was not derived from human beings but was given to him directly through a revelation of Jesus Christ (1:11 – 24). Still, when the apostles heard Paul's gospel, they ratified it as the true gospel (2:1 – 10). In 2:11 – 14 Paul's rebuke of Peter also verifies his apostolic authority, for the Pauline gospel even stands in judgment over Peter when the latter goes astray. Galatians 2:15 – 21 contains in short form the gospel that Paul proclaims. Betz's rhetorical analysis of Galatians pinpoints the centrality of this paragraph, for he labels it as the *propositio*: the central thesis of the letter. Indeed, this paragraph functions as a transition in the letter, for Paul no longer defends his apostolic authority and begins to enunciate the gospel he preaches.

1. Betz, *Galatians*, 113 – 14; Esler, *Galatians*, 139 – 40.
2. So Calvin, *Galatians*, 70.
3. Fung, *Galatians*, 112, but see his qualifications (105); Hays, *Galatians*, 231.
4. For these arguments I am indebted to Joe Rigney's paper written for my Galatians class.
5. Matera, *Galatians*, 90.
6. Betz, *Galatians*, 114.

Main Idea

The central truth in this paragraph is that right standing with God does not come from keeping the law (since everyone sins), but only through faith in Jesus Christ. Thus, all those who revert to the law only display their own sinfulness in returning to a covenant that has passed away, and hence they end up rejecting the grace of God given in the cross of Jesus Christ.

Translation

(See next page.)

Structure

We arrive at perhaps the most significant text in Galatians, in which Paul summarizes his gospel. Hence, this text functions as a hermeneutical key for the remainder of the letter. The argument supports Paul's claim in 2:14 that Peter cannot compel the Gentiles to live like the Jews by in effect forcing them to observe the Mosaic law in order to belong to the people of God.

Paul acknowledges to Peter in 2:15 that he and Peter were not sinful Gentiles outside the covenant but were born as Jews and hence belonged to the covenant people. Nevertheless, they both know as Christians that a person is not right before God not by observing what is commanded in the law, but only through faith in Jesus

Galatians 2:15-21

15	concessive (to 16ab)	For ... even though we are Jews by nature and not sinners from the Gentiles,
16a	assertion	nevertheless, **we know that a person is not justified**
b	contrast (to 16a)	**by works of law, but** / **only by faith in Jesus Christ.**
c	inference (from 15-16a-b)	Therefore, **we also have believed in Christ Jesus,**
d	purpose (of 16c)	in order that we might be justified by faith in Christ, and
e	contrast (to 16d)	not by works of law,
f	basis (of 16d-e)	because by works of law no flesh shall be justified.
17a	simultaneous (to 17b)	And if ... while seeking to be justified in Christ,
b	condition	...we also are found to be sinners,
c	question	**then is Christ a minister of sin?**
d	answer	**By no means!**
18a	condition	For if I build again those things which I have destroyed,
b	basis (of 17d)	**I demonstrate myself to be a transgressor.**
19a	assertion	For I through the law died to the law,
b	purpose (of 19a)	to live to God.
20a	assertion	**I have been crucified with Christ.**
	result (of 19c)	**(As a result) I no longer live,**
b	contrast (to 20a)	**but Christ lives in me.**
c	progression	And the life I now live in the flesh, I live by faith in the Son of God,
d	explanation	who loved me and
e	explanation	gave himself for me.
21a	inference (of 15-20)	(Therefore) **I do not reject the grace of God.**
b	condition	For if righteousness comes through the law,
c	basis (of 21a)	then Christ died for nothing.

Christ (2:16a-b). Therefore, as Jews ("we") they have also put their faith in Jesus Christ so that they can be right with God by faith in Christ instead of on the basis of what is required in the law. For doing what the law commands will never be the basis for justification (2:16c-f) since all fail to keep the law.

In 2:17 Paul proceeds to a new thought, which he most likely also addresses to Peter, since the first person pronoun probably focuses on Peter and Paul as Jews. If Peter and Paul, in seeking to find justification in Christ, are found to be sinners outside the covenant just like the Gentiles, then is Christ responsible for their sin? Paul dismisses such an idea as nonsense (2:17). On the contrary, restoring the law as the basis of one's relationship with God (2:18) would indict them as sinners, for the new age of salvation has arrived and with it the dissolution of the old covenant. Now all believers have died to the law and live to God.

In other words, Paul (along with all believers) has now been crucified with Christ (2:19). His new life is lived in faith in the Christ who gave himself for him on the cross (2:20). It follows, therefore, that if Paul (or any other person) required the Gentiles to keep the food laws, he would be rejecting the grace of God. In returning to the righteousness of the law, he would be teaching that Christ died for nothing (2:21).[7]

Exegetical Outline

I. Introduction: Desertion from Paul's Gospel Is Desertion from the Gospel (1:1 – 2:21)

  A. Greeting: Paul's Apostolic Authority (1:1 – 5)

  B. Problem Explained: Desertion from the Gospel (1:6 – 10)

  C. Paul's Gospel Derived from God, Not People (1:11 – 2:21)

    1. Thesis: source of his gospel was revelation (1:11 – 12)

    2. Thesis support (1:13 – 2:21)

      a. His past hostility (1:13 – 14)

      b. His call from God (1:15 – 17)

      c. His relative obscurity in Judea (1:18 – 24)

      d. Recognition of Paul's authority by pillars (2:1 – 10)

      e. Rebuke of Peter substantiates Paul's authority (2:11 – 21)

        i. Rebuke (2:11 – 14)

        ii. Transition: The Nature of the Gospel (2:15 – 21)

          (1) Righteousness only by faith, not works of law (2:15 – 16)

          (2) Sin does not come from Christ (2:17)

          (3) Sin comes from returning to the law (2:18)

---

7. Silva suggests here that the "for" (γάρ) is adversative (*Interpreting Galatians*, 85), though he goes on to say that it may be causal if ellipsis is present (86).

(4) Believers died to the law at the cross (2:19 – 20)

(5) Believers live by faith in Christ (2:20)

(6) To return to the law is to reject grace of the cross (2:21)

Explanation of the Text

2:15 For even though we are Jews by nature and not sinners from the Gentiles (ἡμεῖς φύσει Ἰουδαῖοι καὶ οὐκ ἐξ ἐθνῶν ἁμαρτωλοί). Paul reminds Peter that they were Jews who were in covenant with God; they were not sinners outside the covenant like the Gentiles.

The words "for even though" do not strictly translate the Greek but represent an interpretation of what Paul said to Peter here. On the one hand, Peter as a Jew had been living like the Gentiles (2:14). On the other hand, by withdrawing from table fellowship he was requiring Gentiles to live like Jews. The "we" (ἡμεῖς) in 2:15 represents Peter and Paul as Jews, and hence we have good reason to think that Paul continues to address Peter here, so that the quotation that began in 2:14 continues.

Peter and Paul were "Jews by nature" (φύσει Ἰουδαῖοι), i.e., they were born as Jews and thus were part of God's covenant people and were recipients of God's covenant promises.[8] Paul does not deny that they were sinners. His point is that they were not sinners in the same way as Gentiles, for the Gentiles were not part of God's covenant people (cf. Eph 2:11 – 12), and hence they did not

receive God's saving promises.[9] Paul focuses on the great privileges he and Peter enjoyed as part of Israel.

2:16a Nevertheless, we know that a person is not justified by works of law (εἰδότες δὲ ὅτι οὐ δικαιοῦται ἄνθρωπος ἐξ ἔργων νόμου). Paul argues that no human being (ἄνθρωπος), whether Jew or Gentile, is declared to be in the right before God by virtue of keeping what the law requires. Even though Peter and Paul were part of God's covenant people as Jews, they know that a person is justified not by works of law but only through faith in Jesus Christ.

Such a statement clearly does not reflect the standard Jewish point of view (cf. 1:13 – 16!), for not all Jews agreed that people were justified by faith in Jesus Christ.[10] The conjunction "but" (δέ), though disputed textually, is probably original,[11] and it should be interpreted as signifying an adversative relation between vv. 15 and 16. Peter and Paul "know" (εἰδότες)[12] as Christians that the old covenant is insufficient, that righteousness does not come through works of law but only through faith in Christ. In other words, Paul appeals here

---

8. So Martinus C. de Boer, "Paul's Use and Interpretation of a Justification Tradition in Galatians 2.15 – 21," *JSNT* 28 (2005): 193.

9. Ultimately, those who are lawless are not in covenant with God; this expression often refers to Gentiles. See 1 Sam 15:18 – 19; Pss 1:1; 9:17; 37:34 – 35; 58:10; Sir 7:16; 9:11; 41:5 – 11; 1 Macc 1:34; 2:44, 48; Tob 13:6; *Jub.* 23:23 – 24; 24:28; *Pss. Sol.* 1:1; 2:1 – 2; 17:22 – 25; *4 Ezra* 3:28 – 36; Luke 6:33.

10. De Boer argues that Paul cites early Jewish Christian tradition in 2:16, perhaps even stemming from the false teachers ("Justification Tradition," 194 – 97). But against this, see Martyn, *Galatians*, 264, n. 158; Ian W. Scott, "Common

Ground? The Role of Galatians 2.16 in Paul's Argument," *NTS* 53 (2007): 425 – 35.

11. Scribes probably deleted "but" (δέ) since the participle connects more smoothly without it (so 𝔓⁴⁶, A, D², Ψ, 𝔐). Furthermore, diverse and early evidence supports its inclusion (ℵ, B, C, D*, F, G, H, 81, 104, 1175, 1241ˢ, 2464, *pc*, lat).

12. Silva argues that the participle here is causal, subordinate to the main verb. See Moisés Silva, "Galatians," in *Commentary on the New Testament Use of the Old Testament* (ed. G. K. Beale and D. A. Carson; Grand Rapids: Baker, 2007), 789. It more likely modifies v. 15, and v. 15 is concessive to the idea in the participle.

to common ground shared by him and Peter. Even though Peter was in effect requiring Gentiles to observe the food laws to belong to God's people, he knows, as a Christian, that no one is right before God by doing what the law requires but only through faith in Jesus Christ.

Peter and Paul both recognize, therefore, that being Jewish grants no saving privileges. Before God they are just ordinary humans (so ἄνθρωπος),

standing in need of God's grace. Two crucial definitions that affect how we interpret the rest of Galatians must be resolved at this point. What does Paul mean by the word "justify" (here δικαιοῦται), and how should we define the phrase "works of law" (ἔργα νόμου)? I will argue that the verb "justify" means "declare righteous," and that "works of law" refers to all that is commanded in the law. Both of these issues warrant an In Depth discussion.

In Depth: The Meaning of Justification in Paul

The verb "justify" (δικαιόω) is used eight times in Galatians, including three times in this verse (cf. also 2:17; 3:8, 11, 24; 5:4). Not surprisingly the other place where the verb is often found is in Romans, where it occurs fifteen times (Rom 2:13; 3:4, 20, 24, 26, 28, 30; 4:2, 5; 5:1, 9, 6:7; 8:30 [2x], 33). This verb refers to God's verdict of not guilty on the day of judgment (Rom 2:13). God's eschatological verdict has now been announced in advance for those who believe in Jesus Christ.[13] Those who have been justified by the blood of Christ will be saved from God's wrath at the eschaton (Rom 5:9). God will announce publicly to the world the verdict of not guilty on the last day, though this verdict already belongs to those who are united with Christ Jesus. God's pronouncement of "not guilty" is hidden from the eyes of the world, and believers receive such a promise by faith.

The forensic and legal character of the term "justify" (δικαιόω) derives from the verbal form of "justify" (ṣdq) in the OT. Judges are to declare the righteous innocent and condemn the wicked (Deut 25:1; cf. 2 Sam 15:4; 1 Kings 8:31–32; 2 Chr 6:23; Prov 17:15; Isa 5:23). Judges do not "make" anyone righteous. They pronounce on what is in fact the case — if they are righteous judges. In other words, the verbal form belongs in the forensic realm, and Paul does not use

---

13. For the most satisfying explanation of the eschatological character of justification, see Richard B. Gaffin Jr., *"By Faith, Not By Sight": Paul and the Order of Salvation* (Waynesboro, GA: Paternoster, 2006), 79–108. Rudolf K. Bultmann identifies the future references to justification (Rom 5:19; Gal 2:17; 5:5) as logical futures ("*Dikaiosynē Theou*," *JBL* 83 [1964]: 15). For recent recognition of the future element of justification, see Paul A. Rainbow, *The Way of Salvation: The Role of Christian Obedience in Justification* (Waynesboro, GA: Paternoster, 2005), 157–74, though he does not explicate as clearly the link between the already but not yet in defining justification. Kwon argues that justification is entirely future (*Eschatology*, 51–77). Kwon rightly argues that the present tense verbs could be gnomic instead of denoting present time, and the eschatological character of justification is clearly a Pauline theme. Still, his one-dimensional explanation of justification fails to convince, for it is clear that Abraham was *already* justified (see 3:6). Moreover, he sustains his thesis by separating too sharply 3:14b from 3:14a when the two clauses together form the climax of the argument (62–63). Furthermore, it is unlikely (against Kwon) that Paul stressed that believers were *already* justified in Romans, while insisting in Galatians that justification is *only future*.

the verbal form to denote a righteousness that transforms us or "makes us" righteous.[14] For example, God will pass judgment on whether Paul is acquitted before the Lord on the judgment day (1 Cor 4:4).

When Paul says doers of the law will be justified (Rom 2:13), a declaration of righteousness is intended. God will pass judgment as to whether people are righteous, i.e., whether they have done what is right and good. If they have lived righteously, according to Rom 2:13, he will declare them to be righteous. This last example, as Westerholm has argued, is the ordinary sense of righteousness.[15] It is ordinary in the sense that it conforms with the way human judges are supposed to conduct themselves. They pass judgment against the wicked, and they pronounce in favor of the righteous.

In Paul, however, we also have what Westerholm labels an extraordinary meaning of righteousness.[16] In this instance, God declares those who are sinners to be in the right before him if they trust in Jesus Christ for their salvation. This is extraordinary because such a verdict violates the normal and just procedure for a judge. Judges who declare the guilty to be righteous violate the standards of justice. Paul, of course, does not think God violates any standard of justice, for Christ bears the curse that sinners deserved (3:10 – 13).[17] Four other arguments support a forensic reading.[18]

(1) The law-court background of "justify" is clear in Rom 8:33 (ESV): "Who shall bring any charge against God's elect? It is God who justifies." On the last day some may bring charges against God's chosen at the divine tribunal, but all charges will be dismissed because God has declared believers to be in the right before him. As the judge, he has declared that they are innocent of all the accusations leveled.

(2) Paul often says that human beings are righteous by faith (e.g., Rom 1:17; 3:22, 26; 4:3, 5, 9, 13; 9:30; 10:4; Gal 2:16; 3:6, 11; 5:5; Phil 3:9).[19] In such contexts

---

14. Against Chris VanLandingham, who defends this view in detail (*Judgment and Justification in Early Judaism and the Apostle Paul* [Peabody, MA: Hendrickson, 2006], 241 – 332). For a discussion and refutation of the view that Paul refers here to transforming righteousness, see Thomas R. Schreiner, *New Testament Theology: Magnifying God in Christ* (Grand Rapids: Baker, 2008), 353 – 62. I also argue there that righteousness should not be defined as covenant faithfulness. The gift of righteousness *fulfills* God's covenant promises, but it should not be equated with his covenant faithfulness. Cf. also Bird, *Saving Righteousness of God*, 35 – 39.

15. Stephen Westerholm, *Perspectives Old and New on Paul: The "Lutheran" Paul and His Critics* (Grand Rapids: Eerdmans, 2004), 263 – 73.

16. Ibid., 273 – 84.

17. Paul unpacks why God is not unrighteous in a number of texts, such as Rom 3:21 – 26; Gal 3:10 – 14; 2 Cor 5:21.

18. De Boer argues that the Jewish Christians understood "justify" (δικαιόω) forensically, but Paul transforms its meaning so that the term in Paul also means "to make righteous," emphasizing God's rectification of those in Christ (de Boer, "Justification Tradition," 205 – 16).

19. Ziesler claims "justify" (δικαιόω) is forensic but "righteousness" (δικαιοσύνη) is transformative (J. A. Ziesler, *The Meaning of Righteousness in Paul: A Linguistic and Theological Enquiry* [SNTSMS 20: Cambridge: Cambridge Univ. Press, 1972]); cf. also Longenecker, *Galatians*, 84 – 85; Bird, *Saving Righteousness of God*, 12 – 18. And yet Bird's comments on

Paul contrasts righteousness by faith with righteousness by works. Righteousness by faith refers to the *gift* of righteousness given to human beings by God. Human beings are not righteous by virtue of doing but believing. The righteousness given to believers, then, is alien since it is not based on anything they have done but on God's work in Christ. This suggests that righteousness as a gift is granted to those who believe.

(3) That righteousness is a forensic declaration is also supported by the link between righteousness and forgiveness. Paul slides easily from justification to forgiveness in Rom 4:1 – 8. David's forgiveness of sins is another way of speaking of his justification — his being in the right before God (4:6 – 8). The idea is not that David is transformed by God; the text calls attention to David's sin and his forgiveness by God, for he blots out his sins and declares him to be in the right.

(4) The idea that righteousness is counted (λογίζομαι) to believers indicates that righteousness is not native to human beings, that it is granted to them by God (Rom 3:28; 4:3 – 6, 8 – 11, 22 – 24; 9:8; Gal 3:6). This argument is strengthened when we add that righteousness is counted to those who believe — not to those who work. God does not "count" sins against those who have put their faith in Christ (2 Cor 5:19). This is a strange reckoning or counting indeed when those who have done evil are considered to be righteous. This fits with the notion, however, that believers have received "the free gift of righteousness" (Rom 5:17 ESV).

Believers are righteous because they are united to Christ in both his death and resurrection.[20] Because they are in Christ, they now enjoy the same vindication that Jesus enjoyed when God raised him from the dead (1 Tim 3:16).

In Depth: The Meaning of "Works of Law"

Before considering the meaning of "works of law," the significance of the preposition (ἐκ) used in the phrase must be assessed. Garlington argues that the preposition has a "partisan" sense, focusing on the group to which one belongs.[21] Thus, the issue is not whether one is justified by doing or believing, according

110 – 11 appear to deny that he thinks righteousness is transformative. The link between the verb and noun in 2:16 and 2:21 and in 5:4 and 5:5 indicates that proposing a different meaning for the noun than the verb is unconvincing. Rightly here Esler, *Galatians*, 149 – 51 (though I do not subscribe to Esler's own view, for he argues that righteousness focuses on social identity and rejects a forensic view, concurring with Wrede and Schweitzer that righteousness is subsidiary in Paul, 153 – 76). It should also be said that I am not denying that there are instances where "righteousness" has an ethical sense in Paul (e.g., Rom 6:13, 16, 18, 19, 20; Eph 4:24). The question being answered here is whether the noun has a transformative meaning in central soteriological texts (e.g., Rom 1:17; 3:21 – 22; 4:3, 5; 9:30, 31; 10:3, 4, 5, 6; Gal 2:21; 3:6, 21; 5:5; 1 Cor 1:30; 2 Cor 5:21; Phil 3:9).

20. See esp. here Bird, *Saving Righteousness of God*, 40 – 59.

21. Don Garlington, "Paul's 'Partisan ἐκ' and the Question of Justification in Galatians," *JBL* 127 (2008): 567 – 89.

to Garlington; the focus is on salvation history. Does one belong to the old era of works of law or to new era of faith in Christ?

Certainly salvation history is part of what Paul communicates here, but Garlington's construal of the preposition is misplaced, and it is more likely that it denotes means. Garlington overemphasizes the distinction between prepositions, as if they are technical terms. In actuality, prepositions are function words, and they often overlap in meaning. We see in 2:16 that Paul alternates between "by means of" (ἐκ) with reference to the law and "through" (διά) with reference to faith in Christ. The differences between the two prepositions should not be pressed.

We see the same phenomenon in Rom 3:30, where Paul shifts from "by means of" (ἐκ) to "through" (διά), arguing that both Jews and Gentiles are saved by means of faith. Most commentators of Romans rightly argue that no exegetical significance should be gleaned from the difference.[22] The precise word that we use to translate the preposition (ἐκ) in English can therefore be overemphasized. Robertson says that the term may denote "occasion" or "cause."[23] English translations such as "by," "when," "from," and even "because" may be appropriate. The significance of the function word must be discerned in context. Lambrecht rightly argues in an article that takes issue with Garlington that the preposition (ἐκ) often signifies "means" or "instrumentality" in Paul; hence, Garlington's interpretation should be rejected.[24] Reading the preposition as designating means fits nicely with Rom 5:1, where Paul says believers "are justified by faith" (δικαιωθέντες … ἐκ πίστεως). Using the English word "by" to translate the construction is, in my judgment, perfectly legitimate. Paul teaches that human beings are not justified by means of the works of law.

Righteousness does not come by works of law, but the meaning of the phrase "works of law" (ἔργα νόμου) is controversial in scholarship today.[25] The genitive could be construed as subjective, "works produced by the law," but such an interpretation reads too much into the phrase.[26] It is probably best to identify the

---

22. Cf. the discussion in Schreiner, *Romans*, 206.

23. A. T. Robertson, *A Grammar of the Greek New Testament in the Light of Historical Research* (4th ed.; Nashville: Broadman, 1934), 598 – 99.

24. Jan Lambrecht, "Critical Reflections on Paul's 'Partisan ἐκ' as Recently Presented by Don Garlington," *ETL* 85 (2009): 135 – 41.

25. For a survey of the term and an analysis, see Hilary B. P. Mijoga, *The Pauline Notion of Deeds of the Law* (Lanham: International Scholars Publications, 1999). Mijoga's own analysis is compatible with what is presented here in some respects, but she wrongly limits the inadequacy of the law to salvation

history. It is virtually a consensus that Paul most often refers to the Mosaic law when using the term "law" (νόμος). See Thomas R. Schreiner, *The Law and Its Fulfillment: A Pauline Theology of Law* (Grand Rapids: Baker, 1993), 33 – 40; Douglas J. Moo, "'Law,' 'Works of the Law,' and Legalism in Paul," *WTJ* 45 (1983): 73 – 100; Stephen Westerholm, "Torah, *nomos*, and Law: A Question of Meaning," *SR* 15 (1986): 327 – 36.

26. Against Paul L. Owen, "The 'Works of the Law' in Romans and Galatians: A New Defense of the Subjective Genitive," *JBL* 126 (2007): 553 – 77. Cf. also Basil S. Davis, *Christ as Devotio: The Argument of Galatians 3:1 – 14* (Lanham: Univ. Press of America, 2002), 72 – 74.

genitive as descriptive, speaking generally of the works demanded by the law.[27] The phrase has been intensely debated, and three main views have been proposed. The phrase refers to (1) legalism;[28] (2) the social boundary markers of the law;[29] or (3) the deeds commanded by the law.[30] Before we comment briefly on the various interpretations, we should note that Paul uses the expression "works of law" eight times in his letters (Rom 3:20, 28; Gal 2:16 [3x]; 3:2, 5, 10). In every instance it is introduced in contexts where the issue of justification or receiving the Spirit is prominent. We also should note that it is invariably contrasted with faith.

Explaining the three most common interpretations further should be helpful. (1) We could paraphrase the legalistic view this way. "Those who rely on the law to gain merit before God are under a curse." The legalistic view argues that "works of law" refers to legalism, so that it has the idea of trying to bribe God or gain his favor or merit his approval on the basis of the works that are accomplished. This view is defective, but we need to be careful in explaining why it is unsatisfactory. It is likely that the Judaizers were attempting to base their standing before God on their obedience to the law (5:4). Still, such a view must be distinguished from a *definition* of the phrase "works of law." The phrase "works of law" does not denote legalism (the desire to gain righteousness on the basis of works performed) in and of itself. "Works of law" refers to the deeds demanded by the law.[31]

---

27. See Daniel B. Wallace, *Greek Grammar beyond the Basics* (Grand Rapids: Baker, 1996), 79. Or it could possibly be an attributive, "the law's works."

28. Daniel P. Fuller, "Paul and 'The Works of the Law,'" *WTJ* 38 (1975): 28 – 42.

29. So James D. G. Dunn "The New Perspective on Paul," *BJRL* 65 (1983): 95 – 122; idem, "Works of the Law and the Curse of the Law (Galatians 3.10 – 14)," *NTS* 31 (1985): 523 – 42; idem, "Yet Once More — 'The Works of the Law': A Response," *JSNT* 46 (1992): 99 – 117; N. T. Wright, *The New Testament and the People of God* (Minneapolis: Fortress, 1992), 238; Garlington, *Galatians*, 149 – 54; Fee, *Galatians*, 84. Wisdom proposes a variant of Dunn's view (*Blessing for the Nations*, 154 – 82, see esp. 182). Though the rationale was different, it is interesting to note that Augustine limited works of law to ritual or ceremonial law (*Augustine's Commentary on Galatians*, 153).

30. So Moo, "'Law,' 'Works of the Law,' and Legalism in Paul," 73 – 100; Stephen Westerholm, *Israel's Law and the Church's Faith: Paul and His Recent Interpreters* (Grand Rapids: Eerdmans, 1988), 106 – 21; Thomas R. Schreiner, "'Works of Law' in Paul," *NovT* 33 (1991): 217 – 44; idem, *DPL*, 975 – 79; de Boer, "Justification Tradition," 197 – 201. Michael Bachmann makes a distinction between the prescriptions of the law instead of fulfilling the law or doing the

law. See Michael Bachmann, "Keil oder Mikroskop? Zur jüngeren Diskussion um den Ausdruck 'Werke des Gesetzes,'" in *Lutherische und Neue Paulusperspektive: Beiträge zu einem Schlüsselproblem der gegenwärtigen exegetischen Diskussion* (ed. Michael Bachmann; WUNT 182; Tübingen: Mohr Siebeck, 2005), 69 – 134; idem, *Anti-Judaism in Galatians? Exegetical Studies on a Polemical Letter and on Paul's Theology* (trans. Robert L. Brawley; Grand Rapids: Eerdmans, 2008), 1 – 18. For two critiques of his position in the same volume, see Robert L. Brawley, "Meta-Ethics and the Role of Works of Law in Galatians," 135 – 59; James D. G. Dunn, "The Dialogue Progresses," 397 – 401. And for an even more pointed and decisive critique of Bachmann's interpretation, see Jacqueline C. R. de Roo, *'Works of the Law' at Qumran and in Paul* (NTM 13; Sheffield: Sheffield Phoenix Press, 2007), 84 – 94. Bachmann's view wrongly drives a wedge between the commands of the law or the prescriptions of the law and doing or keeping the law. It is much more likely that "works of law" refers both to what the law prescribes and the keeping of those prescriptions, rather than what Bachmann thinks, that "works of law" refers only to what is commanded or prescribed by the law.

31. Cf. Calvin, who says that "works of law" refers to the whole law and cannot be restricted to the ceremonial law (*Galatians*, 67 – 68).

(2) The notion that "works of law" refers to the boundary markers of the law is increasingly popular today. This interpretation has gained currency since 1977, when E. P. Sanders wrote his massive *Paul and Palestinian Judaism*.[32] Sanders argued that the Judaism of Paul's day was not legalistic, contrary to the traditional view inherited from the debate between the Reformers and the Roman Catholics. The common pattern in Jewish religion, says Sanders, was covenantal nomism, in which God's people became members of the covenant by God's grace, and they maintained their place in the covenant by obedience. Sanders rejects any notion that the Jews believed that they were saved by the weighing of merits or by the notion that they had to be 51 percent obedient. Through an analysis of rabbinic literature, the Dead Sea Scrolls, the Apocrypha, and the Pseudepigrapha, Sanders defended the idea that Judaism was a religion of grace. Those who identify the Judaism of Paul's day as legalistic read it through the spectacles of the Reformation debate with Roman Catholics.

Sanders's construal of Judaism has been enormously influential and has led many to reassess Paul's theology of the law and justification. The "new perspective" on Paul, whose leading proponent is perhaps James Dunn,[33] has proposed a new understanding of "works of law" and law in Pauline theology. Dunn maintains that "works of law" refers to the entire Mosaic law. He sees, however, a focus on the laws that divide Jews and Gentiles from one another culturally, so that "works of law" brings to the forefront circumcision, food laws, and Sabbath. These laws were "identity markers" or "boundary markers" for Jews. They segregated and distinguished Jews from Gentiles. Dunn concludes that Paul criticized his opponents in Galatia for their exclusivism in which they demanded that Gentiles become Jews. The root problem, then, is not legalism or "activism" or even a failure to keep the law. Paul found fault with his adversaries because of their ethnocentricism, their narrow and sectarian spirit.[34]

The work of Sanders and the "new perspective" have had a salutary impact, in that it was easy previously to caricature Judaism as legalistic. Scholars have been compelled to reexamine the sources to determine what they say. The Judaism of Paul's day was complex and cannot be isolated into a single strand. Still, Sanders oversimplified the evidence. The claim that Judaism was free from all

---

32. E. P. Sanders, *Paul and Palestinian Judaism: A Comparison of Patterns of Religion* (Philadelphia: Fortress, 1977). Rapa seems to argue for a view compatible with what is argued for here, but his work suffers from lack of clarity in distinguishing whether the term means works required by the law or legalistic works. Robert Keith Rapa, *The Meaning of "Works of the Law" in Galatians and Romans* (Studies in Biblical Literature 31; New York: Peter Lang, 2001).

33. See note 29 on p. 159. N. T. Wright has probably been most influential in evangelical circles. For another defense of Dunn's view, see Scot McKnight, *Galatians* (NIVAC; Grand Rapids: Zondervan, 1995), 153 – 55.

34. Dunn does argue, however, that the insights of the "old perspective" are not wrong. See James D. G. Dunn, *The New Perspective on Paul: Collected Essays* (WUNT 185; Tübingen: Mohr Siebeck, 2005), 16 – 26.

legalism cannot be substantiated from the sources. The literature betrays an emphasis on God's grace in some instances and a focus on human obedience in others.[35] Final vindication on the basis of works is evident in some Jewish sources.[36]

(3) This brings us to the third view. The term "works of law" most likely refers to all the works prescribed by the Mosaic law.[37] In support of this, Paul emphasizes in 3:10b the obligation to do all that the law requires, and hence limiting "works of law" to only a part of the law fails to convince.[38] This also fits with 5:3 as well, where Paul reminds the Galatians that those who adopt circumcision are required "to do the whole law," not just part of the law. We should also bring in Rom 3:20 at this point, where Paul affirms that "no one will be declared righteous in his sight by observing the law." Here Paul summarizes the argument of Rom 1:18 – 3:20 as a whole and emphasizes that all deserve judgment since all have sinned and violated God's law (cf. 3:23). It is hardly credible to claim that the Jews were condemned for their bad attitude of excluding Gentiles. They were liable to judgment because they had not kept the entirety of God's law.[39]

35. So Friedrich Avemarie, "Erwählung und Vergeltung: Zur optionalen Struktur rabbinischer Soteriologie," *NTS* 45 (1999): 108 – 26; Mark A. Elliott, *The Survivors of Israel: A Reconsideration of the Theology of Pre-Christian Judaism* (Grand Rapids: Eerdmans, 2000); D. A. Carson, Peter T. O'Brien, and Mark A. Seifrid, eds., *Justification and Variegated Nomism*; vol. 1: *The Complexities of Second Temple Judaism* (Tübingen/Grand Rapids: Mohr Siebeck/Baker, 2001). Simon Gathercole, *Where Is Boasting? Early Jewish Soteriology and Paul's Response in Romans 1 – 5* (Grand Rapids: Eerdmans, 2002). Neusner maintains that the rabbis taught that Israel belonged to God rather than the Gentiles because Israel rejected idolatry and devoted themselves to the law. See Jacob Neusner, "What, Exactly, Is Israel's Gentile Problem? Rabbinic Perspectives on Galatians 2," in *The Missions of James, Peter, and Paul: Tension in Early Christianity* (ed. Bruce Chilton and Craig Evans; NovTSup 115; Leiden: Brill, 2005), 275 – 306. Interestingly, such a perspective fits with Paul's analysis of the Judaism of his day, though Paul, of course, rejects such a theology. VanLandingham also shows some weaknesses in Sanders's construal of Judaism, though he exaggerates the evidence to favor his own thesis and his analysis of the OT is flawed. See VanLandingham, *Judgment and Justification*, 1 – 174.

36. But see Dunn (*New Perspective*, 54 – 63) for a defense of Sanders's covenantal nomism.

37. Such a view is the most natural way of understanding parallels in Qumran literature as well. Against Martin G. Abegg Jr., "4QMMT, Paul, and 'Works of the Law,'" in *The Bible at Qumran: Text, Shape, and Interpretation* (ed. Peter W. Flint; Grand Rapids: Eerdmans, 2001), 203 – 16. Rightly

Ciampa, *The Presence of Scripture in Galatians 1 and 2*, 188 – 91; Joseph A. Fitzmyer, "Paul's Jewish Background and the Deeds of the Law," in *According to Paul: Studies in the Theology of the Apostle* (New York: Paulist, 1993), 18 – 35; de Roo, *Works of Law*, 72 – 81, 94 – 95; Craig A. Evans, "Paul and 'Works of Law' Language in Late Antiquity," in *Paul and His Opponents* (ed. Stanley E. Porter; Pauline Studies 2; Leiden: Brill, 2005), 201 – 26.

38. De Roo's monograph on works of law is immensely helpful in many respects. Still, her own solution is unsatisfying. She suggests that both the Romans and Galatians were relying on the works Abraham performed for justification, pointing out that Abraham's merits were commonly appealed to as the basis of God's mercy in Jewish literature (*Works of Law*, 101 – 28, 139 – 51, 163 – 73, 196 – 215). There are decisive reasons for rejecting this interpretation. (1) Nowhere in Romans or Galatians does Paul indicate that he is engaging in a polemic against Abraham's merits in which his readers trusted for their salvation. Instead, Abraham is presented as a positive example in both letters (Rom 4:1 – 25; Gal 3:6 – 9). (2) Paul writes to *Christians*. Even though some segments of Judaism trusted in Abraham's merits, de Roo provides no reason why Christians would rely on them. (3) De Roo does not explain why Paul would use the phrase "works of law" to refer to Abraham since he did not live under the law. See the exegesis of Gal 3:17 below.

39. This is not to deny that boundary markers were the presenting issue at Galatia. Indeed, B. Longenecker rightly observes that a focus on boundary markers does not exclude the issue of egoism (*Triumph of Abraham's God*, 76, 179 – 83).

2:16b But only by faith in Jesus Christ (ἐὰν μὴ διὰ πίστεως Ἰησοῦ Χριστοῦ). The little phrase translated here is fiercely debated. Before launching into discussion, I will summarize my understanding of the verse thus far. Human beings do not stand in the right before God by observing the law, but only through faith in Jesus Christ.[40]

How should the Greek phrase found here (ἐὰν μή) be translated? The translation adopted above ("but") is unusual, for typically the phrase means "unless" or "if not." If the Greek phrase (ἐὰν μή) is translated as "unless," it seems that Paul argues that a person may be justified by works of law as long as they also have faith in Jesus Christ. But such a view cannot be sustained from the remainder of 2:16 or from elsewhere in Galatians (3:2, 5, 10). Paul emphatically concludes 2:16 by saying that "by works of law no flesh shall be justified." So too, in 3:10 he says that "as many as are of works of law" are cursed. Therefore, it violates clear statements from Paul to say that one can be justified by works of law as long as one also has faith in Christ (cf. also Rom 3:20, 28).

Dunn proposes a variant of this view, suggesting that we catch Paul on the fly, so to speak.[41]

Paul began by saying to Peter that works of the law are insufficient to justify, unless one also has faith. But, as the argument progresses, he goes further and concludes that works of law are excluded in principle. According to Dunn, we see Paul in process, so that he starts his argument by allowing works of law as long as one also has faith, but he ends up excluding works of law altogether. Dunn's suggestion is creative but remarkably speculative. Furthermore, it seems strange that Paul would reproduce for the Galatians a change of mind in the midst of a single sentence![42] If this were so, Paul's both-and position regarding works of law and faith, then followed by his utter rejection of works of law, would confuse the Galatians. And why should they accept his new position in any case? If Paul once held a both-and position, why should not the Galatians do so as well? Dunn's case is too clever by half.[43]

Seifrid tries to solve the grammatical problem by arguing that "works of law" modifies the noun "person" (ἄνθρωπος) instead of the verb "is justified" (δικαιοῦται).[44] The verse then would be translated, "A person of works of the law is not justified unless through faith in Christ Jesus."[45]

---

40. Stanton notes that law and faith in Galatians "function like key musical notes in contrasting thematic phrases which are developed with subtle variations in a movement in a symphony" ("Law of Moses and Law of Christ," 101). He remarks that "2:16 functions as a 'text' which is then expounded at length from many angles throughout the rest of the letter" (101).

41. James D. G. Dunn, "The New Perspective on Paul," in *Jesus, Paul, and the Law: Studies in Mark and Galatians* (Louisville: Westminster/John Knox, 1990), 195 – 197. He also suggests that Paul starts with a softer position so he can move Peter toward his own (*Galatians*, 137 – 40).

42. See the decisive criticisms of Heikki Räisänen, "Galatians 2:16 and Paul's Break with Judaism," *NTS* 31 (1985): 544 – 47.

43. Das's view is similar to Dunn's in some respects. He maintains that the statement here is ambiguous and could be interpreted to defend a more conservative Jewish view or a Pauline view, and Paul proceeds to defend his interpretation. A. Andrew Das, "Another Look at ἐὰν μή in Galatians 2:16,"

JBL 119 (2000): 529 – 39. Against Das, see Debbie Hunn, "Ἐὰν μή in Galatians 2:16: A Look at Greek Literature," *NovT* 49 (2007): 289.

44. Cf. Mark A. Seifrid, "Paul, Luther, and Justification in Gal 2:15 – 21," *WTJ* 65 (2003): 217 – 18; so also Ardel Caneday, "The Faithfulness of Jesus Christ as a Theme in Paul's Theology in Galatians," in *The Faith of Jesus Christ: Exegetical, Biblical, and Theological Studies* (ed. Michael F. Bird and Preston Sprinkle; Peabody, MA: Hendrickson, 2009), 193 – 97. The decision is important for Caneday, for he proceeds to argue that there is only a salvation-historical contrast in the text, not a polarity between works and faith (196 – 202).

45. Seifrid argues for a genitive of source. See Mark A. Seifrid, *Christ, Our Righteousness: Paul's Theology of Justification* (Downers Grove, IL: IVP, 2000), 139 – 46; so also Francis Watson, *Paul and the Hermeneutics of Faith* (London: T&T Clark, 2004), 74 – 76. Martyn identifies it as an "authorial genitive." But he explains it in terms of Christ's "faithful death on our behalf" (*Galatians*, 251). See 251, n. 127.

Seifrid's solution is more satisfactory since it rejects the idea that works of law can play some role in justification. Still, it seems to be an unlikely resolution since in this very verse (2:16) "works of law" clearly modifies the verbs "is justified" (δικαιοῦται) and "we might be justified" (δικαιωθῶμεν). Furthermore, in every other instance where the phrase "works of law" occurs, it modifies a verb (see Gal 3:2, 5, 10; cf. Rom 3:20, 28). Therefore, it seems unlikely that the phrase modifies a noun.[46]

It seems that the best solution is to argue that the Greek phrase (ἐὰν μή) here means "but" instead of "unless" or "if not." Context is the decisive criterion in interpretation, and such a reading is the judgment of many interpreters throughout history who were well acquainted with Greek grammar.[47] Zerwick argues that the construction

(ἐὰν μή) here is equivalent to "but" (ἀλλά).[48] Such a reading for the phrase (ἐὰν μή) is possible, especially since an equivalent construction (εἰ μή) has in some instances an adversative meaning (cf. Rom 14:14; 1 Cor 8:4),[49] and interestingly two of the examples stem from Galatians (1:7, 19).

Understanding the phrase (ἐὰν μή) as adversative could also have a Semitic background. The Hebrew phrase "except" or "but" (*kî ʾim*) often has an adversative meaning (e.g., Deut 7:5; 10:12; Josh 23:8; 1 Sam 2:15; Isa 42:19; Mic 6:8), though it is not translated in the LXX as ἐὰν μή. Interestingly, the Hebrew translation of the New Testament renders the phrase (ἐὰν μή) here as *kî ʾim* (HNT), and the Hebrew is almost certainly adversative here. Hence, an adversative meaning for the construction (ἐὰν μή) is certainly lexically possible, and contextually it is the most probable.

In Depth: What Does Paul Mean by the "Faith of Jesus Christ"?

One controversy follows another in this verse, and scholars dispute vigorously the meaning of the phrase "faith of Jesus Christ" (πίστεως Ἰησοῦ Χριστοῦ).[50] Two main interpretations vie for acceptance: faith *in* Jesus Christ, and the faithfulness *of* Jesus Christ. The phrase is also used in Romans and Philippians, necessitating a wider discussion.

We shall consider first those who translate the phrase "the faithfulness *of*

---

46. Some might argue that "works of law" modifies "as many as" (ὅσοι) in 3:10, but actually the phrase modifies the verb "are" (εἰσίν), so there is no clear instance where the phrase modifies a noun. In Rom 3:20 "works of law" could possibly modify the noun phrase "all flesh" (πᾶσα σάρξ), and if that were the case it would fit Seifrid's solution here. But in context it is clear that "works of law" modifies the verb "shall be justified" (δικαιωθήσεται).

47. See, e.g., ASV, NET, NIV, NRSV, RSV, ESV.

48. Maximilian Zerwick, *Biblical Greek Illustrated by Examples* (Rome: Pontifical Biblical Institute, 1963), 158, §470. Cf. Bruce, *Galatians*, 138.

49. So Räisänen, "Galatians 2:16 and Paul's Break with Judaism," 547.

50. See the 2009 book, *The Faith of Jesus Christ: Exegetical, Biblical, and Theological Studies* (ed. Bird and Sprinkle). In the same volume, see the history of the debate in Debbie Hunn, "Debating the Faithfulness of Jesus Christ in Twentieth Century Scholarship," 15 – 31. Mark W. Elliott surveys the interpretive tradition from the first century to the present. "Πίστις Χριστοῦ in the Church Fathers and Beyond," 277 – 89. Preston Sprinkle cites scholars who defend still a third view and defends it himself in the same book: "Πίστις Χριστοῦ as an Eschatological Event," 165 – 84.

Christ" rather than "faith *in* Christ."[51] The construction is in the genitive — "faith of Christ" (πίστις Χριστοῦ)[52] — so that both "faithfulness of Christ" and "faith in Christ" are grammatically feasible.[53] A number of arguments are presented in support of "faithfulness of Christ":

1. In Rom 3:3 "the faith of God" (τὴν πίστιν τοῦ θεοῦ) clearly means "the faithfulness of God."

2. In Rom 4:12 the phrase in context refers to "the faith of our father, Abraham" (πίστεως τοῦ πατρὸς ἡμῶν Ἀβραάμ).

3. It is argued that the genitive in such constructions is most naturally understood as subjective.

4. If one takes the genitive as objective, "faith in Christ" is superfluous since in the key texts (e.g., Rom 3:22; Gal 2:16; Phil 3:9) Paul already mentions the need to trust in Christ.

5. The "faithfulness of Jesus" is another way of referring to Jesus' obedience, which was necessary to achieve our salvation (Rom 5:19; Phil 2:8).

6. The coming of "faith" refers to redemptive history (3:23, 25), designating the faithfulness of Christ at the key point in salvation history.

7. The focus in Paul's theology is the work of God in Christ, not the human response of faith.

Despite the arguments supporting a subjective genitive, there are still good reasons to prefer an objective genitive, so that Paul refers to "faith *in* Christ":[54]

---

51. E.g., Luke T. Johnson, "Rom 3:21 – 26 and the Faith of Jesus," *CBQ* 44 (1982): 77 – 90; Sam K. Williams, "Again *Pistis Christou*," *JBL* 49 (1987): 431 – 47; Richard B. Hays, *The Faith of Jesus Christ: An Investigation of the Narrative Substructure of Galatians 3:1 – 4:11* (2nd ed.; Grand Rapids: Eerdmans, 2002), 139 – 91; idem, "*Pistis* and Pauline Christology: What Is at Stake?" in SBLSP 1991 (ed. by E. H. Lovering Jr.; Atlanta: Scholars, 1991), 714 – 29; Ian G. Wallis, *The Faith of Jesus Christ in Early Christian Traditions* (SNTSMS 84; Cambridge: Cambridge Univ. Press, 1995); de Boer, "Justification Tradition," 201 – 5; Hung-Sik Choi, "πίστις in Galatians 5:5 – 6: Neglected Evidence for the Faithfulness of Christ," *JBL* 124 (2005): 467 – 90; B. Longenecker, *Triumph of Abraham's God*, 95 – 115.

52. The genitive after "faith" (πίστις) varies from "Jesus Christ" (Ἰησοῦ Χριστοῦ, Rom 3:22; Gal 2:16; 3:22), "Christ" (Χριστοῦ, Gal 2:16; Phil 3:9), to "Jesus" (Ἰησοῦ, Rom 3:26). For the sake of simplicity we shall restrict it to "faith of Christ" (πίστις Χριστοῦ).

53. But see the recent analysis of Stanley E. Porter and Andrew W. Pitts. They argue that semantically and grammatically the objective genitive should be preferred. "Πίστις

with a Preposition and Genitive Modifier: Lexical, Semantic and Syntactic Considerations in the Πίστις Χριστοῦ Discussion," in *The Faith of Jesus Christ: Exegetical, Biblical, and Theological Studies* (ed. Michael F. Bird and Preston Sprinkle; Peabody, MA: Hendrickson, 2009), 33 – 53.

54. See, e.g., Otfried Hofius, *Paulusstudien I* (WUNT 51; Tübingen: Mohr Siebeck, 1989), 154 – 56; J. D. G. Dunn, "Once More *Pistis Christou*," in *SBLSP 1991* (ed. E. H. Lovering Jr.; Atlanta: Scholars, 1991), 730 – 44; Moisés Silva, "Faith versus Works of Law in Galatians," in *Justification and Variegated Nomism*; vol. 2: *The Paradoxes of Paul* (ed. D. A. Carson, Peter T. O'Brien, and Mark A. Seifrid; Grand Rapids: Baker, 2004), 217 – 48; Debbie Hunn, "πίστις Χριστοῦ in Galatians 2:16," *TynBul* 57.1 (2006): 23 – 33; R. Barry Matlock, "Detheologizing the πίστις Χριστοῦ Debate: Cautionary Remarks from a Lexical Semantic Perspective," *NovT* 62 (2000): 1 – 23; idem, "'Even the Demons Believe': Paul and πίστις Χριστοῦ," *CBQ* 64 (2002): 300 – 318; idem, "πίστις in Galatians 3:26: Neglected Evidence for 'Faith in Christ'?" *NTS* 49 (2003): 433 – 39; idem, "Saving Faith: The Rhetoric and Semantics of πίστις in Paul," in *The Faith of Jesus Christ: Exegetical,*

1. The genitive object with "faith" is clear in some instances (Mark 11:22; Jas 2:1).[55]

2. A genitive object with other verbal nouns shows that an objective genitive with the verbal noun "faith" is normal grammatically: e.g., "knowledge of Christ Jesus" (τῆς γνώσεως Χριστοῦ Ἰησοῦ, Phil 3:8).[56] Therefore those who claim that the genitive must be subjective fail to convince.

3. The texts that use the verb "believe" in a verbal construction and the noun "faith" with the genitive are not superfluous but emphatic, stressing the importance of faith to be right with God. Readers hearing the letter read would hear the emphasis on faith in Christ,[57] and thus this interpretation is to be preferred as the simpler of the two options.[58]

4. Paul often contrasts works and human faith in his theology. Therefore, seeing a polarity between works of law and faith in Christ — both *human activities* — fits with what Paul does elsewhere.

5. Nowhere does Paul in speaking of Jesus Christ use the word "faith" (πίστις) to describe his "obedience."

6. The salvation-historical argument fails to persuade as well. Certainly, Gal 3:23, 25 refer to the coming of faith at a certain time in redemptive history. But such an observation hardly excludes faith in Christ, for faith in Christ becomes a reality when he arrives and fulfills God's saving promises. We should not pit redemptive history against anthropology.

7. Nor is the emphasis on faith in Christ somehow Pelagian, as if it somehow detracts from God's work in salvation. A human response of faith does not

Biblical, and Theological Studies (ed. Michael F. Bird and Preston Sprinkle; Peabody, MA: Hendrickson, 2009), 73 – 89; Paul Ellingworth, "A Note on Galatians 2.16," *BT* 56 (2005): 109 – 11; Fee, *Galatians*, 85 – 88. In support of the genitive of source, see Seifrid, "Paul, Luther, and Justification," 218 – 219; idem, *Christ Our Righteousness*, 139 – 46; idem, "The Faith of Christ," in *The Faith of Jesus Christ: Exegetical, Biblical, and Theological Studies* (ed. Michael F. Bird and Preston Sprinkle; Peabody, MA: Hendrickson, 2009), 129 – 46; Jae Hyun Lee, "Against Richard Hays's 'Faith of Jesus Christ'" *JGRChJ* 5 (2008): 51 – 80.

55. For this reading of Mark 11:22, see R. T. France, *The Gospel of Mark* (NIGTC; Grand Rapids: Eerdmans, 2002), 448. He remarks that a subjective reading "is surely forced." An objective genitive is also probable in James. Against Johnson, *James*, 220. Rightly Moo, *James*, 100 – 101; Davids, *James*, 107; Sophie Laws, *A Commentary on the Epistle of James* (HNTC; New York: Harper and Row, 1980), 94; Martin Dibelius, *A Commentary on the Epistle of James* (rev. H. Greeven; Hermeneia; Philadelphia: Fortress, 1975), 127 – 28;

Luke L. Cheung, *The Genre, Composition and Hermeneutics of James* (Paternoster Biblical and Theological Monographs; Carlisle: Paternoster, 2003), 247 – 48.

56. Harrisville shows from a number of Greco-Roman writers that an objective genitive with "faith" (πίστις) was common in classical Greek authors. Roy A. Harrisville III, "Before πίστις Χριστοῦ: The Objective Genitive as Good Greek," *NovT* 41 (2006): 353 – 58.

57. Matlock argues that rhetorical features in the text support an objective genitive as well. R. Barry Matlock, "The Rhetoric of πίστις in Paul: Galatians 2.16, 3.22, and Philippians 3.9," *JSNT* 30 (2007): 173 – 203. For instance, one of the striking features of the verse is that it is characterized by redundancy regardless of one's view of "faith of Christ" here (193).

58. Silva points out that the noun "faith" in Gal 3:2 and 3:5 is followed by the verb "believed" in 3:6. Furthermore, the verbal act of believing is tied to "those of faith" in 3:7 and 3:9, and hence the "expressions allude to the same basic concept." Indeed, "one would need extraordinarily persuasive evidence to the contrary" ("Faith versus Works," 235).

> undercut the truth that God saves, particularly if God grants faith to his own (Eph 2:8 – 9).
>
> Given our long discussion, we must sum up briefly Paul's argument in 2:16. Paul reminds Peter that he must not impose the law on Gentiles, for both he and Peter already recognize that human beings will not be vindicated before the divine tribunal on the basis of their obedience of the law, but only through faith in Christ Jesus.

2:16c-e Therefore, we also have believed in Christ Jesus, in order that we might be justified by faith in Christ and not by works of law (καὶ ἡμεῖς εἰς Χριστὸν Ἰησοῦν ἐπιστεύσαμεν, ἵνα δικαιωθῶμεν ἐκ πίστεως Χριστοῦ καὶ οὐκ ἐξ ἔργων νόμου). Paul now applies what he has just said about human beings in general (see "person" [ἄνθρωπος] earlier in the verse) to himself and Peter as Jews.[59] Even though the word "therefore" is lacking in the Greek, it is implied in the argument. The word "we" (ἡμεῖς) here refers to Peter and Paul as Jews, as members of God's covenant people, Israel (cf. 2:15).[60] They as Jews also believed in Christ Jesus, and hence even as Jews they could only be right with God by trusting in Jesus Christ and not through their observance of the law.

The verb "we believed" (ἐπιστεύσαμεν) provides further evidence that "faith of Christ" (πίστις Χριστοῦ) is an objective genitive, for the simplest interpretation should be preferred, and Paul emphasizes a point that is crucial for the argument so that the readers will not fail to miss it.[61] Paul and Peter as Jews believed in Christ Jesus so that they would be justified (declared to be in

the right before God's tribunal) via their trust in Christ Jesus rather than via their observance of the law. Paul's point is clear. If members of the covenant people (both Peter and Paul) need to put their faith in Christ in order to be right before God,[62] and if they cannot be righteous in God's sight by keeping the law, then it is senseless for Peter to require Gentiles to observe the law in order for them to have a right relationship with God.

2:16f Because by works of law no flesh shall be justified (ὅτι ἐξ ἔργων νόμου οὐ δικαιωθήσεται πᾶσα σάρξ). Paul grounds the claim that Jews, such as Peter and Paul, are only justified by faith in Christ with the proposition that no one anywhere can be righteous before God by doing the law. The reason righteousness does not come by observing the law is because of human sin. Here we should observe that Paul shifts from Jews (see "we" above) to the more general "all flesh" (πᾶσα σάρξ). The Jews, as God's covenant people, cannot stand in the right before God on the basis of observing what the law requires, since no flesh (i.e., no human being—with an emphasis on our

---

59. Matlock rightly observes that Paul moves from the general "person" (ἄνθρωπος) to the particular (Jews, "we," ἡμεῖς) and back to the general ("all flesh," πᾶσα σάρξ). Therefore, "the Jewish Christian experience of the gospel is placed within a common human narrative" ("The Rhetoric of πίστις in Paul," 198 – 99). The citation is from p. 199.

60. So Bruce, *Galatians*, 139.

61. Rightly Silva, "Faith versus Works," 232. Those who favor a subjective genitive argue on the contrary that Paul would not want to be redundant.

62. Bruce rightly argues that the variation between "through" (διά) and "by" (ἐκ) before the noun πίστεως represents stylistic variation (*Galatians*, 139).

fallenness) can be right before God by works of law.

Paul appeals here to Ps 143:2 (142:2 in LXX), "Do not bring your servant into judgment, for no one living is righteous before you" (καὶ μὴ εἰσέλθῃς εἰς κρίσιν μετὰ τοῦ δούλου σου, ὅτι οὐ δικαιωθήσεται ἐνώπιόν σου πᾶς ζῶν).[63] David in this psalm pleads for mercy because he realizes that he cannot stand before God on the basis of his works, but only by virtue of God's mercy.[64] Paul applies what David said to all members of the covenant people, and hence he adds the phrase "all flesh." Furthermore, the word "flesh" emphasizes human fallenness and weakness, signifying further why human beings need forgiveness.

The allusion to Ps 143:2 verifies that righteousness cannot come via works since David acknowledges that judgment is deserved because of his unrighteousness (i.e., sin).[65] Therefore, it anticipates and supports what Paul teaches in Gal 3:10, where he affirms that the curse of the law applies to all since all violate God's requirements. The verb "he shall be justified" (δικαιωθήσεται) most likely refers to the future day of judgment, so that justification is understood as an eschatological event.[66]

Clearly 2:16 is one of the most important verses in all of Galatians. It is packed with some of the most important themes in the letter. Three times Paul asserts that right standing with God does not come by keeping the law but only through faith

in Christ. The redundancy of the verse as a whole supports the idea that we have an objective genitive here ("faith in Christ"). Neither Peter nor anyone else can stand before God on the basis of what they have done. Salvation is of the Lord, and it is received by faith alone.

2:17a-b And if while seeking to be justified in Christ, we also are found to be sinners (εἰ δὲ ζητοῦντες δικαιωθῆναι ἐν Χριστῷ εὑρέθημεν καὶ αὐτοὶ ἁμαρτωλοί). Paul and Peter as Jews have been shown to be sinners before God (just like the Gentiles!), for they sought righteousness in Christ (showing that they were not righteous in themselves) rather than in their observance of the law. Paul probably continues his speech to Peter, for "we" here stands for Jewish Christians, such as Paul and Peter, over against the Gentiles in Antioch. Another reason for thinking Paul continues to address Peter is that what is written here likely reflects the charges brought against Peter by other Jewish Christians.

The meaning of the verse is intensely debated. The verse is typically interpreted in two different ways. In the first view, the charge leveled against Paul and other Jewish Christians is unfounded. They were accused of being sinners since they had abandoned the Torah, but Paul was not a sinner, since he had died and been raised with Christ.[67] The second view, which is favored here, argues that the charges are in fact true. Paul accepts in the "if" clause the reality of the charge. In other

---

63. In defense of the view that Paul cites Ps 143:2 here, see Silva, "Galatians," 790.

64. Ciampa sees an intertextual reference to Gen 15:6 and Hab 2:4 as well here (*The Presence of Scripture in Galatians 1 and 2*, 181–201). Smiles says Paul ignores the historical meaning of the psalm here (*Gospel and Law in Galatia*, 132), but the message of the psalm is that the Lord delivers those who trust in him and find their refuge in him. Therefore, there is no reason to think Paul misreads it. Rightly Silva, "Galatians," 791–92.

65. Silva insightfully comments that the reference here

strengthens the idea that "works of law" refers to the law in general, for surely David's sins here did not consist in exclusion of the Gentiles or focusing improperly on the ceremonial law ("Galatians," 791).

66. So Silva, *Interpreting Galatians*, 173–74; Ciampa, *The Presence of Scripture in Galatians 1 and 2*, 184; Stanton, "Law of Moses and Law of Christ," 104.

67. So Betz, *Galatians*, 119–20; Mussner, *Galaterbrief*, 176–77; Ciampa, *The Presence of Scripture in Galatians 1 and 2*, 202, n. 155; Hansen, *Abraham in Galatians*, 104–6.

words, Peter and Paul had been found to be sinners in seeking to be justified in Christ, and they recognized that they were no better than Gentiles. The only way to be righteous is through faith in Christ.[68]

In the first view, the post-conversion status of Peter and Paul is in view; they were found to be sinners after becoming believers because they had abandoned the law. In the second view, the preconversion status of Peter and Paul is in mind; they were found to be sinners in that they recognized that forgiveness can be found only in Christ. Another way to identify the two views follows. In the first view, the charge that Peter and Paul were sinners is rejected. They were not sinners in rejecting the Torah, for a new era of salvation had dawned in which the Torah was no longer binding. In the second view, Peter and Paul acknowledged that they were sinners, for they confessed that they did not and could not keep the law, but they had found forgiveness for their sins in Christ.

The interpretation that sees Peter and Paul as actual sinners has one major point in its favor: it best explains the use of the word "found." The word "found" (εὑρέθημεν) has a legal and forensic meaning, denoting one's standing before God as Judge and Lord of all. It refers to the verdict pronounced by the Divine Judge, whether one is "found" to be guilty or innocent. (cf. also Sir 44:17, 20; Acts 5:39; 24:5; 1 Cor 4:2; 15:15; Phil 3:9; 1 Pet 1:7; Rev 5:4). Both Peter and Paul as Jews were found to be "sinners" (ἁμαρτωλοί), so that before God they occupied the same status as "sinners from the Gentiles" (ἐξ ἐθνῶν ἁμαρτωλοί, 2:15). Such an interpretation fits with the interpretation proposed for 2:16 above. Paul argues that it is clear

from the OT (Ps 143:2) that no one is righteous by works of law. Instead, the law uncovers human sin.

The interpretation supported here must be explained further. When were Peter and Paul (and by extension all Christian Jews) found to be sinners before God? It was "while [they were] seeking to be justified in Christ." Both Peter and Paul, in turning to Christ, did not try to establish their own righteousness (cf. Rom 10:3) on the basis of the Sinai covenant. They sought instead to stand in the right in Christ before the Divine Judge. The language of "seeking" here points to the day of final judgment, indicating that justification is eschatological.[69]

The phrase "in Christ" (ἐν Χριστῷ) probably denotes union with Christ in light of 2:19 – 20, where believers died to the power of the law when they were crucified with Christ.[70] If Jews like Peter and Paul sought to be vindicated before God on the last day through union with Christ, it follows that as Jews they had no advantage over the Gentiles. They were sinners just like the Gentiles. They testified that the Mosaic covenant was not adequate to gain end-time salvation. Hence, Peter's refusal to have fellowship with Gentiles unless they kept the covenantal regulations contradicted his own experience and theology. For Peter had himself confessed that salvation and forgiveness are found only in Christ, not the Mosaic law.

Others argue for a different reading of the clause. Paul could be understood as saying that he and Peter as Jews were found to be sinners because they were no longer observing the laws of the Mosaic covenant. In other words, in the eyes of their Jewish Christian opponents, they were thought to be sinners because they had abandoned the prescriptions

---

68. So Bruce, *Galatians*, 140–41; Smiles, *Gospel and Law in Galatia*, 147–54. Longenecker holds a variant of this view. Paul responds to the opponents and concedes here that Christians sin (*Galatians*, 89–90).

69. Rightly Martyn, *Galatians*, 254.

70. Longenecker understands it as denoting means "by Christ" (*Galatians*, 89). Others understand "in Christ" as causal (Burton, *Galatians*, 124). Still others see it as instrumental or locative (Fung, *Galatians*, 119; Matera, *Galatians*, 95).

of the Mosaic law.[71] On this reading Paul does not accept the charge being leveled against Peter and himself. The opponents *thought* Peter and Paul sinned in abandoning the law, when in fact they were doing the will of God, for they sought justification in Christ rather than the law. In seeking justification from Christ they abandoned the law and sought forgiveness only in Christ.

This interpretation is possible but is probably not on target.[72] For Paul refers to the status of Jewish Christians before God in the word "we have been found" (εὐρέθημεν, see discussion of this term above). If the second view were true, Paul would have written something like, "we have been accused to be sinners," or, "we have been charged to be sinners." In writing "we are also found to be sinners," Paul emphasizes the place of Jewish Christians before God. Hence they really and truly were sinners before God. As Jewish Christians they sought justification in Christ, for righteousness could not come via the law since they had failed to keep the law and had sinned against God.

Seeing a reference to the actual sin of Peter and Paul does not rule out a salvation-historical dimension of the argument, for by seeking righteousness in Christ rather than the law, Peter and Paul were also acknowledging that the era of the law had ended. Forgiveness of sins was available only in Christ. The salvation-historical implications of seeking justification in Christ are pursued by Paul in the rest of 2:17 – 18.

2:17c-d Then is Christ a minister of sin? By no means! (ἆρα Χριστὸς ἁμαρτίας διάκονος; μὴ

γένοιτο). Paul presses the argument further. If Jewish Christians like Paul and Peter abandoned the Jewish covenant and its regulations and relied on Christ for justification, then is Christ responsible for their sin?[73] Christ would promote sin, according to the opponents, in that the laws of the Mosaic covenant were no longer required. Paul explains in 2:18 why Christ is not a minister of sin.

2:18 For if I build again those things which I have destroyed, I demonstrate myself to be a transgressor (εἰ γὰρ ἃ κατέλυσα ταῦτα πάλιν οἰκοδομῶ, παραβάτην ἐμαυτὸν συνιστάνω). For Paul (or anyone else) to return to the law now that the new age of salvation in Christ has arrived would be fruitless. Salvation cannot be obtained in the old era of the law, and turning to the law again would only reveal Paul's sin. Paul turns the tables on his critics. Christ does not promote sin. It is those who live under the law who are revealed to be transgressors.

Here Paul explains why Christ is not a minister of sin.[74] But what exactly is the argument? We need to look at it piece by piece. The things torn down or "destroyed" refer to the OT law. The verb "I destroy" (καταλύω) is used elsewhere to refer to the abolishing or tearing down of the OT law (cf. Matt 5:17; 2 Macc 2:22; 4:11; 4 Macc 4:20, 24; 5:33).[75] In using the pronoun "I" here, Paul continues to address Peter, but he refers to himself as a representative of the Jewish people. Perhaps Paul universalizes the discussion by referring to himself because he wants to take the spotlight off the conflict between him and Peter.

71. So Burton, *Galatians*, 125.

72. Cf. Lambrecht, "Gal 2:14b – 21," 486 – 87.

73. Garlington says that the sin here is apostasy, but such an interpretation is unlikely if the interpretation offered here is correct (*Galatians*, 162).

74. Lambrecht understands "for" (γάρ) here to be equivalent to another common Greek conjunction (δέ), and hence it has the meaning "but" ("Gal 2,18 – 21," 219). Against this, see

Smiles, *Gospel and Law in Galatia*, 155.

75. Therefore, it seems unlikely that the focus here is on tearing down the old covenant community, which Ciampa suggests (*The Presence of Scripture in Galatians 1 and 2*, 206 – 7), though the two are clearly related logically. Longenecker overemphasizes the "once for-all" character of the aorist tense here (*Galatians*, 91).

If Paul rebuilds the OT law, which is abolished now that Christ has come and a new era in redemptive history has arrived, then he has violated God's will and is to be deemed a transgressor.[76] Hence, for Peter to say, in effect, that Gentiles must observe the OT law to belong to the people of God is contrary to God's will. Reinstituting the law transgresses God's will because it denies that righteousness is in Christ and returns to the old era of salvation history.[77] Therefore, to reach back to the law for righteousness constitutes sin since it denies righteousness is in Christ. The old age was dominated by sin and the law, but the new age in Christ is marked by righteousness and life. This interpretation is preferable because it also explains the ground "for" (γάρ) in 2:19. Paul would prove himself to be a transgressor if he reinstituted the law because he had already died to the law when he died with Christ. The era of the law had ceased with the death and resurrection of Christ.

2:19a For I through the law died to the law (ἐγὼ γὰρ διὰ νόμου νόμῳ ἀπέθανον). Paul died to the the law since Christ ended the era of the law through his death. Christ, who lived under the law and kept it perfectly, died to liberate believers from the law (4:4 – 5).

The speech to Peter likely continues here as Paul explains why reverting to the law and imposing the law on the Gentiles is sinful instead of righteous. The argument here is dense and compact, and hence interpreters differ on the meaning. "I" is used representatively. Paul speaks, not merely as a believer in general, but as a Jewish Christian, though what he says about dying to the law applies by implication to all believers.[78] Peter, in requiring Gentiles to observe the law, is thereby suggesting that the law is necessary to live in a way that pleases God. Paul argues, on the contrary, that such a stance contradicts the cross and the decisive change in redemptive history. No believer (including Jewish believers) is under the law any longer, for believers have now "died to the law." The law no longer exercises authority over them.

But what does Paul mean in saying "I through the law died to the law"? It could mean that he died with reference to the law because he failed to observe what the law commands.[79] Failure to do what the law demands, as Paul teaches elsewhere, leads to death (Rom 7:5 – 25; 1 Cor 15:56). Such an interpretation would explain the words "through the law" (διὰ νόμου) in a meaningful way.[80] The law itself, with its commands, is the means by which death ensues. The verse could be paraphrased as follows, "I died to the law through the commands of the law," with the understanding that the failure to keep the law is implied.

It seems more likely, however, that Paul is arguing in terms of redemptive history here. Believers died to the law when they died with Christ.[81] Such a reading is supported by a parallel text in Romans.[82] We should not impose what Romans says on Galatians, of course. Yet such a compact statement may be explained by what Paul teaches in

---

76. The transgression could consist in Paul's original tearing down of the Mosaic law, which would be the view of the opponents, or in Paul's failure to keep the law after it was reinstated. But Lambrecht is probably correct in saying that both of these options are less likely in this verse, and the transgression here would consist in rebuilding the Mosaic law after Paul has died to the law ("Gal 2,18 – 21," 223, 230 – 36).

77. Longenecker, *Galatians*, 91; Bruce, *Galatians*, 142; Martyn, *Galatians*, 256.

78. Against Kwon, *Eschatology*, 169 – 70.

79. Lightfoot, *Galatians*, 118; Guthrie, *Galatians*, 89; Burton, *Galatians*, 133; George, *Galatians*, 199; Fee, *Galatians*, 91. Bruce seems to argue for both views (*Galatians*, 143 – 44). For a variation of this view, see Cummins, *Crucified Christ*, 216 – 26.

80. Against Dunn, Paul's death to the law did not occur through his persecution of the church (*Galatians*, 143).

81. So Betz, *Galatians*, 122; Hays, *Galatians*, 243.

82. Rightly Witherington, *Galatians*, 188 – 89.

more detail elsewhere: "You also have died to the law through the body of Christ" (Rom 7:4 ESV). Christ's death spelled the end of the reign of the law, signaling the arrival of a new era in the history of salvation. Hence, reinstating the law turns the clock back in redemptive history and thereby teaches that the law rather than Christ is decisive for salvation. Paul likely intends the same truth in saying, "I have been crucified with Christ" (2:19c). In other words, the old self (what humans beings were in Adam) died in being crucified with Christ.

But how does this second interpretation explain the words "through the law"? If Rom 7:4 unpacks how believers died to the law by being incorporated into Christ's death, in what sense did death to the law become a reality "through the law"? It seems that Gal 4:4–5 provides the answer. In a confessional type statement Paul affirms that Jesus as God's Son was "born under the law" (4:4). Even though Jesus was "under the law" and lived in the old era of redemptive history, he was not under the power of sin, for he always did the will of God and kept God's law perfectly. Hence, as the true Son of God and as the sinless one he was qualified to redeem and liberate those who were under the law (4:5).

To put it another way, since Jesus lived under the law, he could free those who lived under the dominion of sin and the law. The reign of the law ended, therefore, "through the law." Jesus in his death took the full penalty of the law upon himself, even though as the sinless one he did not deserve its curse (3:10, 13). By dying under the law he ended the era of the law, and those who have died with Christ share in his victory over the law.

2:19b To live to God (ἵνα θεῷ ζήσω). The purpose of dying to the law is explained. Now that believers

are no longer under the law, they live in the new age of salvation. In Christ the new Adam has arrived and believers are new persons. Again, Rom 7:4 is a helpful parallel. The marriage of believers to the law has come to an end, and now they are, so to speak, married to Christ, so that they will bear fruit for God. To be under the law led to death, but life has arrived with the coming of Christ. Therefore, it makes little sense for Peter to impose the law on the Gentiles, for the old period of redemptive history brought sin and death, but those who have died with Christ are freed from the power of sin and now live to God.

2:19c I have been crucified with Christ (Χριστῷ συνεσταύρωμαι). When did believers die to the law? They died when Christ died, and because believers are united with Christ, they share in his death.[83] The decisive event in salvation history is the death of Christ. The era of the law ended at the cross, and believers died to the law's rule over them when they died with Christ (cf. Rom 7:4).

The polarity between the cross and the law pervades all of Galatians. The latter belongs to the old order and the former to the new age of salvation. Union with Christ in his death spells the beginning of a new life for believers. Peter, however, was denying the significance of the cross by demanding that Gentiles observe the law. If table fellowship with Gentiles depends on observance of the law, then the cross no longer plays the central role in redemptive history, for the law rather than Christ becomes the focus of salvation. Such a view is unthinkable since it trivializes the cross.

2:20a-b (As a result) I no longer live, but Christ lives in me (ζῶ δὲ οὐκέτι ἐγώ, ζῇ δὲ ἐν ἐμοὶ Χριστός). A consequence is now drawn from

---

83. Silva rightly observes that Dunn (*Galatians*, 144) overreads the perfect tense here (see *Interpreting Galatians*, 74, n. 19).

being crucified with Christ. We should not understand the phrase "I no longer live" to denote the suppression of Paul's personality. What Paul means is that the old "I," who he was in Adam, no longer lives. In other words, we have a redemptive-historical statement here. The old age of sin and death has been set aside now that Christ has died.

The language here fits with Paul's claim that the "our old self was crucified with him" (ὁ παλαιὸς ἡμῶν ἄνθρωπος συνεσταυρώθη, Rom 6:6). The phrase "old self" points to who believers were in Adam (cf. also Eph 4:22; Col 3:9). Believers are now a "new self" (καινὸς ἄνθρωπος) in Christ (Eph 4:24; Col 3:10; cf. Eph 2:15).[84] This new reality has dawned precisely because they have died with Christ. The eschaton has dawned at the cross of Christ, and insisting on food laws plunges people back into this "present evil age" (1:4).

The new age of redemptive history is also marked by the indwelling of Christ in believers. Usually Paul emphasizes the indwelling of the Holy Spirit in believers (e.g., Rom 8:9; Eph 2:22; 3:16), but he also on occasion states that Christ dwells in believers (Rom 8:10; 2 Cor 13:5; Col 1:27; Eph 3:17).[85] Again, the verse should not be understood as if the human personality is replaced. The indwelling of Christ signifies the arrival of the new age of redemptive history, the fulfillment of God's saving promises.[86]

Alternatively, Carson argues that Paul refers to the representative significance of Christ for the believer. In other words, the main point of 2:20b is union with Christ in his resurrection (2:20). Thus, to say that Christ lives "in me" (ἐν ἐμοί) is to say that, by virtue of his resurrection, Christ lives in my place.[87] Such a reading is possible, but it seems that the redemptive-historical and existential are not mutually exclusive.[88] Paul often speaks, as noted above, of the indwelling of the Spirit, and hence it seems more likely that he has this notion in mind as well. Later he can speak of "the Spirit of his Son" being sent "into our hearts" (Gal 4:6).[89] And we noticed above that Paul speaks in other texts of Christ dwelling in believers, and hence this meaning should be preferred here.

2:20c-e And the life I now live in the flesh, I live by faith in the Son of God, who loved me and gave himself for me (ὃ δὲ[90] νῦν ζῶ ἐν σαρκί, ἐν πίστει ζῶ τῇ τοῦ υἱοῦ τοῦ θεοῦ τοῦ ἀγαπήσαντός με καὶ παραδόντος ἑαυτὸν ὑπὲρ ἐμοῦ). Paul and all Christians now enjoy the life of the age to come. And yet they still live in the body (the flesh), and hence they live out their lives by faith in Christ, who demonstrated his love by giving himself for his people.

The inauguration of the age to come, i.e., the fulfillment of God's promises at the cross and

---

84. Col 3:10 uses "new" (νέος) rather than "new" (καινός), but the two words are in the same semantic domain, and hence the shift is not significant.

85. Paul likely has in mind the idea that Christ lives in believers by the Holy Spirit. So Gordon D. Fee, *God's Empowering Presence: The Holy Spirit in the Letters of Paul* (Peabody, MA: Hendrickson, 1994), 374; Kwon, *Eschatology*, 177 – 78; Bruce, *Galatians*, 144; Dunn, *Galatians*, 145.

86. See Longenecker's exposition here (*Galatians*, 92 – 93). He uses the word "mystical," but does not mean by it the removal of one's personality. Cf. also Betz, *Galatians*, 124. For a historical glimpse at the mystical tradition, see Riches, *Galatians through the Centuries*, 137 – 43.

87. Carson, *Love in Hard Places*, 166.

88. See Mark A. Seifrid, "Paul does not have merely his inward life in view, but his whole person and history, which has now been manifestly taken up in the cross and resurrection of Christ.... Paul's 'person' is not confined to the inner sanctum of his heart, but includes the entire history of his life, the 'before' and 'after' of his encounter with the Son of God.... Paul's 'person' has been exchanged for that of another with whom he has been united ("Paul, Luther, and Justification," 221). Note Seifrid's use of the words "merely" and "not confined," showing that both the existential and redemptive-historical are in view.

89. Cf. also Longenecker, *Galatians*, 174.

90. "And" (δέ) is continuative here (so Longenecker, *Galatians*, 92).

resurrection (cf. Gal 1:4), does not mean that sin and evil are eradicated. Paul still lives in the body (i.e., the flesh, σάρξ). Paul (with all Christians) is a new person in Christ since the age to come has dawned. Still, his individuality is not obliterated, nor is sin impossible, for he still lives "in the flesh" (ἐν σαρκί).[91] The reference to the flesh is not used in the technical sense of living under the dominion of the former evil age (cf. Rom 8:8 – 9). Here it simply denotes life in the body and should not be equated with living in sin (cf. 2 Cor 10:3).[92] Still, life in the body signals the continuing weakness that marks the old age, indicating that the new age has not arrived in all its fullness.

Paul's new life is not marked by observance of the law, but by faith in Jesus as the Son of God.[93] The pronoun "that which" (ὅ) is an accusative of content, reflecting the meaning of the verb "I live" (ζῶ).[94] The new life is not characterized fundamentally by working for God, but by believing in the Son. Paul does not often designate Jesus as "the Son of God" (Rom 1:4; 2 Cor 1:19; Eph 4:13) or "the Son" (Rom 1:3, 9; 5:10; 8:3, 29, 32; 1 Cor 1:9; 15:28; Gal 1:16; 4:4; Col 1:13; 1 Thess 1:10). In the OT Israel was God's special son (Exod 4:22), and the Davidic king was also God's son (2 Sam 7:14). But Jesus is the true and obedient Son of God, and he also is the true David, the true King of Israel. Son of God also denotes that Jesus is the special and unique Son of God. Though it is disputed, the term points to Jesus' preexistence and hence his distinctive relationship with God.

Paul's faith has a specific referent, for he trusts in Christ, who displayed his love by giving his life for Paul's sake (who is paradigmatic of all believers) on the cross.[95] The language used here is similar to the formulation in Eph 5:2 and 5:25 where Christ's self-giving love is featured. The words here are intensely personal and individualistic. Christ loved "me" and gave himself "for me."[96] Paul sees this love as extending to all Christians, but the individualistic emphasis must not be neglected. Faith in Christ can be sustained only where one is confident in God's love. Love, in this sense, is the fuel of faith.[97] This love finds its roots in the cross, where Christ gave his life "for" Paul. Indeed, the expression "for me" (ὑπὲρ ἐμοῦ) suggests substitution, that Christ died in Paul's place.

2:21 (Therefore) I do not reject the grace of God. For if righteousness comes through the law, then Christ died for nothing (οὐκ ἀθετῶ τὴν χάριν τοῦ θεοῦ· εἰ γὰρ διὰ νόμου δικαιοσύνη, ἄρα Χριστὸς δωρεὰν ἀπέθανεν). Those who require the law for salvation reject God's grace and try to establish a right relationship with God by means of keeping the law. In doing so they deny the significance of Christ's death, and in effect they teach that he died for nothing since they rely on the law rather than Christ for salvation.

It is likely that Paul's concluding words to Peter are found here, and hence 2:21 functions as a summary of the argument. Paul as a Jewish Christian does not reject God's grace, which has been manifested in the self-giving love of Christ on the cross. This grace demonstrates that right standing with God comes through faith in Jesus Christ and not by works of law (see 2:16). Indeed, the summary character of the verse indicates that the noun "righteousness" (δικαιοσύνη) cannot be understood differently from the verb "justify" (δικαιόω).

91. Rightly Machen, *Galatians*, 161.

92. So Bruce, *Galatians*, 145.

93. For a discussion on whether Paul speaks of faith *in* Jesus or the faithfulness *of* Jesus, see comments on 2:16.

94. See Burton, *Galatians*, 138; Longenecker, *Galatians*, 93.

95. Paul likely alludes to Isaiah 53 here (so Harmon, "She Must and Shall Go Free," 133 – 34).

96. "Moreover, this language teaches that each individual justly owes a great debt of gratitude to Christ, as if He had come for his sake alone" (Chrysostom, *Galatians*, 23).

97. Cf. Calvin, *Galatians*, 75.

When Paul refers to righteousness by law, he refers to a declaration of righteousness based on keeping the law.[98]

The term "righteousness" here does not refer to ethical renewal but the pronouncement of the judge based on whether the standards of the law were observed. Paul argues here that righteousness cannot come via the law. If it did, then Christ's death on the cross is superfluous. Christ's self-giving on the cross would be completely unnecessary, for right standing with God would be attained through observing the law rather than by trusting in what God has done in Christ to grant salvation.

Peter's actions relative to the Gentiles sent them the message, whether Peter acknowledged it or not, that the Gentiles must keep the law to be right with God. In so doing, Christ's cross becomes unnecessary for righteousness. If the law suffices, Christ is superfluous. And if the law suffices, grace is nullified. Righteousness is no longer given as a gift; it is attained by human effort. So, either Peter renounces the need to observe the food laws, or he renounces the cross. There is no middle way.

It is almost certain that Peter heeded Paul's advice. Otherwise, Paul would have considered him to be a false brother, and that does not fit what Paul says about Peter in 1 Corinthians (1 Cor 1:12; 3:22; 9:5; 15:5), nor does it fit with Peter's later commendation of Paul (2 Pet 3:15). Further, Paul's appeal to the agreement of the apostles in Gal 2:1 – 10 would be useless if Peter ultimately disagreed with him.

Theology in Application

Right Standing with God

The fundamental issue in these verses is the basis of one's right standing with God. Are human beings right with God on the basis of works or through faith in Jesus Christ and him crucified? The new perspective on Paul argues, however, that boundary markers are the main issue in this text, and hence for them the application is that one is not required to be Jewish or to observe Jewish distinctives to belong to the people of God.

I have argued, however, that such a reading of the text is mistaken. "Works of law" refers to all that is commanded in the law — to all the deeds required by the law. Therefore, the phrase cannot be limited to ethnic distinctives that separate Jews from Gentiles. Paul does not fundamentally consider whether one must be Jewish to belong to the people of God. Instead, he insists that human obedience to commandments cannot function as the basis of a right relationship with the Lord.

It follows, then, that our obedience cannot be the foundation of a saving rela-

---

98. Cf. Betz, *Galatians*, 126.

tionship with God. The gospel proclaimed by Paul is that one is declared to be righteous in God's sight only through faith in Jesus Christ. As human beings we derive our worth from what we accomplish, whether it is in our work, our families, or even our athletic ability. The gospel teaches us, however, that nothing we do renders us righteous before God. There is nothing we can contribute — nothing at all. We must acknowledge that we are naked, miserable, poor, and weak. We live by faith alone, casting ourselves entirely on the grace of God in Jesus Christ our Lord. Christ is our righteousness; his cross is our only hope in the day of judgment. We look away from ourselves and what we have accomplished and cling to Christ alone for salvation.

On occasion it is suggested that this truth is rather obvious and all understand it. But anyone who says such a thing must not be sharing the gospel with unbelievers, for almost without exception they believe that their goodness may qualify them for eternal life. It comes as a rude shock to unbelievers to be told that their only hope is the cross of Christ and the forgiveness and righteousness he gives. Indeed, the gospel shocks us because it undercuts human pride. God sees nothing in us that impresses him. We must forsake all our illusions about our so-called "goodness" and "accomplishments." We must put our trust in Christ crucified rather than leaning on ourselves. We see our utter poverty and find our riches in Christ. If we could be righteous before God based on our works, then Christ died for nothing. The law would be sufficient in teaching us how to live to be saved.

The Law and the Gospel

The law reveals our poverty, and therefore we realize that we need to become a new tree (Matt 7:17 – 19), i.e., we need new life. The old person that we were in Adam must be crucified with Christ. We do not gaze on ourselves to see what good we have accomplished. We never "progress" beyond the gospel. We are reminded every day that our righteousness is found in another. Even as Christians, we are continually reminded of our weakness and sin. If we become bored with the gospel of justification by faith alone, we can be assured that we have become self-deceived about our own goodness, that we are deluded about how good we are. We have forgotten that our life is only in Christ and him crucified.

Martin Luther captured the truth stated above powerfully:

Particularly when you hear an immature and unripe saint trumpet that he knows very well that we must be saved by the grace of God, without our own works, and then pretend that this is a snap for him, well, then have no doubt that he has no idea of what he is talking about and probably will never find out. For this is not an art that can be completely learned or of which anyone could boast that he is a master. It is an art that will always have us as pupils while it remains the master. And all those who do understand and practice it do not boast that they can do everything. On the contrary, they sense it like a wonderful taste or odor that they greatly desire and pursue; and they are amazed that they cannot grasp it or comprehend it as they would like. They hunger, thirst, and yearn for it more and more; and they never tire of hearing about or dealing with it, just as St. Paul himself confessed that he has not yet obtained it (Phil. 3:12). And in Matt 5:6 Christ calls those blessed who hunger and thirst after righteousness.[99]

Mark Galli recently interviewed Rob Bell for *Christianity Today* and asked him to present the gospel on Twitter. Here is how Bell responded:

I would say that history is headed somewhere. The thousands of little ways in which you are tempted to believe that hope might actually be a legitimate response to the insanity of the world actually can be trusted. And the Christian story is that a tomb is empty, and a movement has actually begun that has been present in a sense all along in creation. And all those times when your cynicism was at odds with an impulse within you that said that this little thing might be about something bigger — those tiny little slivers may in fact be connected to something really, really big.[100]

What is astonishing about this definition is that nothing whatsoever is said about human sin and the need for the cross. The most fundamental element of the gospel (cf. 1 Cor. 15:1 – 4) is completely absent. How easy it is to forget the gospel!

99. Martin Luther, "Psalm 117," translated by Edward Sittler in *Selected Psalms III* from *Luther's Works*, vol. 14, edited by Jaroslav Pelikan (St. Louis: Concordia, 1958), 37.

100. Accessed at http://www.christianitytoday.com/ct/article_print.html?id=81195 on September 20, 2009.

Galatians 3:1 – 5

Literary Context

The long argument defending Paul's apostleship stretching from 1:10 – 2:21 has concluded. We saw earlier that 1:10 functions as a transitional verse bridging 1:6 – 9 and 1:11 – 2:21. Interestingly, 2:15 – 21 also functions as a transition to the next major section of the letter (3:1 – 4:11), where Paul defends his gospel theologically over against the Judaizers.

Betz, using rhetorical categories, identifies the section beginning in 3:1 as the *probatio* (proofs for main thesis).[1] Cosgrove argues that 3:1 – 5 is the decisive paragraph in the letter, showing that the Spirit is the primary issue in Galatians. Hence, Cosgrove rejects the notion that justification is central in Galatians or that the presenting issue in the letter centers on what is required *to enter* the people of God. Instead, to him, the central issue is the continued work of the Spirit in the Galatians. Paul exhorts them to *stay in* Christ.[2] I will argue below in 3:3 that such an interpretation misreads what Paul says. Furthermore, the view is flawed because it fails to see the crucial role that 2:15 – 21 plays in the argument, so that it functions as the thesis, or as Betz says, the *propositio* (main thesis) for the remainder of the letter.

Even though Betz's rhetorical analysis of the letter does not succeed, he is not far off the mark in describing 2:15 – 21 as the *propositio*. The fundamental issue in Galatians, and in 3:1 – 5, is justification. The reception of the Spirit, as Paul argues in this paragraph, functions as the decisive evidence that the Galatians are justified by faith.

Paul's argument begins from what is indisputable: the Galatians have received the Spirit. He concludes from this that they are justified by faith instead of by works of law. In addition, the view proposed by Cosgrove misreads the significance of circumcision. The Judaizers followed the standard Jewish view that circumcision was necessary *to enter* the people of God. Circumcison was not conceived in Judaism

---

1. Betz, *Galatians*, 128 – 29.
2. Charles H. Cosgrove, *The Cross and the Spirit: A Study in the Argument and Theology of Galatians* (Macon, GA: Mercer Univ. Press, 1988); so also R. H. Gundry, "Grace, Works, and Staying Saved in Paul," *Bib* 66 (1985): 8 – 9; Scott J. Ha-

femann, "Paul and the Exile of Israel in Galatians 3 – 4," in *Exile: Old Testament, Jewish, and Christian Conceptions* (ed. James M. Scott; JSJSup 56; Leiden: Brill, 1997), 340, n. 29; Witherington, *Galatians*, 175; Fee, *Galatians*, 1, 5 – 6, 81, 107, 120, 171, 201.

or by the Judaizers as necessary *to continue* one's devotion to God. It was required *to belong* to the people of God. Surely the Spirit plays a major role in the letter, but such a judgment overlooks the crucial function of 2:15 – 21 and the summarizing nature of 6:11 – 18.[3]

I. Introduction: Desertion from Paul's Gospel Is Desertion from the Gospel (1:1 – 2:21)

II. Paul's Gospel Defended from Experience and Scripture (3:1 – 4:11)

➡ **A. Argument from Experience: Reception of Spirit by Means of Faith, Not Works (3:1 – 5)**

B. Argument from Scripture: Blessing of Abraham by Faith (3:6 – 14)

C. Argument from Salvation History: Priority of Abrahamic Covenant and Temporary Nature of Mosaic Covenant (3:15 – 4:11)

Main Idea

The Galatians do not need to be circumcised and to observe the works of law in order to belong to the people of God because they have clearly received the Holy Spirit; the reception of the Spirit *is the mark* that signifies that one belongs to the people of God.

Translation

(See next page.)

Structure

The argument in this paragraph is vigorous and pointed. Paul opens with an exclamation (3:1a), and then each of the succeeding units has a rhetorical question (3:1b – 5), which indicates that the Galatians themselves are able to answer the questions posed. In other words, the answers are obvious and plain to anyone with an ounce of perception. Since the argument consists of rhetorical questions,

---

3. Weima rightly sees this as one of the flaws of Cosgrove's work ("Gal 6:11 – 18," 106 – 7). However, Weima overstates his point when he excludes faith and righteousness as central themes by overemphasizing the role of the conclusion of the letter. Nor is it convincing to suggest that righteousness is absent conceptually from 6:11 – 18, for the conclusion of the letter stands as a strong rebuke of the opponents' disobedience (their false righteousness). Furthermore, the cross is inseparably tied to God's saving righteousness (and faith!) in the letter, and hence Weima separates here what should be kept together. Luther was a theologian of the cross because the latter magnified the saving righteousness of God and taught that only faith saves.

Galatians 3:1-5

1a	exclamation	O foolish Galatians!
b	rhetorical question	Who has cast a spell over you, before whose eyes Jesus Christ was publicly proclaimed
c	apposition	as the crucified one?
2a	rhetorical question	I want to learn only this from you: Did you receive the Spirit
b	means	by works of law, or
c	contrast	by hearing with faith?
3a	rhetorical question	Are you so foolish,
b	means *(of 3a)*	in that you are now perfected by the flesh,
c	temporal *(of 3b)*	after you have begun in the Spirit?
4a	rhetorical question	Have you suffered so many things in vain—
b	condition	if indeed they are in vain?
5a	inference *(of 1-4)*	Therefore, does the one who
b	series	supplies you with the Spirit and works miracles among you,
c	means	do it by works of law or
d	contrast	by hearing with faith?

linking words do not connect the verses. The paragraph closes (3:5) with an inference ("therefore," [οὖν]) drawn from 3:1 – 4 (though v. 5 is also set as a rhetorical question).

The paragraph begins with bracing words as the Galatians are identified as "foolish," and Paul asks if they have been bewitched by a spell, since they do not perceive the significance of Christ crucified. Paul tries to undo the bewitchment, so to speak, in 3:2 – 4. Paul has only one question to pose to the Galatians in the examination (3:2). And the answer is easy, for clearly they received the Spirit by faith and not by works of law. And if they have received the Spirit, they are evidently members of Abraham's family and hence do not need to be circumcised. The case against the Judaizers is closed and shut if the Galatians have eyes to see.

Verse 3 follows with another rhetorical question: "Are you so foolish?" Do they now think that the Christian life is begun by the Spirit and completed in the flesh? Surely, they must know that the Christian life continues the way it begins: through faith and by the Spirit! Paul's puzzlement emerges in 3:4. Has the conversion of the Galatians been all for nought? Are they willing to throw away all they have gained? Have they suffered for nothing? Such a state of affairs is inconceivable for Paul.

The paragraph concludes with the main point in 3:5. The Galatians have the Spirit. It is the miracle-working Spirit that has worked powerfully in their midst, and he has done so because the Galatians have believed the gospel, not because they have observed law. Therefore, submitting to the blandishments of the Judaizers is unthinkable.

Exegetical Outline

II. Paul's Gospel Defended from Experience and Scripture (3:1 – 4:11)

→ A. Argument from Experience: Reception of Spirit by Means of Faith, Not Works (3:1 – 5)

1. The Galatians are bewitched (3:1)
2. The Spirit received by faith (3:2)
3. Progress in the Christian life by the Spirit (3:3)
4. The futility of apostasy (3:4)
5. The conclusion: the Spirit's presence by faith (3:5)

Explanation of the Text

3:1a-b O foolish Galatians! Who has cast a spell over you? (Ὦ ἀνόητοι Γαλάται, τίς ὑμᾶς ἐβάσκανεν[4]). The Galatians are upbraided for their foolishness (cf. 3:3), which is an indictment

---

4. Some manuscripts add here τῇ ἀληθείᾳ μὴ πείθεσθαι ("so that you did not obey the truth"), but this is a clear example of assimilation to 5:7.

not of their intellectual capacities but of their moral inclinations.[5] It is as if they have been bewitched, as if someone has cast a spell over them. Hansen rightly points out that the Galatians, like Peter (2:11 – 14), were on the verge of denying the gospel by their actions.[6]

The reference to "Galatians" (Γαλάται) does not necessarily lead to the conclusion that Paul addresses ethnic Galatians, for the term also fits with a general address to the whole province.[7] Thus, the reference to the Galatians fits with, though it certainly does not prove, a south Galatian destination. Paul does not call them "brothers" (ἀδελφοί) as in 1:11, but addresses them more formally and abruptly "to summon them to their responsibility."[8]

Magic attracted people in the ancient world, for it promised control over their lives in an uncertain world.[9] Numerous magical papyri with long strings of invocations have been discovered, showing how ordinary people tried to manipulate their circumstances. Paul does not endorse magic here, but he uses the coinage of the day to express his astonishment (cf. 1:6) at the Galatians' fascination with circumcision (cf. 5:2).[10] It is as if a magician has cast a spell over them, preventing them from seeing what is blatantly obvious, i.e., the significance of the cross of Jesus Christ.[11] Ultimately Paul may be saying that Satan himself stands behind the deception of the Galatians.[12]

3:1b-c Before whose eyes Jesus Christ was publicly proclaimed as the crucified one? (οἷς κατ᾽ ὀφθαλμοὺς Ἰησοῦς Χριστὸς προεγράφη[13] ἐσταυρωμένος;). It is as if a spell has been uttered over the Galatians because they no longer see the significance of the cross of Christ. Their fascination with circumcision and the law deprives the cross of its significance.

Paul "publicly proclaimed" (προεγράφη) the significance of Christ's death. This verb (προγράφω) elsewhere refers to what was written in advance (cf. Rom 15:14; Eph 3:3), but such a meaning does not seem to fit here, for the OT was not written before the Galatians' eyes.[14] The term is also used for written proclamations and public notices, and in this case has the sense of a public proclamation.[15] Hence, it does not mean that

---

5. Rightly Witherington, *Galatians*, 201. Contra S. Elliott, the reference to the Galatians' foolishness (along with other features in this text) does not refer to the castration of the *galli* in their devotion to the mother of the gods (*Cutting Too Close for Comfort*, 335 – 44). The context points toward a Jewish background, and circumcision here is associated with the Mosaic law.

6. Hansen, *Abraham in Galatians*, 109.

7. So Bruce, *Galatians*, 16, 147.

8. Herman N. Ridderbos, *The Epistle of Paul to the Churches of Galatia* (trans. Henry Zylstra; NICNT; Grand Rapids: Eerdmans, 1953), 111.

9. Cf. Clinton E. Arnold, *The Colossian Syncretism: The Interface between Christianity and Folk Belief at Colossae* (Grand Rapids: Baker, 1996), 11 – 20.

10. On the evil eye (suggested in the verb βασκαίνω), see Bruce Longenecker, " 'Until Christ Is Formed in You': Suprahuman Forces and Moral Character in Galatians," *CBQ* 61 (1999): 93 – 97. It is probable that the expression here is metaphorical. So Witherington, *Galatians*, 201 – 4.

11. Susan Eastman argues that the reference to the evil eye echoes Deut 28:53 – 57 and the covenantal curses of Deut 27 – 28. The suggestion is intriguing, but, despite Eastman's arguments, it is no more than a possibility. "The Evil Eye and the Curse of the Law: Galatians 3.1 Revisited," *JSNT* 83 (2001): 69 – 87.

12. Cf. Chrysostom, *Galatians*, 24; Calvin, *Galatians*, 79; George, *Galatians*, 207; Jerome H. Neyrey, "Bewitched in Galatia: Paul and Cultural Anthropology," *CBQ* 50 (1988): 72 – 100.

13. The prepositional phrase "among you" (ἐν ὑμῖν) is added after "publicly proclaimed" (προεγράφη) in the Western text and Majority text (D, F, G, etc.), but it is clearly secondary as the overwhelming support for its exclusion attests (ℵ, A, B, C, P, Ψ, 33*, 81, 104, 365, 630, 1175, 1241ˢ, 1739, 1881, etc.).

14. Basil S. Davis, "The Meaning of ΠΡΟΓΡΑΦΗ in the Context of Galatians 3.1," *NTS* 45 (1999): 196.

15. Lightfoot, *Galatians*, 134; Gottlob Schrenk, "προγράφω," *TDNT*, 1:771. It seems less likely that it refers in this context to pictures that were displayed before the Galatians (but see Betz, *Galatians*, 131).

the crucifixion was physically portrayed in Paul's preaching.[16] Rather, it means that the significance of Christ's cross was vividly communicated when the gospel was announced.[17]

The participle "crucified" (ἐσταυρωμένος) explains that Jesus Christ was proclaimed as the crucified one. Once again the cross takes center stage in Galatians, and Paul hopes that the bewitchment will come to an end and that the Galatians will see again the significance of Christ crucified.

3:2 I want to learn only this from you: Did you receive the Spirit by works of law, or by hearing with faith? (τοῦτο μόνον θέλω μαθεῖν ἀφ' ὑμῶν, ἐξ ἔργων νόμου τὸ πνεῦμα ἐλάβετε ἢ ἐξ ἀκοῆς πίστεως;). Since the Galatians suffered from bewitchment, Paul asks a series of rhetorical questions (3:1 – 4) with the hope that they will be jolted back to reality, so that they will not forsake the gospel. As Betz says, "Rather than presenting it himself, Paul wants to hear it from the Galatians, and thus uses a dialogical device."[18]

The issue can be framed by posing a single question, and hence Paul says he desires to learn only one thing from them. The issue is the reception of the Spirit: did they receive the Spirit through observing the law or through trust in Christ? The word "received" (ἐλάβετε) hearkens back to the time when the Galatians first heard the gospel and became believers. The presence of the Spirit was dramatically and powerfully evident in their lives.[19]

The reference to the Spirit confirms that the conversion of the Galatians is in view, for the Spirit is the sign that one belongs to the people of God (cf. 1 Cor 2:12). At conversion the Holy Spirit is poured out in one's heart (Rom 5:5). Those who belong to Christ and are genuinely Christians have the Spirit dwelling in them (Rom 8:9; cf. 8:14 – 15). Conversely, the natural person does not have the Spirit (1 Cor 2:14). The Spirit authenticates one's salvation and functions as the guarantee that God will complete his saving work (2 Cor 1:22; 5:5; Eph 1:14).

In a similar way, Peter defended the inclusion of Gentiles into the church of Jesus Christ apart from circumcision by appealing to the gift of the Spirit (Acts 15:8; cf. 10:44 – 48). Since Gentiles had the Spirit, circumcision was not required. Paul's argument here is strikingly the same. Since the Galatians have the Spirit, they are clearly Christians and belong to the people of God; hence, circumcision and observing the law are not required to belong to his people.[20]

The issue the Galatians must resolve is whether they received the Spirit by doing the works of the law or through hearing with faith. Paul uses the exact same phrase to express the same contrast in 3:5. The meaning of the phrase "works of law" was discussed in 2:16. There it was argued that the term refers to all that the law requires, though, given the Galatian context, the presenting issue was circumcision.

The phrase "hearing with faith" (ἀκοῆς πίστεως) could be interpreted in various ways.

---

16. Nor does it likely refer to Paul's interpretation of lament psalms as prefigurations of the crucifixion (contra Hays, *Galatians*, 250 – 51).

17. So Longenecker, *Galatians*, 100 – 101. B. Davis argues that the reference is to Paul's own suffering (Gal 4:13; 6:17), and the marks of suffering he endured as an apostle. Cf. also Wilson, *Curse of the Law*, 88; Scott J. Hafemann, "The Role of Suffering in the Mission of Paul," in *The Mission of the Early Church to Jews and Gentiles* (ed. Jostein Ådna and Hans Kvalbein; WUNT 127; Tübingen: Mohr Siebeck, 2000), 174. Against this reading, the subject here is Christ's crucifixion,

and a clear reference to Paul's suffering is lacking. The link Davis attempts to forge to 2:19 – 21 does not succeed, for there Paul does not refer to his suffering but to his union with Christ's death, and the latter was not realized via Paul's suffering but through Christ's death.

18. Betz, *Galatians*, 132.

19. Betz points to 4:6 and says that an "ecstatic experience" is in view here (*Galatians*, 132). Cf. also Dunn, *Galatians*, 153.

20. Against Kwon, who maintains that Paul charges the Galatians with losing the Spirit, so that they have to start all over again (*Eschatology*, 38 – 39).

Diverse interpretations are possible since the noun "hearing" (ἀκοή) can refer to the act of hearing (Matt 13:14; 2 Pet 2:8) or the message heard (John 12:38; Rom 10:16). So too, the noun "faith" (πίστις) may refer to trusting God (Rom 4:5, 9; 1 Thess 1:8 etc.) or to the content of what is believed (Gal 1:23; 1 Tim 4:1, etc.). Therefore, the phrase may be interpreted as (1) hearing with trust;[21] (2) the message heard that demanded faith;[22] (3) the message that enables faith;[23] (4) the message of the faith (i.e., the Christian message); or (5) hearing of the faith (i.e., the Christian message).[24] "Faith" (πίστις) in Galatians typically refers to trust in God, and this meaning dominates in 2:16 – 3:9.[25] Therefore, it seems unlikely that Paul refers to the message of the Christian faith here.[26]

The parallel text in Rom 10:16 – 17, where both nouns are used, supports the notion that trust is the meaning here as well. "For Isaiah says, 'Lord, who has believed (ἐπίστευσεν) our message (ἀκοῇ)?' Hence, faith (πίστις) comes from hearing (ἐξ ἀκοῆς), and hearing (ἀκοή) through the word (ῥήματος) of Christ." There is no doubt that "faith" (πίστις) means "trust" here, for it is parallel to the verb "believed" (ἐπίστευσεν). So, we have further reasons to think that the noun "faith" (πίστις) means trust in Gal 3:2.

The more difficult issue in Gal 3:2 is whether the noun I have translated "hearing" (ἀκοή)

means "hearing" or "message." Indeed, in Rom 10:16 the noun in question (ἀκοή) refers to the message proclaimed, while in 10:17 the act of hearing is in view.[27] The alternation between the two in Rom 10:16 – 17 suggests that the meaning is not greatly affected whichever view we opt for. What is "heard," after all, is the "message" of the gospel. The Galatians received the Spirit "by hearing with faith" or "through the message that required faith." In both cases the emphasis is on faith or trusting God, and what was heard was the gospel. I suspect Paul puts the emphasis on hearing since he contrasts two human activities: doing and hearing. Still, what was heard was the message, so a sharp distinction between the two must not be pressed.

How was the Spirit received? It was not because the Galatians did anything required by the law. In fact, they did not keep the law and its requirements, for they were uncircumcised. They received the Spirit when they heard the gospel preached and placed their faith in the gospel. Believing — not doing — was the pathway to receiving the Spirit.[28]

3:3 Are you so foolish, in that you are now perfected by the flesh, after you have begun in the Spirit? (οὕτως ἀνόητοί ἐστε, ἐναρξάμενοι πνεύματι νῦν σαρκὶ ἐπιτελεῖσθε;). Paul returns to the theme of foolishness first broached in 3:1.

21. So Lightfoot, *Galatians*, 135; Fung, *Galatians*, 132; Hong, *Law in Galatians*, 130 – 31; Sam K. Williams, "The Hearing of Faith: ΑΚΟΗ ΠΙΣΤΕΩΣ in Galatians 3," *NTS* 35 (1989): 82 – 93.

22. Gerhard Kittel, "ἀκοή," *TDNT*, 1:221; Longenecker, *Galatians*, 103.

23. Betz, *Galatians*, 133; H. Wayne Johnson, "The Paradigm of Abraham in Galatians 3:6 – 9," *TJ* 8 (1987): 185 – 88. See also Hays (*Faith of Jesus Christ*, 143 – 49; idem, *Galatians*, 252), but he thinks it is also possible that it is the message that is the Christian faith. For a view similar to Hays, see Martyn, *Galatians*, 284, 286 – 89.

24. Calvin, *Galatians*, 81.

25. See the discussion on "faith in Christ" (πίστις Χριστοῦ) in 2:16 above.

26. Sprinkle argues that it refers to "the report of faith," which means the message of Christ ("Πίστις Χριστοῦ as an Eschatological Event," 210 – 12). But this view suffers from the comparison drawn in Gal 3:6, which emphasizes Abraham's believing, not the message he heard.

27. For a defense of this view, see Schreiner, *Romans*, 566 – 67.

28. Faith, as Calvin argues, is not merely intellectual acceptance but an embracing of Christ and giving oneself to him (*Galatians*, 84 – 85).

He queries whether the Galatians have compounded their foolishness (cf. 1:6) by starting one way and finishing another. Beginning by the Spirit here is another way of speaking of receiving the Spirit in 3:2. The inception of their Christian life was marked by the reception of the eschatological Spirit of promise (cf. Isa 32:15; 44:3; Ezek 11:18 – 19; 36:26 – 27; Joel 2:28). But the Galatians were considering a new strategy, thinking that they could improve on relying wholly upon the Spirit. They were attracted to being "perfected by the flesh."

The word "flesh" (σάρξ) here may be an allusion to circumcision, which involves a cutting of the flesh. Indeed, Jewett suggests that Paul's theology of "flesh" derived from the controversy over circumcision,[29] but this insight, though stimulating, is impossible to verify.[30] Certainly in this context the Galatians' reliance on the flesh manifests itself in their attraction to circumcision. As Betz says, "Ultimately, of course, Paul alludes to the rite of circumcision considered at present by the Galatians."[31]

The term "flesh" here is used in the technical Pauline sense, referring to reliance on the old Adam, the unregenerate person. The opposition between the Spirit and flesh represents the eschatological contrast between this age and the age to come (cf. 1:4), with the flesh representing the old age and the Spirit the age to come.[32] The age to come has penetrated this present evil age, and hence it does not make sense for the Galatians to turn back to the old age now that the new has arrived.

One could argue here that the issue in Galatians was not how to get into the people of God but how to stay in the people of God.[33] We must carefully sort out Paul's view in this matter and distinguish it from the view of the Judaizers. The false teachers were not giving advice about progress in the Christian life, for their view, as in Judaism, was that circumcision was required for *entrance* into the people of God.[34] Therefore, the Judaizers argued that those uncircumcised were not part of the covenant enacted by the Lord (Gen 17:9 – 14; Lev 12:3). The Judaizers argued that the Galatians must be circumcised to belong to the people of God.

Paul, however, believed that the Galatians were Christians because they had already received the Spirit. Hence, he frames the matter in terms of progress in the Christian life. In other words, Paul writes from his perspective; he was not even willing to grant the premise of the false teachers. He assumes that the Galatians are Christians, and thus he describes their desire to be circumcised as a misguided attempt to make progress in the Christian life on the basis of the flesh instead of the Spirit.

We see here as well that the Christian life follows the same course whether the issue is justification or sanctification. It is not as if justification is through the Spirit and by faith, and sanctification is by works and human effort. Both justification

---

29. Robert Jewett, *Paul's Anthropological Terms: A Study of Their Use in Conflict Settings* (Leiden: Brill, 1971), 96.

30. Cf. also Martyn, *Galatians*, 294.

31. Betz, *Galatians*, 134.

32. So Richard B. Gaffin Jr., *Resurrection and Redemption: A Study in Paul's Soteriology* (Phillipsburg, NJ: Presbyterian and Reformed, 1987), 111. See also here the work of W. B. Russell, "The Apostle Paul's Redemptive-Historical Argumentation in Galatians 5:13 – 26," *WTJ* 57 (1995): 333 – 57. Russell, however, overstates his view and unnecessarily diminishes the anthropological dimension of eschatology (so also Garlington, *Galatians*, 184).

33. So Gundry, "Grace, Works, and Staying Saved in Paul," 8 – 9; Fee, *Galatians*, 107. For this view, see also Cosgrove, who argues that the presenting issue in Galatians is not justification or what is required to enter the people of God, but the continued work of the Spirit in the lives of the Galatians (*Cross and the Spirit*, 2, 8 – 15, 32 – 35, 38 – 42, 49 – 51, 86). So also Scott J. Hafemann, "Paul and the Exile," 340, n. 29. Such a reading fails to see the fundamental nature of 2:15 – 21 in the argument, misreads 3:3, and misunderstands as well why circumcision was required (i.e., to enter the people of God).

34. So Nolland, "Uncircumcised Proselytes?" 173 – 94.

and sanctification are due to the Spirit's work and are the result of faith.[35]

3:4 Have you suffered so many things in vain — if indeed they are in vain? (τοσαῦτα ἐπάθετε εἰκῇ; εἴ γε καὶ εἰκῇ).

Another rhetorical question is fired from Paul's arsenal of arguments against the Galatians. Now he asks them as believers whether they have suffered so many things for nothing. The verb used here (πάσχω) could mean "experienced," as many commentators take it, rather than "suffered."[36] Words derive their meaning from context, and thus the reading "experienced" might be correct, and in this case Paul would be referring especially to the powerful work of the Spirit in their midst.

However, this word (πάσχω) elsewhere in the NT means "suffered."[37] Such a reading seems more likely since this is the usual NT meaning of the word. The reading "experienced" is often defended with the claim that the letter says nothing about the Galatians suffering,[38] but 4:29 suggests that they did experience persecution.[39] Further, suffering was a staple of Christian existence, and hence it seems probable that the Galatians were not spared from discrimination and verbal abuse for their newfound faith. What Paul asks here is whether that suffering was in vain, for if they renounced the gospel of Christ and received circumcision, their suffering as Christians had no purpose. Indeed, elsewhere in Paul those who receive the Spirit suffer; hence, there is a closer connection between suffering and the Spirit than is often acknowledged.[40]

Paul's argument turns a sharp corner. In 3:3 he assumes they are Christians and laments the foolishness of trying to progress according to the flesh. Now in 3:4 he contemplates the prospect of their receiving circumcision and concludes that if they do so, they would have suffered in vain. When Paul uses the language of vanity (εἰκῇ, cf. 1 Cor 15:2; Gal 4:11)[41] in soteriological contexts, he teaches that faith is futile if one does not persevere to the end. Failure to continue in the faith will lead to eschatological judgment.

Paul does not make a pronouncement on the fate of the Galatians here. Rather, he warns them about the dangers of succumbing to the blandishments of the Judaizers. Indeed, he closes the verses with a hypothetical statement: "if indeed they are in vain." Paul does not claim that the Galatians' sufferings *were* in vain. He leaves them with a condition. *If* they follow the Judaizers and renounce the gospel, their suffering as new Christians was for nothing. Paul hopes that his warning here will provoke them to reconsider and repent, so that they will obtain the full reward.

3:5 Therefore, does the one who supplies you with the Spirit and works miracles among you, do it by works of law or by hearing with faith?

---

35. Kwon denies that Paul speaks of the need to "continue" in the Spirit by saying that the comment is merely historical, denoting "the before and the after of the outbreak of the crisis" (*Eschatology*, 46–47). But Kwon's observation only works if Paul is teaching that the Galatians must start all over again. On the contrary, Paul does not rule out the legitimacy of their conversion but calls on them to "continue" in the way they started (cf. 5:7–10). Kwon does rightly see here that the Galatians must continue in the faith to receive an eschatological reward.

36. Betz, *Galatians*, 134; Longenecker, *Galatians*, 104; Martyn, *Galatians*, 285; Dunn, *Galatians*, 156; Ridderbos, *Galatians*, 115, n. 5; Fee, *Galatians*, 110.

37. So Lightfoot, *Galatians*, 135; cf. Wilhelm Michaelis,

"πάσχω," *TDNT*, 5:905; Bruce, *Galatians*, 150.

38. So Betz, *Galatians*, 134, n. 64; Silva, *Interpreting Galatians*, 58; Longenecker, *Galatians*, 104.

39. See here Ernst Baasland, "Persecution: A Neglected Feature in the Letter to the Galatians," *ST* 38 (1984): 135–50. See also Cummins, though it is less clear that Paul depicts the opponents to be like the Maccabean oppressors (*Crucified Christ*, 100–106).

40. So Wilson, *Curse of the Law*, 87–88. But against Wilson, it is not clear that the Galatians feared that their suffering placed them under God's curse (ibid., 91–92).

41. See also his use of the term "futility" (κένος) in 1 Cor 15:14; 2 Cor 6:1; Gal 2:2; Phil 2:16; 1 Thess 3:5.

(ὁ οὖν ἐπιχορηγῶν ὑμῖν τὸ πνεῦμα καὶ ἐνεργῶν δυνάμεις ἐν ὑμῖν, ἐξ ἔργων νόμου ἢ ἐξ ἀκοῆς πίστεως;). The paragraph is now summed up with its central theme and with one last rhetorical question. The powerful work of the Spirit has been evident among the Galatians. The present participle is interpreted by some as evidence that the charismatic and powerful work of the Spirit is ongoing,[42] but it may be that Paul describes the impact of his own ministry among the Galatians, for the present tense of the participle does not necessarily indicate ongoing action. The main point, in any case, is that God had given the Spirit to them,[43] and the presence of the Spirit had been manifested among them by works of power.

The dramatic work of the Spirit, however, was not due to their observance of works of law but their hearing the message of the gospel with faith. Since the Galatians have the Spirit, as we saw in 3:2, they are members of the new people of God. They are part of the family of Abraham, and hence they do not need to observe the Torah.

Theology in Application

Relying on Christ

As Christians we need to relearn the gospel every day. We are prone to wander, as the old hymn says, and hence we may act as if a spell has been cast over us. The Christian life is a battle to rely on the gospel, and even as Christians we are inclined to look to ourselves and trust in our own achievements rather than relying solely on the cross of Christ. In our counseling and our preaching and teaching we must summon people over and over to the cross of Christ and call them to look away from themselves and focus on Christ. We may slowly drift from the gospel, just as the Galatians did. The problems Paul addressed in Galatia remind us all that the Christian life cannot be lived on autopilot, that there is a daily struggle to grasp the gospel.

Perseverance in the Spirit

This text also teaches us that the new age has come because God has given us the eschatological Spirit promised in the OT. The Galatians are the people of the new covenant precisely because the Spirit had been poured out in their midst. Furthermore, the Spirit manifested himself in evident ways by doing miracles in their midst. The mark of the Christian community today continues to be the presence of the Spirit in power. Only those who have received the Spirit (Rom 8:9) truly belong to Christ.

We saw above that as believers we are weak and easily led astray by false gospels. Still, we are not left alone in the battle against the flesh. God has given us the Spirit so that by his power and his strength we are enabled to persevere to the end. Hence,

---

42. E.g., Betz, *Galatians*, 135; George, *Galatians*, 214, n. 17; Bruce, *Galatians*, 151. Against this, see Kwon, *Eschatology*, 38.

43. God is clearly the one who does the supplying here, not Paul. Against White, "Rhetoric and Reality in Galatians," 333. Aquinas defended the idea that Paul was the one who gave the Spirit in this verse (so Riches, *Galatians through the Centuries*, 147).

our initial steps of faith will not be in vain, for the Spirit that indwells us will empower us to the end.

Sanctification

One of the most important verses for the Christian life is verse 3. Many believers are taught that justification is by faith alone while sanctification is by faith and works, as if sanctification were a cooperative effort involving both ourselves and the Lord. Such a perspective may be misleading. Believers do not begin the Christian life by faith and through the Spirit and then continue it by works and through the flesh. Sanctification is lived out in the same way as justification (though it does not follow from this that justification and sanctification are the same thing, as too many claim today!). It is by faith alone and through the Spirit alone.

Such a view does not lead to the conclusion that good works are unnecessary, but all good works are the fruit of faith and evidence of the powerful work of the Spirit. Believers please God when they trust him for everything that comes their way, knowing that he has been faithful to forgive their sins and that he will provide everything they need. Paul argues here that progress in the Christian life does not differ from how we began the Christian life. In both instances the believer trusts God and does not rely on the flesh or on any native ability to produce good works.

So, what does sanctification by faith alone look like practically? As believers we must not steal or cheat on our taxes, but we may be tempted to do so when we feel anxious about our finances. But when we walk by faith and trust in the Holy Spirit, we are reminded that the Lord has promised to take care of us and supply all our needs. Therefore, we do not steal because we are trusting in God's provision.

We could say the same thing about sexual sin. Sexual pleasures are intense, but the Lord teaches us that sexual pleasure is to be restricted to marriage and that sexual sin is destructive (cf. Prov. 5:1 – 23; 1 Thess. 4:3 – 8). So, what does it mean to live by faith and the Holy Spirit in this area? We are not called upon to try as hard as we can to avoid sexual sin. Instead, we are called upon to trust God. He loves us, and if we trust him, we will believe that violating his command in this area will damage us and ruin us. Our obedience in this area, in other words, flows from our faith. The great hymn says "trust and obey," but it would be better to rephrase it, for those who trust will obey, and those who disobey show that they don't trust God's goodness or power.

Galatians 3:6 – 9

Literary Context

In 1:10 – 2:21 Paul argues that his gospel is authoritative and independent of the Jerusalem apostles. He received his gospel directly from God through a revelation of Jesus Christ. When the Jerusalem apostles heard his gospel, they ratified it and declared it to be true. The Pauline gospel is so authoritative that Paul rebuked Peter on the basis of it, and 2:15 – 21 explains the substance of the gospel, which is that righteousness is based on the cross of Christ, not via keeping the OT law. Therefore, those who believe in Jesus Christ are justified, not those who attempt to observe the OT law.

In 3:1 – 5 Paul turns directly to the Galatians. He begins by emphasizing that their own experience validates his gospel. They received the Spirit through faith alone, not by their observance of the law. Further, the way they began the Christian life is the way they should continue in it — by the power of the Spirit and in faith. Now in 3:6 – 9 Paul begins to establish his case from the OT, defending his theology in this paragraph from Gen 15:6 and 12:3. In both instances Paul endeavors to prove that believers are children of Abraham.

Main Idea

The main point of this text is reiterated two different ways in 3:7 and 9. The issue before the Galatians is the identity of Abraham's children. The Judaizers claim it is those who are circumcised. Paul counters that believers are the children of Abraham and have received the blessing of Abraham.

Translation

Galatians 3:6-9

6a	action	Just as *"Abraham believed God, and*
b	result *(of 6a)*	*it was counted to him as righteousness."* (Gen 15:6)
7a	inference *(of 6a-b)*	**Know,** therefore, **that those of faith,**
b	apposition *(to 7a)*	**these are the sons of Abraham.**
8a	series *(to 6a)*	And **the Scripture,** because it foresaw that God would justify the Gentiles by faith,
b	inference *(of 8a)*	**proclaimed** the good news beforehand to Abraham
c	content *(of 8b)*	that *"all nations would be blessed in you."* (Gen 12:3)
9	inference *(of 8a-c)*	So then, **those of faith are blessed with the believing Abraham.**

Structure

The paragraph begins with the words "just as" (καθώς), which is difficult to interpret. Is the conjunction loosely connected to the previous paragraph?[1] Or, is the paragraph more closely related to the previous one, so that Abraham is conceived of as having the Spirit? It seems unlikely that Paul would argue that Abraham had the Spirit since the Spirit is conceived of as a gift of the new age that has commenced in Christ. Hence, a looser connection is probably envisioned. Abraham is comparable to the Galatians in that both belonged to God's people by faith.

Abraham is introduced, of course, because he is vital to Paul's argument as the progenitor of Israel. Here Paul argues from Gen 15:6 that Abraham believed God, and *as a consequence* was declared to be in the right before God. The main point, then, follows as an inference in 3:7 (note the inferential "therefore" [ἄρα]). Since

---

1. So Betz, who sees it as an abbreviation of the phrase "just as it is written" (καθὼς γέγραπται) (*Galatians*, 140, n. 13), though Betz acknowledges this abbreviation is not found elsewhere. Longenecker thinks "just as" (καθώς) is used as an *exemplum*, but he does not provide parallel texts to justify his judgment (*Galatians*, 112). Lightfoot suggests that what is missing should be supplied by context, "Surely of faith: and so it was with Abraham" (*Galatians*, 136; so also Silva, *Interpreting Galatians*, 219; cf. also Burton, *Galatians*, 153; Bruce, *Galatians*, 152). Barrett says that the conjunction suggests that the opponents had used Gen 15:6, and Paul now supplies his interpretation ("The Allegory of Abraham," 6).

Abraham was justified by faith, it follows that those who believe, those who have faith, are members of Abraham's family.

Paul adduces a second, similar scriptural argument from Gen 12:3 and 18:18, quoting the great promise that all people groups will be blessed in Abraham. It is vital to observe that Paul quotes Gen 12:3 *after* Gen 15:6. Therefore, Gen 15:6 functions as the lens by which Gen 12:3 is interpreted. Indeed, Paul identifies the promise of universal blessing as the gospel in Gal 3:8, and he interprets this blessing in terms of justification by faith. The blessing of Abraham cannot be separated from those who are the children of Abraham. Paul draws an inference from 3:8 in 3:9 (note the inferential "therefore" [ὥστε]). Only those who have the faith of Abraham enjoy the blessing of Abraham.

Exegetical Outline

   I. Introduction: Desertion from Paul's Gospel Is Desertion from the Gospel (1:1 – 2:21)

  II. Paul's Gospel Defended from Experience and Scripture (3:1 – 4:11)

     A. Argument from Experience: Reception of Spirit by Means of Faith, Not Works (3:1 – 5)

     B. Argument from Scripture: Blessing of Abraham by Faith (3:6 – 14)

➭   **1. Members of Abraham's family by faith (3:6 – 9)**

        a. Righteousness as a consequence of Abraham's faith (3:6)

        b. Conclusion: faith needed to belong to Abraham's family (3:7)

        c. The gospel of universal blessing through Abraham (3:8)

        d. Conclusion: faith needed for Abraham's blessing (3:9)

      2. Curse of law removed only in Christ (3:10 – 14)

Explanation of the Text

3:6 Just as "Abraham believed God, and it was counted to him as righteousness" (καθὼς Ἀβραὰμ ἐπίστευσεν τῷ θεῷ, καὶ ἐλογίσθη αὐτῷ εἰς δικαιοσύνην). Paul teaches here that Abraham's right standing with God was a result of his trust in God. The conjunction "just as" (καθώς), links 3:6 with 3:1 – 5. Scholars dispute the significance of the connection between 3:1 – 5 and 3:6. Can we infer from the use of the conjunction that Paul argues that

Abraham received the Spirit just as the Galatians have? Can we go further and infer from this that the term "righteousness" is not merely forensic but also includes the idea of transformation since those who are righteous have also received the Spirit?

Such conclusions overread the connection between 3:1 – 5 and 3:6. Elsewhere in Paul and the rest of the NT, the gift of the Spirit is considered to be a gift of the eschaton.[2] This is not

---

2. See James M. Hamilton Jr., *God's Indwelling Presence: The Holy Spirit in the Old and New Testaments* (NACSBT; Nashville: Broadman & Holman, 2006).

to say, of course, that the Spirit was not active in the OT, but nowhere else in the OT or the NT do we find the claim that Abraham had the Spirit. It seems the connection between 3:1 – 5 and 3:6 is loose. The point of comparison is that both Abraham and the Galatians exercised faith.[3] It also follows, then, that it is too ambitious to derive a definition of the term "righteousness" by the use of this conjunction. Finding a transformative meaning for righteousness must be established on other grounds. Indeed, I will argue shortly that the context supports a forensic meaning instead.

It is also vital to see that Paul's argument must get to Abraham to settle the matter at hand with the Galatians. The Judaizers almost certainly appealed to Abraham and circumcision (Gen 17:9 – 14) to support their argument that circumcision was required to enter the people of God. Even if the false teachers did not cite Abraham, he is crucial for Paul's argument, for he was the father of the Jewish people and the one to whom the saving promises were made.

Indeed, Jewish tradition emphasized Abraham's obedience rather than his faith. For example, 1 Macc 2:52 says, "Was not Abraham found faithful when tested, and it was reckoned to him as righteousness?" (NRSV).[4] The sacrifice of Isaac recorded in Genesis 22 is merged in 1 Maccabees with Gen 15:6, with the result that Abraham's obedience rather than his faith is featured. The same emphasis on Abraham's faithfulness and obedience emerges in Sir 44:19 – 21:

> Abraham was the great father of a multitude of nations,
> and no one has been found like him in glory.
> He kept the law of the Most High,
> and entered into a covenant with him;
> he certified the covenant in his flesh,
> and when he was tested he proved faithful.
> Therefore the Lord assured him with an oath
> that the nations would be blessed through his offspring;
> that he would make him as numerous as the dust of the earth,
> and exalt his offspring like the stars,
> and give them an inheritance from sea to sea
> and from the Euphrates to the ends of the earth. (NRSV)

Sirach stresses that the blessing of Abraham was given to him because of his obedience. In doing so he reflects, in part, the message of the OT itself (Gen 22:17 – 18; 26:5). What is missing, however, is the crucial role that faith played in Abraham's life.

Such a one-sided focus on Abraham's obedience easily leads to a synergistic understanding that does not accord with the Pauline reading.[5] We read in *Jub.* 23:10, "For Abraham was perfect in all of his actions with the Lord and was pleasing through righteousness all of the days of his life."[6] Abraham's obedience, particularly in the sacrifice

---

3. See Sam K. Williams, "Justification and the Spirit in Galatians," *JSNT* 29 (1987): 92 – 95. Williams argues that justification and the reception of the Spirit are closely connected in Paul, but he also acknowledges that Paul does not say that Abraham received the Spirit, and that justification and life in the Spirit are distinct conceptually (97, 100, n. 13). Still, he rightly concludes that justification necessarily leads to a transformed life, according to Paul (98).

4. De Roo argues that 1 Macc 2:52; Sir 44:19 – 21; and 4Q225 interpret Gen 15:6 as referring to Abraham's *faithfulness* rather than his faith (*Works of Law*), 76, 101 – 2.

5. Hanson argues that Abraham's relationship to the law is portrayed variously in Jewish literature. In some instances (Philo and *Psalms of Solomon*), God's covenant rather than Abraham's obedience receives priority. But in other cases the focus is on obedience to the law. See Hansen, *Abraham in Galatians*, 175 – 99. De Roo argues that the same literature teaches that Abraham was elected because of his obedience (*Works of Law*, 105 – 7).

6. See *The Old Testament Pseudepigrapha: Expansions of the "Old Testament" and Legends, Wisdom and Philosophical Literature, Prayers, Psalms, and Odes, Fragments of Lost Judeo-Hellenistic Works*, vol. 2 (ed. James H. Charlesworth; trans. O. S. Wintermute; Garden City, NY: Doubleday, 1985), 100.

of Isaac, was a common theme in Jewish writings (*Jub.* 16.28; 17.15 – 18.19; 19.8; 24.11; *2 Bar.* 57.1 – 2; *m. ʾAbot* 5:3; Philo, *Abraham* 35 §§191 – 199; Josephus, *Ant.* 1.13.1 – 2 §§223 – 25; 1.13.4 §§233 – 36; Psuedo-Philo, *Bib. Ant.* 40.2; 4 Macc 14:20).

Paul does not discount Abraham's obedience (cf. Rom 4). Nevertheless, in contrast to Jewish Second Temple literature, Paul puts the accent on Abraham's faith.[7] That faith was the fundamental reality of his life. Genesis 15:6 takes center stage in Paul's understanding of Abraham. In Gen 15 Abraham wondered if his only heir would be his servant, Eliezer. The Lord promised him that his offspring would be as numerous as the stars of heaven. Abraham responded to that stunning promise by *believing* in what the Lord said. He did not perform any astonishing works for God but trusted in him. Genesis 15 concludes with the Lord himself, symbolized by fire, passing through the pieces of the animals alone, demonstrating that the covenant would be fulfilled by the Lord alone. Hence, the entirety of Gen 15 focuses on the work of the Lord and Abraham's trust in what the Lord would do on his behalf.

The second clause in 3:6 should be construed as signifying result. As a consequence of Abraham's faith, he was counted as righteous before God. The word "righteousness" (δικαιοσύνη) here does not denote ethical transformation or the infusion of righteousness. Instead, it has a forensic meaning, as the context makes clear. Since Abraham was counted as righteous by believing, there is no idea here of an ethical transformation within him.

The word "counted" (ἐλογίσθη) points to the same conclusion. The verb "count" (λογίζομαι) can refer to something that is reckoned to someone. For example, Phinehas's zeal in killing the Hebrew and the Midianite woman "was counted to him as righteousness" (Ps 106:31 ESV) (ἐλογίσθη αὐτῷ εἰς δικαιοσύνην). Phinehas was counted righteous because he was righteous. In Gen 15:6, however, righteousness is reckoned to Abraham even though it does not belong to him.[8] Abraham was counted as righteous by faith, even though he was not inherently righteous. Righteousness was a gift given to Abraham by virtue of his believing.

Such a reading fits with Paul's explanation of the same text in Rom 4:2 – 5. Abraham was counted as righteous before God even though he was ungodly.[9] Nor does Paul suggest that Abraham's faith *was* his righteousness, as if faith could be considered to be a kind of work that makes one righteous before God. Rather, faith is counted as righteousness because it unites believers to Christ, who is their righteousness.[10] Such a conclusion fits with one of Paul's major themes in Galatians, i.e., that the Galatians' righteousness derives from the cross of Christ.

3:7 Know, therefore, that those of faith, these are the sons[11] of Abraham (γινώσκετε ἄρα ὅτι οἱ ἐκ πίστεως, οὗτοι υἱοί εἰσιν Ἀβραάμ). The particle "therefore" (ἄρα) should be understood

---

7. See also here Longenecker, *Galatians*, 113 – 14.

8. See Brian Vickers, *Jesus' Blood and Righteousness: Paul's Theology of Imputation* (Wheaton: Crossway, 2006), 81 – 83; Fung, *Galatians*, 135. Against Garlington, *Galatians*, 189 – 90. On imputation, see also Martin Luther, *Lectures on Galatians 1535: Chapters 1 – 4*, Vol. 26 of *Luther's Works* (ed. Jarislov Pelikan; St. Louis: Concordia, 1963), 229 – 34.

9. Therefore, justification includes a past reality for both Abraham and the Galatians (contra Kwon, *Eschatology*, 60 – 61).

10. See D. A. Carson, "The Vindication of Imputation: On Fields of Discourse and Semantic Fields," in *Justification: What's at Stake in Current Debates* (ed. Mark Husbands and Daniel J. Treier; Downers Grove, IL: IVP, 2004), 46 – 78. William Perkins held the same position (see Riches, *Galatians through the Centuries*, 163).

11. The word "sons" is intended to refer to both males and females. The word is usually retained in the commentary to conform to Pauline usage.

as inferential here, so that a conclusion is drawn from 3:6.[12] Those who have the faith of Abraham are identified as the children of Abraham. The verb "know" (γινώσκετε) could be an indicative or an imperative, and the meaning does not change dramatically on either scenario.[13] It seems more likely that we have an imperative here, for Paul forcefully calls on the Galatians to realize a truth that has presently evaded them.[14] What is required to be part of Abraham's family, to be counted as his sons? Not circumcision or the other works required by the law. Those who belong to Abraham's family believe just as Abraham did, for Abraham lived before the law was even given. Therefore, his faith was what constituted him as righteous before God. The Galatians, then, do not need to be circumcised to be Abraham's sons. They are already his children if their faith is in Christ Jesus.

It should also be noted that we have a powerful argument supporting the objective genitive reading "faith in Christ Jesus" here. The phrase "those of faith" (οἱ ἐκ πίστεως) is found here and is repeated in 3:9 ("those of faith are blessed"). Furthermore, 3:8 says that "God [justifies] the Gentiles by faith" (ἐκ πίστεως δικαιοῖ τὰ ἔθνη ὁ θεός), which should either be translated that "God justifies the Gentiles by faith," or "God justifies the Gentiles by faithfulness," referring in this latter instance to the faithfulness of Christ. We have a major clue, however, that in every instance Paul refers to "faith" rather than "faithfulness." That clue is the verb "believed" (ἐπίστευσεν) in 3:6. The verb leaves no doubt that the focus is on Abraham's *believing*, not his *faithfulness*.[15]

Moreover, as we noted above, Paul draws a *conclusion* from 3:6 in 3:7.[16] Since Abraham was righteous by believing, it follows that "those of faith" (οἱ ἐκ πίστεως) are also Abraham's children. But then the phrase "those of faith" must refer to those who believe in the same way Abraham believed. Paul's argument would veer off course if he suddenly discussed "faithfulness."[17] No, the Galatians are Abraham's sons if they *believe* as he did. Indeed, every use of "faith" (πίστις) in this context should be interpreted similarly. And it also suggests that the "faith in Christ" phrases in 2:16 and 2:20 should be interpreted the same way. Paul labors to emphasize that it is *faith* and *faith alone* that makes one a child of Abraham.[18]

3:8 And the Scripture, because it foresaw that God would justify the Gentiles by faith, proclaimed the good news beforehand to Abraham that "all nations would be blessed in you" (προϊδοῦσα δὲ ἡ γραφὴ ὅτι ἐκ πίστεως δικαιοῖ τὰ ἔθνη ὁ θεός, προευηγγελίσατο τῷ Ἀβραὰμ

---

12. The inferential conjunction indicates that sonship is the main point in 3:6 – 7. Contra Kwon, *Eschatology*, 79 – 86. Kwon overrides the grammar here (an inferential connection!) to support his contention that realized eschatology is a myth in Galatians.

13. In support of the indicative, see Lightfoot, *Galatians*, 137; Longenecker, *Galatians*, 114; Martyn, *Galatians*, 299.

14. So Betz, who defends the imperative because "it conforms to the parallels in didactic literature" (*Galatians*, 141). Cf. also Bruce, *Galatians*, 155; Dunn, *Galatians*, 162.

15. So too, Hansen, *Abraham in Galatians*, 111.

16. Rightly H. W. Johnson, "Paradigm of Abraham," 190, 192.

17. Caneday rightly sees that Paul is concerned about "spiritual lineage," but he still breaks the most natural connection forged by "therefore" (ἄρα) between 3:6 – 7, which

informs us *how* one becomes a child of Abraham ("Faithfulness of Jesus Christ," 198 – 99).

18. Howard argues that "those of faith" are those who benefit from God's act of faithfulness, but this seems intolerably awkward and ignores the flow of argument between 3:6 and 3:7 (*Paul: Crisis in Galatia*, 57; rightly Hong, *Law in Galatians*, 127 – 28). Hays, on the basis of the citation of Hab 2:4 in 3:11, argues for a reference to the Messiah's faith, seeing Abraham's faithfulness as a foreshadowing of Christ's faithfulness (*Faith of Jesus Christ*, 200 – 202). The interpretation has at least two flaws. First, it is unlikely that 3:11 refers to the Messiah's faith (see commentary on 3:11). Second, even if 3:11 had that meaning, it is exegetically implausible to derive the meaning of "those of faith" in 3:7 from a *later* text. See here Hong, *Law in Galatians*, 128 – 29.

ὅτι Ἐνευλογηθήσονται ἐν σοὶ πάντα τὰ ἔθνη). God promised Abraham that all peoples would be blessed through him. Here Paul argues that this universal blessing is secured through the gospel, and that Gentiles receive this blessing when they are declared to stand in the right before God through their faith in Jesus Christ.

Paul's quotation from the OT represents a merging of Gen 12:3 and 18:18:[19]

> Gen 12:3: "all peoples [tribes] on earth will be blessed through you" (ἐνευλογηθήσονται ἐν σοὶ πᾶσαι αἱ φυλαὶ τῆς γῆς)
>
> Gen 18:18: "all nations will be blessed in him" (ἐνευλογηθήσονται ἐν αυτῷ πάντα τὰ ἔθνη)

By referring to "all nations" Paul demonstrates that it was God's intention from the beginning to bless the Gentiles, as long as they exercised the same kind of faith as Abraham. The Gentiles receive the blessing of Abraham provided that they believe like Abraham.

Hays supports quite a different interpretation. He contends that the words "in you" (ἐν σοί) refer to the faithfulness of Abraham.[20] Abraham points forward to Christ's faithfulness, so that the Gentiles are not blessed by virtue of their faith but Abraham's. There are at least two problems with this reading. (1) The verb "he believed (ἐπίστευσεν) in 3:6, which introduces the paragraph in 3:6, indicates that the focus is on Abraham *believing*, not his faithfulness. (2) Verse 9 teaches that Gentiles are blessed "with" (σύν) the

believing Abraham, not on the basis of Abraham's faith or faithfulness.

Hays is partially right, for Paul's argument here cannot be restricted to Abraham as a paradigm for faith.[21] Abraham's faith also has a redemptive-historical character. The promise that all nations will be blessed in Abraham has a future dimension (Gen 12:3) and points ultimately to Jesus Christ (cf. Gen 3:15; Gal 3:16). Abraham put his faith in the promise of God, and hence his faith was not merely an abstract belief in God but belief in God's promise, which culminates in the coming of Jesus Christ.[22]

The order in which Paul cites the OT here is also instructive. We would expect him to quote Gen 12:3 first and then Gen 15:6. Instead the citations are reversed. As in Rom 4 (cf. Rom 4:2),[23] Gen 15:6 is the foundational text, indicating that Gen 12:3 (and 18:18) must be read through the lens of 15:6. Genesis 12:3 promises that all nations will be blessed in Abraham, and Paul identifies this promissory word as the gospel proclaimed to Abraham in advance.[24] But it is precisely here that Gen 15:6 plays its axiomatic role, for in giving this promise (12:3) to Abraham, Scripture foresaw that God would declare the Gentiles right in his sight by faith.

Nothing in the words of Gen 12:3 forecasted that Gentiles would be blessed in Abraham by believing. Indeed, 12:1 – 5 emphasizes Abraham's *obedience* in *going* to the Land of Promise. Nevertheless, Paul sees in 12:3 a promise of righteousness by faith,

---

19. So Bruce, *Galatians*, 156. Wilcox says it is a "mixed quotation." So Max Wilcox, "'Upon the Tree' — Deut 21:22 – 23 in the New Testament," *JBL* 96 (1977): 96. Collins argues that Gen 22:18 and 26:4 are included as well. C. John Collins, "Galatians 3:16: What Kind of Exegete Was Paul?" *TynBul* 54 (2003): 80 – 81.

20. Hays, *Faith of Jesus Christ*, 203 – 6.

21. See the helpful discussion in H. W. Johnson, "Paradigm of Abraham," 197 – 98.

22. As Jan Lambrecht says, "Abraham's faith too was not without 'christological' content. For he believed in the *promise*

of God (cf. 3,16 – 18 and 21 – 22) and this promise attained its fulfillment precisely in Jesus Christ (3,16). This means that the faith of Abraham and that of the Christians may not be so radically distinguished." *Pauline Studies: Collected Essays by Jan Lambrecht* (BETL 115; Leuven: Leuven Univ. Press, 1994), 287.

23. In Romans, however, Paul also pins his argument on Gen 15:6 preceding Gen. 17 (the circumcision of Abraham). Interestingly, that argument is lacking in Galatians.

24. Against Kwon, who argues that the promise and blessing of justification must be kept distinct in Galatians (*Eschatology*, 103 – 7).

for he interprets it in light of the blessing given to Abraham in 15:6, and hence the Gentiles are not justified through *doing* but by *believing*. As we saw earlier, the key verb "he believed" (ἐπίστευσεν) in Gal 3:6 helps unpack the meaning of the phrase "by faith" (ἐκ πίστεως), suggesting that it means "faith" rather than "faithfulness." Before Paul even cites Gen 12:3, he provides the interpretation of its meaning, so that we read the promise of Abraham in terms of justification by faith.

Nor should we think that the Pauline meaning contradicts Gen 12:1 – 5, even though it calls attention to Abraham's obedience, for Abraham's obedience, according to Paul, Hebrews (Heb 11:8), and James (Jas 2:14 – 26), flows from faith. The prophetic quality of Scripture is also featured in this verse, for it "foresaw" (προϊδοῦσα) and "proclaimed the good news beforehand" (προευηγγελίσατο). Scripture is personified here, so that what Scripture says is what God himself says.[25]

3:9 So then, those of faith are blessed with the believing Abraham (ὥστε οἱ ἐκ πίστεως εὐλογοῦνται σὺν τῷ πιστῷ Ἀβραάμ). The word "therefore" (or, "so then") (ὥστε) is inferential, drawing a conclusion from 3:8. Genesis 12:3 promised that all nations would be blessed in Abraham,

and in Gal 3:8 Paul explains that this blessing becomes a reality when Gentiles are justified by faith. Hence, Paul draws the conclusion here that those who believe enjoy the same blessing that the believing Abraham did.

The Judaizers claimed that the Galatians must be circumcised to become part of Abraham's family and to receive the blessing of Abraham. The two inferential statements, in 3:7 and 3:9, which are parallel in this text, attack both views of the false teachers. The Galatians became part of the family of Abraham when they believed as Abraham did (3:7). *And* the Galatians enjoyed the blessing of Abraham when they believed like Abraham (3:9). The construction "the believing Abraham" (τῷ πιστῷ Ἀβραάμ) could refer to Abraham's *faithfulness* rather than his *faith*. But as we have already argued, such a reading is unlikely contextually, for the paragraph was introduced with Abraham's believing (ἐπίστευσεν), not his faithfulness (3:6). Therefore, what Paul emphasizes here is that the Galatians are blessed *with* (σύν) the believing Abraham. He does not say that they are blessed *in* or *through* Abraham. Indeed, the entire paragraph is repetitive intentionally, stressing that faith makes one a child of Abraham and allows one to receive the blessing of Abraham.

Theology in Application

The Good News of the Gospel

The great Reformation teaching that justification, being right before God, is by faith alone is clearly taught in this text. Abraham was not justified on the basis of his obedience to God. He was declared to be right before God when he believed God's promise. His righteousness came not by working *for* God but by believing *in* God.

The same is true for all of Abraham's genuine children. Right standing with God comes from receiving what God has given us in Christ. This message is the greatest news of all, for Luther was on target in saying that we are *simul justus et peccator*

---

25. See the programmatic essay of B. B. Warfield, "'It Says:' 'Scripture Says:' 'God Says,'" in *The Inspiration and* *Authority of the Bible* (Philadelphia: Presbyterian and Reformed, 1970), 299 – 348.

(justified and at the same time a sinner). As Christians we are aware of the continuing presence of sin in our lives. There is never an excuse for sin, and yet even the most mature Christians continue to sin in multiple ways (Jas 3:2). If we claim that such is not true of our lives, then we do not know ourselves as God knows us. When we realize how far short we fall as believers, the good news that we are justified by faith alone is a great comfort to us, for our righteousness does not reside in ourselves but in Christ risen and crucified.

We need to listen, really listen to the gospel. What messages are you listening to? You can read the Bible and not hear the gospel! The devil may deceive us by telling us:

> You are no good.
> You are a failure.
> You are the greatest.

May we truly listen to the good news of the gospel and hear it with faith. Luther tells the story somewhere of a physician who killed himself because he became convinced that Christ was accusing him before the Father. How tragic, for this thought that battered this doctor's mind was not from God but from Satan. Christ does not accuse us before the Father but pleads for us on the basis of his shed blood. If you think God is condemning you, you are not meditating on the cross and the forgiveness offered to us in Christ.

What a great comfort this truth is, for we are often consumed by our performance. Remarkably, if we feel superior or inferior to others, we are guilty of pride. If we feel superior, we are guilty of pride because we think we are better than other people. If we feel inferior, we are guilty of pride because we can hardly bear the thought that we are worse than other people. We don't want others to see how weak we are and so we blush with shame.

We can apply this to other areas as well. Moral persons take pride in how good they are, that they (unlike others) live virtuous lives. But a person who flouts moral norms may be proud too. They may boast that that are not limited by silly rules like the rest of us. How subtle pride is. We can even become proud of the fact that we are much more sensitive to our pride than others! Our only hope is the gospel, for there we rest on what Christ has done for us instead of boasting in ourselves.

One Way of Salvation in Both Testaments

It is also important to see that righteousness by faith is taught in both the OT and the NT. It is not as if OT saints were right with God on the basis of their works, while NT saints are righteous by faith. Paul argues clearly here that Abraham was justified by faith. Therefore, salvation in both the OT and the NT is by faith alone. There is only one way of salvation.

OT saints, of course, looked forward to the promise, whereas NT believers look back on what Christ accomplished in his death and resurrection. Still, Christ's death and resurrection are the basis of salvation for all. In the OT the sacrifices pointed forward to and anticipated the death of Jesus Christ. OT saints understood that God's promises remained unfulfilled, but at the very least they grasped through the sacrifices that atonement was needed for sin and that the Lord had provided such forgiveness. Perhaps some of them understood that such sacrifices pointed forward to a greater sacrifice. In any case, they were justified by faith and the atonement provided by the Lord.

Faith Is Not a Work That Renders Us Righteous

Finally, it is important theologically to see that Abraham's faith does not constitute his righteousness. Faith cannot be equated with a work that renders one righteous before God. Instead, faith justifies because it unites one with Christ, who is the righteousness of believers. Faith unites believers with Christ, who took the curse on himself for believers (3:13). This is just another way of saying that righteousness is found in Christ alone. Faith is fundamentally receptive and depends on Christ. Such an observation fits with the centrality of the cross in Galatians, for one of the major themes in Galatians is that righteousness is not obtained through circumcision, but only through the cross of Christ.

Why is it important to say that faith is not our righteousness? If it were our righteousness, we would be inclined to boast of our faith. We would subtly think, "At least I was smart enough or virtuous enough to believe." But the gospel does not grant us any credit for believing. We are saved by the imputed righteousness of Christ. Faith saves us because it unites us with Christ, not because our faith is a virtue we can boast in. Luther summarizes the centrality of faith:

> It is a further function of faith that it honors him whom it trusts with the most reverent and highest regard since it considers him truthful and trustworthy. There is no other honor equal to the estimate of truthfulness with which we honor him whom we trust. Could we ascribe to a man anything greater than truthfulness and righteousness and perfect goodness? On the other hand, there is no way in which we can show greater contempt for a man than to regard him as false and wicked and to be suspicious of him, as when we do not trust him.... The very highest worship of God is this that we ascribe to him truthfulness, righteousness, and whatever else should be ascribed to one who is trusted.[26]

We know from everyday life that faith honors the one who is trusted. If you trust your auto mechanic, you honor his integrity. If your coach calls a play and you make

---

26. Martin Luther, "The Freedom of the Christian," in *Three Treatises* (trans. W. A. Lambert; rev. Harold J. Grimm; Philadelphia: Fortress, 1970), 284 – 85.

a scene in front of the crowd so that it is evident that you think the coach's play call is ridiculous, you dishonor your coach.[27] If your doctor diagnoses you with a disease and prescribes medicine, you call into question the doctor's competence if you fail to follow his advice. Faith honors God because it considers him to be trustworthy. So, when the Lord tells us that human anger doesn't produce God's righteousness (Jas 1:20), we show our trust in him by forsaking anger. We are persuaded that God himself has told us that anger will not advance his cause in the world. So, our obedience to him flows from our faith in him.

27. I heard this illustration orally from John Piper.

Galatians 3:10 – 14

Literary Context

Virtually all agree that this paragraph is one of the most important in Galatians. It comes as no surprise, then, that it is also the subject of vigorous debate. Paul began this new segment of the letter by contending that the Galatians belong to God's people because they have received the Spirit (3:1 – 5). He then turned to the OT (3:6 – 14) to defend the view that the Galatians are members of Abraham's family.

The argument in 3:10 – 14 is closely joined to the previous paragraph (3:6 – 9). Paul has just finished an argument in which he contends that the family of Abraham has the faith of Abraham. More precisely, those who *believe* like Abraham participate in the blessing of Abraham. The promise that all nations will be blessed in Abraham (Gen 12:3) has now reached its fulfillment in the justification of Gentiles by faith. Just as Abraham was declared to be in the right before God by faith, so too Gentiles who put their faith in what God has done for them by the cross and resurrection of Jesus Christ are in a right relation with God. The term used to designate this right relation with God is *blessing* (εὐλογ- word group) in 3:8 – 9.

Verses 10 – 14 move the argument in a fresh direction and function as the antithesis to 3:6 – 9. Faith is the pathway to *blessing*, but adherence to the law will lead to a *curse*. The focus in 3:8 – 9 is the Abrahamic *blessing*, but in 3:10 – 13 Paul reflects on the opposite state of affairs, on the *curse* that lies on those who rely on the law for justification. The word "for" (γάρ) at the beginning of 3:10 joins the paragraph commencing here with the paragraph that has just concluded. We can summarize the argument as follows. "Those who trust in God are blessed with the believing Abraham" (3:9). Because faith is the pathway to blessing, it follows that those who rely on the works of law to obtain a right relationship with God are under a curse (3:10).

> I. Introduction: Desertion from Paul's Gospel Is Desertion from the Gospel (1:1 – 2:21)
> II. Paul's Gospel Defended from Experience and Scripture (3:1 – 4:11)
>   A. Argument from Experience: Reception of Spirit by Means of Faith, Not Works (3:1 – 5)
>   B. Argument from Scripture: Blessing of Abraham by Faith (3:6 – 14)
>   1. Members of Abraham's Family by Faith (3:6 – 9)
>   ➡ **2. Curse of Law Removed Only in Christ (3:10 – 14)**
>   C. Argument from Salvation History: Priority of Abrahamic Covenant and Temporary Nature of Mosaic Covenant (3:15 – 4:11)

Main Idea

Paul's main point in the passage is found in 3:14. He argues that in Christ Jesus Gentiles enjoy the blessing of Abraham and that the blessing of Abraham is nothing other than the promise of the Spirit (cf. the emphasis on the Spirit in 3:1 – 5). In 3:10 – 13 he explains why the blessing of Abraham can be obtained only in Christ. Trying to obtain the blessing by "works of law" fails, for the end result will only be a curse since all transgress God's law. The curse of the law is removed only by the cross of Christ, and thus faith is the pathway to blessing.

Translation

(See next page.)

Structure

Paul continues to defend his case from the OT in this text.[1] He begins with the assertion that all those who rely on the law for justification are cursed. He provides the reason ("for," [γάρ]) for this assertion in 3:10b-c by citing Deut 27:26 (supplemented with Deut 28:58), which maintains that those who do not keep the law are cursed. A new but related argument is given in 3:11 (marked by the postpositive "and" [δέ]): justification cannot be obtained by keeping the law. The validity of this assertion is supported by the citation of Hab 2:4 in 3:11b, where the righteous are said to live by faith.

In 3:12, Paul secures his argument with the third assertion, also introduced with "and" (δέ): justification by faith and by law are incompatible. He defends this

---

1. Longenecker argues that Paul's exegesis violates the rules of historical exegesis. He also proposes that Paul responds to misinterpretations from the false teachers (*Galatians*, 110). By way of contrast, I would argue that Paul's exegesis represents a profound and exegetically valid way of reading the OT.

Galatians 3:10-14

10a	assertion	For **as many as are of works of law are under a curse.**
b	basis	For it is written,
c	result	"*Cursed is everyone who does not remain in all the things written in the book of the law so that he does them.*" (Deut 27:26)
11a	assertion	And **that no one is justified by means of the law before God is clear**
b	basis	because
		"*the righteous shall live by faith.*" (Hab 2:4)
12a	assertion	And **the law is not of faith,**
b	contrast	but instead,
		"*the one who does the commandments shall live by means of them.*" (Lev 18:5)
13a	assertion	**Christ redeemed us from the curse of the law**
b	means	by becoming a curse for us,
c	basis (of 13a-b)	for it is written,
		"*Cursed is everyone who hangs on a tree,*" (Deut 21:23)
14a	purpose (of 13a)	so that the blessing of Abraham might come in Christ Jesus to the Gentiles,
b	restatement (of 14a)	so that we should receive the promise of the Spirit through faith.

assertion by quoting Lev 18:5, which shows that one who depends on the law for justification lives on the basis of the law. Therefore, faith is excluded as the pathway for blessing. In other words, vv. 10 – 12 contain three assertions that build to a climax, showing that law and faith are incompatible, and they support the main thesis, namely, those who rely on the law in order to be justified are cursed.

Verses 13 – 14, then, function by way of *contrast* to vv. 10 – 12. Somewhat surprisingly Paul does not use an adversative conjunction to mark the disjunction here. Perhaps he omitted the conjunction to emphasize "Christ," since that is the first word in v. 13. If the law brings a curse, the only way for the curse to be removed is by the cross of Christ. Hence, Paul asserts in v. 13 that Christ redeemed his people from the law's curse. Paul explains the means by which the curse is removed in v. 13b: Christ became a curse for his people. The OT support for this is Deut 21:23, which says that one who hangs on a tree is cursed. The central theme of v. 13 is Christ's redemption of his people.

Why did Christ redeem them? God's intention is articulated in two purpose clauses in v. 14 ("so that" [ἵνα]). He redeemed his people so that the blessing promised to Abraham would become a reality in the lives of Gentiles. Verse 14b most likely restates the blessing of Abraham. Hence, it does not introduce a new purpose clause but is coordinate with the purpose clause in v. 14a (see below). In other words, the blessing of Abraham can also be described as the promised gift of the Holy Spirit.

Exegetical Outline

II. Paul's Gospel Defended from Experience and Scripture (3:1 – 4:11)

  A. Argument from Experience: Reception of Spirit by Means of Faith, Not Works (3:1 – 5)

  B. Argument from Scripture: Blessing of Abraham by Faith (3:6 – 14)

   1. Members of Abraham's family by faith (3:6 – 9)

➡   **2. Curse of law removed only in Christ (3:10 – 14)**

     a. Those who rely on the law are cursed (3:10 – 12)

       i. Because one must obey the law perfectly (3:10)

       ii. Because justification is by faith, not the law (3:11)

       iii. Because the law and faith are incompatible (3:12)

     b. Those who rely on the cross of Christ are blessed (3:13 – 14)

       i. Because Christ redeemed believers from the law's curse (3:13)

       ii. Therefore, believers receive Abraham's blessing (3:14)

Explanation of the Text

3:10a For as many as are of works of law are under a curse (ὅσοι γὰρ ἐξ ἔργων νόμου εἰσὶν ὑπὸ κατάραν εἰσίν). Verse 10a contains the assertion that as many as are of works of law are cursed, which functions as a contrast with the blessing belonging to those who have the faith of Abraham (3:6 – 9). The main purpose in this text is to demonstrate that Gentiles receive the *blessing* of Abraham in Christ Jesus. From the beginning of this paragraph Paul is driving to that conclusion enunciated in 3:14. Conversely, those who rely on the Torah are *cursed*, and hence Paul begins with an assertion: "For as many as are of the works of law are under a curse." We must recall here what was argued (see 2:16) regarding the phrase "works of law" (ἔργα νόμου). Paul refers here to the deeds commanded by the law.[2]

3:10b-c For it is written, "Cursed is everyone who does not remain in all the things written in the book of the law so that he does them" (γέγραπται γὰρ ὅτι Ἐπικατάρατος πᾶς ὃς οὐκ ἐμμένει πᾶσιν τοῖς γεγραμμένοις ἐν τῷ βιβλίῳ τοῦ νόμου τοῦ ποιῆσαι αὐτά). Paul now gives the reason why those who are of works of law are cursed. They stand under a curse because of their failure to keep all that the law requires. Before defending this interpretation in more detail, it should be noted that Paul's attack on the law stands in contrast to what we find in Judaism, where we read, "By three things is the world sustained: by the Law, by the [Temple-] service, and by deeds of loving-kindness" (*m. ʾAbot* 1:2). And *m. ʾAbot* 6:7 says, "Great is the Law, for it gives life to them that practice it both in this world and the world to come."[3]

Verse 10b explains why the curse lies on those who rely on works of law. The "for" (γάρ) introducing v. 10b indicates that we have a reason or basis for the assertion in v. 10a. The reason is summed up in the citation from Deut 27:26. Paul likely alludes to Deut 28:58 as well, which also emphasizes doing "all the words" written in the book of the law ("to do all the words of this law, which are written in this book"). We should note at this point that the paragraph before us condenses in a tightly packed manner Paul's exegesis of OT texts relative to justification. We get a glimpse, presumably, of the kinds of arguments that Paul used in synagogues and other venues when debating with opponents.

As is often the case in Paul, the text tradition of Deut 27:26 fits the LXX rather than the MT. This is especially apparent with the addition of the word "all" (πᾶσιν), which is lacking in the MT. Furthermore, the allusion to Deut 28:58 universalizes what Paul teaches here since it refers to the entire book of the law. Hays says, "The change in wording has the effect of expanding the reference to the canonical Law of Moses as a whole."[4]

The citation from Deuteronomy 27 occurs in a context of blessing and cursing, in which the blessings and cursings of the covenant are rehearsed. In particular, Deut 27:26 occurs in a section in which Moses exhorted the twelve tribes to stand on Mount Gerizim and Mount Ebal to declare covenantal blessings and cursings. In 27:15 – 26 twelve curses are listed. The people will be cursed for idolatry, for dishonoring parents, perverting justice, sexual sin, taking bribes, etc. The last curse in Deut 27:26 capsulizes the whole, functioning as

---

2. Perhaps Paul responds to opponents who cited this text. Wilson, *Curse of the Law*, 62 – 64.

3. I owe these two citations to Betz, *Galatians*, 148.

4. Hays, *Galatians*, 258 ; so also Hong, *Law in Galatians*, 80 – 81.

a summary statement and emphasizing that the curse falls if one does not keep the Torah.

How does the quotation from Deut 27:26 function in Paul's argument?[5] The emphasis in both the Deuteronomic context and in Paul is that the curse applies if one fails to keep God's law.[6] Those who do not do *everything* (cf. also Deut 28:58) enjoined in the law are cursed.

The final clause of the verse "so that he does them" (τοῦ ποιῆσαι αὐτά) is difficult.[7] Note that the article "the" (τοῦ) belongs with the infinitive "to do" (ποιῆσαι), and that the use of the genitive article with the infinitive is conventional. This infinitival clause could be epexegetical to the preceding, or it could also denote a result clause. A decision is difficult, but a result clause seems slightly preferable. In any case, the clause emphasizes further the requirement *to do* what the law commands (cf. again Deut 28:58). We are on firm ground, then, in concluding that the curse applies to those who fail to keep God's law.

We should highlight a special feature in Paul's argument: one must keep "all the things" (πᾶσιν) the law says to avoid the curse. In other words, perfect obedience to the law is required.[8] Some object to this interpretation, complaining that we must supply an implied proposition for Paul's argument to work. The implied proposition is the notion that no one does everything required in the law. I would suggest, then, that Paul's argument works as follows:

> Those who don't do everything required by the law are cursed (v. 10b).
>
> No one does everything required by the law (implied proposition).[9]
>
> Therefore, those who are of the works of law are cursed (v. 10a).

---

5. The Pauline citation here, though it varies from the MT at points, accords with the meaning of Deut 27:26 in the MT. So Silva, "Galatians," 796 – 97.

6. Against the view proposed here, see Andrew H. Wakefield, *Where to Live: The Hermeneutical Significance of Paul's Citations from Scripture in Galatians 3:1 – 14* (SBLABib 14; Atlanta: Society of Biblical Literature, 2003), 67 – 71; cf. Fee, *Galatians*, 118 – 21. Wakefield argues that if Gentiles are in view, they were already under the law's curse and hence could not be cursed any more for relying on the law (69). Wakefield fails to see that the law and Christ are a stark either-or for Paul. If the Galatians *revert* to the law, they return to the cursed state from which Christ has freed them. Wakefield proposes that curse is "integral" to life under law (180). The problem with Wakefield's view, however, is that he does not adequately explain *why* this is the case. The OT text restricts the curse to those who *disobey*.

Gombis argues that those who believe in Christ and remain within the circle of the law are cursed, for if they confess Christ, they are violating the law. It is unclear how this argument actually works. The Judaizers themselves, after all, confessed Jesus as Messiah and observed the law. The Judaizers would fiercely resist the idea that Christ and the law were incompatible. But Gombis maintains, of course, that the law and Christ are incompatible according to Paul. If we follow Gombis, Paul's argument seems to boil down to an assertion regarding the incompatibility of the law and confessing

Christ. But such an assertion, without a textual argument that provides *reasons* for the assertion, would not persuade either the Judaizers or the Galatians. Timothy G. Gombis, "The 'Transgressor' and the 'Curse of the Law': The Logic of Paul's Argument in Galatians 2 – 3," *NTS* 53 (2007): 81 – 93. For the view that the law marks out those who are not of faith and hence does not save, see Michael Cranford, "The Possibility of Perfect Obedience: Paul and an Implied Premise in Galatians 3:10 and 5:3," *NovT* 36 (1994): 242 – 58. Sanders (*Paul, the Law*, 17 – 64) argues that Paul rejects the law on dogmatic grounds. For a critique of his view, see Thomas R. Schreiner, "Paul and Perfect Obedience to the Law: An Evaluation of the View of E. P. Sanders," *WTJ* 47 (1985): 245 – 78.

7. The final word of the verse "them" (αὐτά) refers back to what is written in the book of the law.

8. So Fung, *Galatians*, 141 – 42; George, *Galatians*, 230.

9. Many scholars think this premise is implied. See, e.g., Chrysostom, *Galatians*, 26; Calvin, *Galatians*, 89; Lightfoot, *Galatians*, 137; Burton, *Galatians*, 164 – 65; Schoeps, *Paul*, 176 – 77; Mussner, *Galaterbrief*, 224 – 26; Longenecker, *Galatians*, 118; Otfried Hofius, "Das Gesetz des Mose und das Gesetz Christi," in *ZTK* 80 (1983): 265; Matera, *Galatians*, 123 – 24; Lambrecht, *Pauline Studies*, 281 – 82; In-Gyu Hong, "Does Paul Misrepresent the Jewish Law? Law and Covenant in Gal 3:1 – 14," *NovT* 36 (1994): 177. Against Martyn, *Galatians*, 310 – 11.

The objection that the implied proposition is unstated is hardly a strong one.[10] Paul does not write like a professor of logic, in which each step of the argument is carefully included. He skips steps often, especially when the implied proposition is obvious. Indeed, skipping one of the premises is scarcely surprising, for Aristotle observed that when a premise "is well known, there is no need to mention it, for the hearer can add it himself" (*Rhet.* I.ii.13).[11]

Furthermore, the implied proposition is uncontroversial. The OT also teaches that all human beings without exception sin (cf. 1 Kgs 8:46; Prov 20:9; Eccl 7:20).[12] Some maintain that Paul would not have insisted on perfect obedience since atonement was provided for sin in Judaism.[13] But such an argument would not convince Paul, for now that

Christ has come, OT sacrifices no longer atone. Atonement is reserved for Christ's sacrifice alone. Hence, those who return to the law are restricted to the law covenant and its sacrifices for the forgiveness of sins. Now that Christ has come, however, no atonement is available under the law or its sacrifices. Therefore, the only way to gain life under the law is to keep every provision of the law.[14]

We have now come a crucial point in Paul's argument, for he explains why the curse lies on those of works of law. Contrary to some interpreters, he does not argue that the curse falls on those who do the law.[15] It is the *failure* to do all that is written in the law that condemns, not the desire to keep the law![16] Nor is the curse imposed for having a wrong attitude that excludes Gentiles.[17] Human beings are

---

10. See here the compelling argument of A. Andrew Das, "Galatians 3.10: An Omitted Premise and Credulity," to be published by SBL in a Festschrift in 2010.

11. I owe this reference to Morland, *The Rhetoric of the Curse in Galatians*, 116. See his further discussion, 203 – 10. But, against Morland, the curse is not pronounced because of lack of faith, for this verse zeros in on disobedience. Aune argues that Paul did not derive the enthymeme from Aristotle. David E. Aune, "The Use and Abuse of the Enthymeme in New Testament Scholarship," *NTS* 49 (2003): 299 – 320. The argument presented here does not depend, however, on Paul knowing Aristotle. Debanné rightly remarks that "as long as a Pauline scholar can correctly identify a truncated syllogism in one of the epistles and reconstruct it effectively, whether or not she believes that this scheme comes from Aristotle becomes, in a sense, a secondary issue." See Marc J. Debanné, *Enthymemes in the Letters of Paul* (LNTS 303; London: T&T Clark, 2006), 31 – 32. Debanné sees a number of enthymemes in Galatians. Surprisingly, he does not comment on Gal 3:10 (121 – 66, though see 162).

12. The statement is a general one, and hence cannot be limited to a Pauline comment on the opponents' inability to keep the law (contra Silva, *Interpreting Galatians*, 229 – 32). Nor does Paul only *threaten* his readers with a curse *if* they disobey the law. Contra Christopher D. Stanley, "'Under a Curse': A Fresh Reading of Galatians 3.10 – 14," *NTS* 36 (1990): 481 – 511; J. P. Braswell, "'The Blessing of Abraham' versus 'The Curse of the Law': Another Look at Gal 3:10 – 13," *WTJ* 53 (1991): 76, 78. Rather, Paul contends that no one is able to keep the law.

13. So Hays, who says that the view proposed here is a "ridiculous caricature of Judaism" (*Galatians*, 257).

14. So A. Andrew Das, *Paul, the Law, and the Covenant* (Peabody, MA: Hendrickson, 2001), 113 – 44; idem, *Paul and the Jews*, 46. B. Longenecker rightly argues that Paul as a Christian did not view the law in the same way he did before his conversion (*Triumph of Abraham's God*, 139 – 42).

15. So Schlier, *Galater*, 132 – 33; Lührmann, *Galatians*, 60 – 61. Bruce appears to endorse this view as well (*Galatians*, 159 – 60), though he also argues that the curse comes because the law cannot be kept.

16. Normand Bonneau's solution does not adequately explain the reason Paul gives in 3:10b. Bonneau says that Paul wants to assure the readers that the law cannot curse them because the new age has dawned in Christ, and hence the Galatians are not under the law. He points out that Christ's resurrection overcomes the curse the law pronounced on Christ, and since believers belong to Christ, they are free from the law's curse as well. See his "The Logic of Paul's Argument on the Curse of the Law in Galatians 3:10 – 14," *NovT* 39 (1997): 60 – 80. What Bonneau affirms here is substantially correct, but he fails to explain the particularity of the Pauline argument, for in 3:10, Paul explains why the curse falls on those who are of works of law. And *the reason* he gives is the failure to do all that the law commands.

17. So Dunn, *Galatians*, 172 – 73. See comments under 2:16 for the inadequacies of Dunn's view, and see Dunn (*New Perspective*, 26 – 33, 38 – 41) for further clarification of his views on the matter.

indicted for transgression of the law, for violation of its precepts — not for an ethnocentric attitude.

Nor is the primary sin that is criticized legalism, though the opponents were indeed legalistic. The Judaizers believed that they could be right in God's sight via the law, and this is the heart and soul of legalism. The reason legalism is flawed, however, is rooted in the inability to keep God's law perfectly. Legalism is silly and shallow because it is attempted by people who have not and cannot keep God's commands, and yet somehow they still think they can put God in their debt. Paul does not direct his attention to their wrong attitude of legalism. He shines the spotlight on what can be measured objectively — their transgressions, the fact that human beings fall short of perfection.[18] Some protest that Paul does not demand perfection, but Adam and Eve were banished from the garden, were separated from God, and faced the prospect of death for one sin!

It is increasingly popular to see a reference to the exile in Paul, particularly because of the work of N. T. Wright.[19] Such an interpretation is also defended in Gal 3:10 by James Scott, who notes that the proof text in Deut 27:26 can be traced back to the covenant curses in Deuteronomy.[20] The emphasis, therefore, is shifted from the sins of the individual to the corporate sins of Israel.[21] It is not the case, on this reading, that Paul criticizes individuals for failing to observe the law perfectly. Rather, the focus is on the sin of the nation as the whole. In the context of Deuteronomy, when sin becomes serious enough, it warrants the curses of the covenant manifested supremely in the exile.

This is not the place to interact in detail with Wright's thesis. We should note that Paul himself does not use the language of exile, and hence some reserve about the appropriateness of the term is salutary. Wright is correct in the sense that the covenant promises of the OT were not completely fulfilled. Most of those in Israel would probably agree that this was due, in part, to the nation's sin. Nevertheless, it is unpersuasive to apply the exile theme to Gal 3:10.[22] It should be noted first of all that the sins listed in Deut 27:15–26 all apply to individuals. Nothing is said about a corporate curse on the nation in these verses, but the curse falls on *individuals* who violate the Torah.[23] Even if there is a corporate referent (which is doubtful), individuals are not excluded. As Das says, "The fate of the nation as a corporate whole cannot be abstracted from the conduct of its individual members. The sin of individual Israelites accrues to Israel as a whole."[24]

Second, even if one were to agree that we have a reference to the curse of exile, Paul's readers could

---

18. Against Wolfgang Reinbold, who restricts the text to saying that the law brings a curse because it is contrary to faith. "Gal 3,6–14 und das Problem der Erfüllbarkeit des Gesetzes bei Paulus," *ZNW* 91 (2000): 91–106.

19. Wright, *Climax of the Covenant*, 137–56; Hays, *Galatians*, 258–59.

20. James M. Scott, "'For as Many as Are of Works of the Law Are under a Curse' (Galatians 3.10)," in *Paul and the Scriptures of Israel* (ed. C. A. Evans and J. A. Sanders; JSNTSup 83; Sheffield: JSOT Press, 1993), 187–221; Hafemann, "Paul and the Exile," 342–44. For the view that Paul saw Israel as apostate, just as the prophets did, see Sigurd Grindheim, "Apostate Turned Prophet: Paul's Prophetic Understanding and Prophetic Hermeneutic with Special Reference to Galatians 3.10–12," *NTS* 53 (2007): 545–65. Nor can the sin of apostasy be restricted

to the failure to recognize the new era of salvation history, as Don Garlington argues. "Role Reversal and Paul's Use of Scripture in Galatians 3.10–13," *JSNT* 65 (1997): 85–121.

21. See also Ardel Caneday, who focuses on the corporate sin of Israel and on the epochal and covenantal (rather than individual) character of the curse. "'Redeemed from the Curse of the Law': The Use of Deut 21:22–23 in Gal 3.13," *TJ* 10 (1989): 194–96.

22. See the critique in B. Longenecker, *Triumph of Abraham's God*, 137–39.

23. See here the critique of Kim, *Paul and the New Perspective*, 1–84, 128–64. Cf. also Das, *Paul, the Law, and the Covenant*, 152–53. Das rightly sees an interplay between individuals and the corporate life of the nation in Deut 27–30.

24. Das, *Paul, the Law, and the Covenant*, 152.

have drawn a very different conclusion from the argument. If the exilic curse lies on Israel because it violated Torah, the Gentiles could reason, "We will keep Torah and avoid the curse." If Paul's argument does not contain an argument about the impossibility of keeping the Torah, such a response on the part of the Judaizers and the Galatians would be fitting. Paul's argument has more depth than the exilic interpretation recognizes. He not only claims that people have not kept the law; he also asserts that *they cannot keep the law.*

Third, it is unclear that a reference to Israel's history is intended. Paul does not sketch in here a historical summary of Israel's past. He directs his words to the Galatians, to any who rely on works of law (ὅσοι γὰρ ἐξ ἔργων νόμου εἰσίν), warning them that if they turn to the Torah, they must keep it perfectly to avoid God's curse.[25]

3:11a And that no one is justified by means of the law before God is clear (ὅτι δὲ ἐν νόμῳ οὐδεὶς δικαιοῦται παρὰ τῷ θεῷ δῆλον).

Paul has argued in 3:10 that the curse of the law applies to all who try to be right before God via the law, for God requires perfect obedience, and all fall short of his commands. Verse 11 supplies a second argument, from another angle, to support the same thesis.[26] This verse begins with an assertion in which Paul confidently proclaims that no one can stand in the right before God by means of the law. The phrase "by means of the law" (ἐν νόμῳ)[27] modifies the verb "justified" (δικαιοῦται) and in light of 3:10

refers to the "works of law."[28] The present tense of "justify" should be understood as "gnomic," and so Paul is not emphasizing that they are presently being justified. Rather, he communicates a timeless truth, that no one is ever justified before God by means of the law.

The verb "justify," as most interpreters recognize, is a forensic term here, denoting a right standing before God the judge. Therefore, 3:11a says that no one can obtain right standing before God the judge by means of keeping the law. Verse 10 has already informed us why this is the case — all are cursed by the law because all have sinned. But Paul adds a distinct reason for the assertion in 3:11, drawing upon Hab 2:4 to verify the proposition in 11a. The reason no one can stand in the right before God by means of the works of law is that Habakkuk teaches that the righteous shall live by faith.

3:11b Because "the righteous shall live by faith" (ὅτι ὁ δίκαιος ἐκ πίστεως ζήσεται).

How do we understand Paul's citation of Habakkuk? He introduces it with the word "because" (ὅτι). It is obvious that righteousness is not via the law, for the righteous will gain eschatological life by faith. In this context the verb "shall live" (ζήσεται) must be understood in light of the verb "is justified" (δικαιοῦται),[29] and hence in this context it refers to eschatological life. Such life is obtained not by means of works but through faith.[30]

The LXX translation of Hab 2:4 understands the text to refer to *God's faithfulness* ("the righteous

---

25. Kim rightly remarks that Paul does not confine his critique to *Israel* but to *all people* in 3:10 (*Paul and the New Perspective*, 138–40).

26. Longenecker takes the conjunction (δέ) as adversative (*Galatians*, 118). I follow Betz here, who takes it as continuative (*Galatians*, 146). Betz also argues that Paul's own theology dictates his understanding of Hab 2:4, and that his reading differs from the LXX, the MT, Qumran, and Heb 10:38–39 (147).

27. The preposition (ἐν) is instrumental (so Mussner, *Galaterbrief*, 228, n. 78; Hans-Joachim Eckstein, *Verheis-*

sung und Gesetz: Eine exegetische Untersuchung zu Galater 2,15–4,7 (WUNT 86; Tübingen: Mohr Siebeck, 1996), 134–35.

28. So also Bruce, *Galatians*, 161; Longenecker, *Galatians*, 118.

29. Cf. Bruce, *Galatians*, 162; Hays, *Faith of Jesus Christ*, 150–51.

30. Wakefield argues that Paul refers to life in the covenant rather than eschatological life (*Where to Live*, 169–71). But the context here demonstrates that soteriology is in view, since "live" (ζάω) is paired with "justify" (δικαιόω).

shall live by my faithfulness," ὁ δὲ δίκαιος ἐκ πίστεώς μου ζήσεται), which represents an interpretation remarkably different from Paul's and deviates from the Masoretic Text ("the righteous will live by his faith").[31] The Qumran community understood the text in yet another way: "this concerns all those who observe the Law in the House of Judah, whom God will deliver from the House of Judgement because of their suffering and because of their faith in the Teacher of Righteousness" (1QpHab 8:1 – 3).[32] Such an interpretation is dramatically different from Paul's, for at Qumran law obedience is the pathway to blessing, though it is combined with faith in the teacher of the community.

The text Paul uses differs from the MT in that he drops the third person pronoun "his," though the meaning of the verse is not changed thereby (see also in Rom 1:17). The slight change introduced by Paul suggests that he used the MT or recalled it from memory rather than using the LXX.[33] The author of Hebrews has still a different variation, for he uses the pronoun "my" to modify the substantive "righteous" (Heb 10:38). Still, no significant difference of meaning between Hebrews and Paul is evident, for both emphasize the importance of personal faith. They agree on the meaning of the Habakkuk text over against the LXX and the Qumran interpretations.

Does Paul distort the meaning of Habakkuk in its historical context? Many claim that Habakkuk speaks of human faithfulness rather than faith.[34] Such an interpretation misreads the prophet.[35] Habakkuk predicts a day of judgment when the Chaldeans will punish sinful Judah because the nation has failed to keep God's Torah (1:4 – 11). Such a judgment is a test of faith for the remnant. Will they still believe God's promises, which include a future judgment of Babylon (ch. 2) and a future renewal of the work of the exodus for Israel (ch. 3)? The many allusions to the exodus in Hab 3 indicate the promise of a new exodus, a new deliverance for the people of God. Hence, Habakkuk functions as a paradigm for the people of God. He will continue to trust the Lord even if the fig tree does not blossom and vines are lacking fruit (Hab 3:17 – 18). He will continue to

---

31. The term "righteous" (δίκαιος) is a substantival adjective. It is unlikely that the righteous one is Christ. Contra Hays, *Faith of Jesus Christ*, 151 – 54. See the critique of H. W. Johnson, "Paradigm of Abraham," 190 – 91.

32. The translation is from Geza Vermes, *The Dead Sea Scrolls in English* (3rd ed.; New York: Penguin, 1987), 287.

33. Silva critiques the LXX rendering (*Interpreting Galatians*, 166).

34. Seifrid argues that faithfulness in Hab 2:4 relates to faithfulness to the vision noted in Hab 2:3 (*Christ Our Righteousness*, 37, n. 7), but the antecedent more naturally is found in the third person suffix (cf. "his soul in him," *napšô bô*) that immediately precedes the phrase in Hab 2:4. Rikki E. Watts also maintains that it refers to the trustworthiness of the vision, but argues that the "the righteous are to commit themselves to it" (i.e., the vision) (" 'For I Am Not Ashamed of the Gospel': Romans 1:16 – 17 and Habakkuk 2:4,'" in *Romans and the People of God: Essays in Honor of Gordon D. Fee on the Occasion of His 65th Birthday* [ed. Sven K. Soderlund and N. T. Wright; Grand Rapids: Eerdmans, 1999], 13).

35. For an intriguing explanation of Paul's hermeneutical approach to Hab 2:4, see Watson, *Hermeneutics of Faith*, 112 – 63. Watson rightly rejects a christological reference to the "righteous one" here (see also Watts on the "coming one" in Hab 2:3; "Romans 1:16 – 17 and Habakkuk 2:4," 9 – 10, 13 – 14), but his thesis that Paul drew on Habakkuk for his use of "by faith" (ἐκ πίστεως) elsewhere is undemonstrable. See Watson's "By Faith (of Christ): An Exegetical Dilemma and Its Scriptural Solution," in *The Faith of Jesus Christ: Exegetical, Biblical, and Theological Studies* (ed. Michael F. Bird and Preston Sprinkle; Peabody, MA: Hendrickson, 2009), 147 – 63. For the view that Paul interpreted Hab 2:4 in accord with its historical context, see the illuminating study of Maureen W. Yeung, *Faith in Jesus and Paul: A Comparison with Special Reference to "Faith That Can Move Mountains" and "Your Faith Has Healed/Saved You"* (WUNT 2/147; Tübingen: Mohr Siebeck, 2002), 196 – 212. She goes on to maintain that Paul's understanding of Hab 2:4 was influenced not only by the OT and Jewish tradition but also by Jesus tradition (212 – 25).

trust in and rejoice in God's promise of future salvation.

The canonical context of the book assists us in interpreting Hab 2:4. Like Abraham the people of God are summoned to trust in Yahweh when circumstances conspire against such trust. The fundamental call of Habakkuk is to trust in the Lord.[36] This is not to deny that faithfulness flows from faith, for the former always proceeds from the latter.[37] Faith is the foundation and faithfulness is the superstructure. It follows that Paul is a brilliant interpreter of Habakkuk and does not distort its message but capsulizes it. A right relationship with God is obtained by faith, not by keeping the law.

Another question should be answered relative to the citation from Habakkuk. Is Paul saying that "the righteous by faith shall live"[38] or "the righteous shall live by faith"?[39] Word order does not settle the issue, for the words "by faith" (ἐκ πίστεως) are placed between "the righteous" and "shall live." Probably the prepositional phrase modifies the verb since this is the typical pattern in Greek. If the clause "by faith" (ἐκ πίστεως) modifies the verb (ζήσεται), then the phrase designates means. At the end of the day the difference in meaning between the two interpretations is not as significant as some have claimed.

We should observe as well that the words "shall live" (ζήσεται) refer here to eternal life, not merely to life on earth.[40] Eternal life, or as the first part of the verse expresses it, justification, is by faith. It is difficult to know if the future tense "shall live" (ζήσεται) is significant. Perhaps the future is used because Paul cites Habakkuk and thus does not restrict eternal life to the eschaton. Scholars are debating today the significance of verbal aspect, and Porter argues that none of the tenses have temporal significance, even the future.[41] Others, conversely, maintain that notions of time cannot be excised completely, especially with regard to the future tense.[42] In any case, all agree that the future tense does not necessarily signal future time. Perhaps in this case we should see a gnomic future, for Paul typically understands justification as a present reality (cf. Rom 5:1), and hence the same may be true of "live" here. In saying that justification is a present reality, I am not denying that it is an eschatological gift. Justification is an end-time gift that has invaded the present era.

Others have proposed a different interpretation of the verse. According to this view, in the first part of v. 11, the conjunction (ὅτι) should be translated as "because" instead of "that," and "evident" (δῆλον) is a predicate adjective introducing the second clause. Hence, the verse should be translated, "But because nobody is justified before God by law, it is clear that the righteous

---

36. Cf. Glenn N. Davies, *Faith and Obedience in Romans: A Study in Romans 1–4* (JSNTSup 39; Sheffield: JSOT Press, 1990), 44.

37. Cf. Silva, *Interpreting Galatians*, 165–67. See also the comments of Fung, *Galatians*, 144.

38. Fung, *Galatians*, 143–45; George, *Galatians*, 234, n. 56.

39. See esp. H. C. C. Cavallin, "'The Righteous Shall Live by Faith': A Decisive Argument for the Traditional Interpretation," *ST* 32 (1978): 33–43; cf. Gottlob Schrenk, "δίκαιος," *TDNT*, 2:191, n. 71; Silva, "Galatians," 801–2.

40. Against James D. G. Dunn, *The Theology of Paul the Apostle* (Grand Rapids: Eerdmans, 1998), 152–54, 374–75; Wakefield, *Where to Live*, 174. Nor does Paul speak here of life that is the consequence of justification, as Eckstein

argues (*Verheissung*, 142–43). Instead, justification and life here describe the same reality with different terms. So Bruce, *Galatians*, 163; Silva, "Faith versus Works," 242; Lambrecht, *Pauline Studies*, 283.

41. Porter, *Verbal Aspect*. See also Stanley E. Porter, *Idioms of the Greek New Testament* (Sheffield: JSOT, 1992), 20–28.

42. E.g., Buist M. Fanning, "Approaches to Verbal Aspect in New Testament Greek: Issues in Definition and Method," *Biblical Greek Language and Linguistics: Open Questions in Current Research* (JSNTSup 80; ed. S. E. Porter and D. A. Carson; Sheffield: Sheffield Academic Press, 1993), 58–60; McKay, *A New Syntax of the Verb in New Testament Greek*, 52.

one will attain (eternal) life by faith."[43] Such a reading is certainly possible, and accords with the reading proposed of 3:10 above.[44] Still, the grammatical argument is not decisive.[45] The examples adduced from Greek literature are limited, and a proposed parallel to 1 Cor 15:27 is not compelling, for the structure of the two verses is not the same. It seems more likely that the view defended above is correct, for in every case in 3:10 – 13 the OT citation comes second and functions as proof of the assertion in the first part of the verse.

In addition, the alternate interpretation suggests that Paul's argument is negative, contending that justification is clearly by faith since it cannot come via works. Such a reading clearly coheres with what is said in 3:10, but it seems more likely that Paul makes a *positive* argument here. He is not merely suggesting that since righteousness is not by works, then it must be by faith. Indeed, the Habakkuk citation does not in and of itself show that righteousness does not come via works. Rather, the citation offers a *positive* argument: those who are righteous live by faith.[46] Therefore, it seems more likely that Paul makes a second argument here. Righteousness cannot come via the law, for Scripture teaches we live by faith.

3:12a And the law is not of faith (ὁ δὲ νόμος οὐκ ἔστιν ἐκ πίστεως). Paul explains further why no one can be righteous by the law. Righteousness is not by the law, for the law requires perfect obedience and human performance. Faith, however, looks to what God has done in Christ for salvation, relying on God's work rather than one's own.

The conjunction "and" (δέ) introducing the verse can be either continuative or adversative.[47] Here it is probably continuative,[48] for Paul is piling up three arguments in succession (3:10 – 12) in order to explain why the law cannot save. He claims in 3:11 that human beings cannot be right before God by doing the law since righteousness is by faith alone. Now in 3:12 he asserts that the law is not of faith. The term "law" (ὁ νόμος) refers here to the Mosaic law and likely refers back to the works of law mentioned in 3:10. Paul proceeds to cite Lev 18:5 to say that the law is based on doing rather than believing. The one who does what the law says obtains life via the law.

This is one of the most difficult verses to interpret in the entire Pauline corpus. The reason for this is that the interpretation of the verse reflects one's understanding of the whole of Pauline theology and the relationship between the old covenant and the new. We are reminded that we as interpreters do not simply explain the text in light of the particular paragraph and letter before us. All of us come to the text with a theological worldview that shapes our understanding of the text. Having such a map is not necessarily a disadvantage. Indeed, we all come to the text with preconceptions, and those who claim that they do not have any presuppositions are naïve. Indeed, if we are conscious of our biases, we can test our worldview via the biblical text and reshape our theology.

---

43. So Kim, *Paul and the New Perspective*, 129, n. 4; Witherington, *Galatians*, 234; Frank Thielman, *Paul and the Law: A Contextual Approach* (Downers Grove, IL: IVP, 1994), 127 – 28; B. Longenecker, *Triumph of Abraham's God*, 164; Hays, *Galatians*, 259; Wright, *Climax of the Covenant*, 149, n. 42. See especially Wakefield (*Where to Live*, 162 – 67, 207 – 14), who says that the conjunction (ὅτι, "that" or "because") follows "evident" (δῆλον) about twice as often as it precedes it in first-century Greek.

44. Though Wakefield actually moves in a different direction regarding the meaning of "live." See Wakefield, *Where to Live*, 169 – 71.

45. Wakefield acknowledges that the pattern "is relatively scarce" (*Where to Live*, 165).

46. But see Watts, who argues that the ineffectiveness of the Torah in Hab 1:4 suggests that Habakkuk anticipates the Pauline problem with the law ("Romans 1:16 – 17 and Habakkuk 2:4," 5 – 6, 17).

47. So Longenecker, *Galatians*, 119.

48. Betz, translates it "also" (*Galatians*, 147, n. 88).

When Paul says that the law is not of faith, it is a mistake to read this as a wholesale rejection of the law in the lives of Christians. Paul can speak positively about believers fulfilling the law by the power of the Spirit (Gal 5:13 – 15; cf. also Rom 8:4; 13:8 – 10). He maintains that Christians, through the work of the Spirit, are empowered to keep the law of Christ (Gal 6:2), which can be described as the law of love (5:13 – 14). So what does Paul mean when he says "the law is not of faith"?

We must begin by observing the context, where Paul discusses justification — what is required to be right with God. We must recall that he addresses those who believed that circumcision was mandatory for salvation, that one must keep the law to be justified. Paul rejects any notion that the law is the source of life.[49] One does not become right with God by doing but by believing. Paul has already taught in 3:10 that righteousness by works of law is impossible since the law requires perfect obedience. We must also keep in mind that he writes from the perspective of fulfillment of God's promises in Christ. The covenant with Moses, then, is no longer in force.[50] What makes one right with God with the arrival of the new covenant is faith in Christ — not keeping the commands found in the Sinai covenant.

3:12b But instead, "the one who does the commandments shall live by means of them" (ἀλλ᾽ ὁ ποιήσας αὐτὰ ζήσεται ἐν αὐτοῖς).[51] The conjunction "but" (ἀλλ᾽) is adversative, introducing the OT citation from Lev 18:5.[52] Paul states that those who do what the law requires will live on the basis of their obedience, but, of course, no one can be righteous by law since the law requires perfection. The word "live" (ζήσεται) refers here to eternal life, and hence Lev 18:5 promises eternal life to those who keep the law.[53] The law does not bring life, for human beings are unable to fulfill the required condition.[54] Human sinfulness intervenes.[55] "All have sinned and fall short of the glory of God" (Rom 3:23).[56] Law obedience, then, is contrary to faith since it is predicated on

---

49. Rightly Silva, *Interpreting Galatians*, 187 – 95.

50. Joel Willitts rightly appeals to salvation history to explain what Paul is doing here. See his "Context Matters: Paul's Use of Leviticus 18:5 in Galatians 3:12," *TynBul* 54 (2003): 105 – 22. Unfortunately, Willitts overplays the argument. Sprinkle remarks, "One problem with this approach is that it downplays, or even eradicates, any inherent deficiency in Lev 18:5. In Willitts's view, it seems that the only problem Paul has with adherence to Lev 18:5 is that such adherence is simply past its time." Preston M. Sprinkle, *Law and Life: The Interpretation of Leviticus 18:5 in Early Judaism and Paul* (WUNT 2/241; Tübingen: Mohr Siebeck, 2008), 148. Sprinkle goes on to remark that Willitts fails to see that Hab 2:4 and Lev 18:5, according to Paul, represent two radically different ways to obtain righteousness (148).

51. The word "them" (αὐτοῖς) is ambiguous, having no clear antecedent. The antecedent is clear if one reads Lev 18:5 in the LXX, where it is obvious that the term refers to the commands of the OT law. Even in Galatians the referent to OT commandments is clear if one pauses to think about the sentence. In the phrase "by them" (ἐν αὐτοῖς) the word "them" (αὐτοῖς) refers again to OT commands. The prepositional phrase in this case is one of means, the one who does the law shall live *by means of the law.*

52. I want to express my thanks to Justin Taylor, who interacted with me on this verse, and his helpful comments sharpened my thinking.

53. See the comments in 3:11 on the future tense of "shall live" (ζήσεται).

54. Rightly Calvin, *Galatians*, 91; Lambrecht, *Pauline Studies*, 284. Sprinkle emphasizes that Paul contrasts divine agency (what God does) with human agency (what human beings can accomplish). See *Law and Life*, 148 – 64. Therefore, he rejects the idea that the law does not bring life because it demands perfection. Sprinkle overemphasizes divine agency here since Paul specifically contrasts believing and doing (two human activities). But Sprinkle also notes human disobedience, so the difference between my view and his should not be exaggerated.

55. It is unlikely that Paul thinks of Christ here as the one who keeps the law. Contra C. E. B. Cranfield, *A Critical and Exegetical Commentary on the Epistle to the Romans* (ICC; Edinburgh T&T Clark, 1979), 2.522, n. 2; Hays, *Galatians*, 259 (though Hays sees a subtle and implicit reference here). Rightly Bruce, *Galatians*, 163.

56. Avemarie rejects the notion that perfect obedience is required and posits instead that Paul plays down and ignores the

obeying instead of believing to obtain salvation, on performing what is required instead of trusting God's work in Christ.[57] The attempt, then, to be righteous by keeping the law is fundamentally opposed to believing, to trusting what God has done in Christ for justification.[58]

In Depth: The Meaning of Leviticus 18:5

What is puzzling in Gal 3:12 is Paul's citation of Lev 18:5. Why does Paul relate it to works-righteousness when in its OT context the verse seems to refer to the keeping of the law by those who already enjoy God's covenantal mercies?[59] In other words, the keeping of the law in Lev 18:5 is comparable to Paul's positive statements about law keeping that are found in texts like Rom 8:4; 13:8–10 and Gal 5:13–15. It seems strange, therefore, that Paul relates it to the attempt to obtain righteousness by keeping the Mosaic law.[60] The commands of the Mosaic law were given to a people already redeemed from Egypt, to a liberated people who were already in covenant with Yahweh by his grace. Furthermore, when they transgressed, they could offer sacrifices to obtain forgiveness. Paul, then, appears to cut the verse out of its OT context to support his own theology.

This problem could be resolved by arguing that the Mosaic covenant is not a gracious covenant. From first to last it could be understand as a conditional covenant based on law obedience. If one opts for this solution, then Paul's citation of Lev 18:5 fits with its OT context. This solution should be rejected, however, because it does not accord with the context in Lev 18 (and the rest of the Pentateuch), in which the law is given to a people redeemed from Egypt by God's grace (see Exod 19:3–6; 20:2). To describe the Mosaic covenant as a legalistic covenant misunderstands the Sinai covenant, where God saved his people and then gave them the law.

Another interpretation suggests that Paul refers to his opponents' exegesis of Lev 18:5. Instead of explaining why their interpretation is contextually flawed,

---

soteriological thrust of Lev 18:5. See Friedrich Avemarie, "Paul and the Claim of the Law according to the Scripture: Leviticus 18:5 in Galatians 3:12 and Romans 10:5," in *The Beginnings of Christianity: A Collection of Articles* (ed. Jack Pastor and Menachem Mor; Jerusalem: Yad Ben-Zvi, 2005), 138–41. I would suggest that such a reading does not account as well for the citation of Lev 18:5 as what is proposed here, for Paul does not ignore the soteriology of Lev 18:5. Rather, he explains why the law does not lead to life (human sin intervenes).

57. Martyn argues that Lev. 18:5 stands in fundamental contradiction, in Paul's view, to Hab 2:4. Paul does not harmonize the two texts. Instead, he takes his stand with Hab 2:4 and repudiates what he considers to be the false promise

of Lev 18:5. Martyn, *Galatians*, 328–34. Against Martyn, it is difficult to believe that Paul's scriptural argumentation would convince the Galatians if he arbitrarily chose one OT text over another.

58. The contrast between "believing" and "doing" is clear here (see Betz, *Galatians*, 147–48).

59. For a very helpful history of interpretation that includes Jewish interpretations and the various understandings in church history (including the modern period), see Avemarie, "Paul and the Claim of the Law," 125–37.

60. Note that in Rom 10:5 Paul cites the same verse from Lev 18:5, rejecting the idea that right standing with God comes "from" (ἐκ) the law.

he demonstrates through the whole of his argument that their understanding of the OT is off target. Supporting this interpretation is the practice of the rabbis, who did not usually refute a wrong interpretation by showing that it did not fit the context. Instead, they cited other verses to show that the meaning assigned to the verse in question was incorrect.[61] Such a procedure could possibly fit with what Paul does here. This view is attractive and previously persuaded me,[62] but nowhere else does Paul cite an OT verse refracted through the view of the opponents. He invariably quotes the OT to defend his argument, and it seems likely that he does the same here.

Indeed, in Rom 10:5, where Paul also cites Lev 18:5, he introduces it with the words, "Moses describes [writes]," suggesting that he cites the OT in accord with its meaning — not a misinterpretation. Clearer evidence is needed that Paul responds to a misinterpretation since we have no indication in context that Lev 18:5 is quoted in accord with the opponents' view. Moreover, when one considers the history of Israel, it is evident that they did not continue in the land but were expelled because of disobedience, which is confirmed by the Assyrian (722 BC) and Babylonian (586 BC) exiles. The law per se did not bring life and cannot bring life because of transgression. Israel's experience confirms the Pauline reading of Lev 18:5, for they did not obtain life via the law. Instead, they were cursed because they failed to observe the law.[63]

Paul reads Lev 18:5 redemptive-historically.[64] I have already noted in Gal 3:10 that perfect obedience is demanded from those who place themselves under the law, for atonement provided by OT sacrifices no longer avails with the coming of Christ. Paul returns to that theme here. Perfect obedience was not required under the Sinai covenant, for the law provided forgiveness via sacrifices for those who transgressed.[65] In Paul's view, however (see Gal 3:15 – 4:7), the Sinai covenant was no longer in force. Therefore, those who observe circumcision and the law to obtain justification (5:2 – 4) are turning the clock backward in salvation history.

The coming of Christ spells the end of the Sinai covenant (3:15 – 4:7). Those who live under the law must keep it perfectly to be saved, for in returning to

---

61. Nils A. Dahl, *Studies in Paul*, 159 – 77; Silva, *Interpreting Galatians*, 193 – 94.

62. See Schreiner, *Romans*, 555.

63. For a defense of the Pauline reading of Lev 18:5, see Watson, *Hermeneutics of Faith*, 315 – 36 (though, contrary to Watson, I think perfect obedience is demanded).

64. See James M. Hamilton Jr., "The One Who Does Them Shall Live by Them: Leviticus 18:5 in Galatians 3:12," *The Gospel Witness* (August 2005): 10 – 12. Garlington, however,

makes the mistake of restricting what Paul says to redemptive history (*Galatians*, 198 – 99). Remarkably, he opposes what the text actually says in asserting that "any dichotomy between believing and doing in the Jewish schema is simply off base" (198). The Judaizers probably would have agreed with this judgment.

65. In one sense perfect obedience was required. Otherwise, sacrifices would not be required for infractions of the law.

the law they are forsaking the atonement provided by Christ (2:21; 5:3). Returning to the law is futile, however, for the sacrifices of atonement under the Sinai covenant pointed ahead to the sacrifice of Christ. Hence, animal sacrifices no longer provide forgiveness now that the definitive sacrifice of Christ has been offered (3:13).

One other question needs to be answered in the verse. Life in the context of Lev 18:5 does not refer to eternal life, but to life within the Land of Promise, to a life of blessing within God's covenant on this earth.[66] On what grounds can Paul relate this text to eternal life? The question posed here is too large to answer in a complete way. It is likely that Paul argues typologically, and such typological argumentation is common in the NT. For instance, the inheritance in the land points to and is fulfilled in one's heavenly inheritance — ultimately in the new heavens and earth (Rev 21:1 – 22:5). The judgments of Sodom and Gomorrah anticipate and forecast the eschatological judgment (2 Pet 2:6; Jude 7). It is not surprising that a text that relates to life in the Land of Promise is legitimately applied to eternal life.

Furthermore, we see something similar in targumic traditions. "And you shall keep my statutes and my judgments, which if a man do he shall live by them an everlasting life" (*Tg. Onq.*); "And you shall keep my statutes, and the order of my judgments, which if a man do he shall live in them, in the life of eternity, and his position shall be with the just" (*Tg. Ps.-J.*).[67] Sprinkle, in a thorough study of Lev 18:5 in the OT and Second Temple Judaism, shows that Lev 18:5 in its OT context demanded obedience to the law for life and prosperity in the land (cf. Ezek 20:11, 13, 21; Neh 9:29; see also Ezek 18:9, 17, 19, 21; 33:10, 19), but in some texts in Second Temple literature Lev 18:5 is interpreted as requiring obedience for eternal life (cf. CD III, 15 – 16; 4Q266, 11 I-II, 12; *Pss. Sol.* 14:1 – 5; cf. also 4Q504; Philo, *Prelim. Studies.* 86 – 87).[68] Gathercole also argues that an eschatological reading of Lev 18:5 is evident both in the NT and in Second Temple Judaism.[69] He rightly remarks, "there is an 'eternalization' of the life that, in its original context in Leviticus, would have been understood in terms of lengthened life and prosperity of one's descendents and the nation as a whole."[70]

---

66. See Gordon J. Wenham, *The Book of Leviticus* (NICOT; Grand Rapids: Eerdmans, 1979), 253; John E. Hartley, *Leviticus* (WBC; Dallas: Word, 1992), 293. Cf. also Nicole Chibici-Revneanu, "Leben im Gesetz: Die paulinische Interpretation von Lev 18:5 (Gal 3:12; Röm 10:5)," *NovT* 50 (2008): 105 – 19.

67. Both of these references are reproduced from Longenecker, *Galatians*, 120.

68. See Sprinkle, *Law and Life*, 1 – 130.

69. Simon Gathercole, "Torah, Life, and Salvation: Leviticus 18:5 in Early Judaism and the New Testament," in *From Prophecy to Testament: The Function of the Old Testament in the New* (ed. C.A. Evans; Peabody, MA: Hendrickson, 2004), 126 – 45.

70. Ibid., 140. Gathercole comments on Luke 10:37 here, but his citation reflects his view in Gal 3:12 as well. Wakefield fails to see the typological escalation here, and hence limits the word "live" to the OT context (*Where to Live*, 171, 174 – 75).

3:13a Christ redeemed us from the curse of the law (Χριστὸς ἡμᾶς ἐξηγόρασεν ἐκ τῆς κατάρας τοῦ νόμου). The answer to the crisis posed by 3:10 – 12 is now unfolded. The only way for the curse of the law to be removed is through the redeeming work of Christ. It is difficult to know why Paul does not use an adversative conjunction (e.g., "but," δέ) here. Perhaps the lack of a conjunction focuses on the centrality of Christ as the answer to the human dilemma since "Christ" is the first word in the text.

The curse of the law lies on all people since the law demands perfect obedience. Other scholars argue that the "us" (ἡμᾶς) is limited to the Jews.[71] How could Paul say that Gentiles were under the law's curse since they did not live under the law? Instead, the salvation of the Gentiles is the result of the Lord's redemption of Israel.[72] Though this reading is attractive, it is probably wrong.[73] Paul argues that all are condemned by their failure to observe the law (3:10), and he does not limit the curse of the law only to the Jews in 3:10 but widens it to include all (note "as many as," ὅσοι) those who rely on the law for redemption.[74]

It is also clear from Romans that Paul considers the Gentiles as responsible to do God's will insofar as the law is written on the heart (Rom 2:14 – 15).[75] Further, Paul's reference to "us" in 3:14 raises serious problems for the idea that Paul uses pronouns to distinguish Jews from Gentiles, for it is clear that the Gentiles are included in the "we" in 3:14. Indeed, the heart of Paul's argument is that the Gentiles have received the Spirit (3:1 – 5), and hence 3:14 functions as an inclusio with 3:1 – 5.[76]

Das also observes that the shifting of pronouns in 4:21 – 5:1 does not yield a distinction between Jews and Gentiles. He remarks, "If one were to insist on such distinctions, 5:1 would read, 'For freedom Christ has set us [Jewish Christians] free. Stand firm [you Gentile Christians], therefore, and do not submit again to a yoke of slavery.'"[77] It seems clear that Paul addresses the same group with the first and second person pronouns here. Similarly, when Paul says the Jerusalem above is "our mother" (4:26), he does not limit his words to Jewish Christians, only to include Gentile Christians in 4:28 ("you, brothers").[78] Das rightly concludes that "the first-person pronouns from 3:1 through the end of the letter" are "inclusive of Jewish and Gentile Christians, and the second-person pronouns" are "likewise inclusive but rhetorically pointed toward the addressees."[79]

---

71. So Terence L. Donaldson, "The 'Curse of the Law' and the Inclusion of the Gentiles: Galatians 3:13 – 14," *NTS* 32 (1986): 94 – 112; Matera, *Galatians*, 120; Betz, *Galatians*, 148; Garlington, *Galatians*, 210; D. W. B. Robinson, "The Distinction between Jewish and Gentile Believers in Galatians," *ABR* 13 (1965): 34; Betz, *Galatians*, 148; McKnight, *Galatians*, 156 – 57; Hong, *Law in Galatians*, 78 – 79. Donaldson says that the redemption of Israel is the prerequisite for the redemption of Gentiles.

72. Donaldson finds a precursor and pattern in the promise (in both the OT and Second Temple Judaism) that the Gentiles will share subsequently in the salvation given to Israel ("Galatians 3:13 – 14," 99 – 100). See Isa 2:2 – 4; Mic 4:1 – 4; Isa 56:3 – 8; 60:3 – 4; 66:18 – 24; Zech 2:10 – 13; 8:20 – 23; Zeph 3:9 – 10.

73. In support of a reference to Jews and Gentiles, see Williams, "Justification and the Spirit," 91 – 92; Dunn, *Galatians*, 176 – 77; Fung, *Galatians*, 148 – 49; Bruce says that Rom 2:14 indicates that Gentiles are, in a sense, under the law as well (*Galatians*, 167). Further, the universality of Paul's argument points in the same direction. Dalton sees a reference to pagan Christians. William J. Dalton, "The Meaning of 'We' in Galatians," *ABR* 38 (1990): 38.

74. So Das, *Paul and the Jews*, 124. See also for the same conclusion Norman H. Young, "Pronominal Shifts in Paul's Argument to the Galatians," in *Ancient History in a Modern University*, vol. 2, *Early Christianity in Late Antiquity and Beyond* (ed. T. W. Hillard et al.; Grand Rapids: Eerdmans, 1998), 205 – 15.

75. Again see Das, *Paul and the Jews*, 124.

76. Rightly ibid., 123.

77. Ibid., 126.

78. Rightly ibid., 126. Against Robinson, "Jewish and Gentile Believers," 41 – 42.

79. Das, *Paul and the Jews*, 128.

The genitive "of law" (νόμου) is either a descriptive genitive referring to "the law's curse"[80] or a genitive of source speaking of "curse from the law." Perhaps the former is to be preferred since the latter reads more into the phrase, and it is usually preferable to accept the simplest meaning of the phrase. How can anyone be delivered, therefore, from God's curse since all violate his prescriptions? Paul's answer is that forgiveness is obtained through the cross of Christ, that Christ liberates us from the curse brought by the law.

The verb "redeemed" (ἐξαγοράζω; cf. Gal 4:5), along with its cognates, is central in Pauline theology. The language hearkens back to the exodus, where Yahweh freed his people from Egyptian bondage.[81] Just as the exodus and Passover events (cf. 1 Cor 5:7) speak of Israel's freedom from bondage, so too the cross of Christ is the means by which God saves his people from the law's curse.[82]

3:13b-c By becoming a curse for us, for it is written, "Cursed is everyone who hangs on a tree"

(γενόμενος ὑπὲρ ἡμῶν κατάρα, ὅτι γέγραπται, Ἐπικατάρατος πᾶς ὁ κρεμάμενος ἐπὶ ξύλου).[83] The participle "by becoming" (γενόμενος) is an adverbial participle of means, explaining *how* Christ redeemed his people from the curse of the law, i.e., by becoming a curse for us.[84] The citation from Deut 21:23 is introduced by "for it is written" (ὅτι γέγραπται) as an introductory formula. The word "for/because" (ὅτι) is causal and provides the basis for the claim that Christ was cursed for believers.

Before Paul was converted, he believed the Christian sect was heretical, probably because of its view of the law and the claim that a crucified man was the Messiah. Craigie explains well the meaning of the verse in its OT context (cf. Num 25:4; Josh 10:26 – 27; 2 Sam 21:6 – 9): "Hanging was not a method of execution, but something that was done after the death of a criminal, on the same day. When the man was dead, he would be hanged on a *tree* or a 'wooden post' of some kind; the gruesome sight would then serve as a warning to the

---

80. See Wallace for a discussion of the descriptive genitive (*Greek Grammar*, 79).

81. So Wilson, "Wilderness Apostasy," 556 – 57. Harmon sees an allusion to Isaiah 53 ("She Must and Shall Go Free," 187 – 92). Daniel Schwartz identifies Christ as a Levitical scapegoat. "Two Pauline Allusions to the Redemptive Mechanism of the Crucifixion," *JBL* 102 (1983): 259 – 68. Schwartz's suggestion is possible and certainly fits with Paul's line of thought and the influence of the OT in his thought. Still, the paucity of verbal links raises questions about the link to Leviticus 16. B. Hudson McLean rejects the idea that Christ died as a sacrifice and explains Jesus' death along the lines of the *pharmakos* rituals in the Greco-Roman world. *The Cursed Christ: Mediterranean Expulsion Rituals and Pauline Soteriology* (JSNTSup 126; Sheffield: Sheffield Academic Press, 1996). McLean rightly argues that Paul conceived of Jesus' death in substitutionary terms. Space is lacking to interact fully with his thesis here, but the connections drawn to the Greco-Roman apotropaic *pharmakos* rituals fail to convince, and there are good reasons for seeing Jesus' death in Paul as sacrificial. Davis helpfully summarizes and criticizes both Schwartz and McLean (*Christ as Devotio*, 84 – 105). However, Davis's own proposal, in which the curse

must be read against the Greco-Roman background of the curse tablets and Christ's death in terms of a human *devotio*, fails to convince as well (139 – 98). Paul provides an in-depth explication of the OT Scriptures here. Therefore (against Davis), the background to his meaning must be sought in the OT and Jewish sources, even if there are analogies in Greco-Roman culture.

82. It does not follow, however, that the verb "redeem" is synonymous with the verb "justify" (against Martyn, *Galatians*, 317).

83. Given the variations from the OT text, Wilcox suggests that Paul may have used a different Greek text than the LXX. Wilcox, "Upon the Tree," 86 – 90. The nature of the evidence, however, rules out any clarity on this matter.

84. Against David Brondos, who argues that the curse in the OT citation is not from the law. Further, Brondos wrongly argues that the aorist participle is temporal so that the time of the participle precedes the time of the main verb. "The Cross and the Curse: Galatians 3.13 and Paul's Doctrine of Redemption," *JSNT* 81 (2001): 22. Such a mechanical reading of the participle fails, for aorist participles are not invariably prior to the time of the main verb. See Porter, *Idioms of the Greek New Testament*, 187 – 90.

population of the results of breaking those laws which were punishable by death."[85] Fitzmyer demonstrates that Deut 21:23 was applied in Second Temple Judaism both to those exposed on a tree and those executed by crucifixion (cf. 4QpNah 5 – 8; 11QTemple 64.6 – 13).[86]

We ought not to interpret Paul simplistically here. He knew that a person could be devoted to God and end up being crucified. As a Pharisee Paul was presumably sympathetic to the eight hundred people crucified by Alexander Jannaeus (Josephus, *Ant.* 13.380). It is likely that he viewed at least some of these people as righteous.[87] Thus, Paul is scarcely suggesting that anyone subjected to crucifixion was under God's curse! Still, Paul was sure of one thing. The God of Israel would not allow *the Messiah* to be crucified.[88] That would be an intolerable contradiction, "a stumbling block to Jews" (1 Cor 1:23 ESV). The Messiah would vindicate his messiahship by leading Israel into freedom, by fulfilling God's promises to the people. Hence, before his conversion Paul was convinced that Jesus of Nazareth could not be the Messiah.

Paul, however, failed to grasp a crucial point as long as he rejected Jesus as the Christ. We could say that he did not understand a prepositional phrase! He did not understand that Jesus was cursed "for us" (ὑπὲρ ἡμῶν). Jesus experienced the curse of the law in dying. Those who argue that the law cursed Jesus, but God did not curse him, are mistaken.[89] The law did not function separately from God in pronouncing a curse.[90]

In any case, Jesus did not suffer and die for his own transgressions. He died for the sake of his people. We have here the language of substitution. Some in the past doubted whether this verse taught substitution, thinking that Paul would have used the preposition "instead of" (ἀντί); rather than "on behalf of" (ὑπέρ). Most interpreters now acknowledge that the prepositions "on behalf of" (ὑπέρ) and "instead of" (ἀντί) overlap, and that the former is also used to designate substitution.[91] Nor is it persuasive merely to speak of interchange or representation here, if that language is used to rule out substitution.[92] Paul teaches that Christ took upon himself the curse that sinners deserved, that he stood in their place and absorbed their punishment.[93]

The substitutionary work of Christ is central

---

85. Peter C. Craigie, *The Book of Deuteronomy* (NICOT; Grand Rapids: Eerdmans, 1976), 285.

86. See Joseph A. Fitzmyer, "Crucifixion in Ancient Palestine, Qumran Literature, and the NT," *CBQ* 40 (1978): 493 – 513; cf. Wilcox, "Upon the Tree," 89 – 90.

87. Cf. here Das, *Paul and the Jews*, 47. Contra Paula Fredriksen, the crucifixion of the Messiah probably did account for Paul's rejection of Jesus as Messiah before his conversion. Nor is there any indication, against Fredriksen, that the earliest Christians right from the beginning accepted Gentiles as believers without circumcision. Acts 15 shows that this truth slowly dawned on the church. "Judaism, the Circumcision of Gentiles, and Apocalyptic Hope: Another Look at Galatians 1 and 2," *JTS* 42 (1991): 532 – 64.

88. See the discussion in Bruce, *Galatians*, 166. Against this common reading, see Kelli S. O'Brien, "The Curse of the Law (Galatians 3:13): Crucifixion, Persecution, and Deuteronomy 21:22 – 23," *JSNT* 29 (2006): 55 – 76.

89. Some interpreters reject the notion that Christ was

cursed by God (Duncan, *Galatians*, 100; Bruce, *Galatians*, 165; Fung, *Galatians*, 148; Martyn, *Galatians*, 320 – 21, 325 – 28). George rightly argues that God's curse of Christ is implicit in the verse, and that the doctrine of the substitutionary atonement is here "*in nuce*" (*Galatians*, 241 – 42).

90. Rightly B. Longenecker, *Triumph of Abraham's God*, 144. But Longenecker thinks that the curse was not God's per se since the phrase "by God" is omitted. Rather, the curse of the law is imposed with "God's consent" (145 – 46).

91. See Wallace, *Greek Grammar*, 387.

92. Contra Morna D. Hooker, "Interchange in Christ," *JTS* 22 (1971) 349 – 61; idem, "Interchange and Atonement," *BJRL* 60 (1978): 462 – 81.

93. Rightly George, *Galatians*, 240 – 42. Contra R. G. Hamerton-Kelly, "Sacred Violence and the Curse of the Law (Galatians 3.13): The Death of Christ as a Sacrificial Travesty," *NTS* 36 (1990): 98 – 118. Hamerton-Kelly reads the text in light of the sacred violence theme of René Girard.

to understanding the entire paragraph.[94] It is sometimes objected that the demand for perfect obedience to the Mosaic law is alien to the Sinai covenant. After all, those who sinned under the Mosaic law could offer sacrifice and receive atonement, and hence some interpreters reject the notion that flawless obedience is required.[95] Those who argue in such a way have failed to see a crucial step in Paul's argument. Now in one sense the Mosaic covenant required perfect obedience, and that is why sacrifices were necessary to forgive transgressions. But with the coming of Christ, a new era in the history of salvation has arrived. OT animal sacrifices no longer atone for sin.[96] Therefore, those who place themselves under the law must keep the law perfectly (see 3:10, 12) now that Christ has arrived. By placing themselves afresh under the law, they have repudiated Christ's sacrifice. And OT sacrifices are no longer effective, for that which they pointed to — the sacrifice of Christ — has arrived. Christ is the only means by which the curse of the law can be removed. The Judaizers, who worried so much about release from the law's curse, actually stood under it.

3:14a So that the blessing of Abraham might come in Christ Jesus to the Gentiles (ἵνα εἰς τὰ ἔθνη ἡ εὐλογία τοῦ Ἀβραὰμ γένηται ἐν Χριστῷ Ἰησοῦ). The main purpose of the current paragraph (and all of ch. 3 to this point) now emerges,[97] and the purpose clause is signaled by the term "so that" (ἵνα). The promise of Gen 12:3 — that all nations would be blessed in Abraham — has now become a reality in Christ Jesus (cf. Gal 3:8), not by circumcision or submission to the Mosaic law. In Gal 3:8 – 9 the blessing of Abraham belongs to those who trust in Christ. Conversely, God's curse falls on those who rely on the law for justification (3:10 – 12). Christ Jesus by his substitutionary death removes the curse for all who believe. It follows from this that Gentiles are included in the blessing of Abraham by trusting in Christ instead of through keeping the Torah.

3:14b So that we should receive the promise of the Spirit through faith (ἵνα τὴν ἐπαγγελίαν[98] τοῦ πνεύματος λάβωμεν διὰ τῆς πίστεως). Verse 14b further explicates the nature of the promise of Abraham.[99] The blessing of Abraham can also be described as the promise of the Spirit.[100] The genitive "of the Spirit" (τοῦ πνεύματος) should be take as appositional to "the promise" (τὴν ἐπαγγελίαν),[101] and hence the blessing is to be equated with the gift of the Spirit.

This second "so that" (ἵνα) in v. 14 designates a purpose clause, but is it subordinate to v. 14a, or

---

94. Against Martyn, who consistently separates the triumph in the cross from the forgiveness of sins (*Galatians*, 318, n. 110). Against Martyn, both are true: sin enslaves *and* human beings are guilty of committing it.

95. E.g., Howard, *Paul: Crisis in Galatia*, 53; Daniel P. Fuller, *Gospel and Law: Contrast or Continuum* (Grand Rapids: Eerdmans, 1980), 91 – 92; McKnight, *Galatians*, 154 – 55.

96. For this point, see also Das, *Paul, the Law, and the Covenant*, 144.

97. A number of commentators note that 3:14 summarizes the argument to this point. E.g., George, *Galatians*, 242; Longenecker, *Galatians*, 123.

98. Texts that are mainly Western ($\mathfrak{P}^{46}$, D*, F, G, etc.) support "blessing" (εὐλογίαν) instead of "promise" (ἐπαγγελίαν). The external evidence clearly supports the latter (ℵ, A, B, C, D², Ψ, 𝔐, etc.). Scribes likely inserted "blessing" (εὐλογίαν)

since the term was used earlier in the verse (so Metzger, *Textual Commentary*, 525).

99. Contra Kwon, *Eschatology*, 107 – 17.

100. Kwon argues that the promise of land given to Abraham cannot be equated with the gift of the Spirit. Furthermore, the use of the plural "promises" (Gal 3:16) shows that the promise of the Spirit cannot be identified with the promises given to Abraham since the latter are plural. Indeed, in 3:15 – 29 it is clear that the promise of Abraham is the inheritance and therefore, cannot be equated with the promise of the Spirit (*Eschatology*, 108 – 11). But against Kwon, there is no need to claim that the gift of the Spirit exhausts all that is involved in the promise given to Abraham, but the gift of the Spirit represents one aspect or dimension of the Abrahamic promise.

101. So Williams, "Justification and the Spirit," 92.

is it a coordinate purpose clause, a restatement in other terms of the purpose clause in v. 14a? If it is a separate purpose clause,[102] Paul teaches that Gentiles receive Abraham's blessing so that they then can receive the promise of the Spirit. If the purpose clauses are coordinate and both refer back to the main clause in 3:13, Paul declares that Christ removed the curse of the law so that Gentiles would receive Abraham's blessing, and Abraham's blessing is to be identified with the promise of the Spirit.

The latter interpretation is more convincing for two reasons.[103] (1) We should note the link forged between the righteousness that comes by faith and the gift of the Spirit in Gal 3:1 – 6. This is borne out by the word "just as" (καθώς) introducing 3:6. (2) Paul probably alludes here to Isa 44:3, where the blessing and pouring out of the Spirit are identified according to the simplest reading of the Hebrew parallelism:[104] "For I will pour out water on the thirsty land, and streams on the dry ground; I will pour out my Spirit on your offspring, and my blessing on your descendants." The text from Isaiah adds support to the notion that the blessing of Abraham is equated with the promise of the Spirit, for "blessing" and "Spirit" refer to the same reality.[105]

Paul is now at the conclusion of his scriptural argument. He maintains that since the Gentiles have the Holy Spirit, they enjoy the blessing of Abraham. And if they enjoy the blessing of Abraham, they are members of Abraham's family. And if they are part of Abraham's family by receiving the Spirit, they do not need to submit to circumcision or the law to become part of the people of God.

Theology in Application

Becoming Part of Abraham's Family

In 3:10 – 14 Paul contrasts the curse of the law with the blessing of Abraham. The issue before the Galatians is this: How does one become part of the family of Abraham? The Judaizers insisted that one must receive circumcision and submit to the law. Paul counters in 3:10 – 12 that those who devote themselves to the law will be cursed, for the law demands perfect obedience. The only means by which one can be right with God is through faith.

Paul explicates his view by appealing to proof texts from the OT in 3:10 – 13. What we have here in a compressed form is a summary of the exegetical arguments

---

102. So Betz, who thinks that the second clause presupposes the first (*Galatians*, 152); cf. also Lightfoot, *Galatians*, 140.

103. So Fung, *Galatians*, 151 – 52; Bruce, *Galatians*, 167; Williams, "Justification and the Spirit," 91; Longenecker, *Galatians*, 123.

104. So Hays, *Galatians*, 261. See also Rodrigo J. Morales, "The Words of the Luminaries, the Curse of the Law, and the Outpouring of the Spirit in Gal 3,10 – 14," *ZNW* 100 (2009): 269 – 77. Morales suggests that 4Q504 5.15 – 16 (*Words of the Luminaries*, 270 – 72, 276 – 77) and *T. Jud.* 24:2 – 3 link bless-

ing and the gift of the Spirit with Israel's redemption, and thus reflect dependence on Isa 44:3.

105. For the view that the blessing of Abraham and the promise of the Spirit do not refer to the same reality, see the careful study by Chee-Chiew Lee, "The Blessing of Abraham and the Promise of the Spirit: The Influence of the Prophets on Paul in Galatians 3:1 – 14," PhD diss. (Wheaton, IL: Wheaton College Graduate School, 2010). Nevertheless, the parallelism in Isa 44:3 suggests that the promise of the Spirit was understood by Paul to be at least part of the blessing promised to Abraham.

that Paul presumably used often when preaching to the Jews in synagogues. The curse of the law is removed only through the cross of Christ since Jesus bore God's curse on behalf of his people. Hence, the blessing of Abraham, i.e., the promise of the Spirit, belongs to both Jews and Gentiles who put their faith in Christ. Paul has now proved scripturally that the Gentiles are part of the family of Abraham because they have received the Spirit. He has also demonstrated that observance of the law is not the means by which one becomes part of Abraham's family.

Paul's Broader Purpose

In Galatians Paul argues that Gentiles who trust in Christ are truly members of the people of God.[106] They do not need to be circumcised or keep the Torah to belong to Abraham's family. A number of theological implications can be derived from this paragraph relative to Paul's broader purpose. (1) God demands perfect obedience to be in a right relationship with him. We see this in the garden of Eden. Adam and Eve are separated from God and sentenced to death for one sin. God does not summon them to trust him from that point on and then award them life for their 90 percent obedience. No, their only hope for life is in the promise of a seed who will crush the head of the serpent (Gen 3:15).

It follows, then, that those who pursue the law for justification are destined to fail since the law demands perfect obedience, and all without exception transgress God's standards. The need for perfect obedience and the human inability to attain such is clear even in the Mosaic covenant since animal sacrifices were required for atonement. The need for sacrifices demonstrates that God requires all to obey perfectly, for only by means of sacrifices are sins removed. Moreover, it is clear in the OT that all must offer sacrifices for atonement inasmuch as all without exception sin. With the coming of Christ the new era of salvation-history has arrived, and the Mosaic covenant is abrogated. Therefore, animal sacrifices cannot forgive the sins committed.[107] The only means of atonement is the cross of Christ.

It follows from the above that faith alone is the only way to be right with God. We cannot do anything to merit or earn God's favor. Our works always fall short, and hence we trust what God has done for us in Christ for our salvation. Our salvation is by grace alone through faith alone. Faith is a needy cry for God, while works try to impress God. Faith is a hand reaching out for help, while works insist that no help is needed. Faith trusts that God alone can accomplish salvation, while works smuggle in human effort and cooperation. As Luther said, "trying to be justified by the Law is like counting money out of an empty purse, eating and drinking from an empty

---

106. It is interesting to see how McKnight applies the passage to today since he endorses the new perspective. The application from the time of the Reformation onward is absent. Instead the passage teaches us that we should oppose racial discrimination (*Galatians*, 163).

107. Indeed, such sacrifices never truly purchased forgiveness; they pointed forward to Christ's sacrifice.

dish and cup, looking for strength and riches where there is nothing but weakness and poverty, laying a burden on someone who is already oppressed to the point of collapse, trying to spend a hundred gold pieces and not having even a pittance."[108]

(2) This text also brings to center stage the substitutionary atonement of Christ. Paul clarifies that Christ's atonement, in which he died in place of sinners, is the only hope for believers on the eschatological day of judgment. The doctrine of substitution is repulsive to some and debated by others, but it lies at the very heart of Pauline and biblical theology.[109] It reminds each one of us that we cling to Christ's righteousness alone as our hope on the last day.

(3) The blessing of Abraham is fulfilled in part in the promise of the Holy Spirit. The blessing of Abraham was the missionary promise that all nations would be blessed through Abraham (Gen 12:3). It was unclear when Genesis was written that Abraham's blessing would be fulfilled with the gift of the Spirit. But we saw above that such a connection is implied in Isa 44:3. Furthermore, a number of OT texts indicate that God's promises will only be realized through the coming of the Spirit (e.g., Ezek 11:18 – 19; 36:26 – 27; Joel 2:28). Paul explicitly identifies the blessing of Abraham with the presence of the Spirit here, showing the fulfillment of salvation history.

How to Live in Light of Paul's Message

The truths Paul enunciates to the Galatians still speak to us today. Here I will draw out two of these truths. First, we must relearn the gospel every day. We may think we already understand the gospel and hence can go on to something new. Almost inevitably we begin to think that we are morally superior to others. We begin to compare ourselves with those who are morally deficient to prop up our fragile egos. We forget how radically sinful we are, but the gospel reminds us that God's standard is 100 percent perfection. Sin is so subtle that we can even begin to use our work, a gift of God if we enjoy it, as a way to congratulate ourselves about our virtue. If we are praised regularly in our work, it is easy to begin to think that God is impressed with us as well. Our theology can say that we are all sinners who often fall short, and yet we may live our lives day after day without seriously *thinking* about ourselves as sinners. Therefore, the message of the gospel becomes more and more distant from our real lives. It may become part of our intellectual furniture and yet be removed from how we actually think about ourselves. I am not denying, of course, that God transforms those who belong to him. Still, our sinfulness persists until the day of redemption, and to forget this is to forget the gospel.

Second, we must cling to the cross of Christ alone. Focusing on our sinfulness could depress and discourage us, but God does not intend us to live with a constant

---

108. Luther, *Galatians 1535: Chapters 1 – 4*, 406 – 7.

109. For a robust defense of penal substitution, see Steve Jeffrey, Mike Ovey, and Andrew Sach, *Pierced for Our Trans-gressions: Rediscovering the Glory of Penal Substitution* (Wheaton, IL: Crossway, 2007); see also Schreiner, "Penal Substitution View," 67 – 98.

feeling of failure and condemnation. Our sins should drive us to the cross of Christ, where the full payment was made for our sins. God's love, then, becomes exceedingly precious in the way we think and feel in our everyday lives. We acknowledge our sins daily, but we cling to the cross of Christ as the means by which we are forgiven. Hence, when Satan accuses us, we remind ourselves that we are free from all guilt and condemnation (not because we are so good, but because God is so loving and forgiving).

We live, then, in the joy and freedom of forgiveness. On the one hand, we are conscious of our sin. On the other hand, such knowledge does not cripple us, for the cross is our liberation and freedom from the curse of sin. Faith trusts in what God has done for us in Christ. Depression and discouragement surely have many causes. But one of the main roots of depression is the feeling that we have failed and are unloved. The gospel summons us to reject such feelings and to place our trust in what God says about us. God declares, "You are justified, liberated, and forgiven. I love you." We often feel condemned, but Luther teaches us to fight against feelings of condemnation:

> But battle against that feeling, and say, "Even though I feel myself completely crushed and swallowed by sin and see God as a hostile and wrathful judge, yet in fact this is not true; it is only my feeling that thinks so. The Word of God, which I ought to follow in these anxieties rather than my own consciousness, teaches much differently, namely, that "God is near to the brokenhearted, and saves the crushed in spirit" (Ps. 34:18), and that "He does not despise a broken and contrite heart" (Ps. 51:17).[110]

---

110. Martin Luther, *Galatians 1535: Chapters 1 – 4*, 26.

Galatians 3:15 – 18

Literary Context

We have seen that a new section of the argument begins in chapter 3, with 2:15 – 21 functioning transitionally. Paul's purpose in 3:1 – 14 has been to argue that the Galatians did not need to be circumcised in order to belong to the people of God, the family of Abraham. The argument proceeds as follows: Certainly the Galatians did not need to be circumcised and observe the law to be saved, for they received the Spirit upon conversion, and the Spirit is *the sign* that one belongs to the people of God, that God's eschatological promises are being fulfilled (3:1 – 5). What is required to belong to the family of Abraham or to receive the blessing of Abraham is to have the faith of Abraham (3:6 – 9). Thus, those who believe like Abraham are his sons and daughters and have received the Abrahamic blessing. By contrast, those who attempt to be righteous by works of law are cursed since they fail to do what the law requires and since justification is by faith rather than works (3:10 – 12). The only way to receive the blessing of Abraham, i.e., the promise of the Spirit, is to trust in the death of Christ, for by his death on the cross he redeemed believers from the curse of the law (3:13 – 14).

From 3:15 – 4:11 Paul emphasizes the salvation-historical dimensions of his argument.[1] Why is it that circumcision is no longer required to belong to the people of God? Redemptive history was an implicit part of Paul's argument in the preceding verses, but in 3:15 – 4:11 it comes to the forefront, so that the readers grasp that circumcision was part of the former age and not the new age inaugurated by Jesus Christ. Paul's fundamental argument here is the priority of the Abrahamic covenant. The Mosaic covenant was instituted after the covenant with Abraham, but it does not invalidate the terms of the covenant with Abraham. In other words, there is no straight-line continuity between the Abrahamic and Mosaic covenants. Paul does not conceive of them as the same covenant, for the Abrahamic covenant is marked by promise whereas the Sinai covenant is a law covenant. The two must be distinguished from one another.

---

1. Against Martyn (*Galatians*, 338, n. 157, 342 – 52), who rightly sees the apocalyptic nature of Pauline thought but is unconvincing in trying to wash away any reference to salvation history. Martyn prosecutes his case by severing God from the origin of the law, but such a reading fails to convince. See the exegesis of 3:15 – 20.

Main Idea

The central point in these verses is that the Sinai covenant must be subordinated to the Abrahamic covenant. The two are not on an equal plane, for the promise to Abraham preceded the law given to Moses. Therefore, the inheritance is received via the promise given to Abraham, not by means of the law given to Moses. As a result, circumcision cannot be the pathway to blessing since it accords with the law.

Translation

(See next page.)

Structure

Paul introduces this new paragraph with the word "brothers" (ἀδελφοί), adapting an illustration from everyday human life. Scholars debate whether the reference is to testaments/wills or covenants. I will argue below that Paul had covenants in mind. The theme is illustrated by appealing to human covenants, for once they are ratified, they cannot be annulled or supplemented. In 3:16 – 18 Paul applies, marked by "now" (δέ), what is said regarding human covenants to the covenants God instituted with Abraham and Moses.

The nature of the covenant with Abraham is analyzed in 3:16, for God made promises to Abraham, and not only to Abraham but also to his offspring. Paul clarifies that the offspring is not plural and hence is limited to one particular offspring, i.e., Jesus Christ. In 3:17 Paul considers the role of the Mosaic covenant, stitching the

---

Galatians 3:15-18

15a	introduction	**Brothers, I am speaking humanly.**
b	assertion	**Even in human terms no one rejects or adds to a covenant that has been ratified.**
16a	explanation *(of 15b)*	**Now the promises were spoken** **to Abraham and** **to his offspring.**
b	explanation *(of 16a)*	**He does not say, "and to offsprings,"** **as if referring to many,** but
c	contrast *(to 16b)*	**as to one, "and to your offspring,"**
d	apposition *(to 16c)*	**who is Christ.**
17a	introduction	And **I am saying** this:
b	explanation *(of 17a)*	**The law,** which came four hundred and thirty years later, does not make void a covenant previously ratified by God,
c	result *(of 17b)*	with the result that it nullifies the promise.
18a	condition/basis *(of 17a-c)*	For if the inheritance is by law, **it is no longer by means of promise.**
b	contrast *(from 18a)*	But **God graciously gave it to Abraham through a promise.**

---

argument together with the word "and" (δέ). He emphasizes the temporal interval between it and the covenant made with Abraham, noting that the Sinai covenant was established 430 years later than the Abrahamic. He also stresses that the Abrahamic and Mosaic covenants have a different character, for the Abrahamic is characterized by promise, while the Mosaic is conditional and focuses on law. Hence, the latter covenant cannot annul the former.

The Judaizers would likely reply that the Mosaic covenant would not nullify the Abrahamic, for they were of the same nature. Paul, however, firmly disagrees in 3:18, providing the reason introduced with a "for" (γάρ). If the final inheritance is based on the law (the Mosaic covenant), then the promise of the covenant with Abraham is excluded. Indeed, the promise of grace given to Abraham must stand since it functions as the fundamental covenant. Therefore, the false teachers have gone astray in equating the Mosaic and Abrahamic covenants and in failing to see both the temporal and essential distinctions between the covenants.

Exegetical Outline

II. Paul's Gospel Defended from Experience and Scripture (3:1 – 4:11)

   A. Argument from Experience: Reception of Spirit by Means of Faith, Not Works (3:1 – 5)

   B. Argument from Scripture: Blessing of Abraham by Faith (3:6 – 14)

      1. Members of Abraham's family by faith (3:6 – 9)

      2. Curse of law removed only in Christ (3:10 – 14)

Explanation of the Text

3:15 Brothers I am speaking humanly. Even in human terms no one rejects or adds to a covenant that has been ratified (Ἀδελφοί, κατὰ ἄνθρωπον λέγω· ὅμως ἀνθρώπου κεκυρωμένην διαθήκην οὐδεὶς ἀθετεῖ ἢ ἐπιδιατάσσεται). Paul's language is friendlier here, for he does not label his audience as "foolish" (3:1) but addresses them as "brothers" (cf. 1:11; 4:12, 28, 31; 5:11, 13; 6:1, 18).

He begins with an illustration from everyday human life.[2] Even human beings consider covenants to be unbreakable. Once they are ratified, no one can annul them or add to them. The summary we have proposed, however, makes a number of assumptions about debatable issues in the text. The opening particle (ὅμως) is sharply debated (cf. also 1 Cor 14:7). Some scholars argue that it should be translated "likewise" here, while others translate it "even."[3] Since both interpretations

are possible, the one that makes the best sense in context should be preferred. It seems slightly more plausible to take Paul's argument here as an argument from the lesser to the greater. Hence, he maintains that even in human society (with all its faults and failings) covenants are considered to be binding and unchangeable.

The meaning of the word translated "covenant" (διαθήκη) here is also the subject of controversy. Should it be rendered "will/testament" or "covenant"? Many scholars support the translation "will" or "testament" here, for several reasons.[4] (1) This is the typical meaning of the word in classical literature and the papyri.[5] (2) Since Paul says he speaks "humanly" (lit., "according to man"; κατὰ ἄνθρωπον), he must appeal to the term as it was commonly used in Greco-Roman society.[6] (3) The use of the word "inheritance" also points to a will.[7]

---

2. For the meaning of the expression, "I am speaking according to man," see Longenecker, *Galatians*, 127. Against C. H. Cosgrove, who thinks Paul speaks of a human view in contrast to God's, so that Paul refers to a wrong position of the agitators here ("Arguing Like a Mere Human Being: Galatians 3:15 – 18 in Rhetorical Perspective," *NTS* 34 1988. : 536 – 49). Matera supports Cosgrove's view as well (*Galatians*, 130).

3. For the options, see Bruce, *Galatians*, 169; BDAG, s.v.; Longenecker, *Galatians*, 127.

4. E.g., Bruce, *Galatians*, 169; Martyn, *Galatians*, 338; Longenecker, *Galatians*, 128; Dunn, *Galatians*, 182 – 83;

Johannes Behm, "διαθήκη," *TDNT*, 2:129; S. M. Baugh, "Galatians 3:20 and the Covenant of Redemption," *WTJ* 66 (2004): 54 – 58.

5. See Adolf Deissmann, *Light from the Ancient East: The New Testament Illustrated by Recently Discovered Texts of the Graeco-Roman World* (trans. Lionel R. M. Strachan; 4th ed.; New York: Harper & Brothers, n.d.), 337 – 38.

6. William M. Ramsey, *Historical Commentary on Galatians* (ed. Mark Wilson; repr.; Grand Rapids: Kregel, 1997), 100 – 101; Betz, *Galatians*, 154 – 55; Behm, "διαθήκη," *TDNT*, 2:129.

7. Ramsey, *Galatians*, 100.

(4) The legal terms in the passage point to ratifying and annulling a will.[8]

A decision on the referent of διαθήκη is difficult, but the translation "covenant" should be preferred for a number of reasons.[9] (1) Context is always the most important factor in determining the meaning of a word, and Paul in this context clearly refers to the covenants with Abraham and Moses.[10] It is possible, of course, that Paul moves from the idea of a "will" in human society to a "covenant" when referring to Abraham and Moses, but it is more likely that he retains the same term throughout instead of requiring his readers to switch back and forth between "will" and "covenant."[11]

(2) Wills could be altered, whereas covenants were considered to be immutable.[12] There are several examples of covenants between human beings in the OT that were considered to be unbreakable (Gen 21:22 – 32; 26:26 – 31; 31:44 – 45; 1 Sam 18:3; 20:8; 22:8; 23:18; 2 Sam 3:12).[13]

(3) In both the LXX and the NT the usual referent for the noun used here (διαθήκη) is "covenant."[14]

(4) The use of legal terms does not indicate that the reference is to a will, for legal language is used with covenants as well.[15]

Legal language is used here to explain the nature of covenants. Once they are "ratified" (κεκυρωμένην), one cannot "reject" (ἀθετεῖ)[16] or "add to" (ἐπιδιατάσσεται) them. Paul argues from the lesser to the greater from 3:15 to 3:16. If even human covenants are irrevocable and cannot be supplemented, how much more a covenant given by God. In other words, the covenant with Abraham cannot be revoked by a later covenant, nor can additional stipulations be added to it. The covenant with Abraham stands as it was given originally.

3:16a Now the promises were spoken to Abraham and to his offspring (τῷ δὲ Ἀβραὰμ ἐρρέθησαν αἱ ἐπαγγελίαι καὶ τῷ σπέρματι αὐτοῦ). The covenant with Abraham was characterized by "promises," signifying what God would bring to pass by his grace.[17] The term "promises" calls attention to God's work rather than to what is attained through human effort. The promises

---

8. Behm, "διαθήκη," *TDNT*, 2:129; Betz, *Galatians*, 155 – 56; Martyn, *Galatians*, 338; Witherington, *Galatians*, 243; Baugh, "Galatians 3:20," 55.

9. John J. Hughes, "Hebrews IX 15ff. and Galatians III 15ff.: A Study in Covenant Practice and Procedure," *NovT* 21 (1979): 66 – 91; Lightfoot, *Galatians*, 141 – 42; Burton, *Galatians*, 496 – 505; Leon Morris, *Galatians: Paul's Charter of Christian Freedom* (Downers Grove, IL: IVP, 1996), 109; Scott W. Hahn, "Covenant, Oath, and the Aqedah: Διαθήκη in Galatians 3:15 – 18," *CBQ* 67 (2005): 79 – 86.

10. Ernst Bammel argues that the Jewish custom of *mattenat bari* is in view. Here a donor would give some property to a donee, and the disposition could not be annulled or changed ("Gottes ΔΙΑΘΗΚΗ [Gal iii 15 – 17] und das jüdische Rechtsdenken," *NTS* 6 [1959]: 313 – 19). Against Bammel, see Hughes, "Study in Covenant," 72 – 76.

11. Leon Morris, *The Apostolic Preaching of the Cross* (3rd ed.; Grand Rapids: Eerdmans, 1965), 91; Hughes, "Study in Covenant," 66.

12. Hughes, "Study in Covenant," 70 – 71, 83 – 90. Hughes shows that Egyptian, Greek, and Roman wills could be re-

voked and added to. Therefore, there is no warrant for thinking that Paul refers to a will or testament here.

13. Some scholars argue that "no one" (οὐδείς) in 3:15 means that no one but the testator can revoke the covenant (e.g., Baugh, "Galatians 3:20," 56 – 57; Martyn, *Galatians*, 338, 366 – 67; Schoeps, *Paul*, 182 – 83), but this interpretation is unpersuasive.

14. Hughes, "Study in Covenant," 31 – 32; J. Guhrt, "Covenant," *NIDNTT*, 1:365 – 72; Burton, *Galatians*, 498, 500 – 501.

15. So Gottfried Quell, "διαθήκη," *TDNT*, 2:111 – 18; Hahn, "Covenant," 87. Further, the legal character of the terms used has been exaggerated (so Hahn, "Covenant," 87). But against Hahn, it is unconvincing to restrict the covenant here to the Aqedah covenant of Gen 22:16 – 18 ("Covenant," 90 – 99), particularly because in Gen 15 the covenant depends on God alone, whereas Gen 22 emphasizes Abraham's obedience.

16. Cf. Exod 21:8; Deut 21:14; 1 Chr 2:7; 5:25; 2 Chr 36:13; 1 Macc 6:62; 14:44 – 45; 15:27; 2 Macc 13:25; 14:28.

17. For the close association of promise with the Abrahamic covenant, see Hansen, *Abraham in Galatians*, 128.

given to Abraham included land and universal blessing, and they were given specifically to his "offspring" (Gen 12:1 – 3; 15:1 – 5; 17:4 – 8; 18:18; 22:17 – 18; 26:4).[18] Even though the promises were given to Abraham's offspring, they also forecasted blessing for the whole world through Abraham (cf. Gal 3:8). The promises made to Abraham were confirmed to Isaac (Gen 26:3 – 4) and to Jacob (28:13 – 15; 35:12 – 13).

In light of 3:15 it is clear that the promises given to Abraham constitute the covenant that cannot be repealed or supplemented. We would also expect the word "offspring" to refer to the physical descendants of Abraham, or at least to the elect remnant among Israel (cf. Rom 9:6 – 9), but Paul's additional comments move in a different direction.

3:16b-d He does not say, "and to offsprings," as if referring to many, but as to one, "and to your offspring," who is Christ (οὐ λέγει, Καὶ τοῖς σπέρμασιν, ὡς ἐπὶ πολλῶν, ἀλλ' ὡς ἐφ' ἑνός, Καὶ τῷ σπέρματί σου, ὅς ἐστιν Χριστός). The significance of the word "offspring" is now explored. To whom were these inviolable promises

made? Paul finds significance in the singular form of the word "offspring" (σπέρματι) and distinguishes it sharply from the plural "offsprings" (σπέρμασιν). The distinction drawn is surprising since "offspring" is a collective singular.[19] Nor is Paul ignorant of this fact, for he uses the singular "offspring" (σπέρμα) as a collective just a few verses later (3:29). It is probable that Paul refers here to Gen 13:15 or 17:8 because the inclusion of the word "and" (καί) in the quotation "and to your offspring" (καί τῷ σπέρματί σου) must hearken back to an OT text where the word "and" (καί) is used.[20] Daube makes the same observation, noting that the quotation is found where there is a promise of land pledged to Abraham.[21]

A variety of interpretations have been offered to explain what Paul is doing here. Some claim that Paul's exegesis strayed from the original meaning of the text; hence, it cannot be justified as exegesis and should be categorized as allegory.[22] Similarly, some have in essence argued that Paul bends the text to fit his theology.[23] Daube finds precedence for Paul's interpretation particularly in a midrash on Gen 21:12, where the seed refers to Isaac.[24]

---

18. We should not press the distinction between the singular "promise" (ἐπαγγελία) and the plural "promises" (ἐπαγγελίαι) (see the singular in Gal 3:17, 18, 22, 29; 4:23, 28; Rom 4:13, 14, 16, 20, and the plural in Gal 3:21; Rom 15:8). The singular encompasses the totality of the promises made to Abraham. Cf. Burton, *Galatians*, 181.

19. Max Wilcox demonstrates such by showing that in the Targumim the collective singular "seed" is rendered by the plural "sons." "The Promise of the 'Seed' in the New Testament and the Targumim," *JSNT* 5 (1979): 2 – 16. But for a similar distinction between the singular and plural of the word "seed," see *m. Šabb.* 9:2.

20. So Burton, *Galatians*, 507; Betz, *Galatians*, 157, n. 34; Dunn, *Galatians*, 183; Martyn, *Galatians*, 339. Collins rejects this view since the land does not relate to universal blessing ("Galatians 3:16," 82). Further, he argues that we have an allusion to the biblical text here rather than an exact citation (since Paul uses the word "promise"), and hence an exact match is unneeded (83). Against Collins, the land promise in Paul is interpreted in universal terms (cf. Rom 4:13). Most

important, the presence of "and" (καί) indicates that Paul is quoting the OT text.

21. David Daube, *The New Testament and Rabbinic Judaism* (Peabody, MA: Hendrickson, 1990), 439. Daube also thinks Gen 24:7 is in view.

22. Schoeps, *Paul*, 181.

23. Cf. Burton, *Galatians*, 182 (though Burton ends up saying that the idea is an editorial corruption, 509); J. Christiaan Beker, *Paul the Apostle: The Triumph of God in Life and Thought* (Philadelphia: Fortress, 1980), 51. Byrne says Paul's interpretation is "somewhat bizarre." Brendan J. Byrne, *'Sons of God' — 'Seed of Abraham': A Study of the Idea of the Sonship of God of All Christians in Paul against the Jewish Background* (Rome: Biblical Institute Press, 1979), 159.

24. Daube, *New Testament and Rabbinic Judaism*, 438 – 44. Betz follows Daube in seeing Paul's dependence on midrashic teaching, but he rejects any reference to Isaac since there is no clear reference to Isaac in Gal 3:16, and it is illegitimate to read Gal 3:16 in light of Rom 8:32 (*Galatians*, 157, n. 38 and n. 40).

Daube thinks midrashic influence is substantiated by the following: (1) Paul's use of rabbinic chronology (430 years); (2) the reference to the promise of land for Abraham; (3) the certain fulfillment of the promise; (4) his understanding of the noun "offspring"; and (5) the notion that Isaac prefigured the Messiah. Daube concludes that the reference to a singular with the noun "seed" is defensible from the evidence.

It seems, however, that Paul's interpretation is plausible from the OT apart from the midrashim. The promise of redemption in Gen 3:15, which reaches back to the beginning of the OT story, is not restricted to a collective fulfillment.[25] The word "seed" may refer to a singular person, such as Seth in Gen 4:25. Isaac himself, in the narrative of Genesis, was the singular seed of Abraham (Gen 21:12),[26] and Paul distinguishes elsewhere between Isaac and Ishmael, seeing only Isaac as the true offspring (Rom 9:6–9). Furthermore, the promise articulated in Gen 3:15 is fulfilled through a singular descendant of David.[27] Wilcox has shown that the promised seed of Abraham was related to the promise of an offspring of David who would rule over Israel.[28] Therefore, we have a canonical precedent for the limitation of the seed to a singular, and the reference to David prepares the way for the notion of corporate solidarity.

We see from the OT that the seed narrows from Abraham to Isaac to a son of David. Such a view accords with typology and corporate solidarity as well. Paul interprets the OT text typologically and sees its crowning fulfillment in Jesus Christ.[29] A number of scholars, then, think that Paul employs corporate solidarity here, so that believers become members of God's people through their union with Jesus Christ,[30] for he is the true fulfillment of the promises made to Abraham and David.[31]

Wright argues that the singular indicates a reference to one family rather than to many families.[32] If the Torah was required, there would not be one united human family but a fracturing into many families. In Christ "the people of God are summed up."[33] So, the offspring here refers to Christ representatively or corporately, so that the reference is to one family of God in Christ.

25. Baugh, "Galatians 3:20," 59. So already Geerhardus Vos, *Biblical Theology: Old and New Testaments* (Grand Rapids: Eerdmans, 1948), 54–55. Others argue that Gen 3:15 refers to a singular seed. So C. John Collins, "A Syntactical Note (Genesis 3:15): Is the Woman's Seed Singular or Plural?" *TynBul* 48 (1997): 139–48; T. Desmond Alexander, "Seed," *NDBT*, 769.

26. So Witherington, *Galatians*, 244–45; Hahn, "Covenant," 96–97.

27. Cf. T. Desmond Alexander, "Abraham (Abram)," *NDBT*, 370–71. See the similar argument of Bruce, *Galatians*, 173.

28. Wilcox, "The Promise of the 'Seed,'" 2–20; James M. Hamilton Jr., "The Seed of the Woman and the Blessing of Abraham," *TynBul* 58 (2007): 253–73. Dahl documents a stream of tradition where David's seed (per 2 Sam 7) is singular, designating the Messiah (*Studies in Paul*, 130, n. 12). Cf. also Richard B. Hays, *Echoes of Scripture in the Letters of Paul* (New Haven, CT: Yale Univ. Press, 1989), 85.

29. Lightfoot, *Galatians*, 143. See also Leonard Goppelt, *Typos: The Typological Interpretation of the Old Testament in the New* (trans. Donald H. Madvig; Grand Rapids: Eerdmans, 1982), 138; Ridderbos, *Galatians*, 133–34.

30. Fitting with this conception is Harmon's view that we have an allusion here to Isa 41:8, and the offspring of Abraham finds its fulfillment in the Servant of the Lord ("She Must and Shall Go Free," 199–208).

31. E. Earle Ellis, *Paul's Use of the Old Testament* (Grand Rapids: Baker, 1957), 70–73; Robby J. Kagarise, "The Seed in Galatians 3:16: A Window into Paul's Thinking," *EvJ* 18 (2000): 67–73. See also Richard N. Longenecker, *Biblical Exegesis in the Apostolic Period* (Grand Rapids: Eerdmans, 1975), 123–24; Longenecker, *Galatians*, 132. Hays argues that Paul reads the Bible in light of his christological presuppositions (Hays, *Echoes of Scripture*, 120–21).

32. Wright, *Climax of the Covenant*, 163–68. See also B. Longenecker, *Triumph of Abraham's God*, 57. Cf. Robert L. Brawley, "Contextuality, Intertextuality, and the Hendiadic Relationship of Promise and Law in Galatians," *ZNW* 93 (2002): 104; Hansen, *Galatians*, 102–3.

33. Wright, *Climax of the Covenant*, 174.

Wright's interpretation is fresh and intriguing, but it suffers from deriving the meaning "family" from "offspring" in Gal 3:29 instead of the nearer referent in Gal 3:19, where it clearly refers to Jesus as an individual.[34]

Collins suggests that Paul literally interprets the OT, for Gen 22:17–18 refers to an individual offspring, which is fulfilled in Jesus Christ.[35] Such an interpretation represents an innovative attempt to take Paul's argument seriously as exegesis, even as historical grammatical exegesis. Still, it does not seem convincing, for Paul appeals to Gen 13:15 and 17:8 here, not to Gen 22:17–18. The use of the word "and" (καί) as part of the OT citation "and to your offspring" (καὶ τῷ σπέρματι αὐτοῦ) is lacking in Gen 22:18. If Paul were merely alluding to a text, it is unlikely that he would use the word "and" (καί). The presence of "and" (καί) is a stubborn piece of evidence that calls into question Collins's interpretation, indicating that Paul is actually quoting the OT here. And if he is quoting the OT, he is not referring to Gen 22:17–18, since "and" (καί) is omitted there.

To sum up: Paul reads the Genesis promises in light of the story line of the OT, which narrows the promise down to a son of David and finds its fulfillment in the one man, Jesus of Nazareth. The "offspring" texts should be interpreted, then, in terms of corporate representation. Jesus is *the representative* offspring of Abraham and David and the fulfillment of the original redemptive promise in Gen 3:15. Thus, the promise should be conceived typologically, for the offspring promises have their final fulfillment in Christ, so that the offspring promises in the OT point forward to and anticipate the coming of Jesus Christ.

So why does Paul connect Jesus with the promises to Abraham here? He does so to emphasize that the age of fulfillment has arrived. The promises made to Abraham have become a reality in Jesus Christ. They always pointed to the one offspring, Christ Jesus. Hence, to move backward in salvation history to the Mosaic law and covenant is a serious mistake.

3:17 And I am saying this: The law, which came four hundred and thirty years later, does not make void a covenant previously ratified by God, with the result that it nullifies the promise (τοῦτο δὲ λέγω· διαθήκην προκεκυρωμένην ὑπὸ τοῦ θεοῦ ὁ μετὰ τετρακόσια καὶ τριάκοντα ἔτη γεγονὼς νόμος οὐκ ἀκυροῖ εἰς τὸ καταργῆσαι τὴν ἐπαγγελίαν). The temporal disjunction between promise and law takes center stage here. The Mosaic covenant, which was enacted 430 years after the Abrahamic covenant, cannot invalidate or supersede the provisions of that covenant.

The rabbis did not typically read the Scriptures in terms of its overall story line but mined the OT for truths wherever they were found. It is likely that Paul's opponents maintained that the Mosaic covenant supplemented and "defined" the Abrahamic.[36] Paul argues, however, that the chronology in which the story unfolds is fundamental for reading Scripture rightly. The Abrahamic covenant and its promises preceded the Mosaic covenant (and the giving of the law) by 430 years.[37] The

---

34. Cf. here Das, "the natural reading of the text is an emphatic singular seed in contrast to the plural (or collective) seed. The one seed is Jesus Christ himself. Wright proposes that Jesus is the Messiah who sums up all Israel in himself and thereby rescues the possibility of a collective 'seed' here. The reading seems entirely forced and depends on Wright's understanding of Jesus as Israel's Messiah from other texts. The crucial difficulty to Wright's theory is that he must read the text backward from Gal 3:29." See *Paul, the Law, and the Covenant,* 72–73, n. 9.

35. Collins, "Galatians 3:16," 75–86; idem, "Genesis 3:15," 139–48; T. Desmond Alexander, "Further Observations on the Term 'Seed' in Genesis," *TynBul* 42 (1997): 363–67.

36. So Barrett, "The Allegory of Abraham," 15.

37. In Gen 15:13 the time in Egypt is 400 years, but Paul depends here on Exod 12:40, which says that the time period

covenant with Abraham, then, takes precedence, and the law functions as a subordinate and interim covenant that cannot invalidate the terms of the Abrahamic covenant.[38]

Paul rebuts the view that the Torah is eternal, which was common in Second Temple Judaism (cf. Sir 24:9; Wis 18:4; *4 Ezra* 9:37; *1 En.* 99:2; *Jub.* 3:31; 6:17; Bar. 4:1; *2 Bar.* 77:15; Philo, *Moses* 2:14).[39] Betz also points out here that some Jewish traditions depict Abraham himself as one who observed Torah.[40] The argument Paul makes here would be unnecessary if the covenants with Abraham and Moses were of the same nature and if Abraham observed the Torah. If the covenants were essentially the same, the temporal disjunction between the covenants would be irrelevant. But Paul spies a crucial distinction, for the Abrahamic covenant is characterized by promise and the Mosaic by law.

In other words, the Abrahamic covenant focuses on what God does for his people in saving them, while the Mosaic covenant accents human obedience. The Abrahamic covenant celebrates God's work in delivering his people, whereas the Mosaic summons human beings to keep the law. Paul does not give a complete exposition of the two covenants here, but he does see a fundamental incompatibility. If believers lived under the Mosaic covenant, the promise given to Abraham would be nullified. Human obedience would be the fundamental issue for receiving the promise, and hence circumcision would continue to be required. But

since the law is subsequent to the promise and inferior to the promise, circumcision and observance of the law are not required in order to belong to Abraham's family.

3:18 For if the inheritance is by law, it is no longer by means of promise. But God graciously gave it to Abraham through a promise (εἰ γὰρ ἐκ νόμου ἡ κληρονομία, οὐκέτι ἐξ ἐπαγγελίας· τῷ δὲ Ἀβραὰμ δι᾽ ἐπαγγελίας κεχάρισται ὁ θεός). The discontinuity between the law (the Mosaic covenant) and the promise (the Abrahamic covenant) is further explained here (note the "for" [γάρ]). The final inheritance will not be obtained by observing the law since all violate its provisions. The inheritance is a gift of God's grace — the result of his promise to his people, and it is this promise that God gave to Abraham.

In the OT the term "inheritance" (κληρονομία) and its corresponding verb "to inherit" refers to the Land of Promise pledged to Abraham (Gen 15:3 – 5; 17:8; 21:10; 22:17; 28:4).[41] The term is especially prominent in Joshua in terms of the apportionment of the land (Josh 11:23; 12:6; 13:1; 18:7, 20, 28; 19:1, 8, 9, 10, etc.). The promise of the inheritance cannot be restricted ultimately to Canaan but anticipates inheriting the world (Pss 22:27 – 28; 47:7 – 9; 72:8 – 11; Zeph 3:9 – 10; cf. also Sir 44:21; *Jub.* 22:14; 32:19; *2 Bar.* 14:13; 51:3; *1 En.* 5:7). Elsewhere Paul asserts that Abraham is heir of the world (Rom 4:13). The expectation of a new world, a transformed universe, accords with what

---

was 430 years. The difference in time is of no consequence for the substance of Paul's argument. Longenecker notes how the rabbis and Josephus resolved the difference between the two numbers, seeing the 430 years as the span of the Abrahamic covenant and the inauguration of the Mosaic covenant, and the "400 years as the period Israel spent in Egypt" (*Galatians*, 133). Longenecker concludes that Paul simply transmits the standard view that 430 years elapsed "between the Abrahamic covenant and the Mosaic law" (ibid.)

38. Against Kwon, *Eschatology*, 161 – 68. Kwon doubts

this interpretation since the Galatians can still choose to live under the law. But, against Kwon, this is precisely the point. If the Galatians choose to observe the law, they are living at the wrong time in salvation history. The wavering of the Galatians demonstrates the eschatological tension rejected by Kwon.

39. So Martyn, *Galatians*, 342.

40. Betz, *Galatians*, 158.

41. For a study of inheritance in Paul, see James D. Hester, *Paul's Concept of Inheritance: A Contribution to the Understanding of Heilsgeschichte* (London: Oliver & Boyd, 1968).

we find elsewhere in the NT (Heb 11:10, 13 – 16; 13:14; 2 Pet 3:13; Rev 21:1 – 22:5). To speak of an inheritance, then, is another way of describing the possession of eschatological salvation.[42]

The contrast between law and promise is explained further, where it is clear that Paul does not think that the addition of the Mosaic covenant constitutes a clarification of the covenant with Abraham.[43] They are fundamentally opposed in that the inheritance is obtained through obedience to the law under the Mosaic covenant, whereas it is given through a promise of God under the Abrahamic.[44] The word "no longer" (οὐκέτι) could be understood as temporal, but in this context it is probably logical.[45] The law and the promise are fundamentally opposed. Therefore, if the inheritance is obtained by law, then the promise is eliminated.

The promise, of course, has priority, for God in his grace (note the emphasis on grace in the term "graciously gave," κεχάρισται) gave the promise to Abraham, and Paul has already explained that the Abrahamic covenant has priority.[46] The promise of an inheritance does not depend on observing the Mosaic law or being circumcised. Rather, the promise is a gift of God's grace and is freely bestowed in Christ Jesus. Those who belong to the family of Abraham do not enter into his family by subscribing to the Mosaic law. They are children of Abraham when they are united to Christ Jesus, the offspring of Abraham. Hence, they receive the promise as a gift.

Theology in Application

Continuity and Discontinuity

The importance of reading the story line of the whole Bible comes to the forefront in this chapter. We have a tendency to read the Scriptures apart from the progress of revelation, without paying heed to the unfolding narrative, as if all of Scripture occupies the same place in the landscape of God's plan. This was apparently the way the false teachers read the Scriptures. Commands in the Mosaic law were just as valid as any other part of the scriptural narrative. Such a view, however, fails to see the primacy of the Abrahamic covenant, for it takes precedence as the fundamental covenant with Israel. Therefore, any other covenant that follows is subordinate to the covenant with Abraham.

Such an observation leads to another crucial conclusion. Later covenants, such as the Davidic and new covenants, are harmonious with the Abrahamic covenant

---

42. Kwon rightly emphasizes that the inheritance is exclusively eschatological. Paul does not envision a fulfilled inheritance but restricts the inheritance to the future (*Eschatology*, 130 – 54).

43. For some theological and exegetical reflections on this matter, see T. David Gordon, "Abraham and Sinai Contrasted in Galatians 3:6 – 14," in *The Law Is Not of Faith: Essays on Works and Grace in the Mosaic Covenant* (ed. Bryan D. Estelle, J. V. Fesko, and David VanDrunen; Phillipsburg:

Presbyterian and Reformed, 2009), 240 – 58. I would qualify some of Gordon's statements, but he rightly sees the contrast between the Abrahamic and Sinai covenants.

44. The Pauline argument, then, cannot be restricted to salvation history (contra Garlington, *Galatians*, 217).

45. So Lightfoot, *Galatians*, 144.

46. Kwon translates this clause, "God showed favor to Abraham through the promise" (*Eschatology*, 121).

because they simply elaborate and refine the provisions of God's promise to Abraham. Paul argues, however, that the Mosaic covenant has a different character. This is not to say that the Mosaic covenant was not a covenant of grace or that it bears no relation to the covenant with Abraham. The Lord gave Israel the stipulations of the Mosaic covenant after he redeemed them from Egypt by his grace. Still, the Mosaic covenant promises that the inheritance (the promise of the land) would be gained by obedience, whereas the Abrahamic covenant pledges that God would save his people by virtue of his promise.

When we consider the Mosaic covenant, therefore, we must carefully consider elements of both continuity and discontinuity with the Abrahamic covenant. Here Paul features the discontinuity, and hence those who fail to see such discontinuity between the covenants flatten out the differences in the redemptive-historical timeline and are even in danger of falling into the same error as the false teachers in Galatia, for the latter did not distinguish between the Mosaic and Abrahamic covenants.[47] Thus, they argued that circumcision was necessary for salvation!

Fulfillment of the Promise

Paul also calls attention to the fulfillment of the promise made to Abraham. In other words, the end of the story has arrived. The true and only offspring of Abraham is Christ Jesus. All the other offspring of Abraham failed in one way or another, whether it was Abraham himself, Moses, David, or one of the prophets. Jesus is the perfect offspring of Abraham and the culmination of the narrative that began with the promise of offspring in Gen 3:15.

Every reader knows that all the details of a story take on a different shape and perspective when we know the end of the story. Looking back we realize that Jesus is the only true offspring of Abraham, the only one who faithfully did God's will. He is the one who removed the curse of the law on the cross (3:13). Escape from the present evil age only comes through him (1:4). Failure to see the significance of the cross can only be ascribed to bewitchment (3:1). Those who subscribe to circumcision and law-righteousness do not grasp that righteousness and membership in Abraham's family only come through union with Christ Jesus. The fullness of time has arrived in the cross and believers are freed from enslavement (4:4 – 5). To submit to circumcision turns back the clock in salvation history. It is also an attempt to establish one's own righteousness instead of acknowledging that righteousness only comes through Christ Jesus.

Some people believe that eternal life comes from what we do. But Paul could scarcely be clearer about the difference between the law and the promise, namely, that life comes because of God's promise. Most things in ordinary life are based on

---

47. See here the helpful exposition by Jason Meyer, *The End of the Law: Mosaic Covenant in Pauline Theology* (Nash- ville: Broadman & Holman, 2009).

law. Grades are based on law, on performance, on works. But grades and the gospel are not the same thing. In the gospel God offers himself to us and promises to strengthen us by his grace.

Here we see the sweetness of the gospel from which we derive great comfort. We are not right with God by our obedience but by our faith in God's promise. We receive what he has given to us in Christ Jesus. The law says: Do this. The gospel says: Accept this. When you think of yourself as a widow or widower, a single person, a student, or a wife, mother, husband, father, young person, or child, you can think of many failures in your life. The devil wants to discourage you and tell you that you can never be right with God because of your failures. But the gospel says that we are right with God because of God's promise of life in Christ.

John Piper refers in a sermon to a poem of John Bunyan that beautifully captures the difference between the law and the gospel:[48]

> Run, John, run, the law commands
> But gives us neither feet nor hands,
> Far better news the gospel brings:
> It bids us fly and gives us wings.

48. Accessed at www.desiringgod.org/ResourceLibrary/Sermons/ByDate/1994/862_Long_for_the_Pure_Milk_of_ the_Word/ on October 31, 2009.

Galatians 3:19 – 25

Literary Context

To understand this paragraph, we must follow the line of thought beginning in chapter 3. The Galatians were truly members of God's people because they had received the Spirit of God (3:1 – 5). Further, they were sons of Abraham and had received the blessing of Abraham through faith (3:6 – 9). Those who attempt to be right before God by circumcision and works of law are cursed, whereas those who put their trust in Christ Jesus and his death have received the blessing of Abraham and the promise of the Spirit (3:10 – 14). Beginning with 3:15 Paul focuses on salvation history. The covenant with Abraham is fundamental in the biblical story line, and the covenant with Moses is subsidiary to it since it came later (3:15 – 18). The difference between promise and law is not merely temporal, for the inheritance is a gift in the covenant with Abraham, but it is gained by obedience in the Mosaic covenant. Hence, there is a fundamental opposition between the two covenants.

If the Mosaic covenant is not an extension of the Abrahamic promise, what is the purpose of the law? Paul argues that the law was given to increase transgressions, that it was intended to be in force only until the Messiah came, and that the presence of a mediator shows that it is inferior to the promise (3:19 – 20). But if the law and the promise have such different purposes, does it follow that the law is contrary to God's promises?

Paul's answer is intriguing, for he argues that the law and the promise have different functions. The law could never grant righteousness, but it enclosed all under sin until Jesus Christ came (3:21 – 25). Hence, the law was in force for an interim period in salvation history until the coming of Christ. Now that faith in Christ has come and the promise to Abraham is realized, believers are no longer under the Mosaic covenant and law. And if believers are not under the Mosaic covenant, then circumcision is unnecessary.

Main Idea

The law was not given to secure the promise. Instead, it was given to increase transgressions. Further, the Mosaic law was never intended to be in force forever. It was a temporary custodian until the arrival of the promise, namely, Christ Jesus. Now that faith in Christ has arrived, the era of the Mosaic law has passed away.

Translation

(See next page.)

Structure

Paul has just finished saying that the eschatological inheritance is by promise rather than via the law. The incompatibility of the law and promise leads him to ask why God gave the law at all, and hence the new section is introduced with "then why" (τί οὖν). Paul argues in a compact statement that the law was given to increase transgressions (3:19). Further, the law had a temporary jurisdiction. Now that Jesus the Messiah has arrived, the law is no longer in force. Indeed, the inferiority of the law to the promise is signaled by its transmission through angels to a mediator, whereas the promise was given directly to Abraham by the one God (3:20).

If the inheritance is by promise rather than by law, so that the two are incompatible in terms of gaining life, and if the law was given in such a way as to underline its inferiority, does the law stand in opposition to God's promises (marked by a

Galatians 3:19-25

19a	question	**Then why was the law given?**
b	answer	**It was added on account of transgressions,**
c	time (of 19b)	until the offspring should come for whom the promise was reserved,
d	series (from 19b-c)	having been ordained through angels by the hands of a mediator.
20a	assertion	And a mediator is not for one party,
b	contrast (from 20b)	but **God is one.**
21a	question	Therefore, **is the law contrary to the promises of God?**
b	answer	**By no means!**
c	explanation (of 21b)/condition	For if a law was given that was able to give life, then righteousness would have truly been by the law.
22a	contrast (to 21c)	But **Scripture has imprisoned all under sin,**
b	purpose (of 22a)	in order that the promise might be given to those who believe
c	means (of 22b)	by means of faith in Jesus Christ.
23a	series (to 21-22)/temporal	Now **before faith came, we were held in custody under law,**
b	manner (of 23a)	in that we were shut up to the faith that was about to be revealed.
24a	inference	So then, **the law has become our custodian until Christ,**
b	purpose (of 24b)	in order that we should be justified by faith.
25	restatement (of 24a-b)	And **now that faith has come, we are no longer under the custodian.**

"therefore" [οὖν], 3:21)? From the previous argument we might expect Paul to say, "Yes, indeed." Instead, he categorically rejects such an idea. The law is not contrary to the promises, but it does have a different function. Contrary to the promise, the law cannot produce life (3:21). Instead ("but," [ἀλλά]), Scripture has enclosed all under sin, so that the promise of the eschatological inheritance is given only to those who put their faith in Christ Jesus (3:22).

Therefore, the law functioned as a custodian, a kind of babysitter, until the coming of the promise and faith in Christ Jesus (3:23). The law's jurisdiction was temporary and limited, and now that Christ has come, believers are no longer under its authority (3:24). Like a babysitter, its era of tutelage is over now that the new age of salvation history has dawned (3:24 – 25).

Exegetical Outline

II. Paul's Gospel Defended from Experience and Scripture (3:1 – 4:11)

    A. Argument from Experience: Reception of Spirit by Means of Faith, Not Works (3:1 – 5)

    B. Argument from Scripture: Blessing of Abraham by Faith (3:6 – 14)

        1. Members of Abraham's family by faith (3:6 – 9)

        2. Curse of law removed only in Christ (3:10 – 14)

    C. Argument from Salvation History: Priority of Abrahamic Covenant and Temporary Nature of Mosaic Covenant (3:15 – 4:11)

        1. Addition of law does not nullify promise to Abraham (3:15 – 25)

            a. Interim nature of Mosaic covenant (3:15 – 18)

    →   **b. The purpose of the law (3:19 – 25)**

                i. The law was given to increase sin (3:19a-b)

                ii. The law was in force until Christ came (3:19c)

                iii. The law's inferiority signaled by mediation (3:19d – 20)

                iv. The law is not contrary to God's promises (3:21a)

                v. The law could not produce life (3:21b)

                vi. All imprisoned under sin (3:22)

                vii. The law as custodian (3:23)

                viii. Era of the custodian has ended (3:24 – 25)

        2. Sons of God are Abraham's offspring (3:26 – 29)

Explanation of the Text

3:19a-b Then why was the law given? It was added on account of transgressions (Τί οὖν ὁ νόμος; τῶν παραβάσεων χάριν προσετέθη).[1] If the law is not the primary covenant but is subsidiary to the Abrahamic covenant, and if eschatological salvation is obtained through the promise of the Abrahamic covenant rather than observing the law of the Mosaic covenant, then why did God give the law?[2] It was given, "added" by God (προσετέθη as a divine passive), "for the sake of transgressions," which means that God gave the law to increase transgressions.

Hübner argues that the subject of the passive verb is the angels referred to later in 3:19 and concludes that Paul assigns the giving of the law to evil angels.[3] This view should be rejected for a number of reasons.[4] (1) The passive participle "having been ordained" (διαταγείς) should be construed as a divine passive, indicating that the law was ordained by God. (2) The preposition "through" (διά) with the genitive indicates that the angels were a means through whom the law came, not ultimately responsible for the law. (3) The reference to the angels is in a subordinate clause, and hence they

do not function as the subject. (4) In the clause that immediately follows the verb "promised" (ἐπήγγελται), God is clearly the implied subject.[5] (5) Nowhere else in Pauline theology is the law attributed to evil angels; it is considered to be a good gift of God (Rom 7:12). (6) Such a view clearly contradicts what the OT says about the giving of the law, and Paul assigns divine authority to the OT.

What does Paul mean in saying that the law "was added on account of transgressions"? The word "for the sake of" (χάριν) follows the word "transgressions" (τῶν παραβάσεων) in Greek. That is because the word is postpositive, which means that it occurs after the word it modifies.[6] So, it is translated first but the word it modifies appears first. The phrase is controversial since it is compact, and Paul does not elaborate on its significance. Four interpretations dominate.

(1) The law was given by God to *restrain sin*.[7] According to this reading, the law taught Israel how to live before Christ came.

(2) The law's purpose was to *define sin*.[8] If this view is adopted, 3:19 is similar to Rom 4:15, which says, "Where there is no law, there is no

---

1. There are a number of odd textual variants here. One text adds "for the sake of traditions" (παραδόσεων, D*). Others add the word "actions" (πράξεων, 𝔓46, F, G, it, Irlat, Ambrosiaster, Pseudo-Augustine). These readings make little sense in context and lack significant external evidence. See also Daniel B. Wallace, "Galatians 3:19–20: A *Crux Interpretum* for Paul's View of the Law," *WTJ* 52 (1990): 233–34.

2. The words "why then?" (τί οὖν) are adverbial here. So Wallace, "Galatians 3:19–20," 231–32.

3. Hans Hübner, *Law in Paul's Thought* (trans. James C. G. Greig; Edinburgh: T&T Clark, 1984), 26–27, 82–83. Schoeps does not identify the angels as evil but assigns the law to angels instead of God (*Paul*, 183). Martyn does not attribute the origin to evil angels but argues that God was absent in the giving of the law (*Galatians*, 354, 356–57, 365–68).

4. See Wallace, "Galatians 3:19–20," 235, 240–42; Hong, *Law in Galatians*, 153–55.

5. Against Betz, there is no contradiction with the law being mediated by angels (*Galatians*, 167). The mediation through angels does not deny that the law ultimately stems from God.

6. See Robertson, *Grammar of Greek New Testament*, 647.

7. Chrysostom, *Galatians*, 28; David J. Lull, "'The Law Was Our Pedagogue': A Study of Galatians 3:19–25," *JBL* 105 (1986): 481–98; Linda Belleville, "'Under Law': Structural Analysis and the Pauline Concept of Law in Galatians 3:21–4:11," *JSNT* 26 (1986): 53–78; Brawley, "Promise and Law," 106–8; B. Longenecker, *Triumph of Abraham's God*, 122–28. This view was held by many in the history of the church (so Riches, *Galatians through the Centuries*, 192).

8. Jeffrey A. D. Weima, "The Function of the Law in Relation to Sin: An Evaluation of the View of H. Räisänen," *NovT* 32 (1990): 226–27; Charles H. Giblin, "Three Monotheistic Texts in Paul," *CBQ* 37 (1975): 540.

transgression." The law provides the standard, the measuring stick, by which sin is identified. The law classifies sin as sin in a technical or legal sense. In other words, sin is identified as "transgression" when a specific law is violated. Longenecker defends this view by saying that the notion that the law multiplies sin does not fit with the temporal clause, while the definitional sense accords with the idea of the supervision of the pedagogue, and also explains why those under the law are cursed.[9]

(3) Dunn argues that the law was given *to deal with sin*. In other words, sacrifices were provided in the OT cultus to atone for sin before the coming of Christ.[10]

(4) Despite the attractiveness of the first three views, the view that is the most plausible is that the law was given to *increase sin*.[11] The problem with the first view, that the law was given to restrain sin, is the context of Galatians. Such an admission by Paul would support the view of the Judaizers who argued that the Galatians must be circumcised and keep the law. Surely the opponents must have argued that the law's restraining function was desperately needed among the Galatian Christians. Instead, Paul has already argued that the law curses those who are under its rule since no one can obey it (3:10).[12] Indeed, the law is unable to grant life, and all enclosed within its realm are under the power of sin (3:21 – 22). Furthermore, 4:5 speaks of those who were under law as redeemed or liberated from it, indicating that those who are under law are enslaved to sin. Hence, there is no reason to think that the law is

envisioned as restraining sin here. Quite the opposite. As in Rom 5:20, the law was given to increase transgressions. Such a perspective fits with the history of Israel, for life under law did not lead to a law-abiding society. Instead, sin reigned in Israel, and as a result both the northern and southern kingdoms were sent into exile.

A more attractive solution is that the law was given to *define* sin, and it is possible that both the defining of sin and the expansion of sin are included. Still, it is difficult to see how the law defined sin only until Christ came. The idea that the law increased the reign of sin in Israel until the coming of the Christ, however, fits with the OT story of Israel's life under the law. Furthermore, it was noted above that Paul links being "under law" (cf. 3:23) with being under the power of sin, and hence the upsurge of sin under the law is preferable. By showing that the law could not curb sin, God revealed that the only answer to the power of sin is the coming of the Messiah.[13]

Finally, it is unlikely that Paul emphasizes here that the law provides atonement for sin. Instead, he emphasizes in Galatians that the law does not provide full and final forgiveness, for if forgiveness is truly secured through the law and its sacrifices, then Christ died for nothing (2:21).

3:19c Until the offspring should come for whom the promise was reserved[14] (ἄχρις οὗ ἔλθῃ τὸ σπέρμα ᾧ ἐπήγγελται). The law's reign concluded with the coming of the "offspring" (i.e., Christ), and hence the fulfillment of the promise has been secured. Wright defines "offspring" (σπέρμα) here

---

9. Longenecker, *Galatians*, 138 (but he goes on to say that the meaning cannot be determined with certainty [138 – 39]); cf. Witherington, *Galatians*, 256.

10. Dunn, *Galatians*, 188 – 90.

11. Rightly Calvin, *Galatians*, 100; Betz, *Galatians*, 165 – 66; Hong, *Law in Galatians*, 150 – 51.

12. On Paul's negative understanding of the "under" phrases in Galatians, see Hansen, *Abraham in Galatians*, 130.

13. In response to Longenecker, who sees no reason why God would want to multiply sin before Christ came (*Galatians*, 138).

14. The last part of my translation stems from Baugh, "Galatians 3:20," 59. McKay translates it similarly, "until the seed should come, for whom the promise stands" (*A New Syntax of the Verb in New Testament Greek*, 151).

as "family," but such a translation is difficult to sustain. Christ is the corporate head of the people of God, the only true offspring of Abraham, but that is not quite the same thing as saying that the referent is family rather than Christ.[15]

The first purpose of the law was to multiply transgressions so that it would be evident that the law itself is not the answer to the sin problem. The second comment on the purpose of the law is articulated here: The law was never intended to be in force forever,[16] for it is subordinate to what God had promised.[17] Hence, when the promised offspring arrived, i.e., Jesus the Christ, the law's jurisdiction ended.[18] The law, then, was always intended as an interim arrangement.

What Paul says here is astonishing, for the typical view of Judaism was that the law would last forever. As Bar 4:1 says about wisdom in the Torah, "She is the book of the commandments of God, the law that endures forever" (NRSV; cf. Wis 18:4; Josephus, *Ag. Ap.* 2.277; Philo, *Moses* 2.14). We see again the characteristic salvation-historical teaching of Paul. The law, which preceded Christ's coming, revealed the power and depth of human sin, and thus the greatness of the redemption accomplished in Christ Jesus is set in bold relief.

3:19d Having been ordained through angels by

the hands of a mediator (διαταγεὶς δι' ἀγγέλων ἐν χειρὶ μεσίτου). The subordinate role of the law continues to be Paul's theme, as is shown by its mediation from angels.[19] By way of contrast, the promise was given directly to Abraham, and hence the covenant with Abraham receives priority.[20]

To say that angels were the intermediaries for the reception of the law does not suggest that God was absent when the law was given[21] or even that the angels were actually demonic. The participle "having been ordained" (διαταγεὶς) indicates as a passive participle that God is the one who determined that the law would be transmitted by angels.[22]

The notion that angels were present when the law was given is unclear in the OT, but it may be present in Deut 33:2: "The LORD came from Sinai and dawned from Seir upon us; he shone forth from Mount Paran; he came from the ten thousands of holy ones, with flaming fire at his right hand" (ESV). A reference to angels is clearer in the LXX of this verse, which speaks of the "angels with him" (ἄγγελοι μετ' αὐτοῦ). Another text from which the same tradition may be derived is Ps 68:17. The notion that the law was mediated through angels may be found in Josephus (*Ant.* 15.136)[23] and in Philo (*Dreams* 1.140–44), and it seems clear in *Pesiq. Rab.* 21.8. Other Jewish

---

15. Rightly Baugh, who points out that Wright falls into "illegitimate totality transfer" in seeing "Christ" in 3:16 as referring both to Jesus and the people of God ("Galatians 3:20," 53, n. 17).

16. Rightly Betz, *Galatians*, 168.

17. Against Baugh, it is not evident that the irrevocability of the promise is grounded in an intratrinitarian covenant among the members of the Trinity (Baugh, "Galatians 3:20," 49–70). Nothing is said about a pact among the members of the Trinity here, and we must beware of reading our theology into a text.

18. Rightly Wallace, "Galatians 3:19–20," 239–40.

19. Albert Vanhoye argues that one angel — the angel of God's presence (Acts 7:38) — represented the multitude of angels (7:53), and Moses represented all of Israel. See "Un médiateur des anges en Ga 3,19–20," *Bib* 59 (1978): 403–11; so

also Bruce, *Galatians*, 179. Against Vanhoye, it is unclear that the angel of the presence is in view. The text more naturally refers to Moses as a mediator, and it is unclear that another mediator (the angel of the presence) functioned as a mediator as well. Nor does the text suggest that the law was given through seventy angelic mediators to seventy human mediators as Gaston suggests. Lloyd Gaston, "Angels and Gentiles in Early Judaism and in Paul," *SR* 11 (1982): 65–75.

20. Cf. Burton, *Galatians*, 190–91.

21. As Martyn wrongly argues (*Galatians*, 365).

22. Terrance Callan, "Pauline Midrash: The Exegetical Background of Gal 3:19b," *JBL* 99 (1980): 554.

23. Bandstra defends the notion that angels rather than prophets or priests are in view in *Ant.* 15.136, but he thinks the angels here taught human beings the chief elements of the law prior to Sinai. See Andrew J. Bandstra, "The Law and the

traditions refer to a mediation through a single angel (*Jub.* 1:27; 2:1; 6:22; 30:11–12, 21; 50:6, 13). We find elsewhere in the NT the tradition of mediation through angels (Acts 7:53; Heb 2:2), and hence Paul does not innovate here.

The "mediator" (μεσίτου) in the verse is almost certainly Moses, for he functioned as the one who transmitted the law to Israel.[24] The presence of a mediator suggests the inferiority of the revelation or the weakness of the people.[25] The reference to Moses' hands alludes to the Ten Commandments, which Moses brought down from the mountain with his own hands (cf. Exod 32:15, 19; 34:4, 29). So, Paul emphasizes that the law was given to Moses through angels, and Moses in turn mediated the law to the people.

3:20 And a mediator is not for one party, but God is one (ὁ δὲ μεσίτης ἑνὸς οὐκ ἔστιν, ὁ δὲ θεὸς εἷς ἐστιν). Here Paul contrasts the oneness of God with a mediator (Moses), who stands between two parties (God and the people). The covenant made with Abraham is superior because it is given directly by God in contrast to the mediation between parties that we find in the Mosaic covenant. The genitive "for one" (ἑνός) could also be translated "of one." The difference in meaning between the two expressions is negligible. A mediator is not just "for" or "of" one party. Here Paul reflects on the occasion when Moses mediates between God and the people at Sinai, and he sees the covenant with Abraham as superior since God enacted his covenant directly with Abraham.

The brevity of this verse has puzzled interpreters throughout history. Lightfoot says there are 250 to 300 interpretations.[26] Oepke, drawing on the 430 years of 3:17, mentions 430 different ways of construing the verse (see 3:17).[27] The article with "mediator" (ὁ μεσίτης) may be generic.[28] But it could also be construed as anaphoric, referring back to the mediator of 3:19, who is Moses. Callan maintains that the mediation here is not general but refers to the mediation of Moses.[29] The idea, then, may be that Moses mediated for the angels, which were a plurality.[30] Callan restricts the mediation to angels since Paul refers to the role of angels and not to human beings.[31]

Still, it is likely that Paul has in mind particularly the conveyance of the law to Israel. We saw in the previous verse that the law was given to Israel through the hands of Moses. Hence, the mediatorial role of Moses cannot be restricted to his interaction with angels but should also include his giving of the law to Israel.

Wright suggests that the word "one" here points to one family.[32] The Torah did not produce one

---

Angels: *Antiquities* 15.136 and Galatians 3:19," *CTJ* 24 (1989): 223–40. Still, Bandstra sees some relationship with 3:19 since angels are associated with the law. W. D. Davies argues that prophets are the referent in *Ant.* 15.136. "A Note on Josephus, Antiquities 15:136," *HTR* 47 (1954): 135–140. Francis R. Walton presents evidence that he believes strengthens Davies's general case. See "The Messenger of God in Hecataeus of Abdera," *HTR* 48 (1955): 255–57.

24. Betz, *Galatians*, 170; Fung, *Galatians*, 161; Longenecker, *Galatians*, 140–41. Against many in the history of interpretation who saw a reference to Christ here, such as *Augustine's Commentary on Galatians*, 164, n. 101, 165; Chrysostom, *Galatians*, 28; Calvin, *Galatians*, 102.

25. Contra Baugh, "Galatians 3:20," 53, 64–65. For Jewish traditions that emphasize that mediation was necessary

because of the weakness of Israel, see Callan, "Gal 3:19b," 559–61. Perhaps Paul also alludes to the golden calf incident (Exod 32–34) when Moses functioned as a mediator for Israel (Callan, "Gal 3:19b," 561–64). Israel's sin was more egregious since they violated a law revealed by God himself.

26. Lightfoot, *Galatians*, 146.

27. Albrecht Oepke, *Der Brief des Paulus an die Galater* (3rd ed.; THKNT; Berlin: Evangelische Verlagsanstalt, 1973), 82.

28. Baugh, "Galatians 3:20," 64–65.

29. Callan, "Gal 3:19b," 565–66; cf. Wright, *Climax of the Covenant*, 169.

30. Giblin, "Three Monotheistic Texts in Paul," 540–41.

31. Callan, "Gal 3:19b," 566.

32. Wright, *Climax of the Covenant*, 169–70; cf. also Garlington, *Galatians*, 220–21; Hays, *Galatians*, 267–68.

unified human family since Moses mediated only for Israel. Therefore, the Mosaic covenant separated Israel from the nations, but God's intention was, through Abraham, to bring about one united family. The interpretation is intriguing, but reading the notion of family into the word "one" lacks clear contextual support. If Paul had wanted to make this point, he could have added the word "people" or "nation" to "one."

Lightfoot's interpretation is preferable.[33] A mediator involves at least two parties, and in this context the distance between God and Israel is stressed. Such a view fits with the giving of the law in Exodus, where Moses received the law on the mountain alone and brought it down to Israel (cf. Exod 19 – 34). Mediation also implies a contract between God and Israel. Therefore, the promises of the covenant were dependent on both parties fulfilling their responsibilities. The Sinai covenant failed because Israel did not do what was demanded and broke the stipulations of the covenant. The promise given to Abraham, by contrast, is dependent on God alone. And since it depends on his promise and is not contingent, it will certainly be fulfilled.

The main idea of the verse seems clear in context. On the one hand, the law is inferior to the promise because it required mediation: from God to angels to Moses to the people. On the other hand, the one God spoke directly to Abraham. Hence, the promise is clearly superior to the law. The indirect way that the law came to Israel suggests that it should not be placed on the same plane as the promise.[34]

The declaration that "God is one" recalls one of the fundamental tenets of Judaism, found in the Shema of Deut 6:4. Paul also appeals to the oneness of God in Rom 3:30 to underscore that there is one way of salvation. It is intriguing that both in Romans and here in Galatians the oneness of God is introduced where Paul defends the inclusion of Gentiles into the people of God apart from the law. Since there is one God, there is one way of salvation. Inasmuch as the law did not and could not accomplish salvation, it is inferior to the promise.

3:21a-b Therefore, is the law contrary to the promises of God? By no means! (Ὁ οὖν νόμος κατὰ τῶν ἐπαγγελιῶν τοῦ θεοῦ;[35] μὴ γένοιτο). Paul has argued in the previous verses that the law is subordinate to the promise since the law was instituted 430 years after the covenant with Abraham was established. Furthermore, the promise and the law operated on different principles.[36] Under the promise the inheritance is obtained as a gift of God's grace, whereas under the law the promise is secured through human obedience. Indeed, the law was given to increase transgressions, and it was never intended to be in force forever. Now that Christ has come, the day of its jurisdiction has ended. The inferiority of the law is signaled by its being given through a mediator instead of being given directly by God.

Given this preceding context, we would expect that Paul would agree that the law was contrary to God's promises. But he most emphatically rejects such a conclusion. In what follows, Paul explains how it is that the law and the promises are in accord.

---

33. Lightfoot, *Galatians*, 146 – 47.

34. So also Callan, "Gal 3:19b," 565; Burton, *Galatians*, 190; Longenecker, *Galatians*, 142.

35. The words "of God" (τοῦ θεοῦ) are lacking in some manuscripts (𝔓46, B, d, Ambrosiaster, Marius Victorinus), and the words "of Christ" (τοῦ Χριστοῦ) are substituted by 104. Scribes would incline to add "of God" (τοῦ θεοῦ) after

promises in accord with Rom 4:20 and 2 Cor 1:20 (so Metzger, *Textual Commentary*, 525). Nevertheless, it is likely that the words are original. External evidence for inclusion is significant (א, A, C, D, [F, G], Ψ, 𝔐, etc.).

36. Fee argues that Paul uses the plural "promises" since God reiterated the promise to Abraham more than once (*Galatians*, 131).

3:21c For if a law was given that was able to give life, then righteousness would have truly been by the law (εἰ γὰρ ἐδόθη νόμος ὁ δυνάμενος ζῳοποιῆσαι, ὄντως ἐκ νόμου ἂν ἦν[37] ἡ δικαιοσύνη). When Paul says that the law and the promise do not contradict one another, he is not suggesting that they have the same function. The law and the promise fit together in the economy of God's plan, but they play different roles. The law, though representing God's will, was not a source of life.[38] In Judaism the law was seen as the pathway to life: "the more study of the Law the more life" (*m. ʾAbot* 2:7; cf. Sir 45:5; *4 Ezra* 14:30).[39] A second class, contrary-to-fact condition is used here to explain that the law did not and could not produce life. The law revealed how people should live, but it did not provide the power to enable human beings to live in a way that pleases God. Righteousness would have indeed been through the law if human beings had been able to keep its prescriptions.

That the law and the promise do not have the same function is obvious, for the promise, in contrast to the law, does provide life. Indeed, the promise secures life by grace alone, so that the life bestowed is wholly the work of God. Hence, righteousness (ἡ δικαιοσύνη) — i.e., right standing with God — is by means of the promise. It is clear, therefore, that the harmony of the law and promise cannot be resolved simplistically, for Paul clarifies that the law does not grant life or righteousness, while the promise does. It seems that the law serves the promise in that it reveals that the only way to obtain righteousness is through the cross and grace of Christ. In other words, Luther rightly saw that one of the main purposes of the law was to convict human beings of sin so that they would be driven to Christ.[40]

3:22 But Scripture has imprisoned all under sin, in order that the promise might be given by means of faith in Jesus Christ to those who believe (ἀλλὰ συνέκλεισεν ἡ γραφὴ τὰ πάντα ὑπὸ ἁμαρτίαν, ἵνα ἡ ἐπαγγελία ἐκ πίστεως Ἰησοῦ Χριστοῦ δοθῇ τοῖς πιστεύουσιν). Scripture has shut up all under the power of sin, and hence the promise of the inheritance belongs to those who trust in Jesus Christ. The referent of "Scripture" is debated. Some argue that "Scripture" here is simply another way of describing the law.[41] Nonetheless, Paul does not use "law" here but "Scripture," and the difference is significant given the repetition of the term "law" in the argument thus far.

Others maintain that Paul has in view the Scriptures as a whole.[42] Since Paul nowhere else uses the term "Scripture" without appealing to a particular verse, it may be that he has a particular verse in mind, such as Deut 27:26 cited in Gal 3:10.[43] Still, no particular OT text is clearly cited here, and thus it seems likely that the testimony of the Scriptures as a whole is in view. Scripture here personifies God, indicating that it was God's will that all be imprisoned under sin. Sin is personified here and conceived of as a power that exercises control over human beings. Such a reading is supported by the close parallel in Rom 11:32.[44]

---

37. A number of different variants appear in the textual tradition, but in most instances the meaning remains the same. The variant "by means of the law" (ἐν νόμῳ) (𝔓[46], B) is secondary.

38. See Silva, *Interpreting Galatians*, 192–94.

39. See also Betz, *Galatians*, 174.

40. Cf. also Chrysostom, *Galatians*, 29.

41. Calvin, *Galatians*, 105; Bruce, *Galatians*, 180; Garlington, *Galatians*, 224; Sanders, *Paul, the Law*, 87, n. 6.

42. Morris, *Galatians*, 116; Fung, *Galatians*, 164; Belleville, "Under Law," 56; Hong, *Law in Galatians*, 155; Matera, *Galatians*, 135.

43. Lightfoot suggests Ps 143:2 or Deut 27:26 (*Galatians*, 147–48). Others are persuaded that only Deut 27:26 is in view (Burton, *Galatians*, 195–96; Longenecker, *Galatians*, 144).

44. So Silva, "Galatians," 806. Against Betz, *Galatians*, 175.

The word "all" (τὰ πάντα) is difficult to interpret. If we take the word impersonally, Paul may suggest that Scripture encloses the law, the elements of the world, and the entire old creation under the power of sin.[45] The neuter could also be construed personally (cf. 1 Cor 1:27 – 28), and this may be supported by the emphasis on persons in the context.[46]

What Paul says here confirms the interpretation of the previous verse. The law and the promise are complementary in God's purposes, but such a conclusion does not mean that they function in precisely the same way. The law drives people to the promise, so that they are righteous by faith in Jesus Christ.

Those who support the subjective genitive "faithfulness of Jesus Christ" (πίστεως Ἰησοῦ Χριστοῦ) point to the participle phrase "to those who believe" (τοῖς πιστεύουσιν) and contend that the need for faith is communicated in the participle; hence, the faithfulness of Christ is expressed in the prepositional phrase.[47] That is, referring to faith in Christ twice in one verse would be superfluous. Such a reading is possible but not decisive (see the In Depth article, "What Does Paul Mean by the 'Faith of Jesus Christ'"? at 2:16). The objective genitive should still be favored, for Paul desires to *emphasize* the importance of faith *in* Christ, over against the observance of the law. Such emphasis would especially manifest itself in the oral reading the letter.[48] The promised inheritance is not given to those who observe what the law says but to those who put their trust in Christ Jesus. We see a polarity here between the law versus faith, between doing versus believing. The law is compatible with the promise as long as it moves one toward faith in Christ Jesus

3:23a Now before faith came, we were held in custody under law (Πρὸ τοῦ δὲ ἐλθεῖν τὴν πίστιν ὑπὸ νόμον ἐφρουρούμεθα). The interim character of the law has been at the forefront since 3:15. The law was established 430 years after the promise was made to Abraham (3:17), and it remained valid only until the coming of Jesus, his true offspring (3:19). Here Paul designates the entire period of salvation history until the coming of Christ as "before faith came," saying that the law functioned as the warden before the era of faith.

Paul cannot mean here that faith did not exist at all until the coming of Christ, for he has taught already that Abraham was justified by faith (3:6 – 9; cf. Rom 4:1 – 25). All those who are right with God throughout redemptive history are justified by faith. The coming of faith, in this verse, represents the inauguration of a new era in redemptive history, the time when God was fulfilling his eschatological promises. Faith is portrayed as an objective reality that has now dawned.

Some scholars, perceiving the objective character of faith and the redemptive-historical cast of Paul's argument, maintain that "faith" here must refer to the faithfulness of Jesus Christ.[49] Such an

---

45. See Barrett, *Freedom and Obligation*, 34; Martyn, *Galatians*, 370 – 73.

46. So Betz, *Galatians*, 175, n. 116; Bruce, *Galatians*, 180; Longenecker, *Galatians*, 144 (to exclude any distinctions between peoples); Hong, *Law in Galatians*, 155 – 56.

47. Alternatively, the phrase "by faith in Jesus Christ" (ἐκ πίστεως Ἰησοῦ Χριστοῦ) could modify the noun "promise" (ἐπαγγελία). For a vigorous defense of this reading in support of an objective genitive, see Matlock, "The Rhetoric of πίστις in Paul," 187 – 93. It seems more likely that "by means

of faith in Jesus Christ" modifies the verb "given" (δοθῇ), and since it is conjoined with the participle "those who believe" (τοῖς πιστεύουσιν), the prepositional phrase is added for emphasis.

48. Cf. Silva, "Faith versus Works," 232 – 33, 40.

49. So Choi, "Galatians 5:5 – 6," 474 – 76; Caneday, "Faithfulness of Jesus Christ," 200 – 203. Sprinkle propounds a view similar to the subjective genitive, arguing that the focus is on the Christ event itself rather than his faithfulness ("Πίστις Χριστοῦ as an Eschatological Event," 212 – 15).

argument does not clearly follow, for it wrongly splits redemptive history from anthropology (the impact of the law on human experience), as if the former swallows up the latter. The salvation-historical nature of the text should be highlighted, for a contrast between the age of law and the age of faith is underscored.

What is a reality in this new era of redemptive-history, however, is personal faith in Christ.[50] Abraham and all OT saints believed in God's promise, but now the people of God, at the end of the ages, specifically and particularly put their faith in Jesus Christ. Perhaps we could also say that faith is particularly characteristic of the new age inaugurated by Jesus Christ.[51] This is not to say that faith did not exist in the OT, only that it was limited to a remnant.

The first person plural "we" in this context focuses on Israel since Paul refers to salvation history and to Israel's experience under the law. Still, it does not seem that Gentiles are entirely excluded, for in 4:1–11 Paul lumps the Gentiles with Israel and places them under the law as well.[52] The verb "we were held in custody" (ἐφρουρούμεθα) overlaps in meaning with the verb "imprisoned" (συνέκλεισεν) from 3:22, and the participial form of the same verb immediately follows ("being shut up," συγκλειόμενοι).

These verbal forms can be understood positively or negatively. Some interpreters construe

them positively and think that the point is that the law restrained sin during the era of the Mosaic covenant. The verb here (φρουρέω) means "protect" or "guard" in some contexts (Phil 4:7; 1 Pet 1:5), and the participle "being shut up" (συγκλειόμενοι) could be understood as separating Israel from the influences of sinful Gentiles.[53] Nonetheless, the negative interpretation is more convincing. The parallel expression in 3:22 indicates that all are "imprisoned … under sin,"[54] while here they are said to be held in custody under the law.[55]

The verb "imprison" (συνκλείω) usually has a negative meaning of being enclosed, besieged, or shut up under the hand of an enemy (cf. Jer 21:4; Ps 77:62; 1 Macc 4:31; 5:5; 15:25). Further, Rom 11:32 is an apt parallel where "God has bound all men over to disobedience" (συνέκλεισεν γὰρ ὁ θεὸς τοὺς πάντας εἰς ἀπείθειαν). The phrase "under law" (ὑπὸ νόμον) here in Gal 3:23 invariably refers to the old era of salvation history, referring to the time period in which Israel lived under the Sinai covenant.

In addition, to be under law is also to be under sin. The correlation between being "under sin" and "under law" is suggested by the gliding from the one to the other in 3:22–23. A similar pattern emerges in Rom 6:14–15. Those who live "under law" (the old era of redemptive history) are also under the dominion and power of sin, whereas

---

50. In other words, redemptive history and anthropology (human experience) work together here. So Bruce, *Galatians*, 181; Mussner, *Galaterbrief*, 254–55; Hansen, *Abraham in Galatians*, 134–35.

51. Cf. Betz, *Galatians*, 176.

52. Longenecker argues that "we" here refers to the Jews only (*Galatians*, 145); Dunn, *Galatians*, 198–200; see also Fee, *Galatians*, 137–38. For the notion that Jews and Gentiles are both under the law, see Bruce, *Galatians*, 182; Brice L. Martin, *Christ and the Law in Paul* (NovTSup 62; Leiden: Brill, 1989), 100–103. See also the discussions under Gal 3:13, 4:3, and 4:5.

53. Cf. Norman H. Young, "*Paidagogos*: The Social Setting of a Pauline Metaphor," *NovT* 29 (1987): 150–76; T. David Gordon, "A Note on παιδαγωγός in Galatians 3.24–25," *NTS* 35 (1989): 154.

54. Cf. 2 Cor 11:32; Wis 17:15, and BDAG's comment: "The terminology is consistent w. the Roman use of prisons principally for holding of prisoners until disposition of their cases."

55. So also Hong, *Law in Galatians*, 157. Belleville argues that life under the law is neutral ("Under Law," 60), but Hong rightly observes that she fails to see the import of the parallel between being "under sin" and "under law" (*Law in Galatians*, 157).

those who live in the new age inaugurated by Christ are "under grace," and the tyranny of sin has been defeated. So too, Jesus was born "under law" (Gal 4:4) so that he could liberate those "under law" (4:5) from the "elements of the world" to which they were enslaved (4:3). We should note how Paul connects being "under law," "under sin," and "under the elements of the world" (ὑπὸ τὰ στοιχεῖα τοῦ κόσμου).

In particular, it must be observed that those under the world's elements live in slavery so that sin rules over them. The former age of redemptive history (the Sinai covenant) was an age in which sin ruled over God's people. The equation of being "under law" with being "under sin" is strengthened by 4:21, for those who desire to be "under law" are choosing to be children of the slave woman, Hagar, instead of enjoying the freedom that comes from being the children of the heavenly Jerusalem (4:21 – 5:1). The slavery described most likely denotes life under the dominion of sin. So too, in 5:18 those led by the Spirit are not "under law." Since 5:18 follows on the heels of the conflict between the flesh and Spirit described in 5:17, it seems clear that to be "under law" is to be under the power of sin.

Indeed, the eschatological contrast shines forth brightly, for those who are in Christ have the Holy Spirit, and by the power of the Spirit they no longer live in the old age of death and sin and the law. Some might say that the paradigm does not work since Jesus lived under the law (4:4), but he is the exception that proves the rule. As one who lived under law, he triumphed over the law and over sin and death (cf. 4:5).

The only other place where Paul uses the phrase "under law" is 1 Cor 9:20, where the phrase appears four times. Paul labors to emphasize that even if he chose to live under the law, he was not truly subject to it, but now lives by the law of Christ. Indeed, that those who are "under law" are enslaved to sin is evident, for Paul aims to free them from that condition. It seems clear, then, that Paul's purpose is to speak negatively of being imprisoned by or confined under the law.

Wilson also interprets the phrase "under law" negatively, but he argues from the parallel expression "under a curse" (ὑπὸ κατάραν) in 3:10 that the phrase "under law" in Galatians is shorthand for being under the curse of the law. Wilson argues that this meaning for the phrase is limited to Galatians and that Paul uses the formula ironically in 4:21.[56] Such a reading is possible and fits generally with the interpretation proposed here. Nevertheless, it seems more likely that the formula has a redemptive-historical sense rather than being limited to the curse of the law.[57]

Two arguments make Wilson's view less likely. It is not evident that Paul writes ironically in 4:21. If the verse is interpreted straightforwardly, Paul asks why the Galatians want to live under the old era of redemptive history. Moreover, elsewhere in Paul the phrase does not refer to the curse of the law but the old age in redemptive history (Rom 6:14 – 15; 1 Cor 9:21), and it seems more probable that the phrase has a uniform meaning throughout Paul's letters.

3:23b In that we were shut up to the faith that was about to be revealed (συγκλειόμενοι εἰς τὴν μέλλουσαν πίστιν ἀποκαλυφθῆναι). The law's limited and temporary role in salvation history continues to be emphasized. Israel was confined under the law until the coming of Christ. More specifically, the law ruled until faith in

---

56. Todd A. Wilson " 'Under Law' in Galatians: A Pauline Theological Abbreviation," *JTS* 56 (2005): 362 – 92.

57. Of course, the curse of the law may also fit with the redemptive-historical view. What must be determined is whether the focus is on the curse of the law in the phrase.

Christ was revealed. The words "to be revealed" (ἀποκαλυφθῆναι) emphasize salvation history. Now that a new era has dawned and Christ has come, believers are no longer enslaved to "the present evil age" (1:4). With the coming of Christ, a new age has arrived in which faith in Christ has become a reality.

3:24a So then, the law has become our custodian until Christ (ὥστε ὁ νόμος παιδαγωγὸς ἡμῶν γέγονεν εἰς Χριστόν). The word "so then" (ὥστε), though it can designate result, has an inferential sense here ("so then"). Paul has emphasized from 3:15 on the temporary role that the law played in salvation history, and hence he now draws the threads together of the previous argument. In context the preposition used here (εἰς) should be construed temporally and translated as "until."[58] The law plays an intermediary role in the history of salvation, so that it functioned as the pedagogue or custodian until Christ came.

The key question here is the meaning of the word "custodian" (παιδαγωγός). Pedagogues were typically household slaves (though they could be free persons) and were in charge of children until their later teenage years. A custodian (παιδαγωγός) in the ancient world was not precisely a teacher but more of a child-attendant or babysitter, keeping watch over children during the years of their immaturity. They would teach them morals and manners, attending to them in their daily lives. In ancient literature the pedagogue was both admired and hated. They were supposed to be moral guides for the young, but they did not always live up to the ideal.[59] This is the problem

with interpreting the significance of the custodian in Galatians.

The law could be understood as a pedagogue that restrains and bridles sin, just as the custodian's role was to teach children manners and good behavior.[60] Gordon maintains that the law as a custodian was designed to separate Jews from Gentiles until the coming of Christ, so that the Jews would be protected from corrupting Gentile influences.[61] Similarly, Young focuses on the restrictions of the law for a particular era in the history of salvation, which functioned to segregate Jews from Gentiles until the coming of Christ.[62] Others argue that the law functions as a tutor or teacher, showing that life does not come from keeping the law but only through faith in Jesus Christ.[63] Still others see the point as enslavement under the law.[64]

What makes the issue particularly difficult is that virtually all the interpretations are possible, since the pedagogue could be understood in a variety of ways. The way to solve the impasse is to focus on the context of Galatians. When we attend to the line of Paul's argument in the letter, the meaning of the term "custodian" (παιδαγωγός) comes into sharper profile. I have argued in this commentary that there is no evidence in Galatians for the notion that the law restrains sin. Such was probably the view of the false teachers, the interlopers who visited Galatia and demanded circumcision. Paul argues, on the contrary, throughout the letter that those who are under the law are also under the power of sin. Hence, it is unlikely that the custodian is introduced to emphasize the restraining role of the law.

---

58. So Betz, *Galatians*, 178; Bruce, *Galatians*, 183; Longenecker, *Galatians*, 148 – 49.

59. Young, "*Paidagogos*," 151 – 68.

60. So Lull, "The Law," 486 – 96; Belleville, "Under Law," 53 – 78.

61. Gordon, "παιδαγωγός," 150 – 54. Cf. also Dunn, *Galatians*, 197 – 200. Therefore, Robinson argues that "we" here

refers to Jews only ("Jewish and Gentile Believers," 35).

62. Young, "*Paidagogos*," 150 – 76. See also Michael J. Smith, "The Role of the Pedagogue in Galatians," *BSac* 163 (2006): 197 – 214.

63. Georg Bertram, "παιδεύω," *TDNT*, 5:620 – 21.

64. Hong, *The Law in Galatians*, 160. Martyn sees the pedagogue here as "an imprisoning warden" (*Galatians*, 363).

To say that the law separates Jews from Gentiles for a certain period of salvation history, as Gordon and Young do, is certainly correct. Still, it is questionable in this context whether Paul advances this particular argument. Nowhere else in Galatians do we find an emphasis on the segregating function of the law. The law's role in separating Jews from Gentiles is present by implication (cf. 2:11 – 18), but Paul does not explore this particular feature of the law; that is, he does not reflect on the law's positive function of separating Jews from Gentiles so as to spare Jews from corrupting influences. Instead, he argues that the law should not be imposed on the Gentiles since justification is by faith in Christ. Since Paul does not linger on the law's role in separating Jews from Gentiles, it seems doubtful that this function of the law concerns him here.

The one feature that stands out is that children need a custodian before they arrive at maturity.[65] Paul makes this same point when referring to the guardians and managers in 4:1 – 2. In other words, what comes to the forefront with the word "custodian" (παιδαγωγός) is the interim character of the law. Just as people had a pedagogue only as long as they were children, so too the law was intended to be in force for a limited time in the history of salvation. The Judaizers, who insisted on circumcision, failed to see that the Mosaic law was not designed to be permanent. Therefore, in using the word "custodian" (παιδαγωγός), the precise focus is neither negative or positive. What comes to the forefront is the temporary role of the law. It *functioned* as a kind of babysitter until the fullness of time came.

3:24b In order that we should be justified by faith (ἵνα ἐκ πίστεως δικαιωθῶμεν). It is also the case that the traditional view of the custodian (παιδαγωγός), i.e., the law drives one to faith in Christ, has some support here. Paul has emphasized in 3:15 – 23 that the law encloses and confines all under sin, so that all will be saved through the promise of faith in Christ Jesus. Hence, the law also seems to have the function of displaying the inability of human beings to observe its commands so that it is clearly perceived that the only hope for human beings is faith in Christ Jesus.

The history of Israel portrays the inability of God's people to please him under the Sinai covenant. Living under the pedagogue did not restrain Israel from sin but demonstrated the ability of sin to coopt the law for its own purposes. Now, however, a new era in the history of salvation has commenced. Human beings are declared to be in the right (δικαιωθῶμεν) before God by faith in Jesus Christ. The era of the law has ended.

3:25 And now that faith has come, we are no longer under the custodian (ἐλθούσης δὲ τῆς πίστεως οὐκέτι ὑπὸ παιδαγωγόν ἐσμεν). Paul now draws the conclusion from the preceding argument. Now that faith in Christ has come at this specific time in salvation history, the era of the law, the era of the pedagogue, has ended. The word "no longer" (οὐκέτι) is temporal here rather than logical, so that it emphasizes the dawning of a new era in redemptive history. The phrase "under the custodian" represents another example of an "under" (ὑπό) phrase used in a salvation-historical sense. Indeed, those who are no longer under the pedagogue are no longer under the law, and hence they are no longer under the dominion of sin.

---

65. Cf. R. N. Longenecker, "The Pedagogical Nature of the Law in Galatians 3:19 – 4:7," *JETS* 25 (1982): 53 – 61.

Theology in Application

The Role of the Old Testament

One of the central issues in biblical theology is the role of the law and the Sinai covenant. Paul does not often use the language of covenant when referring to the law, and yet it is clear from 3:15 – 18; 4:21 – 30; and 2 Cor 3:1 – 18 (see esp. 3:14) that the law, in Paul's mind, is part of the Sinai covenant. As part of the Mosaic covenant, the law, according to this section of Galatians, is restricted to a certain era in the history of salvation.

The interim character of the law and therefore of the Mosaic covenant is a distinctive and indeed revolutionary feature in Paul's theology. Before Paul believed in Jesus Christ, he fervently believed what most Jews of his day asserted, that the law remained binding until the end of history. Rabbinic Judaism after the time of Paul also assumed and promoted the continuing validity of the law. Therefore, Paul's notion that the promise to Abraham takes precedence over the law is a striking innovation. He read the OT in terms of its story line and did not conceive of it as a flat entity that could be mined apart from the overall story.

One cannot cite any part of the OT as binding for people today (like circumcision, food laws, tithing, or Sabbath laws) without considering where such commands are in the entire story. The OT as a whole must not be thought of as a gigantic book of Proverbs but must be read and interpreted in light of the unfolding story of redemption. Indeed, Paul makes it clear that the Mosaic law is not binding on believers today, for the Mosaic covenant is no longer the standard for believers.

Of course, all of the OT is part of sacred Scripture and is authoritative for believers. Still, the application of laws in the Mosaic covenant to today must be discerned in light of the entire story of redemption culminating in the coming of Jesus Christ. Clearly some of the commands of the Mosaic covenant are cited as authoritative for believers today (see the discussion of Gal 5:14 and 6:2), but whether and how commands from the OT law apply to today cannot be resolved by simply appealing to a command in the Mosaic law.

Space is lacking here to work out the practical ramifications of this matter in detail. Virtually all those who proclaim the Scriptures argue that circumcision and food laws are no longer binding. But it seems that the same should be said about the Sabbath and tithing, for they are also tied to the Mosaic covenant.[66] Many preachers insist that Christians must tithe today, but in most instances the reasons why this command of the Mosaic covenant is still normative remains unexplained, especially since the tithe went to the priests and was brought to Jerusalem. But it is obvious

---

66. On tithing, see Andreas Köstenberger and David A. Croteau. "'Will a Man Rob God?' (Malachi 3:8): A Study of Tithing in the Old and New Testaments," *BBR* 16 (2006): 53 – 78.

that the OT priesthood is no longer in force today since Christ's Melchizedekian priesthood has arrived (Heb 7:1 – 10:18).

The Role of Law

Another astonishing, at least to Paul's contemporaries, element of his teaching is the notion that the law, instead of restraining sin, provokes and exacerbates it. If immediate punishments follow infractions, then the law, of course, may restrain sin since human beings wish to avoid retribution (cf. Rom 13:1 – 7; 1 Tim 1:8 – 11). Paul does not address the role of the law restraining sin in Galatians (3:19) or Romans (5:20; 7:5, 7 – 25). The typical Jewish view was that the Torah was an agent for moral transformation. Hence, the popular saying, "the more study of the Law the more life" (*m. ʾAbot* 2:7). The notion that the Torah led to life was common in Judaism (Sir 17:11; Bar 3:9; 4:1; Pseudo-Philo, *Bib. Ant.* 23:10; *Pss. Sol.* 14:2 – 3).[67] Certainly Paul must have concurred with such a view before his conversion. As a Christian, however, he was persuaded that the law actually incited human beings to sin, and indeed sin became even more insidious after the onset of the law since it was now colored by rebellion.

Most secular people, and even many religious people, believe that moral education is the pathway to humane living. If we can only succeed in teaching "morals," justice and truth will prevail. The Pauline view of the law and the goodness of human beings is much less optimistic. The law is not the solution but part of the problem. It does not follow, of course, that we should not teach moral principles. Still, any hope that morality is the answer flies in the face of the Pauline gospel. We will not curb the problem with sexual sin by making rules about sexual harassment. Many institutions and places of work have long handbooks on what is permitted and disallowed. Such rules are not necessarily bad, but Paul reminds us that they do not touch the human heart. Human beings may obey laws because they want to avoid getting in trouble, but the law itself grants no power to obey. Only the gospel truly transforms our hearts.

Let us think more about how the law cannot transform us.When I was a child, I hated eating beets. I thought they were absolutely horrid to eat. No command could make me like beets, for I hated them. So too, God's commands can't transform those who hate God. "Can the Ethiopian change his skin or the leopard his spots? Neither can you do good who are accustomed to doing evil" (Jer 13:23). The law can't produce life. It can't change our nature. We cannot by rules and commands produce life.

Let's remember this with children. Rules and commands with immediate punishments can civilize children, and they need civilizing. We can teach them

---

67. Cf. B. Longenecker, *Triumph of Abraham's God*, 120.

manners and insist that they obey and do the right thing when they are small. But let's not equate that with the changing of their hearts. I heard somewhere this analogy: the law is like a cage. If it has bars, it can keep a lion from eating the lamb, but it can't prevent the lion from wanting to eat the lamb. Let's not think that a polite child (which is a good thing) who says "Yes, sir" and "Yes, ma'am" is the same thing as a child who is born again. All of this might cause us to think that the law works against the promise, since it brings death and kills us. But the law is like the stick that drives us to the promise.

The Law and the Promises as Complementary

Finally, the law and the promises are not contradictory but complementary in God's purposes. One could easily conclude from this that the law and the promise have the same function, but Paul clarifies here that complementarity ought not to be confused with identity. The purposes are complementary but distinct. The promise secures the inheritance, whereas the law provides no power for righteousness and life. If the law frustrates the realization of the promise by revealing human disobedience, how does it harmonize with the promise? The law promotes the promise because it reveals to human beings the full extent and power of sin. Hence, the law drives us to Christ and the promise by teaching that the only hope of salvation lies not in ourselves but in Christ crucified.

Consequently, teaching the law remains invaluable, for it punctures human pride and uncovers human sin. Luther rightly saw that one of the purposes of the law was that it convicted human beings of their sin and directed them to Christ for salvation.

> Therefore God must have a mighty hammer [the law] to crush the rocks, and a fire burning in the midst of heaven to overthrow the mountains, that is, to crush that stubborn and perverse beast, presumption. When a man has been brought to nothing by this pounding, despairs of his own powers, righteousness, and works, and trembles before God, he will, in his terror, begin to thirst for mercy and forgiveness of sins.[68]

God uses the law and our failure to keep it to drive us to Christ. The law is a mirror that shows us our sin, and we despair of ourselves and turn to Christ and his cross and resurrection alone for our salvation. So, the law kills us, but we are not left in the state of death. Praise God, he grants us new life and hope in Christ!

---

68. Luther, *Galatians 1535: Chapters 1–4*, 310.

Galatians 3:26 – 29

Literary Context

A new major section of Galatians begins with 3:15. In 3:15 – 18 Paul argues that the law given through Moses does not invalidate the promise made to Abraham. The law is subordinate to the promise inasmuch as it was instituted 430 years after the promise, and the law cannot revoke the terms of the covenant made with Abraham. The law, then, is inferior to the promise because it was given to provoke transgressions, was restricted to the period before the arrival of the "offspring" (Christ), and was given through a mediator (3:19 – 20).

Nonetheless, the law is not contrary to the promises of God (3:21). Rather, it must be understood that the law and the promises have distinct purposes. The law was never designed to bring life but enclosed all under sin so that the promise would be secured through faith in Christ (3:21 – 22). Further, the law was intended to have an interim character from the beginning (3:23 – 25). The law functioned as a custodian until the coming of the promise, and now that the promise of justification by faith has arrived, the custodian is no longer needed.

Galatians 3:26 – 29 supports the notion that the law as pedagogue is now passé since all believers are now God's sons and daughters in Christ through faith. In other words, believers are now Abraham's children through faith and do not live under the terms of the Mosaic law. They are Abraham's offspring by virtue of belonging to Jesus Christ. Jesus Christ, after all, is the one true offspring of Abraham (3:16), and hence those who are baptized into Christ (3:27) and incorporated into Christ (3:26) are part of Abraham's family, whatever their ethnic or class background and whether they are male or female.

Main Idea

The central truth is that believers are the offspring of Abraham by virtue of their union with Christ Jesus. The same truth is communicated in a variety of ways in this paragraph. Believers are all children of God through faith, and they are all one in Christ.

Translation

Galatians 3:26-29

26a	assertion/basis *(of 3:23-25)*	For **you are all sons of God**	
b	sphere	in Christ Jesus	
c	means	through faith.	
27	basis *(of 26a-c)*	For **as many as have been baptized into Christ have put on Christ.**	
28a	inference *(from 27)*	**There is neither Jew nor Greek;**	
b	series	**there is neither slave nor free;**	
c	series	**there is neither male or female.**	
d	basis *(of 28a-c)*	For **you are all one in Christ Jesus.**	
29a	condition	And **if you belong to Christ, you are**	**the offspring of Abraham,**
b	parallel		**heirs according to the promise.**

Structure

The "for" (γάρ) in 3:26 functions as the ground or basis of 3:23 – 25. The law was intended to function as a kind of babysitter or interim custodian until faith in Christ came. Clearly the era of the law has come to an end, for now believers are God's children since they are united with Christ by faith. Verse 27 in turn is the ground (marked by "for" [γάρ]) for 3:26. Believers are united with Christ, for they have been clothed with Christ inasmuch as they are plunged into Christ in baptism.

It follows from their participation in Christ that all believers are one, whether they are Jews or Gentiles, slaves or free, male or female (3:28). Ethnic background, social class, and gender are irrelevant in assessing whether one belongs to Jesus Christ. All those who belong to Christ by faith are part of his family.

Verse 29 brings the argument to a climax. Those who belong to Christ, who is the only true offspring of Abraham, are also part of Abraham's family. They are the true offspring of Abraham. Therefore, they are the heirs that were pledged to Abraham. They are not heirs in accordance with the law but heirs by virtue of the promise of the gospel.

Exegetical Outline

II. Paul's Gospel Defended from Experience and Scripture (3:1 – 4:11)

    A. Argument from Experience: Reception of Spirit by Means of Faith, Not Works (3:1 – 5)

    B. Argument from Scripture: Blessing of Abraham by Faith (3:6 – 14)

        1. Members of Abraham's family by faith (3:6 – 9)

        2. Curse of law removed only in Christ (3:10 – 14)

    C. Argument from Salvation History: Priority of Abrahamic Covenant and Temporary Nature of Mosaic Covenant (3:15 – 4:11)

        1. Addition of law does not nullify promise to Abraham (3:15 – 25)

            a. Interim nature of Mosaic covenant (3:15 – 18)

            b. The purpose of the law (3:19 – 25)

➡   **2. Sons of God are Abraham's offspring (3:26 – 29)**

            a. Sons of God in Christ (3:26)

            b. Clothed with Christ (3:27)

            c. One in Christ (3:28)

            d. Heirs according to promise (3:29)

        3. Argument from slavery to sonship (4:1 – 7)

Explanation of the Text

3:26 For you are all sons of God in Christ Jesus through faith (Πάντες γὰρ υἱοὶ θεοῦ ἐστε διὰ τῆς πίστεως ἐν Χριστῷ[1] Ἰησοῦ). The "for" (γάρ) indicates the ground for 3:23 – 25. Believers are no longer under the law as a pedagogue,[2] for the former age of salvation history is over, and now they are justified by faith.[3] Therefore, they are now God's "sons" (υἱοί). To say that they are God's sons is equivalent to saying that they have reached maturity. It would be equivalent to saying that they have now reached adulthood and have obtained the promised inheritance.

In the OT Israel was God's son (cf. Exod 4:22; Jer 31:9; Hos 11:1; Mal 1:6). The law was in force for a certain period in salvation history and functioned like a babysitter. Now that the time of babysitting has concluded, believers are sons who have obtained the promise. Believers are not only sons but they "all" (πάντες) belong to the people of God.[4] Now that the Christ has come, the door of the promise has swung wide open to include Gentiles who believe.

The promise is not obtained by keeping the Mosaic law but by trusting in Christ Jesus. It is possible that the phrase "in Christ Jesus" functions as the object of faith in this verse.[5] It has been argued previously that "faith in Christ" is a major theme in Galatians. Still, it is probable that the phrase "in Christ Jesus" modifies the verb "are" (ἐστε), for the text emphasizes incorporation into or participation with Christ.[6] In 3:27 believers are "baptized into Christ" (εἰς Χριστὸν ἐβαπτίσθητε), and in 3:28 believers "are ... one in Christ Jesus" (εἷς ἐστε ἐν Χριστῷ Ἰησοῦ), which again highlights union with Christ. Further, 3:29 also calls attention to belonging to Christ (εἰ δὲ ὑμεῖς Χριστοῦ).

Therefore, it seems that Paul teaches here that believers are God's sons because they are united with Christ Jesus, who is the one and only true offspring of Abraham (3:16). They are not God's sons through observing the law but by virtue of being incorporated into Christ.

3:27 For as many as have been baptized into Christ have put on Christ (ὅσοι γὰρ εἰς Χριστὸν ἐβαπτίσθητε, Χριστὸν ἐνεδύσασθε). The "for" (γάρ) supports and grounds the truth that all believers are God's sons if they are united with Christ by baptism.[7] Paul emphasizes here incorporation into Christ or participation with Christ. Believers are clothed with Christ since their baptism. Elsewhere Paul speaks of believers being "clothed" (ἐνδύω) with the "new self" (cf. Eph 4:24; Col 3:10). Before being united with Christ human beings are "clothed," so to speak, with the old Adam. But at

---

1. A few manuscripts delete "in" (ἐν), so that the text reads "Christ Jesus" (Χριστοῦ Ἰησοῦ), but this clearly represents assimilation to the genitive "Christ Jesus" after "faith" elsewhere in the letter.

2. The second person plural is taken by some to be a distinct turn to Gentile Christians over against the first person references to Jewish Christians (e.g., Betz, *Galatians*, 185), but I have argued earlier that this is unlikely. See the discussion under 3:13, 23; 4:3, 5.

3. In support of this understanding of "for" (γάρ), see Fung, *Galatians*, 170. Justification has always been by faith, of course, in both the OT and the NT. In the OT era, however, few believed, in contrast to the new age in which both Jews

and Gentiles are united with Christ by faith.

4. "All" here is emphatic. So Lightfoot, *Galatians*, 149; Longenecker, *Galatians*, 151; Martyn, *Galatians*, 375.

5. Longenecker, *Galatians*, 151 – 52; Luther, *Galatians 1535: Chapters 1 – 4*, 351.

6. Lightfoot, *Galatians*, 149; Betz; *Galatians*, 185 – 86; Bruce, *Galatians*, 184; Hansen, *Abraham in Galatians*, 136; Fee, *Galatians*, 139.

7. Many scholars believe that some part or the whole of 3:26 – 28 represents pre-Pauline tradition. So Betz, *Galatians*, 181 – 85; Longenecker, *Galatians*, 154 – 55; Martyn, *Galatians*, 378 – 80. Even if this is the case, it does not affect the interpretation of these verses in their present context.

baptism they have been plunged into or immersed with Christ.[8]

Most scholars agree that baptism was by immersion in NT times, and hence it functions as a vivid picture of being incorporated into Christ.[9] Those baptized into Christ have been baptized into his death and resurrection (Rom 6:3 – 6; Col 2:12). Therefore, the old self has been crucified with Christ (Rom 6:6). Here Paul emphasizes that those who were plunged into Christ at their conversion are now clothed with him (cf. also Rom 13:14; Eph 4:24; Col 3:10). Hence, they are clearly God's sons since they belong to Christ and have a new identity. Sonship does not depend on circumcision, for the old era has now passed. It all hangs on whether one is united with Christ as the only true offspring of Abraham (3:16).

It should be noted that Paul does not argue against circumcision in Galatians by saying that baptism replaces circumcision as an initiation rite.[10] Therefore, even though baptism and circumcision are both initiation rites, they are not analogous in every respect. We see both continuity and discontinuity between circumcision and baptism. If Paul believed that baptism merely replaced circumcision, he almost surely would have made such an argument in Galatians, for it seems that such a declaration would have settled the debate over circumcision in Galatia decisively. Instead of focusing on baptism, however, Paul stresses that faith in Christ is what qualifies one to be a member of God's people.[11]

3:28 There is neither Jew nor Greek; there is neither slave nor free; there is neither male or female. For you are all one in Christ Jesus (οὐκ ἔνι Ἰουδαῖος οὐδὲ Ἕλλην, οὐκ ἔνι δοῦλος οὐδὲ ἐλεύθερος, οὐκ ἔνι ἄρσεν καὶ θῆλυ· πάντες γὰρ ὑμεῖς εἷς ἐστε ἐν Χριστῷ Ἰησοῦ[12]). All believers are united in Christ regardless of their ethnic background, their social class, or their gender. Here we have one of Paul's most famous statements, though it is common also to think it is derived from a pre-Pauline confession.[13] To interpret the text via its alleged pre-Pauline shape is precarious. Even if the saying is pre-Pauline, which is a matter of speculation that cannot be settled by modern scholarship, it is imperative that we interpret its meaning in context, for the issue in all of Galatians, and particularly in chapter 3, is who belongs to the family of Abraham. Who are the true sons and daughters of Abraham?

Paul argues that one's ethnic background, social class, and gender are irrelevant in determining whether one is a child of Abraham. The first pair is particularly relevant for the Galatian situation,

---

8. Baptism here is not merely a metaphor. Against Dunn, *Galatians*, 203 – 4; Garlington, *Galatians*, 229; Debbie Hunn, "The Baptism of Galatians 3:27: A Contextual Approach," *ExpTim* 115 (2005): 372 – 75. Paul refers here to water baptism. So Bruce, *Galatians*, 185. Robert H. Stein shows that the attempt to separate water baptism from Spirit baptism fails to understand that water baptism is part of the complex of initiation events describing conversion. "Baptism and Becoming a Christian in the New Testament," *SBJT* 2 (1998): 6 – 17. See Fee's helpful observations on baptism as well (*Galatians*, 141).

9. Cf. here the comments of Longenecker, *Galatians*, 155.

10. Rightly Longenecker, *Galatians*, 156; George, *Galatians*, 277.

11. See here *Believer's Baptism: The Covenant Sign of the New Age in Christ* (ed. Thomas R. Schreiner and Shawn D. Wright; Nashville: Broadman & Holman, 2007).

12. The reading of NA[27] has strong support ($\aleph^2$, B, C*, D, Ψ, 33, 1739*vid, etc.) and should be accepted as original. Some texts read "one" (ἕν) "perhaps with some allusion" to 1 Cor 12:12 (Metzger, *Textual Commentary*, 526). A couple of manuscripts ($\mathfrak{P}^{46}$, A) have the genitive "Christ" (Χριστοῦ), which is translated "you belong to Christ."

13. So Martyn, *Galatians*, 374. For a concise survey of the history of interpretation relative to male and female up to 1987, see Dennis Ronald MacDonald, *There Is No Male and Female: The Fate of a Dominical Saying in Paul and Gnosticism* (HDR 20; Philadelphia: Fortress, 1987), 1 – 16. For MacDonald's own contribution, see 17 – 62, 113 – 32; cf. also Riches, *Galatians through the Centuries*, 209 – 13. For a short survey of possible parallels, see Bruce, *Galatians*, 187.

for one became part of the Jewish people by receiving circumcision. The circle around God's people for the Judaizers was bounded by the law and circumcision, and hence the children of Abraham, in their view, were essentially Jewish. Paul moves in a radically different direction. The children of Abraham are those who belong to Christ, who is the only true offspring of Abraham (3:16). Those who are incorporated into Christ (3:26) by faith and who are clothed with Christ through baptism are his children.

Hence, there is a fundamental unity among all those who are members of God's people. As coheirs of the promise of Abraham, Jews are not superior to Gentiles, those who are free are not more important than slaves, and men are not worth more than women. All those who are united to Christ are equal as members of Abraham's family. It may be the case that males and females are introduced here because females could not be circumcised, and hence Paul emphasizes their oneness in Christ.[14]

Equality as members of Abraham's family does not rule out all social distinctions.[15] Paul is not negating all distinctions between Jews and Gentiles.[16] They are one in Christ, and yet they are still distinct and identifiable social groups. In Rom 9 – 11 a future salvation for ethnic Israel is promised, but such a promise does not contradict the unity of Jews and Gentiles in Christ. Clearly, there are social implications to the unity of Jews and Gentiles in Christ. One concrete illustration of their unity is their eating together as brothers and sisters in the Lord. Furthermore, the unity in Christ of slaves and free would manifest itself socially. The church should not be marked by social classes and cliques.

Nevertheless, what Paul meant by such unity must be discerned by reading all that he wrote. The new relationship between Philemon and Onesimus functioned as a kind of charter for the way slaves and masters should treat one another as Christians (Philemon). Nevertheless, Paul did not demand that Philemon free Onesimus, though he may hint that such an outcome would be desirable. Elsewhere Paul did not require Christian masters to liberate their slaves but instead encouraged slaves to serve their masters well (1 Tim 6:1 – 2). He did not call for the abolition of slavery but encouraged believers to serve Christ in the way they worked for their masters and admonished masters to treat their slaves fairly (cf. Eph 6:5 – 9; Col 3:22 – 4:1; Titus 2:9 – 10). Slaves should gain their freedom if possible (1 Cor 7:21), but Paul was not greatly concerned about whether one is free. What concerned him was whether one fulfilled one's calling before God in whatever social situation one found oneself (1 Cor 7:17 – 24).

The unity and oneness that belong to slave and free in Christ, then, did not rule out the existence of slavery in Paul's day, though such teaching

---

14. So Troy W. Martin, "The Covenant of Circumcision (Genesis 17:9 – 14) and the Situational Antitheses in Galatians 3:28," *JBL* 122 (2003): 117 – 21 (though Martin overemphasizes the role of Gen 17:9 – 14 and underemphasizes Gen 1:26 – 27). See also Ben Witherington III, "Rite and Rights for Women — Galatians 3.28," *NTS* 27 (1981): 595, but against Witherington, we lack clear evidence that the opponents demanded that women get married (593 – 604).

15. Contra a common view expressed by many. See, e.g., Betz, *Galatians*, 189 – 200. Betz goes so far as to say Paul nullifies both "*social* differences" and "*biological* distinctions" (195, italics his).

16. Troy Martin rightly says, "This verse does not proclaim the absolute abolition of these distinctions but only their irrelevance for participation in Christian baptism and full membership in the Christian community" ("The Covenant of Circumcision," 122). See also his comments (121) where he acknowledges that maleness and femaleness are not abolished but are "irrelevant for entering into the community of faith." Martin also remarks, "Later interpreters who use Gal 3:28 to develop idealistic notions of the body of Christ as a reality that completely erases all distinctions and inequalities take Gal 3:28 far beyond its situational context" (124).

led to the eventual abolition of slavery as Christian values took stronger root in society. Paul, of course, never endorses slavery as a social system, but it it would have been fruitless for him to lead a social revolution against slavery.[17] In any case, we must beware lest Paul's statement in 3:28 becomes untethered from the rest of what he wrote, so that it is wrested from its context and becomes the pretext for modern social agendas.

Such a danger is especially present when it comes to males and females. The beautiful unity of men and women in Christ must not be missed.[18] Women are equally members of the family of Abraham with men, and there are clearly social implications that can be drawn from their unity. The social implications, however, must also include what Paul wrote elsewhere. Paul affirms the oneness of males and females in Christ, but he does not claim that maleness and femaleness are irrelevant in every respect. If one were to draw such a conclusion, then Paul would not object to homosexuality, but it is clear that he thinks homosexuality is sinful (Rom 1:26 – 27; 1 Cor 6:9; 1 Tim 1:10). In the same way, the equality of men and women in Christ does not cancel out, in Paul's mind, the distinct roles of men and women in marriage (Eph 5:22 – 33; Col 3:18 – 19; Titus 2:4 – 5) or in ministry contexts (1 Cor. 11:2 – 16; 14:33 – 36; 1 Tim 2:9 – 15).[19]

3:29 And if you belong to Christ, you are the offspring of Abraham, heirs according to the promise (εἰ δὲ ὑμεῖς Χριστοῦ, ἄρα τοῦ Ἀβραὰμ σπέρμα ἐστέ, κατ᾽ ἐπαγγελίαν κληρονόμοι). Paul now not only ties the threads together of 3:26 – 28 but also reminds the readers of his main thesis in all of chapter 3. The major issue throughout the chapter is who belongs to the family of Abraham. Who are Abraham's true sons and daughters?[20] Who are his true offspring? Paul has already clarified that the only genuine son of Abraham is Christ himself (3:16). The law could not produce true sons of God, for the law only precipitated more sin. Therefore, the only way one can legitimately be called the offspring of Abraham is if one belongs to Christ. Union with Christ, being clothed with Christ, and being baptized into Christ are all different ways of portraying the same reality. The heirs of Abraham are those who belong to Jesus Christ by faith.

In other words, as Paul has argued throughout chapter 3, the inheritance does not come via the law but via the promise. Gentiles do not become members of Abraham's family, nor do they receive the inheritance, by observing the law. The inheritance is theirs by faith in Christ. The inheritance is secured by God's gracious promise, and hence it is received by faith alone.

---

17. For further discussion, see Schreiner, *New Testament Theology*, 794 – 800.

18. Female circumcision of the clitoris is practiced in some societies but was never considered to be part of circumcision in Jewish circles.

19. Contra Bruce, *Galatians*, 189 – 90. For a feminist reading, see Tatha Wiley, *Paul and the Gentile Women: Reframing Galatians* (New York: Continuum, 2005). For the inadequacy of such treatments, see Richard W. Hove, *Equality in Christ? Galatians 3:28 and the Gender Dispute* (Wheaton, IL: Crossway, 1999). For a fuller evaluation of the issue of women in

ministry, see Thomas R. Schreiner, "Women in Ministry: Another Complementarian Perspective," in *Two Views on Women in Ministry* (ed. J. R. Beck; Counterpoints Series; Grand Rapids: Zondervan, 2005), 265 – 322.

20. Kwon fails to see that 3:26, 28 and 3:29 are basically parallel statements (*Eschatology*, 88 – 90). Such a misjudgment seems to stem from his insistence on seeing only future eschatology in Galatians (99). He is right that sonship is distinct from being an heir, and that the latter is the climax in 4:7 (92). Still, sonship is indissolubly connected with the inheritance, and Paul emphasizes that the Galatians are *already* sons.

Theology in Application

The Equality of All Believers in Christ

One remarkable truth in this paragraph is the equality of all believers in Christ. In both the ancient world and the modern world, some people are inevitably considered "more important" than others. Jews generally considered themselves to be superior to Gentiles because they were God's covenant people. Free people tended to look down on slaves, and men were inclined to disparage women. As human beings we long for something that makes us feel superior to others, and hence we may appeal to our race, our class status, or our gender.

In the United States we have the horrible legacy of whites enslaving, abusing, and demeaning blacks. On the one hand, immigrants have often been welcomed to our shores, and yet, on the other hand, they have often been scorned as unsophisticated and uneducated. One reason the feminist movement arose in our culture (though the historical roots are too complex to trace out here) can be ascribed to misogyny of men who failed to grant respect, honor, and dignity to women as human beings.

Jesus Christ taught that believers would be known by their love for one another (John 13:34 – 35). One of the marks, we hope and pray, of our churches is love for all fellow believers regardless of their ethnic background, social class, or gender. Paul did not propose a social program to advance such love. Instead, he argued that all believers were fundamentally equal in Christ. As human beings we are all enslaved to sin, and therefore we have known the bondage that sin brings. Nevertheless, we have found salvation through the one man, Jesus Christ, and therefore he is our all in all. Paul does not call believers to be unified. Instead, we *are* unified in Christ (cf. also Eph 2:14 – 18), and we are to maintain the unity that is already ours (Eph 4:3). If we are humbled and cast down to the dust by our own sins, our hearts are prepared to love others and to see other believers from all backgrounds as fellow travelers.

The solution to problems of race and class and gender is found in the gospel. Some might claim that such an assertion is simplistic, but such a response is itself superficial, for it fails to see the profundity and depth of the gospel. To make such a claim, of course, does not mean that any proposals are being made here regarding social programs or political platforms. My discussion here is limited to the church of Jesus Christ, which is the orbit in which Paul celebrates unity. If believers are able to influence the public sphere, they should do so with the wisdom, prudence, and skill granted to them by God.

Evangelical Feminism?

Galatians 3:28 has been featured as the charter verse for evangelical feminism and the claim that all church offices are open to women and that there are no role differences between husbands and wives. A full-fledged discussion of the issue is impossible here since books and articles continue to pour forth on the matter. Still, as was pointed out in the commentary, the context of Paul's affirmation must not be neglected. In saying that all are one in Christ, the central issue is who belongs to Abraham's family. As brothers and sisters in Christ all are one, whether male or female, Jew or Greek, slave or free.

Paul is scarcely arguing that whether one is male or female is insignificant in any sense. Otherwise, as was pointed out above, homosexuality would not be proscribed as sin. Nor would Paul assign particular roles to men and women in the home and the church. Philosophically some find it impossible to believe that men and women could be equal in Christ and have different roles. But we must beware, as Luther warned regularly during the Reformation, of letting Aristotle or any other philosopher reign over the biblical text.

I just witnessed to some Mormons two days ago who found the doctrine of the Trinity to be philo-sophical nonsense. Some think the doctrine of the two natures of Christ is irrational as well. How can one person be fully God and fully man? I am not suggesting that anything in our faith is contradictory and irrational, but I am suggesting that even if some truths are beyond our finding out, we must submit ultimately to Scripture instead of limiting ourselves to what seems reasonable to us.

Incidentally, I think a robust philosophical defense can be made of the notion that women and men are equal in essence and different in role.[21] In any case, Jesus Christ submitted himself to the Father (cf. 1 Cor 15:28) and is equal to him in essence, dignity, and value. Hence, to say that a different role requires a lesser dignity flies in the face of Trinitarian teaching. We must beware of demeaning women and slighting their many gifts. Men have much to repent of in their treatment of women. But we must also avoid wrenching texts out of context and reading a program out of them that was never intended by the author.

---

21. See Steven B. Cowan, "The Metaphysics of Subordination: A Response to Rebecca Merrill Groothuis," *JBMW* 14 (2009): 43 – 53.

Galatians 4:1 – 7

Literary Context

From 3:15 to this point in the argument Paul has argued for the limited and temporary duration of the Mosaic law. He began by asserting the priority of the Abrahamic covenant and the subsidiary nature of the Mosaic (3:15 – 18), and hence the latter cannot cancel out the stipulations of the former. The law was intended to be in force only until Christ came, and it functioned as custodian or a babysitter until the promise of righteousness by faith in Christ arrived on the scene (3:19 – 25). Believers are no longer under the law, for they are now God's sons, united with Christ by faith (3:26). Therefore, all believers are one in Christ and recipients of the promise made to Abraham (3:27 – 29).

Galatians 4:1 – 7 restates from another angle the content of 3:15 – 29. The era under the Mosaic law and covenant is conceived of as a time of slavery (4:1 – 3). However, a new period in the history of salvation has now become a reality with the coming of Jesus Christ, and he has liberated his people from the slavery they were subjected to under the Mosaic law (4:4 – 5a). Therefore, believers in Jesus Christ are now God's "sons"; indeed the gift of the Spirit demonstrates they are sons, and as sons they are heirs of the promise made to Abraham (4:5b – 7). This section, then, concludes in the same way as 3:26 – 29. Believers through Christ Jesus are sons and heirs of the promise made to Abraham, so that observance of the Mosaic law is unnecessary.

Main Idea

Believers are no longer enslaved under the elements of the world but have been freed by Christ Jesus from its power. Thus, they are now sons of God and heirs of the promise; therefore, reverting to the Mosaic law would be senseless since they have now obtained what the law could never grant.

Translation

(See next page.)

Structure

This passage is split into three sections. (1) Paul begins with an illustration in 4:1 – 2 that is introduced with the words "now I say" (λέγω δέ). When an heir is still a minor, he has to wait until maturity to receive the inheritance. In the interval his status is no different from a slave's, and he lives under the supervision of others.

(2) Paul applies the illustration to his readers in 4:3 – 5, drawing the comparison with the words "thus also" (οὕτως καί). Believers were also enslaved during the time of their infancy (i.e., when they were under the Mosaic law) to the elements of the world. But the days of immaturity have come to an end. Now the fullness of time has arrived — the realization of God's saving promises in Christ. As one who lived under the law, God's Son liberated and freed those who were enslaved under the law, so that believers could be God's sons.

(3) The implications of 4:3 – 5 are drawn for the readers in 4:6 – 7, introduced with "and" (δέ) in 4:6 and concluded with "therefore" (ὥστε) in 4:7. The evidence that the readers are truly God's children is that they have received the Spirit, and

Galatians 4:1-7

1a	assertion/temporal	Now I say, as long as an heir is a minor he is no different from a slave,
b	concessive	even though he is master of all.
2a	contrast (to 1a–b)	But **he is under guardians and managers**
b	temporal (to 2a)	until the appointed time of the father.
3	comparison (to 1–2)	Thus also when we were minors, we were enslaved under the elements of the world.
4a	event/contrast (to 3)	But **when the fullness of time came, God sent forth his Son,**
b	description	who was born of a woman,
c	description	who was born under law,
5a	purpose (of 4a–c)	to redeem those under law,
b	purpose (of 5a)	so that we should receive adoption as sons.
6a	basis (for 6b)	And
		because you are sons,
b	event	**God sent forth the Spirit of his Son into our hearts crying, "Abba, Father."**
7a	inference from 6a-b	Therefore, **you are no longer** a slave but a son.
b	condition	And if you are son, you are also an heir through God.

hence they call on God as their beloved Father. And since they are sons, they are no longer slaves but heirs of God's promises, heirs of the promises made to Abraham.

Exegetical Outline

II. Paul's Gospel Defended from Experience and Scripture (3:1 – 4:11)

   A. Argument from Experience: Reception of Spirit by Means of Faith, Not Works (3:1 – 5)

   B. Argument from Scripture: Blessing of Abraham by Faith (3:6 – 14)

   1. Members of Abraham's family by faith (3:6 – 9)

   2. Curse of law removed only in Christ (3:10 – 14)

   C. Argument from Salvation History: Priority of Abrahamic Covenant and Temporary Nature of Mosaic Covenant (3:15 – 4:11)

   1. Addition of law does not nullify promise to Abraham (3:15 – 25)

   a. Interim nature of Mosaic covenant (3:15 – 18)

   b. The purpose of the law (3:19 – 25)

   2. Sons of God are Abraham's offspring (3:26 – 29)

➡ **3. Argument from slavery to sonship (4:1 – 7)**

   a. The illustration: a slave while a minor (4:1 – 2)

   b. Application of illustration (4:3 – 5)

   i. Enslaved under the elements (4:3)

   ii. Sending of Son in fullness of time (4:4)

   iii. Liberation of those under law (4:5)

   c. Implication of illustration: sons and heirs (4:6 – 7)

   4. The folly of reverting to the law (4:8 – 11)

Explanation of the Text

4:1 Now I say, as long as an heir is a minor he is no different from a slave, even though he is master of all (Λέγω δέ, ἐφ᾽ ὅσον χρόνον ὁ κληρονόμος νήπιός ἐστιν, οὐδὲν διαφέρει δούλου κύριος πάντων ὤν). Paul provides here an illustration from everyday life regarding the reception of an inheritance.[1] A minor, practically speaking, occupies the same position as a slave until he receives

---

1. In support of a reference to Roman law, see Trevor J. Burke, *Adoption into God's Family: Exploring a Pauline Metaphor* (NSBT 22: Downers Grove, IL: IVP, 2006), 46 – 71; Francis Lyall, "Roman Law in the Writings of Paul — Adoption," *JBL* 88 (1969): 458 – 66. Longenecker thinks Paul refers to a Greco-Roman practice that is now unknown to us. Betz says Paul may be reflecting the law in some of the provinces, or that he modifies the illustration to make his point (*Galatians*, 202 – 4). Scott argues that Paul refers to bondage in Egypt under Egyptian taskmasters. James M. Scott, *Adoption as Sons of God: An Exegetical Investigation into the Background of* υἱοθεσία *in the*

Pauline Corpus (WUNT 2/48; Tübingen: Mohr Siebeck, 1992), 140 – 48. Scott etches in the lines too firmly here. For instance, he understands the time appointed by the father as the time between the promise to Abraham and the exodus; "minor" to refer to Israel during the time of Exodus; "heir" to Israel as the inheritors of the promise to Abraham; and "lord of all" to the fulfillment of the promise to Abraham that Israel would rule the world. It seems doubtful that such specific connections can be forged, but a general reference to exodus and second exodus traditions is likely (cf. also here Arnold, "Returning to the Domain of the Powers," 64).

the inheritance. The word "heir" (κληρονόμος) ties into Paul's argument, for the issue in Galatians turns on who will receive the inheritance promised to Abraham. The translation reveals that the Greek word is best translated "minor" (νήπιος) instead of "infant." A minor is one who has not yet reached the age to receive the inheritance.

Even though the minor is destined to become an heir, he has not yet attained that status while still a child. Paul anticipates his application of the illustration in 4:3 in comparing the future heir to a "slave" (δούλου), for there is no reason why one should identify a future heir as a slave![2] The reference to slavery forecasts the state of living under the law (4:3 – 5), which is characterized by bondage rather than freedom. Paul bends the illustration of a minor, then, to articulate the theme he deems fitting for the Galatians.

4:2 But he is under guardians and managers until the appointed time of the father (ἀλλὰ ὑπὸ ἐπιτρόπους ἐστὶν καὶ οἰκονόμους ἄχρι τῆς προθεσμίας τοῦ πατρός). The interval between the promised inheritance and its realization is featured here, for a minor is under supervision until he receives the inheritance. Longenecker correctly notes that Paul underscores the same point that was made regarding pedagogues.[3] The words "guardians and managers," according to most scholars, refer to governmental officials in the Hellenistic world. If Paul draws on a practice from Greco-Roman culture, he does not attempt to portray accurately the custom,[4] but crafts the illustration, as we saw with the reference to slavery in 4:1, to fit the point he desires to drive home.[5]

If Paul draws generally on exodus traditions, as Scott proposes, our inability to locate the practice in the Greco-Roman world is explained. But it must be admitted that it is difficult to demonstrate conclusively that Paul draws on exodus traditions, and hence our attempt to solve the background of the Pauline statements does not lead to any easy resolution. Perhaps Paul interweaves exodus and Greco-Roman traditions here.

In any case, the free application of the illustration is confirmed by 4:4 – 5, for unlike in 4:1 – 2, the son does not belong to the family by birth but is adopted.[6] The time designated by the father in

2. Rightly Kwon, *Eschatology*, 134 – 35.

3. Longenecker, *Galatians*, 162.

4. See Martyn, *Galatians*, 386. In Roman law a child was under a tutor (ἐπίτροπος) until the age of fourteen and a curator (κουράτωρ) until the age of twenty-five. See Hester, *Paul's Concept of Inheritance*, 18 – 19, 59. But the problem here is that Paul does not use the term "curator" (κουράτωρ) but "manager" (οἰκονόμος), and the latter term is not used to designate control over a minor but one who is a manager of a master's estate and household (cf. 1 Kgs 4:6; 16:9; 18:3; Luke 12:42; 16:1). Rightly Burton, *Galatians*, 212; Hong, *Law in Galatians*, 161. In support of a Hellenistic custom, see Witherington, *Galatians*, 282 – 83; Derek R. Moore-Crispin, "Galatians 4:1 – 9: The Use and Abuse of Parallels," *EvQ* 60 (1989): 203 – 23. Longenecker notes that others have tried to find parallels in both Greek and Semitic inheritance laws, but the problem with such solutions is that "ancient inheritance laws — whether Roman, Greek, or Semitic — assumed the death of the testator before coming into effect" (*Galatians*, 163). Such a solution does not work here, for Paul does not

envision the guardians (or God!) as dying before one obtains the inheritance.

Ramsey located the practice in the Phrygian cities of south Galatia. He argued that Seleucid legal practices are referred to here (*Galatians*, 130 – 31). The problem with Ramsey's solution is that the laws to which he appeals appear five hundred years after Paul (Longenecker, *Galatians*, 163 – 64). Three other problems exist with Ramsey's solution according to Longenecker: (1) the death of the father is not required in Paul for the son to receive the inheritance; (2) in contrast to the legal practice to which Ramsey appeals, the time is set by the father (not by the supervisor or curator); (3) in Paul the two terms "guardian" (ἐπίτροπος) and "manager" (οἰκονόμος) are likely synonymous (*Galatians*, 163 – 64).

5. For the various attempts to explain the cultural and legal system Paul had in mind, see Longenecker, *Galatians*, 162 – 64, who concludes that Paul adapts the illustration to suit his own purposes.

6. See here Hafemann, "Paul and the Exile," 334.

the illustration points to the time when the father grants the inheritance to the son. Paul applies the decision of the father to give the inheritance to his son to God's control of history and the realization of his saving promises. Such a theological viewpoint does not fit as well with Greco-Roman law and strengthens the case that Paul works from exodus traditions, where Israel was redeemed and adopted as God's son.[7] Scott, however, tries to tie the elements of Gal 4 too specifically to the OT. It is more satisfactory to say that Paul uses exodus and second exodus traditions more generally here and combines them in a general way with Greco-Roman practices.[8]

4:3 Thus also when we were minors, we were enslaved under the elements of the world (οὕτως καὶ ἡμεῖς, ὅτε ἦμεν νήπιοι, ὑπὸ τὰ στοιχεῖα τοῦ κόσμου ἤμεθα δεδουλωμένοι). Paul now applies the illustration to his readers, teaching them that they were also enslaved to the spiritual forces and powers of this world before the coming of Christ.[9] "We" (ἡμεῖς) here could be restricted to the Jews,[10] but since Paul speaks of the world's elements, he probably includes both Jews and Gentiles.[11] As Das notes, the Gentiles are warned against

returning to the elements in 4:9, and hence they must be included in those who were previously enslaved to them and subsequently liberated according to 4:3 – 5.[12] The word "minors" (νήπιοι) forms a link with 4:1, as does the word "enslaved" (δεδουλωμένοι). The period of infancy and immaturity refers to the era of salvation history when the Mosaic law was in force. According to Paul, the reign of the law has ceased with the coming of Christ.

The meaning of the word "elements" (στοιχεῖα) is fiercely debated. When the word "world" (κόσμου) is added (i.e., "elements of the world," στοιχεῖα τοῦ κόσμου), it invariably refers to the physical elements that make up the world, whether earth, air, fire, or water (Plato, *Timaeus* 48B; Diogenes Laertius 7.134 – 135; 4 Macc 12:13; Philo, *Decalogue* 31; *Creation* 146; 2 Pet 3:10, 12).[13] The term "elements" (στοιχεῖα) alone also refers to the fundamental elements of a matter, whether of science, art, etc.,[14] and hence the term can be understood to denote the elementary or fundamental principles or rules of life (Philo, *Alleg. Interp.* 7.790C; Xenophon, *Mem.* 2.1.1; Plutarch, *Lib. Ed.* 16.2).[15] Still another possibility is that the elements

---

7. Scott, *Adoption as Sons of God*, 121 – 86; Hafemann, "Paul and the Exile," 330 – 49; Wilson, "Wilderness Apostasy," 560 – 63. Wilson rightly sees echoes of exodus traditions and threats about going back to Egypt, but he goes too far in saying that the Galatians are in the wilderness. Paul warns them about falling prey to apostasy, but he does not declare that they have fallen away from Christ.

8. Arnold, "Returning to the Domain of the Powers," 64. Cf. also here some of Hafemann's modifications of Scott's view ("Paul and the Exile," 334 – 38).

9. Martyn says we have in this section "the theological center of the entire letter" (*Galatians*, 388).

10. So Longenecker, *Galatians*, 164; Belleville, "Under Law," 68; Bruce, *Galatians*, 193; Donaldson, "Curse of the Law," 95 – 98; Garlington, *Galatians*, 236; Robinson, "Galatians 3:13 – 14: Jewish and Gentile Believers," 36 – 38; Fee, *Galatians*, 146.

11. So Betz, *Galatians*, 204; Burton, *Galatians*, 215; Scott,

Adoption as Sons of God, 155 – 57.

12. Das, *Paul and the Jews*, 125.

13. See Richard DeMaris, "Element, Elemental Spirit," *ABD*, 2.445; Eduard Schweizer, "Slaves of the Elements and Worshipers of Angels: Gal 4:3, 9 and Col 2:8, 18, 20," *JBL* 107 (1988): 455 – 68; Frank Thielman, *From Plight to Solution: A Jewish Framework for Understanding Paul's View of the Law in Galatians and Romans* (NovTSup 61; Leiden: Brill, 1989), 80 – 83; Dietrich Rusam, "Neue Belege zu dem στοιχεῖα τοῦ κόσμου (Gal 4,3.9; Kol 2,8.20)," *ZNW* 83 (1992): 119 – 25; Josef Blinzer, "Lexikalisches zu dem Terminusτὰ στοιχεῖα τοῦ κόσμου bei Paulus," in *Studiorum Paulinorum Congressus Internationalis Catholicus*, vol. 2 (AnBib 17 – 18; Rome: Pontifical Biblical Institute, 1961), 429 – 43.

14. Blinzer, "στοιχεῖα τοῦ κόσμου," 430 – 31.

15. So Lightfoot, *Galatians*, 167; Burton, *Galatians*, 510 – 18; Longenecker, *Galatians*, 165 – 66; Matera, *Galatians*, 149 – 50, 155 – 56; Witherington, *Galatians*, 284 – 86;

refer to angelic powers, to demonic forces that rule unbelievers (*T. Sol.* 8:1 – 2; 18:1 – 2).[16]

The phrase is also used in Gal 4:9 and Col 2:8 and 20, and in every instance scholars defend the various views presented above. Supporting a reference to the demonic powers is the personal nature of the language in Gal 4:8 – 9, where the elements are conjoined with turning back to idols. Elsewhere idols are identified as demons in Paul's thought (1 Cor 10:19 – 22).[17] Furthermore, in Colossians the false teachers made much ado about angels (cf. Col 1:16; 2:10, 15, 18), and hence there are good contextual reasons to see a reference to angels. There is no clear reference, however, to "elements" (στοιχεῖα) referring to demons until after the NT era.[18]

A good argument can also be made for a reference to the fundamental principles or elementary principles in both Galatians and Colossians.[19] The law is clearly center stage in Galatians, and Paul refers to specific traditions and regulations in Col 2:8 and 2:21 – 23. Nevertheless, in terms of usage, the phrase "elements of the world" (στοιχεῖα τοῦ κόσμου) has a long history of referring to the elements that make up the world: earth, air, fire, and water. Obviously, such a literal definition would make little sense in context, but metaphorically it could denote this present world order — the old creation.

A decision is remarkably difficult, and good arguments can be made for every position. Perhaps defining the term as the elements that make up the world should be preferred since this is the most common meaning of the term in Greek literature. Such a view may include the worship of the elements, for we see in Wis 13:1 – 5 that the elements were also adored:

> For all people who were ignorant of God were
>   foolish by nature;
> and they were unable from the good things that
>   are seen to know the one who exists,
> nor did they recognize the artisan while paying
>   heed to his works;
> but they supposed that either fire or wind or
>   swift air,
> or the circle of the stars, or turbulent water,
> or the luminaries of heaven were the gods that
>   rule the world.
> If through delight in the beauty of these things
>   people assumed them to be gods,
> let them know how much better than these is
>   their Lord,

Belleville, "Under Law," 67 – 69. Belleville does not equate the rudimentary principles and the law. She sees them as parallel but not identical; cf. also Gerhard Delling, "στοιχεῖον," *TDNT*, 7:685. Andrew J. Bandstra identifies the "elements" (στοιχεῖα) with the law and flesh that oppose God (*The Law and the Elements of the World: An Exegetical Study in Aspects of Paul's Teaching* [Grand Rapids: Eerdmans, 1964], 57 – 68).

16. Betz, *Galatians*, 204 – 5. Reicke sees a reference back to the angels of Gal 3:19 who gave the law. Bo Reicke, "The Law and This World according to Paul," *JBL* 70 (1951): 261 – 63. But if the "elements" (στοιχεῖα) are identified as angels, they are evil angels in contrast to the good angels who mediated the law. Rightly Arnold, "Returning to the Domain of the Powers," 61 – 62.

17. Some argue that the "elements" (στοιχεῖα) refer to heavenly bodies and the elements that comprise the world, and hence represent "*demonic forces*" (italics Hong, *Law in Galatians*, 165). So also Betz, *Galatians*, 204 – 5; Barrett,

Freedom and Obligation, 39; Sanders, *Paul and Palestinian Judaism*, 554. But see Arnold's lucid and strong argument supporting the view that the "elements" (στοιχεῖα) are demonic powers. "Returning to the Domain of the Powers," 55 – 76. Martyn has a very helpful discussion of "elements" (στοιχεῖα), but his own solution that postulates a polarity between Jew/Gentile, sacred/profane, and law/no-law is too complex to be probable (*Galatians*, 395 – 406).

18. But Arnold claims that the arguments from a late date are not decisive since the term is used in Greek magical papyri, and the traditions from these papyri likely hearken back to the first century AD or even before this date. See also *T. Sol.* 8:1 – 2; 18:1 – 2 and *2 En.* 16:7, which may contain evidence for an early date for the term. See Arnold, "Returning to the Domain of the Powers," 58 – 59. But against this, see Blinzer, "στοιχεῖα τοῦ κόσμου," 435 – 36, 438 – 39.

19. So Longenecker, *Galatians*, 165 – 66, though he argues that the specific nuance must be discerned in context.

for the author of beauty created them.

And if people were amazed at their power and
working,

let them perceive from them

how much more powerful is the one who formed
them.

For from the greatness and beauty of created
things

comes a corresponding perception of their
Creator.[20] (NRSV; cf. also Wis 7:17 – 19)

Indeed, demonic powers may be included in the meaning inasmuch as they ruled over the elements of the old creation (cf. Eph 2:2; 6:12).

In any case, Paul clearly sees the elements ruling during the period in which the Mosaic law was in force.[21] The use of the "under" (ὑπό) phrase calls to mind the other references to the law in Galatians (see 3:10, 22, 23, 25; 4:2, 4, 5, 21; 5:18). They lived under slavery, so that to be under the law is to be under the power of sin.[22] Some scholars argue that Paul thinks here of Israel's exile under sin, where its failure to keep the law resulted finally in being dispelled from the land. A direct reference to exile is lacking here. Still, a reference to the exile accords with the subject at hand, for those who were under the law in the history of Israel did not find freedom but were enslaved to sin.

4:4 But when the fullness of time came, God sent forth his Son, who was born of a woman, who was born under the law (ὅτε δὲ ἦλθεν τὸ πλήρωμα τοῦ χρόνου, ἐξαπέστειλεν ὁ θεὸς τὸν υἱὸν αὐτοῦ, γενόμενον ἐκ γυναικός, γενόμενον ὑπὸ νόμον). Now a new era has arrived in salvation history with the arrival of God's Son, who was truly human and lived under the law. Many scholars detect a pre-Pauline confessional formula in these verses (4:4 – 5).[23] Paul may draw on such a confession here, but it is doubtful that he did. The presence of *hapax legomena* is too thin of a reed on which to base any conclusions, nor does the switch in pronouns indicate the use of tradition since the alternation of pronouns is common in Galatians.

Finally, the substance of what is said here fits with the main themes of Galatians. Deliverance from the law comes only through the cross of Christ, and those who are redeemed are God's sons. Indeed, the expression "under law" itself suggests that Paul's hand is at work here, as does "adoption" (4:5), since the latter term does not occur in the LXX and is found only in the Pauline writings in the NT.

The time under the Mosaic law is compared to when one is a minor, and Paul does not stop there

---

20. Even though the author does not use the word "elements" (στοιχεῖα) here, the idea of the "elements" is clearly present. See here Martinus C. de Boer, "The Meaning of the Phrase τὰ στοιχεῖα τοῦ κόσμου in Galatians," *NTS* 53 (2007): 204 – 24.

21. Nancy L. Calvert maintains that in Gal 4:1 – 10 Paul draws on Jewish traditions relating to Abraham's rejection of idolatry and argues that devotion to the law functions as idolatry. See her "Abraham and Idolatry: Paul's Comparison of Obedience to the Law with Idolatry in Galatians 4.1 – 10," in *Paul and the Scriptures of Israel* (ed. C. A. Evans and J. A. Sanders; JSNTSup 83; Sheffield: JSOT Press, 1993), 222 – 37. Since Abraham is not even mentioned in these verses, it is unclear that Paul draws on Abrahamic traditions here.

22. Arnold says that Paul does not *"equate"* being under the elements with being under the law, but speaks "in terms

of close *association*" ("Returning to the Domain of the Powers," 68, italics his). Perhaps Donaldson's reading is even more satisfying, for he argues that "under law" is a subset of being "under the elements." Therefore, the two are not precisely equivalent ("Galatians 3:13 – 14," 96 – 97, 104). So also Johannes Woyke, "Nochmals zu den 'schwachen und unfähigen Elementen' (Gal 4.9): Paulus, Philo und die στοιχεῖα τοῦ κόσμου," *NTS* 54 (2008): 231. Such a view would seem to fit with Rom 7:7 – 25, where the good law is employed for an evil purpose by the power of sin. If "the elements of the world" include a reference to demonic powers, Paul may be saying that demons have used the law (because of human sin) to enslave human beings. Against this, see Hafemann, "Paul and the Exile," 346 – 47.

23. E.g., Betz, *Galatians*, 205 – 7; Longenecker, *Galatians*, 166 – 70.

but compares it to slavery, to subjugation to the elements of the world. So too, the realization of the inheritance, the growing up and maturity of the child, is compared to the fulfillment of God's promises in redemptive history, to the sending of God's Son, Jesus Christ.[24] "The fullness of time" emphasizes the realization of God's saving promises (cf. Mark 1:15). In Eph 1:10 God has so designed history that his plan "for the fullness of the times" (lit. trans. of τὸ πλήρωμα τῶν καιρῶν) was to unite all things in Christ. Now that Christ has come, "the fulfillment of the ages has come" (τὰ τέλη τῶν αἰώνων κατήντηκεν, 1 Cor 10:11). Jesus came at "the appointed time of the Father" (Gal 4:2), for God sent him as his Son at the right time in the history of salvation.

Scholars debate whether the formula "God sent" (cf. Rom 8:3) implies the preexistence of the Son. When God sends wisdom or knowledge or a spirit of confusion, the preexistence of such qualities is not in view. Nevertheless, the sending of the Son is distinct from God's sending wisdom or knowledge, for the latter are abstract entities and the Son is personal.[25] Hence, it seems likely that the preexistence of the Son is implied here.

To say that Jesus was "born of a woman" is not an allusion to the virgin birth,[26] for in Job 25:4 a similar expression is used ("born of woman," γεννητὸς γυναικός) to describe the birth of human beings (cf. also Matt 11:11; Job 14:1; 15:14; Josephus, *Ant.* 7.21; 16.382). Instead, the formula used here emphasizes Jesus' full humanity.

Not only was Jesus fully human; he also lived under the law. Those who live under the law, as noted previously, live under the dominion and tyranny of sin. Jesus, however, is the exception that proves the rule. He is the true offspring of Abraham (3:16), the true Israel (cf. Exod 4:22), the true Son of God. He lived obediently to God's law, whereas all others violated God's will.[27] As the one who lived under the law, he took the curse of the law on himself (3:13) so that he could liberate and free those who were captivated by the power of sin.

4:5 To redeem those under law, so that we should receive adoption as sons (ἵνα τοὺς ὑπὸ νόμον ἐξαγοράσῃ, ἵνα τὴν υἱοθεσίαν ἀπολάβωμεν). God's plan that human beings would be delivered from the power of sin has been realized in the sending of his Son. He has redeemed "those under law" so that believers are now God's "sons." Paul consistently depicts the power of sin with the "under" phrases in Galatians. Those who are "under law" (3:23; 4:4) are "under a curse" (3:10), and "under sin" (3:22), and "under [a] custodian" (3:25), and "under the elements" (4:3). Sin has placed people under its tyranny and mastery.

As noted in v. 4, Jesus lived under the law and took its curse on himself as the true and perfect Son of God, and hence he redeemed and freed those who were under the authority and dominion of sin.[28] The verb "redeem" (ἐξαγοράζω) hearkens back to 3:13,[29] where Paul used the same verb to denote that liberation from the law came because

---

24. Hafemann ("Paul and the Exile," 340) rightly sees the redemptive-historical character of what Paul says here, but he wrongly concludes that there is no existential dimension to the text and hence rules out any polarity between "works" and "faith."

25. Contra James D. G. Dunn, *Christology in the Making: A New Testament Inquiry into the Origins of the Doctrine of the Incarnation* (2nd ed.; Grand Rapids: Eerdmans, 38 – 45); cf also Longenecker, *Galatians,* 167 – 70; Betz, *Galatians,* 206 – 7; Martyn, *Galatians,* 406 – 8. In support of preexis-

tence, see Matera, *Galatians,* 150; Lightfoot, *Galatians,* 168; Bruce, *Galatians,* 195; Hans-Christian Kammler, "Die Prädikation Jesu Christi als 'Gott' und die paulinische Christologie: Erwägungen zur Exegese von Röm 9,5b," *ZNW* 92 (2003): 176; Fee, *Galatians,* 148 – 49.

26. Against Calvin, *Galatians,* 118.

27. So Longenecker, *Galatians,* 171 – 72.

28. Cf. Bruce, *Galatians,* 196.

29. The language of redemption also alludes to exodus traditions. See Scott, *Adoption as Sons of God,* 172 – 73.

Jesus took the law's curse upon himself. Therefore, this verse points to Jesus' substitutionary death on behalf of sinners and also indicates that the liberation of those under the law came at the cost of Jesus' life.

Those who are freed and redeemed from slavery to sin are adopted as God's children.[30] The word "adoption" (υἱοθεσία) is unique to Paul in the NT (cf. Rom 8:15, 23; 9:4; Eph 1:5). Many scholars contend that the term is borrowed from the Roman world.[31] Scott makes a strong argument for a Jewish background, but resolving this issue is unnecessary for grasping the main point of the text.[32] Believers are now adopted as God's children through the cross-work of Jesus Christ.

The first person plural here ("we should receive," ἀπολάβωμεν) functions as strong evidence that Paul does not use the first person plurals in Galatians to refer only to the Jews.[33] The whole point of the argument in Galatians is that Gentiles are now adopted into God's family as his children, that they are the offspring of Abraham because they are incorporated into Christ. As Burke says, "God's family comprises solely adopted sons and daughters — there are no natural-born sons or daughters in his divine household."[34] Paul's argument here would be intolerably awkward if the first person plural were restricted only to Jews. Instead, he envisions Gentiles (like the Jews) to be under

the law, in the sense that they too lived under the dominion of sin. Now in Christ Jesus they have been adopted as children of God. Das rightly observes that Paul's flow of thought only works if Gentiles are included in the "we." The "we" who have been adopted (4:5) are the same group as the "you" (4:6) who are God's sons.[35]

4:6 And because you are sons, God sent forth the Spirit of his Son into our hearts crying, "Abba, Father" (Ὅτι δέ ἐστε υἱοί, ἐξαπέστειλεν ὁ θεὸς τὸ πνεῦμα τοῦ υἱοῦ αὐτοῦ εἰς τὰς καρδίας ἡμῶν[36] κρᾶζον, Αββα ὁ πατήρ). The fundamental proof and evidence that the Galatians are truly God's adopted sons is that God has given them the Holy Spirit, and their sonship is expressed by their acclamation that God is their Father.

Paul returns here to the theme of 3:1 – 5, where the powerful presence of the Spirit marks the Galatians out as members of the people of God. Just as God "sent" his Son (4:4), he has also "sent" the Spirit. Paul likely draws on second exodus themes of God's deliverance of his people from Isa 48:16 – 17, for there Isaiah speaks of the sending of the Messiah, God's Spirit, and God's work of rescuing his people.[37] The close relationship between the Father, the Son, and the Spirit is reflected in the phrase "the Spirit of his Son."

The logic of Paul's argument seems strange, for he seems to suggest that first believers become

---

30. The second "so that" (ἵνα) clause is not coordinate with the first (against Matera, *Galatians*, 150), and so here the pattern is distinct from what we find in 3:14.

31. E.g., Hester, *Paul's Concept of Inheritance*, 57 – 61; Betz, *Galatians*, 202; Bruce, *Galatians*, 192.

32. Scott, *Adoption as Sons of God*.

33. Rightly Dalton, "'We' in Galatians," 40. Longenecker agrees, but he bases his view on the dubious foundation that Paul cites a confession in 4:4 – 5 (*Galatians*, 172), which is, as noted above, improbable. For the contrary view, see Betz, *Galatians*, 208 (who sees a "Jews first, then Gentiles" pattern); Bruce, *Galatians*, 197; Matera, *Galatians*, 150; B. Longenecker, *Triumph of Abraham's God*, 92 – 93.

34. Burke, *Adoption into God's Family*, 89.

35. Das, *Paul and the Jews*, 125. "The view that he [Paul] has only Jews in mind leads to chaos, particularly in verses 5 – 6." So Williams, *Galatians*, 110 – 11.

36. A second person plural pronoun "your" (ὑμῶν) fits with the second person plural verb (ἐστε) and is supported particularly by the Majority Text. Still, it is clear that the first person plural "ours" (ἡμῶν) is original ($\mathfrak{P}^{46}$, ℵ, A, B, C, D*, F, G, P, 104, 1175, 1241ˢ, 1739, 1881, 1962, 2464, etc.). Cf. also Fee, *Galatians*, 151, n. 58.

37. So G. K. Beale, "The Old Testament Background of Paul's Reference to 'the Fruit of the Spirit' in Galatians 5:22," *BBR* 15 (2005): 10 – 11.

God's sons and then God sends the Spirit to them to confirm the sonship that already exists. It is mistaken, however, to derive a chronological order from what Paul says here.[38] The main point in this paragraph is that believers are sons and heirs. Hence, the verse begins with the declaration that believers are God's sons. They are truly members of Abraham's family.

Paul introduces the sending of the Spirit to confirm that they are truly the sons of God.[39] He is not intending to say that the Spirit being given *after* sonship is a reality. The point is that the Spirit *confirms, authenticates, and ratifies* their sonship. What we have here is language similar to Rom 8:15 – 16. "You received the Spirit of sonship. And by him we cry, '*Abba*, Father.' The Spirit himself testifies with our spirit that we are God's children" (cf. also Rom 8:9; Phil 1:19).

The verb "cry out" (κράζω) denotes "a loud or earnest cry" (cf. Matt 9:27; Acts 14:14; Rom 9:27).[40] The Spirit works charismatically, so that believers gladly exclaim that God is their beloved Father.

Probably the word "Abba," the Aramaic term for "Father," derives from the term that Jesus himself used in addressing God (cf. Mark 14:36),[41] signifying that God is the loving and dear Father of those who believe in Jesus the Christ. And the Galatians know they are truly believers, for the Spirit confirms it in their hearts.[42]

4:7 Therefore, you are no longer a slave but a son. And if you are a son, you are also an heir through God (ὥστε οὐκέτι εἶ δοῦλος ἀλλὰ υἱός· εἰ δὲ υἱός, καὶ κληρονόμος διὰ θεοῦ[43]). The word "therefore" (ὥστε) is an inferential conjunction that draws a conclusion from the entire section, bringing the illustration that commenced in 4:1 to a close.[44] Believers are no longer minors, living in the old age of redemptive history, slaves under the tyranny of sin. They have now reached full adulthood as God's sons. They have been redeemed from the law and have received the gift of the Holy Spirit. Since they are sons, they are also heirs. The promises of Abraham are theirs.

---

38. Longenecker argues that sonship and receiving the Spirit both occur at the same time in Paul, and hence arguments over chronology miss the point (*Galatians*, 173).

39. Especially helpful here is Betz, *Galatians*, 209 – 10. He remarks, "Paul bases his argument with the Galatian readers upon the fact that they too have experienced the Spirit (3:2 – 5); what they are in doubt about is whether or not they are 'sons of God' already now" (210).

40. Longenecker, *Galatians*, 174.

41. See Joachim Jeremias, *The Prayers of Jesus* (SBT 2/6; London: SCM), 1967: 11 – 67; idem, *New Testament Theology: The Proclamation of Jesus* (trans. John Bowden; New York: Scribner's, 1971), 61 – 68. See the summary and evaluation of Jeremias's views in Marianne Meye Thompson, *The Promise of the Father: Jesus and God in the New Testament* (Louisville: Westminster John Knox, 2000), 21 – 34. Betz follows Luther and Augustine in saying that the bilingual use of "Father" indicates the "bilingual character of the early church," which includes both Jews and Gentiles (*Galatians*, 211).

42. See esp. here Calvin, *Galatians*, 121.

43. A great variety of readings exist here as recorded by Metzger (*Textual Commentary*, 526 – 27): (1) heir "of God" (1962, etc.); (2) an heir "on account of God" (διὰ θεόν, F, G, 1881, *pc*); (3) an heir "through Christ" (81, 630, *pc*, sa); (4) an heir "through Jesus Christ" (1739ᶜ); (5) an heir of "God through Christ" (𝔐, ℵᶜ, C², D, K, P, 88, 104, 614*, etc.); (6) an heir "of God through Jesus Christ" (326, 614ᶜ, 2127, 2495, etc.); (7) an heir "through God in Christ" (copᵇᵒ ᵐˢ); (8) "an heir of God and co-heir with Christ" (Ψ, 1984, 1985, etc.). The diverse readings are due to "the unusual and unexpected expression" (*Textual Commentary*, 526), and there is significant support for the "heir through God" (𝔓⁴⁶, ℵ*, A, B, C*, 33, 1739*ᵛⁱᵈ).

44. Betz says it is surprising that Paul shifts to a second person singular here, suggesting that it may derive from the style of the diatribe (*Galatians*, 211, n. 96). Perhaps Paul wanted to emphasize the need for each reader to take the truth personally.

Theology in Application

Trusting in the God Who Does Right

Many of the themes in this section have already been emphasized previously in Galatians. The importance of salvation history is featured once again. Hence, we need constantly to keep in mind where a text belongs in the biblical story line when we interpret its significance for today. All of Scripture is inspired and authoritative, but the application of a text to contemporary life must be informed by the larger story.

Further, we see in this text that God planned the whole of redemptive history. In his own wisdom he determined when the Son would be sent into the world. As human beings we may wonder why God sent his Son in the time and place he did. Why Palestine? Why the first century? Perhaps the Roman peace (*Pax Romana*) and the Roman network of roads are part of the answer. In the last analysis, however, we must admit that we know too little to understand why God has planned history as he has. Only the Lord of history comprehends its purposes.

Only one who grasps both the concrete events and the big picture of history can explain why God sent his Son when he did. God himself, of course, is the only one who has such infinite knowledge. We are all limited by our finite perspective, by our limited vision. Hence, we finally must trust in a sovereign and loving God, believing that he does all things well and that he, as the judge of all the earth, always does what is right (Gen 18:25).

If God rules over history, we can trust him with the particulars of our lives as well. We may agonize about particular sufferings in our lives: health problems, circumstances that are difficult, or the timing of the death of loved ones. Usually we don't understand such hard things. Even though we don't fully grasp why sufferings happen to us, we cling to the promise of God's love for us (Rom 8:31 – 39), and we trust that he will strengthen us for whatever comes our way.

Privileges of Being God's Adopted Children

Believers also enjoy the privilege of being God's sons and daughters. No privilege is greater than being part of God's family. Those who belong to his family are also his heirs. So many in our society today come from families that are dysfunctional, and every family is defiled by sin. Every human family (Eph 3:15), however, points to a greater family and to a perfect Father, a Father who loves us and out of love for us sent his own Son for our salvation. He has freed us from the sin that enslaves us and granted us his Spirit, so that we can embrace him as our beloved Father.

Perhaps you as a reader grew up in a family where you were unloved or even abused. It can be difficult, coming from such a background, to understand what it means for God to be your Father. You need to remind yourself daily as you meditate on God's Word that God is very different from your father (and perhaps your mother as well). Soak yourself in the truth that God loves you and that you have a thrilling future and a hope. Ask the Holy Spirit to reveal to you the true nature of your Father in heaven, so that you gladly give yourself to him. And meet with a Christian counselor to be helped in your journey.

Many families in American society, especially among Christians, have adopted children.[45] Such adoptions specially testify to the gospel, for believers who adopt children include them as part of their family, and they long for such children to know the love of God in Jesus Christ our Lord. So too, by nature and birth, we are not part of God's family but are children who deserve God's wrath (cf. Eph 2:3). How great is the love of God, for he sent his Son to liberate us from sin. But the love of God did not stop with justification and liberation. We are not only justified, but we also have all the rights and privileges of children. We are deeply and dearly loved as the children of God.

Perhaps you are young Christian parents and you have never thought of adopting children. I am not saying that it is God's will that you do so. My wife and I did not do so. But what a wonderful ministry! Many children who are adopted come from unbelieving cultures. What a privilege it is to adopt them into your family and to raise them in the nurture and admonition of the Lord, so that they come to know the gospel of Jesus Christ. The book by Russell Moore, noted in the previous footnote, provides practical advice and gives powerful incentives to consider adoption.

---

45. For a powerful book on adoption, see Russell D. Moore, *Adopted for Life: The Priority of Adoption for Christian Families and Churches* (Wheaton: Crossway, 2009).

Galatians 4:8 – 11

Literary Context

Galatians 4:8 – 11 functions as the conclusion of the long argument from redemptive history that began in 3:15, but here Paul applies what he has taught to the Galatians. Dahl rightly sees that 1:6 – 4:11 comprises a major section in the letter.[1] Paul has labored to demonstrate that believers are no longer under the Mosaic covenant and the law and that they live in the days when the promise given to Abraham has been fulfilled. Therefore, in both 3:26 – 29 and 4:1 – 7 he emphasizes that believers belong to the family of Abraham. They are God's sons and heirs. In 4:8 – 11, however, Paul explains why he fears that his apostolic labors may be in vain. The Galatians are relapsing back into paganism, but in a most remarkable way, for their relapse manifests itself in their desire to subject themselves to the Mosaic law.

I. Introduction: Desertion from Paul's Gospel Is Desertion from the Gospel (1:1 – 2:21)

II. Paul's Gospel Defended from Experience and Scripture (3:1 – 4:11)

A. Argument from Experience: Reception of Spirit by Means of Faith, Not Works (3:1 – 5)

B. Argument from Scripture: Blessing of Abraham by Faith (3:6 – 14)

C. Argument from Salvation History: Priority of Abrahamic Covenant and Temporary Nature of Mosaic Covenant (3:15 – 4:11)

1. Addition of Law Does Not Nullify Promise to Abraham (3:15 – 25)

2. Sons of God Are Abraham's Offspring (3:26 – 29)

3. Argument from Slavery to Sonship (4:1 – 7)

➡ **4. The Folly of Reverting to the Law (4:8 – 11)**

Main Idea

If the Galatians embrace the Mosaic law after their conversion, Paul's apostolic labors have been in vain.

---

1. Dahl, "Paul's Letter to the Galatians," 133.

Translation

Galatians 4:8-11

8a	basis *(of 8b)*	But	formerly when you did not know God,
b	assertion		**you were enslaved to those beings which are not gods by nature.**
9a	contrast *(to 8a-b)*	But	now that you have come to know God, or rather
b	qualification *(of 9a)*		you have been known by God,
c	rhetorical question		**how can you return again to the weak and poor elements to which you desire** ↵
			to be enslaved again?
10	assertion		**You are observing days and months, and seasons and years.**
11	exclamation		**I fear for you lest somehow I have labored for you in vain.**

Structure

In 3:26 – 29 and 4:1 – 7 the Galatians' sonship and promise of being heirs is celebrated. In 4:8, however, Paul recalls their former life as unbelievers. Here we find the contrast between the old life and the new with the words "formerly" (τότε, 4:8) and "now" (νῦν, 4:9). Since they did not know the one true God, they lived under bondage to false gods. Verse 9 functions as a contrast to v. 8. The Galatians are no longer subservient to the gods they served formerly. They have come to know God in a saving way.

Paul immediately introduces a qualification, for the emphasis is not on their choice in knowing God but on God's knowing them. Still, Paul fears that their so-called "com[ing] to know God" has been for nothing. They are relapsing to serve the elements they left behind. Verse 10 moves the argument in an astonishing direction. We would expect from 4:8 – 9 that the Galatians are literally resuming worship of false gods, but 4:10 explains that their setback manifests itself in an observance of the Jewish calendar. Apparently Paul equates living under the law with a reversion to paganism. The inconstancy of the Galatians renders Paul uncertain about their spiritual state. He speculates from the state of affairs in 4:8 – 10 that all his work may have been in vain (4:11).

Exegetical Outline

II. Paul's Gospel Defended from Experience and Scripture (3:1 – 4:11)

   A. Argument from Experience: Reception of Spirit by Means of Faith, Not Works (3:1 – 5)

   B. Argument from Scripture: Blessing of Abraham by Faith (3:6 – 14)

Explanation of the Text

4:8 But formerly when you did not know God, you were enslaved to those beings which are not gods by nature (Ἀλλὰ τότε μὲν οὐκ εἰδότες θεὸν ἐδουλεύσατε τοῖς φύσει μὴ οὖσιν θεοῖς). Before believers knew God — i.e., before they were converted — the Galatians were enslaved to false gods. One of the key themes that ties together Paul's argument from redemptive history in this section of the letter is "slavery." Life "under law" is characterized as one in which human beings lived under the dominion and tyranny of sin. Believers were "imprisoned … under sin" (3:22 ESV), "held captive under the law" (3:23 ESV), "enslaved under the elements of the world" (4:3), but now they are freed from the bondage that previously ensnared them (4:5) and are no longer slaves (which implies they previously were slaves, 4:7).

As unbelievers they were enslaved to false gods.[2] They served idols rather than the true and living God (1 Thess 1:9), though these so-called gods were not truly gods. Elsewhere he observes that idols are not genuine (1 Cor 8:4). Still, behind idols are demonic powers (1 Cor 10:19 – 20), and though demons are not gods, they still exercise power over people, which fits with the claim that the Galatians were enslaved to false gods before their conversion.[3]

The reason for this subjugation to false gods is explained in the temporal participial phrase — "when you did not know God" (οὐκ εἰδότες θεόν). The fundamental error of unbelievers is their failure to know and praise and thank God, and hence they turn instead to self-worship and adulation of the creature rather than the Creator (cf. Rom 1:21 – 25; cf. 1 Cor 1:21). The sexual sin of Gentiles, says Paul in Romans (Rom 1:24 – 27), flows from their not knowing God. Apparently, those who do not know God give worship to someone or something else instead of to the one and only true God.

4:9a-b But now that you have come to know God, or rather you have been known by God (νῦν δὲ γνόντες θεόν, μᾶλλον δὲ γνωσθέντες ὑπὸ θεοῦ). A beautiful picture of conversion is drawn here

---

2. As Betz observes, Paul has no interest in describing the different gods the Galatians served. "He prefers to lump them all together under the heading of 'the elements of the world'" (*Galatians*, 213).

3. Betz (*Galatians*, 215) and Bruce (*Galatians*, 202) incline to the view that false gods were only a projection of the human imagination, but they fail to explain how 1 Cor 10:19 – 20 fits with 1 Cor 8:4 – 6.

(cf. 1 Thess 1:9), as Paul contrasts "then" (τότε, 4:8) and "now" (νῦν)—their former lives and their new life in Christ. Then they did not know God, but when the Galatians were converted, they came to know God.[4] Such knowledge is not merely abstract and impersonal but has a personal and warm dimension, for they exclaim that God is their beloved Father (4:6). They sense his nearness and love for them, since they are now his children.

Still, the accent cannot rest on their knowing God, and hence Paul qualifies his initial statement. Even though it is true that believers have come to know God, there is a deeper reality that explains why they know God's saving love, namely, God's knowledge of them. God's knowledge of his people hearkens back to the Hebrew verb "know" (*yādaᶜ*), where God's knowledge refers to his choosing of someone—the setting of his affection upon someone.[5] Hence, he "knew" Abraham by choosing him to be the father of the Jewish people (Gen 18:19). He "knew" Israel and chose them out of all the people groups on earth (Amos 3:2). He "knew" Jeremiah before he was born and hence appointed him to be a prophet (Jer 1:5).[6] So too, the Galatians have come to know God because God knew them first, because he loved them and graciously chose them to be his own.[7]

4:9c How can you return again to the weak and poor elements to which you desire to be enslaved again? (πῶς ἐπιστρέφετε πάλιν ἐπὶ τὰ ἀσθενῆ καὶ πτωχὰ στοιχεῖα οἷς πάλιν ἄνωθεν δουλεύειν θέλετε;). Paul is startled that the Galatians are turning back to their old ways, and he apparently thinks that devotion to the Mosaic law is just another form of paganism! The word "return" (ἐπιστρέφω) is often used for conversion to Christ (Acts 3:19; 9:35; 11:21; 14:15; 15:19; 26:18, 20; 2 Cor 3:16; 1 Thess 1:9; 1 Pet 2:25), but here the term is turned on its head and used for "converting back" to paganism, for renouncing the faith (cf. 2 Pet 2:22) and reverting to false gods.[8]

On the one hand, Paul is "astonished" (1:6) and "at a loss" (4:20) that the Galatians would desire to return to that which is weak and impoverished. Indeed, they are on the brink of trading liberty for slavery, freedom for bondage. As in 4:3 the "elements" (στοιχεῖα) are linked with bondage. Seeing the "elements" here as spiritual powers, as "elemental spirits," makes good sense in that the Galatians are returning to the gods they previously served. On the other hand, perhaps Paul is simply saying that they are subjecting themselves to the things of this world, though it seems more likely that demonic powers are in view.[9] In any case, the Galatians' desire for bondage is inexplicable and irrational.[10] What is astonishing is that Paul equates subjection to Torah with paganism.

---

4. Against Betz, the language of knowing is not gnostic here (*Galatians*, 215 – 16).

5. See here S. M. Baugh, "The Meaning of Foreknowledge," in *Still Sovereign* (ed. Thomas R. Schreiner and Bruce A. Ware; Grand Rapids: Baker, 2000), 183 – 200.

6. Different verbs for "knowing" are used in Greek, but the verbs overlap semantically. The Hebrew verb is the same in every instance.

7. For an excellent theological and pastoral reflection on being known by God, see Brian S. Rosner, "'Known by God': The Meaning and Value of a Neglected Biblical Concept," *TynBul* 59 (2008): 207 – 30.

8. Kwon rightly perceives that Paul speaks of apostasy here, but he wrongly concludes that the Galatians no longer know God (*Eschatology*, 39 – 40). Kwon, however, fails to read the letter with appropriate rhetorical balance. Therefore, he takes all the statements about the Galatians' defection seriously (37 – 42), but he tends to explain away any statements that indicate that the Galatians still belong to God. See, e.g., the commentary under 5:10.

9. See the discussion under 4:3.

10. Wilson ("Wilderness Apostasy," 561 – 63) intriguingly suggests that their desire to be enslaved echoes Israel wanting to return to Egypt (cf. Exod 14:10 – 12; 16:3; 17:3; Num 14:2 – 4).

One can only imagine the shock the Pauline assertion would have given the Judaizers![11]

4:10 You are observing days and months, and seasons and years (ἡμέρας παρατηρεῖσθε καὶ μῆνας καὶ καιροὺς καὶ ἐνιαυτούς). The Galatians are beginning to observe the OT calendar. Some scholars argue that the reference here is to a pagan calendar, since Paul indicts the Galatians for their reversion to false gods and for turning back to their former way of life. It seems more likely, however, because of the context of the entire letter, that the readers are being criticized for observance of the OT calendar and hence for devotion to the OT law.

The "days" refer especially to observance of the Sabbath,[12] though other special days may also be in mind. Burton is likely correct in cautioning us from being too specific in distinguishing the four terms from one another.[13] Paul piles up terms to designate the Galatians' observance of the Jewish calendar. Betz argues that the Galatians were not observing the law but describes their lifestyle if they actually decided to keep the law.[14] Still, it is most natural to read the text to say that the Galatians were actually observing the OT calendar, though they had not yet submitted to circumcision.[15]

Perhaps we have an allusion here to Gen 1:14, where the words "seasons" (καιρούς) and "days" (ἡμέρας) and "years (ἐνιαυτούς) appear. The same concern for observing certain days and feasts arises in Rom 14: 5 and Col 2:16. In both instances Gentiles were apparently attracted to the OT law. One of the most surprising themes of this section becomes clear here. Paul compares devotion to the Mosaic law to reverting to paganism. The Galatians before their conversion to Christ were devoted to false gods (4:8), yet Paul sees their attraction to Judaism as equivalent to paganism.[16]

4:11 I fear for you lest somehow I have labored for you in vain (φοβοῦμαι ὑμᾶς μή πως εἰκῇ κεκοπίακα εἰς ὑμᾶς). The Galatians desire for and attraction to the Mosaic law raised questions about the Galatians' end-time salvation. It also called into question the efficacy of Paul's apostolic labors. Perhaps Paul's work was in vain (cf. 3:4). If the Galatians strayed from the gospel of grace, their only hope was an eschatological curse (1:8 – 9), for those who trust in the law are cut off from Christ (5:2 – 4).

We see elsewhere in the Pauline writings that only those who continue in the faith will receive the eschatological inheritance. Hence, Paul contemplates the possibility that his work will be futile if those whom he evangelized do not persevere (1 Cor 15:2; Phil 2:16; 1 Thess 3:5). Such a warning is designed to awaken the Galatians from their lethargy and to call them back to the Pauline gospel.[17]

---

11. Cf. Betz, *Galatians*, 216 – 17; Hays, *Galatians*, 287.

12. So Dunn, *Galatians*, 227; Garlington, *Galatians*, 249.

13. Burton, *Galatians*, 234. Cf. Longenecker, *Galatians*, 182; Martyn, *Galatians*, 416 – 17. Thornton rightly sees that Jewish observances are in view, but it is less clear that "months" refers to new moons, which in turn, according to Thornton, are related to "the elements of the world" (τὰ στοιχεῖα τοῦ κόσμου). See T. C. G. Thornton, "Jewish New Moon Festivals: Galatians 4:3 – 11 and Colossians 2:16," *JTS* 40 (1989): 97 – 100.

14. Betz, *Galatians*, 217 – 18. Betz, in fact, argues that what Paul describes does not represent Judaism but paganism. Arnold rightly observes that Betz mistakenly interprets the opponents as if "we are dealing with a more magical-mystical form of Judaism." Arnold, "Returning to the Domain of the Powers," 74.

15. Longenecker, *Galatians*, 181 – 83; Bruce, *Galatians*, 205 – 6; Dunn, *Galatians*, 227 – 29; Fung, *Galatians*, 193.

16. Rightly Longenecker, *Galatians*, 181.

17. As Chrysostom says, "the wreck has not happened, but I see the storm big with it" (*Galatians*, 31).

Theology in Application

This paragraph assists us in putting together a theology of conversion. Before one becomes a believer, one is enslaved (4:8) to that which is not the true God. Elsewhere Paul teaches that unbelievers are enslaved to sin (Rom 6:6, 17, 19 – 20). They are dead in trespasses and sin, under the dominion of the world and the devil, and carried along by their fleshly desires (Eph 2:1 – 3). Therefore, conversion is described as redemption (Gal 4:4 – 5), as being freed from the mastery and tyranny of sin (Rom 6:14, 18, 22). Such liberation is the work of the Lord, and hence all praise belongs to him for the stunning deliverance accomplished.

Paul also describes conversion here in terms of knowing God (4:9). Believers are no longer alienated from the God of the universe. Marvellously and wondrously we are said to know him, and surely that also means that we love him. A new relationship has commenced, a new love has dawned, a new Lord is the passion of our lives. Conversion is not marked merely by doing what God commands; it manifests itself in an intimacy with God, a love for the Lord Jesus Christ (Eph 6:24).

Yet knowing God cannot finally be attributed to the initiative of believers. Before believers come to know God in a saving way, the Lord knew them first. He sets his covenantal favor on them and has elected them to be his children. The doctrine of election is the subject of controversy in evangelical circles, and various views are expressed. Paul regularly reminds believers of their election to grant them comfort and strength and to remind them that all praise belongs to God for their salvation. Salvation is not ultimately due to human choice or exertion (Eph 1:4; Rom 9:10 – 23), but it is the work of the sovereign Lord.

The scriptural writers do not attempt to justify the ways of God in choosing only some for salvation, for God is holy, just, and good. The salvation of any should lead to praise, for no one deserves to be saved. If salvation is truly gracious and merciful, God's choice of some is stunning. If our hearts are cold and distant, perhaps we have ceased to think of the grace given us as a gift; perhaps we think God "should" save us. If so, grace is no longer grace for us.

At the same time we see the complexity of conversion in 4:8 – 11. Paul wonders if he has labored in vain over the Galatians (4:11). He contemplates the possibility that they are not truly converted at all. Genuine conversion cannot be restricted to a onetime event in the past. Those who are saved demonstrate their new life by continuing in faith until the last day. Their perseverance in faith functions as the evidence that they have truly come to know God. Therefore, the grace of God can never become an excuse for license. Those who are truly saved demonstrate such by clinging to the cross of Christ until the end.

Galatians 4:12 – 20

Literary Context

If we sum up the argument thus far, Paul has argued for his apostolic authority and the truth of his gospel in 1:1 – 2:21. Galatians 2:15 – 21 functions as a transition to the next major section of the letter, where the vital question is who belongs to the family of Abraham. In 2:15 – 21 Paul argues that right standing with God comes by faith rather than works of law. Indeed, the Galatians belong to the people of God. The Spirit, which is the mark of being a Christian, has been given to them by faith rather than by their observance of the works of law (3:1 – 5). Believers are the children of Abraham and enjoy the blessing of Abraham, for they share the faith of Abraham (3:6 – 9). Those who attempt to be righteous by works of law will be cursed, but the blessing of Abraham and the promise of the Spirit belong to those who put their trust in Christ, who removed the curse of the law by taking it upon himself (3:10 – 14). Furthermore, the Mosaic law is a temporary covenant, and it is subsidiary to the covenant with Abraham (3:15 – 25); hence, believers are no longer under its authority. They are now God's sons and heirs, not by observing the law but through faith in Christ and by virtue of union with Christ (3:26 – 4:7). Still, Paul worries about the Galatians, for they are reverting to their pagan past through their devotion to the Mosaic law (4:8 – 11).

The first imperative calling the Galatians to action occurs in 4:12,[1] and those who emphasize epistolary conventions argue from this that we have the beginning of a new section here (4:12 – 6:10), which can be designated as the request section of the letter.[2] Since the Galatians are Abraham's children and belong to God's people, and since the law is no longer in force, they should live in freedom from the law, just as Paul is no longer subject to the law. Betz rightly sees the friendship theme as

---

1. There is an imperative in 3:7, but it is not a call to action.
2. Dahl, "Paul's Letter to the Galatians," 133 – 39; Longenecker, *Galatians*, 184 – 87. Longenecker argues that a number of epistolary conventions are used here that signal a new
section. But though Longenecker rightly sees a major break
in the letter here, his claim that 4:12 – 5:12 addresses matters

raised by Judaizers and 5:13 – 6:10 the issue of libertinism is
unpersuasive (*Galatians*, 187). Paul's concern remains the
same throughout the letter. Callan, in his study of the style of
Galatians, also sees 4:12 – 6:10 as a new section, which commences the exhortation section of the letter ("Style of Galatians," 513).

central here,[3] even though friendship does not capture all that Paul does here since he is also the founder of the Galatian churches and functions as an authority.[4]

The new section is marked by a verb of appeal, "I beseech" (δέομαι).[5] All commentators recognize the different character of the argument here, and some have suggested that Paul departs from logical argumentation and relies on emotions and personal experience.[6] Such a judgment overreaches because it neglects the argument that undergirds the text. Instead of arguing from Scripture or salvation history, Paul rehearses his history with the Galatians and makes his case from his relationship with them, appealing to them to live in accord with the model he provided instead of following after the Judaizers, who have acted with improper motives. Furthermore, the argument is not devoid of theology. As B. Longenecker in particular recognizes, "At stake, in Paul's mind, is Christian character enlivened by the Spirit and evidenced within human relationships."[7]

I. Introduction: Desertion from Paul's Gospel Is Desertion from the Gospel (1:1 – 2:21)

II. Paul's Gospel Defended from Experience and Scripture (3:1 – 4:11)

III. A Call to Freedom from the Law and Freedom in the Spirit (4:12 – 6:10)

➡ **A. Live in Freedom from the Law: Argument from Friendship (4:12 – 20)**

B. Stand in Freedom: Argument from Allegory (4:21 – 5:1)

Main Idea

The imperative to become like Paul (4:12) functions as the central truth in the text. Paul no longer lives under the Mosaic law, and the readers should not do so either.

Translation

(See next page.)

---

3. See Betz, *Galatians*, 220 – 237. Betz cites many parallels to demonstrate the friendship theme. For some qualifications of Betz's view and an emphasis on Paul's frankness in rebuking the Galatians, while assuring them of his friendship, see White, "Rhetoric and Reality in Galatians," 307 – 49.

4. Rightly Matera, *Galatians*, 163.

5. So Dahl, "Paul's Letter to the Galatians," 134; Hansen says, "This request is the decisive turning point in the letter" ("Paradigm of the Apocalypse," 144). So also, Hafemann, "Role of Suffering," 166; Dieter Mitternacht, "Foolish Gala-

tians? — A Recipient-Oriented Assessment of Paul's Letter," in *The Galatians Debate: Contemporary Issues in Rhetorical and Historical Interpretation* (ed. Mark D. Nanos; Peabody, MA: Hendrickson, 2002), 408. The focus is on freedom from the law, and so there is not, as Mitternacht claims (419 – 23), an exhortation here to join Paul in suffering. Rightly Hafemann, "Role of Suffering," 169, n. 12.

6. Burton, *Galatians*, 235; Schlier, *Galater*, 208; Mussner, *Galaterbrief*, 304.

7. B. Longenecker, "Until Christ Is Formed in You," 106.

Galatians 4:12-20

12a	command	**Become as I am,**
b	basis *(of 12a)*	because I also have become as you are, brothers, I beseech you.
c	assertion	**You have not wronged me in any way.**
13	concessive *(to 14a)*	But **you know that I preached the gospel to you formerly** because of weakness ⌖ of the flesh.
14a	assertion	And **you did not despise your temptation in my flesh.**
b	series *(to 14a)*	**Neither did you spit upon me,**
c	contrast *(to 14a-b)*	but **you received me** as an angel of God,
d	apposition *(to 14c)*	as Christ Jesus.
15a	inference *(from 12c-14d)*/rhetorical question	Therefore, **where is your blessing?**
b	basis *(of 15a)*	For **I testify to you that you would have given me your eyes**
c	means *(of 15b)*	by plucking them out if it were possible.
16a	inference *(of 12c-15c)*/rhetorical question	So then, **have I become your enemy**
b	basis *(of 16a)*	because I speak the truth to you?
17a	explanation *(of 16a-b)*	**They are not zealous for you in a good way,**
b	alternative *(to 17a)*	but **they wish to shut you out,**
c	purpose *(of 17b)*	in order that you might be zealous for them.
18a	explanation *(of 17a-c)*	Now **to be zealous for the good** **is always good, and**
b	series *(from 18a)*	**not only when I am present with you,**
19a	exclamation	my children, for whom I am suffering birth pangs again
b	temporal	until Christ is formed in you!
20a	series *(from 19a-b)*/wish	And **I wish I were present with you now**
b	purpose *(of 20a)*	so that I could change my voice,
c	basis *(of 20a-b)*	for I am at a loss over you.

Structure

The first imperative calling the Galatians to action opens this paragraph and constitutes the central point of 4:12 – 20.[8] The Galatians must become like

---

8. Cf. Longenecker *Galatians*, 186. The paraenetic section of the letter has been identified as beginning with 4:12; 4:21; 5:1; 5:2; 5:7; 5:13 (so Matera, "Gal 5.1 – 6.17," 80, who depends on Merk here). Matera argues that the variation of opinion as to the beginning of the paraenesis suggests that a firm dis-tinction between paraenesis and theology is misplaced (Matera, "Gal 5.1 – 6.17," 80 – 81). Matera rightly warns us against drawing too firm a line between theology and exhortation. Nevertheless, it does seem significant that the first imperative calling the Galatians to action in the letter is here.

Paul — free from the Mosaic law, for Paul, though Jewish, has become as they are, i.e., free from the law (4:12).[9]

Verses 12c – 14 give reasons (introduced by "because" [ὅτι]) why the Galatians should become like Paul and free themselves from the law. In doing so they will recapture how they treated Paul when he first proclaimed the gospel to them. Even though he suffered from a physical ailment, they recognized he was God's messenger to them; it was as if Christ Jesus himself spoke to them. Hence, as in 3:1 – 5, Paul wonders if they have forgotten the "blessing" of the Spirit they received from his ministry (4:15).

The climatic statement in 4:15 is introduced by an interrogative and an inferential conjunction ("where then," [ποῦ οὖν]). The Spirit was given through Paul's suffering, not in spite of it, and hence the Galatians would have gladly given him their eyes if they were able to do so. The blessing will be lost, however, if they now view the truth of the gospel that Paul proclaimed as the words of an adversary (4:16).

A vital part of the truth of the gospel Paul communicates is the evil of the intruding teachers (4:17 – 18). Their zeal is not for the gospel but for their own advancement and praise (cf. 6:12 – 13). Hence, Paul longs for the Galatians to return to their zeal for the gospel he preaches, even though he is currently absent. Paul functions as a mother who gave birth to the Galatians, but now he fears their premature death by miscarriage and longs for Christ to be formed in them (4:19). His perplexity and astonishment over their attraction to a false gospel continue (1:6; 3:1, 3; 4:9).

Exegetical Outline

---

9. Cf. Susan Eastman, who sketches in the dynamic relational and personal factors that inform Paul's exhortation. *Recovering Paul's Mother Tongue: Language and Theology in Galatians* (Grand Rapids: Eerdmans, 2007), 25 – 60.

Explanation of the Text

4:12a-b Become as I am, because I also have become as you are, brothers, I beseech you (Γίνεσθε ὡς ἐγώ, ὅτι κἀγὼ ὡς ὑμεῖς, ἀδελφοί, δέομαι ὑμῶν). Paul entreats the Galatians to become as he is: free from the Mosaic law. I intentionally translated the text somewhat awkwardly to reflect the order of the words in the Greek text. We expect the vocative "brothers" (ἀδελφοί) to occur first in the sentence, but the imperative is thrust at the beginning for emphasis. Indeed, the first imperative calling the Galatians to action is found here, coming after Paul has explained in depth the reasons why the Galatians must not submit to circumcision or subject themselves to the Mosaic law.

Here Paul urges the Galatians to imitate him, to live as he does, and this clearly means that they are not to live under the Mosaic law.[10] It is ironic that Paul, even though he is Jewish, exhorts the Gentiles here to live as he does so that they are not enslaved to the law.[11] The reason Paul gives for the command (see the causal ὅτι) is that he has become like the readers. In other words, Paul, so to speak, has become like the Gentiles, i.e., free from the law. Hence, it makes no sense for them as Gentiles to live like Jews and to submit to the OT law.

Paul's love and warmth for his readers manifests itself in the word "brothers" and in his entreaty to them ("I beseech you"). He commands them as one who longs for their growth and their maturation (cf. 4:19). If they follow Paul's advice here, Christ will be fully formed in them.[12] Eastman rightly observes that becoming like Paul means that the Galatians will face suffering. They will face resistance from the false teachers and continue to suffer for the cross (3:4; cf. 4:29).[13]

4:12c You have not wronged me in any way (οὐδέν με ἠδικήσατε). The friendly relations between Paul and the Galatians now come to the forefront as Paul recalls his initial proclamation of the gospel. Their warm reception of Paul did not merely represent their kindness and humanity but also has theological significance, for Paul came as an apostle, as one who proclaimed the gospel.[14] Hence, their response to Paul signified their reaction to Christ himself. Even though the Galatians did not wrong Paul when he was first with him, circumstances have now changed.[15]

4:13 But you know that I preached the gospel to you formerly because of weakness of the flesh (οἴδατε δὲ ὅτι δι᾽ ἀσθένειαν τῆς σαρκὸς εὐηγγελισάμην ὑμῖν τὸ πρότερον). The welcome Paul received among the Galatians was remarkable because his presence among them was not attractive. He apparently suffered from sickness

---

10. So Chrysostom, *Galatians*, 31; Dahl, "Paul's Letter to the Galatians," 134; Betz, *Galatians*, 222 – 23; Matera, *Galatians*, 159; Longenecker, *Galatians*, 189. Longenecker rightly remarks that what Paul says here indicates that the Galatians have not yet fallen away.

11. Against Bruce, who thinks that Paul simply communicates a paternal concern for the Galatians (*Galatians*, 208). Paul, of course, is willing to live under the law in some situations to win law-abiding Jews to faith in Christ (1 Cor 9:19 – 23). See here Acts 16:3; 18:18; 21:20 – 25.

12. So also B. Longenecker, "Until Christ Is Formed in You," 100 – 101. R. Longenecker says that "I beseech" (δέομαι)

informs the remainder of 4:12 – 20 (*Galatians*, 190).

13. Eastman, *Paul's Mother Tongue*, 108 – 10.

14. Martyn says that Paul reflects on the period after their conversion and before the opponents arrived (*Galatians*, 420). It is not clear that we have an ironic question here. Against White, "Rhetoric and Reality in Galatians," 340.

15. Burton, *Galatians*, 238; Longenecker, *Galatians*, 190; Matera, *Galatians*, 159; Betz, *Galatians*, 223. Burton lists other possible interpretations: (1) they are not wronging Paul but Christ; (2) they are not injuring Paul but themselves. (238). It seems more likely, however, given what Paul says next, that he reflects back on when he first visited the Galatians.

when he proclaimed the gospel to them.[16] Hays suggests that Paul needed "to recuperate from being flogged, beaten, or stoned,"[17] and a number of interpreters now argue that his physical problem was due to his suffering as an apostle.[18] But the phrase "because of weakness of the flesh" is more naturally understood as referring to sickness rather than persecution.[19] Therefore, most scholars think that Paul refers to a *bodily* ailment or sickness rather than his being persecuted.

Scholars who think Paul refers to sickness have attempted to identify the disease from which Paul suffered.[20] Some suggest eye disease since Paul in short order says that the Galatians were willing to give him their own eyes (4:15). The expression, however, need not be literal and could simply convey with a striking picture the Galatians' willingness to endure any sacrifice to assist Paul. Others have suggested that the malady was epilepsy or malaria, and the list goes on and on. Any attempt to identify the disease lands us in the territory of conjecture since we lack sufficient information to draw a conclusion.

Paul's sickness, however, was not a liability for the spread of the gospel. Rather, he considered it to be a *corollary* of Christ's sufferings. In other words, Paul did not think his diseases and sufferings should be separated from his calling as an apostle. The weakness of Paul, manifested in sickness, was the pathway by which Christ's strength was manifested through him (2 Cor 12:7 – 10). Indeed, Paul regularly teaches that his sufferings were the means God used for the dissemination of the gospel (e.g., 2 Cor 1:3 – 11; 2:14 – 15; 4:7 – 12; 11:23 – 29; 13:4; Col 1:24 – 29).[21] God's regular pattern is to display his strength in and through the weakness of his servants. Therefore, Paul's sickness and suffering are not astonishing or surprising to him but precisely what he expects (Acts 9:16).[22]

4:14 And you did not despise your temptation in my flesh. Neither did you spit upon me, but you received me as an angel of God, as Christ Jesus (καὶ τὸν πειρασμὸν ὑμῶν[23] ἐν τῇ σαρκί μου οὐκ ἐξουθενήσατε οὐδὲ ἐξεπτύσατε, ἀλλὰ ὡς

---

16. Hafemann rightly argues that Paul speaks here of his sickness ("Role of Suffering," 168 – 69).

17. Hays, *Galatians*, 294.

18. Cf. Mitternacht, "Recipient-Oriented," 422; A. J. Goddard and S. A. Cummins, "Ill or Ill-Treated? Conflict and Persecution as the Context of Paul's Original Ministry in Galatia (Galatians 4:12 – 20), *JSNT* 52 (1993): 93 – 126; Eastman, *Paul's Mother Tongue*, 100 – 108; Hays, *Galatians*, 293 – 94. For a contrary view, see B. Longenecker, "Until Christ Is Formed in You," 106, n. 36. Martin argues that Paul refers here to the weakness of the flesh *of the Galatians*, and that the temptation in Paul's flesh in 4:14 refers to Paul's own circumcision. See Troy W. Martin, "Whose Flesh? What Temptation? (Galatians 4.13 – 14)," *JSNT* 74 (1999): 65 – 91. But the first singular verb "I preached the gospel to you" (εὐηγγελισάμην) more naturally suggests that the weakness accords with the subject of the verb (i.e., Paul). So, it is likely that Paul would have used the pronoun "your" (ὑμῶν) if the Galatians' flesh were in view. Furthermore, it is more natural to take "flesh" in both 4:13 and 4:14 as referring to the same person (i.e., Paul; see here Hafemann, "Role of Suffering," 168 – 69, n. 11). We have no evidence in the letter that the Galatians were put off by Paul's circumcision.

19. So David Alan Black, "Weakness Language in Galatians," *GTJ* 4 (1983): 28 – 33; Hafemann, "Role of Suffering," 168 – 70. Hafemann rightly says that "Paul's weakness *grounds* his preaching, whereas persecution is its *consequence*" (169 – 70).

20. See the history of interpretation in Lightfoot (*Galatians*, 185 – 91), and the surveys in Bruce, *Galatians*, 208 – 9; Longenecker, *Galatians*, 191.

21. See here the work of Hafemann, "Role of Suffering," 170 – 72, and particularly his work, *Suffering and the Spirit: An Exegetical Study of II Cor. 2:14 – 3:3 within the Context of the Corinthian Correspondence* (WUNT 2/19; Tübingen: Mohr Siebeck, 1986).

22. Eastman demonstrates that Paul's life replicates in many respects the suffering of the prophets (*Paul's Mother Tongue*, 63 – 88).

23. For Paul to speak of "your temptation" is rather surprising, and as the harder reading it should be accepted as original. Moreover, it has good external support (א*, A, B, C², D*, F, G, 33, etc.) To relieve the awkwardness, some scribes inserted "my" (μου) instead of "your" (ὑμῶν) (𝔓⁴⁶, Cᵛⁱᵈ, Dᶜ, Ψ, 𝔐), or they inserted "the" (τόν) after "temptation" (πειρασμόν) and omitted the pronoun (א², 81, 104, 326, 1241ˢ, 2464).

ἄγγελον θεοῦ ἐδέξασθέ με, ὡς Χριστὸν Ἰησοῦν).
Paul's weakness was almost certainly a physical
malady or sickness of some kind, for he locates
it again, as in 4:13, in his flesh, which almost
certainly means his body. Such weakness was a
temptation to the Galatians, for it seemed to be
a sign that Paul's message was not from God, for
surely a divine message would be accompanied
by the strength rather than the weakness of the
messenger.

Nevertheless, the Galatians were granted spiritual perception, for they did not reject or loathe
Paul for his suffering.[24] The language of spitting
may suggest "they did not spit in order to protect
themselves ... warding off illness and the influence of the demonic."[25] Instead, they realized that
he was God's messenger in and through his suffering, that Christ Jesus was speaking through
him.[26] Just as the Galatians heard with faith the
message of Christ crucified (3:1–2), they also
realized that the message proclaimed by Paul,
weakened as he was, was the message of salvation. Hence, their response to Paul is "a clear
demonstration of Christian character already at
work with the Galatians.... It evidenced the Spirit
at work within them already when encountering
Paul."[27]

4:15a Therefore, where is your blessing? (ποῦ[28]
οὖν ὁ μακαρισμὸς ὑμῶν;). This rhetorical question

hearkens back to the Galatians' conversion and
their initial relationship with Paul. When Paul
came with sickness, they welcomed him with joy,
and his presence was accompanied by blessing.
What is the blessing Paul has in mind here? Possibly he refers to blessing in general, so that it refers
to a sense of joy and contentment[29] or honor,[30] or
righteousness by faith (Rom 4:6, 9).[31] But B. Long-
necker is likely correct in arguing that Paul has
in mind God's "redemptive activity," and particularly the work of the Holy Spirit in their midst.[32]
In Rom 4:6–9 "blessing" (μακαρισμός) refers to a
work of God himself in the lives of the readers (cf.
Gal 3:14). Hence, Paul probably returns again to
the subject of 3:1–5, where he emphasizes that the
Galatians received the Spirit by faith instead of via
the works of law.

**4:15b For I testify to you that you would have
given me your eyes by plucking them out if it
were possible** (μαρτυρῶ γὰρ ὑμῖν ὅτι εἰ δυνατὸν
τοὺς ὀφθαλμοὺς ὑμῶν ἐξορύξαντες ἐδώκατέ μοι).
As noted above, some think this verse confirms
that Paul suffered from some kind of eye disease.
Such a diagnosis is uncertain, for the expression is
more likely a vivid way of saying that the Galatians
were willing to give what was precious to them for
Paul's benefit. In any case, Paul highlighted the
initial warmth of the relationship between himself and the Galatians. Their joy at receiving the

---

24. Hafemann suggests that the Judaizers may have argued that Paul's suffering shows that he was under the law's
curse ("Paul and the Exile," 355).

25. B. Longenecker, "Until Christ Is Formed in You," 102;
cf. Hafemann, "Role of Suffering," 173.

26. Cf. Betz, *Galatians*, 226. It is unclear that *the* angel of
the Lord is in view (against Fee, *Galatians*, 165–66).

27. B. Longenecker, "Until Christ Is Formed in You," 102.
B. Longenecker argues (against Betz, *Galatians*, 221) that we
have more than friendship here. For the Galatians response
to Paul shows "God's transforming power already at work
within them" (102).

28. The Majority Text and a few other witnesses read

"what" (τί), but the textual tradition overwhelmingly supports "where" (ποῦ).

29. So Bruce, *Galatians*, 207, 210; Lightfoot, *Galatians*,
175–76; Longenecker, *Galatians*, 192; Martyn, *Galatians*,
421; Matera, *Galatians*, 160, 164.

30. Ridderbos, *Galatians*, 167; Betz, *Galatians*, 227. Hays
says Paul "is asking what happened to the word of blessing
they once pronounced on him" (*Galatians*, 294).

31. So Dunn, *Galatians*, 235.

32. So B. Longenecker, "Until Christ Is Formed in You,"
97, 103; cf. also Wilson, *Curse of the Law*, 86; Hafemann, "Role
of Suffering," 182, n. 36..

Spirit was so great that they were happy to suffer themselves if only they could assist Paul in some way. Such love for Paul confirms that they had truly received the Spirit.

4:16 So then, have I become your enemy because I speak the truth to you? (ὥστε ἐχθρὸς ὑμῶν γέγονα ἀληθεύων ὑμῖν;). The change in Paul's relationship with the Galatians is nothing short of astonishing. Only their turning from the gospel can account for their defection from him.[33] Therefore, opposition to Paul is equated with rejection of the gospel (the truth Paul spoke to them), just as their warm reception of Paul indicated their acceptance of the saving message. It must be recognized, of course, that Paul asks a rhetorical question here. He does not accuse the Galatians of being enemies but asks whether the situation has reached the stage where he has now become an opponent instead of a friend; he hopes that his strong words will bring them to their senses, so that they will align themselves again with Paul.

4:17 They are not zealous for you in a good way, but they wish to shut you out, in order that you might be zealous for them (ζηλοῦσιν ὑμᾶς οὐ καλῶς, ἀλλὰ ἐκκλεῖσαι ὑμᾶς θέλουσιν, ἵνα αὐτοὺς ζηλοῦτε). The zeal of the Judaizers is acknowledged, but zeal is not pleasing to God if unaccompanied by knowledge (Rom 10:2 – 4). Therefore, there is a kind of missionary zeal with which God is not pleased. The Judaizers had a desire to remove the Galatian believers from the church.[34] These teachers surely claimed that they desired to *include* the Galatians in the true people of God, but in fact, they were *excluding* them from God's people if the Galatians followed them.[35]

Three times in this letter Paul refers to the desires (θέλουσιν) of the false teachers. They longed to make a good showing in the flesh (6:12) and to have the Galatians circumcised so they could boast in them (6:13). Here they desire to turn the Galatians away from Paul so that the Galatians will show zeal for them as teachers. The Judaizers, in contrast to Paul, had an ardent desire to be praised and honored. Their motives are corrupted by a longing for adulation. The Galatians are faced with a choice: either they follow the Judaizers or Paul; either they show zeal for the true gospel or the false gospel that requires circumcision.

4:18 Now to be zealous for the good is always good, and not only when I am present with you (καλὸν δὲ ζηλοῦσθαι ἐν καλῷ πάντοτε καὶ μὴ μόνον ἐν τῷ παρεῖναί με πρὸς ὑμᾶς). Zeal, of course, is a commendable quality, as long as it is directed to the right object. If one is zealous for what is good, one's life will be pleasing to God. In other words, Paul was not jealous for his own reputation. If others had arrived in Galatia, preached the gospel, and strengthened the Galatians in the faith, he would have rejoiced.[36]

4:19 My children, for whom I am suffering birth pangs again until Christ is formed in you! (τέκνα μου, οὓς πάλιν ὠδίνω μέχρις οὗ μορφωθῇ Χριστὸς ἐν ὑμῖν). The striking image in this verse

---

33. So Bruce, *Galatians*, 211; Matera, *Galatians*, 161. Against Betz, who does not think the truth of the gospel is designated in the term "speaking the truth" (ἀληθεύων) (*Galatians*, 229).

34. Betz thinks instead Paul merely speaks of friendship, and hence the text should not be read in such a theological way (*Galatians*, 231). In favor of the reading here, see Schlier, *Galater*, 212 – 13; Smiles, *Gospel and Law in Galatia*, 66 – 67.

35. C. C. Smith sees a reference to the "excluded lover"

here. "ἐκκλεῖσαι in Galatians 4:17: The Motif of the Excluded Lover as a Metaphor of Manipulation," *CBQ* 58 (1996): 480 – 99; cf. also Hays, *Galatians*, 295. But B. Longenecker rightly notes that the verb for such a nuance is "shut off from" (ἀποκλείω) instead of "shut out" (ἐκκλείω) as we have here ("Until Christ Is Formed in You," 97, n. 13).

36. So Martyn, *Galatians*, 423. Thus, the good Paul has in mind is the gospel (so Garlington, *Galatians*, 258).

jolts us awake.[37] Paul, as a man, is in labor, gasping in pain as one about to give birth. We then expect the next part of the verse to speak of the birth of the Galatians, but strikingly Paul shifts the image again. Now he speaks of Christ as the one who is to be born and the Galatians as the mother! The mixing of metaphors is almost certainly intentional and is designed to shake the Galatians out of their spiritual lethargy. Paul's labor pains indicate that the Galatians need to be converted all over again.[38]

As in 4:9 Paul fears that the Galatians are reverting (or better "converting") again to paganism. Paul portrays himself here (cf. 1 Thess 2:7) as their spiritual mother, but as one who needs to endure again birth pangs for a second time. Elsewhere Paul portrays himself as the spiritual father of his converts (1 Cor 4:15; 1 Thess 2:11; Phlm 10). The suffering of birth pangs is often used in the OT in terms of the day of the Lord (Isa 13:6 – 8; Jer 6:24; Mic 4:10; cf. *1 En.* 62:4; *2 Bar.* 56:6; *4 Ezra* 4:42).[39] We find birth pangs in eschatological-apocalyptic texts in the NT as well (Matt 24:8; Mark 13:8; Rom 8:22; 1 Thess 5:3; Rev 12:1 – 2). Hence, Gaventa is correct in detecting an "apocalyptic expectation" in Paul's language.[40] The labor pains that Paul endures as an apostle characterize this present age. When Paul speaks of his labor pains, he has in mind his suffering as an apostle,[41] for his apostolic sufferings are a corollary to the gospel and the means by which the gospel became a reality among the Galatians.

The word "again" (πάλιν) recalls the suffering Paul endured when he first evangelized the Galatians, and now such suffering must apparently be repeated since the Galatians are tempted by a subversive gospel. Those who have received the Spirit face fierce attacks on their faith and must be urgently warned against apostasy. Eastman sums up her careful study of birth pangs by saying that

> it seems wisest to see that the bold metaphor of Gal 4:19 draws on a rich textual tradition that includes Jer 8:21, Isa 42:14, and Isa 45:10. The apostle's cry reminds the Galatians that his labor is also God's labor, and that God is the one who has power to bring from conception to birth, from beginning to completion. Furthermore, this creative power cannot be divorced from the suffering of God and its embodiment in the apostle's missionary preaching.[42]

In this instance, the reality of their birth will be evident when Christ takes shape in them, when they reach a stage where it is evident that they will not turn away from Christ.[43] Gaventa relates this to their crucifixion with Christ (2:20), which is a fitting parallel, for those who have died with Christ have also been raised with him and enjoy eschatological life.[44] Paul speaks of the formation of Christ rather than the birth of the Galatians to call attention to the supernatural work of God.[45] Paul is not only speaking of the Galatians

---

37. See Beverly R. Gaventa, "The Maternity of Paul," in *The Conversation Continues: Studies in Paul & John in Honor of J. Louis Martyn* (ed. Robert T. Fortna and Beverly R. Gaventa; Nashville: Abingdon, 1990), 189.

38. Wilson remarks that they need "rebirth" (*Curse of the Law*, 87). The language used here should not be unduly pressed to say that the Galatians are now damned in Paul's eyes and literally need to be reconverted.

39. I owe these references to Gaventa, "The Maternity of Paul," 193.

40. Ibid., 191 – 94.

41. See Eastman, *Paul's Mother Tongue*, 97 – 126. Even though I think Eastman incorrectly identifies Paul's "weak-

ness of the flesh" as his suffering persecution (see comments on 4:13 – 14), she rightly sees that Paul's suffering becomes the pathway for the gospel.

42. Ibid., 123. For Eastman's discussion of suffering birth pangs, see 111 – 23.

43. Cf. the discussion in Martyn, *Galatians*, 426 – 31.

44. See Gaventa, "The Maternity of Paul," 195 – 96. She rightly rejects the idea that Paul speaks here of the Galatians' moral formation or a right doctrine about Christ.

45. Ibid., 197. Note that the subject of the passive "is formed" (μορφωθῇ) is "Christ." See Eastman, *Paul's Mother Tongue*, 94 – 95.

individually, for the phrase "in you" (ἐν ὑμῖν) also refers to the growth of the Galatians as a church.[46]

These two ideas — i.e., a reference to both individual and corporate growth — are not mutually exclusive.[47] Paul's anxiety over the Galatians is evocative of 2 Cor 11:28 – 29: "Besides everything else, I face daily the daily pressure of my concern for all the churches. Who is weak, and I do not feel weak? Who is led into sin, and I do not inwardly burn?" The weakness of the Galatians affects Paul so that he is worried and angry (cf. Gal 5:12) about their future. He longs for the day when anxiety is a thing of the past and the Galatians have reached maturity.

4:20 And I wish I were present with you now so that I could change my voice, for I am at a loss over you (ἤθελον δὲ παρεῖναι πρὸς ὑμᾶς ἄρτι καὶ ἀλλάξαι τὴν φωνήν μου, ὅτι ἀποροῦμαι ἐν ὑμῖν). The letter to the Galatians cannot replace a face-to-face encounter in which Paul can engage the Galatians in conversation.[48] If he were present with them, he could respond in the dynamics of everyday life to each issue they raise. Since he is absent from them, however, he must resort to writing, not knowing how they will react. Perhaps the change of voice is reflected in the next section, where he wages a different kind of argument, an allegorical one, to try to persuade the readers.[49] In any case, Paul was deeply puzzled over the Galatians' attraction to Judaism and the OT law. He was not completely sure what to say, and yet his feelings of perplexity did not paralyze him. He continues to prosecute his case in subsequent verses.

Theology in Application

Brothers and Sisters Who Love One Another

Paul's argument from friendship reminds us that believers are bound together as brothers and sisters who love one another. Christians not only acknowledge a common confession; they are also part of a new family bound together by cords of love. Therefore, Paul reminds the Galatians of the love they expressed to him, recalling them to their former affection. One of the great attractions of the church is the love and service shown for one another. As fellow believers we are one body. Hence, our love is not limited to those who share our same education, race, or social class. We are to show concern and care for all, so that unbelievers will know we are Christians by our love (John 13:34 – 35).

As Christians we are hesitant to say, "Be like me." Naturally all of us think of our many faults. I don't want someone to imitate me in everything! But isn't it also true that if Christ has changed us, that we can and should call upon people to imitate us? If we are following Christ, it is right and proper to call on others to follow Christ as we are (cf. Eph 4:32 – 5:2). Indeed, God typically uses others to draw us after Christ, so that we love him more. Most of us were converted through the life and words of a Christian we admired. Or, we have grown spiritually through a believer who has invested in our lives. Are you living in a way that you are a godly influence on others?

---

46. So Gaventa, "The Maternity of Paul," 196.
47. Rightly Betz, *Galatians*, 234 – 35; Bruce, *Galatians*, 212.
48. Cf. Betz, *Galatians*, 236.
49. Cf. ibid., 236 – 37, 240.

Progress through Suffering

The progress of the gospel is accompanied by the suffering of its messengers. Such has been the story throughout church history, and God intended that it be so. When the world sees that Christians are willing to suffer and die for their faith, it understands that something incredibly precious (i.e., someone wonderfully delightful) is at stake. Tertullian rightly said that the blood of the martyrs is the seed of the church, that the church advances as it proclaims a crucified Lord and lives a crucified life. The beauty of Christ is reflected in the humble and glad suffering of its messengers. No one delights in suffering inherently, but if suffering begets complaining and grumbling, the distinctiveness of the Christian faith is lost. It is the gladness and courage of the messengers, despite the pain in their bodies, that heralds the goodness of the gospel to the world.

Exercising Patience and Love

This section also instructs us that ministers and fellow Christians must be patient with one another. The Christian life is not necessarily marked by straight-line growth. Believers can be waylaid and set off course by any number of things. Love responds to people where they are, not where we might hope them to be. Love is anchored in the real world, tackling the problems people face, and it does not give up on others when they are not where we expect or hope them to be. At the same time, love longs for the perfecting of the one loved. When we love others, we call them to love Christ with all their hearts and souls. We accept them where they are, while also calling them to scale new heights. Therefore, love cannot be confused with sentimentality, for there is also a stringency in it, summoning others to continued growth in Christ.

We see here that lack of spiritual growth in others can bring us great anguish and pain. We can be perplexed and confused about how to help them along. Like Paul, we don't know what to say next. We wonder, what is the best approach? What will be effective? Those of us ministering don't always have all the answers. But like Paul, we keep praying. We keep trying. We keep hoping. We don't become angry and upset. We pray to have the same affection as Paul and we exhort them as "little children." We exhort those who are struggling because we love them, and we realize that there is a struggle in the Christian life.

Such affection and love does not mean that there is not church discipline. We discipline those who refuse to follow the Lord and turn their backs on him. But we give people time to repent and to turn to the Lord. We exhort them so that Christ will be formed in them.

Do you have that kind of ministry to others? Are there any whom you are discipling or praying for and anguishing over? Let us rest in the gospel. Let us look to Christ to change them. Let us look to the broken body and the shed blood as their hope and ours.

CHAPTER 17

Galatians 4:21 – 5:1

Literary Context

After Paul's substantative theological argument against the Judaizers in 3:1 – 4:11, the tone of the letter changes with the argument from friendship in 4:12 – 20. There the first imperative in the letter appeared (apart from 3:7), in which Paul summoned the Galatians to become as he is, i.e., to live free from the Jewish law. Thus, we are prepared for exhortations to close out the rest of the letter, and exhortations do appear in 4:30 and 5:1.

Still, 4:21 – 5:1 in some ways returns to the previous part of the letter in that Paul argues against returning to the Mosaic law. It is not always possible to distinguish sharply one section of the letter from another. Betz, therefore, identifies this section as part of Paul's *probatio* (proofs that defend the main thesis) before the exhortation section of the letter begins.[1] Nevertheless, as Longenecker notes, imperatives are found in this section, signifying that the exhortation that began in 4:12 continues.[2] Paul continues to urge his readers to live in freedom from the OT law. Hence, the text climaxes with an exhortation to freedom in 5:1.

The tone of the letter changes here, for Paul uses an allegory to make his case. Perhaps the allegorical nature of the argument represents the change of voice spoken of in 4:20. Scholars debate whether we have a strict allegory here.[3] Some contend that the passage should be identified as an allegory in the Philonic sense, where one thing stands for another, and the biblical text is sundered from the historical context in which it was birthed. Others maintain that the text should be classified as typology, even though Paul uses the word "allegory." They argue that Paul's exegesis of the text, though creative, is rooted in the OT, and fits with a salvation-historical reading.[4]

---

1. Betz, *Galatians*, 238 – 40.

2. Longenecker, *Galatians*, 199. Supporting the idea that 4:21 – 31 belongs with the request section is Hansen, *Abraham in Galatians*, 141 – 54. But Hansen's contention that the Galatians are commanded to remove the false teachers from the church is not persuasive (see comments under 4:30 and 5:9).

3. For a helpful discussion of the term along with cautions

about reading a later meaning into it, see Andrew T. Lincoln, *Paradise Now and Not Yet: Studies in the Role of the Heavenly Dimension in Paul's Thought with Special Reference to His Eschatology* (SNTSMS 43; Cambridge: Cambridge Univ. Press, 1981), 13.

4. Cf. Charles H. Cosgrove, "The Law Has Given Sarah No Children (Gal 4:21 – 30)," *NovT* 29 (1987): 221, n. 12; Ellis, *Paul's Use of the Old Testament*, 130.

Perhaps it is justified to identify the text as typological allegory.[5] On the one hand, the first and last part of the text are typological (4:21 – 23 and 4:28 – 30), for Isaac as the son of promise was born in accord with the power of God, whereas the birth of Ishmael represented a human attempt to fulfill the promise. On the other hand, it is difficult to see how Hagar in any historical sense anticipates the covenant at Sinai, and hence Paul exploits the Hagar narrative allegorically. A table helps us to see the contrasts in the text.[6]

Abraham's son of the slave woman (Ishmael)	Abraham's son of the free woman (Isaac) (4:22)
Born of the flesh	Born of the promise (4:23)
Mount Sinai = Hagar = slavery (4:24)	
Present Jerusalem = slavery (4:25)	Jerusalem above = free = our mother (4:26)
Children of the barren and desolate one (4:27)	Children of the one with the husband
	You = children of promise = Isaac (4:28)
Born of flesh ... persecutor	Born of Spirit (4:29) ... persecuted
Cast out son of slave	Son of free woman will inherit (4:30)
We are not children of slave woman	But children of free woman (4:31)

On the one hand, a connection is drawn between Ishmael, the flesh, Hagar, Mount Sinai, the Jerusalem of Paul's day, and slavery to sin.[7] On the other hand, the polar side of this is Isaac, God's promise, the Jerusalem above, the work of the Spirit, freedom, and the inheritance. If the argument is not strictly typological, neither is it arbitrary. It is apparent in reading Genesis that Abraham and Sarah resorted to human wisdom and strength in having a son through Hagar (Gen 16). Hence, the second part of this passage (4:24 – 27) is rightly identified as allegory, and then Paul draws the application in 4:28 – 5:1.

Perhaps Paul resorts to this argument here to try to startle his readers into seeing in a fresh way the folly of reverting to the law. Reliance on the law represents leaning on the flesh and hence results in slavery and expulsion from the inheritance. Paul reminds his readers that those who trust in God's promise (rather than in the law) have great hope because they rely on the work of the Holy Spirit. Those who have received the Holy Spirit are free from slavery and will receive the inheritance.

5. Betz says we have here "a mixture of what we would call allegory and typology" (*Galatians*, 239). Verses 22, 23, 28 – 30 fit with typology, whereas 4:24 – 27 are allegorical. See also the helpful discussion in Lincoln, *Paradise*, 13 – 14; Hansen, *Abraham in Galatians*, 210 – 11.

6. Longenecker detects a chiasm here (*Galatians*, 213), but the order of the text does not precisely fit his arrangement.

7. Cf. George's two columns, though he adds items that are not expressly stated in the text (*Galatians*, 342).

Main Idea

Paul drives to the conclusion of the argument in 4:31 and 5:1. Believers are children of the free woman, not the slave woman. And since they are now free in Christ, they must not return again to the slavery of living under the law (5:1).

Translation

(See next page.)

Structure

Scholars dispute the structure of the text. For example:

- Davis divides the text into three sections:[8] (1) introduction (4:21 – 23); (2) the focus of the argument (4:24 – 27); and (3) the conclusion (4:28 – 5:1).[9]
- Fung sees four sections: (1) the facts (4:21 – 23); (2) the spiritual meaning (4:24 – 27); (3) the application to the Galatians (4:28 – 30); and (4) the summary and appeal (4:31 – 5:1).[10]
- George identifies three sections: (1) historical background (4:21 – 23); (2) figurative meaning (4:24 – 27); and (3) the personal application (4:28 – 31).[11]
- Cosgrove maintains the text ends with 4:30 and sees three sections: (1) introduction (4:21); (2) the allegory (4:22 – 27); and (3) the warning (4:28 – 30).[12]

Most agree that the text is divided into at least three sections that begin with 4:21, 4:24, and 4:28. The issue is where the last section concludes. It seems to me that Davis's analysis is the most promising. The argument concludes with the exhortation to stand in freedom in 5:1. Galatians 5:1 functions as a transitional verse. It concludes this section and leads into the next section. The call to stand in freedom and resist the bondage of the law (5:1) functions as the conclusion to 4:21 – 31, since the allegory is designed to lead to a response from the Galatians.

The text begins with a rhetorical question, introduced with the words "tell me" (λέγετέ μοι). Paul queries whether the Galatians' desire to live under the law actually accords with what the law says (4:21). Beginning in 4:22 he unpacks ("for," γάρ) what the law (i.e., the Scriptures) says about living under the law. The text is

---

8. My structure of the section and the claim that 4:24 – 27 should be identified as allegorical fit with Davis's analysis of the text. My only substantive disagreement relates to 4:21 – 23 and 4:28 – 30, which are identified as typology here, whereas Davis rejects the idea that these verses are typological. See Anne Davis, "Allegorically Speaking in Galatians 4:21 – 5:1," *BBR* 14 (2004): 161 – 74. On the matter of allegory, see also

Steven Di Mattei, "Paul's Allegory of the Two Covenants (Gal 4.21 – 31) in Light of the First-Century Hellenistic Rhetoric and Jewish Hermeneutics," *NTS* 52 (2006): 102 – 22.

9. Contra Cosgrove, "Gal 4:21 – 30," 223, 226, 232.

10. Fung, *Galatians*, 204 – 17.

11. George, *Galatians*, 334 – 48.

12. Cosgrove, "Gal 4:21 – 30," 219 – 35.

marked by polarities and opposites. The two sons of Abraham (Isaac and Ishmael), born from the free woman (Sarah) and the slave woman (Hagar) respectively, are contrasted (4:22). The latter's son was born according to the flesh and the former's son by the Spirit (4:23).

Paul explains the birth of these two sons allegorically, seeing in them two different covenants (4:24). Hagar represents the covenant enacted at Mount Sinai, which is still operative in the Jerusalem of Paul's day since Jerusalem remains in bondage to sin (4:24–25). The second covenant remains unnamed. Paul proceeds to speak of the heavenly Jerusalem, which is identified as the mother of believers and enjoys freedom (4:26). Willits argues that 4:27 grounds all of 4:24–26,[13] but it seems more likely that the "for" (γάρ) grounds 4:26. Israel in exile (Isa 54:1) is compared to a barren woman who does not have children, and yet as a miracle of God's grace her children will multiply far beyond what is expected (4:27). The law did not produce genuine children of Abraham; such children are the fruit of the work of the Holy Spirit.

Paul approaches the conclusion of his argument by using the words "and you" (ὑμεῖς δέ, 4:28) to apply the allegory to his readers; he sees this prophecy fulfilled in Gentile believers, who are children of promise like Isaac (4:28).[14] Just as Ishmael persecuted Isaac long ago, so the Judaizers were persecuting those born of the Spirit in Galatia (4:29). Paul then reminds the Galatians what Scripture teaches in quoting Gen 21:10 in Gal 4:30.[15] He is not asking the Galatians to expel the Judaizers from Galatia. Instead, he wants them to listen to what the law says. The Scripture says that only the son of the free woman will inherit the promise. Therefore, if the Galatians listened to the law, they will not pay heed to Judaizers.

Paul draws an inference in 4:31, marked by "therefore" (διό).[16] What we have here is the conclusion to the argument thus far, though it restates what Paul said in 4:28.[17] The Galatians are children of the free woman, Sarah, not the slave woman, Hagar. Galatians 5:1 is transitional but also draws out the main point from 4:21–31. No conjunction is used between 4:31 and 5:1, suggesting perhaps the close relationship between the two verses. The Galatians have been set free in Christ (5:1).[18] Therefore, they must continue in that freedom and not fall into the bondage of accepting circumcision for salvation (5:1).

---

13. So Joel Willitts, "Isa 54,1 and Gal 4,24b–27: Reading Genesis in Light of Isaiah," *ZNW* 96 (2005): 201. Even less likely is Harmon's view that it grounds 4:22–26, for Harmon fails to see that 4:24 introduces a new section ("She Must and Shall Go Free," 234).

14. Longenecker says that "Paul now spells out the consequences of his argument as set out in vv 22–27" (*Galatians*, 216).

15. Willitts argues that 4:30–5:1 is the main point of the text. "Isa 54,1 and Gal 4,24b–27," 198.

16. Against Cosgrove, the "therefore" (διό) makes most sense as a conclusion, not as an exhortation ("Gal 4:21–30," 232).

17. Cf. also Longenecker, who remarks that 4:31 is "somewhat redundant" to what we find in 4:28 (*Galatians*, 218). Longenecker goes on to identify 4:31 as the conclusion of all of 4:21–30.

18. Scholars debate whether 5:1 belongs to this section. Supporting its inclusion here are Willitts, "Isa 54,1 and Gal 4,24b–27," 188, n. 1; Martinus C. de Boer, "Paul's Quotation of Isaiah 54.1 in Galatians 4.27," *NTS* 50 (2004): 371–72, n. 5.

Galatians 4:21-5:1

21	rhetorical question	Tell me, those who want to be under the law, do you not listen to the law?
22a	basis *(of 21)*	For it is written that Abraham had two sons:
b	description *(of 22a)*	one from the slave woman and
c	series	one from the free woman.
23a	explanation *(of 22a-c)*	Now the son from the slave woman was born according to the flesh,
b	contrast *(to 23a)*	but the son from the free woman was born by means of a promise.
24a	explanation *(of 22-23)*	Now these things are an allegory:
b	explanation *(of 24a)*	that is, **these women represent** **two covenants:**
c	explanation *(of 24b)*	the one from Mount Sinai who bears children for slavery is Hagar.
25a	series *(from 24c)*	Hagar represents Mount Sinai in Arabia, and
b	series	she corresponds to the present Jerusalem,
c	basis *(of 25b)*	for she is in slavery with her children.
26a	contrast *(to 24c-25c)*	But
		the Jerusalem above is free, and
b	progression	she is our mother.

27a	basis *(of 24-26)/* exclamation	For **it is written,** *"Rejoice, O barren one who does not give birth.*
b	series	*Break forth and shout, O one without birth pangs,*
c	basis *(of 27a-b)*	*because the children of the desolate are more than* *the children of the one who has a husband."* (Isa 54:1)
28	progression *(from 26-27)*	And **you, brothers, are children of promise according to Isaac.**
29	comparison	And **just as formerly the one being born according to the flesh persecuted the one being born according to the Spirit, thus also now.**
30a	contrast *(to 29)*	But **what does the Scripture say?**
b	exhortation	*"Cast out the slave woman and her son,*
c	basis *(of 30a)*	*for the son of the slave woman will not inherit with the son of the free woman."* (Gen 21:10)
31a	inference *(from 21-30)*	Therefore, **brothers, we are not children of the slave woman,**
b	contrast *(to 31a)*	but **we are children of the free woman.**
1a	series *(to 31a)*	**Christ set us free for freedom.**
b	inference *(to 1a)*	Therefore, **stand fast,**
c	series	and **do not be subject again to a yoke of slavery.**

Exegetical Outline

Explanation of the Text

4:21 Tell me, those who want to be under the law, do you not listen to the law? (Λέγετέ μοι, οἱ ὑπὸ νόμον θέλοντες εἶναι, τὸν νόμον οὐκ ἀκούετε;). The verse is rich with irony. The Galatians want to live under the Mosaic law, but if they actually understood the law (i.e., the Scripture), they would realize that their desire to place themselves under the Sinai covenant is off-kilter. In 4:20 Paul expressed perplexity and said he wished he could adapt what he says to speak to the readers. Perhaps the allegory in this text represents that adaptation, a new form of the argument that will capture the Galatians' minds and hearts.

It is instructive that the Galatians are described as wanting "to be under the law," which is most naturally seen as an address to the Galatian congregation.[19] Apparently they did not think that circumcision alone would suffice. They fully intended to keep the whole law, which was signified by their adherence to the OT calendar (4:10).[20] The use of "under law" (ὑπὸ νόμον) signals Paul's estimation of their desire, for those who place themselves under the law are also subjecting themselves to the power of sin and are living in the old era of redemptive history. Therefore, the Galatians should listen to what the "law," i.e., the Scripture says.[21] For if they did so, they would understand that living under the law constitutes a fatal mistake.

In any event, in the subsequent verses Paul attempts to explain that living under the law is not in accordance with what Scripture itself teaches. Barrett argues that Paul appeals to Hagar and Sarah here because the false teachers appealed to Sarah to say they were the true sons of Isaac. The Judaizers would have linked Hagar with the

---

19. Dunn, *Galatians*, 245; Longenecker, *Galatians*, 206.

20. Therefore, this verse suggests that they had not yet fully placed themselves under the OT law. So Longenecker,

Galatians, 206 – 7.

21. Paul distinguishes here between the Torah and Scripture. So Betz, *Galatians*, 241.

Gentiles, who were uncircumcised.[22] Barrett says the plain meaning of the text supports the Judaizers, not Paul.[23] But his conclusion is faulty, for Paul's argument in this section is that the OT law must be read in light of the story line of Scripture as a whole. If Scripture is read carefully, it becomes clear that those who were under the Mosaic law lived in bondage to sin, and freedom has only come about with the proclamation of the gospel.[24]

4:22 For it is written that Abraham had two sons: one from the slave woman and one from the free woman (γέγραπται γὰρ ὅτι Ἀβραὰμ δύο υἱοὺς ἔσχεν, ἕνα ἐκ τῆς παιδίσκης καὶ ἕνα ἐκ τῆς ἐλευθέρας). It is immediately evident that the second use of "law" (τὸν νόμον) in 4:21 refers to Scripture, since Paul appeals to the OT. He does not cite specific verses but appeals to the scriptural tradition as found in Genesis.

Abraham has already played a significant role in the letter, and now Paul appeals to Abraham's role as the father of two different sons by two different wives. The sons and the wives are not named here, but they are Ishmael and Isaac, and Hagar and Sarah respectively. In fact, Paul never identifies Ishmael and Sarah by name here, only Isaac and Hagar. He does not focus on the names of the women here but their social status.[25] Hagar was a slave and Sarah was free, and Paul spies spiritual significance in their status.

4:23 Now the son from the slave woman was born according to the flesh, but the son from the free woman was born by means of a promise (ἀλλ' ὁ μὲν ἐκ τῆς παιδίσκης κατὰ σάρκα γεγέννηται, ὁ δὲ ἐκ τῆς ἐλευθέρας δι' ἐπαγγελίας). The words "slave" and "free" continue to be important, for Paul does not name the mothers but designates them again as slave and free. What comes to the forefront is the birth of the two sons. The son of the slave woman Hagar (i.e., Ishmael) was born in accord with natural processes, whereas the son of Sarah (i.e., Isaac) was born in accord with God's promise.

Ishmael's birth "according to the flesh" (κατὰ σάρκα) is interpreted by some as a neutral comment, as if Paul were simply thinking of the birth of Ishmael in biological terms.[26] The contrast, however, between the flesh and the promise and the flesh and the Spirit in 4:29 suggests that Paul intends the deeper theological meaning of the word "flesh," so that "flesh" refers to what human beings are in Adam. Such a reading fits the Genesis narrative as well. Abraham and Sarah's attempt to have a child via Hagar signaled a lack of faith on their part — a human attempt to fulfill the promise (Gen 16).

The birth of Isaac, by contrast, could not be attributed to human effort or agency in any sense of the word. The promise that Sarah and Abraham would themselves have a son was so stunning that they both laughed in disbelief upon hearing it (Gen 17:17; 18:12 – 15). Moreover, Abraham tried to convince the Lord that Isaac was unneeded, that it was sufficient for him if the promise were fulfilled through Ishmael (Gen 17:15 – 21). The Lord rejected Abraham's request and declared that the

---

22. Barrett, "The Allegory of Abraham," 6, 9 – 10. Cf. also Bruce, *Galatians*, 218. Others maintain that since Ishmael was circumcised, the teachers may not have appealed to this text. So Cosgrove, "Gal 4:21 – 30," 221, 223; Andrew C. Perriman, "The Rhetorical Strategy of Galatians 4:21 – 5:1," *EvQ* 65 (1993): 33.

23. Barrett, "The Allegory of Abraham," 10. The opponents probably said that the Abrahamic covenant was rede-

fined by the Mosaic covenant (15).

24. Paul is generalizing here and does not include the remnant in the OT who trusted in the Lord and obeyed him.

25. Eastman says that Sarah remains unnamed to emphasize that the multitude of children are due to God's promise, not natural ability (*Paul's Mother Tongue*, 144 – 46).

26. So Bruce, *Galatians*, 217.

covenant would be through Isaac, not Ishmael, even though Ishmael would receive other blessings as Abraham's son.

Paul's illustration is astonishing, for surely the Judaizers saw themselves as descendants of Isaac! Paul, however, identifies them as the descendants of Ishmael and sees the Galatian converts as sons of Isaac. Those who rely on the law and human effort to be right with God are not the children of the covenant, whereas those who rely on the free promise given in Christ Jesus are the true covenant children.

4:24a Now these things are an allegory (ἅτινά ἐστιν ἀλληγορούμενα). The verb "to speak allegorically" (ἀλληγορέω) occurs only here in the NT and the LXX, though both Josephus and Philo used the term, and the practice of allegorizing texts was common in Greek literature, especially in the application of Homer's writings. Some scholars maintain that Paul uses allegory here rather than typology.[27] Allegory may be defined as assigning a meaning to the biblical text that does not fit with its historical context.[28] For instance, seeing a connection between Hagar and the Sinai covenant is scarcely obvious when one reads the OT narrative. Further, it could be claimed that at Sinai Israel was liberated from Egypt, and yet Paul links it with slavery. Others argue that the OT text is used typologically, even though Paul uses the word "allegory."[29] In other words, Paul's use of the OT does not represent the kind of arbitrary allegory that we find in Philo or that we find later in Origen or Clement of Alexandria.

Probably the best solution is to see a combination of typology and allegory. Paul argues typologically with reference to Isaac and Ishmael,

especially in 4:21 – 23 and 4:28 – 30. Hence, his reading of the text fits with his salvation-historical understanding of the Scriptures as a whole. There are clearly, however, allegorical elements in the argument, particularly in 4:24 – 27. The fundamental reason for seeing the text as having an allegorical component is the identification of Hagar with the Sinai covenant. Such a move does not comport with typology, where there is historical connection between the type and its fulfillment. It is difficult to see how Hagar functions as a historical type of the Sinai covenant. Paul introduces the connection, then, to startle the readers, so that they will see the truth of his gospel from a different angle.

4:24b-c That is, these women represent two covenants: the one from Mount Sinai who bears children for slavery is Hagar (αὗται γάρ εἰσιν δύο διαθῆκαι, μία μὲν ἀπὸ ὄρους Σινᾶ εἰς δουλείαν γεννῶσα, ἥτις ἐστὶν Ἁγάρ). The verb "are" (εἰσιν) here should be translated "represent," for Hagar and Sarah "are" not literally two covenants. In the allegory they represent two covenants, which are radically different from one another. It seems clear that Paul writes allegorically at this point rather than typologically, for it is difficult to see how Hagar historically anticipates the Sinai covenant. Still, the correspondence Paul sees between Hagar and the Sinai covenant is not arbitrary, for the destiny of the Ishmaelites corresponds to the destiny of those who lived under the law, in that both ended up being slaves to sin. Paul stimulates the reader to see in a fresh way the liability of the Sinai covenant.

Strictly speaking, the second covenant remains unnamed, but given the discussion in 3:15 – 18, it

---

27. Witherington, *Galatians*, 321 – 27; Davis, "Allegorically Speaking," 161 – 74.

28. Paul is not claiming, therefore, that the story was intended allegorically by the author of Genesis. Rather, he

interprets the account allegorically, and he probably does so in response to the opponents. So Barrett, "The Allegory of Abraham," 6, 10; Longenecker, *Galatians*, 209 – 10.

29. Lightfoot, *Galatians*, 180; Bruce, *Galatians*, 217.

is possible that the covenant with Abraham is in view.[30] Other scholars argue that the reference here is to the new covenant in contrast with the old.[31] Probably the new covenant is in view here, but the new covenant fulfills the covenant made with Abraham, so we should not exaggerate the difference between these two options. The citation of Isa 54:1 in Gal 4:27 signals the eschatological fulfillment of the covenant enacted with Abraham.[32]

The term "one" (μία) could refer to Hagar or the Sinai covenant, and it seems that the focus is on the covenant at Sinai established with Moses and Israel.[33] Even though Israel's redemption and freedom from Egypt were celebrated at Sinai (Exod 19:3 – 4; 20:2), Paul associates slavery with Sinai. The reader of Exodus may be astonished at such an interpretive move, given the emphasis on God's redemption in Exodus. Still, the reader of Galatians is scarcely surprised since Paul has argued throughout Galatians that the law does not free from sin but enslaves. The law as part of the old age does not liberate the people of God from sin.

Nor is Paul's reading of the OT arbitrary. The exodus events celebrate Israel's liberation from Egypt, but even in the Pentateuch Israel's failure to keep the Torah becomes a prominent theme, and Moses prophesies that Israel will definitively break the covenant. And that story line does not change as we progress through the OT narrative. Both Israel and Judah land in exile because of their failure to keep the Mosaic covenant.

Solid grounds exist, then, for the claim that the law kills instead of making alive (2 Cor 3:6). What is startling is the connection drawn between Hagar and Sinai. The link, of course, is slavery. Just as Hagar was Sarah's slave and Ishmael did not receive God's covenantal promises, so too Israel's life under the law was marked by slavery to sin.

4:25 Hagar represents Mount Sinai in Arabia, and she corresponds to the present Jerusalem, for she is in slavery with her children (τὸ δὲ Ἁγὰρ Σινᾶ ὄρος ἐστὶν ἐν τῇ Ἀραβίᾳ, συστοιχεῖ δὲ τῇ νῦν Ἰερουσαλήμ, δουλεύει γὰρ μετὰ τῶν τέκνων αὐτῆς). Paul sees a correspondence between Hagar and Mount Sinai, and then draws a connection between Hagar and the Jerusalem of his day, since he sees the Jews of his day as enslaved under the law.

Before we can comment in more detail on the meaning of the verse, the text must be established. In some manuscripts "Hagar" is omitted, and so the sentence reads, "And Mount Sinai is a mountain in Arabia." It is likely, however, that "Hagar" is original, and scribes omitted it because of the oddness of the assertion.[34] Moreover, to say that Mount Sinai is a mountain in Arabia is quite prosaic.[35] Further, to add a reference to Hagar is the harder reading.[36]

If we accept the inclusion of Hagar, the use of the article "the" (τό) is puzzling, since Hagar is feminine. Perhaps the article modifies "mount" (ὄρος), though the article is rather distant from the noun in this case, and hence this seems unlikely. Betz argues that the article designates

30. Ridderbos, *Galatians*, 175 – 76; Bruce, *Galatians*, 218; Dunn, *Galatians*, 249; Witherington, *Galatians*, 331 – 32; Hays, *Echoes of Scripture*, 114 – 15. Martyn contends that the term "covenant" is used for the sake of the argument and that no historical covenants are in view precisely (*Galatians*, 453 – 56).

31. Betz, *Galatians*, 243; Lincoln, *Paradise*, 16; Longenecker, *Galatians*, 211; Willitts, "Isa 54,1 and Gal 4,24b – 27," 199.

32. Willitts, "Isa 54,1 and Gal 4,24b – 27," 199 – 200, n. 30.

33. So Perriman, "Galatians 4:21 – 5:1," 35; Willitts, "Isa 54,1 and Gal 4,24b – 27," 198.

34. Some witnesses support this reading with "for" (γάρ) (𝔐, sy, bo^mss), but most support it with "now" (δέ) (A, B, D, 323, 365, 1175, 2464, *pc*). A decision between "for" (γάρ) and "now" (δέ) is difficult since the external evidence is rather evenly divided. The internal evidence, however, favors the inclusion of "now" (δέ). As Metzger notes, the inclusion of "for" (γάρ) could account for the accidental omission of "Hagar" (Ἁγάρ) in some witnesses (*Textual Commentary*, 527).

35. So Longenecker, *Galatians*, 198, 211; Martyn, *Galatians*, 437 – 38.

36. So Betz, *Galatians*, 245.

Hagar; Paul is focusing on her name and identifies it with Mount Sinai.[37] In other words, Paul forges a connection between the name "Hagar" and the Arabic word for "rock" (ḥadjar). Betz notes that the word "rock" in Arabic is "used in references to mountains in the Mount Sinai area."[38]

One of the problems with this view is that the name "Hagar" in Hebrew "is similar (but not identical) to a Semitic word meaning 'rock' or 'crag' in Arabic."[39] Most who favor the solution think that such a detail would not deter Paul as he pursues an allegory. The solution, however, seems forced, and it is hard to see how the Galatians would have seen a connection based on the Arabic language. The best possibility is that the article refers to the sentence as a whole.[40] It calls attention to Hagar,[41] and the verb "is" (ἐστίν) should be translated as "represents."[42] On this reading Paul is not saying that Hagar is literally Mount Sinai in Arabia. Instead, he writes allegorically, drawing a correspondence between Hagar and Mount Sinai.

This solution should be favored because it is much simpler than the option proposed above, and it fits with how allegory works. The verb "corresponds" (συστοιχεῖ)[43] also indicates that Paul is drawing parallels between Sinai and past and present circumstances.[44] What is new here is the

reference to Arabia in relationship to Hagar. Perhaps Paul is suggesting that the Judaizers are still in the wilderness. They have never entered into the promised inheritance, but they still live in slavery as Hagar and Ishmael did.

Supporting the above interpretation is the link drawn between Hagar, Sinai, and the present Jerusalem. Older scholarship tended to understand the present Jerusalem as a reference to non-Christian Jewish opponents.[45] It is more likely, however, that the Judaizers are in view.[46] Such an identification fits with Paul's major concern throughout the letter. Still, the older view is not without merit, for the problem with the Judaizers was that they had not broken with Judaism sufficiently.[47] The Judaizers desired to impose the OT law on Gentile converts, and clearly such theology accords with the standard Jewish view that Gentiles cannot be proselytes without being circumcised.

Paul continues to emphasize the theme of slavery. The present Jerusalem, along with her children, is enslaved. The standard Jewish view was that the law is the pathway to liberation and freedom, but Paul argues that it ends up enslaving and captivating people, for the law demands obedience and does not grant any power to keep its precepts. It slays but does not grant life.[48]

---

37. Betz, *Galatians*, 244–245, n. 65. Against this, see Perriman, "Galatians 4:21 – 5:1," 37.

38. Betz, *Galatians*, 245.

39. So Bruce, *Galatians*, 219.

40. C. F. D. Moule, *An Idiom Book of New Testament Greek* (2nd ed; Cambridge: Cambridge Univ. Press, 1963), 110.

41. Cf. BDF § 267 (1).

42. For this translation, see Bruce, *Galatians*, 219.

43. Cosgrove rightly says that Hagar is the subject of the verb ("Gal 4:21 – 30," 228 – 29).

44. The emphasis on Sinai and the OT law excludes, contra S. Elliott (*Cutting Too Close for Comfort*, 258 – 86), any allusion here to the Mountain Mother or Mother of the gods familiar to those living in Anatolia.

45. Bruce, *Galatians*, 220; Jewett, "Agitators," 339. But see more recently Lambrecht, "Abraham and His Offspring," 528.

46. Longenecker, *Galatians*, 217; George, *Galatians*, 347. Against Bachmann, *Anti-Judaism in Galatians?* 85 – 100. Martyn identifies Jerusalem here as the church in Jerusalem, arguing that Paul proclaimed a different gospel from the one preached in Jerusalem. On Martyn's reading, Paul also has in mind the false brothers of Gal 2:3 – 5, who were part of the Jerusalem church. See Martyn, *Galatians*, 459 – 66. Martyn's reconstruction depends on his interpretation of 2:1 – 10, which I argue veers off course (see comments on 2:1 – 10).

47. Betz sees both Judaism and the Jewish-Christian teachers as standing under Paul's indictment here (*Galatians*, 246 – 47; see esp. 251, n. 123 where Jewish Christians are identified "as Jews in the religious sense").

48. It is less likely that Paul has in mind Israel's political subjugation under Rome. Contra Hays, *Galatians*, 303 – 4.

4:26 But the Jerusalem above is free, and she is our mother (ἡ δὲ ἄνω Ἰερουσαλὴμ ἐλευθέρα ἐστίν, ἥτις ἐστὶν μήτηρ[49] ἡμῶν). The earthly Jersualem stands in contrast to the Jersualem above, for the latter is free, and it is this Jerusalem that stands as the mother of believers in Jesus Christ. Believers are citizens of the heavenly city.

In constructing the allegory, in which a relation is forged between Sinai and Hagar, Paul's eye is on "the present Jerusalem," and he is thinking of those opposed to his gospel. Hence, when he picks up the other side of the contrast, he does not mention Sarah or name the second covenant. He immediately contrasts the earthly Jerusalem with the Jerusalem above.

Elsewhere in the NT the heavenly Jerusalem (cf. Heb 12:22; Rev 3:12; 21:2, 10; cf. *2 Bar.* 4:2) represents the heavenly city that awaits believers.[50] The Jerusalem above, according to Paul, is the eschatological Jerusalem that has reached down into the present evil age.[51] Even though the heavenly Jerusalem had not arrived in its fullness, the age to come had invaded the present evil age, so we have an example here of Paul's already but not yet eschatology.[52] It also seems likely that Paul believed that the arrival of the Jerusalem above reflects an inauguration and partial fulfillment of the new covenant promise of a new creation (Isa 65:17; 66:1 – 11).[53]

In Isa 66:7 – 11, which is in the same context as the promise of the new creation, Zion is portrayed as a mother in labor, and the birth of her sons will spell the fulfillment of God's saving promises.[54] The Jerusalem on high is identified as the "mother" of believers.[55] The mother of believers here is not the church but the heavenly Jerusalem, showing that believers in Christ, both Jews and Gentiles, are citizens of the heavenly city.[56] Just as Sarah was the mother of Isaac, so believers are begotten in the new age of the Spirit. They are not slaves like the Judaizers but free sons by virtue of the Spirit's work.[57]

4:27 For it is written, "Rejoice, O barren one who does not give birth. Break forth and shout, O one without birth pangs, because the children of the desolate are more than the children of the one who has a husband" (γέγραπται γάρ, Εὐφράνθητι, στεῖρα ἡ οὐ τίκτουσα, ῥῆξον καὶ βόησον, ἡ οὐκ ὠδίνουσα· ὅτι πολλὰ τὰ τέκνα τῆς ἐρήμου μᾶλλον ἢ τῆς ἐχούσης τὸν ἄνδρα). Isaiah 54:1 is introduced to support Paul's argument in Gal 4:26, showing that the Gentile Christians in Galatia are the children of the Jerusalem above, for

---

49. The word "of all" (πάντων) follows "mother" (μήτηρ) in ℵ², A, C³, 0261ᵛⁱᵈ, 𝔐, and some other Western traditions. Nonetheless, it is clearly secondary. The external evidence from both the Alexandrian and Western tradition for its omission is strong (𝔓⁴⁶, ℵ*, B, C*, D, F, G, Ψ, 6, 33, 1241ˢ, 1739, 1881, 2464, 2495, etc.). Furthermore, the addition universalizes the text in accord with Rom 4:16 (cf. Metzger, *Textual Commentary*, 528).

50. Cf. Longenecker, *Galatians*, 214; Witherington, *Galatians*, 334 – 35. Against Martyn, it is unlikely that the contrast is between the Jerusalem church and the heavenly Jerusalem (*Galatians*, 459 – 66). Martyn's argument is linked with his view that the false brothers (Gal 2:3 – 5) made inroads with James — a view I find unconvincing (see comments on 2:1 – 14).

51. See Ps 87, where Zion is the mother of those born from many places outside Israel. See also 2 Esd 10:7, "For Zion, the mother of us all, is in deep grief and great distress" (NRSV).

See also *4 Ezra* 10:25 – 28; *2 Bar.* 4:2 – 6.

52. So also Lincoln, *Paradise*, 21 – 22.

53. Note how Paul says the Jerusalem above is "our mother." Therefore, Paul is not arguing here that the children of the free woman are his children as if he is Sarah. Contra Witherington, *Galatians*, 339; rightly Susan G. Eastman, "'Cast Out the Slave Woman and Her Son': The Dynamics of Exclusion and Inclusion in Galatians 4.30," *JSNT* 28 (2006): 317.

54. See *4 Ezra* 10:7, and the discussion in Longenecker, *Galatians*, 215.

55. Cf. Willitts, "Isa 54,1 and Gal 4,24b – 27," 205.

56. Rightly Betz, *Galatians*, 248.

57. Betz maintains that the opponents would have rejected the idea that Gentiles could be members of the heavenly Jerusalem (*Galatians*, 248). But Cosgrove rightly observes that the argument should be more nuanced. The opponents would not object to Gentiles being members if they were circumcised (Cosgrove, "Gal 4:21 – 30," 224, n. 25).

they are the children of the barren woman from whom no children were expected. Miraculously and supernaturally they have new life.

The link between the Isaiah passage and the previous verses is Sarah's barrenness.[58] Nor is Sarah's barrenness a minor theme in Genesis, for her inability to bear children impinges on the fulfillment of God's promise that Abraham would have offspring, and the same theme reappears in the lives of Isaac and Rebekah (Gen 25:21) and Jacob and Rachel (Gen 30:1). The context of Isaiah is one of return from exile. Israel is like a barren woman whose children have been lost to exile.[59] The Lord promises, however, to return her to the land, where she will multiply and prosper. Israel in exile is likened to a wife abandoned by her husband (the Lord). But a new day is dawning, and the Lord will have compassion on Israel again. The day of judgment has ended, and God's "covenant of peace" will be established (Isa 54:10). Jerusalem as a city will be made of precious and beautiful stones, and no one will harm her.[60]

Paul sees the fulfillment of this "covenant of peace" in his day. The return from exile has arrived

in the gospel of Jesus Christ. The Lord has poured out his grace on his people. The pattern in Sarah's life has been replicated. The child borne by Hagar came naturally, and it seemed to Abraham and to Sarah to represent the fulfillment of the promise. Nevertheless, it was the miraculous child, Isaac, who was the true fulfillment of God's promise. So too, when Israel's future seemed to be desolate, when all hope of her future was given up because of exile, the Lord promised to restore her children.

The ultimate fulfillment of this promise has become a reality, not in the physical return of Israel from exile, but in the conversion of Gentile Christians in places like Galatia. The law did not produce God's children, for those under the law were enslaved by sin. The law puts to death, but the gospel proclaimed by Paul brings freedom. Further, the gospel produces true children for the Lord — children of the promise like Isaac. Therefore, the Gentiles of Galatia should exult with joy because they are the fulfillment of the promise; they are the true children of the Lord.

4:28 And you, brothers, are children of promise according to Isaac (ὑμεῖς[61] δέ, ἀδελφοί, κατὰ

---

58. Cf. Barrett, "The Allegory of Abraham," 12; Karen H. Jobes, "Jerusalem, Our Mother: Metalepsis and Intertextuality in Galatians 4:21 – 31," *WTJ* 55 (1993): 302 – 3. Willitts criticizes Jobes for overlooking the role of Isa 54:2 – 17 in her intertextual analysis of Gal 4:27 and Isa 54:1 (Willitts, "Isa 54,1 and Gal 4,24b – 27," 191, n. 11). Also Jobes plays the LXX off against the MT (Jobes, "Jerusalem, Our Mother," 306), maintaining that the former is the basis for Paul's intertextual argument, but Willitts rightly argues that when one considers Isaiah 54 as a whole "the prophecy remains consistent in both traditions" ("Isa 54,1 and Gal 4,24b – 27," 192, n. 13).

59. See here Jobes's explication of the theme of barrenness and restoration in Isaiah ("Jerusalem, Our Mother," 299 – 320). Israel as "God's corporate people" is in view "personified by the city of Jerusalem or Zion" (so Willitts, "Isa 54,1 and Gal 4,24b – 27," 194).

60. The barren woman of Isa 54:1, then, "is a figurative characterization of Jerusalem." So Willitts, "Isa 54,1 and Gal 4,24b – 27," 193, and it should not be identified as Sarah (contra Betz, *Galatians*, 249). Harmon suggests that Hagar can

legitimately be said to have a husband on the basis of Gen 16:3 ("She Must and Shall Go Free," 238 – 39). He then argues that the husband of Hagar here represents the law, and hence Isa 54:1 represents two different stages in Israel's experience — one under law and the other forecasting God's eschatological work (237 – 40). The eschatological focus is clearly present here, but it is doubtful that Abraham as Hagar's husband would represent the law, for Paul separates Abraham from the era of the law in Galatians.

61. As Metzger remarks, scribes inserted "we" (ἡμεῖς) and "are" (ἐσμέν) (א, A, C, D², Ψ, 062, 𝔐, lat, syr, cop^sa) to conform the text with the first person plural in 4:26 and the verb "are" (ἐσμέν) in 4:31 (*Textual Commentary*, 528). Alexandrian and Western witnesses support NA²⁷ (𝔓⁴⁶, B, D*, F, G, 0261^vid, 6, 33, 365, 1175, 1739, 1881, *pc*, b, sa, Ir^lat, Ambrosiaster). Furthermore, the first person plural removes the rhetorical force of Paul using the second person plural to address his Gentile readers. Against Robinson, who accepts the variant ("Jewish and Gentile Believers," 44). Rightly Fee, *Galatians*, 183, n. 7.

Ἰσαὰκ ἐπαγγελίας τέκνα ἐστέ). Paul begins here to apply the allegory directly to his readers.[62] The Judaizers would most certainly have considered the Galatians to be Ishmaelites (not true children of the covenant) if they refused to be circumcised. Paul applies the allegory in a counterintuitive way. The Galatian Christians are like Isaac, and they are the true children of Sarah. They are the recipients of the promise, for they are children by virtue of the work of the Holy Spirit.

4:29 And just as formerly the one being born according to the flesh persecuted the one being born according to the Spirit, thus also now (ἀλλ᾽ ὥσπερ τότε ὁ κατὰ σάρκα γεννηθεὶς ἐδίωκεν τὸν κατὰ πνεῦμα, οὕτως καὶ νῦν). Just as Ishmael persecuted Isaac, the Judaizers were persecuting those who have been given new life by the Spirit in Galatia. The word "and" (ἀλλ᾽) here does not signify a contrast but "provides a transition to the next argument."[63] If the Galatians are Sarah's true children, then how does one classify the Judaizers, who came to Galatia and insisted on circumcision? Surely they saw themselves as true sons of Sarah and Abraham. Paul, however, compares them to Ishmael, who ridiculed and persecuted Isaac (cf. Gen 21:9).[64]

Therefore, the Judaizers' insistence on circumcision does not represent the work of God's Spirit wooing Gentiles into the fold. Instead, the evangelistic work of the Judaizers in Galatia was nothing less than persecution (cf. 3:4).[65] Just as Ishmael's

birth was explicable solely on natural terms (Gen 16), representing a fallible human attempt on the part of Abraham and Sarah to secure the promise, so too the Jewish adversaries are of the flesh — from the present evil age (1:4). They resist the Galatians because the latter have been born of the Spirit.

The polarity between the Spirit and the flesh is stark. The Galatian Christians are part of the age to come. They have the Jerusalem above as their mother. They are men and women of the Spirit. Therefore, they must resist the blandishments of the Judaizers, who are spiritually dead and who want to impose the slavery of the law and circumcision on them.

4:30 But what does the Scripture say? "Cast out the slave woman and her son, for the son of the slave woman will not inherit with the son of the free woman" (ἀλλὰ τί λέγει ἡ γραφή; Ἔκβαλε τὴν παιδίσκην καὶ τὸν υἱὸν αὐτῆς, οὐ γὰρ μὴ κληρονομήσει ὁ υἱὸς τῆς παιδίσκης μετὰ τοῦ υἱοῦ τῆς ἐλευθέρας). The Galatians must listen to the scriptural narrative regarding Isaac and Ishmael, for it speaks to their situation, informing them that those who belong to the slave woman will never receive the inheritance.[66]

When Ishmael ridiculed Isaac, Sarah was provoked, seeing Ishmael as a rival to her son. Hence, she demanded that Abraham remove Ishmael and Hagar from the household, for the inheritance belonged only to Isaac (Gen 21:10). Abraham

---

62. Rightly Betz, *Galatians*, 249; Longenecker, *Galatians*, 216; Jobes, "Jerusalem, Our Mother," 301. Cosgrove argues that this is not the conclusion to the argument ("Gal 4:21 – 30," 222 – 23), but he operates with a false dichotomy when he concludes that life in the Spirit rather than status is in view here (234). Actually, in this verse Paul emphasizes status by declaring that they are Isaac's children. Contra also Perriman, who joins 4:28 with 4:26 – 27 ("Galatians 4:21 – 5:1," 31).

63. So Betz, *Galatians*, 249.

64. The meaning of the Hebrew in Gen 21:9 is disputed.

Some see Gen 21:9 as innocent playing. For the various Jewish traditions, see Bruce, *Galatians*, 223 – 24.

65. Cf. Martyn, *Galatians*, 445. Against Mitternacht ("Recipient-Oriented," 427), who identifies the opponents as Jews from Galatia.

66. Bruce says Paul treats the word as Scripture even though Sarah's words were unreasonable (*Galatians*, 224 – 25). But, against Bruce, Gen 21:12 indicates that the Lord affirmed Sarah's demand. So even if Sarah's motivations were evil (which is entirely possible), her words represented God's intention.

hesitated to do what Sarah requested, for he loved his son Ishmael (21:11). Still, the Lord ratified what Sarah said, and Abraham was ordered to carry out her request, "Whatever Sarah says to you, do as she tells you, for through Isaac shall your offspring be named" (21:12 ESV). The inheritance was only through Isaac, not Ishmael. Only Isaac was the son of the promise.

How does this OT text apply to the Galatians? Traditionally the text has been understood to refer to the exclusion of Jews from the people of God.[67] This view has been seriously challenged in recent years. More recently scholars have argued that it was the Judaizers who were to be removed from Galatia and cast out of the church.[68] Such a view is possible, but it seems unlikely since Paul does not give such advice anywhere else in the letter but consistently appeals to the Galatians not to listen to the outside teachers, who have come with another gospel.

It seems more likely that the focus here is on Paul's desire that the Galatians *listen* to the biblical word addressed to Abraham.[69] We see from the OT that those who are sons of the slave woman will not receive the inheritance.[70] Only the sons

of Sarah, those who are children of promise, will receive the inheritance. Therefore, Paul is not enjoining the Galatians to remove the false teachers from the church. He is reminding his readers with the scriptural word that those who put themselves under the Sinai covenant will not receive the inheritance. The Galatians are not exhorted to expel the false teachers; rather, they are encouraged to remain in the sphere of the promise, for only those who are children of Sarah will receive the inheritance.

4:31 Therefore, brothers, we are not children of the slave woman, but we are children of the free woman (διό,[71] ἀδελφοί, οὐκ ἐσμὲν παιδίσκης τέκνα ἀλλὰ τῆς ἐλευθέρας). In essence, Paul restates in other terms the conclusion drawn in 4:28.[72] Here we have an inference from the entirety of the previous argument (4:21 – 30), as the "therefore" (διό) makes clear. Since the Galatians were born of the Spirit instead of the flesh, they were children of the Jerusalem above rather than of Hagar and were thereby children of the promise. Therefore, they are children of the free woman, belonging to the heavenly rather than the earthly Jerusalem.

---

67. E.g., Burton, *Galatians*, 262, 267 – 68.

68. Martyn says that the *slave woman* who must be expelled represents the opponents, and *the son* is restricted to those in Galatia who have fallen prey to the theology of the adversaries (*Galatians*, 446). In support of the idea that the false teachers are to be removed from the church, see Longenecker, *Galatians*, 217; Hays, *Echoes of Scripture*, 126; Matera, *Galatians*, 178 – 79; Garlington, *Galatians*, 282; Lincoln, *Paradise*, 28 – 29; Witherington, *Galatians*, 338 – 39. But Eastman notes Jews "cannot be expelled from a community to which they do not belong in the first place" ("Galatians 4.30," 312). Others see both Jews and Jewish Christians (the opponents) as excluded. So Lightfoot, *Galatians*, 184; Dunn, *Galatians*, 258; Hansen, *Abraham in Galatians*, 145 – 46; Willitts, "Isa 54,1 and Gal 4,24b – 27," 206 – 7. It is unconvincing to posit that Paul speaks here of throwing out the Sinai covenant (contra Di Mattei, "Gal 4.21 – 31," 121).

69. So Eastman, who argues that the Galatians overheard the divine word spoken to Abraham and thereby received illu-

mination regarding their situation ("Galatians 4.30," 309 – 36). Confirming her view is the second person singular imperative instead of the second person plural imperative. The latter is used elsewhere in Galatians when the congregation is admonished to do something. Thus the imperative is to be construed as a warning for the Galatians themselves. For a similar view, see Perriman, "Galatians 4:21 – 5:1," 41. But against Perriman, 4:30 should not be seen as the purpose of the entire text. The main point in 4:21 – 31 is reiterated in 4:28 and 4:31: the Galatians were like Isaac, children of the free woman.

70. Less likely is the view that Paul has in view angelic agents who will do the excluding at the eschaton. So Barrett, "The Allegory of Abraham," 13; Bruce, *Galatians*, 225.

71. A number of different readings exist here, but all of them support a concluding statement. The external evidence supports NA[27] (ℵ, B, D*, H, 0261, 33, 365, 1175, 1739, 1881, *pc*, sa, Marcion).

72. Betz sees this as the conclusion not only of this paragraph but of all of 3:1 – 4:30 (*Galatians*, 251).

5:1a Christ set us free for freedom (τῇ ἐλευθερίᾳ ἡμᾶς Χριστὸς ἠλευθέρωσεν). The purpose of Christ's work is summarized with this short pungent statement. Christ liberated his people so that they may enjoy the freedom of the gospel. The placement of 5:1 is disputed. Some see it as the conclusion to the previous section.[73] Others claim that it introduces the exhortation section.[74] More likely, the verse is transitional, so it functions both as the conclusion to 4:21 – 31 and represents a bridge to the next section.[75]

The dative "for freedom" (τῇ ἐλευθερίᾳ) is probably a dative of purpose,[76] though it may alternatively refer to sphere or realm.[77] Freedom versus slavery dominates the argument in 4:21 – 31, and 5:1 functions as a transition between 4:21 – 31 and 5:2 – 6. For the Galatians to submit to circumcision and adopt the OT law is to return to the Sinai covenant, which is one of slavery. They will effectively put themselves into Ishmael's family rather than Isaac's. Surely the Judaizers argued the opposite! Paul argues strenuously that they must continue in the freedom from the law that was theirs at the inception of their Christian lives (cf. 2:4). This freedom was won for believers by Christ through his redeeming work (explained in 3:13 and 4:5).[78]

5:1b-c Therefore, stand fast, and do not be subject again to a yoke of slavery (στήκετε[79] οὖν καὶ μὴ πάλιν ζυγῷ δουλείας ἐνέχεσθε). We have a prime example here of the indicative and imperative in Pauline theology. Since the Galatians are free from the law in Christ, they must stand in that freedom.

The law is elsewhere described as a "yoke" in Jewish literature (cf. Sir 51:26).[80] Paul departs from the standard Jewish view, which saw the law as an agent of liberation, in identifying it as a yoke that enslaves. Peter's words about the law at the Jerusalem Council are similar: "Now, therefore, why are you putting God to the test by placing a yoke on the neck of the disciples that neither our fathers nor we have been able to bear?" (Acts 15:10 ESV). Christ frees and liberates believers, but the law enslaves and holds captive all those who are under its dominion. Therefore, for the Galatians to subject themselves to circumcision and the law is foolish and fatal.[81]

This passage concludes, then, with the main point in an exhortation. The Galatians must stand fast in their freedom and resist the pressure to submit to circumcision and the law. Since they belong to the Jerusalem above and to the free woman and are the inheritors of the eschatological promises and recipients of the Holy Spirit, they must enjoy the freedom that is already theirs.

---

73. Lightfoot, *Galatians*, 185; Bruce, *Galatians*, 226. Hays thinks it summarizes the message of chapter 4 and "encapsulates the message of the letter in a single powerful slogan" (*Galatians*, 306).

74. Burton *Galatians*, 269 – 70; Betz, *Galatians*, 253, 255; Cosgrove, "Gal 4:21 – 30," 232; Matera, *Galatians*, 180.

75. Cf. Longenecker, *Galatians*, 223 – 24; Fee, *Galatians*, 186. Martyn sees it as the conclusion of 4:21 – 31 (*Galatians*, 468).

76. Betz, *Galatians*, 255 – 56; Longenecker, *Galatians*, 224.

77. Martyn, *Galatians*, 447. It is less likely that it should be construed as instrumental (Bruce, *Galatians*, 226).

78. So Jan Lambrecht, "Abraham and His Offspring: A Comparison of Galatians 5,1 with 3,13," *Bib* 80 (1999): 530.

79. A remarkable variety of readings exist here, probably, as Metzger says, to soften the abruptness of the text (*Textual Commentary*, 528). The variant readings stem from the Western and Majority Text traditions, and it is most likely that the text attested by the Alexandrian tradition and by NA[27] should be accepted.

80. See Karl H. Rengstorf, "ζυγός," *TDNT*, 2:896 – 901; Bruce, *Galatians*, 226.

81. Wilson emphasizes that the apostasy contemplated here echoes Israel's desire to return to Egyptian bondage ("Wilderness Apostasy," 565).

Theology in Application

Liberation from Sin

Paul's use of allegory is pressed into the service of eschatology here. Contrasts dominate the passage: the present Jerusalem versus the Jerusalem above, the slave and the free woman, the old and new covenant, slavery and freedom, the flesh and the Spirit, and being cast out and receiving the inheritance. The problem with the Judaizers is that they wanted to turn the clock back in salvation history.

But their fault was not merely chronological. It is not as if their only problem was that they didn't know what time it is. The era of the law is one of slavery to sin. Freedom and life only come through Christ and the Jerusalem above. Those who are part of the old era are dominated by the flesh instead of the Spirit. Hence, Paul's problem with Judaism was not, contrary to Sanders, merely that it is not Christianity. Returning to the law is fatal for Paul because it lands one under the dominion of sin, so that one is subjugated to its tyranny.

Liberation from sin, therefore, can never come from the law or from education in moral principles. If swift punishment is meted out, the law can restrain the outward expression of sin. Still, it does not cure the desires of the heart. The only true cure for sin is death, where the old person dies with Christ and a new person is born. When one's mother is the Jerusalem above, the new eschatological era in Christ, a new freedom becomes a reality. Believers are joined to Christ and love Christ. Of course, the struggle with sin persists since believers live in the interval between the already and not yet. Still, the dominion of sin has been broken through Jesus Christ.

What do most people mean by "freedom"? They define freedom as doing what you want to do. If you want to take a day off work, you take the day off. If you want to go hiking, you go hiking. If you want to marry Jane, you marry Jane, provided, of course, that Jane wants to marry you.

Understanding freedom, however, is more complex than immediately meets the eye. When my dad was young, he decided he wanted to smoke cigarettes. He enjoyed them immensely. He did what he wanted to do when he started smoking. He loved cigarettes so much that he eventually smoked three packs a day. As he grew older, he became more concerned about his health. He decided he wanted to stop smoking. But he found it incredibly difficult to stop. He even enrolled in a one-week treatment program, where among other things they tried shock treatment to wean him off the desire to smoke. But the shock treatment did not work. He smoked the day he came out of the treatment.

Smoking began for my dad as a choice, but later he was enslaved by it. Indeed, he could never shake the habit. And eventually he contracted cancer and emphysema. Even when he had an oxygen tank at the end of his life, he still smoked. My dad thought he was free when he began to smoke, but he ended up being a slave of the habit. The same principle is true, of course, is many different arenas of life. We can begin by choosing to eat candy three times a day. But later our body begins to crave candy all day long.

Living under Grace

But we also need to remind ourselves that if we are Christians, we are already free. We are called to live out the freedom that is already ours and not to turn back to slavery. We are to live under grace instead of under the law. What are some signs that we are living under grace? One sign is that we are not devastated when we are criticized or snubbed by others. If we are devastated, we are still subtly living by the law, for our god is receiving the approval of others. We are living by grace if we can rest in being passed over for a job that we thought we should have received. If we live by the law and focus on ourselves, we become resentful and angry because we have been passed over. But if we live by grace, we rest in God's purposes, even if we think others made a mistake.

What if you are trying to be free and you are not changing at all? One possibility is that you are not a Christian. One pastor told me that in his counseling with men struggling with pornography that non-Christians could not ever win victory over it, and this was one of the signs to him that a person was not truly a believer. If you are an unbeliever, you will never be free from your slavery until you turn to Christ and ask him to liberate you from your sin by his grace and give him control of your life. But things aren't so simple for Christians either. For we see in this very passage that Christians are tempted to go back under the law and return to the slavery from which they were freed. So, matters are complex, for believers struggle with sin as well, and yet God has promised that believers will enjoy substantial, significant, and observable victory over sin (even if Christians will not in this life enjoy perfection).

CHAPTER 18

Galatians 5:2 – 6

Literary Context

Some scholars begin the exhortation section of the letter at 5:13. Such a division is plausible, but actually the exhortations begin, as noted previously, in 4:12, and in 5:2 – 12 those exhortations continue. In this section, for the first time in the letter, Paul turns his attention explicitly to the major issue facing the Galatians, namely, whether to receive circumcision,[1] and he warns them in no uncertain terms about the danger of submitting to circumcision.[2] Galatians 5:1 functions as a transitional verse between 4:21 – 31 and 5:2 – 6, and hence Paul continues to exhort the Galatians to stand fast in freedom. Freedom will be their portion only if they refuse to submit to the demand of the Judaizers, who insist on circumcision for salvation.

I. Introduction: Desertion from Paul's Gospel Is Desertion from the Gospel (1:1 – 2:21)

II. Paul's Gospel Defended from Experience and Scripture (3:1 – 4:11)

III. A Call to Freedom from the Law and Freedom in the Spirit (4:12 – 6:10)

    A. Live in Freedom from the Law: Argument from Friendship (4:12 – 20)

    B. Stand in Freedom: Argument from Allegory (4:21 – 5:1)

    C. Resist the Dangerous Message of Bondage (5:2 – 12)

→   **1. It Involves the Requirement of Circumcision (5:2 – 6)**

       2. Its Perpetrators Will Be Judged (5:7 – 12)

Main Idea

If the Galatians submit to circumcision, they cut themselves off from Christ and salvation, for they remove themselves from the only means by which they can be forgiven of their sins. Those who live by faith through the Spirit will receive the eschatological gift of righteousness.

---

1. See also Dahl, "Paul's Letter to the Galatians," 136; Matera, "Gal 5.1 – 6.17," 79 – 80.

2. The warning shows we have an exhortation here (contra Martyn, *Galatians*, 468).

Translation

> ## Galatians 5:2-6
>
> | | | |
> |---|---|---|
> | 2 | warning | **Behold I, Paul, say to you** that if you receive circumcision, Christ will not profit you at all. |
> | 3 | assertion | And **I testify again to every man** who receives circumcision that he is a debtor ✍ |
> | | | to do the whole law. |
> | 4a | assertion | You, who are attempting to be justified by law,   are severed from Christ; |
> | b | assertion | you   are fallen from grace. |
> | 5a | assertion | For **we are waiting for the hope of righteousness** |
> | b | agency *(of 5a)* | through the Spirit |
> | c | means *(of 5a)* | by faith. |
> | 6a | basis *(of 5a-c)* | For **in Christ Jesus** neither circumcision nor uncircumcision means anything, but |
> | b | contrast *(to 6a)* | faith working through love (means everything). |

Structure

A solemn warning introduces this paragraph, where Paul threatens the Galatians if they receive circumcision. The initial words, "Behold I, Paul, say to you" (Ἴδε ἐγὼ Παῦλος λέγω ὑμῖν), commence a new section and underline the importance of what Paul writes. As Baugh says, "The staccato style of the Greek and of the thoughts in Galatians 5:1 – 6 is notably abrupt and direct. There is no luxurious, unfolding periodic style.... Instead, Galatians 5:1 – 6 is unvarnished, direct, heartfelt appeal, warning, and testimony, because the audience's actions carry the gravest of consequences."[3] The Galatians will either trust in circumcision or in Christ; no middle ground exists. If they choose the former, they have no profit from the latter.

The argument continues in 5:3, and again the verse is introduced solemnly, "And I testify" (μαρτύρομαι δέ). The matter before the Galatians cannot be restricted to circumcision. If they adopt circumcision, they place themselves in debt to the whole law. In other words, they must keep the whole law to obtain eschatological salvation. The word "again" recalls 3:10, and hence the argument here is that placing themselves under the law is an intolerable burden since perfect obedience is required, and such obedience is impossible.

Paul reiterates what is at stake with a general truth in 5:4. In addition, he clarifies what is at stake. Those who are considering circumcision are attempting to be

---

3. S. M. Baugh, "Galatians 5:1 – 6 and Personal Obligation: Reflections on Paul and the Law," in *The Law Is Not of Faith: Essays on Works and Grace in the Mosaic Covenant* (ed. Bryan D. Estelle, J. V. Fesko, and David VanDrunen; Phillipsburg: Presbyterian and Reformed, 2009), 265.

justified by means of the law. To trust in the law for righteousness, however, severs one from Christ. If they look to the law for righteousness, they are no longer in the realm of grace. An adversative conjunction does not separate 5:4 and 5:5, but we clearly have a contrast between the two verses, for now Paul describes those who belong to God. They are waiting for the eschatological hope of being declared righteous. They do not, however, trust in the law. They are relying on the Spirit and waiting in faith (cf. 3:1 – 5).

The final verse (5:6) explains why ("for," γάρ) believers anticipate the hope of righteousness through the Spirit and by faith. They realize that in Christ circumcision and, for that matter, uncircumcision are irrelevant for salvation. Faith alone receives the promise, but it is never a faith that is alone. It is a living and dynamic faith that produces love.

Exegetical Outline

   III. **A Call to Freedom from the Law and Freedom in the Spirit (4:12 – 6:10)**
       A. Live in Freedom from the Law: Argument from Friendship (4:12 – 20)
       B. Stand in Freedom: Argument from Allegory (4:21 – 5:1)
       C. Resist the Dangerous Message of Bondage (5:2 – 12)
  ➡   **1. It involves the requirement of circumcision (5:2 – 6)**
           a. Paul's warning (5:2)
           b. The impossible obligation (5:3)
           c. The consequence (5:4)
           d. The contrast (5:5)
           e. Its irrelevance (5:6)
        2. Its perpetrators will be judged (5:7 – 12)

Explanation of the Text

5:2 Behold I, Paul, say to you that if you receive circumcision, Christ will not profit you at all (Ἴδε ἐγὼ Παῦλος λέγω ὑμῖν ὅτι ἐὰν περιτέμνησθε, Χριστὸς ὑμᾶς οὐδὲν ὠφελήσει). If the Galatians get circumcised, they will lose any saving benefit that comes from Christ. For the first time in the letter the issue of circumcision in Galatia is dealt with directly. In 2:3 – 5 Paul recounted the desire of false brothers to impose circumcision on Titus in Jerusalem. Certainly that decision in Jerusalem was recounted for the sake of the Galatian readers. Still, Paul holds off against mentioning the attraction of circumcision directly in Galatia until here, where he vigorously exhorts the readers not to receive the rite.

The exhortation comes at this juncture in the letter because Paul has now completed the theological foundation (2:16 – 5:1) by which the Galatians will be able to grasp the rationale for his command and the seriousness of the issue. The fact that the imperative grows out of the indicative, besides being typical of Paul's writings, also yields another insight. The discussion of the law and circumcision in Galatians are part and parcel of the same question. The Galatians' desire to be circumcised reflects a desire to be under the law as a whole (4:21). Therefore, all that Paul wrote about the law in 2:15–5:1 applies to circumcision.

The introduction to Paul's strong assertion in 5:2 is solemn and serious. The words "Behold I, Paul, say to you" as an introduction underscore that the words that follow are of immense weight. As Betz says, "he mobilizes his whole authority as an apostle."[4] The issue before the Galatians cannot be waved off as a difference of opinion on an inconsequential matter. According to Paul their final destiny is at stake, and hence he reminds his readers at the outset that he speaks authoritatively as an apostle of Jesus Christ.

The verb "receive circumcision" (περιτέμνησθε) could be understood as a middle ("you yourselves receive circumcision") or a passive ("you receive circumcision"), but in both instances the meaning remains the same. If they submit to the knife, they will find no profit in Christ at the final judgment.[5] The verb "will profit" (ὠφελήσει) refers to the final judgment here.[6] Elsewhere the same verb "profit" (ὠφελέω) appears in another context pertaining to circumcision. Circumcision only "profits" (ὠφελεῖ) if one keeps the entire law (Rom 2:25). Those who are circumcised and fail to observe the law become like uncircumcised Gentiles, i.e., outside of God's covenant people.

Paul argues in Romans that no one performs the whole law (cf. 3:9–20), and hence circumcision does not have any saving benefit. In the same way here, if the Galatians think they find "profit" or "benefit" in circumcision for salvation, there is no saving benefit that accrues to them in Christ. If they rely on circumcision for salvation, they cannot lean on Christ for the same. No middle way exists between circumcision and Christ. If the Galatians turn to circumcision, they lose Christ and all his benefits.

5:3 And I testify again to every man who receives circumcision that he is a debtor to do the whole law (μαρτύρομαι δὲ πάλιν[7] παντὶ ἀνθρώπῳ περιτεμνομένῳ ὅτι ὀφειλέτης ἐστὶν ὅλον τὸν νόμον ποιῆσαι). Those who submit to circumcision must keep the entire law perfectly in order to enjoy eschatological salvation, and such flawless obedience is impossible. The solemnity of the previous verse continues,[8] for here Paul bears witness, as in a courtroom situation, about those who accept circumcision.[9]

The meaning of this compact statement is disputed. Some have argued that the Galatians desired to receive circumcision as the pathway to Gnostic libertinism, thinking that the rite freed them from all other moral obligations.[10] Hence, Paul informs them of the consequences of their decision. The fatal defect with this view is that any evidence supporting gnostic false teachers in Galatia is lacking.[11]

Others suggest that the Galatians did not realize that accepting circumcision meant that they must also keep the remainder of the law. Paul informs them, then, of the implications of their decision. Such a view, however, fails to convince, nor

---

4. Betz, *Galatians*, 258.

5. Rightly Betz, *Galatians*, 259; Garlington, *Galatians*, 297. Against Judith M. Gundry Volf, who sees no reference to final judgment. *Paul and Perseverance: Staying in and Falling Away* (Louisville: Westminster John Knox, 1990), 209.

6. Rightly Witherington, *Galatians*, 367. Contra Longenecker, *Galatians*, 226. Longenecker fails to see the eschatological thrust of the paragraph in 5:5 and misinterprets the aorist verbs in 5:4 (see exegesis of 5:4).

7. The word "again" (πάλιν) is missing in a few manuscripts, which are mainly Western, but the external evidence for its inclusion is decisive. Perhaps a few scribes omitted it because it was not clear to them where Paul had said this previously.

8. The particle "and" (δέ) is continuative here (so Longenecker, *Galatians*, 226).

9. We have an oath formula here. Cf. Betz, *Galatians*, 259.

10. Schmithals, *Paul and the Gnostics*, 33–34, 38.

11. See the introduction.

does it truly advance Paul's argument in the letter. The Galatians could have very well responded by insisting that they had every intention of keeping the rest of the law. What Paul viewed as a debt they may have embraced with joy. Presumably that is how the Judaizers would have responded to this kind of argument. If the Galatians did not find circumcision to be an intolerable burden, presumably they would not find the remainder of the law to be such either.

Moreover, it is unlikely that the Galatians separated circumcision from the remainder of the law. We saw in 4:10 that they were observing some of the days of the OT calendar, and thus the notion that they were informed only about circumcision is unlikely. Further, in 4:21 the Galatians are described as those who desired to be under the law as a whole, which suggests that they did not limit themselves to circumcision.

A better interpretation links 5:3 to 3:10.[12] The word "again" (πάλιν) here does not clearly refer to 5:2,[13] for the content of the two verses is different. Galatians 5:2 simply asserts that those who receive circumcision receive no profit from Christ. Nothing is said about an obligation or debt to keep the law. It makes more sense to think that Paul reverts to the crucial argument of 3:10, where he insisted that one must keep the entire law to avoid the curse of the law, implying at the same time that no one could observe the law flawlessly.[14] Paul thus

reminds the readers again of the burden of placing themselves under the law.[15] If they are circumcised, they stand in debt to the entire law.[16] One cannot merely observe part of the law, as James also testifies (Jas 2:10 – 11), for it will scarcely do to observe some of its precepts and ignore others.

Paul's argument has even more teeth than what we find in James, for the obligation here relates to salvation. Putting onself under the law is a burden because perfect obedience is required to be right with God.[17] Insofar as the animal sacrifices of the OT do not avail now that Christ has come, the Galatians' only hope if they place themselves under the law is to keep every part of it without fail.[18] Such obedience is, of course, impossible, and hence the Galatians must not adopt circumcision, for to do so places them in the impossible situation of needing to keep the whole law to be saved.

5:4 You, who are attempting to be justified by law, are severed from Christ; you are fallen from grace (κατηργήθητε ἀπὸ Χριστοῦ, οἵτινες ἐν νόμῳ δικαιοῦσθε, τῆς χάριτος ἐξεπέσατε). Paul continues to threaten the Galatians here. If they try to be justified by the law by being circumcised, they will be cut off from Christ and will have abandoned the Christ of the gospel. The aorist verbs "severed" (κατηργήθητε) and "have fallen" (ἐξεπέσατε) have a gnomic sense.[19] Therefore,

---

12. So Betz, *Galatians*, 260 – 61.

13. Against Bruce, *Galatians*, 229; Longenecker, *Galatians*, 226; Martyn, *Galatians*, 469; Matera, *Galatians*, 181.

14. So Baugh, "Galatians 3:20," 63.

15. Garlington notes a play on words between 5:2 ("it will not profit," ὠφελήσει) and 5:3 ("debtor," ὀφειλέτης) (*Galatians*, 298, n. 11).

16. Rightly Betz, *Galatians*, 259 – 61; Bruce W. Longenecker, "Defining the Faithful Character of the Covenant Community: Galatians 2.15 – 21 and Beyond," in *Paul and the Mosaic Law* (ed. James D. G. Dunn; Tübingen: Mohr Siebeck, 1996), 91, n. 42; Baugh, "Galatians 5:1 – 6 and Personal Obligation," 270 – 75. Against Dunn, *Galatians*, 266 – 67.

17. In support of the notion that perfect obedience is required here, see Barrett, *Freedom and Obligation*, 63; Hong, *Law in Galatians*, 109. Against Bruce, who thinks Paul kept the whole law (Phil 3:6), but was condemned anyway (*Galatians*, 231). For a view similar to Bruce here, see Matera, *Galatians*, 189.

18. Surprisingly Hays misses this point, failing to see that Paul sees no efficacy in OT sacrifices now that Christ has come (*Galatians*, 312).

19. For a similar explanation, see Lightfoot, *Galatians*, 204. Alternatively, the verbs could be taken as proleptic aorists (so Bruce, *Galatians*, 231). Longenecker's explanation is awkward here. He tries to read the aorist verbs as designating

Paul does not declare here that the Galatians *have* definitively fallen from grace.[20] The exhortations in this letter to resist the false teachers in the letter do not fit if the Galatians have already succumbed to the heresy.

It seems more likely, then, that Paul asserts what will be the case *if* the Galatians revert to the law.[21] Such an interpretation fits the context since in 5:2 Christ will be useless to the Galatians *if* they submit to circumcision. It seems that the two verbs in 5:4 should be construed similarly so that Paul reflects on what will happen if the Galatians apostatize.[22] Again, Paul leaves no room for compromise. They will be estranged from Christ and will fall from grace.

Christ and grace are mutually exclusive here, so that the Galatians will either follow Christ and the gospel or accept circumcision and the law. Opposed to Christ and grace is the law and circumcision. Those who attempt to derive their justification from the law are severed from Christ and cut off from grace, for they are attempting to accomplish their own salvation instead of trusting in the grace and mercy of Christ.

The verb "justify" (δικαιοῦσθε) in this context must be understood as conative or tendential, indicating that they are attempting to be justified by the law, not that they actually are justified by the law. Clearly Paul believed that justification by the

law is impossible (3:11). It also seems that we have further evidence for the verb "justify" (δικαιόω) being forensic. If human beings could keep the law, they would be declared righteous by means of it. The keeping of the law would not *make* them righteous but would be the basis of the declaration, if such law obedience were possible. But law and grace are polar opposites. The law tries to find righteousness by doing and obeying; grace and Christ bestow righteousness as a gift. If the Galatians accept circumcision, they abandon grace and Christ.

5:5 For we are waiting for the hope of righteousness through the Spirit by faith (ἡμεῖς γὰρ πνεύματι ἐκ πίστεως ἐλπίδα δικαιοσύνης ἀπεκδεχόμεθα). The eschatological hope of believers is the final declaration of righteousness on the last day. In the interim believers wait for that end-time declaration in reliance on the Holy Spirit and place their trust in Christ. The "for" (γάρ) here does not connect easily with 5:4. An unstated contrast between 5:4 and the beginning of 5:5 is assumed.[23] Perhaps the unstated idea is that true believers will not be cut off from Christ nor will they defect from grace.

Galatians 5:5, then, provides the reason or ground for such. Instead of relying on obedience to the law for righteousness, believers wait for

---

the past and the present tense verb ("you are attempting to be justified," δικαιοῦσθε) as denoting the present (*Galatians*, 228). A more satisfactory understanding of verbal aspect recognizes that verbs should be construed in light of aspect rather than time. Whether aorist verbs denote past time must be discerned in context, and the context here shows that past time is not in view.

20. Contra Baugh, "Galatians 5:1–6 and Personal Obligation," 270.

21. Kwon rightly says, "Paul proleptically visualizes the terrible consequences of their behavior" (*Eschatology*, 47).

22. Against Fee, who suggests that falling from grace does not refer to losing eschatological salvation (*Galatians*, 189). Eastman interprets the verbs in 5:3 and 5:4 (and the exhor-

tation in 6:1) as perhaps suggesting that some of the Galatians had received circumcision ("Galatians 4.30," 329–31). If Eastman is correct, then the Galatians would still be saved if they renounced dependence on circumcision for salvation. It is more probable, however, that Eastman relies too heavily on tense in interpreting the verbal forms. Recent studies in verbal aspect have taught us that aspect rather than tense is fundamental in interpreting verbal forms. Therefore, the present tense in 5:3 and the aorist forms in 5:4 do not necessarily signify present and past time respectively.

23. Paul does not restrict his words here to Jewish Christians. Contra Longenecker, *Galatians*, 229; Witherington, *Galatians*, 369.

the eschatological gift of righteousness by faith.[24] They do not attain righteousness by doing or obeying but through believing in God's promises in Christ Jesus. Further, they do not rely on the flesh or self-effort but on the Holy Spirit.

The verb "wait for" (ἀπεκδεχόμεθα) is always used to denote eschatological realities in Paul (Rom 8:19, 23, 25; 1 Cor 1:7; Phil 3:20; cf. Heb 9:28). The eschatological focus of the text is confirmed by the word "hope" (ἐλπίδα). Believers do not base their hope on their obedience but in faith cling to what God has done for them in Christ. Such looking away from oneself to Christ is the work of the Spirit, and it cannot be produced by mere human willpower. The Holy Spirit transforms human beings so that they put their trust in God's saving work instead of relying on themselves.

The word "righteousness" (δικαιοσύνη) should be understood forensically here, for it is likely that it has the same meaning as the verbal form found in 5:4.[25] A difficult matter here is how to construe the genitive noun "righteousness" (δικαιοσύνης). The genitive could be understood as a genitive of source, so that the hope comes from the righteousness that already belongs to believers now.[26] The advantage of this reading is that it fits with Paul's emphasis on righteousness being a gift that believers already possess, which is a prominent theme in his writings. But as Moo points out this interpretation does not seem to make much sense:

> First, if "righteousness" in this verse refers to the believer's "past" justification, then the object of our eager anticipation is simply "hope," in the sense of "what we hope for." But after this verb we expect a more specific object than this. "We are eagerly awaiting what we hope for" is close to being a nonsensical tautology — especially in a context where there has been no previous mention of hope or the content of that hope.[27]

Righteousness is much more likely appositional.[28] The hope believers await *is* the final verdict of righteousness. Such a reading does not contradict the truth that believers are righteous now, nor should it be read as implying that justification is a process of renewal. Rather, the eschatological verdict differs from what God pronounces in history in that on the last day God's verdict is announced before the whole world.[29] Believers are already righteous before God by virtue of their union with Christ Jesus. Still, their righteousness is hidden from the world and will only be unveiled on the last day. Indeed, the righteousness of believers is hidden to some extent even to them since they grasp it now by faith. On the last day, however, their righteousness will be undeniable both to themselves and to the whole world.

---

24. Kwon argues that "by faith" (ἐκ πίστεως) modifies "through the Spirit" (πνεύματι) rather than "we wait for" (ἀπεκδεχόμεθα) (*Eschatology*, 181), so that Spirit is given by faith. Such a reading is possible, but prepositional phrases more often modify verbs, and therefore the interpretation proposed above should be retained.

Choi argues that "by faith" (ἐκ πίστεως) refers here to Christ's faithfulness ("Galatians 5:5 – 6," 479 – 82). His argument depends on seeing the previous references to "faith of Christ" (πίστις Χριστοῦ) as referring to Christ's faithfulness, which, as was argued in the commentary on 2:16, is doubtful.

25. So Moo, unpublished article. VanLandingham's suggestion that righteousness refers to the character of the future age does not fit with Pauline usage elsewhere in the letter, nor with the present context, where the issue is justification (*Judgment and Justification*, 318 – 19).

26. So Fung, *Galatians*, 224 – 27; Matera, *Galatians*, 182; Fee, *Galatians*, 190.

27. Moo, unpublished. Moo points to other texts where justification is likely a future reality: Rom 5:19; 8:33; Gal 2:17.

28. Silva suggests either an objective genitive or one that is appositional (*Interpreting Galatians*, 182). Martyn favors the appositional (*Galatians*, 472). See also Kwon, *Eschatology*, 66; Hays, *Galatians*, 313, n. 241.

29. Barrett says that the initial verdict of justification is "confirmed" on the last day. See his entire discussion, *Freedom and Obligation*, 63 – 65.

5:6 For in Christ Jesus neither circumcision nor uncircumcision means anything, but faith working through love (means everything) (ἐν γὰρ Χριστῷ Ἰησοῦ οὔτε περιτομή τι ἰσχύει οὔτε ἀκροβυστία, ἀλλὰ πίστις δι᾽ ἀγάπης ἐνεργουμένη). Neither circumcision or uncircumcison has any significance. The life that pleases God is characterized by trust in God and Christ, and love for others is the fruit or result of that faith.

Verse 6 functions as the ground or basis for 5:5. Righteousness is a gift given on the last day. It is obtained not on the basis of works but through faith alone. It is not the work of the flesh, for the flesh falls short of God's requirements, and hence only a supernatural work of the Spirit avails. Therefore, circumcision plays no role in obtaining eschatological righteousness, for no work of the law counts before God as the basis of justification.[30]

At the same time, no one should be proud of his uncircumcision either. If one recognizes that circumcision or any other work does not constitute one as righteous, one could perversely become proud of his uncircumcision. Human beings could congratulate themselves on their spiritual insight, thinking that they must have great spiritual perception to remain uncircumcised. But there is no spiritual advantage to uncircumcision per se. What matters is whether one is clinging to Christ in faith,[31] whether one sees that righteousness is found only in him.

The Galatians could fall prey to pride in what they did (circumcision) or in what they did not do (uncircumcision). In both instances the focus remains on human accomplishments or perception. Faith, however, looks entirely away from oneself and grasps Christ for righteousness. Faith, of course, is not a nullity. It is living and active and powerful. It expresses itself in love. The participle "working" (ἐνεργουμένη) should be construed as a middle here, so that faith is the root and love is the fruit.[32]

Love, then, is not the basis of justification but the fruit of faith, the result of faith. The statement is somewhat ambiguous, for "through love" could be construed as if love was the means by which faith became a reality. But the priority of faith in Paul suggests that love is the result of faith. This interpretation is confirmed by Gal 5:22, where love is the fruit of the Spirit, and therefore those who trust in Christ and embrace him as Lord show that faith in love.[33]

Two similar statements occur elsewhere in Paul. In Gal 6:15 he says, "For neither is circumcision anything, nor is uncircumcision anything, but a new creation is everything." Such a statement fits well with the assertion in 5:6, but the new creation replaces "faith working through love." In other words, faith is the result of God's new creation work; it cannot be attributed to the autonomous work of human beings but is a creative and miraculous work of God.

The other place is 1 Cor 7:19: "Circumcision is nothing and uncircumcision is nothing. Keeping

---

30. As Betz says, neither circumcision or uncircumcision has "the power to achieve ... salvation and righteousness before God" (*Galatians*, 263, n. 94).

31. Against Choi, there is no reference to the faithfulness of Christ here ("Galatians 5:5 – 6," 482 – 89).

32. So Bruce, *Galatians*, 232 – 33; Matera, *Galatians*, 183. Garlington's own explanation is ambiguous. It is unclear if he means that faith expresses itself in love or if faith is actually animated by love. Note his expressions: "faith ... impelled by love" (*Galatians*, 304); "an activist faith with love

as its energizing agent" (305); "expresses itself in love" (305); "faith *working itself out* through love" (306, n. 24, italics his); "faith working through love" (307). Some of these statements suggest that faith is formed by love (a traditionally Roman Catholic view — so Aquinas and Trent [see Riches, *Galatians through the Centuries*, 250, 258 – 59]). For the contrary view of Luther, Calvin, and Perkins, see Riches, *Galatians through the Centuries*, 254 – 55, 257, 260.

33. So Calvin, *Galatians*, 152.

God's commands is what counts." Does this contradict Gal 5:6 and 6:15? It could be construed in such a way, but surely a sympathetic reading finds an inner harmony. If faith expresses itself in love in Gal 5:6, such a notion is not far from saying that faith keeps God's commands. In other words, keeping God's commands is the consequence of faith, the result of being a new creation. Such obedience is not the basis of justification, but the result of justification and an expression of the new life granted to believers. Those who do not manifest love or who do not keep God's commands show that they do not have genuine faith and that they are not part of the new creation.

Theology in Application

Only One Way

In our postmodern and relativistic world, we are apt to accept different ways to God as equally legitimate. What is striking and perhaps even shocking here is Paul's complete rejection of circumcision and the Torah as the way to God. Christ and the law are not compatible for Paul but polar opposites. Either one clings to Christ and the righteousness he gives, or one is damned. Salvation cannot be divided between the work of Christ and human accomplishment.

If keeping the law leads to salvation, then Christ is superfluous. If what human beings do becomes the basis of salvation, then praise and honor redound to those who perform the required works. But if salvation is the work of Christ, he receives the praise and honor for redeeming his people. Paul categorically rejects human works because they rule out the importance and centrality of Christ. They make the work of Christ a cipher. They deprive him of his glory, and human idolatry rather than God's glory takes center stage.

Warning against Apostasy

Another striking feature of the text is the warning against apostasy. Paul warns the readers that if they accept circumcision, they will no longer derive any benefit from Christ. In other words, if they receive circumcision, they will be lost forever. Arminians understandably interpret these warnings to teach that believers can lose their salvation. Too often Reformed believers ignore such warnings altogether. I would argue that the warnings are the means God uses to preserve the faith of those whom he has chosen. Those who fall away demonstrate that they did not truly belong to God (1 John 2:19), but it does not follow from this that the warnings are addressed only to false believers. They are directed to the entire church, and God uses the severity of the warnings to remind believers of the need to keep trusting God until the end.

We may fall into the danger of abstracting the warnings from their reality by reading them in terms of an *ordo salutis* instead of reading them in terms of the history of redemption. If we contemplate the strong admonitions in Scripture from a viewpoint that transcends history, they can easily be thought of as superfluous. If, however, we grasp that warnings and admonitions are means God uses to preserve believers, the function of the warnings is preserved. The first hearers, and all readers since, should take the warning with utmost seriousness. If we rely on the law for salvation and thereby renounce Christ, there is no hope for salvation on the last day. The severity of the warning is intended to provoke readers to keep trusting Christ until the end, so that they do not turn to other gods for deliverance.

We could easily think that the bracing warning here falls prey to a kind of works righteousness. Such a conclusion would constitute a dramatic misreading of the Pauline intention. For what Paul calls for here can be summarized in two words: faith alone. In other words, apostasy in this context manifests itself as a reliance on circumcision and works of law. Hence, in calling on the readers to persevere, Paul summons them to keep trusting God. Perseverance is not conceived of as an arduous human work that receives God's blessing. Rather, it clings to Christ alone in faith, forsaking any trust or reliance on oneself. Those who belong to God know that their only hope of righteousness is in Christ.

Apostasy in Galatians constitutes reliance on one's own works, while those who persevere realize afresh every day that they are naked, miserable, and weak, and therefore they must rely on Christ and his righteousness alone for life. Faith looks eagerly ahead to the last day when the righteousness that is now ours through Christ is declared to the world and confirmed to us. Believers are now righteous by faith, but the world does not know that God counts believers as righteous in Christ, and believers themselves rely on God's promise that the final declaration is coming. Faith awaits that day in confidence, knowing that the eschatological verdict has already been announced in advance for those who trust in Christ.

Finally, to say faith alone saves does not mean that faith is alone. Faith embraces Christ and all of his benefits, and so it issues in love and every kind of good work. Love is the fruit of faith, the expression of a vibrant and living faith.

What if one were to object: "But I don't need a warning like this, because I am a true Christian and I will never fall away from Christ. He has promised to keep me by his grace"? I agree in part. He has promised to keep you by his grace. But the warnings are one of the means God uses to keep us in the good way of trusting in Christ. Warnings are not opposed to promises, but are one of the means God uses to fulfill his promises. Just like road signs keep us driving safely onto the highway, so warnings remind us to keep putting our trust in Christ.

Recently we had some friends staying with us, and they parked a rented van in back of our driveway. I joked that one day when pulling out of our garage I would hit it. One day our family had to go somewhere in a hurry. We jumped in the van and I backed up quickly. Suddenly our son, John, yelled out, "Dad. Stop!" I slammed on the breaks and missed the van that was parked out back. I had completely forgotten about it being there! John's warning was the means by which I avoided an accident. That's how God's warnings work too. They prevent us from falling away from Christ.

But how does a warning like this fit with the gospel? For it says that if we fall away from Christ, we will be damned. Doesn't this fill us with fear and impel us to trust in ourselves and to rely on our own works? God forbid! Do you see here that the Lord warns us against trusting in our righteousness and in our works? We have already seen that the sin that he warns the Galatians about is returning to the law and their own righteousness, about trusting in themselves rather than Christ. Paul isn't teaching works-righteousness but just the opposite. He encourages the Galatians to turn away from the law and to keep clinging to Christ, to keep trusting in Christ.

The warning, then, should not turn us to a kind of obsessive perfectionism but just the opposite. Paul warns us to trust in the cross alone for our salvation, to find our righteousness in Christ alone, to turn away from ourselves to God. The warning can be expressed this way: Don't trust in yourself but trust in Christ. Look to him alone. He is your hope, your strength, and your shield. Don't trust in your strength, your intellect, your wisdom, or your accomplishments. Look only to Christ.

Our future hope of righteousness also provides comfort. Luther is on target when he says:

> This is a very important and pleasant comfort with which to bring wonderful encouragement to minds afflicted and disturbed with a sense of sin and afraid of every flaming dart of the devil . . . your righteousness is not visible, and it is not conscious; but it is hoped for as something to be revealed in due time. Therefore you must not judge on the basis of your consciousness of sin, which terrifies and troubles you, but on the basis of the promise and teaching of faith, by which Christ is promised to you as your perfect and eternal righteousness.[34]

---

34. Luther, *Lectures on Galatians 1535: Chapters 1 – 4*, 21.

19

Galatians 5:7 – 12

Literary Context

The exhortation section commences in 4:12. Paul has explained from the Scriptures why the Galatians should not submit to the law in 3:1 – 4:11. He then forcefully applies those truths in the exhortation portion of the letter. The Galatians should become like Paul and live free from the law (4:12 – 20). They need to stand in the freedom they have gained in Christ (4:21 – 5:1).

In 5:2 – 4 the Galatians are urgently warned not to submit to circumcision, for to do such will separate them from Christ and will lead to final judgment. By way of contrast, those who live by faith and through the power of the Spirit will receive the eschatological verdict of righteousness. They eagerly await by faith the consummation of what God has promised (5:5). Living by faith is not animated by opposition to circumcision (5:6). Whether one is circumcised or uncircumcised remains insignificant. What matters is a genuine faith that expresses itself in love.

The argument shifts in 5:7 – 12 from the Galatians themselves to the adversaries who brought them a novel message. Paul emphasizes the deleterious effect of the opponents and declares that they will certainly face judgment. Still, he has confidence that the Galatians themselves will not be swayed. They will withstand the assault from the false teachers.

Finally, Paul turns to himself. It is scarcely the case that he himself advocates circumcision, for if he promoted such, he would escape persecution. Paul wishes that the opponents who are so enamored with circumcision and the cutting of the flesh would go the whole way and emasculate themselves. Paul emphasizes the judgment of the Judaizers in this paragraph so that the Galatians will not submit to their message, for if the Galatians follow the opponents, they will face the same judgment as the Judaizers. Therefore, 5:7 – 12 functions as an implicit exhortation to resist the false teachers.

I. Introduction: Desertion from Paul's Gospel Is Desertion from the Gospel (1:1 – 2:21)

II. Paul's Gospel Defended from Experience and Scripture (3:1 – 4:11)

III. A Call to Freedom from the Law and Freedom in the Spirit (4:12 – 6:10)

   A. Live in Freedom from the Law: Argument from Friendship (4:12 – 20)

   B. Stand in Freedom: Argument from Allegory (4:21 – 5:1)

   C. Resist the Dangerous Message of Bondage (5:2 – 12)

      1. It Involves the Requirement of Circumcision (5:2 – 6)

➡   **2. Its Perpetrators Will Be Judged (5:7 – 12)**

   D. Live Out Freedom in the Spirit (5:13 – 6:10)

Main Idea

Paul's central point here is that the encouragement to be circumcised is not from God. It stems from messengers who will themselves be judged on the final day. Nor is there any credibility to the claim that Paul has promoted circumcision. Despite all the clamor over circumcision, Paul remains confident that the Galatians will not succumb to the blandishments of the opponents.

Translation

Galatians 5:7-12

7a	assertion	**You were running well.**
b	rhetorical question	**Who hindered you**
c	result	so that you did not obey the truth?
8	assertion	**This persuasion is not from**
		the one who called you.
9	assertion	**A little leaven leavens the whole lump.**
10a	assertion	**I am persuaded in the Lord with reference to you that you will think no other way,**
b	contrast *(to 10a)*	but **the one disturbing you will bear his judgment,**
c	expansion *(of 10b)*	whoever he is.
11a	rhetorical question	And **I, brothers, if I still preach circumcision, why am I still persecuted?**
b	basis *(of 11a)*	For then the stumbling block of the cross has been removed.
12	exclamation	**I would that those who trouble you mutilate themselves.**

Structure

The Galatians were contemplating circumcision in contrast to the flying start they had as new believers. This section is loosely connected. Betz says, "The new section is freer, appearing like a rambling connection of pointed remarks, rhetorical questions, proverbial expressions, threats, irony, and, climaxing it all, a joke of stark sarcasm."[1] Hence, we are not surprised to see that structural markers that tie the verses together are infrequent.

The impetus for retrenchment from the gospel had come from outside teachers. The rhetorical question in 5:7 stimulates the readers to ask themselves why they were tripped up. In 5:8 – 9 Paul goes on the attack with short and pungent sentences. The Galatians had not received a message from God; rather, it was false teachers who wielded an infectious and pernicious influence, and hence they must not be tolerated. Despite the threat from the outside, Paul is convinced that the Galatians will keep running on the right path. They will not finally defect from the gospel (5:10a).

The opponents, however, will face certain judgment for attempting to trip them up. Nor can it be plausibly asserted that Paul is on the side of the opponents, as if he still promotes the message of circumcision (5:11). The persecution he constantly faces demonstrates that he proclaims the message of the cross. The opponents are nothing if not exasperating, and hence Paul muses that if they are so fascinated with the cutting of the genitals, they might as well go the entire way and cut off their male members.

Exegetical Outline

III. A Call to Freedom from the Law and Freedom in the Spirit (4:12 – 6:10)

    A. Live in Freedom from the Law: Argument from Friendship (4:12 – 20)

    B. Stand in Freedom: Argument from Allegory (4:21 – 5:1)

    C. Resist the Dangerous Message of Bondage (5:2 – 12)

        1. It involves the requirement of circumcision (5:2 – 6)

➡   **2. Its perpetrators will be judged (5:7 – 12)**

            a. They are interlopers (5:7)

            b. They are not God's messengers (5:8)

            c. Their pernicious influence (5:9)

            d. They will not succeed in winning over the Galatians (5:10)

            e. Their misrepresentation of Paul (5:11)

            f. Paul's prophetic exclamation (5:12)

    D. Live Out Freedom in the Spirit (5:13 – 6:10)

---

1. Betz, *Galatians*, 264. But against Betz, 5:12 is not appropriately identified as a joke.

Explanation of the Text

5:7 You were running well. Who hindered you so that you did not obey the truth? (Ἐτρέχετε καλῶς· τίς ὑμᾶς ἐνέκοψεν τῇ ἀληθείᾳ μὴ πείθεσθαι;). The Galatians began the race well as Christians, but someone cut in on them during the race. We saw in 3:1–5 that they received the Spirit by faith instead of relying on works of law. Running well, in other words, means that they responded to the gospel with trust in its message, relying on Christ rather than their own accomplishments.

Nevertheless, the race is long, and they are now in danger of stumbling. With a rhetorical question Paul asks who cut in on them during the race.[2] Their progress has been hindered so that they are in danger of not obeying the truth. Hays rightly observes, "Paul's choice of verb almost certainly carries a witty double entendre: the missionaries have 'cut in' on them by demanding to cut the flesh of their foreskins."[3]

The "truth" (ἀληθεία) here refers to the truth of the gospel. We might expect Paul to say that they do not believe in or trust in the truth of the gospel instead of obeying it. The importance of such obedience is found elsewhere in Paul (cf. Rom 10:16; 15:18). All obedience, however, is rooted in faith (cf. Rom 1:5; 16:26). Faith is the root and obedience is the fruit (1 Thess 1:3). Paul has already emphasized that faith expresses itself in love (5:6). Another way of putting it is that obeying the truth means believing the truth. Here John and Paul are

similar, for we find in John that the work God requires is believing (John 6:28–29). Outsiders have brought the Galatians to the brink of defection.[4]

5:8 This persuasion is not from the one who called you (ἡ πεισμονὴ οὐκ[5] ἐκ τοῦ καλοῦντος ὑμᾶς). Paul now passes judgment on those who hindered the Galatians as they were running the race. How should the interlopers be assessed? They should be categorically rejected, for they are not from God. In a pithy sentence Paul pronounces his verdict on the Judaizers. The passion of their missionary zeal has convinced some that the opponents must be proclaiming a divine message. Their influence in Galatia, however, does not suggest that they have God's imprimatur.[6] The reference to God's calling (καλοῦντος) is reminiscent of Gal 1:6, where even though the Galatians have been called by God, they are defecting. The God who has powerfully called the Galatians to faith is not, Paul affirms, speaking through the opponents.

5:9 A little leaven leavens the whole lump (μικρὰ ζύμη ὅλον τὸ φύραμα ζυμοῖ[7]). The evil introduced by the Judaizers will spread to the whole church if it is uncontained. This same phrase is used in a church discipline context, where the Corinthians are exhorted to remove the man committing incest from the church (1 Cor 5:6).

It is less clear that we have a church discipline context in Galatians. Paul does not command the Galatians to expel the false teachers per se,[8]

---

2. Cf. ibid., 264.

3. Hays, *Galatians*, 315.

4. The singular is generic here, and those who hindered the Galatians are the opponents, not Satan (contra Betz, *Galatians*, 264), though Satan lies behind the opponents.

5. The omission of "not" (οὐκ) is attested only by a few manuscripts and is clearly secondary. The omission turns the statement into a positive assertion about God or Paul as

a persuader.

6. Betz may be right here in suggesting that the ultimate "persuader" is the devil (*Galatians*, 265, n. 121). Cf. also Bruce, *Galatians*, 234.

7. A secondary but interesting variant from Western texts substitutes "adulterates" (δολοῖ) for "leavens" (ζυμοῖ).

8. Rightly Fee, *Galatians*, 194. Contra Hansen, *Abraham in Galatians*, 146; Hays, *Galatians*, 315.

probably because they are not members of the church but have come from the outside. Rather, he underscores the adverse influence of the false teachers. The Galatians must not succumb to their teaching; otherwise, the deviant theology will spread. Paul does not explicitly call on the Galatians to expel the teachers from the community, but he does exhort them not to submit to their theology.

5:10a I am persuaded in the Lord with reference to you that you will think no other way (ἐγὼ πέποιθα εἰς ὑμᾶς ἐν κυρίῳ ὅτι οὐδὲν ἄλλο φρονήσετε). Despite the presence and influence of the adversaries and the remarkable collapse of the Galatians upon hearing the teachers, Paul remains confident (πέποιθα)[9] that the Galatians will ultimately persevere on the right course, for the Lord who began the good work in them will bring it to completion (cf. Phil 1:6). Apparently Paul is convinced that his warnings will be just the tonic that the Galatians need to come to their senses. Though they have been staggered by the false teachers, he is convinced in the Lord that they will not ultimately be persuaded by them. They will find their footing and resist the deviant gospel that the teachers have been attempting to impose on them.

The incredibly strong warning in 5:2–4 is now balanced by the word of assurance. Perhaps it is better to say that the warning actually becomes a means of assurance, for Paul is persuaded that the Galatians will heed his admonitions and continue on the road of faith.[10] But we should add here that

Paul's assurance does not rest on any recent good news from Galatia or confidence in the Galatians themselves. His confidence rests in the Lord, whose grace will sustain the Galatians to the end.[11] Lightfoot remarks that "ἐν κυρίῳ ['in the Lord'] here denotes not the object of the writer's confidence but the sphere in which it is exercised."[12]

5:10b-c But the one disturbing you will bear his judgment, whoever he is (ὁ δὲ ταράσσων ὑμᾶς βαστάσει τὸ κρίμα, ὅστις ἐὰν ᾖ). The opponents, by contrast, will not escape judgment. They will experience God's eschatological retribution for creating havoc in the Galatian churches. Jesus himself said something rather similar: "Woe to the world because of the things that cause people to sin! Such things must come, but woe to the man through whom they come!" (Matt 18:7).

The singular "the one disturbing" (ὁ ταράσσων) is used here with reference to the opponents, while the plural "those disturbing" (οἱ ταράσσοντες) occurs in 1:7. Perhaps the leader of the Judaizers is denoted here with the singular participle.[13] It is also possible, however, that the singular form is generic, denoting the adversaries as a whole;[14] this seems more probable.

In any case, the future phrase "will bear judgment" (βαστάσει τὸ κρίμα) assures the Galatians that those who annoy them with a deviant gospel will not be spared on the last day.[15] The verb "will bear" (βαστάσει) is also used with reference to the final judgment in 6:5, where each believer will "bear" his or her own load before God on the final day. In the present verse, of course, the focus is on

---

9. Dahl observes here that we have an epistolary statement of confidence ("Paul's Letter to the Galatians," 138–39). He rightly emphasizes that Paul is convinced that his letter will have the right effect on the Galatians. Against Longenecker, the perfect tense here should not be read in terms of the past (*Galatians*, 231). It denotes here Paul's present confidence.

10. Betz's comments here fail to reflect Paul's confidence (*Galatians*, 267).

11. Rightly Bruce, *Galatians*, 235; Martyn, *Galatians*, 475; Dunn, *Galatians*, 277.

12. Lightfoot, *Galatians*, 206; cf. Garlington, *Galatians*, 313.

13. So Betz, *Galatians*, 267; Fee, *Galatians*, 195.

14. So Bruce, *Galatians*, 235–36; Longenecker, *Galatians*, 232; Hays, *Galatians*, 316.

15. In support of an eschatological judgment, see Longenecker, *Galatians*, 232.

the adverse consequences that will be the portion of the false teachers.

Some have construed the words "whoever he is" as if Paul does know the identity of the leader among the false teachers.[16] It seems that Paul is rather well informed about what is happening in Galatia. Instead of confessing ignorance about the leader's identity, he emphasizes God's impartiality in judgment. No one who teaches falsely will receive an exemption from God's judgment. Their reputation or stature is irrelevant. If they introduce destructive teaching into the church, they will not be spared on the last day.

5:11a And I, brothers, if I still preach circumcision, why am I still persecuted? (ἐγὼ δέ, ἀδελφοί, εἰ περιτομὴν ἔτι[17] κηρύσσω, τί ἔτι διώκομαι;). What Paul says here is a matter of dispute, for we lack the necessary historical information to determine what he has in mind.[18] Apparently some maintained that he continued to promulgate circumcision, but this is contradicted, says Paul, by the fact that he is being persecuted. First, it could refer to Paul's pre-Christian preaching, but we lack evidence in either Paul or Judaism that proselytizing Gentiles was common.[19]

Second, Howard suggests that the agitators were unaware that Paul opposed circumcision.[20]

He thinks that the opponents said that Paul had not explained to the Galatians all that was necessary for Christian discipleship, but he fully intended to supplement what he had first taught them. This interpretation fails to convince. I have already argued that the adversaries attacked Paul's apostolic authority, and hence they did not have such a sunny view of his person (cf. 1:1; 1:10 – 2:21). It is difficult to believe that the content of Paul's gospel was such a well-kept secret. Furthermore, Paul's words about persecution (5:11) suggest that the charge was hypocrisy. The opponents claimed that Paul did not proclaim the necessity of circumcision because he wanted to curry the favor of the Galatians.

Third, the most likely view is that the opponents accused Paul of inconsistency, in that he preached circumcision among the Jews. We know from the circumcision of Timothy (Acts 16:3) that Paul had no problems with Jews receiving circumcision as long as it was not required for salvation.[21] Even if Timothy's circumcision was in the future relative to the date of Galatians, it probably signals Paul's practice relative to Jewish Christians. Circumcision was acceptable for social and cultural reasons as long as it was not required for salvation. The Galatian opponents likely charged Paul with

---

16. Bruce, *Galatians*, 236.

17. Probably "still" (ἔτι) was removed by some scribes because they questioned whether Paul *had ever* preached the necessity of circumcision. In any case, the omission obviously represents a secondary reading.

18. For the various possibilities, see Betz, *Galatians*, 268 – 69; Dunn, *Galatians*, 278 – 80.

19. See Scot McKnight, *A Light among the Gentiles: Jewish Missionary Activity in the Second Temple Period* (Minneapolis: Fortress, 1991).

20. Howard, *Paul: Crisis in Galatia.* A view that is similar in some respects is proposed by Winger. Winger claims that the Pauline opponents ate unclean food with the Gentiles in Galatia and hence did not keep the entire law; they "did not attack Paul directly" (567); they did not grasp Paul's stance on the law; they preached the law as the solution to

the problem of the flesh; and they buttressed their authority by appealing to their relation to the church in Jerusalem. See Michael Winger, "Act One: Paul Arrives in Galatia," *NTS* 48 (2002): 548 – 67. Winger is probably correct in saying that the opponents appealed to Jerusalem and perhaps they brought in the law to counter the flesh. It is difficult to believe, however, that the opponents ate unclean food. If such were the case, it is difficult to see why they believed circumcision was necessary. Further, against Winger, it is unlikely that they did not understand Paul's view of the law, and that they did not counter Paul. I argue in this commentary (see the introduction) that there are solid reasons for thinking that they opposed Paul directly and that they understood his view on the law.

21. Fee dates Galatians later and hence sees a reference to the circumcision of Timothy here (*Galatians*, 195).

hypocrisy and a desire to avoid conflict in leaving out the requirement to be circumcised. But they failed to represent Paul's view fairly, for he always, after his conversion, refused to circumcise if it was required for salvation (2:3 – 5).

5:11b For then the stumbling block of the cross has been removed (ἄρα κατήργηται τὸ σκάνδαλον τοῦ σταυροῦ). The word "then" (ἄρα) here should be understood as an inferential particle, so that Paul is drawing a conclusion from the previous statement. If Paul proclaimed the necessity of circumcision, he would have certainly avoided persecution, for then the scandal of the cross would be eliminated. Circumcision nullifies the scandal of the cross because it establishes righteousness based on human ability. If righteousness comes by the law, then the goodness of human beings is celebrated and promoted.

The cross, however, rejects any and all human attempts to be right with God. Righteousness is found only in what Christ Jesus has done for sinners. The message of the cross is a scandal or a stumbling block because it is an affront to human pride. Human beings take umbrage in being told that even their best works are stained with evil, that everything they do is insufficient to be right with God, and that the only basis for right standing with God is the cross of Jesus Christ.

5:12 I would that those who trouble you mutilate themselves (ὄφελον καὶ ἀποκόψονται οἱ ἀναστατοῦντες ὑμᾶς). The exclamation here is shocking. The opponents are characterized as troublemakers (cf. the verb ἀναστατόω also occurs in Acts 17:6; 21:38). This fits with what Paul has said about them earlier in the letter (1:7; 5:10). The trouble they inflict comes from their preoccupation with circumcision. Paul wishes that they would go the whole way with the knife and emasculate themselves. The verb "mutilate" (ἀποκόπτω) is used in the LXX of the cutting off of the penis (Deut 23:1; 23:2 LXX).[22] Paul now considers the covenantal rite of circumcision to be no better than a pagan cutting.

We see the same sentiment in Phil 3:2, where circumcision is no longer a sign of dedication to God but is dismissed as mutilation. Any attempt to derive right standing with God by human effort is nothing other than paganism, according to Paul (cf. Gal 4:3, 8 – 9), and hence it must be resisted both root and branch. Those who are so taken with circumcision as a means to enter the people of God are actually cutting themselves off from God's people.[23]

Theology in Application

Responding to False Teachers

What has precipitated the Galatians' wavering with reference to the gospel are false teachers who have come from the outside proclaiming a variant message. Difficulties in the Christian life come from within and without. Here we see that the Galatians' defection does not stem from their own doubts about the Pauline gospel. Others have come from the outside and have raised questions about the legitimacy of Paul's teaching.

---

22. If this is the case, Paul refers here not to castration but the removal of the penis. So Hardin, *Galatians and the*

Imperial Cult, 7.

23. Cf. Barrett, *Freedom and Obligation,* 70.

Often difficulties arise in the Christian life when believers begin to doubt the truth of the gospel. Deviant teachings abound, and intellectual objections to the Christian faith seem to have no end. Part of what it means to persevere is to continue to believe in the gospel despite the objections that are constantly raised against it. Persistence in faith takes place in the midst of trials and difficulties. Faith battles through the uncertainties and perplexities raised by life and continues to trust Christ to the end. Though many cast aspersions on the gospel, though close friends may depart from the faith that has been handed down once-for-all (Jude 3), faith continues to cling to Christ and to reject all false gospels. True believers know that trials are God's appointed means for reaching the Jerusalem that is above.

Recently there have been a number of books promoting atheism. Christopher Hitchens, journalist and author, has written a book titled *God Is Not Great*. The British scientist Richard Dawkins has recently authored a book titled *The God Delusion*. Sam Harris, who has a PhD in neuroscience, has in the last three years written two books: *The End of Faith* and *Letter to a Christian Nation*. How should we respond?

The first thing to say is that such books should not worry or trouble us. As Christians we should not have a fortress mentality. There is no need to panic when people question our faith. There is nothing new under the sun. We have weathered attacks like these for a long time. We should not fear to read books like this, as long as we are aware of the compelling responses to what they have written.

For example, ChristianityToday.com has a six-part discussion and debate between the atheist Christopher Hitchens and Douglas Wilson. You can go online and read those. I think you would be struck by how the Christian, Douglas Wilson, wins the debate decisively. Hitchens can never explain why something is good rather than evil. Wilson asks Hitchens again and again to do so, but Hitchens either avoids the question or comes up with nothing.

Furthermore, you should know that Dawkins' book has come in for scathing criticism, even by some who are secularists. The quality of his book has not impressed people. As for Sam Harris, Doug Wilson has also written a response titled *Letter from a Christian Citizen*. We can be confident that the Christian faith is true. One of my favorite quotes comes from Edith Schaeffer, who was asked why someone should believe in the Christian faith. Her reply was, "Because it is true." Not because it works, or it makes us feel better, but because it is true.

Confidence in the Lord

Paul's word of assurance in 5:10 provides confidence that the Lord will finish the good work he has begun (Phil 1:6). The Lord saves and continues to preserve until the end those whom he has called. Therefore, the confidence of believers is not ultimately in themselves but in the Lord, who summoned them to himself. Believers look away from themselves to Christ and trust his promise that he will keep all those who have entrusted their lives to him. When believers turn inward and contemplate their own resources, they know that they do not have the wherewithal to continue in the faith. In many texts, of course, believers are exhorted to continue to the end and to remain immoveable in the things of the Lord. Ultimately, however, assurance of obtaining a heavenly reward comes from the Lord himself. He strengthens his own so that they do not turn from the Lord who rescued them from this present evil age (1:4).

If believers proclaim the cross of Jesus Christ, persecution will come. The extent of persecution varies depending on circumstances and culture. In some instances, persecution may take the form of verbal abuse, harsh criticism, and discrimination. In other situations, believers may be physically abused, tortured, and even put to death.

The fundamental root of all persecution is resistance to the gospel. The world despises the cross, for the cross pronounces a thunderous no to all human goodness. The cross lays us bare before God and exposes our wickedness and evil. The cross reminds us that the solution to the human problem is death and resurrection, while we as human beings think that we can be reformed and transformed with education and civilizing influences. When the message of the cross breaks upon the human consciousness, we either repent or are enraged at such an affront to our egos. We long for a gospel that commends us, makes us feel good about ourselves, and exalts us. The cross, however, renounces human potential. It teaches us to relinquish our hope that human beings can construct a just and good society. The new creation only comes through the cross, but the cross is not the last word; the last word is resurrection.

20

Galatians 5:13 – 15

Literary Context

The heart and soul of Paul's argument against the opponents has been completed. Paul has defended his apostolic authority (1:1 – 2:21), for in doing so he has defended his gospel. He has also argued in some detail against the theology of the Judaizers (3:1 – 4:11). He longs for the readers to become as he is (4:12) — free from the law. He warns them about the devasting consequences of submitting to circumcision (5:2 – 4). Outsiders have caused the trouble, and yet Paul remains confident that the Galatians will not depart from the gospel (5:10). Apparently, he believes his exhortations will prevent them from capitulating to the view of the false teachers.

In the section from 5:13 – 6:10 Paul continues to exhort his readers (the exhortation section began in 4:12). Now Paul particularly warns his readers against libertinism so that their liberty in Christ does not become an excuse for licentiousness. What precipitates Paul's instructions here? It has occasionally been suggested that two different opponents are in view in Galatia, so that 1:1 – 5:12 is directed against legalists and 5:13 – 6:10 to libertines. Few scholars, however, have believed that such a partition is convincing. Evidence for two sets of adversaries is scarcely clear, and other explanations for the inclusion of 5:13 – 6:10 are more persuasive.[1] Some have suggested, more plausibly, that Paul anticipates a possible overreaction to his teaching on freedom from law. Freedom from law does not mean freedom from all moral obligations. Life in the Spirit expresses itself in service to others.

Betz intriguingly suggests another possibility that is compatible with what is said above. The Judaizers made significant inroads among the Galatians because the Galatians had already, before the Judaizers arrived, misunderstood the Pauline gospel. The Galatians had misconstrued what it meant to live in the Spirit and had yielded in significant ways to the flesh.[2] Hence, the Judaizers appealed to a felt need for moral order and discipline among the Galatians. In the main substance of the letter, Paul dismantles the theology of the Judaizers. He must also, however, coun-

---

1. For a fuller discussion of the possibilities set forth here, see the introduction.

2. Betz, *Galatians*, 8 – 9, 273; cf. Bruce, *Galatians*, 240; Longenecker, *Galatians*, 238.

ter the problem that gave the teachers a foothold in Galatia in the first place, and hence at the end of the letter he explains that true life in the Spirit does not lead to libertinism.

Betz's reconstruction is certainly possible, but it suffers from lack of evidence, since Paul gives us no indication that the Galatians struggled with libertinism before the arrival of the Judaizers. And he reminds them that he warned them about the danger of libertinism previously (5:21), before the Judaizers ever arrived. Another solution seems to be more promising. The notion that Paul wants to dissuade the Galatians from an overreaction is plausible, demonstrating Paul's pastoral wisdom as he anticipates a possible extreme response to the letter.

It is also possible that Paul's argument moves in another direction. Life under the law actually leads to the reign of sin, for the law does not restrain sin but increases it. Therefore, the solution to moral disorder is not the law but the Spirit. Faith is never a cipher that sits idle, but it invariably produces a life pleasing to God.

I. Introduction: Desertion from Paul's Gospel Is Desertion from the Gospel (1:1 – 2:21)

II. Paul's Gospel Defended from Experience and Scripture (3:1 – 4:11)

III. A Call to Freedom from the Law and Freedom in the Spirit (4:12 – 6:10)

    A. Live in Freedom from the Law: Argument from Friendship (4:12 – 20)

    B. Stand in Freedom: Argument from Allegory (4:21 – 5:1)

    C. Resist the Dangerous Message of Bondage (5:2 – 12)

    D. Live Out Freedom in the Spirit (5:13 – 6:10)

➡   **1. Freedom Expressed in Love (5:13 – 15)**

       2. Living by the Spirit Instead of the Flesh (5:16 – 24)

Main Idea

Believers are free from the law in Christ, but true freedom expresses itself in serving and loving others, not in satisfying selfish desires. Such freedom represents the fulfillment of the OT law.

Translation

(See next page.)

Galatians 5:13-15

13a	assertion	For, **brothers, you were called for the purpose of freedom,**
b	qualification *(of 13a)*	only **do not use your freedom as an opportunity for the flesh,**
c	contrast *(to 13b)*	but **become slaves of one another through love.**
14a	basis *(of 13a-c)*	For **the whole law is fulfilled** **in one word,**
b	explanation *(of 14a)*	namely, in the word,
c	comparison *(of 14b)*	*"You shall love your neighbor as you love yourself."* (Lev 19:8)
15a	condition	But if you bite and devour one another,
b	exhortation	**beware lest you are consumed by one another.**

Structure

The "for" (γάρ) in 5:13 probably functions to introduce a new section.[3] The Galatians have been summoned by God to freedom from the law. Others argue that the "for" reaches back to 5:1, where Paul proclaims that Christ set us free for freedom.[4] In terms of content, we can see that 5:13 fits nicely with 5:1. But it seems unlikely that the "for" here reaches back so many verses. The call to freedom fits well with 5:2 – 12, for the demand that the Galatians receive circumcision is bondage. Indeed, it puts them under a debt (5:3), and such oppression does not square with the freedom that is theirs in Christ.

Still, this freedom must be rightly understood. It does not function as an excuse for satisfying selfish desires but expresses itself paradoxically in serving one another in love. Verse 14 functions as the ground for 5:13 ("for," [γάρ]). Believers are to serve one another in love because such service fulfills the OT law. In particular it fulfills the admonition in Lev 19:18 to love one's neighbor as oneself. In 5:15 Paul again contrasts love with actions that divide the church. If the Galatians turn against each other and resort to harsh criticism and judgmental attitudes, they will destroy the church.

Exegetical Outline

III. A Call to Freedom from the Law and Freedom in the Spirit (4:12 – 6:10)
A. Live in Freedom from the Law: Argument from Friendship (4:12 – 20)
B. Stand in Freedom: Argument from Allegory (4:21 – 5:1)
C. Resist the Dangerous Message of Bondage (5:2 – 12)

---

3. So Fee, *Galatians*, 203.   4. So Longenecker, *Galatians*, 238 – 39.

Explanation of the Text

5:13a For, brothers, you were called for the purpose of freedom (Ὑμεῖς γὰρ ἐπ᾽ ἐλευθερίᾳ ἐκλήθητε, ἀδελφοί). In a ringing statement Paul says that believers are called by God to be free, and he thinks especially of freedom from the law. The word "for" (γάρ) seems to function as a transitional particle here, introducing this new section and relating generally to the previous verses that warn the Galatians against falling prey to a message that enslaves them. The Judaizers were unsettling and disturbing the Galatians, but the Galatians were not called by God to be troubled over whether they were observing the OT law. When God effectually called them, he summoned them to freedom.

The prepositional phrase "for freedom" (ἐπ᾽ ἐλευθερίᾳ) should be understood here as denoting purpose.[5] In summoning the Galatians to himself, the Lord called them to be free from the OT law, and in particular, the requirement of circumcision.[6] The burden of attempting to be right with God on the basis of one's obedience no longer applies to believers, for they enjoy the freedom of being redeemed from the curse of the law through the crosswork of Jesus Christ (3:13; 4:4 – 5). Hence, they live in freedom and joy as God's children. It should also be noted that the Galatians are identified as

"brothers," in contrast to the opponents, who were the focus of the previous paragraph.

5:13b Only do not use your freedom as an opportunity for the flesh (μόνον μὴ τὴν ἐλευθερίαν εἰς ἀφορμὴν τῇ σαρκί). The word "only" (μόνον) signals a qualification of the previous statement so that it is not misunderstood. The freedom to which believers are called must not be distorted or debased by the flesh. The "flesh" here stands for the old age of redemptive history, the identity of human beings in Adam. Believers, of course, are no longer in Adam but in Christ, and yet they live in the period between the times in the history of salvation so that living in accord with the flesh is still a possibility. They must not deceive themselves so that their freedom in Christ becomes a pretext for the flesh. Elsewhere in Paul we see that sin used the law as a "bridgehead" for its further operations (ἀφορμή, Rom 7:8, 11). Here the concern is that freedom may be abused and become an occasion for the selfish will to dominate.

5:13c But become slaves of one another through love (ἀλλὰ διὰ τῆς ἀγάπης[7] δουλεύετε ἀλλήλοις). The freedom to which the Lord called the Galatians was never intended to become an excuse for selfish desire or the furtherance of sin. True

---

5. See BDF §235 (4); Bruce, *Galatians*, 240; Longenecker, *Galatians*, 239.

6. The passive verb "you were called" (ἐκλήθητε) indicates that God is the one who has done the calling. So Betz, *Gala-*

tians, 271 – 72; Longenecker, *Galatians*, 238.

7. A secondary but fascinating Western reading speaks of "love of the Spirit," perhaps motivated by Gal 5:22, where Paul speaks of love as the fruit of the Spirit.

freedom manifests itself as slavery (δουλεύετε), as serving one another in love.

Hays writes that "this formulation comes as a shocking paradox."[8] Freedom suggests to human beings an open door to fulfill natural desires, but subjection to such desires is not freedom but slavery. True freedom liberates believers from their selfish will so that they find joy in serving others. Freedom manifests itself as love,[9] as a desire to fulfill the needs of others. As Wilson notes, what Paul says here picks up the exodus story, where the Lord freed Israel so that they would serve him (Exod 4:23; 19:4 – 6; 20:1 – 6; Lev 25:42).[10] The redemption believers enjoy liberates them to pursue goodness so that they serve others with gladness.

5:14 For the whole law is fulfilled in one word, namely, in the word, "You shall love your neighbor as you love yourself" (ὁ γὰρ πᾶς νόμος ἐν ἑνὶ λόγῳ πεπλήρωται,[11] ἐν τῷ Ἀγαπήσεις τὸν πλησίον σου ὡς σεαυτόν). The word "for" (γάρ) indicates that the basis for 5:13 is now provided. It is fitting for the freedom of believers to express itself in loving service to others, for such loving service fulfills the message of the OT law.[12]

It is astonishing that Paul speaks here of fulfilling the OT law after emphasizing in such detail that believers are no longer under the OT law.[13] In 5:3 Paul has just stated that believers ought not to receive circumcision because if they do so they are obligated to keep the whole law. Here he turns around and says that the entire law is fulfilled in loving one another, and he cites Lev 19:18.[14] Is there a contradiction here, as Räisänen asserts?[15] Does Paul affirm freedom from the law in 5:3, and then in opposition to all that he has said in the letter, insist on an obligation to keep the law in 5:14?

Such a claim of contradiction should be rejected, for it is improbable that Paul had forgotten what was said in 5:3. Indeed, Paul has emphasized freedom from the law throughout the letter (even in 5:11!), and hence it is scarcely possible that it has left his consciousness. When we compare the two verses, the differences between them are striking. (1) For instance, 5:3 focuses on "debtor" (ὀφειλέτης), but in 5:13 Paul emphasizes "freedom" (ἐλευθερία). In 5:3 doing the whole law is a burden, but in 5:14 fulfilling the whole law accords with freedom.

(2) Verse 3 focuses on "doing" (ποιῆσαι) the law, whereas 5:14 refers to "fulfilling" (πεπλήρωται)

---

8. Hays, *Galatians*, 321.

9. Against Longenecker, the article "the" (τῆς) does not revert to 2:20 or even 5:6 (*Galatians*, 241). The article is simply being used with an abstract noun here.

10. Wilson, "Wilderness Apostasy," 566 – 68.

11. The Western and Majority Text types read a present tense here (πληροῦται), and a few manuscripts read "sums up" (ἀνακεφαλαιοῦται) to harmonize with Rom 13:9, but the reading in NA[27] is surely original ($\mathfrak{P}^{46}$, ℵ, A, B, C, 062, 0254, 33, 81, 104, 326, 1175, 1241^s, 1739, etc.).

12. Betz in his commentary adduces a number of parallels between this section (5:13 – 6:10) and Hellenistic literature, but Barclay demonstrates that many of the alleged parallels do not accord with the subject matter of Galatians (*Obeying the Truth*, 170 – 77). Indeed, Betz veers rather dramatically off course in saying that we do not have "a specifically Christian ethic" in Galatians, so that Paul simply reproduces "what would be expected of any other educated person in the Hellenistic culture of the time" (*Galatians*, 292). The focus on the

fulfillment of the OT law, the Holy Spirit, the cross, and the new creation indicate, on the contrary, that Paul sees in the lives of believers the fulfillment of the eschatological promises found in the OT. Therefore, it is incorrect to rule out any reference to the Mosaic law here (rightly Wilson, *Curse of the Law*, 100 – 104).

13. Hübner argues that 5:14 does not refer to the Mosaic law since this would contradict 5:3, and contends that 5:14 should be understood ironically, with the result that the law is reduced to the command to love one another (*Law in Paul's Thought*, 36 – 37). But against this view, Paul clearly refers to the Mosaic law in 5:14, and it is scarcely apparent that the reference is ironic. Hong solves the dilemma by saying that 5:3 refers to the law in terms of the Mosaic covenant, while 5:14 refers to the law in terms of God's will (*Law in Galatians*, 172 – 73).

14. Against Hays, there is no suggestion that Lev 19:18 is construed as a promise here (*Galatians*, 324).

15. Heikki Räisänen, *Paul and the Law* (Philadelphia: Fortress, 1986), 113 – 14.

the law.[16] Doing the law is required for justification and is unattainable, while fulfilling the law is the consequence of justification and the result of the Spirit's work.[17]

(3) Furthermore, the expression "the whole law" is distinct in 5:3 and 5:14, for the former has "the entire law" (ὅλον τὸν νόμον) while the latter has "the whole law" (ὁ πᾶς νόμος).[18]

(4) Finally, the context of the two statements must be distinguished, for the requirement of doing the whole law appears in a context where the Galatians were threatened with judgment if they submitted to circumcision. The fulfilling of the entire law occurs in a context where true freedom expresses itself in serving others through love.

It is somewhat surprising that Paul does not follow Jesus in seeing the fulfillment of the whole law in terms of love for God and for neighbor (Matt 22:34 – 40). Instead he restricts himself to love of neighbor and sees in it the fulfillment of the whole law. Perhaps the focus is on loving neighbors because social relationships dominate this section of Galatians. The mark of love is the ability of believers to get along with one another.

Furthermore, there is ample biblical teaching supporting the notion that love for God manifests itself in love for others. The biblical citation stems from Lev 19:18 and conforms exactly to what is written there. The text does not suggest that human beings need to learn to love themselves before they can love others.[19] Instead, it *assumes* that we love ourselves, in that we invariably seek our own interests. Love, then, seeks out the interests of others and pursues their best.

The various commands of the law, insofar as they relate to interaction with human beings, are summarized in this command.[20] Commands like "do not steal" and "do not murder" and "do not commit adultery" are simply ways of saying, "show love to the neighbor" (cf. Rom 13:8 – 10). Indeed, no rule book could ever summarize all that is involved in loving others, for life is too varied and complex to codify how love expresses itself.

Those who are free from the law, however, and empowered by the Holy Spirit live a life of love.[21] Love does not go around the moral norms of the law, nor does it violate them, but it does transcend them. Indeed, the call to love probably reflects "the law of Christ" (6:2), and Christ himself modeled that love in his self-giving for his people (2:20). So too, believers live out the law of Christ when they give themselves for the good of others.

5:15 But if you bite and devour one another, beware lest you be consumed by one another (εἰ δὲ ἀλλήλους δάκνετε καὶ κατεσθίετε, βλέπετε μὴ ὑπ᾽ ἀλλήλων ἀναλωθῆτε). Freedom must not be equated with dissension and squabbling, for that

---

16. See here Stephen Westerholm, "On Fulfilling the Whole Law (Gal 5:14)," *SEÅ* 51 – 52 (1986 – 87): 233 – 37. Cf. also Betz, *Galatians*, 275; Wilson, *Curse of the Law*, 107 – 12. Still, Westerholm wrongly says that Gal 5:14 is not a command (235), and underestimates the role of commands and "doing" in Pauline theology.

17. Garlington disputes the distinction between "fulfilling" and "doing" the law (*Galatians*, 232). Contra Wilson, it is not clear that Paul calls for the fulfillment of the law here to avoid incurring the curse of the law (*Curse of the Law*, 104 – 16). The connection posited by Wilson is never clearly enunciated by Paul. Paul does speak of the necessity of righteousness to enter the kingdom (5:21) and to avoid eschatological corruption (6:8), but not to prevent them from receiving the law's curse.

18. I actually translate the two the same in the commentary, but give a different translation here to highlight the different contexts in which the phrases occur.

19. Rightly Fee, *Galatians*, 205.

20. Martyn conceives of the law here differently, seeing Christ as the subject of the verb "fulfill" and thus as the one who has brought the law to completion (*Galatians*, 490 – 91). For further explication of his view, see 503 – 24.

21. Therefore, the fulfillment of the law fulfills the new covenant prophecy of Jer 31:31 – 34 and the promised gift of the Holy Spirit (Isa 32:15; 44:3; 59:21; Ezek 11:19; 36:26 – 27; 37:14; 39:29; Joel 2:28 – 32). See here Wilson, *Curse of the Law*, 110.

would tear the church apart. When we examine the exhortations in Galatians, a focus on social relationships is evident, and that is borne out by this verse as well. The Galatians are admonished in colorful terms not to turn into animals that gnaw at and eat one another.[22] The word "bite" (δάκνετε) is often used in the OT of serpents (Gen 49:17; Num 21:6, 8, 9; Deut 8:15; Eccl 10:8, 11; Am 5:19; 9:3; Jer 8:17). If these texts are echoed here, Paul sharply distinguishes between life in the Spirit and that which is "demonic." The Galatians must never think that freedom opens the door for fierce criticism and hatred for others. If poisonous speech erupts and remains unchecked, the church will be undone and destroyed. It will internally implode unless such hatred is checked. The Spirit liberates believers to restrain evil; it does not give free reign to evil impulses.

Theology in Application

Freedom versus Natural Desire

True freedom must never be equated with natural human desires. Human beings as sons and daughters of Adam conceive of freedom as the removal of all constraints so that we are able to do whatever we want. Freedom for Paul, however, cannot be equated with natural desire, for the latter is the product of the flesh and a human will turned upon itself.

Human beings are truly free when they are no longer under the dominion of natural desires. Freedom does not come by giving into selfish desire but, paradoxically enough, is found when believers serve others. Those who are constrained by natural desires are not free but slaves, whereas those who live in love are liberated to serve others, so that slavery to the will of God is perfect freedom. Such freedom will only be perfectly realized in the new creation, for then believers will always and only desire to do the will of God. Perfect submission to God's will means perfect freedom.

Our deepest desires are realized when we do God's will, and we will see even more clearly in the age to come than we do now that submission to our own selfish desires was a terrible bondage. In the present evil age, however, we have the first-fruits of the Spirit, and hence we experience in part the freedom of the new creation and the joys of obedience to God.

We can become enslaved to something by emphasizing our freedom. Some Christians go to movies that they cannot handle but excuse it by emphasizing their freedom. Others become enslaved to alcohol by emphasizing their freedom, and suddenly they find themselves getting drunk. Others may even defend smoking marijuana by emphasizing their so-called freedom. I have heard a person even defend looking at pornography by appealing to freedom. Truly the siren song of freedom can become a platform for the flesh.

---

22. Russell argues that the Judaizers were falling into the sins proscribed here. "Galatians 5:13 – 26," 341 – 42. But against this, see Betz, who also rightly remarks that Paul's language here is "hyperbolic" (*Galatians*, 277).

What is true freedom? Paul tells us what true freedom is. We are living by grace if we don't become angry when we disagree with one another. If we shout and yell to win arguments, we are not secure in the gospel. We have to prove we are right. But if we live by grace, we can firmly state the truth and even restate it if necessary and leave the results to God.

The True Purpose of OT Law

Love fulfills the true purpose of the OT law. On the one hand, believers are no longer under the Mosaic law and its prescriptions. On the other hand, believers by the Spirit now fulfill what the law intended. Neither Paul nor any other writer operates strictly with the ceremonial, civil, and moral divisions in the law that are familiar to us from church history.[23] It is not as if the ceremonial and civil laws have passed away and the moral law is still binding on believers. Instead, Paul argues that the Mosaic covenant and the law as a whole have passed away.

Still, it does not follow that there is only discontinuity between the OT and the NT. Life in the Spirit also represents the fulfillment of the OT law. The Mosaic covenant and the OT law point to Christ and are fulfilled in Jesus Christ. The law is both abolished and fulfilled in Christ. In order to trace out the lines of continuity and discontinuity, we must read the Scriptures in terms of the unfolding story of God's redemption. The OT law must be read in light of the fulfillment that has dawned in Jesus Christ, for he is the sovereign interpreter of the law (cf. Matt 5:17 – 48).

We see from the NT witness that the OT law pointed to Christ in a number of ways, and that there is continuity between many of the moral norms in the OT and the command to love one another. It is clear from Rom 13:8 – 10, which is remarkably parallel to Gal 5:14, that love manifests itself in keeping the commandments. No one can claim to love and then commit adultery, murder, steal, or covet. Such moral norms help us to discern the contours of love so that love does not become a plastic thing that is twisted to fit selfish desire.

Love, of course, can never be exhausted by moral norms, for no moral rule book can comprehend the thousand decisions that must be made every day. Here love and the prompting of the Spirit constitute the guide for believers. But even if love cannot be exhausted by moral norms, neither does it ignore such norms. Moral rules are not the whole of love or even the heart of love, but they are still part of love. After all, one could still be enslaved to selfish desires and refrain from murder, adultery, and stealing. Therefore, love must stand as the heart and soul of a biblical ethic, and it can never be completely codified or detailed in a modern day Mishnah. Love asks how others can be served and edified in a way that accords with the gospel of Jesus Christ.

---

23. Against *Augustine's Commentary on Galatians*, 205, 207.

If you are a husband, you are free if you ask yourself, "How can I serve my wife and make her stronger in the Lord?" If you are a wife, you ask, "In what ways can I support and affirm my husband, so that he is strengthened spiritually?" And we can all ask: "How can I serve others in the body of Christ? What would the Lord have me do? What can I do with my life that will help others mature spiritually or bring them to faith in Christ?" If you are saying to yourself, "That doesn't sound like freedom but slavery," then you don't know what true freedom is. You are still enslaved to your own selfish desires.

Galatians 5:16 – 24

Literary Context

The exhortation section of the letter, which began in 4:12, continues. The Galatians are to follow Paul's example by living in freedom from the Mosaic law (4:12 – 20). They are to stand in the freedom that is theirs in Christ (4:21 – 5:1). They must not submit to circumcision and must resist the inducements to do so from the false teachers (5:2 – 12). They were called to freedom, and such freedom manifests itself in serving one another in love (5:13 – 15).

Now Paul clarifies further what it means to be called to freedom and what it means to live in accordance with love.[1] Such a life becomes a reality only through the power of the Holy Spirit. This section can be divided into three subsections. (1) Yielding to the Spirit enables believers to triumph over the flesh and the law (5:16 – 18). (2) The consequences of life in the flesh and life in the Spirit are easy to discern (5:19 – 23). (3) Those who belong to Christ have put to death the desires of the flesh (5:24).

---

1. Alternatively, Russell thinks δέ introduces a contrast to 5:15 ("Galatians 5:13 – 26," 343).

Main Idea

The desires of the flesh are not absent from believers but threaten them constantly. Nevertheless, believers are now able to conquer the flesh and its desires through the power of the Holy Spirit. Nor is it unclear whether one is yielding to the flesh or the Spirit, for one's life demonstrates whether the flesh or the Spirit reigns.

Translation

(See next page.)

Structure

Under literary context it was noted that this unit can be divided into three subsections (see the Literary Context). Each section warrants further analysis. (1) The section begins, much like 5:2, with the words, "Behold I ... say" (λέγω δέ). Verse 16a exhorts us to live in the Spirit, and v. 16b specifies the result of doing so, namely, that those who live in the Spirit will not carry out the desires of the flesh. Verse 17, however, explains ("for," [γάρ]) that life in the Spirit is not easy, for the flesh and the Spirit are diametrically opposed to one another. Still, v. 18 explains that such a state of affairs is not the final word, for those who are led by Spirit are no longer under the realm of the law and hence are no longer subject to the power of sin.

(2) Whether one is living in the flesh or the Spirit is no great mystery (5:19 – 23). The concrete actions and attitudes that are expressed indicate the source of one's earthly life. The two main units here are introduced by "now" (v. 19) and "but" (v. 22) (marked by δέ ... δέ). The works of the flesh are generally grouped into four categories: (a) the first three items refer to sexual sins; (b) the fourth and fifth vices focus on the failure to honor and worship God; (c) the sixth through the thirteenth vices concentrate on social vices, on sins that disrupt community life; these are clearly emphasized since more of these sins are listed than those in other categories; and (d) the last two vices relate to a dissolute life of drinking and carousing. The vice list is not comprehensive, and Paul remarks that he could have listed other sins. The vice list ends with a strong warning that those who practice the works of the flesh will not inherit God's kingdom.

Verses 22 – 23 stand in contrast with the vice list and contain a virtue list. Here nine elements in the fruit of the Spirit are listed. Love stands at the head of the list, but the list as a whole does not fall into a discernible pattern like the vice list. Paul closes this section by noting that no law stands against these virtues. That is, the law does not produce such a transformed life; rather the gift of the new age — the Holy Spirit — strengthens believers to live in such a way.

Galatians 5:16-24

16a	exhortation	And **I say, walk by the Spirit,**
b	result	and **you will not fulfill the desire of the flesh.**
17a	basis *(of 16a-b)*	For **the flesh desires against the Spirit,**
b	series	and **the Spirit desires against the flesh.**

| c | basis *(of 17a-b)* | For **these are opposed to one another,** |
| d | purpose *(of 17c)* | so that you cannot do what you desire. |

| 18 | contrast *(to 17a-d)*/condition | But **if you are led by the Spirit, you are not under the law.** |

| 19a | series *(from 16-18)* | Now **the works of the flesh are evident, and**   they are: |
| 19b-21a | list | |

sexual immorality,
impurity,
sensuality,
idolatry,
sorcery,
enmities,
strife,
jealousy,
bursts of rage,
selfish ambition,
dissensions,
factions,
envying,
drunkenness,
carousing, and
things like these,

b	series	and **I am telling you**
		about these things in advance,
c	comparison *(to 21b)*	just as I told you before,
d	explanation *(of 21bc)*	that those who practice these things will not inherit ⤵
		the kingdom of God.

| 22-23a | contrast *(to 19-21)*/list | But **the   fruit of the Spirit is** |

love,
joy,
peace,
patience,
kindness,
goodness,
faithfulness,
gentleness, and
self-control,

23b	series *(from 22-23a)*	and **there is no law against such things.**
24	series *(from 23)*	And **those who belong to Christ Jesus have crucified the flesh with its passions** ⤵
		and desires.

(3) Finally, the section concludes with an indicative statement. Believers triumph over the flesh because they have crucified the flesh's desires (5:24). Presumably this death was accomplished when they were crucified with Christ (2:20). Therefore, the flesh was dethroned by the cross of Christ instead of by the law of Moses.

Exegetical Outline

III. A Call to Freedom from the Law and Freedom in the Spirit (4:12 – 6:10)

    A. Live in Freedom from the Law: Argument from Friendship (4:12 – 20)

    B. Stand in Freedom: Argument from Allegory (4:21 – 5:1)

    C. Resist the Dangerous Message of Bondage (5:2 – 12)

    D. Live Out Freedom in the Spirit (5:13 – 6:10)

        1. Freedom expressed in love (5:13 – 15)

➡   **2. Living by the Spirit instead of the flesh (5:16 – 24)**

            a. Yield to the Spirit (5:16 – 18)

                i. To conquer the flesh (5:16)

                ii. Because the battle is fierce (5:17)

                iii. To be free from the law (5:18)

            b. Marks of the flesh and the Spirit (5:19 – 23)

                i. The works of the flesh (5:19 – 21b)

                    (1) Sexual sins (5:19b)

                    (2) Refusal to worship God (5:20a)

                    (3) Social sins (5:20b – 21a)

                    (4) Sins of revelry (5:21b)

                    (5) Eschatological warning (5:21c)

                ii. Fruit of the Spirit (5:22 – 23)

            c. The crucifixion of the flesh (5:24)

        3. Caring for One Another by the Spirit (5:25 – 6:5)

Explanation of the Text

5:16 And I say, walk by the Spirit, and you will not fulfill the desire of the flesh (Λέγω δέ, πνεύματι περιπατεῖτε καὶ ἐπιθυμίαν σαρκὸς οὐ μὴ τελέσητε).[2] If believers want to conquer the flesh, they must continually yield to the Holy Spirit. Paul's emphatic introduction could suggest a new direction in the argument (cf. 3:17, 4:1; 5:2)[3] and perhaps even a contrast to 5:15. One could also see the argument as unpacking further what it means to serve one another through love in 5:13 – 15,[4] which is the view favored here. It is less certain that Paul responds here to the false

---

2. My thanks to Nick Nowalk, who wrote an outstanding paper on Gal 5:16 – 18 for my class, and his work was of significant help to me in this section.

3. Witherington, *Galatians*, 393.

4. So Ronald Lutjens, " 'You Do Not Do What You Want': What Does Galatians 5:17 Really Mean?" *Presb* 16 (1990): 110.

teachers.[5] Instead, Paul now clarifies further the nature of true freedom.

Slavery consists in capitulating to the desires of the flesh, while freedom comes from yielding to the Holy Spirit.[6] Freedom is ultimately not attainable by human potentiality; it is a supernatural work of the Holy Spirit.[7] So too, serving others in love cannot be accomplished by those who are still in Adam, for those who remain under the dominion of the flesh. Such loving service becomes a reality only through the power of the Holy Spirit. The word "walk" (περιπατεῖτε) denotes the need to submit to the Spirit day by day. There is a tension in the verse between divine enablement and human choice. On the one hand, believers must choose to live by the Spirit, while on the other hand, the Spirit empowers believers to live a life pleasing to God.

The last clause in the verse is translated in the RSV as follows: "and do not gratify the desires of the flesh." The RSV, then, interprets both clauses as imperatives, calling on believers to yield to the Spirit and to resist the flesh. Such a reading of the second clause is, however, almost certainly mistaken.[8] The emphatic subjunctive clause ("you will never fulfill," [οὐ μὴ τελέσητε]) should not be construed as an imperative here but as a promise.[9] If believers live in the Spirit, then they will not put into practice the desires of the flesh. The desires of the flesh will be thwarted and conquered as long as the Galatians yield to the Holy Spirit.

Believers are not immune to the desires of the old Adam. They still beckon them and are immensely attractive, but believers triumph over those desires as they walk in the Spirit.

5:17a-b For the flesh desires against the Spirit, and the Spirit desires against the flesh (ἡ γὰρ σὰρξ ἐπιθυμεῖ κατὰ τοῦ πνεύματος, τὸ δὲ πνεῦμα κατὰ τῆς σαρκός). The reason it is so crucial to walk in the Spirit is now explained. A great battle wages in the hearts of believers.[10] Believers are indwelt by the Holy Spirit, and hence the promised gift of the age to come is now theirs. And yet the present evil age has not passed away (1:4). The flesh remains a reality as well, and its desires are not absent. Furthermore, the desires of the flesh are implacably opposed to the things of the Spirit. Nonetheless, the continuing desires of the flesh are not the whole story. Believers are also indwelt by the Holy Spirit, and the Spirit within them impels them to righteousness, so that believers have powerful desires for goodness as well.

5:17c-d For these are opposed to one another, so that you cannot do what you desire (ταῦτα γὰρ[11] ἀλλήλοις ἀντίκειται, ἵνα μὴ ἃ ἐὰν θέλητε ταῦτα ποιῆτε). What is latent in the first part of the verse is expressed clearly here. The Spirit and the flesh stand in opposition to each other, so neither the desires of the flesh nor the desires of the Spirit are actualized. Even though Christians enjoy the life of the age to come through the Holy Spirit, a battle

---

5. Contra Martyn, *Galatians*, 492; Hays, *Galatians*, 325.

6. Contra the suggestion of Russell, the desire of the flesh here cannot be limited to circumcision ("Galatians 5:13 – 26," 343) but refers to the desires of the flesh more comprehensively. The vice list in 5:19 – 21 demonstrates that the desires of the flesh go beyond the intent to be circumcised.

7. Longenecker says that "the dative πνεύματι suggests both origin and instrumentality" (*Galatians*, 244). Martyn is correct that Paul is not speaking of the commencement of life in the Spirit, or appealing to human ability (*Galatians*, 535), though Martyn appears to diminish the role of human

responsibility here.

8. So Barclay, *Obeying the Truth*, 111, n. 10; Witherington, *Galatians*, 393; Martyn, *Galatians*, 492; Bruce, *Galatians*, 243.

9. Rightly Betz, *Galatians*, 278.

10. It is not clear (against Russell, "Galatians 5:13 – 26," 349) that Paul addresses "the dynamic at work on Christians who become a part of the Judaizers' communities and attach themselves to Israel."

11. The Majority Text and a few other manuscripts support the reading δέ (ℵ², A, C, D², Ψ, 0122, 𝔐), but γάρ is most likely original (𝔓⁴⁶ᵛⁱᵈ, ℵ*, B, D', F, G, 33, lat).

with the flesh remains. The flesh and the Spirit vie against one another constantly so that temptations continue to harass believers.[12]

The last clause in this verse is particularly nettlesome. It could be read a number of different ways. (1) The Spirit and flesh are opposed to one another, and the result is that believers cannot do what the Spirit impels them to do.[13] This view should be rejected. It mistakenly reads 5:17 as if it were similar to Rom 7:14 – 25, whereas the two texts must be distinguished, for the latter says nothing about the Holy Spirit! Further, this view does not explain how 5:17 functions as a ground for 5:16. The argument as a whole (5:16 – 18) does not propound such a pessimistic view of the Christian life, as if Christian existence is marked by constant frustration regarding doing the will of God.[14]

(2) The second view is quite creative, for it sees a parenthesis in the verse. "For the flesh desires what is contrary to the Spirit (and the Spirit what is contrary to the flesh, for they are in conflict with each other) in order that you might not do what you want."[15] The central problem with this view is that it is scarcely apparent that a parenthesis exists. The proposal fails because it is too clever and sophisticated.

(3) Another interpretation says that the Spirit and flesh are opposed to one another, and the result is that the flesh is unable to fulfill its desires.[16] This interpretation is much more probable than the first two, and if adopted, Paul would be emphasizing the victory over the flesh accomplished by the Holy Spirit. This interpretation, however, is not the most natural way to read the text, and it diminishes unduly the flesh's role in the verse.[17] If Paul had intended such a view, it seems that he would have said "so that you cannot do what the flesh desires."

(4) The battle between the flesh and Spirit produces a stalemate, so neither the flesh nor the Spirit fulfills its desires.[18] This view suffers from the same problem as some of the others above, for it does not explain the optimism of 5:16 and 5:18, and 5:17 ends up taking both of these verses hostage.[19]

(5) Believers cannot remain neutral in the struggle between the flesh and the Spirit.[20] The "so that" (ἵνα) here is construed as result rather than purpose. This is how most commentators construe this clause.[21]

(6) Perhaps the best explanation understands "so that" (ἵνα) here to denote purpose.[22] Paul gives the reason why the flesh and Spirit resist one another, i.e., so that the desires of the flesh will not become a reality and so that the desires of the Spirit will not be realized. With the coming of the Spirit, a new eschatological reality has dawned.

---

12. Martyn limits what Paul says to only some of the Galatians, to those who have submitted to the message of the agitators (*Galatians*, 495, 540), but this is improbable. There is no evidence that Paul restricts his remarks here to only some of the Galatians.

13. Ridderbos, *Galatians*, 203 – 4. Some interpreters maintain that we have the same conflict found in Rom 7:14 – 25. E.g., Calvin, *Galatians*, 163; Longenecker, *Galatians*, 246; George, *Galatians*, 387.

14. See Barclay, *Obeying the Truth*, 113.

15. Lutjens, "Galatians 5:17," 115; so also J. J. Kilgallen, "The Strivings of the Flesh … (Galatians 5:17)," *Bib* 80 (1999): 113 – 14.

16. Duncan, *Galatians*, 167 – 68; Guthrie, *Galatians*,

135 – 36; Eastman, *Paul's Mother Tongue*, 164 – 65; Fee, *Galatians*, 209 – 10.

17. So Matera, *Galatians*, 207.

18. So Burton, *Galatians*, 300 – 302; Betz, *Galatians*, 279 – 82. Though Betz sees a stalemate in 5:17, he argues that 5:18 removes the stalemate.

19. Barclay, *Obeying the Truth*, 114.

20. Ibid. 115 – 17. Cf. also Matera, *Galatians*, 200, 206 – 7; Hays, *Galatians*, 326.

21. See, e.g., Fung, *Galatians*, 250 – 51; Martyn, *Galatians*, 494; Lambrecht, "Galatians 5:17d," 521. A few, however, construe it as purpose (e.g., Longenecker, *Galatians*, 245 – 46; Dunn, *Galatians*, 299; Witherington, *Galatians*, 394 – 95).

22. I am relying on the comments here of Nick Nowalk.

A conflict between the flesh and the Spirit has ensued, explaining why it is so vital for believers to walk in and to be led by the Spirit. Therefore, walking in the Spirit is not the same thing as coasting along in a fair breeze, for the flesh wars against the Spirit and the Spirit wars against the flesh. Still, Paul is fundamentally optimistic here, claiming that as one walks by the Spirit and is led by the Spirit, there is substantial, significant, and observable victory over the flesh.

5:18 But if you are led by the Spirit, you are not under the law (εἰ δὲ πνεύματι ἄγεσθε, οὐκ ἐστὲ ὑπὸ νόμον). The "but" (δέ) here should be construed as adversative. Even though there is a great conflict between the flesh and the Spirit, those who led by the Spirit triumph over sin because they are no longer under the law. Verse 18 provides the resolution to the problem of 5:17, restating what we find in 5:16.[23] Hays nicely summarizes the primary thrust of Galatians 5:16 – 18: "The central point of vv. 16 – 18, then, is that the Spirit provides strong leadership and direction in a world that is described as an eschatological war zone."[24]

The Spirit's empowering presence grants believers the ability to conquer the desires of the flesh. The word "if" should be read as conditional and should not be translated as "since."[25] The condition beckons the readers to fulfill the hypothesis. The word "led" (ἄγω) is used elsewhere of being guided by the Holy Spirit (Rom 8:14; cf. Luke 4:1), of being led by idols (1 Cor 12:2), of women being moved by their sinful desires (2 Tim 3:6), or of people being brought to repentance (Rom 2:4).

The point here is not so much specific guidance for daily decisions as it is being directed by the Spirit to live a life that pleases God. Paul may well draw here on Isa 63:11 – 15, which refers to God's end-time leading of his people by his Spirit.[26]

Those who are impelled by the Spirit are not "under the law." It might seem that freedom from the law means that those who are directed by the Spirit transcend moral norms; they are free to do whatever they wish whether it accords with moral norms or not. The verses that immediately follow indicate that Paul is not teaching antinomianism. Whether one is guided by the flesh or the Spirit can be discerned objectively (cf. 5:19 – 23).

Paul makes a salvation-historical argument here, for those who are led by the Spirit do not belong to the old era of redemptive history when the law reigned.[27] To be "under law," as was noted previously (see also 3:23; 4:21), is to be "under a curse" (3:10), "under sin" (3:22), "under the custodian" (3:25), "under guardians and managers" (4:2), "enslaved under the elements of the world" (4:3), and in need of redemption (4:4 – 5). If one is "under law," then one is not "under grace" (Rom 6:14 – 15).

Paul's argument here is illuminating and fits with what he says in Romans 6 as well. Those who are directed by the Spirit are no longer under the law, and therefore they no longer live in the old era of redemptive history under the reign of sin. Freedom from law does not, according to Paul, mean freedom *to sin*; it means freedom *from sin*. Conversely, those who are under the law live under the dominion of the sin. Hence, for the Galatians

---

23. Against Longenecker, *Galatians*, 246. Rightly Lutjens, "The ἵνα-clause of v. 17 sets out the problem of which v. 18 is the resolution" ("Galatians 5:17," 116). So also Dunn, *Galatians*, 300.

24. Hays, *Galatians*, 327.

25. Against Longenecker, *Galatians*, 246.

26. So Beale, "Fruit of the Spirit," 13 – 14; Harmon, "She Must and Shall Go Free," 294 – 98.

27. This is contrary to Wilson, who thinks that Paul teaches here that the believers are not under the curse of the law (*Curse of the Law*, 117 – 20). It has been argued earlier that the phrase "under law" (contra Wilson) does not refer to the curse of the law. See the exegesis of 3:22 earlier. Indeed, in sketching out the various views of this verse, Wilson fails to note the redemptive-historical view advocated here.

to subjugate themselves to the message of the Judaizers would be a disaster, for it would open the floodgates for the power of sin to be unleashed in the Galatian community. The answer to the dominion of sin is the cross of Christ and the gift of the Spirit. If the Galatians follow the Spirit, they will not live under the tyranny of sin and the law.

5:19 Now the works of the flesh are evident, and they are: sexual immorality, impurity, sensuality (φανερὰ δέ ἐστιν τὰ ἔργα τῆς σαρκός, ἅτινά ἐστιν πορνεία, ἀκαθαρσία, ἀσέλγεια). Identifying the works of the flesh does not demand extraordinary spiritual discernment. It is not a secret disclosed to a gnostic elite. Instead, those things that issue from the flesh are obvious and clear to anyone with an ounce of discernment. The term "flesh" (σαρκός) here is a genitive of source, specifying that evil works stem from the old Adam. Vice lists are common in Pauline literature, and they function to delineate qualities that are not pleasing to God and not in accord with life in the Spirit. The first three vices here focus on sexual sin. Indeed, Paul uses the same three terms (with a different order) to designate sexual sin in 2 Cor 12:21.

The word "sexual immorality" (πορνεία) is used with the term "impurity" (ἀκαθαρσία) in Eph 5:3 and Col 3:5. The term "sexual immorality" (πορνεία) is a general term for sexual sin that is often used in the NT to denote sexual malfeasance.[28] We need to remember in a vice list that the terms used are not necessarily sharply distinguished from one another, and hence there is overlap among the three words that designate sexual sin here.

The word "impurity" (ἀκαθαρσία) is not remarkably common in Paul (nine occurrences), but it often denotes sexual sin (Rom 1:24; 2 Cor

12:21; Eph 5:3; Col 3:5; 1 Thess 4:7), and perhaps in the other instances as well (Rom 6:19; Eph 4:19; 1 Thess 2:3). The word focuses on the defilement and filthiness generated by sexual sin.

The final term, "sensuality" (ἀσέλγεια), is also a common word used for sexual sin (Mark 7:22; Rom 13:13; 2 Cor 12:21; 1 Pet 4:3; 2 Pet 2:2, 7, 18; Jude 4) and emphasizes the lack of restraint and unbridled passion of sexual license. It "throws off all restraint and flaunts itself."[29] Those who are deceived may think following their sexual passions is equivalent to following the Spirit, but such actions flow from the selfish will rather than the work of the Holy Spirit.

5:20a Idolatry, sorcery (εἰδωλολατρία, φαρμακεία). The next two sins are grouped together because they both focus on the refusal to worship the one true God. The fundamental sin in Pauline theology is the failure to praise and thank God for his goodness and to turn to the worship of idols (εἰδωλολατρία), to the worship of the creature rather than the Creator (Rom 1:21 – 25). Coveting is idolatry (Col 3:5), for it reveals desires that rule in human hearts, so that the thing desired takes precedence over God.

Sorcery or magic (φαρμακεία) is regularly condemned in Jewish literature (Exod 7:11, 22; 8:14; Isa 47:9, 12; Rev 18:23; cf. Wis 12:4; 18:13), for instead of trusting in God, people try to manipulate circumstances to bring about the end they desire. Sorcery, then, turns one from trust in the living God to dependence on other sources.

5:20b – 21a Enmities, strife, jealousy, bursts of rage, selfish ambition, dissensions, factions, envying, drunkenness, carousing, and things like these (ἔχθραι, ἔρις, ζῆλος, θυμοί, ἐριθείαι,

---

28. It cannot be restricted to sexual sin within marriage. Against Martyn, *Galatians*, 496; Bruce Malina, "Does *Porneia* mean Fornication?" *NovT* 14 (1972): 10 – 17. Rightly,

Joseph Jensen, "Does *Porneia* Mean Fornication? A Critique of Bruce Malina," *NovT* 20 (1978): 161 – 84.

29. Bruce, *Galatians*, 247.

διχοστασίαι, αἱρέσεις, φθόνοι, μέθαι, κῶμοι, καὶ τὰ ὅμοια τούτοις). Social sins that disrupt the community predominate in the vice list.[30] Eight different words describe the sins that foment discord in the church. Six of the eight terms are plurals. The terms overlap in meaning so that we cannot always distinguish sharply how one term differs from another.

The word "enmities" (ἔχθραι) occurs only here in a Pauline vice list, denoting the hatred that lies at the root of discord.[31] We note that a plural form appears here. Longenecker says, "Greek abstract nouns are often, though not always, used in the plural to signify manifestations or demonstrations of the quality denoted in the singular, and thus to mean 'displays of' or 'actions expressing' that quality."[32]

"Strife" (ἔρις) is a more common term in Pauline vice lists (Rom 1:29; 13:13; 2 Cor 12:20; 1 Tim 6:4; cf. also 1 Cor 1:11; 3:3; Phil 1:15; Titus 3:9), focusing on the contention that divides people from one another.

The word "jealousy" (ζῆλος), along with "strife," is the only other singular among the social sins listed. The term often has positive content, signifying zeal and passion for God or what is right (Rom 10:2; 2 Cor 7:7, 11; 9:2; 11:2; Phil 3:6), but it may also refer to jealousy that is consumed by self-glorification (Rom 13:13; 1 Cor 3:3; 2 Cor 12:20; cf. Jas 3:14, 16).

"Bursts of rage" (θυμοί) comes from a word for anger that is common in the OT. Paul uses it occasionally in vice lists (see also 2 Cor 12:20; Eph 4:31). It refers to savage flashes of anger that are poured out on others, to an uncontrolled temper that leaves in its wake people who are the object of one's vituperation.

"Selfish ambition" (ἐριθεῖαι) nowhere occurs in the LXX, but it is found on six other occasions in the NT (Rom 2:8; 2 Cor 12:20; Phil 1:17; 2:3; Jas 3:14, 16).[33] Selfish ambition brings discord, for it does not focus on the good of others but grasps after honor and praise for oneself.

"Dissensions" (διχοστασίαι) is an infrequent term (cf. 1 Macc 3:29; Rom 16:17), that calls attention to the division and fragmentation in a community as a result of sin.

"Factions" (αἱρέσεις) may be used to denote a sect, whether in a good or bad sense, as we find in the book of Acts (Acts 5:17; 15:5; 24:5, 14; 26:5; 28:22). The term cannot be distinguished sharply from "dissensions," and in some instances probably stands for false teaching (e.g., 2 Pet 2:1). Here the focus lies on a selfish exclusiveness and "party spirit" (so RSV) that creates division where there should be none (cf. 1 Cor 11:19).

"Envying" (φθόνοι) is found in other Pauline vice lists (Rom 1:29; 1 Tim 6:4; Titus 3:3; cf. Phil 1:15), and it concentrates on the desire to possess what others have, so that one is not satisfied with the gifts God has given. "It is the grudging spirit that cannot bear to contemplate someone else's prosperity."[34]

Two words are used to designate a dissolute lifestyle where one remains unconstrained by moral norms: "drunkenness" (μέθαι) and "carousing" (κῶμοι). We find a similar pairing in Rom 13:13, and 1 Pet 4:3 is also similar to what we find in Galatians. Those who give themselves over to revelry and wild parties demonstrate that they are still under the control of the old Adam rather than living in the new age inaugurated by Jesus Christ.

---

30. Cf. Barclay, *Obeying the Truth*, 152–53; Wilson, "Wilderness Apostasy," 569; Hays, *Galatians*, 327.

31. B. Longenecker warns about overreading the distinction between sorcery and enmity since the former was motivated by the latter. "Until Christ Is Formed in You," 98–99, 98, n. 17.

32. Longenecker, *Galatians*, 253.

33. For this meaning, see Longenecker, *Galatians*, 256.

34. Bruce, *Galatians*, 249.

The phrase "things like these" indicates that the vice list is partial and does not represent an exhaustive list of sins.

5:21b-d And I am telling you about these things in advance, just as I told you before, that those who practice these things will not inherit the kingdom of God (ἃ προλέγω ὑμῖν, καθὼς προεῖπον ὅτι οἱ τὰ τοιαῦτα πράσσοντες βασιλείαν θεοῦ οὐ κληρονομήσουσιν). Doing the works of the flesh cannot be dismissed as inconsequential, for Paul warns the Galatians that those who make a practice of doing such will not inherit the eschatological kingdom.[35] Instead, they will face judgment on the final day along with the rest of the wicked (6:8).

Paul does not invariably use "kingdom" (βασιλεία) to refer to the final day, for in some contexts the focus is on the present dimension of the kingdom (Rom 14:17; 1 Cor 4:20; Col 1:13; 4:11?), but often the term refers to the end-time kingdom (1 Cor 6:9 – 10; 15:24, 50; Eph 5:5; 1 Thess 2:12; 2 Thess 1:5; 2 Tim 4:1, 18). In 1 Cor 6:9 – 10 and Eph 5:5, the parallels with Gal 5:21 are especially prominent, since both texts conjoin inheritance and the kingdom. Further, both 1 Cor 6:9 – 10 and Eph 5:5 identify sins that exclude people from the eschatological inheritance. Clearly, such a theme is a staple of the Pauline proclamation.[36]

Indeed, as this verse demonstrates, the Galatians had been orally informed previously about the consequences of giving reign to the works of the flesh. The terrible consequence of these vices is reiterated most solemnly here. Righteousness by faith instead of works of law must not lead to a life of sin. Those who are justified by God's grace are also empowered by the Spirit to live in a new way. If the works of the flesh dominate, then no eschatological reward will be received. Good works are not the basis of justification, but they are most certainly, though still imperfect and partial, a consequence of justification.[37]

5:22 – 23a But the fruit of the Spirit is love, joy, peace, patience, kindness, goodness, faithfulness, gentleness, and self-control (ὁ δὲ καρπὸς τοῦ πνεύματός ἐστιν ἀγάπη, χαρά, εἰρήνη, μακροθυμία, χρηστότης, ἀγαθωσύνη, πίστις, πραΰτης, ἐγκράτεια[38]). The vice list is now contrasted (adversative conjunction "but" [δέ]) with a virtue list. The list has no discernible order apart from love appearing first.[39] The godly qualities are the fruit of the Spirit, i.e., they are not the product of the old Adam or human strength.[40] The word "fruit" in the singular may indicate that the fruit of the Spirit is unitary.[41] As Betz says, "They do not represent qualities of personal behavior which man can elect, cultivate, and appropriate as part of his character."[42] Alternatively, fruit may simply be a collective noun.[43]

Believers are not called upon to summon up the strength within them, for their new way of life is supernatural, stemming from the powerful work

---

35. Russell makes the mistake here of turning a warning or an admonition into an ontological statement ("Galatians 5:13 – 26," 350 – 51), so that he ends up saying that Paul refers here to Israel and the Judaizers. Paul does believe that those who proclaim a false gospel will be cursed (1:8 – 9), but this text functions as a *warning* for believers, not a declaration regarding the spiritual state of opponents.

36. Against Betz, who thinks it stands in tension with Paul's theology (*Galatians*, 285).

37. Calvin remarks that those who do not repent will not inherit the kingdom (*Galatians*, 166).

38. A few manuscripts add the word "purity" (ἁγνεία) and a few others "endurance" (ὑπομονή), but such readings are clearly secondary.

39. Against Betz, *Galatians*, 287 – 88.

40. The use of the word "fruit" does not in itself indicate a divine work, for Paul also uses the term "fruit" for evil behavior (cf. Rom 6:21), and hence the supernatural character here is evident from the focus on the Holy Spirit. Cf. Barclay, *Obeying the Truth*, 120; Bruce, *Galatians*, 251; Longenecker, *Galatians*, 259 – 60.

41. So Betz, *Galatians*, 286; Matera, *Galatians*, 202.

42. Betz, *Galatians*, 286.

43. So Fee, *Galatians*, 217.

of the Holy Spirit.[44] Believers did not receive the Spirit by doing the works of the law but by hearing the gospel with faith (3:2, 5). Still, those who have the Spirit are not rendered inert and lifeless. The Spirit is better than the law because a life pleasing to God is the result of his work. Hence, it is clear that the word "Spirit" (πνεύματος) is a genitive of source.[45] "Law may prescribe certain forms of conduct and prohibit others, but love, joy, peace, and the rest cannot be legally enforced."[46]

The first fruit listed is "love," (ἀγάπη), and this is scarcely surprising since love is *the* mark of new life in Christ according to Paul (cf. 1 Cor 13). Indeed, the love of believers for others is rooted in the love of God poured out in their hearts through the Holy Spirit (Rom 5:5). Any genuine love flows from the Spirit (Rom 15:30; Col 1:8), though such love can also be traced to the Father (Rom 8:39; 2 Cor 13:14; Eph 1:4; 2:4) or the Son (Rom 8:35; 2 Cor 5:14; 13:14), showing the Trinitarian character of God's love. Love is the heart and soul of the Pauline ethic, for it is love that fulfills the law (Rom 13:8–10; Gal 5:14).

The problem with spiritual gifts in Corinth can be traced to lack of love, as the sublime 1 Cor 13 reveals. Indeed, the root problem with the quarrels over foods can also be attributed to a failure to love (Rom 14:1–15:6; 1 Cor 8:1–11:1). Elsewhere when the virtues of the Christian life are described, Paul begins with love (Rom 12:9), and Col 3:14 may mean that love is the bond that holds all the virtues together. Giving to help others in need

flows from love (2 Cor 8:7, 8, 24), and the goal of the whole of the Christian life can be characterized as love (1 Tim 1:5). Love may be defined as giving oneself for others so that they are encouraged and strengthened to give themselves more fully to God.

Joy (χαρά) is also a work of the Holy Spirit (cf. Rom 14:17) and cannot be attributed to human ability. The theme of joy is especially prominent in Philippians (Phil 1:4, 18, 25; 2:2, 17, 18, 28, 29; 3:1; 4:1, 4, 10), where sacrificing for the unity of fellow believers is emphasized. Believers are called upon to rejoice in all circumstances (1 Thess 5:16), trusting that God is working all things together for their good. Sorrow is the portion of believers in this life, but even sorrow is mingled with joy (2 Cor 6:10) since God grants grace even in the deepest pain.

"Peace" (εἰρήνη) is commonly used in the opening of Pauline letters.[47] Paul conjoins it with joy elsewhere (Rom 14:17; 15:13), and such peace is the result of the Spirit's work (Rom 14:17). Christ Jesus has brought peace to both Jews and Gentiles via the cross (Eph 2:14, 15, 17). Peace should rule in the Christian community (Col 3:15).

"Patience" (μακροθυμία) is used elsewhere in Pauline virtue lists (2 Cor 6:6; Eph 4:2; Col 3:12; 2 Tim 3:10). It is the work of the Spirit of God when one endures difficult situations and people without losing one's equanimity.

The word "kindness" (χρηστότης) appears elsewhere in virtue lists (2 Cor 6:6; Col 3:12), but it is particularly used of God's kindness in offering or providing salvation through Christ Jesus (Rom

---

44. Perhaps Paul echoes the OT, where Israel bears fruit for Yahweh (Ps 80:8–18; Isa 5:1–7; 27:2–6; Jer 2:21; 11:16; 12:10; Hos 14:6). So David S. Dockery, "Fruit of the Spirit," *DPL*, 317. Barclay suggests that Paul may see eschatological promises from the OT fulfilled in the work of the Spirit (*Obeying the Truth*, 121). Beale argues more specifically that Isa 57:15–19, with echoes from Isa 32:15–18, is in view, and perhaps Isa 11:1–5 and 44:2–4 as well ("Fruit of the Spirit," 1–38; cf. also Harmon, "She Must and Shall Go Free," 284–94). Even if one does not follow Beale here, the reference to the Spirit indicates

that Paul draws on the promise of the Spirit from the OT and thereby emphasizes the new creation work of God.

45. Betz says the context suggests that "the 'fruit of the Spirit' presupposes man's active involvement" (*Galatians*, 287). It is clear from 5:25–6:10 that external commands do not contradict life in the Spirit. Rightly, T. J. Deidun, *New Covenant Morality in Paul* (AnBib 89; Rome: Biblical Institute, 1981), 88–217, 251–58; Barclay, *Obeying the Truth*, 229.

46. Bruce, *Galatians*, 255.

47. See comments on 1:3.

2:4; 11:22; Eph 2:7; Titus 3:4). Believers imitate God and Christ whenever they are generous to others, but especially in extending benevolence to those who are not loving in return.

"Goodness" (ἀγαθωσύνη) should not be distinguished sharply from kindness, and it appears in Paul in only a few instances (Rom 15:14; Eph 5:9; 2 Thess 1:11). Those who have the Spirit of God are strengthened to live lives of moral beauty, and their decency shines forth in a world blighted by evil.

The word translated "faithfulness" (πίστις) often means "faith" in Paul, but in a virtue list such as this it almost certainly means "faithfulness"[48] (Titus 2:10) and perhaps in a few other texts as well (1 Tim 4:12; 6:11; 2 Tim 2:22; 3:10; Titus 2:2). Those led by the Spirit are loyal and dependable, and one can count on them to fulfill their responsibilities.

Another virtue inspired by the Spirit is "gentleness" (πραΰτης). This term also appears in other Pauline virtue lists (Eph 4:2; Col 3:12; Titus 3:2). Those who sin should be reproved gently (6:1), and gentleness characterized Jesus Christ (2 Cor 10:1). Unbelievers should be gently corrected in the hope that they will repent (2 Tim 2:25). Forceful and harsh behavior is not the mark of the Spirit's work, but meekness and gentleness reflect a transformed heart.

"Self-control" (ἐγκράτεια) is a rare word in the NT (Acts 24:25; 2 Pet 1:6; cf. also 4 Macc 5:34).[49]

The verbal form is used in 1 Cor 7:9 and 9:25. Those who have self-control are able to restrain themselves unlike those who are dominated by the desires of the flesh.

5:23b And there is no law against such things (κατὰ τῶν τοιούτων οὐκ ἔστιν νόμος). The meaning of this short phrase is difficult. The phrase "such things" (τῶν τοιούτων) is probably neuter (referring to the fruit of the Spirit) rather than masculine (referring to people).[50] Paul could mean that no law prohibits the fruit of the Spirit, and hence no one can find fault with such virtues.[51] Or, perhaps the point is that the law can never produce these godly qualities, but such is the result of the Spirit's work. It is possible that both ideas are in view here. We have seen consistently in Galatians that the law cannot produce righteousness (3:21), and in 5:18 that those who are led by the Spirit are not under the law. In other words, those under the law are under the dominion of sin. The Spirit, then, produces fruit that the law cannot create.[52]

5:24 And those who belong to Christ Jesus have crucified the flesh with its passions and desires (οἱ δὲ τοῦ Χριστοῦ Ἰησοῦ[53] τὴν σάρκα ἐσταύρωσαν σὺν τοῖς παθήμασιν καὶ ταῖς ἐπιθυμίαις). Believers do not need the law to restrain their behavior. Since they belong to "Christ Jesus" (Χριστοῦ Ἰησοῦ is a genitive of possession), they have put to death

---

48. So Betz, *Galatians*, 288; Bruce, *Galatians*, 254; Longenecker, *Galatians*, 262.

49. Against Betz, it is not evident that "self-control" is the "climax" of the list of virtues (*Galatians*, 288). Betz draws this conclusion because he interprets the virtues listed here from the standpoint of Greek ethics.

50. R. A. Campbell, " 'Against Such Things There Is No Law'? Galatians 5:23b Again," *ExpTim* 107 (1996): 271 – 72. Campbell argues that the verse means that the law is not against such people, i.e., the law does not condemn those who walk in accord with the fruit of the Spirit. Against Campbell, it is unclear that the phrase "against such" (κατὰ τῶν τοιούτων) relates to the condemnation stemming from the law, for nowhere else does Paul speak of the law's condemna-

tion with the preposition "against" (κατά).

51. Cf. Ridderbos, *Galatians*, 208; Barclay, *Obeying the Truth*, 122 – 24; Hong, *Law in Galatians*, 185; Longenecker, *Galatians*, 263.

52. Contra Wilson, it is not persuasive to say that Paul refers here to the curse of the law being set aside. *Curse of the Law*, 117 – 20.

53. Determining whether "Jesus" (Ἰησοῦ) is original is difficult. It seems that scribes would be inclined to include it for liturgical purposes, and yet it is absent in many manuscripts (𝔓⁴⁶, D, F, G, 0122ᶜ, 𝔐, latt, sy). On the other hand, the witnesses for its inclusion are impressive (ℵ, A, B, C, P, Ψ, 0122*, 33, 104*, 1175, 1241ˢ, 1739, [1881], *pc*, co), and hence I slightly favor its inclusion.

the desires of the flesh. It is surprising that Paul uses an active verb that emphasizes that believers themselves have crucified the flesh. When did they slay the flesh with its desires? Given the context of all of Galatians Paul is scarcely suggesting that the Galatians crucified the flesh autonomously. Such a notion flies in the face of the whole of the letter. Those who are in Adam and in the flesh do not have the resources to crucify it.

Surely, the verb "crucified" functions as the clue for interpreting this verse. It points the reader back to Gal 2:20, where believers are said to be crucified with Christ.[54] The crucifixion of the flesh, then, occurred at conversion, when believers died with Christ. Perhaps the active form of the verb

"crucified" is used to indicate that believers have chosen to be aligned with Christ at conversion, that they said no to their life in Adam and in the flesh when they put their faith in Christ. The death of the flesh signals the inauguration of a new age — their deliverance from the present evil age (1:4).

The death of the flesh does not mean that believers do not feel the tug of fleshly desires (5:17). Still, the flesh has been dealt a decisive blow at the cross. The passions and desires of the flesh are not absent, but they no longer rule and reign. Those who walk by the Spirit and who are led by the Spirit find themselves, even though imperfectly and partially, triumphing over the passions of the flesh that formerly dominated them.

Theology in Application

The Conflict

The new age of the Spirit has arrived, and believers are no longer in the old Adam. They have crucified the flesh with its desires, and they now belong to Christ Jesus. Still, believers live in the interval between the already and not yet. Desires for sin are not absent, and sometimes such desires are incredibly strong (5:17). They are so intense that warfare between the flesh and Spirit takes place in believers.[55]

Such conflict in the lives of believers is reflected elsewhere (Rom 8:13; Col 3:5; 1 Pet 2:11). Therefore, the Christian life is not an ethereal existence in which the conflicts of this world are left behind. Believers do not "float" into a new sphere that cuts them off from the pressures and desires of the present evil age. Desires for evil still afflict us and bedevil us. It is far too simplistic, then, to say that believers must "let go and let God," or to promise that the fight against sin will vanish in this life if a certain formula for spiritual victory is applied. The war against the world, the flesh, and the devil continues until the day of death.

The word about conflict is immensely practical. If the conflict between the flesh and the Spirit is strong in our life, we should not become discouraged and think that we aren't Christians if we are engaged in a struggle against sin. The opposition

---

54. For a contrary view, see Kwon, *Eschatology*, 174 – 77.

55. On the flesh and Spirit conflict in Paul with a helpful history of interpretation, see Barclay, *Obeying the Truth*, 178 – 215. Barclay interprets the terms in light of Pauline eschatology and focuses on the social dimension of the terms

as well. See the helpful work of Russell, who argues that flesh and Spirit must be interpreted in light of redemptive history (Russell, "Galatians 5:13 – 26," 333 – 57), though he underestimates the anthropological dimension of Pauline thought.

between the flesh and the Spirit is the normal Christian life, which is not marked by perfection but by war. Luther reminds us about the nature of the conflict, emphasizing that it should never be confused with perfection:

> Anyone who would know this art well [living by the Spirit] would deserve to be called a theologian. The fanatics of our day, who are always boasting about the Spirit, as well as their disciples, seem to themselves to know it superbly. But I and others like me hardly know the basic elements of this art, and yet we are studious pupils in the school where this art is being taught. It is indeed being taught, but so long as the flesh and sin remain, it cannot be learned thoroughly.[56]

No Room for Pessimism

We must not think, however, that Paul's view of the Christian life is fundamentally pessimistic. The gift of the new age, the Holy Spirit, now belongs to believers. Believers who live by the Spirit will not carry out the flesh's desires. Those who yield to the Spirit will not live under the dominion of law and sin. A new quality of life (5:22 – 23) is the result of the Spirit's work. The old age no longer reigns over believers. The old Adam has been crucified with its passions and desires, so that the flesh no longer enslaves believers.

In other words, believers enjoy a substantial, significant, and observable victory in their new life in Christ. Since believers live in the interval between the already and not yet, perfection is not their portion. Yet believers now have the firstfruits of the Spirit and are a new creation (2 Cor 5:17), and hence Paul is fundamentally optimistic about the new life that is possible for saints.

An Objective Criterion

The vice and virtue lists provide an objective criterion for life in the Spirit or life in the flesh. Thereby Paul counters spiritual enthusiasm that claims to live by the Spirit, while one's life is marked by "the works of the flesh." The life of the Spirit is not a great mystery, if one means by mystery that we cannot tell if one is following the Spirit. The fruit of the Spirit is impossible to produce for the sons and daughters of Adam, but they are not hard to discern. Where there is sexual sin, self-absorption and self-worship, strife and quarreling, and dissolute lives under the control of drugs and alcohol, the flesh is in control. Where there is love, harmony, joy, forgiveness, and kindness, we see the power of the Spirit.

The Galatians are not called upon to work at being more virtuous. They are summoned to walk in the Spirit and to be led by the Spirit. Living in a way that pleases God is the fruit of his miraculous work, not the result of self-effort, though human beings are called upon to walk in the Spirit and yield to the Spirit.

---

56. Luther, *Galatians 1535: Chapters 1 – 4*, 342.

22

CHAPTER

Galatians 5:25 – 6:5

Literary Context

The exhortation section that began in 4:12 continues. Paul has called on the readers to imitate him and free themselves from the law (4:12 – 20), to stand in their freedom in Christ (4:21 – 5:1), to resist the inducements of the false teachers (5:2 – 12), and to live in love by the Spirit, resisting the desires of the flesh (5:13 – 24). A new paragraph probably begins here, so that 5:25 – 26 belong with 6:1 – 5 rather than 5:19 – 24.

A decision on this issue is difficult, for the reference to the Spirit could suggest that these verses fit with the previous section. Furthermore, one could argue that the term "brothers" in 6:1 introduces a new section.[1] Despite these arguments, putting 5:25 – 26 with the next section is preferable. The word "brothers" may open a new section (1:11; 3:15; 4:12; 5:13), but in some cases the term does not commence a new paragraph (4:28, 31; 5:11), and hence this argument is not decisive.

What inclines me to see 5:25 – 26 with the next section is the emphasis on community and caring for one another that informs 5:25 – 6:5.[2] As will be noted in the exegesis in 6:1, it seems that this verse is tied particularly closely to 5:26. Instead of provoking and envying one another, believers are to watch over and restore those who sin.[3] The divisions between the various sections in the exhortation are not airtight, for in both 5:13 – 24 and 5:25 – 6:10 Paul teaches that believers carry out the admonitions only by walking in the Spirit.[4]

---

1. Cf. Longenecker, *Galatians*, 264 – 65.

2. Cf. Betz, *Galatians*, 254 – 55, 291. The verses may also be transitional. So David W. Kuck, " 'Each Will Bear His Own Burden': Paul's Creative Use of an Apocalyptic Motif," *NTS* 40 (1994): 290.

3. So Jan Lambrecht, "Paul's Coherent Admonition in Galatians 6,1 – 6: Mutual Help and Individual Attentiveness," *Bib* 78 (1997): 41.

4. Contra Betz, who argues that the admonitions here do not indicate a Christian ethic (*Galatians*, 292). Rightly Martyn, *Galatians*, 545.

Main Idea

Believers are not to compete with one another but to support one another and bear one another's burdens. At the same time believers must realize that they will stand alone before God and bear responsibility for their actions on the last day.

Translation

(See next page.)

Structure

Exhortations permeate these verses. Discerning the structure of this section and the following one (6:6 – 10) is not easy, and some scholars maintain that a perceptible structure is not evident inasmuch as the text seems to be characterized by unrelated maxims.[5] Barclay, however, rightly sees a structural unity to 5:25 – 6:10, noting an alternation between individual responsibility and community accountability. In other words, Paul's remarks remind believers to care for one another.[6]

The "if" (εἰ) in 5:25 is intended to provoke the readers to answer affirmatively. They do live by the Spirit, and hence they should continue to keep in step with the Spirit. In 5:26 the Galatians are urged to forsake conceit, which manifests itself in provoking and envying one another. We see again that social sins come to the

---

5. Betz, *Galatians*, 292.

6. Barclay, *Obeying the Truth*, 149 – 50. Matera follows Barclay here (*Galatians*, 217 – 18).

Galatians 5:25-6:5

25a	condition	If we live by the Spirit,
b	exhortation	**let us also keep in step with the Spirit.**
26a	exhortation	**Let us not become conceited,**
b	manner	in that we provoke one another, and
c	series	envy one another.
1a		**Brothers,**
	concessive	even if anyone is overtaken in any trespass,
b	exhortation	**you, who are spiritual, should** **restore such a one in a spirit of gentleness,**
c	series	and **look to yourself,**
d	purpose	so that you too will not be tempted.
2a	exhortation	**Bear one another's burdens,**
b	manner	and in this manner **you will fulfill the law of Christ.**
3a	basis *(of 2a-b)*	For if anyone thinks he is something,
b	concessive *(to 3a)*	even though he is nothing,
c	consequence to condition *(3a-b)*	**he deceives himself.**
4a	exhortation	And **each one should examine his own work,**
b	result	and then **he will have boasting** with reference to himself only, and
c	contrast *(to 4b)*	not with reference to another.
5	basis *(of 4)*	For **each one will bear his own load.**

forefront in the text. Concern for fellow believers must be the mark of the Christian community instead of provoking and envying one another.

The word "brothers" (ἀδελφοί) begins chapter 6, but the use of this term does not necessarily designate a new section (cf. 5:11; 6:18). If any are detected to be in sin, they should be restored, though those who admonish must be gentle and avoid becoming entrapped in sin themselves (6:1). Perhaps 6:1 functions as a specific illustration of 6:2, as the fourth exhortation in the text is given. Believers are to carry the burdens of one another. As a result of doing such, they fulfill Christ's law, which is most likely the law of love. The "for" (γάρ) linking 6:2 and 6:3 is difficult. Perhaps the point is that those who live isolated lives and do not assist others thereby demonstrate their arrogance.

If 6:1 – 3 emphasize helping fellow believers, 6:4 – 5 remind believers of their individual responsibilities. Ultimately each person must examine his or her own work before God, and he or she will receive the reward on the last day for the work accomplished (6:4). Verse 5 grounds v. 4 (see the "for," γάρ), giving the reason why everyone should examine his or her own work. At the end of the day, each one will bear his or her own load before God. Each one will stand before God alone on the day of judgment.

Exegetical Outline

III. A Call to Freedom from the Law and Freedom in the Spirit (4:12 – 6:10)

    A. Live in Freedom from the Law: Argument from Friendship (4:12 – 20)

    B. Stand in Freedom: Argument from Allegory (4:21 – 5:1)

    C. Resist the Dangerous Message of Bondage (5:2 – 12)

    D. Live Out Freedom in the Spirit (5:13 – 6:10)

        1. Freedom expressed in love (5:13 – 15)

        2. Living by the Spirit instead of the flesh (5:16 – 24)

        3. Caring for one another by the Spirit (5:25 – 6:5)

            a. Keep in step with the Spirit (5:25)

            b. Refuse conceit (5:26)

            c. Restore those sinning (6:1)

            d. Bear another's cares (6:2)

            e. Beware of pride (6:3)

            f. Test one's own work (6:4)

            g. Remember the final judgment (6:5)

        4. Doing good by the Spirit (6:6 – 10)

Explanation of the Text

5:25 If we live by the Spirit, let us also keep in step with the Spirit (εἰ ζῶμεν πνεύματι, πνεύματι καὶ στοιχῶμεν). Believers live by virtue of the Holy Spirit, and hence they must also march in step with and obey that same Spirit. The word "if" (εἰ) should not be translated "since."[7] The condition is intentional, for Paul wants the Galatians to ask themselves if they do indeed live by the Spirit. He expects, of course, that they will answer affirmatively, but as interpreters we should pay heed to the grammar of the text instead of leaping ahead to the expected affirmation.

The word "live" (ζῶμεν) refers to eschatological life that now belongs to believers. If the Galatians have such life by means of the Holy Spirit, they are summoned to keep in line with the Spirit, to keep in step with the Spirit. Therefore, believers are again summoned to live the Christian life in the same way they began it (cf. Gal 3:3).[8]

The verb "keep in step with" (στοιχέω) is found only four other times in the NT, three of them in Paul (Acts 21:24; Rom 4:12; Gal 6:16; Phil 3:16). It is in the same semantic range as the verb "walk" (περιπατέω), and it emphasizes that believers should continue to stay in line with the Spirit.[9] "However, 'to live by the Spirit' cannot possibly mean one's idle possession of it or exclusion by it from the daily struggle of life."[10] Perhaps the verb functions as a contrast to the elements (στοιχεῖα) in 4:3 and 4:9, so that here Paul contrasts the new

---

7. Contra Longenecker, *Galatians*, 264 – 65; Garlington, *Galatians*, 350.

8. So Dunn, *Galatians*, 317.

9. Cf. Bruce, *Galatians*, 257.

10. Betz, *Galatians*, 293.

creation life of the Spirit with the old creation of the elements.[11] Believers enjoy life in the Spirit now, but they must continue to march in tune with the Spirit.[12] Life in the Spirit is not on automatic pilot, for the battle against the flesh continues (5:17), so that believers must continue to walk by the Spirit (5:16) and be led by the Spirit (5:18).

5:26 Let us not become conceited, in that we provoke one another, and envy one another (μὴ γινώμεθα κενόδοξοι, ἀλλήλους προκαλούμενοι, ἀλλήλοις φθονοῦντες). What it means to keep in step with the Spirit is now explained more concretely. The Galatians are exhorted not to give way to arrogance or pride. The term "conceited" (κενόδοξος) occurs only here in the NT, though the related word "conceit" (κενοδοξία) is found in Phil 2:3. Here Paul forbids pride, which manifests itself in irritating and inflaming others, so that quarrels and fighting ensue.

The "verb προκαλέομαι ['provoke'] … is used of mutal challenges to combat or athletic contest."[13] Believers are not keeping in step with the Spirit if they are irritating and aggravating others, if they goad others to anger and frustration. From pride also comes envy, so that one is embittered at the success and happiness of others, or one rejoices at the misfortunes of others. If believers serve one another in love, they will not give way to envy.[14]

6:1a-b Brothers, even if anyone is overtaken in any trespass, you, who are spiritual, should restore such a one in a spirit of gentleness (Ἀδελφοί, ἐὰν καὶ προλημφθῇ ἄνθρωπος ἔν τινι παραπτώματι, ὑμεῖς οἱ πνευματικοὶ καταρτίζετε τὸν τοιοῦτον ἐν πνεύματι πραΰτητος). Those who are tripped up in sin should be gently restored by fellow believers. Instead of becoming arrogant and irritating and envying one another, believers should exercise concern and love for others, so that their goal is to build one another up. Instead of rejoicing that others have fallen, Paul exhorts the Galatians to restore those who have fallen into sin. The word "restore" (καταρτίζω) is used of rebuilding walls (Ezra 4:12, 13) and of mending fishing nets (Matt 4:21). Restoration to spiritual health and vitality is in view here.

It is difficult to ascertain the nuance of the verb "is overtaken" (προλημφθῇ) here. It could simply mean detected in sin by others, but it seems more likely that it denotes one who has been overtaken in sin by surprise.[15] Even though believers have life in the Spirit, they still inhabit this present evil age (1:4), and hence sin attacks them in unanticipated ways. Paul is not suggesting that those who commit such trespasses are simply unwilling victims. They bear full responsibility for their sins. Still, Paul envisages situations in which believers sin in unplanned and unexpected ways — hence, the need for restoration. It seems likely that what Paul describes here generally accords with the first step of church discipline in Matt 18:15 – 20. One who becomes aware of another's sin should privately speak to the offender in order to restore him or her to fellowship with Christ.

Those who are "spiritual" (οἱ πνευματικοί) are called upon to care for and restore those who have

---

11. Hays, *Galatians*, 328 – 29.

12. For this meaning of "keep in step with" (στοιχέω), see Betz, *Galatians*, 293 – 94. The word could also mean that believers should conform to or agree with the Spirit (see Delling, στοιχεῖον," *TDNT*, 7:669).

13. Bruce, *Galatians*, 257.

14. So Kuck, "Each Will Bear His Own Burden," 291.

15. Rightly Garlington, *Galatians*, 356. Gerhard Delling,

"προλαμβάνω," *TDNT*, 4:14; Fung, *Galatians*, 284; Fee, *Galatians*, 230. Eastman suggests that they may have received circumcision, but Paul holds out the possibility of forgiveness if they repent ("Galatians 4.30," 329 – 31), but the warning in Gal 5:2 – 4 makes this improbable. Against Martyn there is no temporal idea here, as if Paul suggests that they are caught in sin "before it is possible to escape notice" (*Galatians*, 546).

fallen. The "spiritual" do not constitute an elite group of Christians,[16] nor does Paul restrict himself to a portion of the congregation.[17] All of the Galatians received the Spirit when they heard the message of the gospel (3:2, 5). They enjoy Abraham's blessing, for they have received the promise of the Spirit (3:14). God has given them his Spirit because they are his sons (4:6), and they live by the Spirit (5:25). Therefore, as those who are walking by the Spirit (5:16), are led by the Spirit (5:18), and are keeping in step with the Spirit (5:25), they are to reestablish those who have fallen.

Furthermore, they are to restore them gently and meekly. Here we see another indication that 6:1 qualifies 5:26. A gentle and humble spirit does not provoke one who has sinned but treats that person with dignity, and such gentleness is the fruit of the Spirit (5:23).[18] Those who envy others find joy in the sins of others since the faults of others are on full display and they look better by comparison. But one who truly loves others and is walking in the Spirit approaches them with firmness (since they have sinned) mingled with humility (so that they are treated gently).

6:1c-d And look to yourself, so that you too will not be tempted (σκοπῶν σεαυτόν μὴ καὶ σὺ πειρασθῇς). Paul elaborates on what humility involves. One does not focus on the sins of others, provoking and discouraging them because they have fallen. Instead, those who restore the fallen remain humble because they remember their own fallibility and propensity to sin.[19] They realize that they too may be tempted and fail. Today they are reinstating one who has sinned, but tomorrow they may need to be reinstated. Recognition of one's own failures will keep believers from triumphalism or arrogance.

6:2 Bear one another's burdens, and in this manner you will fulfill the law of Christ (Ἀλλήλων τὰ βάρη βαστάζετε καὶ οὕτως ἀναπληρώσετε τὸν νόμον τοῦ Χριστοῦ). The command here represents a general exhortation to carry one another's burdens.[20] In light of 6:1, it could refer to helping and sustaining others when they sin. The admonition, however, is stated broadly, and it seems unlikely that it should be limited only to bearing the sins of others,[21] especially since believers have a variety of burdens that cannot be equated with sin, such as persecution, financial difficulties, sickness, and the like.

Others have suggested that the burdens here are financial, so that believers are called upon to help believers in financial need.[22] Again, such a reading is too specific, for it is unclear that the law of Christ refers to a specific admonition from Jesus to help fellow believers financially. The exhortation reads as a wide-ranging call to help in the struggles of other believers.[23]

When believers bear the burdens of others, they "fulfill the law of Christ." An alternative

---

16. Against this, Barrett suggests that Paul may ironically refer to those who believed they were spiritual (*Freedom and Obligation*, 79; so also Dahl, "Paul's Letter to the Galatians," 128; Bruce, *Galatians*, 260). Stott wrongly limits what Paul says here to mature Christians. John R. W. Stott, *The Message of Galatians* (London: IVP, 1968), 161.

17. Rightly Barclay, *Obeying the Truth*, 157; Longenecker, *Galatians*, 273; Martyn, *Galatians*, 546; Witherington, *Galatians*, 422.

18. Cf. Garlington, *Galatians*, 357; Fee, *Galatians*, 231 – 32.

19. Some think the temptation is to commit the same sin as the one who has fallen (so Dunn, *Galatians*, 321). Others

argue that the sin is the temptation to become proud (so Bruce, *Galatians*, 260). The warning seems to be rather general and may include both (so Hays, *Galatians*, 332).

20. "This more general injunction includes the precept of v. 1" (Bruce, *Galatians*, 260).

21. Rightly Lambrecht, "Galatians 6,1 – 6," 44. Contra Hofius, "Das Gesetz des Mose und das Gesetz Christi," 282; Matera, *Galatians*, 214; Mussner, *Galaterbrief*, 399; Garlington, *Galatians*, 361; Kuck, "Each Will Bear His Own Burden," 292.

22. So J. G. Strelan, "Burden Bearing and the Law of Christ: A Re-examination of Galatians 6:2," *JBL* 94 (1975): 266 – 76.

23. Rightly Bruce, *Galatians*, 261.

textual reading has the imperative "you must fulfill" (ἀναπληρώσατε) Christ's law. Metzger summarizes well, however, why the future is preferable:

> Although the aorist imperative ["you must fulfill"] ἀναπληρώσατε is strongly supported (א A C Dᵍʳ K P Ψ 614 1739 syrʰ arm *al*), the future tense appeared to the Committee to be slightly preferable on the basis of early and diversified external attestation ($\mathfrak{P}^{46}$ B G and most ancient versions), as well as transcriptional probability (scribes would be likely to conform the future to the preceding imperatives, "restore" [καταρτίζετε] ver. 1) and "bear" [βαστάζετε].[24]

In Depth: The Law of Christ

Paul's wording here echoes Gal 5:14, where we also find the ideas of fulfillment and the law ("for the whole law is fulfilled in one word," ὁ γὰρ πᾶς νόμος ἐν ἑνὶ λόγῳ πεπλήρωται).[25] Here the fulfillment is not of the Mosaic law but the law of Christ.[26] So too, in Gal 5:14 the law points to the fulfillment of the law in Christ.

Some maintain that the use of the word "law" here is dictated by the opponents, with Paul reformulating their expression, speaking of Christ's law (νόμος) rather than the Mosaic law.[27] Others think that the words of Jesus form a new Torah for believers.[28] Such a view is sometimes linked to the rabbinic view that the law would cease when the messianic age was inaugurated.[29] Surely, the words of Jesus were authoritative for early Christians, and there are a number of citations and allusions to his teaching in Paul's writings.[30]

Still, we should not restrict the law of Christ to the words of Jesus. Even though there are many allusions to Jesus' teaching in Paul, he infrequently introduces them explicitly as the words of Jesus. If Christ's oral teachings were the new law for Paul, we would expect that he would cite Jesus' teachings often and explicitly. The notion that the messianic age would spell the end of the Torah is not clearly taught in rabbinic literature. At most it teaches that a few

---

24. Metzger, *Textual Commentary*, 530.

25. For a survey of interpretation of "law of Christ," see Barclay, *Obeying the Truth*, 126 – 35; Schreiner, "Law of Christ," *DPL*, 542 – 44.

26. But see the discussion below for the role of the Mosaic law.

27. Betz thinks Paul uses the term polemically (*Galatians*, 300 – 301).

28. W. D. Davies, *Paul and Rabbinic Judaism* (4th ed.; Philadelphia: Fortress, 1980), 142 – 44; C. H. Dodd, "ENNOMOS CHRISTOU," in *Studia Paulina in honorem J. de Zwaan* (Haarlem: Bohn, 1953), 96 – 110; A. Feuillet, "Loi de Dieu, Loi du Christ, et Loi de l'Esprit d'apres Les Epîtres Paulinennes," *NovT* 22 (1980): 45 – 57.

29. See Albert Schweitzer, *The Mysticism of Paul the Apostle* (trans. William Montgomery; repr.; New York: Seabury, 1986), 187 – 92; Schoeps, *Paul*, 171 – 73.

30. Dale Allison, "The Pauline Epistles and the Synoptic Gospels: The Pattern of the Parallels," *NTS* 28 (1982): 1 – 32; Peter Stuhlmacher, "Jesustradition im Römerbrief: Eine Skizze," *TBei* 14 (1983): 240 – 50; Michael Thompson, *Clothed with Christ: The Example and Teaching of Jesus in Romans 12.1 – 15.13* (JSNTSup 59; Sheffield: JSOT Press, 1991).

rather peripheral commandments would be altered and that a more complete understanding of the Torah would be realized.[31]

A similar view is that the law of Christ fits with the Zion Torah. According to this view, the Mosaic law is abolished while the Zion Torah is established. The Zion Torah hails from Zion (Isa 2:1 – 4; Mic 4:1 – 4) and is eschatological (Jer 31:31 – 34) and universal.[32] This view rightly sees discontinuity between the law in the old covenant and the new. It is questionable, however, whether the OT texts adduced point to a new law from Zion.[33]

Others see a reference to law as principle,[34] but in a section of the letter including moral exhortations it seems that a reference to "law" fits better than the word "principle." The similar phrase "under Christ's law" (ἔννομος Χριστοῦ) in 1 Cor 9:21 suggests that we do not have a direct response to the opponents here. Rather, in a striking phrase (cf. 5:14), Paul focuses on the fulfillment of the law in Christ, though it is possible that such an expression came in response to Jewish opponents who trumpeted the Mosaic law.

The law, according to Paul, must be interpreted christocentrically, so that it comes to its intended completion and goal in Christ.[35] The "law of Christ" is equivalent to the law of love (5:13 – 14),[36] so that when believers carry the burdens of others, they behave as Christ did and fulfill his law.[37] In this sense Christ's life and death also become the paradigm, exemplification, and explanation of love.[38]

---

31. For a careful sifting of the evidence, see W. D. Davies, *Torah in the Messianic Age* (Philadelphia: SBL, 1952). For a decisive argument contrary to such a view, see Peter Schäfer, "Die Torah der messianischen Zeit," *ZNW* 65 (1974): 27 – 42.

32. Harmut Gese, *Essays on Biblical Theology* (Minneapolis: Augsburg, 1981), 80 – 92; Peter Stuhlmacher, *Reconciliation, Law, and Righteousness* (Philadelphia: Fortress, 1986), 110 – 33, esp. 114 – 17.

33. See Martin Kalusche, "'Das Gesetz als Thema biblischer Theologie'? Anmerkungen zu einem Entwurf Peter Stuhlmachers," *ZNW* 77 (1986): 194 – 205; Heikki Räisänen, "Zionsstora and Biblische Theologie: Zu einer Tübinger Theorie," in *The Torah and Christ* (Helsinki: Finnish Exegetical Society, 1986), 337 – 65.

34. Räisänen, *Paul and the Law*, 80; Sanders, *Paul, the Law*, 15, n. 26; Burton, *Galatians*, 329 (principle of love); Bruce, *Galatians*, 261.

35. Still, it must not be forgotten that the law of Christ fulfills the intention of the Mosaic law. So B. Longenecker, *Triumph of Abraham's God*, 85 – 87; Stanton, "Law of Moses and Law of Christ," 116; B. Longenecker, "Defining the Faithful Character of the Covenant Community," 92; Hong, *Law*

in *Galatians*, 173 – 83; Sanders, *Paul, the Law*, 97 – 98; Barclay, *Obeying the Truth*, 132. Hong emphasizes that the Mosaic law is fulfilled in its true intention, and such fulfillment of the law does not involve the keeping of every single commandment of the law, so that the laws that created a nationalistic breach between Jews and Gentiles (like circumcision) are abolished. See the invaluable survey by Todd A. Wilson, "The Law of Christ and the Law of Moses: Reflections on a Recent Trend in Interpretation," *CurrBR* 5 (2006): 123 – 44. Wilson suggests a close connection between the Mosaic law (per Gal 5:14) and the law of Christ.

36. So Karl Kertelge, "Gesetz und Freiheit im Galaterbrief," *NTS* 30 (1984): 390 – 91. Against this, see Hong, *Law in Galatians*, 176, for he says that love is the means by which the command of 5:14 is fulfilled, and hence cannot be the content of the command.

37. Against Winger, who limits the law of Christ to life in the Spirit and rules out any norms in the law of Christ. Michael Winger, "The Law of Christ," *NTS* 46 (2000): 537 – 46.

38. So Hans Schürmann, "'Das Gesetz des Christus' (Gal 6,2): Jesus Verhalten und Wort als letzgültige sittliche Norm

6:3 For if anyone thinks he is something, even though he is nothing, he deceives himself (εἰ γὰρ δοκεῖ τις εἶναί τι μηδὲν ὤν, φρεναπατᾷ ἑαυτόν). Those who are proud are warned about the self-delusion of thinking that they are something. The logical relationship between this verse and 6:2 is a bit elusive. What does carrying the burdens of others have to do with pride? We actually have another piece of evidence that 5:26 belongs to this section, for it also warns against conceit. Those who are conceited and proud are consumed with themselves rather than others.

Such an observation provides a clue for understanding the "for" (γάρ) that links 6:2 and 6:3.[39] Those who do not help others in their struggles, who live lives of splendid isolation, are guilty of pride. They think they are something when they are nothing.[40] Or perhaps Paul thinks of those who are proud because they think they are "immune to temptation," and hence they need not worry about their own failings but can devote their lives to helping others.[41] Arrogance cuts people off from the lives of others, but it is also deceitful, for those who are proud are impressed with themselves, when in actuality they are nothing. Those who help others in their spiritual struggles must be conscious of their own sins, and thereby they will not fall prey to the deception that they are part of the spiritual elite.

6:4 And each one should examine his own work, and then he will have boasting with reference to himself only, and not with reference to another (τὸ δὲ ἔργον ἑαυτοῦ δοκιμαζέτω ἕκαστος, καὶ τότε εἰς ἑαυτὸν μόνον τὸ καύχημα ἕξει καὶ οὐκ εἰς τὸν ἕτερον). On the one hand, believers who are marching in step with the Spirit must show concern for others. They fulfill Christ's law of love when they bear the burdens of others and when they restore with gentleness and humilty those who sin. They violate Christ's paradigm of self-giving when they are blighted by pride and irritate one another. What it means to follow the Spirit is to live in community with others, to care for the needs of others.

On the other hand, believers are responsible before God individually for their own lives. Hence, Paul calls on them to assess and examine their lives carefully and realistically (cf. Rom 12:3).[42] They are not to deceive themselves by overestimating what they have accomplished. If their self-examination accords with reality, then they can legitimately boast with reference to themselves.

The idea that believers can boast in their own

---

nach Paulus," in *Neues Testament und Kirche. Festschrift für Rudolf Schnackenburg* (ed. J. Gnilka; Freiburg: Herder, 1974), 282 – 300; Richard B. Hays, "Christology and Ethics in Galatians: The Law of Christ," *CBQ* 49 (1987): 268 – 90. Hays has modified his view, seeing in addition a reference to the fulfilling of Torah, which fits with what is being argued here (*Galatians*, 333). Hofius understands the law of Christ in light of the sin-bearing work of the Servant in Isaiah. "Das Gesetz des Mose and das Gesetz Christi," 262 – 86. Hofius rightly reminds us that Christ embodies the law of love in his atoning work. Still, it must be observed that no direct reference to Christ's death is stated.

39. Contra those who link it with 6:1. So Lightfoot, *Galatians*, 216; Lambrecht, "Galatians 6,1 – 6," 46. If sense can be made of the relationship between 6:2 and 6:3, then we should not skip to 6:1. Kuck argues that the link is both with 6:1 and 6:2 ("Each Will Bear His Own Burden," 292), but such a solution is unnecessarily complicated. Fee thinks Paul reverts to 5:26 here (*Galatians*, 233 – 34).

40. So Longenecker, *Galatians*, 276; Witherington, *Galatians*, 426. Against Barrett, the verb "think/seem" (δοκέω) does not indicate that Paul has in mind the pillar apostles (*Freedom and Obligation*, 80 – 81).

41. So Martyn, *Galatians*, 549. Matera says that "the context suggests a sense of pride after restoring a fellow believer, or a sense of immunity from a similar failure in one's own life" (*Galatians*, 214).

42. Against Martyn, it is unclear that the work Paul has in mind here can be limited to preaching the gospel (*Galatians*, 550).

work sounds exceedingly strange, especially since Paul has emphasized throughout Galatians that believers are righteous by faith rather than works (cf. also Rom 3:27 – 28; 4:2 – 5). Has Paul forgotten what he has taught throughout the letter and fallen back into a works-oriented ethic? We should note here that the construction is future, "he will have boasting" (τὸ καύχημα ἕξει), and it probably refers to the final judgment, to the day when the Lord assesses each person's work.[43] Therefore, the boasting that is commended here does not relate to this life but to the life of the age to come, and in that day all vain and conceited boasting will disappear.

Furthermore, we see in the context that the boasting envisioned is a result of the Spirit's work in believers (5:16, 18, 22 – 23, 25; 6:8). It is the result of the new creation (6:15). Hence, the boasting is not autonomous here. Paul may be calling the Galatians away from comparing themselves to one another so that they will assess their own lives before God.[44]

Witherington proposes another and rather convincing interpretation of the last clause in the verse. He argues that the the phrase "with reference to another" (εἰς τὸν ἕτερον) does not denote comparison.[45] Instead what Paul criticizes is "the all too common practice of boasting about (and taking credit for) someone else's accomplishments or actions."[46] This would fit with 6:13, where the opponents boast in the circumcision of the Galatians. Believers will only be able to praise God for the work he has done in their own lives, and they will not be able to claim any credit for what God has accomplished in others.

6:5 For each one will bear his own load (ἕκαστος γὰρ τὸ ἴδιον φορτίον βαστάσει). Verse 5 functions as the ground (see "for," γάρ) for 6:4. One will only boast about his or her own work on the day of judgment, for on that day each one will carry his own load before God.

The saying here could be construed as a general maxim that relates to everyday life.[47] If the verse is interpreted as a kind of proverbial saying, Paul merely says that even though we are to help one another as believers and bear each other's burdens, we finally carry our own load in this life. In other words, we are responsible for our own behavior.

Nevertheless, the future tense "will bear" (βαστάσει) suggests that the final judgment is in view. Such an interpretation fits with 6:4 where the future tense also points to the final reward. Furthermore, 6:7 – 9 clearly refer to the last judgment, and Paul uses the verb "will bear" (βαστάσει) with reference to the last judgment in 5:10.[48] Finally, the "for" (γάρ) that links 6:5 to 6:4 indicates that we do not have an individual maxim here.[49]

Paul emphasizes in this paragraph, then, that believers are to support and help one another with the burdens and cares of life. At the same time they must recognize that they will stand alone before God on the day of judgment, that they will not be judged with relation to what others have done but what they themselves have accomplished. The different word for "load" (φορτίον

---

43. Against Witherington, *Galatians*, 427. Others take it as a logical future. So Longenecker, *Galatians*, 277.

44. So, e.g., Kuck, "Each Will Bear His Own Burden," 293 – 94; Lambrecht, "Galatians 6,1 – 6," 48.

45. Witherington, *Galatians*, 428. But against Witherington, I think eschatology is in view here.

46. Ibid., 428, n. 40.

47. In that case the future tense "shall bear" (βαστάσει) is

gnomic. So Betz, *Galatians*, 303 – 4; Burton, *Galatians*, 334; Witherington, *Galatians*, 429. Against Lambrecht, who takes it as imperatival ("Galatians 6,1 – 6," 50).

48. Matera, *Galatians*, 22; Kuck, "Each Will Bear His Own Burden," 296; Garlington, *Galatians*, 369; Hays, *Galatians*, 335. The load one must bear relates to the whole of life, not merely gospel proclamation (against Martyn, *Galatians*, 550).

49. Rightly Kuck, "Each Will Bear His Own Burden," 294.

instead of βάρη in 6:2) should not be construed as a significant clue regarding the meaning of the verse. As Burton says, "no sharp distinction can be drawn" between the two words.[50]

Theology in Application

Caring for Others in Humility

As Westerners we live individualistic lives, and such individualism is mediated to us through our culture. We learn from this paragraph that life in the Spirit is community life. Often we in the West identify a fruitful Christian life with private prayer and reading of Scripture, while scarcely giving any thought to serving other believers. A life that is pleasing to Christ is humble and not self-absorbed and conceited. One indication that we are puffed up with ourselves is if we provoke and annoy others when we are present with them. Similarly, if we are cast down by the success of others and long to surpass them in glory and honor, we betray the pride in our hearts.

Instead of being caught up with ourselves, we are called to care for others. What it means to live in the church of Jesus Christ is to help others as they face the difficulties of life. How can we help other believers financially? Who in the church is lonely and needs a visit? Who needs to be counseled and strengthened? Who is sick and in need of assistance?

Caring for others cannot be restricted to words of comfort. We see from 6:1 that we are to confront those who are in sin. Sometimes love demands that we speak a word that is hard and difficult. Tolerating evil in the church may appear to be loving since it flies under the banner of "unconditional acceptance." But such tolerance cannot be equated with love since it does not confront an evil that will surely spread (cf. 5:9), and such evil will surely destroy the perpetrator.

We must beware of thinking of ourselves as the righteous. Our correction of others will smell of conceit unless we sense that we ourselves are deeply flawed and are as prone to sin as anyone. If we put ourselves on a pedestal, we cannot humbly serve others by correcting them. Perhaps it is most helpful to think of parents and children. We correct our children (it is hoped!) because of our intense love for them, because we so long for them to be all that God has called them to be.

A Delicate Balance

A delicate balance exists between community and individual responsibility. Those who desperately need help from others may identify themselves as victims and refuse to be accountable for their own behavior. We may become so focused

---

50. Burton, *Galatians*, 334.

on community life that we forget about our own lives and decisions. Therefore, we are reminded that our final reward will be given after an assessment at the final judgment (6:4 – 5).

In other words, the Lord will judge us individually for what we have done as believers. In the Western world we are prone to individualism, but believers from the East have told me that they are often too fearful to go against the consensus. All of us are responsible for our decisions and actions before God, and we must live our lives with the knowledge that we will be judged on the final day for what we have done with our lives, that we will bear our own load.

23

Galatians 6:6 – 10

Literary Context

The exhortation section of Galatians (4:12 – 6:10) concludes here. Galatians 6:4 – 5 ended by stressing that each one will stand alone before God, who will render final judgment on every person. Galatians 6:6 – 10 returns to the theme of community responsibility, emphasizing in particular helping others financially, especially fellow believers. Part of what it means to march in step with the Spirit (5:25) is to care for the practical needs of other believers. Those who fulfill the law of Christ (6:2) are those who follow the example Christ set of self-giving love for others (5:14). Such love manifests itself in caring for the concrete needs of others.

Main Idea

Verse 10 captures the central truth of this paragraph. Believers are to do good to all people but particularly to other believers. The good in view here is especially supporting others financially, caring for their practical needs in everyday life.

Translation

Galatians 6:6-10

6	exhortation	**The one being taught the word should share**
		in all good things
		with the one who teaches him.
7a	exhortation	**Do not be deceived;**
b	basis *(of 7a)*	**God is not mocked.**
c	basis *(of 7b)*	For whatever a person sows **he will also reap.**
8a	explanation *(of 7c)*	Namely, **the one who sows to his own flesh will reap corruption** from the flesh, but
b	contrast *(to 8a)*	the one who sows to the Spirit will reap eternal life from the Spirit.
9a	exhortation	And **let us not lose heart in doing good,**
b	basis *(of 9a)*	for **we will reap** in due time,
c	condition	if we do not grow weary.
10a	inference *(from 6-9)*/exhortation	Therefore, **let us do good to all,**
b	temporal *(to 10a)*	while we have opportunity,
c	qualification *(of 10a)*	especially to those who are members of the household of faith.

Structure

The section begins with a community exhortation (6:6). Those who are instructed in the word of the gospel should provide financial help for those who teach them. The verse could be seen as an isolated maxim.[1] Conversely, one can argue that we have an entirely new section here in which the focus is on financial obligations.[2] One can accept this latter view and, at the same time, say that Paul here resumes the emphasis on corporate responsibility after emphasizing personal accountability in 6:4 – 5.[3]

The command to assist teachers is vitally important, for believers are prone to be deceived (6:7a). And they must beware of deceit since God will not be mocked (6:7b). We know that God will not be mocked because (γάρ) he will judge all on the basis of what they accomplish (6:7c). Paul unpacks what he means by this in 6:8. The one who lives according to the flesh will experience final judgment ("corruption"), whereas the one who lives in accord with the Spirit will enjoy eternal life.

Now that Paul has explained the importance of the exhortation in 6:6, he returns to the main point in 6:9 – 10. Believers should not become lax in doing good, which

---

1. Ridderbos, *Galatians*, 216.
2. Burton sees a reference to finances in 6:6 and more general admonitions through 6:10 (*Galatians*, 334).

3. Cf. Barclay, *Obeying the Truth*, 163; Lambrecht, "Galatians 6,1 – 6," 53 – 54.

in this context focuses on helping others materially, for those who assist others will receive a final reward on the day of judgment (6:9). The passage is summarized with an inferential conjunction ("therefore," ἄρα οὖν) in 6:10. Believers should do good to (i.e., help financially) all people, but priority is given to those who belong to the family of God. Fellow believers should be the first to receive assistance.

Exegetical Outline

III. A Call to Freedom from the Law and Freedom in the Spirit (4:12 – 6:10)

    A. Live in Freedom from the Law: Argument from Friendship (4:12 – 20)

    B. Stand in Freedom: Argument from Allegory (4:21 – 5:1)

    C. Resist the Dangerous Message of Bondage (5:2 – 12)

    D. Live Out Freedom in the Spirit (5:13 – 6:10)

        1. Freedom expressed in love (5:13 – 15)

        2. Living by the Spirit instead of the flesh (5:16 – 24)

        3. Caring for one another by the Spirit (5:25 – 6:5)

➡   **4. Doing good by the Spirit (6:6 – 10)**

           a. Support teachers financially (6:6)

           b. God will judge what we do (6:7)

           c. How we sow determines whether we live or die (6:8)

           d. A call to persistence in helping others (6:9)

           e. An exhortation to help all, especially believers (6:10)

  IV. Final Summary (6:11 – 18)

Explanation of the Text

6:6 The one being taught the word should share in all good things with the one who teaches him (Κοινωνείτω δὲ ὁ κατηχούμενος τὸν λόγον τῷ κατηχοῦντι ἐν πᾶσιν ἀγαθοῖς). One of the prime indications of life in the Spirit, according to Paul, is concern for one another, which is manifested in practical ways. Here he focuses on the responsibility of those who receive instruction to support financially their teachers. The word for "teach" (κατηχέω) occurs twice in this verse and in six other instances in the NT (Luke 1:4; Acts 18:25; 21:21, 24; Rom 2:18; 1 Cor 14:19). The teachers here

are not identified by a title such as "elder" (e.g., 1 Tim 5:17, 19; Titus 1:5) or "overseer" (Phil 1:1; 1 Tim 3:2; Titus 1:7). Paul focuses on the function of the leaders, for they exercise leadership by faithfully teaching the congregation. Perhaps this dimension of the leaders' role is highlighted because false teachers had disturbed the Galatians.

The teachers instruct in "the word" (τὸν λόγον), and this expression refers to the gospel (cf. 1 Cor 1:18; 2:4; 15:2; 2 Cor 1:18; 2:17; 4:2).[4] Those being taught are exhorted to support financially those who teach the word, presumably so that the

---

4. The "word" refers here to the gospel message as a whole. So Longenecker, *Galatians*, 278; Burton, *Galatians*, 337.

teachers can invest the requisite time and energy for study and proclamation. The term "should share" (κοινωνείτω) in both the verbal (Rom 12:13; Phil 4:15) and nominal forms (Rom 15:26; 2 Cor 8:4; Phil 1:5; cf. 1 Tim 6:18) elsewhere describes generous giving (Rom 12:13; Phil 4:15). So too, "good things" in other instances refers to possessing the things necessary to live (e.g., Deut 28:11; Luke 12:18 – 19; 16:25; Sir 22:23).[5] Those who benefit from the instruction of teachers should support them, for as Paul teaches elsewhere, those who receive spiritual benefit should share their material blessings with those who have benefited them (Rom 15:26 – 27).[6]

6:7 Do not be deceived; God is not mocked. For whatever a person sows he will also reap (Μὴ πλανᾶσθε, θεὸς οὐ μυκτηρίζεται. ὃ γὰρ ἐὰν σπείρῃ ἄνθρωπος, τοῦτο καὶ θερίσει). Paul uses the phrase "do not be deceived" on two other occasions (1 Cor 6:9; 15:33; cf. also Jas 1:16). In both instances he is worried about the eschatological inheritance of those whom he warns. Such Pauline exhortations must not be disregarded or taken lightly, for God will not stand for being scorned. He will punish those who spite him.

The last clause explains why God does not tolerate disparagement (see "for," γάρ). God has built a principle into the world that one will reap what one sows. The agricultural image is used here of the final judgment.[7] The words "sowing" and "reaping" in this context refer especially to generosity in giving.[8] The two terms are used to refer

to generous giving and in reference to the final judgment in 2 Cor 9:6 as well: "The point is this: whoever sows (ὁ σπείρων) sparingly will also reap (θερίσει) sparingly, and whoever sows (ὁ σπείρων) bountifully will also reap (θερίσει) bountifully" (ESV).

It is probably the case that what Paul says in 6:7 cannot be limited to giving, that we have a principle that sums up life as a whole. Still, the focus is on giving.[9] Those who live for the sake of others and for the glory of God will receive an eternal reward. As v. 8 indicates, they will receive eternal life. Such good works cannot be the ultimate basis of life eternal, for Galatians has shown that salvation is a gift of God granted by grace alone. It seems best to say that such good works constitute evidence that one has been transformed by God's grace.[10]

6:8 Namely, the one who sows to his own flesh will reap corruption from the flesh, but the one who sows to the Spirit will reap eternal life from the Spirit (ὅτι ὁ σπείρων εἰς τὴν σάρκα ἑαυτοῦ ἐκ τῆς σαρκὸς θερίσει φθοράν, ὁ δὲ σπείρων εἰς τὸ πνεῦμα ἐκ τοῦ πνεύματος θερίσει ζωὴν αἰώνιον). The term translated "namely" (ὅτι) here can also be translated "because," providing a reason God is not mocked.[11] But it seems more likely that the term is explanatory, further explaining what is meant by the last phrase in 6:7,[12] a person will reap what he sows. If we adopt such an interpretation, the ὅτι should be translated "namely" or "that is."

---

5. Against Fee, who fails to see that in context Paul refers to financial support (*Galatians*, 236).

6. Hurtado departs from the text in seeing a specific reference to support for the Jerusalem collection here, when it is clear that the support is for teachers in the Galatian congregation ("Jerusalem Collection," 53 – 55).

7. So Betz, *Galatians*, 307.

8. Rightly Hurtado, "Jerusalem Collection," 53, but against Hurtado, the connection with v. 6 makes it unlikely that the Jerusalem collection is in view here (55).

9. Cf. here Martyn, *Galatians*, 552.

10. Rightly de Roo, *Works of Law*, 130 – 33. Kwon rejects this formulation, saying that good works are a condition and not evidence (*Eschatology*, 190, 218 – 19). Against Kwon, there is no necessary contradiction to say that they are a condition in the sense that good works function as the necessary evidence of new life.

11. So Betz, *Galatians*, 308.

12. So Longenecker, *Galatians*, 280 – 81.

Further confirmation of this interpretation comes from the repetition of the verbs "sow" (σπείρω) and "reap" (θερίζω) from 6:7, so that the nature of the sowing and reaping in 6:7 is unpacked here. Two different kinds of sowing are envisioned. One either sows to the flesh, or one sows to the Spirit. The flesh-Spirit opposition points to the eschatological contrast that informs all of Galatians. Those who sow to the flesh demonstrate that they belong to the present evil age (1:4) and will perish, while those who sow to the Spirit demonstrate that they are part of the new creation and will receive eternal life (6:15). The "flesh" represents the "old Adam" with its corrupt desires and longings. The word "his own" (ἑαυτοῦ) suggests that even though believers are part of the new creation, they are not entirely free of the flesh and its enticements until the day of the resurrection. Sowing to the flesh in this paragraph means that one uses one's worldly goods for one's own advantage and in accord with selfish desires.

Sowing to the Spirit is likely another way of speaking of walking in the Spirit (5:16), being led by the Spirit (5:18), and marching in step with the Spirit (5:25). If Paul were speaking of the human spirit here, he likely would have repeated the words "his own" (ἑαυτοῦ) with reference to the Spirit. The absence of the phrase "his own" and the emphasis on the Holy Spirit elsewhere in this context indicate that the Holy Spirit is in view. Those who sow to the Spirit produce the fruit of the Spirit (5:22 – 23). In this context, such sowing to the Spirit manifests itself in generous giving to others.

Though what one does with one's possessions is primarily in view, it seems likely that what Paul says here reflects a wider principle as well, so that sowing to the flesh involves all actions that are evil. Betz rightly sees that one sows to the flesh "in placing one's hope for salvation upon circumcision and obedience to the Jewish Torah, a move which would result in missing salvation altogether."[13] Further, "the works of the flesh" (5:19 – 21) manifest themselves in those who sow to the flesh, and sowing to the Spirit includes all that is lovely and good, as is summarized in "the fruit of the Spirit" (5:22 – 23).

Not only are there two different kinds of sowing, but two contrasting results are also envisioned. Those who sow to the flesh "will reap corruption" (θερίσει φθοράν). The future tense "will reap" points to the last judgment. What is the nature of the corruption in view here? It could merely be a general term, indicating lack of fruitfulness in this life or the failure to receive rewards above and beyond eternal life (with eternal life itself being secured). But the contrast indicates that corruption refers to final destruction and final judgment, for those who sow to the Spirit "will reap eternal life" (θερίσει ζωὴν αἰώνιον). Since "eternal life" is contrasted with "corruption," the latter means that one will not enjoy the life of the coming age, while the former refers to the eschatological reward of life that is promised to those who sow to the Spirit.[14] Paul's gospel of grace in Galatians does not countenance moral laxity. Righteousness is not based on works, but those who do not practice good works will not receive the final inheritance.[15] The Pauline gospel of grace does not provide a foundation for license.

6:9 And let us not lose heart in doing good, for we will reap in due time, if we do not grow weary (τὸ δὲ καλὸν ποιοῦντες μὴ ἐγκακῶμεν, καιρῷ γὰρ ἰδίῳ θερίσομεν μὴ ἐκλυόμενοι).The Galatians are exhorted not to become discouraged in doing good,

---

13. Betz, *Galatians*, 308; cf. Lührmann, *Galatians*, 117.

14. Rightly Betz, *Galatians*, 308 – 9.

15. Against VanLandingham, who says that obedience "causes salvation" (*Judgment and Justification*, 209). In Paul's theology obedience is necessary for salvation and the evidence of salvation but never the basis for salvation.

for they will reap a reward on the last day. In several other places in Paul, readers are admonished not to lose heart (ἐγκακέω, 2 Cor 4:1, 16; Eph 3:13; 2 Thess 3:13; cf. Luke 18:1). Here the Galatians are encouraged not to become fainthearted in doing good.

"Doing good" (καλὸν ποιοῦντες) here focuses particularly on the giving of money and resources to alleviate the suffering or to meet the needs of others. The parallel in 2 Thess 3:13 is remarkable, and it bears the same meaning. After rebuking the idle and instructing the Thessalonians not to give to those who refuse to work, since the former must supply their own needs through useful work, Paul says, "And as for you, brothers, never tire of doing what is right." Both the verb "lose heart" and the idea of "doing good" match the text in Galatians.

It seems clear in the context of 2 Thess 3:13 that "doing good" means that the Thessalonians must continue to help those in financial need, even though they must not support those who refuse to work. So too, the Galatians are exhorted to continue to be generous in helping others and not to grow lax in such giving. Perhaps we can say again that "doing good" goes beyond helping others financially,[16] but the latter seems to be the focus of the Pauline exhortation.

As in 6:7 – 8 Paul reminds the Galatians of the eschatological reward. At the right time, a time known only to God and not disclosed to the Galatians or anyone else, those who have given generously will reap a reward. "Time" (καιρός) refers

here to the final judgment (cf. 1 Cor 4:5),[17] as the future "will reap" (θερίσομεν) confirms, for the verb "reap" also points to the final judgment 6:7 – 8.[18] The reward is reserved for those who do not become disheartened, and hence Paul exhorts the Galatians to continue to march in step with the Spirit by showing beneficience to others.

6:10 Therefore, let us do good to all, while we have opportunity, especially to those who are members of the household of faith (ἄρα οὖν ὡς καιρὸν ἔχομεν,[19] ἐργαζώμεθα[20] τὸ ἀγαθὸν πρὸς πάντας, μάλιστα δὲ πρὸς τοὺς οἰκείους τῆς πίστεως). The paragraph concludes with a strong inferential conjunction, literally translated "therefore then" (ἄρα οὖν). Hence, the main point of 6:6 – 10 is capsulized here. The term "opportunity" (καιρός) does not refer to the final judgment but to the opportunity to do good while life lasts (cf. Eph 5:16; Col 4:5).

The "good" in view here is particularly helping others materially,[21] so that their needs for everyday life are supplied. The limited resources of believers are acknowledged in the recognition that it is not possible to meet all needs. Indeed, a hierarchy is established, so that a priority is assigned to those who are fellow believers ("members of the household of faith"). Still, believers should also work to meet the needs of others as well, for if they have resources, they should do good to "all" — and the "all" includes unbelievers.

---

16. So Betz, *Galatians*, 309; Longenecker, *Galatians*, 281.

17. So Betz, *Galatians*, 309. He rightly sees that Paul warns them against "destroying salvation" (310) and proceeds to say, "Therefore, *maintaining* that freedom is the condition for reaching the fulfillment of salvation in the hereafter" (310). Betz emphasizes that this new life is different from the works of the law because it is the result of the Spirit's work. The believer must "not let himself get bored with and tired of the 'good'" (310).

18. Contra Longenecker, *Galatians*, 282, and Martyn, who relates it to the gift of the Spirit (*Galatians*, 554).

19. A few manuscripts read the subjunctive "let us have" (ἔχωμεν), but it is common to confuse the o and ω, and scribes would be prone to mistakenly include a subjunctive, given the subjunctives in 6:9 – 10.

20. Here a few scribes include the indicative "we do/work" (ἐργαζόμεθα), but as Metzger says, "intrinsic probability as well as significant external attestation favors the hortatory subjunctive in the context" (*Textual Commentary*, 530).

21. Betz is also correct in saying that it probably denotes "the fruit of the Spirit" (*Galatians*, 311).

Theology in Application

Giving to Assist Others

The importance of giving in order to assist others is highlighted by the attention Paul spends on it in this brief letter (6:6 – 10; cf. 2:10). We see a similar theme in 1 Tim 5:3 – 16. Here believers are commanded to support widows who are related to them. The failure to lend such support is considered a denial of the faith, and Paul identifies those who refuse to help needy widows in their families as worse than unbelievers (1 Tim 5:8). In other words, those who do not assist family members in need are not authentic believers. The text on widows confirms the principle of hierarchy seen in Gal 6:10. Believers should use their resources to help their families first. If extra funds are available, they should give to the church. Remaining resources should be given to assist those outside the circle of faith who are in need.

Generous giving is not optional according to Paul. It is a prime indication that one is walking in the Spirit (5:16), being led by the Spirit (5:18), and sowing to the Spirit (6:8). Indeed, we could say that generosity is one of the fruits of the Spirit, even though it is not listed in 5:22 – 23. Surely the list of the fruit of the Spirit is not comprehensive.

The importance of helping fellow believers is also emphasized by Paul's concern for the collection for the poor saints in Jerusalem. The collection was a major issue for Paul, as 1 Cor 16:1 – 4; 2 Cor 8:1 – 9:15; and Rom 15:22 – 29 attest. What it means to live in the Spirit is to demonstrate concern and care for others, and supplying physical needs is the most concrete way to do so. Hence, Paul ties how believers spend their money to their future eschatological reward. Those who are generous will receive eternal life on the last day, while those who are stingy and self-absorbed will face judgment.

Support for Teachers

It should also be noted that those who teach the gospel must be supported financially (6:6). This same teaching is reflected often elsewhere in the NT (cf. Matt 10:10; Luke 10:7; 1 Cor 9:14; 1 Tim 5:17 – 18). If at all possible, churches should support financially at least one person who can devote himself to preaching and teaching the Word of God (cf. Acts 6:4).

If this was true in NT times, it is no less true today. In our complex world, preachers of the Word need to study sufficiently so that they can preach faithfully and relevantly to the flock. Applying the message of Scripture to the myriad of issues we face today is not an easy task. Therefore, study and diligence are required of those who proclaim the Word. What preachers need, above all, is time to engage in such study and reflection. Hence, the financial assistance of believers in the congregation is of the utmost importance, for it frees pastors to attend to the ministry of the Word and prayer (cf. Acts 6:4).

It is amazing how we often find money for what we value. If we value going out for dinner, we often scrape up the money to do so. If we value an iPod or a computer, we often spring forth the money to buy what we want. So supporting at least one pastor is an indication of what we value in life. It testifies to how important teaching of the Word is in a congregation. We must remember that private Bible study is not the focus in the NT, though it is a good thing. What the NT emphasizes is the faithful public teaching of the Word, so that there is doctrinal harmony in the congregation.

We also know this principle of reaping what we sow from ordinary life. Our car was starting with difficulty, but we kept delaying bringing it in. One day it did not start, and then we had to have it towed and had to pay extra for not acting more quickly. If we eat more than we should, it may show up on our bodies as extra pounds. When we lived in Minnesota, I was driving too fast on a day when the road was slightly icy, and I slid into a car that was in front of me. Paul applies this same principle to our spiritual lives. If we invest in the things of the flesh, we will face judgment; but if we invest in the things of the Spirit, we will enjoy eternal life.

CHAPTER 24

Galatians 6:11 – 18

Literary Context

Galatians 6:11 – 18 should be categorized as a letter closing. The exhortation section has concluded with 6:10, and Paul now touches on several major themes of the letter. Cosgrove underestimates the role of the conclusion when he says that "the postscript itself affords no immediate entrée into the inner logic of the epistle."[1] The central themes of the letter are touched upon in the conclusion so that the Galatians are reminded of what is at stake in the controversy.

By contrast, Betz overstates his case in saying that that the postscript "contains the interpretive clues to the understanding of Paul's major concerns in the letter as a whole and should be employed as the hermeneutical key to the intentions of the Apostle."[2] Nevertheless, he rightly sees that the conclusion plays a major role in interpreting the letter, and we must not follow Cosgrove in shunting it aside. Betz identifies this section as the *peroratio* (summary and conclusion) and says this is the "last chance to remind the judge or the audience of the case, and it tries to make a strong emotional impression upon them."[3]

Paul's letters typically conclude with a prayer for grace (6:18). What is striking here is that two verses earlier we also have a prayer for peace and mercy (6:16). Still, most of the elements of the conclusion are unique to Galatians and are best explained by the situation addressed in the letter.

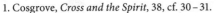

---

1. Cosgrove, *Cross and the Spirit*, 38, cf. 30 – 31.
2. Betz, *Galatians*, 313. So also Weima, "Gal 6:11 – 18,"

92 – 93; Longenecker, *Galatians*, 286 – 89.
3. Betz, *Galatians*, 313.

Main Idea

Many of the major themes of the letter are summarized in the conclusion. Paul teaches that the cross of Christ is the decisive turning point in history so that the new creation is inaugurated. Hence, those who are still advocating circumcision have denied the cross and belong to the present evil age (1:4).

Translation

(See next page.)

Structure

Weima notes various unique features of this section of the letter.[4] (1) Paul emphasizes the importance of the conclusion by writing in large letters (6:11) and introduces the section with the exclamation "see" (ἴδετε). (2) The closing statements are much longer than usual (6:12 – 15). (3) "The peace benediction (v. 16) is conditional."[5] (4) The term "Israel of God" (6:16) is unusual. (5) The tone of 6:17 is "caustic." (6) Paul includes the typical grace benediction (6:18), but personal greetings are absent and there is no expression of praise or thanksgiving in a concluding doxology.

The conclusion of the letter commences with Paul taking up the reed pen, authenticating the letter and underscoring its contents by writing in his own hand (6:11). In 6:12 – 13 he reminds the Galatians one last time of the danger of the opponents. Their motives for promoting circumcision, Paul asserts, are not sincere. They desire to avoid the persecution of the cross (6:12). Paul supports the assertion in 6:12 by claiming that the agitators themselves do not observe the law ("for," γάρ, 6:13). They promote circumcision only to advance themselves.

The centrality of the cross comes to the forefront again in 6:14, which is scarcely surprising since circumcision points to the cross and is fulfilled in the cross.[6] By way of contrast to the opponents, Paul does not boast in himself but only in the cross (6:14). Through the cross the present world has been crucified to Paul, and Paul (and all believers) has been crucified to the world. The enticements of the world no longer hold the same grandeur they did previous to Paul's conversion.

In 6:15, because (see "for," γάρ) of the cross of Christ, neither circumcision nor uncircumcision matters anymore. What matters is the new creation inaugurated through the cross of Christ. Those who grasp the significance of the new creation march in step with it and acknowledge that circumcision and uncircumcision are

---

4. Weima, "Gal 6:11 – 18," 90 – 91.

5. Weima notes that none of the other final peace benedictions in Paul are conditional (ibid., 91, n. 2).

6. For the centrality of the cross in the postscript and the letter, see ibid., 104.

Galatians 6:11-18

11	exclamation	**See with what large letters I am writing to you in my own hand.**
12a	assertion	**Those who want to make a good showing in the flesh try to compel you to be circumcised,**
b	purpose (of 12a)	only so that they will not be persecuted because of the cross of Christ.
13a	basis (of 12a-b)	For those who are circumcised do not keep the law themselves,
b	contrast (to 13a)	but they want you to be circumcised
c	purpose (of 13b)	so that they might boast in your flesh.
14a	contrast (to 13a-b)/desire	But may I never boast, except in the cross of our Lord Jesus Christ,
b	series (to 14a)	through which the world has been crucified to me, and
c	series (to 14b)	I am crucified to the world.
15a	basis (of 14a-c)	For neither is circumcision anything,
b	series (to 15a)	nor is uncircumcision anything, but
c	contrast (to 15a-b)	a new creation is everything.
16a	prayer wish	And for those who shall keep in step with this rule, may peace and mercy be upon them, even upon the Israel of God.
b	explanation (of 16a)	
17a	conclusion	From now on let no one cause me trouble,
b	basis (of 17a)	for I bear the marks of Jesus on my body.
18a	prayer wish	**May the grace of our Lord Jesus Christ be with your spirit, brothers.**
b	exclamation	**Amen.**

insignificant in and of themselves. They see clearly that only the new creation matters. Hence, Paul prays that those who follow this "rule" (κάνων) will enjoy God's peace and mercy, and that this peace and mercy will be the portion of the Israel of God — the church of Jesus Christ (6:16).

With the dawning of the new creation and the centrality of the cross, Paul concludes (see the words "from now on," τοῦ λοιποῦ) with the wish that no one will trouble him any further (6:17). After all, Paul's physical suffering for the gospel indicates the centrality of the cross in his life. Finally, the letter ends appropriately with a wish for grace (6:18).

Exegetical Outline

   III. A Call to Freedom from the Law and Freedom in the Spirit (4:12 – 6:10)

➡ IV. **Final Summary (6:11 – 18)**

     A. The Importance of the Conclusion (6:11)

     B. The Opponents' Desire to Avoid Persecution (6:12)

     C. The Opponents' Desire for Adulation (6:13)

     D. Boasting Only in the Cross (6:14)

     E. Centrality of the New Creation (6:15)

     F. Peace and Mercy for the Israel of God (6:16)

     G. Paul's Sufferings for the Cross (6:17)

     H. Prayer Wish: Grace (6:18)

Explanation of the Text

6:11 See with what large letters I am writing to you in my own hand (ἴδετε πηλίκοις ὑμῖν γράμμασιν ἔγραψα τῇ ἐμῇ χειρί). The conclusion of the letter is marked by Paul taking the reed pen from the amanuensis and writing the conclusion in his own hand.[7] We see elsewhere that Paul concludes the letters with his own signature, so to speak (cf. 1 Cor 16:21; Col 4:18; 2 Thess 3:17; Phlm 19). In the other letters such a signature comes virtually at the end. In Galatians, however, Paul recapitulates one more time many of the major themes of the letter before closing. The large letters are not due to Paul's poor eyesight or hands that are deformed, or to a crucifixion! They signify the importance of the conclusion, provoking the readers to pay special heed to Paul's final thoughts.[8]

6:12 Those who want to make a good showing in the flesh try to compel you to be

---

7. Gordon J. Bahr argues that Paul's own writing commences in 5:2. See "The Subscriptions in the Pauline Letters," *JBL* 87 (1968): 35. Longenecker, however, points out that in Greek epistles we find shorter subscriptions (Richard N. Longenecker, "Ancient Amanuenses and the Pauline Epistles," in *New Dimensions in New Testament Study* [Grand Rapids: Zondervan, 1974], 290 – 91).

8. Rightly Betz, *Galatians*, 314; Weima, "Gal 6:11 – 18," 90 – 91, n. 1; Longenecker, *Galatians*, 290. See Weima for the other views mentioned here.

circumcised, only so that they will not be persecuted because of the cross of Christ (ὅσοι θέλουσιν εὐπροσωπῆσαι ἐν σαρκί, οὗτοι ἀναγκάζουσιν ὑμᾶς περιτέμνεσθαι, μόνον ἵνα τῷ σταυρῷ τοῦ Χριστοῦ[9] μὴ διώκωνται[10]). Paul indicts the motives of the opponents, saying that they promoted circumcision to avoid persecution. The Judaizers precipitated the letter by disturbing the Galatians with their promotion of circumcision (1:7; 5:2 – 4, 10). Only now does Paul directly state that advocacy for circumcision hails from the opponents.

Significantly, the word "compel" (ἀναγκάζουσιν) appears for the third time in the letter. In 2:3 – 4 it was the false brothers who attempted to "compel" Titus to receive circumcision, but Paul stoutly resisted them to preserve the truth of the gospel. Peter behaved like the false brothers in requiring Gentiles to observe Jewish food laws (2:11 – 14), and in doing so he was in effect "compelling" them (2:14) to become Jews to join the people of God. Therefore, the use of the word "compel" here indicates that the opponents in Galatia are no different from false brothers.[11]

Nor does Paul commend them for their good intentions and sincerity. He indicts their motives, claiming that they wanted to advertise the circumcision of the Galatians "to make a good showing in the flesh." They longed for the praise and adulation of others according to Paul. At the same time the circumcision of the Galatians would protect the Judaizers from persecution. No Jewish opponent could say that they refuse to keep the law, for they could present the circumcision of the Galatians as evidence of their fidelity to the law.[12] Jewett thinks the persecution stemmed from Zealots.[13] Evidence is lacking, however, to verify such a precise identification. As Esler points out, persecution of believers existed in the 30s without Zealot participation.[14] Similarly, Muddiman remarks that it is plausible that the Judaizers feared Jewish opponents even if they are not technically identified as Zealots.[15]

Paul insists that their avoidance of persecution reflects their dismissal of the cross of Christ. One is righteous either by circumcision or by the cross as far as Paul is concerned — either by the law or by Christ. By promoting circumcision these opponents avoided the offense of the cross (cf. 5:11).[16] At the same time they lost any benefit in what Christ has done (5:2 – 4). One cannot trust in circumcision and the cross at the same time, for the cross assigns salvation to the Lord, while circumcision focuses on human obedience.

6:13 For those who are circumcised do not keep the law themselves, but they want you to be circumcised so that they might boast in your

---

9. "Jesus" (Ἰησοῦ) is added in a few manuscripts, but it is almost certainly secondary and was probably added for liturgical reasons.

10. The textual evidence is divided between the indicative and subjunctive here, but fortunately the meaning remains unaffected.

11. As many commentators note, the verb "compel" (ἀναγκάζουσιν) here is conative. E.g., Fung, *Galatians*, 302, n. 12; Longenecker, *Galatians*, 291; Matera, *Galatians*, 225.

12. The persecution would likely stem from failure to abide by the Torah. See Betz, *Galatians*, 315 – 16.

13. Jewett, "Agitators," 340 – 41. Jewett has been followed by Bruce, *Galatians*, 269; Longenecker, *Galatians*, 291; Weima, "Gal 6:11 – 18," 97.

14. Esler, *Galatians*, 74. See also the criticisms of Fung, *Galatians*, 6 – 7.

15. Muddiman, "Anatomy of Galatians," 259 – 60. Some are tempted to dismiss what Paul says here as rhetoric, but Muddiman rightly concludes that Paul would undermine his own case if he inaccurately criticized his opponents (260). Still, Muddiman goes too far in saying that the opponents did not argue passionately for circumcision and devotion to Torah (264 – 67). They were not libertines, and the most plausible reading is that they argued for submission to Torah. Paul simply uncovers their motives for doing so.

16. The dative "cross" (τῷ σταυρῷ) is likely a dative of cause here. So Bruce, *Galatians*, 269; Moule, *Idiom Book*, 45; Wallace, *Greek Grammar*, 167 – 68; Turner, *Syntax*, 242.

flesh (οὐδὲ γὰρ οἱ περιτεμνόμενοι[17] αὐτοὶ νόμον φυλάσσουσιν ἀλλὰ θέλουσιν ὑμᾶς περιτέμνεσθαι, ἵνα ἐν τῇ ὑμετέρᾳ σαρκὶ καυχήσωνται). In 6:12 Paul argued that the agitators' insistence on circumcision came from ignoble motives. They were not genuinely devoted to the law. In actuality they wanted to avoid persecution. In 6:13 Paul supports the charge further (see the "for" [γάρ] linking the verses together).[18] Even though the opponents have been circumcised, they themselves do not keep the law.[19]

It is difficult to know precisely what Paul has in mind here. Is he saying that they were attempting to keep the law but they failed to do so? Such a reading fits with the Pauline teaching about the impossibility of observing the law elsewhere (3:10; 5:3; Rom 1:18 – 3:20).[20] Or Paul may be saying that they violated the law because of their desire to boast in the flesh of their converts.[21] Jesus criticized the Pharisees on both scores in Matthew 23 — for their failure to keep the law themselves and for their base motives. If one adopts the second view, the devotion of the Judaizers to the law stemmed from their desire to look impressive in the eyes of others.

Still, it seems somewhat more likely that Paul speaks here not of their motives (he indicted their

motives in 6:12) but of their failure to do what the law says (the first view above). Paul's criticisms here, then, are similar to what Jesus said in Matthew 23, so that the Judaizers are censured for the motives of their hearts (6:12) and their objective disobedience (6:13). When Paul speaks of their failure to keep the law, it seems more likely that he is not focusing on their motives. Such disobedience to the law is evident in objective ways — in the transgressing of specific commandments. In other words, Paul has in mind something rather similar to his words about the Jews in Rom 2:17 – 24.

The opponents are designated here as "those who are circumcised" (οἱ περιτεμνόμενοι). Some have concluded from the present tense that the opponents were Gentiles who had recently submitted to circumcision.[22] Such an interpretation overreads the present tense of the participle. The present participle does not necessarily point to *present time*.[23] Instead, it is a general designation, referring to those who are circumcised as a class. Here it refers to the opponents, who were almost certainly Jewish.[24]

6:14 But may I never boast, except in the cross of our Lord Jesus Christ, through which the world

---

17. The perfect tense "those who have been circumcised" (περιτετμημένοι) is supported by significant textual evidence (𝔓[46], B, F, [G], L, Ψ, 6, 365, 614, 630, 1175, 2495, etc.). The present tense per NA[27] also has significant support (ℵ, A, C, D, K, P, 33, 81, 104, 1241[s], etc.). The reading in NA[27] should be accepted, for scribes would be more likely to use a perfect tense in order to emphasize the past circumcision of the opponents.

18. But see Betz, who says that the second "for" (γάρ) "may simply mark a sequence" (Betz, *Galatians*, 316, n. 40).

19. Burton argues that the reference is to the converts of the Judaizers in Galatia (*Galatians*, 351 – 53). Such a view should be rejected, because the "for" (γάρ) ties together vv. 12 – 13. What is fatal for Burton's view is the verb "they want" (θέλουσιν), for it clearly refers to the opponents, as even Burton admits. It is much more natural to think the same subject is in view with both the verbs "keep" (φυλάσσουσιν) and "want" (θέλουσιν) (so Fung, *Galatians*, 304).

20. So Hong, *Law in Galatians*, 108.

21. So Barrett, *Freedom and Obligation*, 87. For Hardin's unlikely suggestion as to the meaning of the verb, see the In Depth discussion on whether Galatians is written against the empire in the introduction. Against A. B. du Toit, Paul's language is not merely hyperbolic here. "Galatians 6:13: A Possible Solution to an Old Exegetical Problem," *Neot* 28 (1994): 157 – 61.

22. Munck, *Paul and the Salvation of Mankind*, 87 – 90; Schoeps, *Paul*, 65. Longenecker rightly remarks that it is hard to conceive of Gentiles facing danger of persecution from Jews (*Galatians*, 292).

23. Cf. here Barrett, *Freedom and Obligation*, 57; Hong, *Law in Galatians*, 117 – 18; Martyn, *Galatians*, 549; Howard, *Paul: Crisis in Galatia*, 17.

24. See the introduction for further discussion.

has been crucified to me, and I am crucified to the world (ἐμοὶ δὲ μὴ γένοιτο καυχᾶσθαι εἰ μὴ ἐν τῷ σταυρῷ τοῦ κυρίου ἡμῶν Ἰησοῦ Χριστοῦ, δι᾽ οὗ ἐμοὶ κόσμος ἐσταύρωται κἀγὼ κόσμῳ). In contrast to the opponents, who were self-absorbed and engaged in devotion to the law to win the praise of others, Paul prays that he might boast only in the cross of Christ. Those devoted to the law boast in what they have accomplished and in their works, even though they disobey the law. Those who boast in the cross put all their confidence in what Christ has done for them. They acknowledge that salvation is wholly of the Lord.

The cross of Jesus Christ has introduced the new creation (6:15). The present evil age no longer rules over those who have been delivered by the cross.[25] Those who boast in the cross understand that the law does not bring righteousness; the cross kills the old person and introduces a new reality (2:21). The curse of the law has been removed by Christ's taking the curse on himself (3:13), and hence those who boast in the cross rejoice in their deliverance from the elements of the world and their freedom from the law (4:3 – 5). The relative pronoun "which" (οὗ) likely refers back to the cross here instead of to Jesus Christ, for the cross has spelled death to the old world order for Christians.[26] The world no longer rules over them, and they are no longer beholden to the world.[27]

It is legitimate to speak of Christians in general here, for surely Paul's experience reflects the experience of all believers. The answer to the problem of humanity is death, but the death of believers is in the cross of Christ, for they have been crucified with him (2:20),[28] so that the passions and desires of the flesh have now been crucified (5:24).

6:15 For neither is circumcision anything, nor is uncircumcision anything, but a new creation is everything (οὔτε γὰρ[29] περιτομή τί ἐστιν οὔτε ἀκροβυστία ἀλλὰ καινὴ κτίσις). The "for" (γάρ) here grounds 6:14. Since the world has been crucified to Paul (and by extension to all Christians), whether one is circumcised or not is utterly irrelevant. What is remarkable is that circumcision is assigned to the old world order, to the old creation rather than the new creation. The law is part of the old age, while the cross inaugurates the new age. The centrality of the new creation functions as an envelope with the introduction to the letter, where the death of Christ delivers from the present evil age (1:4).[30] The new creation has dawned, in other words, through the cross of Christ.[31]

We see the same dynamic in 2 Cor 5:14 – 21. There Paul also features the new creation, and

---

25. The "world" functions as the antonym to "the new creation." So Fung, *Galatians*, 306 – 7; Weima, "Gal 6:11 – 18," 102 – 3.

26. Cf. Calvin, *Galatians*, 184; Lightfoot, *Galatians*, 223; Longenecker, *Galatians*, 294. If the pronoun (οὗ) refers to "Jesus Christ" (Ἰησοῦ Χριστοῦ) rather than "cross" (σταυρῷ), the interpretive difference is minimal, since Christ is the crucified one (so Betz, *Galatians*, 318; Weima, "Gal 6:11 – 18," 103).

27. The world here refers to the arena in which trust is placed in circumcision and observance of the law. Cf. Hong, *Law in Galatians*, 86.

28. Therefore, the focus here is still on what God has done in Christ. So Martyn, *Galatians*, 564.

29. A number of texts here harmonize with Gal 5:6 so that the beginning of the verse reads "for in Christ Jesus neither

[circumcision ... nor uncircumcision]" (ἐν γὰρ Χριστῷ Ἰησοῦ οὔτε) and "means" (ἰσχύει) is substituted for "is" (ἐστιν). Since scribes tended to harmonize, and there is significant textual support for NA[27], the reading in the text should be accepted.

30. The contrast with "world" suggests a reference to the new creation rather than merely a new creature. Contra Lightfoot, *Galatians*, 224; Ridderbos, *Galatians*, 226. So Weima, "Gal 6:11 – 18," 102, n. 32. There is probably an allusion to the new heavens and new earth of Isa 65:17 and 66:22 here. Cf. Hays, *Echoes of Scripture*, 157 – 59.

31. Kwon rightly sees that Paul exhorts believers to walk in accordance with the new creation, but against Kwon there is the notion of an already but not yet here (*Eschatology*, 173 – 74). Paul encourages the Galatians to live in accord with the new creation that has dawned.

again it is tied inextricably to the cross of Christ. The new creation has been inaugurated in Christ and will be consummated at the eschaton, when the groaning that characterizes the old creation will pass away (Rom 8:18 – 22).

Remarkably, in the midst of a great conflict over circumcision, Paul does not elevate uncircumcision either. Those who find significance in uncircumcision belong to the old world order as well. There is no particular virtue in uncircumcision, which explains why Paul was willing to circumcise Timothy (Acts 16:3). If circumcision is practiced for cultural reasons and not to achieve salvation, observing it is up to one's individual conscience.

Verse 15 parallels both 5:6 and 1 Cor 7:19. The faith that expresses itself in love (5:6) is now a reality because the new creation has dawned. The ability to keep God's commands is a reality in the new creation (1 Cor 7:19). Eschatology, then, plays a vital role in Galatians, for the Judaizers were attached to the old age and failed to see that the new has come. Their error, however, was not merely eschatological; there were anthropological corollaries and causes, for those who are attached to the old age cling to it because they desire to establish their own righteousness instead of receiving the righteousness from God (cf. Rom 10:3).

6:16 And for those who shall keep in step with this rule, may peace and mercy be upon them, even upon the Israel of God (καὶ ὅσοι τῷ κανόνι τούτῳ στοιχήσουσιν, εἰρήνη ἐπ' αὐτοὺς καὶ ἔλεος καὶ ἐπὶ τὸν Ἰσραὴλ τοῦ θεοῦ). Paul now adds a prayer wish for those who will walk by the rule that he has just enunciated in 6:15. The rule he has in mind is the preeminence of the new creation, which leads to the conclusion that both

circumcision and uncircumcision are irrelevant.[32] Paul uses the verb "march in step with" (στοιχέω), which he used with reference to walking in step with the Spirit in 5:25 (cf. also Phil 3:16). Those who keep in step with the Spirit also keep in step with the new creation.[33]

The link between the Spirit and the new age is scarcely surprising since the Spirit is the gift of the new creation. Indeed, in Isa 32:12 – 18 the pouring out of the Spirit spells the coming of the new creation:

> Beat your breasts for the pleasant fields,
>> for the fruitful vines
> and for the land of my people,
>> a land overgrown with thorns and briers —
> yes, mourn for all houses of merriment
>> and for this city of revelry.
> The fortress will be abandoned,
>> the noisy city deserted;
> citadel and watchtower will become a wasteland forever,
>> the delight of donkeys, a pasture for flocks,
> till the Spirit is poured upon us from on high,
>> and the desert becomes a fertile field,
>> and the fertile field seems like a forest.
> Justice will dwell in the desert
>> and righteousness live in the fertile field.
> The fruit of righteousness will be peace;
>> the effect of righteousness will be quietness
>> and confidence forever.
> My people will live in peaceful dwelling places,
>> in secure homes,
>> in undisturbed places of rest.

The text from Isaiah shows the transformation of the wilderness and fields (the new creation) that will arrive when the Spirit is poured out on God's people.

---

32. The standard, then, is not merely the new creation (Martyn, *Galatians*, 567; Matera, *Galatians*, 226), but the entire statement in 6:15 (Betz, *Galatians*, 319; Longenecker, *Galatians*, 296 – 97). For the new creation here, see Martyn, *Galatians*, 570 – 74.

33. Betz glosses the verb here as "follow or conform to" (*Galatians*, 320 – 21).

Paul prays that God's peace and mercy will belong to those who walk according to the rule of the new creation. Conversely, those who do not live in such a way stand under a curse (1:8 – 9).[34] This is the only text in Paul where we have peace and mercy together without any mention of grace (cf. 1 Tim 1:2; 2 Tim 1:2), though a grace prayer wish concludes the letter in 6:18. Perhaps he prays for peace because of the disruption and disturbance caused by the agitators (cf. also 1:3). He prays for mercy because he casts his eye on the final judgment, for what is needed from God on that day is not what is deserved but his beneficient mercy.

In Depth: Israel of God

The last words of Gal 6:16, "even upon the Israel of God" (καὶ ἐπὶ τὸν Ἰσραὴλ τοῦ θεοῦ), could be interpreted to refer to ethnic Israel or to the church of Jesus Christ. Scholars dispute whether Paul refers (1) to a remnant of Jewish believers within the church of Jesus Christ,[35] or (2) to Gentile believers (along with Jewish believers) who constitute the new people of God — the new and true Israel.[36] If the reference is to ethnic Israel, it is limited to Jewish believers in Christ, for it is "the Israel *of God*," not merely ethnic Israel.[37] Burton argues that the order of the words in the benediction supports a reference to ethnic Israel, for if, says Burton, Paul had the church in mind, "mercy" would precede "peace,"[38] and he sees peace as the petition for the church, while mercy is the request for unredeemed Jews.[39]

Richardson argues that peace belongs to those who conform to the rule, while mercy relates to a distinct group: the Israel of God.[40] He also contends that "Israel" does not denote the church until the writings of Justin Martyr in AD 160.[41] Finally, Johnson argues that the conjunction used here (καί) almost certainly means "and," indicating that ethnic Israel is in view.[42]

It is unlikely that the dispute can be resolved on the basis of grammar alone. Köstenberger cautiously suggests that the nouns "peace" and "mercy" belong

---

34. So Betz, *Galatians*, 321.

35. So, e.g., S. Lewis Johnson Jr., "Paul and 'the Israel of God': An Exegetical and Eschatological Case-Study," in *Essays in Honor of J. Dwight Pentecost* (ed. Stanley D. Touissaint and Charles H. Dyer; Chicago: Moody Press, 1986), 181 – 96; W. S. Campbell, "Israel," *DPL*, 441 – 42; Robinson, "Jewish and Gentile Believers," 45 – 47; Mussner, *Galaterbrief*, 417; Peter Richardson, *Israel in the Apostolic Church* (SNTSMS 10; Cambridge: Cambridge Univ. Press, 1969), 74 – 84; Gottlob Schrenk, "Was bedeutet 'Israel Gottes'?" *Jud* 5 (1949): 81 – 94. Schrenk's fundamental argument is that Israel always refers to ethnic Israel, and Paul concludes by referring to ethnic Jews who belong to the Lord. Bachmann argues that the reference is to ethnic Israel, and it should not be limited

to Jewish Christians. See Bachmann, *Anti-Judaism in Galatians?* 101 – 23.

36. See, in the discussion below, the scholars who support this view.

37. So Burton, *Galatians*, 358; Bruce, *Galatians*, 275; Mussner, *Galaterbrief*, 417; Richardson, *Israel*, 82.

38. So also Richardson, *Israel*, 76 – 80.

39. Burton, *Galatians*, 358.

40. Richardson, *Israel*, 74 – 84. Richardson paraphrases his view as follows, "May God give peace to all who will walk according to this criterion, and mercy also to his faithful people Israel" (84).

41. Richardson, *Israel*, 9 – 32, 83, n. 2.

42. S. Johnson, "Paul and 'the Israel of God,'" 187 – 88.

to the same implied "to be" verb, so that the Israel of God is not a distinct ethnic entity.[43] Furthermore, the conjunction here (καί) may also be construed as ascensive (meaning "even"), and hence to identify the church as God's Israel is exegetically possible, though such an issue must be resolved by context.[44] It is true that in most instances in Paul "Israel" refers to ethnic Israel (Rom 9:6, 27, 31; 10:19, 21; 11:2, 7, 25, 26; Eph 2:12; Phil 3:5), though the referent in the second use in Rom 9:6 and in Rom 11:26 is debated. The predominant usage is not of great significance, however, for most of the uses are in Rom 9 – 11, where the context makes clear that Paul is discussing the fate of ethnic Israel.[45]

Furthermore, in 1 Cor 10:18 Paul speaks of (lit.) "Israel according to flesh," which at least suggests that there may be a contrast between Israel according to the flesh and Israel according to the Spirit, and the latter could possibly include Gentile Christians. The term "Israel" is not decisive in any case, for context as always must be determinative, and here the arguments for Israel referring to the church of Jesus Christ, made up of both Jews and Gentiles, are compelling.

The key question in Galatians is whether one must become a Jew and be circumcised to belong to the people of God. Must one receive circumcision to belong to the family of Abraham? The false teachers argued that circumcision and observance of the law were required to be part of Abraham's family. But Paul has argued throughout the letter that circumcision is unnecessary and that those who put their faith in Christ belong to the family of Abraham. When he speaks of "the Israel of God" at the conclusion of the letter, where he rehearses the major themes of the letter, he is driving home the point that believers in Christ, members of the new creation, are the true Israel.[46]

Such an interpretation fits with the whole of the letter, for believers in Christ are the true sons of Abraham. But if they are Abraham's children and belong to

---

43. Andreas Köstenberger, "The Identity of the ΙΣΡΑΗΛ ΤΟΥ ΘΕΟΥ (Israel of God) in Galatians 6:16," *Faith and Mission* 19 (2001): 13. Also, Köstenberger argues, contra Burton (*Galatians*, 357), that the order of the words ("peace" before "mercy") is not determinative. The pattern in the opening of the Pauline letters should not be imposed on the closings, which have "more variety" ("Galatians 6:16," 14). Richardson's claim (*Israel*, 79 – 81; cf. also Betz, *Galatians*, 322) that Paul relied on the nineteenth benediction of *Shemoneh Esreh* is implausible, given the late date of the tradition (So Köstenberger, "Galatians 6:16," 14). Beale observes that the AD 70 – 100 edition of that benediction lacks the key term "mercy," and hence the alleged parallel is hardly secure. See G. K. Beale, "Peace and Mercy Upon the Israel of God; The Old Testament Background of Galatians 6:16b," *Bib* 80 (1999): 207 – 8.

44. For an ascensive use of the conjunction (καί), see Turner, *Syntax*, 335; Köstenberger, "Galatians 6:16," 12 – 13; Beale, "Israel of God," 206 – 7, n. 8; Charles A. Ray Jr. "The Identity of the 'Israel of God,'" *The Theological Educator* 50 (1994): 106 – 8, 112 – 14.

45. We must beware of imposing the context of Rom 9 – 11 on Gal 6:16. So Nils A. Dahl, "Der Name Israel: Zur Auslegung von Gal 6,16," *Jud* 6 (1950): 161; Köstenberger, "Galatians 6:16," 14.

46. The decisive arguments for this view were expressed by Dahl, who interacts particularly with Schrenk (Dahl, "Der Name Israel," 161 – 70). For others who share Dahl's view, see Longenecker, *Galatians*, 298 – 99; Weima, "Gal 6:11 – 18," 105; Martyn, *Galatians*, 574 – 77; Köstenberger, "Galatians 6:16," 3 – 24.

his family, then they belong to the Israel of God. It would be highly confusing to the Galatians, after arguing for the equality of Jew and Gentile in Christ (3:28) and after emphasizing that believers are Abraham's children, for Paul to argue in the conclusion that only Jews who believe in Jesus belong to the Israel of God.[47] By doing so a wedge would be introduced between Jews and Gentiles at the end of the letter, suggesting that the latter were not part of the true Israel. Such a wedge would play into the hands of the opponents, who would argue that to be part of the true Israel one must be circumcised.[48]

Instead, Paul confirms one of the major themes of the letter. All believers in Christ are part of the true Israel, part of God's Israel.[49] This fits with what Paul says elsewhere when he says believers are the true circumcision (Phil 3:3). Since believers in Christ are the true family of Abraham and the true circumcision, they are also part of the true Israel.

Beale offers another argument for seeing a reference to the church in "Israel of God": the OT background.[50] He suggests that Isa 54 functions as the background, and particularly 54:10, where God's mercy and peace are promised to Israel. Further, the peace and mercy for Israel results in a new creation (cf. 54:11 – 12), which Paul emphasizes in Gal 6:15. Beale suggests that the mercy and peace promised to Israel will be the portion of eschatological Israel — the new Israel composed of Jews and Gentiles.

New creation themes are clearly present here, and so Paul may be hearkening back to Isa 54 and other texts with new creation themes. Scholars may dispute whether the connection to 54:10 is established since the words "peace and mercy" in Gal 6:16 are not in the same order in Isa 54:10. The case would be more convincing if more verbal parallels could be adduced. In any case, the decisive argument for seeing the church as the Israel of God is the argument of Galatians as a whole.

6:17 From now on let no one cause me trouble, for I bear the marks of Jesus on my body (Τοῦ λοιποῦ κόπους μοι μηδεὶς παρεχέτω, ἐγὼ γὰρ τὰ στίγματα τοῦ Ἰησοῦ ἐν τῷ σώματί μου βαστάζω). The words "from now on" (τοῦ λοιποῦ) are temporal, introducing a concluding statement in the letter.[51] They are also tied to the previous verses. Now that the new creation has been inaugurated,

---

47. Cf. also Beale, "Israel of God," 207.

48. Cf. Longenecker, *Galatians*, 298; Weima, "Gal 6:11 – 18," 105.

49. Ulrich Luz notes that the role of Jewish Christians or ethnic Israel is never raised in Galatians (*Das Geschichtsverständnis des Paulus* [BEvT 49; Munich: Chr. Kaiser,

1968], 285).

50. Beale, "Israel of God," 204 – 23. He evaluates other proposals on 207 – 8.

51. So Bruce, *Galatians*, 275; Betz, *Galatians*, 342, n. 122. It is also possible that the construction could be taken as logical rather than temporal. So Longenecker, *Galatians*, 299.

no one should trouble Paul with the requirements and regulations of the old creation by trying to impose the law on his converts.[52]

Paul grounds (γάρ) what he has to say in his sufferings. The marks inflicted on him because he belonged to Jesus Christ function as evidence that he was part of the true Israel. In the Greco-Roman world such marks were put on slaves as tattoos to signify ownership or to designate that one was dedicated to a god or under its protection.[53] But Paul does not think of tattoos here, for it is improbable that he would accept a mark prohibited by the OT (Lev 19:28).[54] Nor is it clear that the marks stem from eye trouble or that Paul thinks of his imminent martyrdom. The marks refer to "the physical wounds and scars left on his body as a result of the various sufferings he experienced as an apostle."[55]

The physical marks of circumcision belong to the old world and have no saving significance. Circumcision is utterly irrelevant before God (5:6; 6:15). The marks on Paul's body, however, belong to him because of the proclamation of the cross (5:11), and the opponents had no such marks since they avoided persecution because of their refusal to proclaim the scandal of the cross (5:11).[56] Paul's marks are the only ones that matter because they point to the cross.

The use of the word "bear" (βαστάζω) confirms that the cross is in view.[57] In Luke the verb is used of disciples who must carry their own cross daily (Luke 14:27), and in John it is used of Jesus, who carried his own cross to his execution (John 19:17). Paul as an apostle of Jesus Christ suffers for the sake of the gospel; the marks on his body

authenticate his apostolic ministry. His suffering (cf. 4:12 – 14) did not disqualify him for ministry. Indeed, his suffering was a corollary of Christ's suffering, though it was not of the same nature, since only the death of Jesus delivers from the present evil age (1:4), brings righteousness (2:21), removes the curse of the law (3:13), and redeems from the elements of the world and from the power of the law (4:3 – 5). Paul now challenges the Galatians with the import of his suffering, and Betz captures well the reason Paul writes the letter as a whole:

> Thus the letter to the Galatians reenacts the apostolic parousia and the Christianization of the Galatians. The difference is that at the beginning they were confronted as to whether or not they should accept the "gospel of Christ," while now they are asked to remain loyal to it and not bring upon themselves the curse of apostasy.[58]

6:18 May the grace of our Lord Jesus Christ be with your spirit, brothers. Amen (Ἡ χάρις τοῦ κυρίου ἡμῶν Ἰησοῦ Χριστοῦ μετὰ τοῦ πνεύματος ὑμῶν, ἀδελφοί· ἀμήν). Galatians concludes fittingly with the prayer wish that the grace of Christ will be the portion of the believers in Galatia. Paul typically includes such a prayer wish at the conclusion or near the conclusion of his letters (Rom 16:20; 1 Cor 16:23; 2 Cor 13:14; Eph 6:24; Phil 4:23; Col 4:18; 1 Thess 5:28; 2 Thess 3:18; 1 Tim 6:21; 2 Tim 4:22; Titus 3:15; Phlm 25). The grace benediction in Galatians does not match exactly any other letter, though it is closest to Phil 4:23 and Phlm 25, for in both those instances Paul prays for grace to be with the spirit of his readers. The

---

52. Cf. Betz, *Galatians*, 324.

53. For a valuable survey of the use of the term, see Otto Betz, "στίγμα," *TDNT*, 7:657 – 64.

54. Rightly Weima, who surveys other suggestions made ("Gal 6:11 – 18," 97 – 98). Cf. also Betz, *Galatians*, 324. Though perhaps he is suggesting that he is Christ's slave (so Hays,

Galatians, 347).

55. Weima, "Gal 6:11 – 18," 98. So most commentators.

56. So ibid., 99.

57. So Betz, *Galatians*, 325.

58. Ibid., 325.

word "spirit" (πνεύματος) here designates the whole person, so that it does not make a great difference whether the text says "grace be with you," or "grace be with your spirit."

Three features stand out here in v. 18: (1) the addition of the word "our" (ἡμῶν), so that it is *our* Lord Jesus Christ"; (2) the addition of the word "brothers";[59] and (3) the final "amen." Items one and two suggest that Paul wanted to assure the Galatians that they were part of the family of God,

the true children of Abraham. Jesus Christ is their Lord, and thus they truly belong to the people of God. Furthermore, they are "brothers," and hence genuinely part of God's family. The "amen" confirms and ratifies the prayer of grace.[60] Galatians focuses on the grace of God in Christ and insists that righteousness cannot be derived from the law. Paul concludes by reminding the Galatians of the power of such grace, and he prays that such grace will continue to be unleashed in their lives.

Theology in Application

The New Creation

What matters in life, Paul reminds us here, is the new creation. Our future inheritance does not involve a disembodied existence. We will not float on clouds in the sky in an ethereal and immaterial sphere. We will be raised from the dead and enjoy the coming physical new heavens and new earth (2 Pet 3:13; Rev 21:1; cf. Isa 65:17; 66:22). The curse that blights the present world (Gen 3:17 – 19) will be lifted, and "sorrow and sighing will flee away" (Isa 35:10). The groaning of the present creation will cease, and the liberty promised to the children of God and to the created order will dawn (Rom 8:18 – 25). The promise of a new creation teaches us that issues like circumcision and uncircumcision do not ultimately matter. Rituals and human practices are not fundamental; what is important is whether someone is a new creation in Christ (2 Cor 5:17).

In addition, the teaching on the new creation shows us that our work in this world is significant. The created world is not a necessary evil. It is the good and beautiful work of God, and hence our work in this world has significance. Every painting, every building, every meal made, and every work of landscaping image the work of our Creator and must not be dismissed as insignificant. The current world order is passing away. Ecclesiastes reminds us that there is a futility in our work in this world.

There is both continuity and discontinuity with the world to come, and hence we must not think that our labor in this world will ever bring in the new heaven and new earth. Any utopian scheme is destined to fail before the arrival of the new

---

59. As Betz points out, this is the only Pauline benediction with the word "brothers" (*Galatians*, 325).

60. Betz argues it was not original and was added later "by the church" (*Galatians*, 325); there is no evidence to support

this hypothesis, and we might expect the same to be added to all the Pauline letters if Betz were correct, but it occurs only in Rom 16:27 and 2 Tim 4:18.

creation. We must beware of the siren song of human perfectability, which sings the chorus that we can enjoy paradise during the present evil age. As believers we are to be optimistic but realistic, full of faith and hope without denying the curse that still rests on the present world.

The Israel of God

Paul makes it clear in Galatians that believers are the children of Abraham and the true circumcision. They are the true Israel of God (6:16). Is this a supersessionist view that leaves Israel behind? Space is lacking to investigate all the issues adequately here, but we must integrate what Paul says about Israel in Galatians with Rom 9 – 11.

Of course, that text is the subject of exegetical debates as well![61] Here I can only state my conclusion: Paul promises that there is a future, end-time salvation of ethnic Israel. Does such a promise contradict what Paul teaches in Galatians and in Ephesians, where the church of Jesus Christ consists of both Jews and Gentiles united in Christ (Eph 2:11 – 22)? Does Paul inconsistently reintroduce a special place for Israel after repudiating such in Galatians? Is Israel promised a salvation apart from the gospel? The answer to all of these questions is no. The future salvation of Israel does not contradict the unity of Jews and Gentiles in Christ, for Jews who are saved become part of the church of Christ. When Jews put their faith in Jesus Christ, they do not become part of a new entity, but belong to the new assembly of the redeemed along with their Gentile brother and sisters.

Nor is there any salvation of Israel apart from the gospel. The future salvation of Israel will occur when they put their faith in Jesus Christ as Savior and Lord. But is there favoritism here? Certainly not! The salvation of anyone is due to God's electing grace according to Rom 9 – 11. Why God chooses some and not others is hidden in the counsel of his will. If God has decided to show mercy to a great number of Jews at the end of history, that is his prerogative.

As believers, then, we celebrate our unity in Christ Jesus. We are brothers and sisters in the family of God. We are one body and belong to one another. Therefore, we are called upon as believers to love and care for one another, to bear one another's burdens as Paul instructs us in Galatians (6:2). May the world see that we are Jesus' disciples by our love for one another (John 13:34 – 35)!

---

61. For my understanding of these chapters, see Schreiner, *Romans*, 469 – 638.

Themes in Galatians

Galatians is intensely theological. The Judaizers were demanding that the Gentiles in Galatia who responded to the Pauline gospel get circumcised in order to belong to the people of God. Paul responds to the Galatians with what we could call "theological flurry." In his counterattack we see his view of God, Christ, the Spirit, the human plight apart from Christ, the gospel, justification by faith, the cross, the law, the inbreaking of the eschaton, the new life of believers, and his view of the people of God. The topics Paul covers are almost breathtaking in their breadth and their significance. Naturally Galatians does not represent a full-fledged exposition of any of these themes, but Paul primes the pump in ways that are illuminating.

God

As a Jew nutured in the OT and as one who saw the gospel fulfilling OT revelation, Paul confesses that there is only one God (3:20). Hence, the importance of the Shema for Paul is evident (Deut 6:4). The one God is the Creator of all and the Sovereign One. Since he is Lord of all, Paul pledges his truthfulness before God (1:20) and emphasizes that the aim of life is to glorify God (1:5, 24) by living for him (2:19) and pleasing him (1:10).

God's sovereignty and power are revealed in his raising Christ from the dead (1:1) and by his rule expressed in the coming kingdom (5:21). Indeed, he is working out his will in history. He chose to reveal Christ to Paul on the Damascus road and called him to be an apostle (1:1, 15–16). In the same way, he chose that Christ's death would liberate human beings from the evil of the present age (1:4), determining at what time in history he would send his Son for the redemption of the world (4:4–5).

Just as God called Paul on the Damascus road, so too he has called believers to faith in Christ (1:6). God's call is effectual and powerful, demonstrating that he takes the initiative in knowing and choosing those who are saved (4:9). God works out his saving plan in history by sending both his Son (2:20; 4:4) and his Spirit (4:6) for the redemption of human beings. Therefore, believers are now sons of God through Jesus Christ (3:26; 4:6). God is their dear Father (1:1, 3, 4) and they come to him confidently and joyfully in prayer because he is their Father (4:6). Salvation is of the Lord, and thus grace and peace come from him (1:3; 2:20; 3:18; 6:18). God justifies those who trust in him for salvation (3:6, 8), and those who are justified and saved know God (4:8 – 9) and belong to his assembly (1:13) — the true Israel (6:16).

Since God is sovereign, he is not mocked; those who refuse to obey him will face judgment on the last day (5:21; 6:7 – 8). He will judge according to the truth since he is not moved by human reputation (2:6).

Christ

Paul uses the title "Christ" about thirty-eight times in Galatians (depending on text-critical decisions). The title has not lost its significance for Paul. For Jesus to be the Christ means that he fulfilled the covenant made with David (2 Sam 7) and that he is the Anointed One, the Messiah of Israel. Paul uses the name "Jesus" seventeen times. Eight times he is identified as "Jesus Christ" and eight times as "Christ Jesus." Perhaps the former slightly emphasizes his humanity and the latter his messiahship.

Paul also identifies Jesus as God's Son. God revealed his Son to Paul on the Damascus road (1:16), and Paul lives by faith in God's Son, who demonstrated his love by giving his life for Paul (2:20). Jesus' sonship is also connected to his work on the cross in 4:4 – 5, and we have a fascinating Trinitarian-type statement in 4:6, for Paul mentions God who sent the Spirit, and the Spirit is said to be the "Spirit of his Son." Jesus is not only God's Son but he is the Lord of all (1:3, 19; 5:10; 6:14, 18), and hence should be venerated just as God is venerated.

Jesus clearly shares the same stature as God. Like God he called Paul to be an apostle (1:1), and grace and peace come from him (1:3; 6:18). Paul considers himself Christ's slave, for he saw Christ on the Damascus road (1:12, 16), and hence he lives to please him, just as he lives to please God (1:10). Salvation comes through believing in Jesus Christ (2:16; 3:22), and the gospel that Paul proclaims is focused on Jesus as the Christ (1:7).

Believers are incorporated into Christ (1:22; 2:4, 17; 3:14, 26, 28; 5:6), and they have died with Christ (2:19), been baptized into him (3:27), and are clothed with him (3:27). Indeed, Christ lives in believers (2:20) and is formed in believers (4:19). The fundamental question is whether believers belong to Christ (3:29; 5:24), for if they do, they are Abraham's offspring and the power of the flesh has been dethroned in their lives. Those who are cut off from Christ by relying on circumcision for salvation will be damned (5:2, 4).

We sketch in below the centrality of the cross of Christ in Galatians. Salvation does not come through circumcision but through the work of Jesus Christ on the cross. It is Christ Jesus who has set believers free (2:4; 5:1). The gospel is Christ's gospel (1:7), and his grace is revealed in it (1:6). Believers are called upon to fulfill his law (6:2). The Sinai law is no longer required now that Christ has come (3:24), for Jesus is the climax of salvation history since he is the true offspring of Abraham (3:16).

Plight of Humanity

Galatians does not systematically chart out the plight of human beings. Yet one of its main themes is that righteousness does not come by works of law but only through faith in Jesus Christ (cf. 2:16; 3:2, 5, 10). Why can't righteousness by obtained by works of law? Paul's argument cannot be restricted to salvation history, though that is certainly part of the answer. Works of law belong to the Sinai covenant, which has expired now that Christ has come. But Paul also argues that works of law do not bring righteousness because of human sin. A careful reading of 3:10 and 2:16 (see the commentary) indicates that God demands perfection, but human sin intervenes, preventing anyone from being right with God through obedience. Human beings stand under a curse because of sin (3:10). If human beings try to gain righteousness via the law, they will only confirm their own sinfulness (2:17 – 18).

The giving of the law did not remedy human sinfulness but exacerbated it, for the law was given to increase transgressions (3:19). The "under" phrases in Galatians illustrate the bleakness of the human condition. Human beings are "under a curse" (3:10), "under sin" (3:22), "under law" (3:23; 4:5, 21; 5:18), "under a custodian" (3:25), and "under the elements of the world" (4:3). All of these phrases are mutually interpretive, and hence to be "under law" is to belong to the old age of salvation history, where one is under the power of sin and under a curse.

Indeed, Paul says that those who are "under the elements" (4:3) and those who live under the law are enslaved. Hence, in the allegory of the two women, those who are under the law are compared to the slave Hagar. The law imprisons those who are under its authority (3:22 – 23). Therefore, human beings need to be freed by Jesus Christ, for he is the only one who can liberate and redeem those under the law (3:13; 4:5). The reference to "the elements" (4:3, 9) also indicates (see the commentary) that human beings are enslaved by spiritual powers — to spiritual beings ("gods," 4:8) who hold them in thrall. In other words, they are not only subjugated to sin but to demons.

Paul does not ultimately place blame on the law. The law simply illustrates the sin and evil of human beings. They are enslaved to sin and to spiritual powers and have no ability to extricate themselves; hence, they desperately need the saving work of God in Jesus Christ in order to be saved, for before salvation they were in bondage "to the present evil age" (1:4). The old "I" must die, and it does so by being crucified with Christ (2:19 – 20; 5:24; 6:14) in order to live to God.

Truth of the Gospel

Twice Paul refers to "the truth of the gospel" in Galatians (2:5, 14). On the first occasion the false brothers are indicted, who insinuated themselves into a meeting in Jerusalem to try to compel the circumcision of Titus (2:3 – 5). Paul resisted the imposition of circumcision to preserve the truth of the gospel. Paul also argues that Peter threatened the truth of the gospel, for in effect he was compelling Gentiles in Syrian Antioch to become Jews by refusing to eat with them unless they followed the food laws.

Not only does the phrase "truth of the gospel" link these two events (2:5, 14), but Paul also uses the verb "compel" (2:3, 14) to describe both incidents. Peter must be distinguished from the false brothers, for his actions did not stem from conviction but hypocrisy. Nevertheless, Peter's refusal to eat with the Gentiles had the same practical effect as the pressure stemming from the false brothers. Both the false brothers and Peter were saying that one had to observe the Mosaic law in order to be saved.

These two accounts assist us significantly in defining the truth of the gospel. The truth of the gospel is that one is justified not by works of law but only through faith in Jesus Christ (2:16). It is no accident that Paul unpacks this truth in his encounter with Peter, for the salvation of Gentiles in Antioch was at stake. The problem with the Judaizers in Galatia was that they proclaimed a false gospel and perverted the true gospel (1:6–7). We saw in the introduction that what the Judaizers required for entrance into the people of God was circumcision along with a promise to keep the entire Mosaic law. Such a "gospel," Paul asserts, warrants an anathema (1:8–9), an eschatological curse. Paul was particularly called to preach the gospel to the Gentiles (1:16; 2:7). He identifies this gospel in 3:8 as the universal blessing promised to Abraham (Gen 12:3). But as I argued in the commentary, the gospel proclaimed in advance to Abraham is explained in terms of justification by faith through the lenses of Gen 15:6.

It seems clear, then, that the truth of the gospel is that human beings are saved not through the works of the law but by faith in Jesus Christ. They put their trust in Jesus' atoning death on their behalf and are thereby declared to be right with God.

Justification by Faith

One of the central themes in Galatians is that justification is by faith alone. In former days Protestants were well acquainted with this theme, but now it seems to have lost its luster, and some are even wondering if the Reformation might be over. The new perspective on Paul and our postmodern times have sowed doubts in the minds of many. Is justification truly a central element in the Pauline gospel? Is it really important enough to warrant division in the Christian community?

If the biblical text is to continue to function as our authority, we need to hear afresh the truth of justification by faith alone, and we need to recapture Luther's confidence that the Holy Spirit speaks clearly with assertions so that we are spared from skepticism. Postmodernism, when it denies a clear word from God, functions as a kind of hermeneutical atheism in which the truths of Scripture can never be mediated to human beings who live in a certain cultural and historical location. I will not defend at length the theological judgments enunciated here since they are argued for in the commentary.

Justification does not play a minor role in the letter. The Judaizers apparently were orthodox in their Christology and believed that Jesus was the Messiah and the Son of God. Still, Paul charges them with propounding another gospel and threatens them with final judgment for their deficient soteriology (1:6–9). In the same way, some in Jerusalem tried to force Titus to be circumcised, saying it was required in order to belong to the people of God (2:3–5). Again, we have no indication that they were off-base theologically in any other area, and yet Paul identifies them as false brothers (2:4). Surely many Christians today would demure from such a strong judgment. But if we distance ourselves from Paul when he writes soteriologically, then it seems that his writings are bereft of all authority, and human judgments rather than the Scriptures become supreme.

As Paul reminds Peter, every true Christian knows, even if they were nurtured in the Torah from childhood on, that justification does not come from works of law but through faith in Jesus Christ (2:15–16). I argued in the commentary that there are good reasons to conclude that the verb "justify" and the noun "righteousness" are both forensic. They refer to the verdict of God as the Divine Judge that those who trust in God stand in the right before God, that they are acquitted rather than guilty. This righteousness belongs to believers because they are united with Christ in his death and resurrection (cf. 1:4; 2:16–20; 3:13, 26–28; 4:4–5; 5:24; 6:14).

If right standing with God may be obtained through obeying the law, then Christ died for nothing (2:21). Justification by grace alone through faith alone is the heart of the gospel (3:6, 8, 11, 24). If righteousness is obtained by human performance, then salvation is a human work (3:12), and the free and powerful grace of God is compromised. Indeed, if works secure right standing with God, then human beings should receive adulation and praise for what they have accomplished. Paul insists, on the contrary, that justification is entirely God's work, and hence all the praise and honor go to God alone for our salvation. Faith receives the gift that God has given through Jesus Christ and his work on the cross, whereas works obtain righteousness on the basis of human achievement.

Another truth relative to justification is that justification is fundamentally eschatological (2:17; 5:5). Justification is God's end-time pronouncement that those who trust in Christ rather than in themselves are declared to be not guilty. Still, the eschatological verdict has been declared ahead of time, so that those who trust in Christ crucified and risen are now free from God's condemnation. This verdict is grasped by faith and is not observable. Believers can fall into doubts and trials and can question whether they are truly right with God, and so they must grasp by faith each day the Christ in whom is their righteousness. On the day of judgment, however, God's verdict for the justified will be declared to the entire world, and what believers grasp now by faith will be sealed and secured in a way that will remove all doubts.

Centrality of the Cross

Justification and the cross are inextricably intertwined. The Galatians' temptation to undergo circumcision demonstrated a shocking misunderstanding of the role of the cross. Paul wonders if the Galatians had been bewitched or had a spell cast over them so that they no longer grasped the significance of Christ crucified (3:1). We must not make the mistake of thinking the cross is central only where Paul uses the term "cross," as if a word study approach will suffice. The theology of the cross in Galatians is present wherever Paul speaks of the death of Christ, and the cross is introduced in a variety of ways in the letter.

From the inception of the letter, the theme of Christ's death is introduced. The opening of the Pauline letters is typically brief, but Galatians is one of the letters that stands apart. In addition, the opening is distinctive in that Paul explicates the significance of Christ's death (1:4), for in no other opening does Paul even mention the death of Christ. Therefore, we rightly conclude that it is fundamental for interpreting the letter. Paul explains that Christ gave himself for believers to "deliver" them "from the present evil age" (1:4). The eschatological significance of Christ's death is underlined, in that it inducts one into the age of promise. What worries Paul is that the Galatians were falling backward in salvation history, for they were entranced with the demand that they should be circumcised and observe the law. Paul reminds them that the purpose of Christ's death is to free them from the old order, and that includes the regulations of the Sinai covenant.

The cross plays a bookends role in the letter, for just as Paul begins the letter by featuring the freedom won in the cross, so too he closes the letter by underlining the significance of the cross. Paul's only boast is in Christ's cross, by which he is crucified to the world and the world is crucified to him (6:14). Once again the cross and eschatology are inseparable. Just as the cross liberated believers from the present evil age (1:4), so too it crucifies attachment to this world (6:14). The opponents boasted in circumcising converts and took pleasure in external accomplishments because they lived to win the applause of others (6:12 – 13). They lived for comfort in order to avoid persecution. The cross severs a love affair with the world and grants a person (by grace!) a desire to boast only in the cross. A new reality — a new age — has begun through the cross, and Paul summons the Galatians and all believers to find their joy only in the cross and to renounce any boasting in human accomplishments.

Those who rely on obedience to the law in order to be right with God nullify the cross (2:21), for if righteousness can be attained through human performance and obedience, there was no need for Christ to die. Christ's death does not function primarily as an example of devotion to God, nor does it fundamentally summon human beings to imitate the narrative of Jesus' life, as if the purpose of the cross were to call us to imitate Christ. Such a theme is not absent in Paul (6:2) and the remainder of the NT. Still, if such a theme becomes predominant, the fundamental purpose of the cross is obscured, and the evil of human beings is slighted.

The only solution to sin and death is the death of the Son of God. Death and sin can only be conquered by Christ's taking the curse of the law upon himself (3:13) — the curse that human beings deserve because of their sin (3:10). In other words, human beings are enslaved to sin (4:3) since they are under a curse (3:10), under the power of sin (3:22), under a pedagogue (3:23, 25), and under the law (4:21; 5:18). The wonder of the cross is that Christ acts as our representative and substitute, taking on himself the punishment we deserve. As one who was born under the law (4:4) and who always kept the law, he freed those who lived under the law (4:5). The cross of Christ shouts "No!" to human ability and performance; it does not promote self-esteem but God-esteem. It renounces human righteousness (5:11) and salutes God's righteousness. The cross, as noted above, is fundamental to justification.

Paul could have argued that circumcision no longer applies since it is replaced by baptism. Remarkably he never makes that argument. His rejection of circumcision lies at a deeper and more fundamental level. The replacement for circumcision is the cross of Christ. Those who receive circumcision for salvation no longer profit from Christ (5:2), for in embracing circumcision they deny Christ and his benefits.

The Gift of the Spirit

Certainly the Holy Spirit plays a central role in Galatians, though Cosgrove mistakenly assigns 3:1 – 5 and the Holy Spirit as the main theme in the letter.[1] Instead, the Spirit constitutes the evidence that believers are right with God (3:1 – 5) and that they are truly sons of God (4:6). The Spirit functions as the unmistakable evidence that the new age has arrived and that the era of promise has begun. The Judaizers demanded that the Galatians receive circumcision to be inducted into the people of God. But Paul instructs the Galatians that they must chase away any doubts about whether they belong to God and repudiate the demand for circumcision. The Spirit's presence was dramatically and charismatically evident in the Galatians' lives (3:1 – 5), and hence there can be no doubt that they belonged to the people of God (cf. Acts 15:7 – 11).

The Galatians did not receive the Spirit by doing what the law commands but by placing their trust in the gospel of Christ crucified. In other words, Paul emphasizes that the Spirit is a consequence of believing in the gospel, assuring the Galatians that they were part of God's true Israel (6:16). The opponents disputed whether the Galatians were part of Abraham's family since they were not circumcised as

---

1. See comments on 3:3.

Abraham was. Paul strikes back by stressing that the Galatians enjoyed the blessing of Abraham because they had received the Holy Spirit (3:14). And those who enjoy the blessing of Abraham most certainly belong to his family.

Justification and the Spirit are correlative realities as well; hence, separating them too rigidly is misleading. Both justification and the Spirit are gifts of the new age. And if the gift of the Spirit, on the one hand, is a fruit of justification and a consequence of belief, it is also the case, on the other hand, that those who believe are born of the Spirit (4:29). New life cannot be generated by human beings, for they are "flesh" and belong to the old Adam, which is under the dominion of sin and death. The only hope for life, then, is the regenerating work of the Spirit. The Spirit both produces new life and is received as a gift of that same life.

The Spirit also plays a vital ethical role in Galatians, for the Galatians are exhorted to walk by the Spirit (5:16), be led by the Spirit (5:18), march in step with the Spirit (5:25), and sow to the Spirit (6:8). Thereby they can produce the fruit of the Spirit (5:22 – 23) and conquer the flesh in its contest with the Spirit (5:17). A life that is pleasing to God cannot be accounted for on the basis of human potential or effort. Such a life is supernatural and the fruit of the Spirit's work. Persevering in faith does not depend on human beings working their hardest but is the result of faith that the Spirit provides (3:3; 5:5).

Paul does not limit the Spirit's work to the inception of one's new life. Rather, the Spirit empowers believers so that they are enabled to please God in the warp and woof of everyday life. The power of the new life is supernatural, and yet believers are exhorted to yield to the Spirit, to sow to the Spirit, to march in step with the Spirit, and to walk in the Spirit. Life in the Spirit cannot be conceived of as a kind of spiritual floating in the air, where believers are caught up in spiritual ecstasy and passively let the Spirit move them. Instead, believers are summoned to give themselves daily to the Spirit so that he can work powerfully in them.

Already-Not Yet Eschatology

All of the themes explored here are interrelated, and hence we have already touched upon the eschatological character of Galatians. Beker, in his important book on apocalyptic in Paul, maintained that Galatians lacked such an apocalyptic character, and hence he saw Galatians as an exception to the apocalyptic focus in Paul.[2] But Martyn has rightly corrected Beker on this score and has shown that apocalyptic, which I am using synonymously here with the word eschatology, plays a prominent role in Galatians.[3]

We have already seen the importance of eschatology in the topics touched on above. Justification is an eschatological verdict that has been declared in advance

---

2. Beker, *Paul the Apostle*, 58.

3. See Martyn, "Apocalyptic Antinomies," 410 – 24.

of the last day. This is not to say that the verdict announced now only refers to a future reality. Believers are already justified, and yet at the same time they await the final declaration on the day of judgment when the verdict that God has already announced becomes public (5:5).

In the same way, the cross of Jesus Christ has launched believers into the age to come, even though they live in the present evil age (1:4). In other words, the new exodus promised in the OT has become a reality through Jesus as the crucified and risen Lord (Isa 40:3 – 11; 42:16; 43:2, 5 – 7, 16 – 19; 48:20 – 21; 49:8 – 11; 51:10 – 11). The resurrection in Jewish thought also signals the end of the old evil age and the coming of the new age of peace and plenty (cf. Isa 26:19; Ezek 37:1 – 14; Dan 12:2 – 3).

The resurrection is not a prominent theme in Galatians, and yet it appears in the first verse of the letter (1:1), signifying that the age to come has invaded the present age. The old evil cosmos has lost its hold over believers through the cross of Jesus Christ (6:14). Therefore, believers now belong to the new creation (6:15). The new creation has not been consummated (Isa 65:17; 66:22), but it has been inaugurated through the work of Jesus Christ. As argued above, the gift of the Holy Spirit represents the arrival of the new creation (Isa 32:15; 44:3; Ezek 11:18 – 19; 36:26 – 27; Joel 2:28). The Spirit is a gift of the last days, and his presence and indwelling among the Galatians shows that the final days have begun.

Eschatological contrasts dominate Galatians, so that we have a contrast between the old age of the flesh and the new age of the Spirit. The flesh in Paul represents the old age and who human beings are in Adam, whereas the Spirit signifies the inbreaking of the age to come. We see the same eschatological contrast between the law and the gospel. The Mosaic law belongs to the former era and believers are no longer under the law (see esp. 3:15 – 4:7). To be under the law is to be enslaved to the power of sin (3:10, 22, 23, 25; 4:3, 21 – 31; 5:18). Such slavery belongs to the former age. Now that the gospel of Christ (a fulfillment of the promise of the new exodus! Isa 40:9; 52:7) is proclaimed, the age of the law is obsolete. Believers live in the era of the cross, the resurrection, and the gift of the Spirit. Second Corinthians 5:17 rightly summarizes Galatians: "If anyone is in Christ, he is a new creation. The old has gone; the new has come!"

The discontinuity between the old and the new has led some to conclude that Paul has no room for salvation history in Galatians.[4] Surely, Galatians emphasizes the discontinuity between the law and the promise in many ways. The Mosaic covenant is identified as an interim covenant that was never intended to be in force forever (3:15 – 4:7). It had a temporary and intermediate role in God's purposes. Nevertheless, the gospel also fulfills the promises and blessings made to Abraham

---

4. So Martyn, *Galatians*, passim. For a fuller discussion of this matter, though I would not subscribe to all of his conclu- sions, see B. Longenecker, *Triumph of Abraham's God*.

(3:8 – 9, 14). Indeed, I argued in the exegesis of 4:21 – 5:1 that the message Paul proclaimed fulfills both the Abrahamic covenant and the new covenant, and hence the gospel instantiates the saving promises found in the OT.

There is both continuity and discontinuity between the OT and the NT. It is not as if Paul sees only apocalyptic disruption between the two, even if there is not a neat, straight-line continuity in the history of salvation. Even in the case of the law, Paul does not teach that the law is contrary to God's promises (3:21). God had a salvation-historical purpose for the law as well, for the law revealed to Israel and to all human beings that righteousness cannot be obtained through human performance and obedience. Luther rightly saw, even if this theme can be exaggerated, that the law prepares people for the gospel.

Therefore, at the end of the day, the law and the gospel work together, and both fit harmoniously into the one plan of God. In other words, it was part of God's salvation-historical plan for the Sinai covenant to have a temporary function; he intended that there be an apocalyptic disruption between the old covenant and the new. It is crucial to see, then, that the OT law is no longer binding on believers. The stipulations of the Mosaic covenant were intended for Israel under the old covenant, and with the coming of Christ, that age has ended.

The Law and the Covenant

The word "law" is used thirty-two times in Galatians. Virtually all commentators agree that the vast majority of these uses (at the very least twenty-nine of the thirty-two) refer to the Mosaic law. The exceptions are the reference to law as Scripture in the second use in 4:21, the reference to "the law of Christ" in 6:2, and perhaps the reference to law in 5:23.

Paul uses the term "works of law" six times in Galatians (three times in 2:16 and also in 3:2, 5, 10). In every instance he argues that righteousness or the reception of the Spirit is not by works of law. Indeed, he contrasts works of law and faith in every instance. I argued in the commentary that the phrase "works of law" does not refer fundamentally to boundary markers, nor does it designate legalism. It refers to all the actions commanded in the law. In other words, "works of law" refers to the law as a whole and does not, contrary to the new perspective, focus on the sociological features of the law that separate Jews from Gentiles. Human sin makes it impossible for righteousness and the Spirit to be given via works of law, for no one does what the law commands (2:16; 3:10; 5:3; 6:13). God demands perfect obedience, and human beings are under a curse because they fail to do what God commands.

The law, then, is opposed to faith (2:16; 3:2, 5, 10, 11, 12; 18; 5:2 – 6). The law focuses on what God demands and calls for human performance. Faith, however, looks away from the human subject and finds its righteousness in Christ crucified and risen. The law, if it could be kept, would exalt human beings and their virtue, but faith exalts

Christ as the one who liberates human beings from their bondage. Therefore, the only solution to the problem of the law is death. When human beings belong to Christ, they share in his death and resurrection (2:19 – 20; 3:26 – 28; 5:24; 6:14 – 15). They belong to the new creation, which is inaugurated with Christ's resurrection (1:1, 4).

The focus on the new creation, Christ's resurrection, and the overlapping of the ages (1:4) helps us see that the law must be understood as part of the old creation, the old covenant — the past age that is no longer normative. Paul's argument is not only anthropological (human beings don't obey), but also salvation-historical (the time period in which the law was in force has passed away). Paul uses the phrase "under law" (3:23; 4:4 – 5, 21; 5:18; cf. Rom 6:14 – 15; 1 Cor 9:20) in a salvation-historical sense. It refers to the old age in which the Mosaic covenant was in force, but now that era has passed away with the coming of Christ.

Another way of putting this is to say that the law is part of the Mosaic covenant. As Paul explains in 3:15 – 18, the law and the Mosaic covenant were always intended to be an interim arrangement. The law was given 430 years after the covenant with Abraham, and the law and its covenant could not nullify the provisions of the Abrahamic covenant. Paul does not argue that the covenants are the same. He detects great significance in the temporal gap between the covenants, and he also argues that the covenants are different in nature (3:18); that is, the Abrahamic covenant focuses on promise, while the Mosaic covenant stresses human obedience.

Why was the law given if the covenant with Moses is distinct from the covenant with Abraham (3:19)? Paul argues that God ordained that the law increase transgressions (see the commentary). Those who are "under law" (see above) are also "under sin" (3:22) and "under a curse" (3:10) and "enslaved under the elements of the world" (4:3). The allegory of Sarah and Hagar indicates that those who live under the law are in bondage (4:21 – 5:1). So Paul does not argue that the law restrains sin in Galatians (that was the position of the Judaizers!), nor is his point that the law segregated Jews from Gentiles (even though that point is true). The law defines sin, but it does more than this. It enclosed and imprisoned Israel under sin (3:22 – 23). Such a statement incidentally is borne out by Israel's history. Both the northern kingdom, Israel, and the southern kingdom, Judah, were sent into exile because of their inability to keep the Mosaic law. The law did not diminish sin but maximized it.

Paul argues, however, that believers are no longer under the law now that Christ has come. Christ lived under the law (obeying God in contrast to Israel) and freed those under the law from the dominion of the law (4:4 – 5). Christ is the promised seed predicted in the covenant with Abraham (3:16), and the law and the Mosaic covenant were in force only until the seed (Christ) arrived (3:19). The law and the Mosaic covenant functioned as the custodian and babysitter until Christ came, but now that he has come, the era of the law has passed away (3:24 – 25). The age of infancy and being a minor has ended, and the era of being sons and daughters of God has arrived (4:1 – 7).

I am not suggesting, incidentally, that the Mosaic covenant was legalistic. The Lord by his grace liberated Israel from Egyptian bondage. He carried them on eagles' wings and brought them to himself (Exod 19:4; 20:1). Even though God graciously liberated Israel from Egyptian bondage, it seems from reading the story of the exodus and NT commentary on it (1 Cor 10:1 – 12; Heb 3:12 – 4:11) that most of Israel was unregenerate, and hence they were unable to keep God's law. God did not plant the law in their hearts; that was the gift of the new covenant (Jer 31:31 – 34; cf. Ezek 11:18 – 19; 36:26 – 27). This is not to deny that there was a remnant that pleased God, but still the majority of the nation was not truly saved.

God intended the Mosaic law and covenant, then, to be in force for a limited time in the history of salvation. Paul argues in Galatians that the function of the law, in contrast to the promise, is to reveal sin. Now that Christ has come, believers are no longer under the law. Its time period has ended. Those who put themselves under the law have to keep it perfectly, because the forgiveness provided by OT sacrifices is no longer valid. Only the sacrifice of Christ removes the curse that comes from disobeying the law (3:13). But those who live under the old covenant are repudiating Christ's sacrifice and hence are cutting themselves off from the forgiveness he grants (cf. 5:2 – 4). Thus, the only way they can be right before God is if they keep the law perfectly, but such perfection is impossible. As a result, all those who rely on the law for salvation are under a curse (2:16; 3:10; 5:3: 6:13).

Oneness of Jews and Gentiles

The presenting issue in Galatians is circumcision. Must Gentiles submit to circumcision to belong to the people of God? The Judaizers conceived of God's people in terms of the Mosaic covenant. In other words, the people of God are fundamentally Jewish. According to the Judaizers, believers in Jesus Christ become part of Israel in the same way believers did under the Mosaic covenant — by receiving circumcision. Paul, however, departs dramatically from this reading. We have already seen above that the Judaizers failed to understand justification, the significance of the cross, the gift of the Spirit, and the place they occupied in salvation history. The Judaizers wanted to turn the clock back and live in the old evil age, and unfortunately the Galatians were enticed by their proposal. The Judaizers were convinced that believers in Jesus Christ must receive circumcision to belong to Abraham's family and to receive Abraham's blessing.

What is striking is how Paul's eschatological view reshapes his understanding of Israel. Who are the children of Abraham? What does it take to belong to Abraham's family? Paul argues forcefully in 3:6 – 14 that the blessing of Abraham and membership in Abraham's family are accessed by faith alone. Only those who believe like Abraham are the children of Abraham. The Judaizers almost certainly argued that circumcision would bring God's blessing, but Paul plots a dramatically different course. He argues that those who attempt to be part of the family of God through the law and circumcision are cursed (3:10 – 12). The only pathway into the people of God is through the crucified Christ (3:13 – 14). Those who turn to circumcision cut themselves off from Christ and grace (5:2 – 4).

The true family of Abraham, then, consists in believers in Jesus Christ. They have received the true circumcision in the cross of Jesus Christ. The new perspective on Paul has failed to understand the relationship between law and grace in Judaism and in Paul, but it has rightly perceived that the true and new Israel is not fundamentally nationalistic or ethnocentric.

When Paul invokes a blessing on the Israel of God (6:16), then, he certainly thinks of the church of Jesus Christ. To limit God's Israel to Jewish believers who are circumcised would contradict everything Paul has argued for in the letter, where he has emphasized that those who trust in Christ are members of Abraham's family and the true circumcision. If Paul introduced a division between Jewish and Gentile believers at this juncture, it would have been deeply confusing to the Galatian believers, for they were swayed by the Judaizers because they wanted to be part of the Israel of God. What Paul affirms at the close of the letter is that Gentile Christiains are part of God's Israel, for they have been delivered by the cross of Christ from the present evil age (1:4), they are part of the new creation (6:15), they have received the end-time verdict of "not guilty," and the gift of the Spirit has been granted to them. They are part of God's Israel through faith in Jesus Christ.

Freedom in Christ to Obey

Galatians particularly emphasizes the freedom of believers from the Mosaic law. As noted above, believers are no longer under the law. The Mosaic covenant has passed away since it was intended to be in force only until the coming of Jesus Christ. Hence, believers are not subject to what is codified in the Mosaic law, whether it commands circumcision, Sabbath keeping, tithing, food laws, and the like.

And yet are not believers still required to love one another (Lev 19:18) and to observe many of the Ten Commandments, so that murder, adultery, stealing, lying, and coveting are still wrong for believers? Paul himself lists many of these commands in describing what love is in Rom 13:8 – 10. Furthermore, in Eph 6:2 Paul commends the command to honor one's parents. How do we account for this? Some have said that Paul simply contradicts himself, but this is hardly convincing. When Paul speaks of fulfilling the law (5:14), he could scarcely have forgotten that he said a few verses earlier that we are free from the law (5:1). Nor does Paul carve out a nice and simple distinction between the civil, ceremonial, and moral law. He clearly teaches that the entire law has passed away.

If the law is abolished, how do we explain Paul's appealing to parts of the law for the moral life? The question is difficult, and hence there have been various explanations throughout history, including the idea that Paul distinguishes between the moral and ceremonial law. Perhaps a better solution is to say that the law of Christ is authoritative for believers (6:2). This law is fundamentally the law of love (5:14), so that believers live for the benefit of their neighbors. Part of what it means to show love is to refrain from adultery, murder, stealing, and so on. These moral norms are not authoritative because they are part of the Mosaic law; rather, they are authoritative because they are part of Christ's law, since they are universal moral norms.

Paul emphasizes in Galatians that the curse falls on all people because of their inability to observe the law (3:10; 5:3). God demands perfect obedience, and all human beings fall short of his requirements and hence stand under God's judgment. Unbelievers are enslaved to sin (4:3, 21–31) and are not freed from such slavery via the law. In Second Temple Judaism the law was thought to lead to life, but Paul argues that the law actually increases transgressions (3:19). Instead of being the answer, the law has become part of the problem. The only solution to sin is the cross of Christ, as was argued above, and now believers are no longer under the law.

Paul's emphasis on the temporary character of the Mosaic covenant and the weakness of the law might lead us to think that Paul is unconcerned about the moral life. But such a judgment is premature. Human beings cannot obtain righteousness on the basis of their good works, and yet those who walk by the Spirit (5:16), are led by the Spirit (5:18), march in step with the Spirit (5:25), and sow to the Spirit (6:8) manifest the fruit of the Spirit (5:22–23). They still battle the flesh and struggle with sin daily (5:17), and yet a new kind of life is lived, not on the basis of one's autonomous resources, but by virtue of the supernatural work of the Holy Spirit.

Indeed, this new way of living is not optional. Those who practice the works of the flesh (5:19–21) and sow to the flesh (6:8) will not enter God's kingdom on the last day. Does this contradict Paul's emphasis on grace and the free salvation granted through the gospel? The new obedience of believers cannot be understood as the basis of their end-time reward, for perfection is required on this score, and all fall short. Even the new obedience of believers, animated by the Spirit, is partial and fragmentary, and it hence cannot stand as the basis of a relationship with the Lord. Therefore, it seems best to conclude that the obedience of believers functions as necessary evidence that they belong to the Lord, that it is the fruit and expression of the new life. What Paul says on this score is captured in 5:6, where he refers to "faith working through love." True faith leads to a life of love, and that life of faith and love is empowered by the Holy Spirit.

Danger of Apostasy

Galatians features the freedom of the gospel and liberation from the bondage of the law through the cross of Jesus Christ. Yet Paul threatens the Galatians with eschatological judgment if they deny the gospel and receive circumcision (1:8–9;

5:2 – 4). If they turn from the gospel and commit apostasy, they will be damned. Is this threat a new legalism that contradicts the freedom of the Pauline gospel? Are Paul's threats the reintroduction of a law that is even stricter than the law he rejects as a basis for salvation? In order to understand Galatians, we must understand the nature of apostasy in the letter.

The apostasy about which Paul warns the Galatians is a return to the law for righteousness and salvation. Hence, those who turn from the gospel cease trusting in Christ and his cross and rely on their own righteousness and obedience to gain the final inheritance. Apostasy in Galatians, in other words, constitutes self-righteousness instead of relying on God and Christ for righteousness. The Galatians would commit apostasy if they denied the efficacy of the cross and relied on their own observance of the law. It follows, then, that apostasy does not represent a new kind of legalism. Apostasy consists in a refusal to trust in Christ and a turn to self-righteousness. In other words, this is the essence of apostasy! Clinging to Christ and the gospel, by the power of the Spirit, is the only antidote.

Conclusion

Paul's theology in Galatians is profound and at points complex. The significance of Christ's work on the cross is unpacked in a unique way. We see the centrality of justification and the cross and the gospel, which helps us to understand the depths of human sin and the heights of God's love. At the same time Paul emphasizes eschatology: the new age has arrived with the death and resurrection of Christ. With the coming of the new creation, the Mosaic covenant and law have passed away. The Spirit as the gift of the new age has been given and empowers believers to obey the Lord. Still, believers live in the overlapping of the ages. They are warned not to fall back into the old evil age by submitting to circumcision (1:4; 5:2 – 4). They must continue the way they started: by walking in the Spirit and trusting in Christ (3:2, 3, 5; 5:5 – 6, 16, 18, 25; 6:8).

Scripture Index

1 Corinthians

Subject Index

Author Index